SALTERS HORNERS ADVANCED PHYSICS

PHYSICS

A2

Student book

Heinemann

Heinemann Educational Publishers
Halley Court, Jordan Hill, Oxford OX2 8EJ
A division of Reed Educational and Professional Publishing Ltd
Heinemann is a registered trademark of Reed Educational & Professional Publishing Ltd

OXFORD MELBOURNE AUCKLAND
JOHANNESBURG BLANTYRE GABORONE
IBADAN PORTSMOUTH NH (USA) CHICAGO

First published 2001
Published as trial edition 1999

ISBN 0 435 62892 5

04 03 02 01
10 9 8 7 6 5 4 3 2 1

Edited by Anne Trevillion and Geoff Priddle

Typeset and Illustrated by Tech Set Ltd, Gateshead

Cover design by Philip Parkhouse, Design Consultancy

Printed and bound in Spain by Edelvives

Acknowledgements

The authors and publishers would like to thank the following for permission to use photographs:

Transport on Track:
p2: figure 1a Milepost 92 1/2, figure 1b Milepost 92 1/2; **p5:** figure 2 Alvey and Towers, figure 3a Channel Tunnel Publications; **p13:** figure 13 Milepost 92 1/2; **p16:** figure 15 Alvey and Towers; **p19:** figure 17 Corbis; **p30:** figure 32 Milepost 92 1/2; **p32:** figure 34 Milepost 92 1/2; **p42:** figure 48 Gareth Boden; **p45:** figure 52 Railnews; **p49:** figure 58 Railnews; **p50:** figure 59 S.P.L.; **p53:** figure 61 Milepost 92 1/2

The Medium is the Message:
p64: figure 1 Airbus Industrie; **p66:** figure 2 Corbis; **p68:** figure 4 ESTEC; **p69:** figure 6 Airbus Industrie; **p69:** figure 7 Airbus Industrie; **p70:** figure 9 Gareth Boden; **p71:** figure 11 Cumulus; **p84:** figure 28a Chris Butlin, figure 28b Chris Butlin; **p86:** figure 31 Chris Butlin; **p88:** figure 32 Tony Stone; **p90:** figure 38 Gareth Boden; **p94:** figure 43 GEC Marconi, figure 44 Cumulus; **p95:** figure 45 S.P.L., figure 47 Gareth Boden; **p99:** figure 51 Airbus Industrie; **p100:** figure 52 British Aerospace, figure 53a Peter Gould/Cumulus, figure 53b Photodisc; **p101:** figure 54 GEC Marconi; **p106:** figure 60 Gareth Boden; **p108:** figure 61 Gareth Boden; **p111:** figure 69 Corbis; **p113:** figure 71 Airbus Industrie; **p115:** figure 73 Science and Society

Probing the Heart of Matter:
p122: figure 1a S.P.L., figure 1b S.P.L.; **p125:** figure 2 Corbis; **p126:** figure 3 S.P.L.; **p127:** figure 4 CERN; **p131** figure 5a John Cleare Mountain Camera Picture Library, figure 5b Allsport/Mike Hewitt, figure 5f Stable Micro Systems, figure 5g Colorsport, figure 5j S.P.L./NASA, figure 5k Tony Sherborne; **p133:** figure 7 S.P.L.; **p134:** figure 8 Corbis; **p138:** figure 10 Ronald Grant, figure 11 S.P.L., figure 13 S.P.L.; **p142:** figure 14 S.P.L.; **p163:** figure 38 CERN; **p165:** figure 40a Corbis, figure 40b Corbis; **p170:** figure 43 S.P.L.; **p172:** figure 45 Empics; **p173:** figure 47 Empics; **p174:** figure 48 Cumulus; **p182:** figure 55 S.P.L., figure 56 CERN; **p194:** figure 1a Rex features, figure 1b Rex Features

Build or Bust:
p194: figure 1 (three pictures) Rex Features; **p196:** figure 2 Corbis; **p211:** figure 17 Corbis; **p214:** figure 22 Corbis; **p216:** figure 24 Corbis; **p228:** figure 34 Gareth Boden; **p230:** figure 36 Corbis, figure 37 Gareth Boden; **p248:** figure 52 Photodisc; **p251:** figure 54 Corbis

Reach for the Stars:
p266: figure 1a NASA; **p266:** figure 1b S.P.L., figure 1c S.P.L.; **p269:** figure 2 S.P.L.; **p273:** figure 5 S.P.L., figure 6 NASA; **p277:** figure 10a SOHO, figure 10b SOHO; **p279:** figure 13 Corbis, figure 14 Corbis; **p280:** figure 15 S.P.L.; **p283:** figure 17 S.P.L.; **p286:** figure 20 S.P.L.; **p291:** figure 22 Corbis; **p292:** figure 23 S.P.L.; **p293:** figure 25 S.P.L.; **p294:** figure 26 Science and Society Picture Library; **p296:** figure 28 J.E.T.; **p297:** figure 29 Corbis; **p297:** figure 30 S.P.L.; **p301:** figure 31 S.P.L.; **p303:** figure 34 S.P.L.; **p304:** figure 35a Corbis, figure 36 S.P.L.; **p306:** figure 37a S.P.L, figure 38 Photodisc; **p308:** figure 40 S.P.L.; **p309:** figure 41 Corbis; **p315:** figure 48 Goodricke College, York; **p317:** figure 50 S.P.L.; **p321:** figure 53a S.P.L., figure 53b Corbis; **p329:** figure 57 S.P.L.; **p333:** figure 59 S.P.L.; **p336:** figure 63 S.P.L., figure 64 S.P.L.; **p338:** figure 66 Corbis; **p340:** figure 68 Corbis; **p341:** figure 69 S.P.L., figure 70 S.P.L.; **p345:** figure 75 Corbis; **p248** figure 78 Fred Hoyle and Martin Rees courtesy of Corbis; **p350:** figure 80 Corbis; **p354:** figure 84 S.P.L.; **p357:** figure 86e NASA, figure 86f S.P.L.; **p366:** figure 93 Photodisc; **p368:** figure 94a S.P.L., figure 94b S.P.L.

Picture research by Peter Morris

The authors and publishers would like to thank the following for permission to reproduce copyright material:

p12: figure 11 copyright IRSE. The Institution of Railway Signal Engineers is the professional institution for all those engaged in railway signalling and telecommunications; **p31:** figure 33 reproduced by permission of the Nuffield Foundation; **p36:** figure 38 courtesy of Pico Technology, *www.picotech.com*; **p82:** figures 25 and 26 Chris Butlin; **p207:** figure 15 Seismic Wave program by Alan L. Jones, State University of New York at Binghamton. *http://www.geol.binghamton.edu/faculty/jones*; **p229:** figure 35 Chris Butlin; **p252:** figure 55 originally published as 'The acoustics of concert halls' in Physics World, May 1997, pages 33–37.

The publishers have made every effort to trace the copyright holders, but if they have inadvertently overlooked any, they will be pleased to make the necessary arrangements at the first opportunity.

Contributors

Many people from schools, colleges, universities, industries and the professions have contributed to the Salters Horners Advanced Physics project.

Central team

Andy Butlin, York College (technical support)
Chris Butlin
Nancy Newton (Secretary)

Elizabeth Swinbank (Director and General Editor)
David Waddington

Advisory committee

Prof. Frank Close
Prof. Cyril Hilsum F.R.S.
Prof. Sir Derek Roberts F.R.S. (Chair)
Prof. Robin Millar

CERN, Geneva, and Rutherford Appleton Laboratory
Unilever and University College, London
University College, London
University of York

Sponsors

AEA Technology	Corus UK Ltd	Pilkington	The UK Steel Industry Education Programme
British Nuclear Fuels	Esso UK	The Salters Company	The University of York
British Telecom	The Horners Company	Smiths Industries	Urenco

A2 authors

Jonathan Allday	The King's School, Canterbury	Maureen Maybank	Argyll
Chris Butlin	University of York	David Neal	John Leggott College, Scunthorpe
Tony Connell	Wilberforce College, Hull	Kerry Parker	Sheffield College
Howard Darwin	John Leggott College, Scunthorpe	David Sang	Bognor Regis
Nick Fisher	Rugby School	Tony Sherborne	Sheffield Hallam University
Alasdair Kennedy	Rugby School	Carol Tear	York
Averil MacDonald	University of Reading	Nigel Wallis	York

We would also like to thank the following for their advice and assistance with the development of the A2 materials.

Clive Avery	AEA Technology Rail	Christine Long	Porsche Cars Great Britian Ltd
Andrew Bunce	BAe Warton	Mark E. Lutman	University of Southampton Institute of Sound and Vibration Research
David Davidge	Imperial College, London		
Mike Evans	Focus Exploration	Trevor Mason	BAe Fulton
Richard Gostling	AEA Technology Rail	Justin Smith	Wokingham Borough Council
Jane High	GEC Marconi Avionics	Gareth & Louise Tear	York
		Andrew West	Formerly Caistor Grammar School

Contents

How to use this book

Context-led study

Welcome to the second year of the Salters Horners Advanced Physics course.

Each unit in the course starts by looking at particular situations in which physics is used or studied, and then develops the physics you need to learn to explore this 'context'.

We have tried to select contexts to give you some idea of how physics can help improve people's lives, how physics is used in engineering and technology, and how physics research extends our understanding of the physical world at a fundamental level. These will show you just some of the many physics-related careers and further study that might be open to you in the future.

Within each unit, you will develop your knowledge and understanding on one or more areas of physics. In later units, you will meet many of these ideas again – in a completely different context – and develop them further. In this way, you will gradually build up your knowledge and understanding of physics and learn to apply key principles of physics to a variety of contexts.

About this book

Each unit includes the following features:

Main text

This presents the context of each unit and explains the relevant physics as you need it.

Within the main text, some words are printed in **bold**. These are key terms relating to the physics. We suggest that you make your own summary of these terms (and others if you wish) as you go along. Then you can refer back to it when you revisit a similar area of physics later in the course and when you revise for exams.

Activities

The text refers to many *Activities*. These include practical work, the use of information technology (e.g. CD-ROMs and the Internet), reading, writing, data handling and discussion. Some activities are best carried out with one or more other students, others are intended for you to do on your own. For some activities, there are handout sheets giving further information, details about apparatus and so on.

Questions

You will find plenty of *Questions* in this book. Some are to do as you go along and at the end of each main section. The answers to these questions are given at the end of each teaching unit. Once you have had a go at a question, check your answer. If you have gone wrong, use the answer (and the relevant part of the book chapter) to help you sort out your ideas. Working in this way is not cheating! Rather, it helps you to learn.

Maths notes

Maths references in the main text will direct you to the *Maths notes*, which are to help you with the maths needed in physics. This may involve calculations, rearranging equations, plotting graphs, and so on. You will probably have covered most of what's needed at GCSE, but you may not be used to using it in physics.

The *Maths notes* at the end of the book summarise the key maths ideas that you need in the course, and show how to apply them to situations in physics.

Study notes

These notes in the margin are intended to help you get to grips with the physics – for example, they indicate links with other parts of the course.

Further investigations

Some time in the second year of this course, you will spend two weeks on a practical project exploring a topic of your own choice as part of your coursework unit. You will be asked to research some background information on your chosen topic, plan and carry out your laboratory work, and write a report. You might already have some topic in mind that arose from your AS work. We have included some further suggestions under the heading *Further investigations*, but any question that intrigues you could form the basis of your project.

Achievements

At the end of each unit you will find a list of *Achievements*. This is a summary of the key points that you have covered in that unit, and shows you what you can expect to be tested on in the exams. (It is copied from the Exam Specification.) Look through the *Achievements* when you check back over your work after finishing a unit. If there is anything that looks unfamiliar, or that you think you have not properly understood, consult your teacher and the explanations in this book. To help you build on your earlier work, the *Achievements* from the AS part of the course are listed on pages 425–429 of this book.

TRANSPORT ON TRACK

(a)

(b)

Figure 1 *(a) Stephenson's* Rocket, *(b)* Eurostar

Why a unit called Transport on Track?

In 1825 George Stephenson's steam-powered *Locomotion* (developed from his famous *Rocket*) drew the world's first passenger/goods train from Stockton to Darlington, a 37-mile journey, at an average speed of only 12 miles per hour. One can now travel from Britain to France in roughly 20 minutes (Figure 1).

This desire to improve and extend the rail transport system has constantly tested scientists and engineers. The rails themselves needed to be made strong enough to cope with the weight of fully loaded trains, while incorporating designs to limit the effect of expansion. Engine and coach production has had to make use of new techniques of propulsion and new materials of construction to become faster and cleaner. Finally and most importantly, increasing train speeds, passenger numbers and service density (number of trains required per time interval) have necessitated continuous advances in the area of railway safety, using the foremost technologies of the day. As Clive Avery, a research engineer at AEA Technology Rail in Derby, puts it, "People see the running of trains as being a very simple process, yet the science and technology involved in propelling them, and keeping them safe, is staggering".

Rail enthusiasts claim that this millennium will see the birth of a new railway age, as environmental worries and road congestion force trains back under the spotlight. The extraordinary technical success of the Channel Tunnel, and the trains that thread their way at speed through its fifty confined kilometres, is said to have marked the beginning of this new era.

Overview of physics principles and techniques

This unit builds on your understanding of basic electrical circuits and conservation of momentum gained from earlier units. After a review of dc electricity, ideas about magnetism will be extended; this will lead into electromagnetism and the laws of electromagnetic induction. Transformer theory will also form part of this section. The importance of digital signals will be emphasised, since they are fundamental to situations involving feedback and control, and you will investigate circuits containing capacitors and resistors.

In the course of this unit you will be involved in a wide range of practical activities, many of which will have an electrical and electronic basis. You will also use spreadsheets to model situations involving the motion of trains, and a circuit-modelling application to test circuit designs.

In this unit you will extend your knowledge of

- dc circuits from *Technology in Space* and *Digging Up the Past*;

- energy and momentum conservation from *Higher, Faster, Stronger*, *Technology in Space* and *Spare Part Surgery*;

- signals from *The Sound of Music*.

In other units you will do more work on

- momentum and magnetic fields in *Probing the Heart of Matter*;

- exponential changes in *The Medium is the Message* and *Reach for the Stars*;

- capacitance and signals in *The Medium is the Message*;

- kinetic energy and work in *Reach for the Stars*.

▮ *Getting on track*

At the end of this unit, you will be asked to write either a newspaper article about safety in rail transport or a technical advertisement selling some of the technology that is used to make trains safe. The following short article, compiled from items published in *Snippets* and in *Electronics Education*, provides you with some initial information and sets the scene for the unit.

1.1 Tunnel trains

ACTIVITY 1   **Getting on track**

Read this article on Tunnel trains, and think which aspects of physics you might expect to find being used in each of the four areas mentioned. Use the Internet to find out more information about Channel Tunnel trains and other modern rail systems.

The *Eurostar* train in Figure 1(b) carries hundreds of people on board, all of whom hope to arrive safely at their destination. It is half a kilometre long and has roughly the mass of a thousand small cars; and yet it can travel at 300 kilometres per hour ($83 \, \mathrm{m \, s^{-1}}$). When moving at speed, it has enough energy to raise itself and its contents to the top of the Eiffel Tower. Each of its electrically powered locomotives needs to be equivalent to 20 Formula One racing cars.

Figure 2 shows *Le Shuttle*. This train is three quarters of a kilometre long and it can travel at 140 kilometres per hour ($39 \, \mathrm{m \, s^{-1}}$). At this speed, it needs one and a half kilometres to stop. It contains hundreds of vehicles: cars, lorries, coaches and their passengers. To cope with passenger demand, there is generally a similar train not far behind it, and one in front.

Both *Eurostar* and *Le Shuttle* travel through a narrow tunnel 7.6 m wide, only slightly wider than the train itself (Figure 3). The Channel Tunnel actually consists of three separate tunnels, each 50 km long. There are two rail tunnels, one for traffic in each direction, and a central service tunnel. They were bored, largely through chalk, at an average depth of 45 m below the sea bed; for most of its length the Channel Tunnel runs through the virtually impermeable stratum of chalk marl (Figure 4).

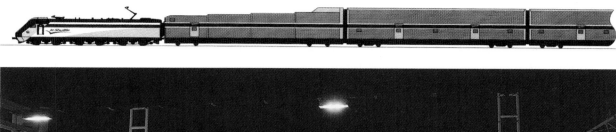

Figure 2   Le Shuttle *locomotives are the most powerful electric railway locomotives in the world. Each passenger-vehicle shuttle has one at each end*

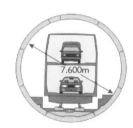

7.600m

Figure 3   *The Channel Tunnel*

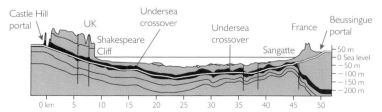

Castle Hill portal
UK
Shakespeare Cliff
Undersea crossover
Undersea crossover
Sangatte
France
Beussingue portal

50 m
0 Sea level
−50 m
−100 m
−150 m
−200 m

0 km   5   10   15   20   25   30   35   40   45   50

Figure 4   *Geological cross-section showing the Channel Tunnel*

The Channel Tunnel was designed as a quick and reliable route for passengers and freight between Britain and continental Europe. *Le Shuttle* trains, specially designed and constructed for the Tunnel, run between purpose-built terminals at each end of it. *Eurostar* trains provide a fast link to the continent – London to Paris in 2 hours 20 minutes. To meet the demand for cross-Channel transport, the Eurotunnel company need to send 24 trains through the tunnel per hour, possibly even rising to 30 per hour in the future. These trains will be travelling at up to 160 kilometres per hour, forcing air pressure pulses in front of them that generate high winds, making it impossible to work in the tunnels. In the entry and exit sections of the Tunnel, trains will be travelling over gradients as steep as 1 in 90.

The facts and statistics presented above pose obvious safety problems:

- How can the vast energies of these trains be dissipated safely as the train is slowed?

- How can we ensure that the trains will not collide with each other, or anything else?

- How can we ensure that if a train breaks down in the dangerous, isolated environment of the Channel Tunnel, where access is very difficult, it can be started again and moved to safety?

To solve these problems, some of which affect all modern railway systems, sophisticated engineering techniques are used. For example, in the Channel Tunnel, an automated electronic signalling system is employed to produce very close gaps between trains. This involves a technically advanced sensing system to ensure the position and speed of each train in the system is known exactly at all times. Despite the complexity of modern rail safety systems, you will find their principles of operation are firmly based in fundamental physics, and often straightforward to understand.

This unit looks at some of the physics behind making high-speed, high-momentum trains acceptably safe. It focuses on four areas:

- *Signalling* The technique of detecting a train and thereby providing signals to indicate its presence.

- *Stopping and starting* Bringing trains to halt in an acceptably safe time or distance interval; and starting them moving again, if necessary on a gradient.

- *Sensing* Automatically detecting the speed of a train to enable safe intervals to be computed and applied.

- *Structure* How to make trains 'crashworthy' – that is, able to undergo collisions, with as little damage and danger to passengers as possible.

2 Signalling

2.1 Short circuits and train safety

Early days

Reliable signalling is important for the safety of passengers on today's railways, but in the early days of rail travel, safety could only be ensured by having large time gaps between trains. Getting information about hazards, breakdowns, etc., back to other trains on the line was very difficult. The earliest solution was to use railway policemen who gave hand signals in a similar fashion to the way traffic police do today. At night time, they held up coloured lights instead. As rail traffic increased, more policemen were needed. This put up the costs of running a railway, so a system was needed that required one person to operate several signals. An early hand-operated signal on the Great Western Railway (GWR, or affectionately known as God's Wonderful Railway) was the 'disc and crossbar'. With its red disc facing the driver, the indication was 'all clear', but if the crossbar showed, the train had to stop. At night time, the disc and crossbar had lights attached; red for 'stop' and white for 'all clear'. This idea of using coloured lights became the norm for both day and night-time signalling and is still the main method used today.

Track circuit signalling – how it works

The route followed by a train is set from a control centre or signal box. Its exact position along that route needs to be communicated to other train drivers on the same track. This is done by signals, set by the train itself, providing a **short circuit** across the rails through its wheels and axles – this is called 'track circuiting'. The track is divided up into electrically insulated 'blocks', and whenever a train is in a block, it activates signals behind it to inform other trains that the block is occupied. In 'three-aspect' signalling, three colours of light are used. The idea is that the train automatically puts the signal closest behind it at red ('stop'), and the previous signal at yellow ('caution – start braking'). A green light indicates all-clear, meaning that the next two sections, at least, are free of trains (see Figure 5).

When dealing with electricity, you may well have been told that it is essential to avoid short circuits. These circuits (having negligible resistance and excessive current) can flatten batteries, blow fuses, cause fires and generally stop things from working properly, so it can be a surprise to find them used as a method of setting signals.

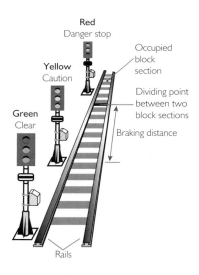

Figure 5 *Three-aspect signalling*

ACTIVITY 2   Short circuits on the line

Set up a model of a railway line from the circuit diagram in Figure 6 and note the ammeter reading before adding a short circuit. Note how a brief short circuit between the two rails affects the current. The granite bed is called the ballast. See what happens to the current if the ballast is slightly salty and damp. Write a statement about short circuits and the effect of ballast on the signalling circuit.

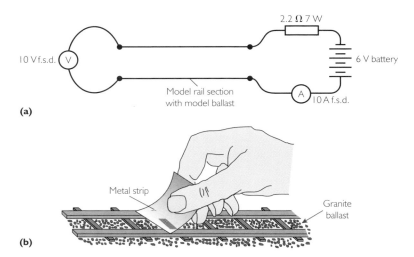

Figure 6 *Model track circuit: (a) circuit diagram, (b) one way to short-circuit it*

The **electromagnetic relay** is one of the main devices used to control a signal in a track circuit system. It is an enclosed mechanical switch that can use one electrical circuit to operate another, electrically isolated, circuit. The relays shown in Figure 7 are only for two-aspect signalling (red and green lights only), but interconnection between additional relays would enable three-, four- and five-aspect signals to operate.

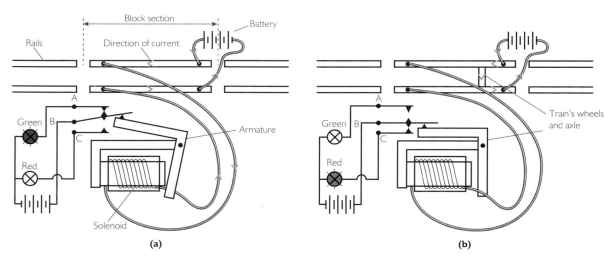

Figure 7 *Signals (a) with relay current high and (b) with relay current low*

With no train on a section of track electric current flows along the rails into the solenoid of the relay (Figure 7a). This makes the solenoid into an **electromagnet**, which causes it to attract the soft-iron armature. The armature's movement closes the switch contacts A and B. The green lamp's circuit is now complete and it lights.

With a train on the track (Figure 7b), the situation is different. The short circuit through the train's wheels and axles causes a fall in the potential difference across them and the relay. There is now only a small current in the relay, so its solenoid magnetic field is not strong enough to attract the armature. The switch contacts B and C now spring back together and the red lamp comes on as its circuit is now complete.

Notice that this system is fail-safe; if there was a power failure to the relay solenoid, the signal would set itself to the safest position, i.e. red, in order to stop all traffic. All signalling systems have to be fail-safe.

What can go wrong?

If, for any reason, the train can't short-circuit the lines, it can't be detected. Alternatively, if the lines are short-circuited by something other than the train, signals will falsely be set to stop. Examples of each of these conditions occurring might include:

- Torrential rain making the ground and sleepers more conductive (low ballast resistance) so that the two rails short-circuit.

- Leaves on a track, whose waxy surface coatings are good insulators, preventing a short circuit occurring.

- Very rusty rolling stock or track. (Rust is iron oxide, which conducts badly.) In normal use this is not a problem as friction between the wheels and the rails soon removes the corrosion.

- Where the track is adjacent to the sea or in undersea tunnels. In clean, dry, well-insulated conditions track-to-track or 'ballast' resistance should be around 100 ohms per km. Moist, saline conditions can reduce this to 0.5 ohms per km.

- A train coming off the rails, but blocking the track. There would be no short circuit and so the track would appear unoccupied. (To deal with this eventuality the guard's van contains a length of thick copper cable with a large clip at each end. If such an accident had occurred, the guard would clip this cable across the track to short-circuit it.)

Even safer systems for the future

More modern, and even safer, systems of signalling have now been devised, and are gradually being installed around the world. Some control the train remotely. The system for controlling *Le Shuttle* trains through the Channel Tunnel is very sophisticated, although it still follows the idea of fixed block sections. The difference is that the speed and position of a train are automatically sensed and the driver receives an in-cab display of a required speed for the end of the next block.

Another modern approach, which uses radio communications between train and control centre, can still be thought of as involving blocks, but with the block moving as a sort of 'safety envelope' (Figure 8). The control centre allocates each train its own particular safety envelope and no envelopes are allowed to

Study note

See part 4, *Sensing speed*.

overlap. The big advantage of individual trains 'carrying' their own safety envelope is that slower trains can have smaller envelopes, thus increasing the line capacity – i.e. the number of trains occupying a particular length of track at any one time.

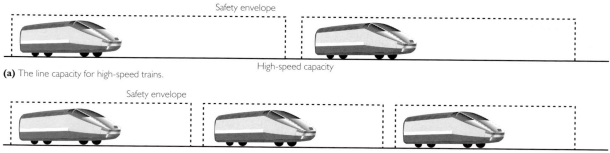

(a) The line capacity for high-speed trains.

(b) The line capacity for slower freight trains. It is higher than for high-speed trains because of the smaller braking distances

Figure 8 *Safety envelopes*

Use questions 1 to 5 to check your understanding of Activity 2 and the passage you have just read.

QUESTIONS

1 What do you understand by the term, 'electrically insulated blocks'?

2 A solenoid is a coil of wire along a straight axis. How does passing electric current through a solenoid alter its properties?

3 Track circuit signalling is said to be 'fail-safe.' Explain what you think this means with reference to the two-aspect signalling shown in Figure 7.

4 Explain why 'leaves on the line' or a rusty coating to the rail can be a serious problem for train safety.

5 In new and future train signalling systems, each train will be assigned a safety envelope based on a calculation of its theoretical deceleration curve.

(a) The deceleration curve calculated does not use the shortest practically possible time to stop the train. Suggest a reason for this.

(b) Explain why freight trains can operate in smaller envelopes.

(c) What is the advantage of having smaller envelopes?

2.2 *Exploring track circuits*

Why should a short circuit in parallel with the relay cause a drop in potential difference? If there were no other resistance in the circuit, the pd across the combination would be the same as the supply voltage. The key point is that there is another resistance in series with the relay, so the circuit is really a potential divider (Figure 9). Adding very low resistance(s) (a short circuit) in parallel with the relay alters the way in which the supply voltage is 'shared'.

Study note

You might wish to look back at work you did in the AS units *Technology in Space* and *Digging Up the Past* and refer to Maths note 3.3 *Reciprocals*.

The pd across the relay-plus-short-circuit is small, so there is only a small current in the relay. Activity 3 and questions 6 and 7 illustrate what happens.

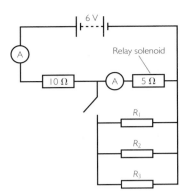

Figure 9 *Track circuit*

ACTIVITY 3 Modelling a track circuit

Use a computer simulation or work with components to model and explore a simple track circuit for two-aspect signalling.

QUESTIONS

6 A 6 V supply provides the current to operate a relay solenoid of resistance 5 Ω as shown in Figure 9. Unfortunately other resistances R_1, R_2 and R_3 may occur in parallel with the relay.

(**a**) Without these extra resistances, calculate the current drawn from the supply and the pd across the relay.

(**b**) If the resistors are all present and $R_1 = R_2 = R_3 = 5\,\Omega$:
   (**i**)   What is the new circuit resistance?
   (**ii**) How much current is now drawn from the supply?
   (**iii**) What is the new pd across the 5 Ω relay?
   (**iv**) What is now the current in the relay?
   (**v**)   Comment on any problem that might arise as a result of additional resistors in parallel with the relay.

7 Figure 10 shows a model track circuit. *R* is a series variable resistor used to regulate the current and voltage in the parallel part of the circuit.

(**a**) If the relay is to have a pd of 6 V across it, what resistance value of *R* is required?

(**b**) If the variable resistor is set as suggested in part (**a**), what is the electric current through the relay?

(**c**) What is the current through the variable resistor in this situation?

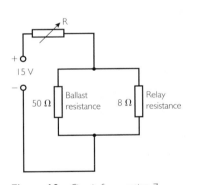

Figure 10 *Circuit for question 7*

Near the sea, or within the Channel Tunnel, damp, saline (salty) conditions between the rails can be a problem because salt water is a good electrical conductor. If there is enough of it around, it can lower the ballast resistance to a level sufficient to deactivate the track circuit relay and indicate the presence of a train erroneously. The more complex track signals used in the Channel Tunnel can also be disrupted.

ACTIVITY 4 Trouble between the tracks

In Activity 3, you found the minimum ballast resistance required to deactivate a track circuit relay and give a false signal. Determine the resistivity of damp, salty kitchen towel and hence make an estimate for the effect of salt water on railway ballast.

Study note

You might need to look back at the AS unit *Digging Up the Past* for a reminder of resistivity.

Further investigations

Measure the electrical conductivity of leaves, or rust, and see how that might affect track circuit signalling.

Explore how the contact resistance between track and train might be affected by the weight of the train.

2.3 Summing up part 2

This part of the unit has mainly involved revision of work from AS about dc electric circuits.

ACTIVITY 5 | Summing up part 2

Before you move on to later parts of this unit, make sure you know the meaning of all the terms printed in bold in part 2.

QUESTIONS

8 Figure 11 shows a record of a test done on a track circuit in 1909, when track circuit signalling was first being investigated by railway engineers. The 'lorry' being tested is an open wagon on the rails. Figure 12 represents the test on a diagram.

C obbe/09

Mr Holt

Derby August 12th/09

Automatic signalling Keighley – Steeton.
Platelayers lorry on track circuit

In accordance with Superintendent's verbal instruct-ions, a platelayer's lorry was tested on the Utley – Steeton Down Line track circuit, on Friday August 6th.

The voltmeter was connected from rail to rail, and fluctuations noted each time the lorry was run on to track circuit.

The lorry was first tested light, and weight gradually increased.

Test

Weight on lorry.	Voltage rail to rail with lorry on track.	
	Minimum.	Maximum.
Light	·5	·68
100 lbs	·5	·69
200 lbs	·5	·7
400 lbs	·5	·7
1000 lbs	·4	·7
2000 lbs	·25	·66
2500 lbs	·16	·6
3000 lbs	·16	·6
3500 lbs	·15	·5

Test commenced at 5.0. am. Track every dry. Rails bright and clean, with frequent traffic. Weather Fine. (Brilliant sunshine)

Figure 11 *Extract from engineer's records*

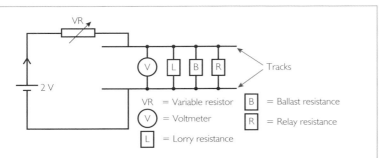

Figure 12   *Circuit diagram for the test*

(**a**) If the voltmeter reads 0.5 V, what is the voltage across the relay?

(**b**) If the voltmeter reads 0.5 V, what is the voltage across the variable resistor?

(**c**) Why is there a maximum and minimum voltage for each load?

(**d**) What happens, in general, to the voltage measured from track to track as the load is increased?

(**e**) From your answer to (**d**), what must happen to the resistance, L, from track to track across the lorry?

(**f**) Suggest a reason for your answer to (**e**).

(**g**) What problems may arise from trains with very light loads?

3 *Stopping and starting*

3.1 *The technical challenge of* Eurostar

Moving and stopping the massive *Eurostar* trains (Figure 13) has proved an enormous technical challenge. It has required the application of intriguing uses of electromagnetism plus an understanding of dynamics. The following passage sets the scene for this part of the unit.

Figure 13   *A Eurostar locomotive*

Supplying electricity

The *Eurostar* service runs through three European countries and each one has a different electrical power supply. This means that the trains have to be able to collect their supply either from the 'third rail' on the ground or via a pantograph from an overhead cable. The demands of imposed restrictions on axle loads means that the power developed in the new motors has to be 50% higher than in any previous locomotive for less weight.

Brakes

In the 19th century mechanical braking was used for wagons and trains. While a mechanical lever coupled to a brake shoe could stop a wagon fairly quickly, it required great force and long levers when used on a train. Each coach had a separate mechanical brake, so that when a train went down hill the brakemen had to run along the top of the train turning a cranking wheel to set the brakes on each coach, and repeat the process to turn the brakes off. A single mechanical system is impossible because trains are so long and made of separate freight wagons or passenger coaches. The invention of the air brake eventually solved this problem for the railways and is a system still in use. A simple high-pressure air hose could easily be connected or disconnected between coaches and the system could be supplied from a single high-pressure air pump in the locomotive.

Even when *Eurostar* is slowing down quite gradually, it needs a braking power of many megawatts. To achieve this braking power the train uses three braking systems. Air lines operate the conventional friction action of disc brakes (just as in a car) on the passenger coaches, while on the locomotive two types of electric braking are available. Knowledge of the stopping distances required by these new trains is essential if the signals are to be put at suitable intervals along the line.

Motors

Eurostar has ac traction motors rated at 1400 kW with two motors per locomotive. Each drive system includes a power conversion unit to change a dc or ac fixed voltage supply into an ac supply of variable voltage and variable frequency. Domestically we run hair dryers, electric drills, etc., using motors of a type called commutator motors, and they will run very effectively on 50 Hz ac. But these applications only need a few hundred watts. *Eurostar* needs much, much more. The more powerful ac motors are generally of a type called induction motors. The winding on a static part generates a rotating magnetic flux that induces current in copper bars in a rotating part. These currents react with the changing flux to produce rotation. The copper bars look like the sort of exercise wheel given to hamsters or pet mice and, presumably for this reason, ac induction motors are often called 'squirrel cage motors' (see Figure 14).

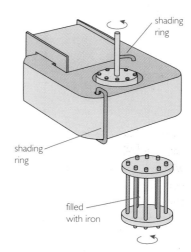

Figure 14 *An induction motor*

Forces

A high force of friction between the wheels and the track enables a large driving force or tractive effort to be developed. For *Eurostar* up to 5.6 MW of power can be provided using two locomotives. This gives around 400 kN of tractive effort to start the train off.

3.2 *Moving theory*

In this section we will consider the motion of trains as they start and stop. This will involve building on the basic theories and equations of motion that you met in the AS unit *Higher, Faster, Stronger*.

QUESTIONS

9 (**a**) If the *Eurostar*, mass 750 tonnes, is subject to a net tractive (pulling) force of 400 kN, what is its acceleration?

(**b**) What power is required to produce this acceleration when the train reaches a speed of 10 m s^{-1}?

Back to Newton

The link between force, mass, and acceleration given by the equation $F = ma$ was probably presented to you as Newton's second law, which is true, but it is a limited interpretation of what Newton meant. We now explore the wider significance of that law.

Newton himself did not mention the word acceleration but said something to the effect that the rate of change of motion is proportional to the size of the force producing it.

Working from the familiar equation,

$$F = ma$$

we can establish the nature of that 'rate of change of motion'. Substituting for a gives:

$$F = m\frac{\Delta v}{\Delta t} = \frac{m(v - u)}{\Delta t}$$

where the velocity changes from u to v in time Δt. Expanding the bracket:

$$F = \frac{(mv - mu)}{\Delta t}$$

$$F = \frac{\Delta(mv)}{\Delta t} \tag{1}$$

Now we have a force that is equal to a rate of change of something that is represented by *mass × velocity*. This is much more in line with Newton's original meaning. The quantity, *mass × velocity*, is a vector quantity known as **momentum**. Momentum is usually given the symbol p, and has SI units kg m s^{-1}.

Equation (1) can be further simplified to:

$$F = \frac{\Delta p}{\Delta t} \tag{1a}$$

Study note

Here we are using symbols F, u, v and p to represent the magnitudes of vector quantities.

If Δp and Δt are small this can give an instantaneous value for force, written:

$$F = \frac{\mathrm{d}p}{\mathrm{d}t} \tag{1b}$$

When Newton's second law is expressed in terms of momentum change we do not have to assume that the mass remains constant. If the mass changes from an initial value of m_1 to a final one of m_2:

$$\Delta mv = (m_2 v - m_1 u)$$

This widens the application of Newton's second law to cover, for example, a steam train carrying its own coal for fuel (not a complication needed for *Eurostar* trains as they run on electricity).

Another rearrangement gives us:

$$F\Delta t = \Delta(mv) = \Delta p \tag{2}$$

This relationship is used so frequently that the product of force and time has gained its own name. It is called the **impulse** of a force and is particularly useful when analysing impacts since the force and time of an impact must be the same for both participants. It can be expressed in words as:

$$\text{impulse} = \text{change in momentum}$$

Note that impulse and momentum are both vector quantities, so the direction as well as magnitude should be included.

We are now able to address such important questions as 'how much force is needed to stop a train?'. Use equations (1) and (2), and other equations of motion, to answer questions 10 to 15.

QUESTIONS

10 What are two possible SI units for impulse and momentum?

11 A railway coach of mass 50 tonnes is in motion at $+20\,\mathrm{m\,s^{-1}}$. Calculate the change in momentum needed to produce each of the following final velocities ($1\,\mathrm{t} = 1000\,\mathrm{kg}$):

(**a**) $v = +40\,\mathrm{m\,s^{-1}}$, (**b**) $v = -20\,\mathrm{m\,s^{-1}}$, (**c**) $v = 0\,\mathrm{m\,s^{-1}}$.

12 A $1.2\,\mathrm{t}$ car accelerates from 0 to $25\,\mathrm{m\,s^{-1}}$ in $10\,\mathrm{s}$. Calculate (**a**) the change in momentum, (**b**) the tractive force applied (ignore any drag due to air resistance, etc.), (**c**) the distance travelled and (**d**) the power of the engine.

13 A *Shuttle* train (Figure 15) has mass of $2400\,\mathrm{t}$, i.e. 2000 times greater than the car in question 12. To achieve the same performance it would require a power 2000 times greater, i.e. $75\,\mathrm{MW}$, but it is pulled by power units rated at only $5.6\,\mathrm{MW}$. Why is this sufficient?

Figure 15   Le Shuttle

14 A fully laden *Eurostar* of 750 tonnes leaves the tunnel at $44\,\text{m}\,\text{s}^{-1}$ and takes 14 min to get to its top speed of $83\,\text{m}\,\text{s}^{-1}$.

(**a**) What tractive force was required?

(**b**) How many times smaller is the tractive force required to give the same acceleration to a train of mass 250 tonnes?

(**c**) How does your value for the tractive force compare with the braking force required to slow down the same train as it enters the Tunnel on the way back? (Ignore friction and drag.)

(**d**) For both *Eurostar* and the lighter train, drag at high speeds is about 40 kN. What difference does that fact make to your answers to (**a**) and (**b**)?

15 Suppose a train must come to a halt in 60 s.

(**a**) Find the braking force required to do this inside the Tunnel, where the maximum speed is $44\,\text{m}\,\text{s}^{-1}$, when the train is (**i**) a fully loaded *Shuttle*, mass 2400 tonnes and (**ii**) a *Eurostar*, mass 750 tonnes.

(**b**) Above ground the top speed of *Eurostar* is $83\,\text{m}\,\text{s}^{-1}$. If it stops in 3 min, what net braking force must be applied?

(**c**) In question 14 you calculated tractive forces. Compare the sizes of the forces required from the engine to those needed by the brakes.

Stopping distances

Once the brakes are applied to a fast-moving train it still takes some time to come to a stop, during which the train can move a considerable distance. Information about the probable stopping distance is critical for normal service in order to ensure that the train stops exactly alongside its platform. It is also important in deciding on the positions of signals. This type of question can be tackled using force and momentum and other equations of motion, but another approach, using energy, is more direct.

Imagine that a train of mass m is moving, at an initial speed u, before it is brought to a standstill by a force, F, acting in the opposite direction to its motion. All the kinetic energy, E_k, of the train is transferred by the work of the resultant braking force. We can use

work done = energy transferred

and

work done = force × distance moved in direction of force

Let Δs be the distance covered while the brakes are applied. Since the force acts along the direction of motion, we have

$$-F\Delta s = \Delta E_k = \left(\frac{1}{2}mv^2\right) - \left(\frac{1}{2}mu^2\right)$$

Since the final kinetic energy of this train is zero

$$-F\Delta s = -\frac{1}{2}mu^2 \qquad (3)$$

Study note

You met this idea in the AS unit *Higher, Faster, Stronger*. You might wish to refer back to that earlier work now.

Rearranging equation (3), the stopping distance for a known brake system can be calculated from:

$$\Delta s = \frac{mu^2}{2F}$$

QUESTIONS

16 (a) Calculate the stopping distance for a *Shuttle* train that is partly loaded and has a mass 2100 tonnes; it is stopped from a speed of 40 m s^{-1} by a braking force of 1.2 MN.

(b) A *Eurostar*, mass 750 t, is travelling at 80 m s^{-1} and must stop within 1500 m. What force is required?

(c) If there is a drag force of 40 kN at a speed of 80 m s^{-1}, suggest what difference that would make to your answers to (a) and (b).

17 (a) How long would it take the *Eurostar* in question 16 to come to rest?

(b) What would its acceleration be?

18 (a) The speed of a train is doubled. What is the change in (i) its momentum and (ii) its kinetic energy?

(b) Suppose two trains are travelling at the same speed but one has twice the mass of the other. What is the ratio of (i) their momenta and (ii) their kinetic energies?

We could go on with all the possible combinations of initial speed, mass of train and distance to station, and calculate the braking force required to stop in time. It would require far too many hours at your calculator. In Activity 6 you will let a computer take the strain.

ACTIVITY 6 **Stop the train**

Set up spreadsheets to calculate the braking forces required to stop a *Eurostar* train within a specified distance or time. The initial speed could be anything up to 300 km h^{-1}. Analyse any patterns that you find by plotting graphs from your spreadsheets.

So far, we have dealt only with situations involving trains. However, the same approaches can be used to analyse the motion of any object – as is the case in Activity 7, which uses data from the Highway Code.

In the Highway Code there is a table of stopping distances for cars travelling at different speeds (Figure 16). It is there to inform drivers on the correct distance to allow between themselves and the vehicle in front in case they have to make an emergency stop. The figures include an allowance for a delay between recognising danger and applying the brakes – the thinking time.

Shortest stopping distances

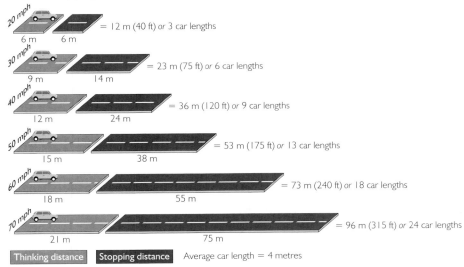

20 mph
6 m   6 m   = 12 m (40 ft) *or* 3 car lengths

30 mph
9 m   14 m   = 23 m (75 ft) *or* 6 car lengths

40 mph
12 m   24 m   = 36 m (120 ft) *or* 9 car lengths

50 mph
15 m   38 m   = 53 m (175 ft) *or* 13 car lengths

60 mph
18 m   55 m   = 73 m (240 ft) *or* 18 car lengths

70 mph
21 m   75 m   = 96 m (315 ft) *or* 24 car lengths

| Thinking distance | Stopping distance | Average car length = 4 metres |

Figure 16   *Table of stopping distances from the Highway Code*

ACTIVITY **7**   **Highway Code**

Use the information from Figure 16 and set up a spreadsheet or use your calculator to find out the values assumed for thinking time, acceleration and braking force for a typical car.

Data:
30 mph $\approx$ 13 m s^{-1}
Mass of typical car $\approx$ 1 t

An uphill struggle

It is important that Channel Tunnel trains do not get stuck – especially not underground. The engine specifications for Channel Tunnel trains particularly mention that the two locomotives must be able to restart the train from rest with an acceleration of 0.13 m s^{-2} up the steepest slope on the track (Figure 17). This section has a gradient of 1 in 90. If one locomotive fails the other must still be able to restart the train, albeit at a reduced speed.

In such a situation, the forces do not all act along the same direction. In order to analyse what's going on, you need to resolve force vectors into components.

Study note

You met components of vectors in the AS unit *Higher, Faster, Stronger*. You might wish to look back at this work before you tackle questions 19 and 20.

Figure 17   *Hauling a train uphill*

QUESTIONS

19 (**a**) How much tractive force is required to give the specified acceleration to a fully loaded *Shuttle* on the flat against a constant friction force of 40 kN? (*Shuttle* mass 2400 t.)

(**b**) If the train stops on a slope of 1 in 90 how much forward tractive force does it need to exert to stay still, i.e. just stop rolling back? (Use $g = 9.8\,\mathrm{N\,kg^{-1}}$.)

(**c**) Combine your answers to determine the total force needed to accelerate the train from rest (with the required acceleration) on this slope.

(**d**) Using equation (2) find how much time it takes for the train in (**c**) to reach a speed of $44\,\mathrm{m\,s^{-1}}$. Check that you get the same answer using $v = u + at$.

(**e**) (**i**) If a single locomotive has a tractive force of 400 kN what acceleration can it produce on the slope?

(**ii**) How long is it before the *Shuttle* speed reaches $44\,\mathrm{m\,s^{-1}}$?

(**iii**) How far has it travelled?

20 Suppose a *Shuttle* loses all engine power at the lowest point in the Channel Tunnel when it is travelling at $44\,\mathrm{m\,s^{-1}}$ and has 25 km to travel along a 1 in 90 slope to get up and out.

(**a**) Assuming no friction, would the train be able to free-wheel to the surface?

(**b**) If the drag forces average 30 kN, how far will the free-wheeling train travel?

3.3 *Motors*

In section 3.1 we mentioned that *Eurostar* depended on electrical motors and brakes to operate at its extremely high speeds. The motors and braking systems of Channel Tunnel trains exploit electricity and magnetism to generate an **electromagnetic force** that drive motors and to recover some the energy 'lost' during braking.

Study note

Brakes are the subject of section 3.4.

ACTIVITY 8 **Brush up on magnetism**

Use some permanent magnets and a current-carrying coil to review your knowledge of the nature and behaviour of magnetic fields.

In an electric motor, the magnetic effect of a current is used to drive and maintain the rotation of the wheels. Activities 9 and 10 build up the basic principles behind the working of an electric motor.

ACTIVITY 9 **An electromagnetic force**

Use the arrangement shown in Figure 18 to explore the force on a current-carrying conductor when it is in a magnetic field. Use a top pan balance to measure the size of the force between an electric current in a wire and a magnetic field (Figure 19). Vary the conditions to show how the size of the force varies with the length of wire, the strength of field and the size of the current.

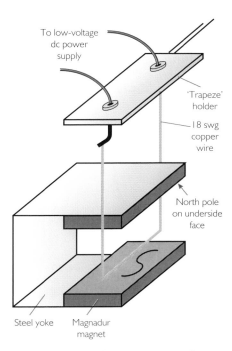

Figure 18 *Demonstrating the direction of an electromagnetic force*

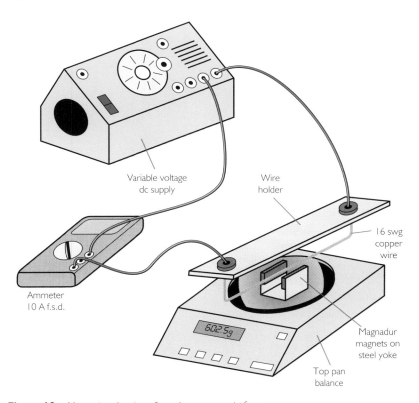

Figure 19 *Measuring the size of an electromagnetic force*

The results of the first part of Activity 9 are usually expressed in a rule known as **Fleming's left-hand rule**. The thumb and first two fingers of the left hand are held so that they are all at right angles to each other, like the corner of a box (see Figure 20). If the **f**irst finger points in the direction of the magnetic **f**ield and the se**c**ond finger points in the direction of the **c**urrent, then the thu**m**b shows the direction of the **m**otion and therefore of the force.

The size of the force

Several factors determine the size of the force: the strength of the magnet, the size of the current and the length of the wire. Experiments such as the second part of Activity 9 lead to the conclusion that the size of the force, F, on a wire is proportional to:

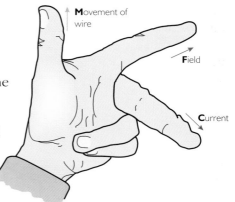

Figure 20 *Fleming's left-hand rule*

- the current, I, in the wire,
- the length of wire, ℓ, that lies within the magnetic field,
- the strength of the magnetic field.

and that F is a maximum when the current is at right angles to the field and zero when the current and field are parallel. The force still acts in a direction that is at right angles to both the current and the field, but its magnitude decreases as the angle between field and current is reduced.

When the field and current are at right angles, the relationship could be written as

$$F = kI\ell m$$

where k is a constant of proportionality and m represents the strength of the magnets. In practice, though, this relationship is used to *define* what we mean by the strength of the magnetic field and, rather than introducing an extra constant, we express it as

$$F = BI\ell \qquad\qquad (4)$$

where the symbol B represents the **magnetic flux density** (loosely speaking, the 'strength' of the field). The SI unit of magnetic flux density is the tesla, T (named after Nikola Tesla, 1856–1943, Croatian-American physicist). $1\,\text{T} = 1\,\text{N}\,\text{A}^{-1}\,\text{m}^{-1}$. A field of $1\,\text{T}$ containing a wire of length $1\,\text{m}$ carrying $1\,\text{A}$ at right angles to the field will produce a force of $1\,\text{N}$ on the wire. How large is a tesla? Very large as it happens. The magnetic field of the Earth is typically about $50\,\mu\text{T}$ and most laboratory solenoids produce a few mT at their centres.

We use the term **magnetic field** to describe the three-dimensional region of space where the magnet has some influence, but the term 'flux density' requires some explanation, as 'flux' is a word generally associated with flow – you met it in the AS unit *Technology in Space*, where it was used to describe the 'flow' of energy associated with radiation. The same word is used to describe the flow of fluids. The formal language to describe electromagnetism was developed by Michael Faraday (1791–1867), and he adopted the term flux because there are some similarities between the mathematical descriptions of magnetic field patterns and fluid flow patterns. If you think of a magnetic field plotted out by field lines, then B represents the density of these lines – where the lines are closer together the magnetic flux density is higher. Loosely speaking, the magnetic flux density is related to the number of lines crossing a given area.

Angles

To see how the size of the force varies with angle between field and current, we need to note that magnetic field and current are both vectors – they have direction as well as size. Imagine a magnetic field acting vertically down into this page. Now add an imaginary wire running along the foot of the page. If the current goes left to right the wire will want to move up the page (as described by Fleming's left-hand rule). Now let the side of the page lift up so your imaginary 'wire' slopes uphill at an angle θ to the vertical. Only the component of magnetic field at right angles to the wire, $B \sin \theta$, produces a force. The component $B \cos \theta$ is parallel to the wire and ineffective. (Alternatively, you can think of the current being resolved into components $I \sin \theta$ and $I \cos \theta$ perpendicular and parallel to the field – it comes to the same thing.) See Figure 21. The full version of equation (4) now becomes

$$F = BI\ell \sin \theta \qquad\qquad (4a)$$

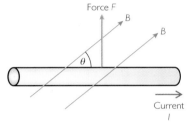

Figure 21 *Angles and the electromagnetic force*

─ QUESTIONS ───

21 There is a current in each of the wires shown in Figure 22. State the direction of the force on the wire in each case.

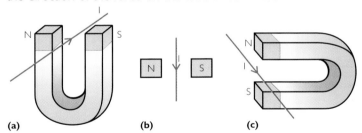

(a)　　　　**(b)**　　　　**(c)**

Figure 22 *Diagram for question 21*

22 The flux density between the poles of a powerful electromagnet is 2 T. What is the force exerted on 10 mm of wire carrying 4 A when the wire is (**a**) at right angles to the field, (**b**) parallel to the field and (**c**) at an angle of 30° to the field?

23 A horizontal wire of length 100 mm lies perpendicular to the field between the poles of a magnet. When a current of 5.0 A is passed through the wire, it is pushed vertically upwards. A rider of mass 15 g placed on the wire just brings it back to its original position. Calculate the mean magnetic flux density between the poles of the magnet ($g = 9.8 \, \text{N kg}^{-1}$).

A force that just kicks a wire into or out of a horseshoe magnet is not sufficient to move a train from Waterloo to Brussels. The wheels have to keep turning for hours, driven by forces acting to produce a turning effect – a **torque**. Figure 23 and Activity 10 show how a force on a wire can produce a torque that will maintain the rotation of an axle. This is the basis of a simple electric motor.

When a wire is wound into a coil and the current switched on the two faces have magnetic poles. Freely suspend such a coil and place it at an angle to a magnetic field, and the pull of attraction between opposite poles will turn the coil. That is the first stage of a continuously moving motor. Unfortunately the turning stops once the coil faces its opposite poles. This problem goes away if the current then reverses, since the poles are then on the opposite faces of the coil and the coil has to move on. In the following activity you will look at motors. The paper clip version maintains rotation by inertia – the coil turns past the place where it is facing the poles because it is moving rapidly and there is nothing to stop it. The more elaborate split ring version is more similar to the construction of working motors.

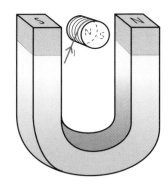

Figure 23 *A current-carrying coil in a magnetic field*

ACTIVITY 10 **A simple electric motor**

Construct a simple motor such as one of those shown in Figure 24. If you are working with other groups of students, compete to see whose motor can rotate for more than 30 s.

Motors have their own vocabulary: armature, split ring commutator, brushes, etc. Use this activity to make sure that you know and recognise them.

As an optional extension, use the motor demonstration program at this website:

http://home.a-city.de/walter.fendt/phe/electricmotor.htm

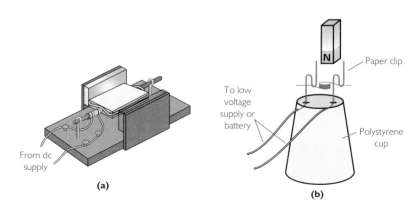

Figure 24 *Simple electric motors: (a) the Westminster model, (b) the paper clip model*

┌ QUESTION ───────────────────────────

24 The *Eurostar* demands very large forces from its motors (around 400 kN). Assume the engineers have designed a modified motor of the sort you have met in Activity 10. Using equation (4), make estimates for the necessary sizes of the quantities involved if the forces are to be anything approaching the right order of magnitude. (There is one extra quantity you need to include – think back to the construction of the coils.)

3.4 Brakes

The motor effect can get *Eurostar* going but doesn't look promising as a means of stopping a train. And, as you have seen, it takes just as much force to give a negative acceleration as a positive one. Activity 11 shows you how it is possible to make magnetic brakes. Such a braking system was considered for the *Advanced Passenger Train* but at the time was not found to be effective.

ACTIVITY 11	**Eddy current braking**

Use the apparatus shown in Figure 25 to explore the strange effects of magnetic brakes.

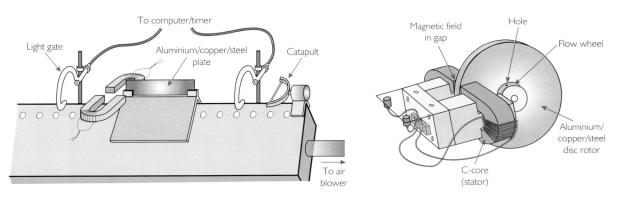

Figure 25 *Diagrams for Activity 11*

In Activity 11 you saw examples of **eddy current** braking. Many lorries and coaches use this method for their initial braking at high speed. In a wire circuit the path of the electrons is clearly round the wire but, if the conducting material is a whole thick sheet of metal, the possible loops for a flow of electrons are not so clear. Indeed, in the changing situations we are talking about here, the eddies of current change path from one minute to the next (Figure 26), just like the swirls of water (eddies) in a fast-moving river.

Each temporary current loop produces its own magnetic field and hence gives rise to forces of attraction and repulsion between it and the external magnet. But how do the eddy currents arise in the first place? In order to produce a current, an emf is required. One way to provide an emf is to use a battery or a solar panel, but

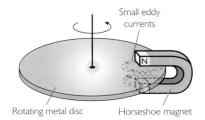

Figure 26 *Eddy currents*

as you will see in Activity 12, an emf can also be produced using magnetism – this effect is called **electromagnetic induction**, and the emf and current thus produced are often referred to as an **induced emf** and an **induced current**.

ACTIVITY 12 **Electromagnetic induction**

Use the apparatus shown in Figure 27 to show how a current can be induced in a wire using magnetism. Explore the factors that affect the size of the induced emf and current.

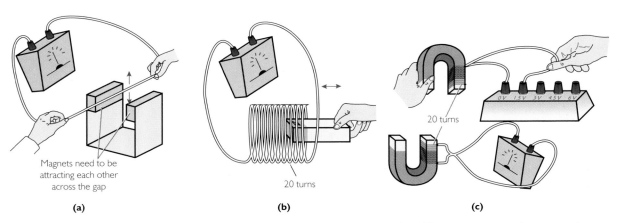

Figure 27 *Demonstrations of electromagnetic induction: (a) moving a wire in a magnetic field, (b) moving a magnet relative to a coil, (c) changing a magnetic field in a coil.*

We can now describe some of the properties of electromagnetic induction, i.e. when there is relative motion between a conductor and a magnetic field an electromotive force is induced in the circuit. In each case there is an induced emf when there is a change in the magnetic field around the wire and the size of the induced emf, $\mathscr{E}$, is proportional to:

- the strength of magnetic field
- the rate at which the wire or coil is moved, or the rate at which the magnet is moved
- the number of wire loops or turns on the coil.

The emf changes direction if the magnet is reversed, or the direction of movement is reversed.

In the third part of Activity 12 you saw that an emf can be induced in one solenoid when the current in another, nearby, solenoid is changed. Again, the key point is that an emf is induced in the first solenoid because it is in a changing magnetic field – only now the change is made electrically rather than by moving a magnet or the coil.

Laws of electromagnetic induction

We can make the above descriptions more formal using Faraday's way of describing magnetic fields. Think first of the situation when an emf is induced by moving a magnet into a single loop of wire

(Figure 28), and picture the magnet's field lines. When the magnet is some distance from the loop, only a few lines thread through the loop, but as the magnet approaches the coil, the field within the loop becomes stronger – more lines thread through the loop. Faraday expressed the 'amount of field' within a loop in terms of the **magnetic flux** enclosed by (or 'linking') the loop. For a (flat) loop square-on to the field direction,

magnetic flux = magnetic flux density × area of loop

Flux is usually given the symbol Φ (the Greek letter phi), so in symbols:

$$\Phi = BA \tag{5}$$

where A is the area of the loop. If you think of B as the number of magnetic field lines per square metre, then Φ is the total number of lines enclosed by the loop. The SI unit of magnetic flux is the weber, Wb. $1\,\text{Wb} = 1\,\text{T}\,\text{m}^2 = 1\,\text{N}\,\text{A}^{-1}\,\text{m}$. Magnetic flux density is sometimes expressed in units of $\text{Wb}\,\text{m}^{-2}$ rather than tesla – the two are exactly equivalent.

If the normal to the loop makes an angle θ to the field as in Figure 28(b), then equation (5) becomes

$$\Phi = BA \cos\theta \tag{5a}$$

The size of the induced emf

Faraday noted that the size of the emf, $\mathscr{E}$, induced in a loop is proportional to the rate at which the flux within the loop is changed; this relationship is known as **Faraday's law of electromagnetic induction** and is written mathematically as

$$\mathscr{E} \propto \frac{\Delta\Phi}{\Delta t} \tag{6}$$

If a coil contains N turns (N loops) of wire, then an emf is induced in each loop; as the loops are connected in series, the net emf from the whole coil is multiplied by N, and equation (6) becomes

$$\mathscr{E} \propto \frac{\Delta(N\Phi)}{\Delta t} \tag{6a}$$

$N\Phi$ is called the **magnetic flux linkage**. For a coil with more than one loop, Faraday's law states that the size of the induced emf is proportional to the rate of change of flux linkage. Flux linkage is sometimes given the unit weber-turns to distinguish it from the flux through a single loop – but N is just a number so 1 weber-turn has the same dimensions as 1 weber.

In SI units, i.e. with Φ in webers, t in seconds and $\mathscr{E}$ in volts, the size of the emf is *equal* to the rate of change of flux linkage – not merely directly proportional. However, there is one important point that we have not yet included, and that is the direction of the induced emf (and hence of the induced current). Here, an energy argument is useful.

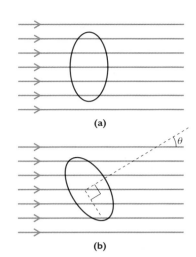

Figure 28   *A single loop of wire in a magnetic field (a) square-on (b) at an angle*

Study note

The normal is a line at 90° to the plane of the loop. You met the term in the AS unit *The Sound of Music* in the context of reflection and refraction at a surface.

Maths reference

Dimensions
See Maths note 2.5

The direction of the induced emf

People have long searched for a perpetual motion machine, i.e. one that needs no input of energy to keep on turning for all eternity. It's a pipe dream, of course. At first sight the demonstration of induction in Activity 12 appears to offer untold riches. For example, in a bicycle dynamo, movement of a coil inside a magnet produces an emf that drives a current through the coil which, from Activity 10, you know will make it rotate inside the magnet. As the coil moves faster, it will generate a larger emf, which in turn will drive a larger current making the coil rotate faster still... and so on... A small initial movement would produce runaway motion, apparently generating kinetic energy out of nothing. So what is the catch? It is that the emf is, in practice, always induced in a direction such that any forces will oppose the motion that produces it. A wire moving into the magnet is slowed down by a repelling action. A coil rotating clockwise is opposed by a torque that is trying to rotate it anti-clockwise.

Lenz's law sums up the situation. 'The direction of the current induced in a conductor by moving it relative to a magnetic field is such that its own field opposes the motion.' Mathematically, Lenz's law is expressed by inserting a minus sign into equation (6):

$$\mathscr{E} = -\frac{\Delta(N\Phi)}{\Delta t} \qquad (6b)$$

thus producing an expression that encapsulates both Faraday's and Lenz's laws. In calculus notation:

$$\mathscr{E} = -\frac{\mathrm{d}(N\Phi)}{\mathrm{d}t} \qquad (6c)$$

The change in flux linkage can be brought about by a change in any or all of N, B or A. If only one of these is changed, then we can rewrite equation (6) in yet more ways. Changing B only:

$$\mathscr{E} = -NA\frac{\mathrm{d}B}{\mathrm{d}t} \qquad (6d)$$

changing A only:

$$\mathscr{E} = -NB\frac{\mathrm{d}A}{\mathrm{d}t} \qquad (6e)$$

or changing N only:

$$\mathscr{E} = -\Phi\frac{\mathrm{d}N}{\mathrm{d}t} \qquad (6f)$$

QUESTIONS

25 Show that the SI units on the left-hand side of equation (6) (any version) are the same as those on the right.

26 A magnetic flux of 10 Wb passes through a coil of 50 turns. The flux decreases to zero over 2.0 s. What would be the size of the emf induced in the coil?

27 A 10 turn coil has a cross-sectional area of 0.03 m². It is placed so that the plane of the coil is perpendicular to a field of magnetic flux density 2 T. It is then rotated through 90° in 0.2 s so that it lies parallel to the field. What size emf would be induced in the coil?

28 If large currents are turned on or off near your radio you may hear a crack or a click. Suggest an explanation for this.

Another look at electromagnetic induction

We started by considering a single wire loop that can be extended to make a coil with many turns, but equation (6) also applies to all other ways of inducing an emf. In Figure 27(c), changing the current on one solenoid changes the magnetic flux linking the other solenoid; in Figure 27(a), the movement of the wire between the poles of a magnet changes the flux linking the circuit made by the wire and the meter. It is sometimes useful, too, to consider an isolated section of wire as shown in Figure 29, moving in a magnetic field. The wire is straight, has a length ℓ, and moves at velocity v in a direction that is at right angles to its length and to the direction of a uniform field B. Notice the symbol that represents the field (or any other vector) directed into the page; think of an arrow travelling away from you – you see its feathers, which are represented by a cross. A field (or other vector) directed towards you out of the page would be represented by a dot in a circle (the tip of the arrow).

Imagine that the wire is connected in a circuit. In a time Δt, the wire moves through a distance $v\Delta t$, and so the area of the circuit changes by an amount

$$\Delta A = \ell v \Delta t$$

The motion will thus give rise to an emf which, from equation (6e) with $N = 1$, is given by

$$\mathcal{E} = -\frac{B\ell v \Delta t}{\Delta t} = B\ell v \tag{7}$$

This emf could be detected as a potential difference by a voltmeter connected between the ends of the wire. If the wire is connected into a complete circuit, the induced emf will give rise to an induced current whose size will depend on the emf and on the resistance of the circuit.

Inspection of Figure 29 and a consideration of Lenz's law provides us with another useful way of predicting the direction of the induced emf and current. We know that the electromagnetic force due to the induced current must oppose the motion, i.e. it must act to the left on Figure 29. Using Fleming's left-hand rule with the first finger pointing into the page and the thumb pointing to the left shows that the current must be flowing towards the top of the page.

The direction of the induced current can be deduced directly, using **Fleming's right-hand rule** (see Figure 30). Now the thumb points in the direction of the motion giving rise to the induced current, and the first and second fingers have the same meaning as in Fleming's left-hand rule. But it is easy to confuse left and right

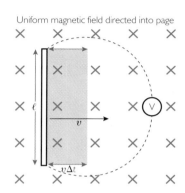

Uniform magnetic field directed into page

Figure 29 *Moving an isolated wire in a magnetic field*

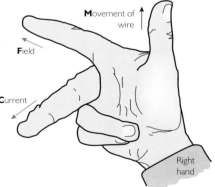

Figure 30 *Fleming's right-hand rule*

and forget which hand to use in which situation, so it might be wise just to remember the left-hand rule for the motor effect, and use Lenz's law to deduce the direction of an induced current.

29 Imagine an aeroplane as two metal conductors (the fuselage and wing tip to wing tip) connected together in the shape of a cross. What are the electromagnetic consequences as it flies towards the Earth's magnetic north pole?

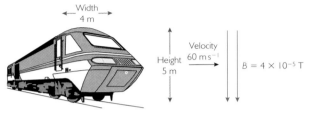

30 At a certain location, the Earth's magnetic flux density has a vertical component of 4×10^{-5} T. The metal body of a train is 4 m wide and 5 m high, and the train is moving at $60\,\text{m s}^{-1}$ (see Figure 31).

(**a**) State the direction of any induced emf and current resulting from moving across the vertical component of the Earth's magnetic field.

(**b**) Calculate the size of the induced emf that is likely to develop.

Figure 31 *A moving train for question 30*

Back to brakes

We are now in a position to explain eddy current braking such as you saw in Activity 11 when a metal disc rotated in a magnetic field. The motion of the metal in the field induces emfs in the disc that vary according to the local flux density and the speed of the motion. The net effect is to drive eddy currents in the disc. These currents, plus the external magnetic field, give rise to electromagnetic forces that, by Lenz's law, must oppose the motion, i.e. they retard the disc.

31 (**a**) A bicycle brake operates by a block of rubber being pressed against the rim of the wheel. It is a contact brake. Is an eddy current brake a contact brake?

(**b**) Is an eddy current brake any use as a parking brake? Explain.

32 In designing an eddy current brake, how would you design the disc so as to ensure that the induced currents were large?

33 From a given speed, any braking system must allow strong or gentle braking. Suggest one way to get this kind of control from eddy current braking.

Electromagnetism is used to good effect in designing braking systems in modern trains. The following short article from the June 1992 issue of *Rail News* describes the braking systems on a class of trains known as 465 (Figure 32).

Brakes save wear and tear

Trains have three braking systems: three-step air braking, rheostatic braking and regenerative braking, electric braking being selectable.

Figure 32 *A Class 465 train*

Air brakes are standard three-step automatic electrically controlled 'energise to release' air brakes with enhanced emergency braking.

Rheostatic braking is an electric braking system. When braking is selected the traction motors are made to act as generators, producing current which is fed to braking resistances (rheostats) similar to electric fire elements. They glow and produce thermal energy when current is passed through them. Generating current in this way produces a retarding effect on the traction motor armatures, which acts through the traction motor gearing to individual wheels and slows them down. Thus the kinetic energy of the train is converted into thermal energy. The rheostatic circuits ensure that the braking effect produced in the motors matches the braking rate selected by the driver.

As speed falls, however, the retarding effect diminishes. Special circuitry – electronic on the Class 465 – detects this and makes up the shortfall in braking effect by progressively blending in the air brakes.

Regenerative braking operates on a similar principle to rheostatic braking but with the difference that the current produced by the motors is fed back into the third rail and used to power other trains. If there are no trains to accept the current, the braking circuitry detects this and switches to rheostatic braking.

Regenerative braking uses a dynamo to 'recover lost energy' by generating a current while braking. Figure 33 shows a circuit in which a motor, when connected to a power supply, turns a flywheel. If no power is connected to it, the motor runs as a dynamo as long as it is rotated by something. Activity 13 demonstrates this.

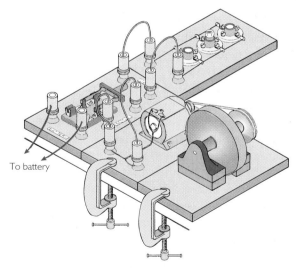

To battery

Figure 33   *Circuit for demonstrating regenerative braking*

ACTIVITY 13   **Electrical braking**

Use the apparatus shown in Figure 33 to demonstrate regenerative braking. First allow the flywheel to reach a steady speed, then switch off the power and allow it to free-wheel to a stop. Repeat, but this time connect the circuit through the light bulb when the power is switched off. Note any differences, and explain them in terms of energy transfer.

3.5 Getting the voltage right

The European challenge

At the time of writing (2000) the trains from Waterloo to France
and Belgium have to cope with the vagaries of an electrical power
supply system that is radically different in the three countries. The
line from London to the Tunnel is not yet a high-speed line so its
third rail provides 750 V dc, not the main-line higher voltages. In
France and in the Tunnel it is 25 000 V ac. In Belgium the supply is
taken from an overhead line – this time at 3000 V dc. Add to these
problems the fact that the motors themselves run at 1500 V, and
we have another problem for physics to solve.

Flexible power conversion equipment is needed to convert the
electricity into a suitable supply of 1500 V. First the voltage size is
adjusted, then the ac to dc bit is addressed. When regenerative braking
is used the whole problem goes into reverse and the generated power
has to be returned to the power lines at a suitable voltage.

This is done with the help of **transformers** (Figure 34). A
transformer is a device consisting of two electrically insulated coils,
of differing numbers of turns, both wound on the same common
laminated (layered) iron core that passes through the centre of
each coil, often forming a complete loop. In Activity 12 a changing
magnetic field in one solenoid induced a current in a nearby
solenoid. It was a case of a sudden surge and that was that.
But if the magnetic field is produced by an alternating current
in one solenoid, the magnetic field also changes continuously
and so produces a continuous but alternating current in the
second solenoid. To get the largest effect possible the
solenoid coils are wound one on top of the other. This means
that all the field from the first solenoid threads through the
second, thus increasing the flux linkage between the two
solenoids, which is further improved by using a core of
so-called soft iron (see Figure 35).

The primary solenoid has N_p turns and is connected to an input
voltage, V_p. An output voltage of V_s is obtained from the secondary
coil, where the number of turns is N_s. Activity 14 illustrates the
relationship between the voltages, currents, powers and the turns
ratio N_p/N_s.

Figure 34 *Transformer used in a rail
power supply*

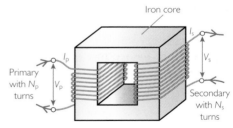

Figure 35 *A transformer circuit*

Build circuits with C-cores and coils or with the software *Crocodile
Clips* to produce transformers and investigate the relationships
between input and output voltage, current and power.

Study note

The term 'soft' here refers to magnetic
properties. Soft iron can easily be
magnetised or demagnetised. (It is not soft
like putty.)

In Activity 14 you probably found that the ratio of the voltages equals the ratio of the numbers of turns

$$\frac{V_s}{V_p} = \frac{N_s}{N_p} \tag{8}$$

If N_s is greater than N_p this gives a **step-up transformer**, whereas a **step-down transformer** has N_s less than N_p.

In an ideal transformer, the transfer of energy from primary to secondary will be 100% efficient, so the output power is the same as the input power

$$V_p I_p = V_s I_s \tag{9}$$

Comparing equations (8) and (9) shows that

$$\frac{I_s}{I_p} = \frac{N_p}{N_s} \tag{10}$$

so a step-up transformer steps up the voltage but steps down the current. However, as you probably saw in Activity 14, a real transformer has an output power less than the input power and so the current ratio is less than predicted.

One reason for this is the core design. For 100% efficiency, all the magnetic flux from the primary should link the secondary coil; in practice this may not quite be the case. Also, not all the input power will be 'transformed' into electrical output power.

Some energy is wasted in heating the coils, and some in producing motion as parts of the transformer are repeatedly attracted to one another and released – this produces the characteristic low-frequency hum that you may have noticed in Activity 14. Question 37 identifies another way in which energy can be wasted in a transformer.

QUESTIONS

35 In France the electricity supply is at 25 kV, in Belgium it is 3000 V, but the motors require 1500 V. If the primary has 1000 turns, how many turns are required in the secondary coil for each country?

36 The Railtrack supply of 750 V is converted to ac and then stepped up for the 1500 V motors. The motor power is 1200 kW.

(**a**) What is the turns ratio?

(**b**) What is the primary current?

37 (**a**) When investigating the magnetic field of a coil carrying alternating current, a student notices that an iron nail on which the coil is wound becomes very hot. Explain the source of this heating. (Hint: look back to your work in section 3.4 of this unit.)

(**b**) The iron cores used for solenoids and transformers are normally laminated, i.e. made from thin layers of iron glued together, rather than from solid iron. Use your answer (**a**) to suggest a reason for this.

3.6 Summing up part 3

This has been a long part of the unit. After some revision work on mechanics in which you were introduced to the idea of momentum and reviewed your knowledge of vectors, you met two important areas of the physics of electricity and magnetism. You saw how a current-carrying wire can experience an electromagnetic force in a magnetic field, and how a changing magnetic field can give rise to electromagnetic induction.

Activities 15 and 16 are designed to take you back through some of the ideas you met earlier and at the same time they give you an opportunity to extend your knowledge of electromagnetism.

ACTIVITY 15 **More electromagnetism**

Explore some more examples of electromagnetism and electromagnetic induction. In each case, describe and explain your observations using *at least three* of the terms printed in bold in part 3 of this unit.

ACTIVITY 16 **Induction motor**

Construct and investigate an induction motor. Compare its operation with that of the motor that you used in Activity 10.

QUESTIONS

38 Imagine a situation where engineers were ignorant of the effects of electromagnetic induction and the Channel Tunnel was allowed to be lined with hoops of metal connected together. A *Eurostar* motor, as you have seen, has magnets as a vital element in its motor construction and is going to rush towards the tunnel at $44 \, \text{m s}^{-1}$. Why would this cause problems?

39 An aeroplane is travelling horizontally with a velocity of $268 \, \text{m s}^{-1}$ in a region where the vertical component of the Earth's field is $4.1 \times 10^{-5} \, \text{T}$ and the horizontal component is $1.8 \times 10^{-5} \, \text{T}$. If the wing span is $47 \, \text{m}$, find the size of the emf induced between the wing tips.

40 A rectangular coil with 100 turns, 5.0 cm by 8.0 cm, hangs in a vertical plane with a north–west to south–east orientation. A horizontal magnetic field of size $3.5 \, \mu\text{T}$ is aligned due north.

(**a**) What flux passes through the coil's area?

(**b**) What is the flux linkage through the coil?

(**c**) If the magnetic field through the coil collapses to zero in $0.10 \, \text{ms}$, find the size of the emf induced in the coil.

4 *Sensing speed*

In part 2 you saw how signals could be set by the train. It is no use having signals unless they are seen and acted upon by the drivers. The problem is to how get information to a fast-moving object reliably under all conditions. The key elements in the solution are the design of sensors and the electronics to decipher the outputs.

The driver of a train has access to computer-generated information about the journey. This is shown on a screen and includes a three-digit number, which is either a maximum allowable speed (if all is clear) or a target speed for the end of the block section (if slowing down is required). If a signal is flashing, it means that there will be a new signal at the beginning of the next block section, thus giving the driver some forewarning of a required change. For each block a new target speed is set. A graph modelling the projected journey ahead is shown in Figure 36 above the sequence of signals. This shows a *Shuttle* train that needs to be brought to rest from $140 \, \text{km h}^{-1}$.

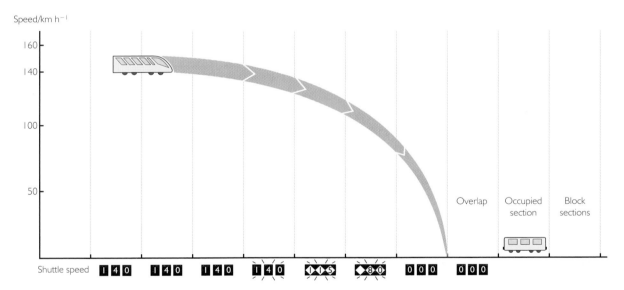

Figure 36 *Slowing down* Le Shuttle

The most important task of a driver is to control the train's speed, for example in anticipating a steep bend, the approach to a station or the speed limits of the Channel Tunnel. Speed is continuously monitored directly on the train and if the driver exceeds a maximum speed or ignores a target speed, automatic braking comes into effect operated by the on-board computer. Measuring speed is the subject of this part of the unit.

4.1 *Making and counting pulses*

You will probably have had some experience at GCSE using light gates to measure the linear speed of vehicles. Activity 17 introduces a similar method using magnetism.

ACTIVITY **17** **Sensing train speed**

Use a system of magnets and coils, such as shown in Figure 37, to show how electromagnetic induction can be used to sense the speed and acceleration of a model train. Figure 38 shows some typical results for you to analyse if you are unable to obtain your own.

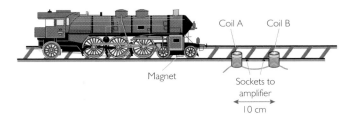

Figure 37 *An arrangement for sensing the speed of a model train*

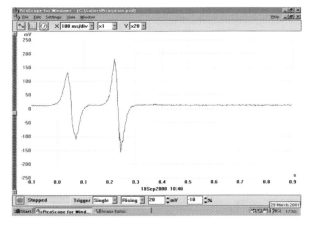

Figure 38 *Output from coils in Activity 17 displayed on Pico Technology Picoscope*

The arrangement in Activity 17 illustrates some basic principles of the inductive speed sensors used on trains, but because a practical speed sensor must have all its parts on the train, some modification is required. Each train has a coil set close to an axle, carrying a current that generates a magnetic field. A toothed wheel connected to the train's axle rotates close to the coil. As each metal tooth passes the coil it disturbs the coil's magnetic field, which in turn has the effect of briefly altering the current. This produces a series of current pulses – essentially a stream of digital (high/low) signals. The more pulses per unit time, the faster the train is moving. See Figure 39.

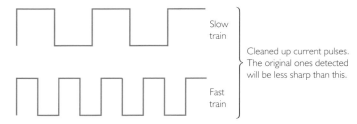

Figure 39 *Speed signal code*

Using the toothed wheel, the speed of a train can be automatically sensed by electromagnetic induction effects that create a series of current pulses. If the current is fed through a resistor, the pulses will produce a voltage signal. The pulses will start life as a fairly small, indistinct signal that can be 'sharpened' and amplified by electronic techniques as shown in Figure 40. You will see this as part of Activity 18.

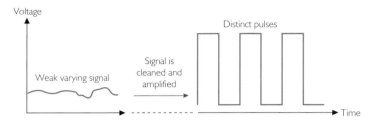

Figure 40   *Sharpening and amplifying the pulses*

ACTIVITY **18**   **Counting pulses**

Use *Alpha Kit* electronic component boards to make a model to demonstrate the use of a pulsed signal to determine a speed.

To get from a series of pulses to a speed we simply have to count the number of pulses occurring over a set time period. The way that pulses are counted is illustrated in Figure 41.

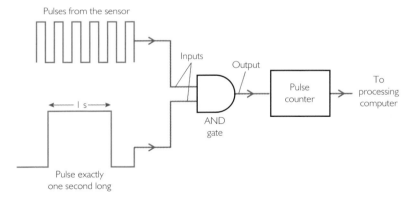

Figure 41   *Counting pulses*

The pulses from the sensor, together with a simultaneous voltage signal that stays high for exactly one second, are fed into a simple electronic device called an AND gate. (Both of these voltage signals are digital signals – signals that can only have one of two possible values, high/low represented as 1 and 0.)

The AND gate only gives a high output signal when both of its inputs are high. The result is that a pulse-train lasting exactly one second appears at the AND gate's output.

Connected to this output is an electronic pulse counter that will record the number of pulses that it receives during the one-second interval. This information can be sent as a digital signal to the rest of the processing electronics and then the counter can be reset, ready to receive the next burst of pulses.

4.2 Timing

In measuring speed electronically, one very important requirement is the ability to generate a voltage pulse that is exactly one second long. To do this, we can use devices called **capacitors**, which can store electric charge and release it at a precisely known and predictable rate. Such devices are the subject of this section.

Introducing capacitors

Capacitors are components that can store electrical charge. The simplest capacitor design consists of two parallel metal plates separated by an air gap, so capacitors are symbolised as two parallel lines, one of which may be shown as an open plate or with a positive sign to indicate which terminal of the capacitor should be connected nearest to the positive terminal of a power supply (see Figure 42).

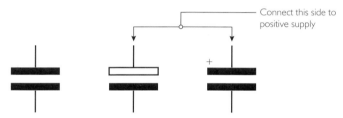

Figure 42   *Capacitor symbols*

Capacitors

Explore the way the current in a circuit changes as various capacitors are charged from a battery and then discharged using the circuit shown in Figure 43.

For a circuit as shown in Figure 44, when the switch is closed charge flows on to one side of the capacitor from the battery; an equal amount flows away from the other side of the capacitor into the other battery terminal. Charge flows until the potential difference across the plates becomes the same as that across the battery. The capacitor then has a charge $+Q$ on one side and $-Q$, on the other; in a sense it 'stores' a charge Q (though perhaps 'separates' would be a better word). The charge that a capacitor can store is proportional to the battery voltage:

$$Q \propto V$$

The ratio Q/V is constant, and is defined to be the **capacitance**, C, of the capacitor

$$Q = CV \tag{11}$$

Capacitance is the amount of charge stored per unit potential difference across the plates. The SI unit of capacitance is the farad,

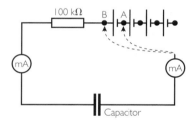

Figure 43   *Diagram for Activity 19*

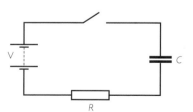

Figure 44   *Capacitor circuit*

F (named after Michael Faraday). $1\,F = 1\,C\,V^{-1}$. One farad is a very large capacitance. Capacitances generally range between 1 picofarad (pF) and 10 000 microfarads (μF).

If potential difference or voltage across the capacitor plates is too high, the insulation (called dielectric) between the plates may start to fail and start to conduct. For this reason capacitors are marked with a maximum working voltage above which the capacitor should not be operated.

Charging and discharging

In order to see how a capacitor can be used in a timing circuit, it is important to know what happens to voltage and current in a capacitor–resistor circuit as the capacitor accumulates charge and releases it. In Activity 20 you will investigate charging and discharging experimentally using a large-valued capacitor and resistor, which will slow down the changes in the circuit sufficiently so that they can be easily observed.

ACTIVITY **20** **Slow charge and discharge**

Observe the way voltages and currents change as a capacitor charges and discharges.

ACTIVITY **21** **Modelling charge and discharge**

Use *Crocodile Clips* to investigate more closely how the charging and discharging of a 100 μF capacitor through a 100 kΩ resistor affects the current and voltage in the circuit, and to see how capacitance and resistance values determine the time of charging and discharging.

In Activities 20 and 21, you have seen graphs representing the charge and discharge of a capacitor. They belong to a family of graphs known as **exponentials**. Many naturally occurring changes are exponential, as you will see when you study the units *The Medium is the Message* and *Reach for the Stars*. One important characteristic of an exponential discharge (or decay) graph is that *the changing quantity changes by equal fractions in equal times*. You should have seen this when you found the times for the voltage to halve, halve and halve again.

We will look at various ways in which the shape of a capacitor discharge graphs can be described mathematically; they are all equivalent to one another.

Figure 45 shows a capacitor, C, discharging through a resistor, R. The capacitor behaves rather like a cell with a changing terminal potential difference. This pd, V, is related to the charge, Q, stored on the capacitor.

$$V = \frac{Q}{C}$$

(equation 11)

Maths reference

SI prefixes
See Maths note 2.4

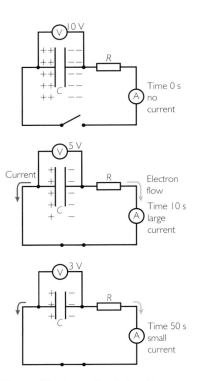

Figure 45 *A capacitor discharging through a resistor*

As the capacitor discharges, Q decreases and hence V also decreases. Since we also know that the current, I, in the resistor is related to the pd, we can write

$$I = \frac{V}{R} = \frac{Q}{RC} \qquad (12)$$

Since Q is decreasing, I must also be decreasing. Remembering that current is the rate of flow of charge

$$I = \frac{\Delta Q}{\Delta t}$$

we can write

$$\frac{\Delta Q}{\Delta t} = -\frac{Q}{RC} \qquad (13)$$

The negative sign indicates that the charge is decreasing with time.

If we are dealing with very small time intervals, we can use calculus notation

$$\frac{\mathrm{d}Q}{\mathrm{d}t} = -\frac{Q}{RC} \qquad (13a)$$

Equation (13) says that *the rate of flow of charge is proportional to the charge itself*. This is another important characteristic of exponential discharge. Equation (13) is actually equivalent to the 'equal fractions in equal times' pattern, as you can see by rearranging it:

$$\frac{\Delta Q}{Q} = -\frac{\Delta t}{RC} \qquad (13b)$$

This version tells us that the fraction $\dfrac{\Delta Q}{Q}$ is directly proportional to the time interval Δt.

ACTIVITY 22 **Exponential discharge**

Examine the discharge curve shown in Figure 46 and verify that it is exponential.

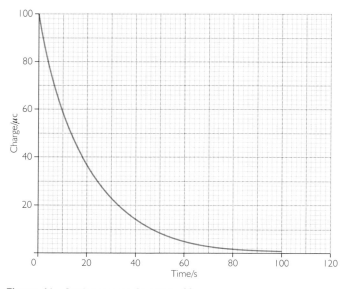

Figure 46 *Discharge curve for Activity 22*

Equation (13) describes a capacitor discharge curve by telling us how the gradient at any one time is related to the stored charge at that time. But it does not tell us directly how much charge is stored at any one time, or answer the most commonly asked questions like: 'how much charge is left after 0.5 s?' For this, we need another equation, which can be derived from equation (13) using calculus:

$$Q = Q_0 e^{-t/RC} \qquad (14)$$

Here Q_0 is the charge stored when $t = 0$, and e is a number known as the exponential number that arises from the maths: e $\approx$ 2.718. We can use equation (14) to tell us how the voltage and current change as well. Substituting $Q = CV$ (equation 11) and cancelling C, we get

$$V = V_0 e^{-t/RC} \qquad (15)$$

Then similarly using $I = \dfrac{V}{R}$ and cancelling R, we get

$$I = I_0 e^{-t/RC} \qquad (16)$$

In other words, the voltage and current also decrease exponentially.

Study note

If you are familiar with calculus you can show that the 'equal fractions in equal times' pattern can always be described by an expression such as equation (14).

Maths reference

Exponential changes
See Maths note 9.1

Exponential functions
See Maths note 9.2

QUESTIONS

41 (**a**) A 100 μF capacitor is discharged through a 250 kΩ resistor for 20 s. What fraction of its original charge will remain stored at this time?

(**b**) Initially the pd across the plates was 10 V. How much charge remained stored after the 20 s?

42 (**a**) By inspecting equation (13), argue convincingly that RC must have dimensions of time (and hence SI units of seconds).

(**b**) A capacitor, C, discharges through a resistor, R. What fraction of the starting voltage (or charge) will remain across the capacitor after a time equal to RC?

If you answered question 42 correctly, you should have seen that approximately 0.37 (or 37%) of the initial voltage or charge will remain on a capacitor after a period of time equal to RC. The time RC is called the **time constant** of the discharge and is used as a measure of how fast the resistor–capacitor combination discharges. It is sometimes represented by the Greek letter τ 'tau': $\tau = RC$.

As the charge and voltage drop by 37% in each interval of τ, we can argue that they never actually reach zero. In practice, provided the time interval is several times τ, we can say the capacitor is fully discharged. Question 43 and Activity 23 illustrate this.

ACTIVITY **23** **One step at a time**

Use a spreadsheet to examine the discharge of a capacitor over a succession of small time intervals.

43 (**a**) What percentage of a capacitor's initial charge will remain after 3 time constants?

(**b**) A student claims that a discharging capacitor is 'effectively fully discharged' after 5 time constants. Do a calculation and comment on this viewpoint.

44 Figure 47 shows a timing circuit. When the push-switch is pressed, the capacitor charges almost instantly. When the switch is released, it discharges more slowly through the resistor. As it does so, the voltage at the output falls as the pd across the capacitor falls.

(**a**) What is the voltage at the output after the push-switch is pressed?

(**b**) What is the time constant for the resistor–capacitor combination?

(**c**) What will be the output voltage after 5 s?

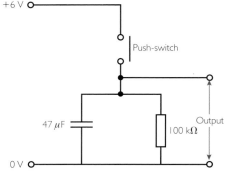

Figure 47 *Timing circuit for question 44*

An electronic timer

In question 44 you saw how a simple capacitor circuit might be used to produce a set time delay. In this section, we look at a small, electronic integrated circuit (chip), the 555 timer, which uses capacitor charge/discharge in a more versatile timing device.

An integrated circuit (IC) is simply a package that includes an array of electronic components miniaturised to fit on a single silicon 'chip'. The 555 IC is a very cheap and versatile chip that works on any dc supply from 5 to 15 V and can give out or take in a current up to 200 mA (see Figure 48). It is particularly useful as a simple timing device since it can easily be adapted to form part of either an **astable** or a **monostable** circuit.

An astable circuit has no stable output states. It continually switches from its first state to its second state, and back again. The two states are usually a high voltage and zero volts. (An example of an astable circuit would be that operating the flashing lights warning of a train or on a pedestrian crossing.) The 555 chip is used to control the switching period.

A monostable circuit has one stable output state. This means the output will never leave that state unless it is switched, and when changed to the other state it is unstable and will return eventually to the first, stable, state after a pre-determined time delay. (An example of a monostable circuit might be the timing circuit to set a video recorder to switch on to record a chosen programme.) The 555 chip is used to set the length of the time delay.

It is not necessary to know the details of how the 555 IC works; it is sufficient to know that the eight pins are organised as shown in Figure 49. The 555 IC contains the equivalent of 40 resistors and transistors, and needs just an external resistor or two and a capacitor to make up the final circuit. It is these external

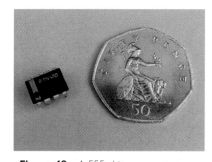

Figure 48 *A 555 chip*

components that are used to set the required time delays (monostable) or time periods (astable).

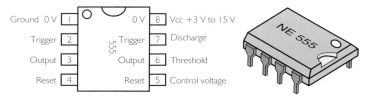

Figure 49   *The pins on a 555 chip*

Figure 50 shows how to connect a 555 chip to form a monostable circuit. When push-switch, S, is momentarily pressed, the stable zero volts output of the monostable goes 'high' – close to the supply voltage, V_S. It then stays high for a certain time period, T, before falling back to zero volts. The time period is determined by the size of resistor R and capacitor C; it is controlled by how fast C charges through R. The time period, T, can be approximated to a reasonable degree of accuracy by the formula:

$$T = 1.1\,RC$$

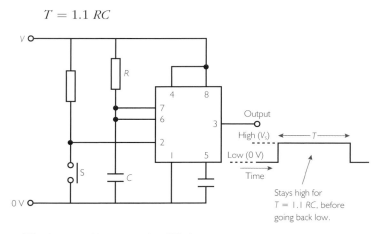

Figure 50   *A monostable circuit with a 555 chip*

ACTIVITY **24** **Modelling a 555 monostable circuit**

Use *Crocodile Clips* to model the operation of a monostable circuit incorporating a 555 chip.

Near the start of this part of the unit we considered a method of counting pulses to determine the speed of a train and said that it was necessary to create a voltage pulse exactly one second long. Now that we have the means to do this accurately, we are in a position to go back to our model with a greater understanding.

ACTIVITY **25** **Counting revolutions**

Either re-assemble the *Alpha* apparatus used in Activity 18 and make sure you understand how the boards illustrate the functions of parts of the speedometer, or model a counting circuit with *Crocodile Clips*.

4.3 Summing up part 4

In this part of the unit you have learned about capacitors and about some properties of exponential graphs, and seen how the discharge of a capacitor can be used to control a timing circuit.

ACTIVITY 26 **Summing up part 4**

Check through your work from this part of the unit and make sure you know the meaning of all the terms highlighted in bold.

QUESTIONS

45 A model rail enthusiast wants to create a block signalling system that gives a red light when a train is occupying one section of track, and give a green light 10 seconds after the train has left the block. The circuit is shown in Figure 51.

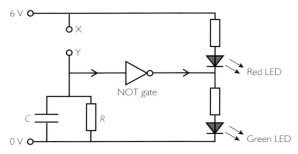

Figure 51 *Model railway circuit for question 45*

X and Y are connected to each of the metal tracks in the 'block' to be monitored.

The NOT gate turns an analogue (continuously varying) input voltage into a digital output signal. If the input voltage to the NOT gate is above 1.5 V, the output is low (close to 0 V), and if the input is below 1.5 V the output is high (around 6 V).

The LEDs (light-emitting diodes) emit light only when the potential *decreases* in the direction of the arrow that forms part of their symbol.

(**a**) Explain how the circuit works.

(**b**) Show that, for a time delay of 10 s, $RC \approx 7.2$ s.

(**c**) Suppose the circuit was made with $R = 1000$ kΩ and $C = 10 \, \mu$F. Comment on whether this would produce a time delay that was too short or too long.

---

5 Structure and safety

5.1 How safe is the Channel Tunnel?

Train passengers want to get to their destination on time and in safety. As trains move ever faster and travel in more extreme conditions the potential for danger increases, but so does the skill of the engineers applying physics in the modern world.

Despite what some people think, flooding is not a major concern as the amount of sea water actually seeping into the tunnel is very slight; some of it evaporates and pumps remove the rest. Fire is the biggest worry and there is a complex system of fire detection, suppression and smoke control in place. In the case of a fire, the passengers would be sealed off and would breathe recycled air until the fire was under control.

General wear and tear is also a concern. High speeds and heavy loads deform and move the track under a train. Tiny kinks and dips develop and become exaggerated with time, like potholes in roads. Eventually they can lead to the train swaying about (which disturbs the passengers) and, if left for a very long time, they could cause a derailment. *Eurostar* reduces the problem of wear by being lighter than traditional trains. Axle loads are limited to 17 tonnes and the line is maintained every single night so that the high-speed service can continue.

The lighter weight may be ideal for track maintenance but seems to offer poor protection in the event of hitting something or being hit. In fact, you have already seen one advantage of reducing the mass of a train in part 3. It makes it easier to stop a train before it collides with anything dangerous; less force is required.

The manufacturers use materials that may be light but are also strong and so resist deformation. But, most important of all, the locomotives and coaches incorporate sophisticated impact-absorbing structures. These designs are the result of the British Rail Research's Crashworthy Development Programme. To protect passengers in a collision this team has constructed trains with collapsible zones in the ends of the coaches. Hydraulic couplers will now sheer off at high-speed impact and slide back into the undercarriage. Each cab and coach end has special anti-climber bars fitted to prevent riding up in a crash. Winston Rasaiah, project engineer, says, 'With crash damage restricted to collapsible zones the passenger compartment remains intact' (see Figure 52).

Figure 52 *Modified coach after collision*

We need to be able to predict the likely damage caused by moving objects and for that we need to know the sizes of any forces involved, and also the energy transferred. This part of the unit deals with both those aspects of collisions.

5.2   *Forces in collisions*

A train crash can be caused by many different events. Here we focus on collisions between two trains that are unfortunately on the same track. A theory of collisions will enable you calculate the likely outcome of such a meeting or to deduce the speeds just prior to impact.

ACTIVITY 27 **Observing collisions**

Observe some collisions between trolleys on a runway or between airtrack vehicles. Include situations where one vehicle is initially at rest and when both are initially moving towards one another. Include some collisions in which the two vehicles become coupled together and some in which they bounce off one another. Notice what happens to the velocities after impact. Try altering the mass of one or both vehicles.

In Activity 27 you probably noticed that, if the moving mass is increased (as when a moving vehicle couples to a stationary one and they both move off together), the velocity decreases. Also, if two vehicles of equal mass approach one another with equal speeds, they come to rest when they couple together. Mass and velocity are both important when it comes to determining the outcome of a collision, and so are the material properties of the colliding vehicles (do they bounce, stick together or crumple?). To gain more insight into what happens, we need to use Newton's laws of motion and the concept of momentum that you met in part 3 of this unit. If one train meets another train we may have situations like the one shown in Figure 53.

Figure 53   *Two trains about to collide – the rear train is travelling faster*

For all collisions the impact forces on the two bodies during the collision are equal and opposite and last for equal times. This is a direct application of Newton's third law and is always true, regardless of whether the two bodies bounce apart or stick together. In part 3 you met the impulse of a force ($F\Delta t$). Both objects in a collision experience the same impulse during the impact. In Figure 53, unequal amounts of damage may be caused by the force of the collision but the force will be of equal size on each train. The *Eurostar* will experience a force of magnitude F to the left and the steam train a force of the same magnitude to the right; both forces will act for exactly the same time interval Δt.

As you saw in part 3, the change in momentum of a moving object (*mass* × *velocity*) is related to the impulse

$$F\Delta t = \Delta(mv) \qquad \text{(equation 2)}$$

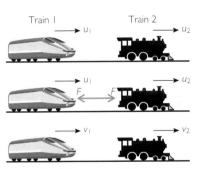

Figure 54   *Two trains colliding*

Since the forces at impact act in opposite directions, the changes in momentum produced are also in opposite directions (remember that both force and momentum are vector quantities). Let the magnitudes of the initial velocities be u_1 and u_2, final velocities v_1 and v_2, as shown in Figure 54 for trains 1 and 2 with masses m_1 and m_2.

For train 1

$$-F\Delta t = m_1 v_1 - m_1 u_1$$

For train 2

$$F\Delta t = m_2 v_2 - m_2 u_2$$

So

$$-(m_1 v_1 - m_1 u_1) = m_2 v_2 - m_2 u_2$$

which can be rearranged to give

$$m_1 u_1 + m_2 u_2 = m_1 v_1 + m_2 v_2 \qquad (17)$$

Equation (17) can also be written using p to represent momentum:

$$p_1 + p_2 \text{ before collision} = p_1 + p_2 \text{ after collision} \qquad (17a)$$

and also generalised to a system consisting of more than two interacting objects

$$\sum p = \text{constant} \qquad (17b)$$

(in words: the sum of all the momenta remains constant).

The terms on the left of equation (17) represent the total momentum of the system before the impact, and those on the right the total momentum of the system afterwards. This is very important! Expressed in words, *the total momentum of a system remains constant provided no external forces act on the system*; this is the **principle of conservation of linear momentum**. ('Linear' means it applies to objects moving in a straight line.) It applies to *all* interactions without exception. The idea of a system is important. For the duration of the impact the only forces that count must be between the two trains. In Activity 27, you should have found that the velocities before and after impact were (approximately) as described by equation (17).

Explosions

At first sight an explosion is very different from a collision, but this is another event where the principle of conservation of momentum can be applied. When a gun fires a shell forward the gun recoils backward. The two forces produced by the explosion have to be equal but opposite in direction. This means the impulses are equal for gun and shell, and so the total momentum of the gun–shell system is unchanged (see Figure 55).

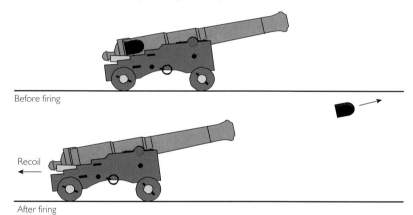

Before firing

Recoil

After firing

Figure 55 *An explosion*

QUESTIONS

46 A 5 tonne wagon runs into the back of a stationary 41 tonne *Eurostar* locomotive and gets jammed there. They move off together at $5\,\text{m}\,\text{s}^{-1}$. How fast was the wagon travelling before the collision?

47 As shown in Figure 56, two railway coaches are about to collide head on. After the collision the 90 tonne mass moves on in the same direction at a velocity of $30\,\text{m}\,\text{s}^{-1}$. What is the velocity of the 20 tonne mass after the collision?

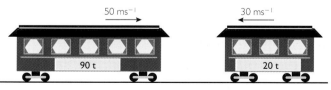

$50\,\text{ms}^{-1}$ $30\,\text{ms}^{-1}$

90 t   20 t

Figure 56 *Diagram for question 47*

48 A party trick is to let the air out of a balloon and watch it fly all over the room. How is this an example of an 'explosive' collision?

Impulse and momentum change

The principle of conservation of momentum is useful for analysing the situation immediately before and after a collision. But if we want to know about possible safety implications, we need to know something about the forces that act during the collision. You have already met useful expressions for this:

$$\text{impulse} = F\Delta t$$

and

$$F = \frac{\Delta p}{\Delta t} \qquad \text{(equation 2)}$$

If the impact time is known, then the (average) force acting can be found. Activities 28 and 29 and questions 49 to 52 illustrate this.

ACTIVITY 28 **Forces in collisions**

Use the *Multimedia Motion* CD-ROM that you met in the AS unit *Higher, Faster, Stronger* to explore the forces acting in various impacts. For example there is a soccer sequence where you can step through the frames to find how long the foot is in contact with the ball. There are also sequences showing collisions between airtrack vehicles. The *Data* button gives you access to values for subsequent speeds, and the mass of the ball can be found using the *Text* button. Additional help is available through the *Help* screen.

ACTIVITY 29 **Force–time graphs**

Use a force–time grapher to log and plot graphs of forces acting during collisions and explosions. Investigate some of the situations suggested in the user guide. Plot force–time graphs and comment on their shapes.

QUESTIONS

49 A snooker ball is struck by a cue. Figure 57 shows the force–time graph for the shot from the point of view of the ball.

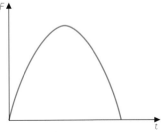

Figure 57   *Diagram for question 49*

(**a**) Draw the force–time graph for same event for the cue.

(**b**) What information can you obtain from the area under such a graph?

(**c**) What shape graph would you get for uniform acceleration?

50 When you catch a hard cricket ball it hurts less if you pull your cupped hands back at impact. Why does this work?

51 A hole in a water pipe leading from a tanker in the Channel Tunnel allows 70 kg of water to escape every second in a horizontal jet moving at 30 m s^{-1}. The jet strikes the tunnel wall and then falls to the ground.

(**a**) What horizontal force does the wall exert on the water?

(**b**) What is the horizontal force on the wall?

52 Suppose the arrival of a hurricane is predicted for the Channel area with winds speeds of 120 mph. The forces on the side of a *Eurostar* train are known for a 60 mph gale. Will the hurricane forces on the same train be **A** the same, **B** twice as large, **C** three times as large, or **D** four times as large?

5.3 *Energy in collisions*

There is another useful way to look at what happens in a collision. Figure 58 shows test coaches that have been damaged in a collision. Each coach experiences a force, and the force does work producing some plastic deformation of the structure, so in a **plastic collision** there is a net loss of kinetic energy (though energy overall is conserved). On the other hand, an **elastic collision** is one in which there is no net loss of kinetic energy – any energy that is temporarily stored due to elastic deformation is recovered as kinetic energy as the colliding objects spring apart.

Study note

This might remind you of some ideas you met in the AS units *Good Enough to Eat* and *Spare Part Surgery*, where you considered elastic and plastic deformation of materials.

Figure 58 *Result of collision between two test coaches*

Mathematically, an elastic collision can be described as follows:

$$\frac{1}{2}m_1u_1^2 + \frac{1}{2}m_1u_2^2 = \frac{1}{2}m_1v_1^2 + \frac{1}{2}m_1v_1^2 \tag{18}$$

or

$$E_{k1} + E_{k2} \text{ before} = E_{k1} + E_{k2} \text{ after} \qquad (18a)$$

where E_k represents kinetic energy and the other symbols have the same meanings as in equation (17). For a system consisting of more than two elastically interacting objects, equation (18) can be written in a more general form:

$$\sum E_k = \text{constant} \qquad (18b)$$

From the viewpoint of a safety engineer, which type of collision is more desirable – elastic or plastic? How can trains or cars be designed to be 'crashworthy'?

From the perspective of train crashes the chances of an elastic collision are remote and positively undesirable. Bits rebounding all over the place would be a nightmare in an accident. The whole point of crashworthiness is that kinetic energy must be absorbed in ways that do as little damage as possible. One way to achieve this is to make the outer parts of a vehicle from a material that readily undergoes plastic deformation, such as is done for the 'crumple zones' of cars, while surrounding the passengers with a strong and fairly rigid structure.

In some situations, though, elastic collisions are desirable, as in some items of sports equipment; a tennis racket that can return a demon serve with little loss of kinetic energy is very desirable (Figure 59). You may have seen a desk toy called Newton's cradle, which also relies on collisions being elastic in order that the ball-bearings can continue to bounce back and forth for a long time.

Figure 59 *A tennis racket at full stretch*

ACTIVITY 30 **Impact forces and crumple zones**

Using the apparatus shown in Figure 60, explore the forces that arise during collisions.

The sharpened dowel rod provides a means of estimating the force involved in the impact. Impacts will throw the dummy onto the spike, which penetrates the Plasticine. Note the depth of penetration. To obtain a value for the force, pull the dummy onto the spike using a thread fastened to a force meter. Obtain enough readings to plot a graph of force against depth of penetration. Explore the effects of colliding at different speeds, changing the mass of the trolley and having a crushable front to the trolley.

Study note

In order to do Activity 30 and some of questions 53 to 55, you will probably need to look back at part 3 of this unit, and possibly at the work you did in the AS unit *Higher, Faster, Stronger*.

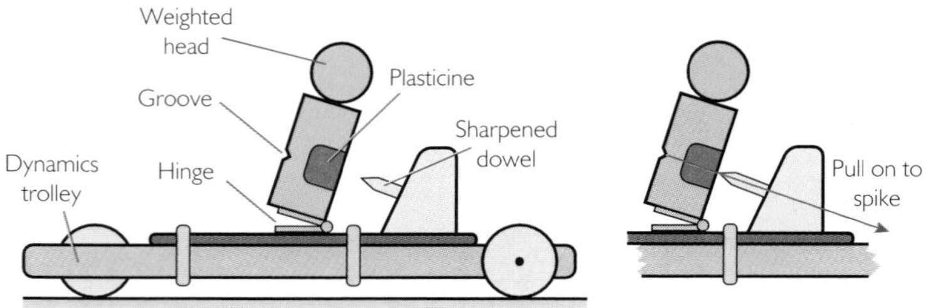

Weighted head

Plasticine

Groove

Sharpened dowel

Dynamics trolley

Hinge

Pull on to spike

Figure 60 *Apparatus for Activity 30*

QUESTIONS

53 The new collapsible front on trains mentioned in section 5.1 provides for a total of 1 MJ energy absorption in a deformation length of 1 m at each end of the locomotive and further energy absorption at the interfaces between coaches. A multiple unit of 24 tonnes is built to this specification.

(**a**) What is the approximate acceleration as the front of the locomotive deforms? Comment on the size of your answer and the likely effect of this acceleration on people within the vehicle.

(**b**) If a 750 tonne *Eurostar* has the same features, what is its acceleration on deforming?

54 In part 1 of this unit it was stated that the kinetic energy of *Eurostar* at full speed ($83 \, \mathrm{m\,s^{-1}}$) is almost exactly that required to raise its 750 tonnes from the ground level to top of the TV aerial at the top of the Eiffel Tower, which is 318 m high.

(**a**) Calculate the energies involved to show how close 'almost' is to having enough energy to do this ($g = 9.8 \, \mathrm{N\,kg^{-1}}$).

(**b**) In practice, could the *Eurostar* be made to rear straight up in the air to such a great height? (Imagine this taking place outside the tunnel!)

55 Examine some of the collisions from questions 46 and 47 and Activities 27 and 28 to see whether they were elastic.

5.4 *Coming together*

In this part of the unit, you have seen how collisions can be analysed in terms of force and impulse and in terms of energy transfer. The questions and activities in this section combine both approaches and thus provide you with an opportunity to review your knowledge and understanding.

ACTIVITY 31 | **Summing up part 5**

Check through your work on this part of the unit and make sure you know the meaning of all the terms printed in bold.

ACTIVITY 32 | **Crashworthy?**

At a press conference, after a nasty railway accident, a railway engineer was asked why his trains weren't built to be as strong as it is physically possible to build. He replied 'our trains are as strong as is necessary to withstand normal service loads but we use clever engineering at the ends of the vehicles to disperse energy by structural collapse while maintaining the integrity of the occupied zone'.

Explain in your own words what he meant, using at least three of the terms printed in bold in this part of the unit.

┌─ QUESTIONS ──────────────────────────────────

56 A man of mass 70 kg stands on a trolley of mass 330 kg that rolls smoothly on frictionless rails. The man fires a rivet gun in a direction parallel to the rails. The gun contains 50 g rivets that leave the gun at a speed of 20 m s^{-1} relative to the trolley.

(**a**) How does firing a single rivet affect the speed of the man-plus-trolley?

(**b**) If the gun fires continuously at a rate of 2 rivets per second, calculate the speed of the trolley after the first minute.

(**c**) Which acquires more kinetic energy per minute, rivets or man-plus-trolley?

(**d**) The man gets a warning of an on-coming train, 5 km away, approaching at a constant speed of 10 m s^{-1}. Can he get up enough speed to escape?

└──

6 *Journey's end*

6.1 *On track*

In this unit, you have encountered several areas of physics: mechanics, electromagnetism and dc electricity. You have met some important fundamental physical laws and principles: momentum conservation, and Faraday's and Lenz's laws. And you have used a mathematical description of a common type of naturally occurring change: exponential decay. The following activities, and the questions in the next section, are designed to help you look back over your work from this unit.

ACTIVITY **33** | **Tracking the physics**

You learned something about each of the following in this unit. Look back through your work and make brief notes under each heading, listing the examples that were used in the unit and noting any ways in which the ideas were developed or refined. Add cross-references to earlier units where you met the same areas of physics. You could add references to later units when you have studied them.

- *DC circuits*   Potential divider, resistivity

- *Capacitors*   Behaviour in dc circuits, charge and pd, exponential discharge, time constant

- *Digital signals*   Pulse counting and timing devices

- *Electromagnetism*   Magnetic flux and flux density, electromagnetic force, electromagnetic induction, transformers

- *Mechanics*   Momentum and impulse, kinetic energy, elastic and plastic collisions

---

ACTIVITY 34 | Hold the front page

Watch a train-crash video. *Either* act as a reporter for a non-specialist publication and write an article on train safety or the nature of the collision you have observed, *or* act as a member of a company that makes and sells devices that help make trains safe, and produce a technical advertisement for one of your products.

ACTIVITY 35 | Down the tubes

Observe a small cylindrical magnet being dropped down three different vertically mounted tubes: a plastic tube much wider than the magnet; a plastic tube just wider than the magnet; and a copper or aluminium tube just wider than the magnet. Explain your observations.

ACTIVITY 36 | Runaway train

In this activity, a model train is allowed to run, out of control, down an inclined track and is brought to rest by an energy-absorbing buffer. Hold a competition to see who can construct the safest buffer. Use your knowledge of dynamics and of capacitor circuits to analyse your results and to hence test your structures as fully and quantitatively as possible.

Further investigations

- Explore ways in which cracks in rails might be detected and located.
- Investigate the effectiveness of seatbelts or airbags.

6.2 Questions on the whole unit

The following passage shows how the physics you have just learned is applied in modern rail signalling systems that involve digital signals and, with questions 57 to 62 that follow, is intended to help you look back over your work from this the unit.

Sensing and signalling

France's legendary high-speed TGV trains (Figure 61), and all trains using the Channel Tunnel, use a sophisticated form of in-cab signalling known as TVM (Transmission Voie-Machine, or 'track to train transmission'). This system uses fixed block sections of track, each about 1.5 km or less in length, and the train is detected by short-circuiting a signal.

In addition, TVM sends information to the train driver about the block of track along which it is travelling. These include fixed properties such as the block length, its gradient and the maximum allowable speed within it, and variable properties that depend on the presence of other trains or obstacles, such as the target speeds at the end of the current block section and at the end of the following block.

Figure 61 *A French TGV*

TVM uses computers, some of which are based around a microprocessor such as found in many personal computers. There are track-side computers, controlling stretches of track about 15 km long, as well as computers on board each train. An electrical signal containing the properties of the block section in which the train is moving is sent along the rails and detected by the train. The train's computer combines this signal with a signal representing its own speed, in order to display relevant information in the cab and, if necessary, apply automatic braking. The whole process can be summarised in a flowchart as shown in Figure 62.

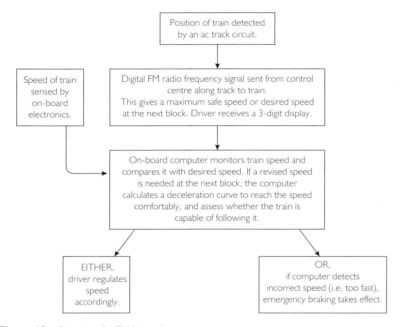

Figure 62 *Flowchart for TVM signalling*

The signal

The electrical signal that travels along the rails of each block to the train is an alternating current (Figure 63). Alternating current (ac) is current which continually changes its size and also reverses its direction repeatedly – the electrons in the circuit oscillate to and fro.

There can be as many as 27 much higher frequency signals superposed onto the fundamental frequency which carries them. (This process of modulation is covered in more detail in the unit *The Medium is the Message*.) Each of the higher 'modulating' frequencies can be either present or not, represented by a 1 or a 0. Thus, the train receives a 27-bit digital signal containing all the information representing each block-section's properties (Figure 64).

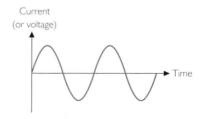

Figure 63 *An ac signal*

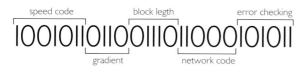

Figure 64 *Decoding the 27-bit digital signal*

Sensing the signal

As you saw in part 2, the train axles form part of the track circuit. In TVM, the first axle of the locomotive contains sensor coils that respond to the signals. The varying current in these coils induces an emf in sensor coils mounted beneath the train (just in front of the axle) – the method of detection is called inductive coupling. This sensor coil current is then fed into the electronics to be decoded.

As you read in part 4 there is another coil, with a pre-existing current, which is used to sense the speed of the train. This gives a direct signal into the driver's cab.

The future – complete automation?

With TVM and all modern signalling techniques, a central computer is used to assess and display the status of all trains in a particular region. The software used, written in a special computer language, is so reliable that, statistically, the average time between dangerous failures is estimated to be over 1 million years. With such impressive reliability, we might ask why the driving of a train is not completely automated. The current thinking is that any present system does not have enough adaptability built in to cope with unexpected situations. Hence, it is considered desirable to 'retain a human in the loop'.

QUESTIONS

57 (**a**) What characteristics of any block of rail track are needed by a train's on-board computer to calculate a safe speed?

(**b**) What other information is needed by the computer?

58 (**a**) What do you understand by 'the frequency of an ac signal'?

(**b**) What is the frequency of the ac mains provided to most homes?

(**c**) Suggest what is meant by 'audio frequency ac'.

59 How does the signal sent down the track provide digital information?

60 How is energy transferred from the track signal to the train's sensor coils?

61 What do you think the phrase, 'dynamic interaction between magnetic fields and electric charge', means?

62 Why may complete automation of trains never be realised?

6.3 *Achievements*

Now you have studied this unit you should be able to:

- recall and use the expression $p = mv$, and apply the principle of conservation of linear momentum to problems in one dimension (3.2, 5.2)*;

- relate net force to rate of change of momentum in situations where mass is constant (3.2, 5.2);

- understand and apply the principle of conservation of energy, and determine whether a collision is elastic or inelastic (5.3);

- recognise and use the expression $F = BI\ell \sin \theta$ (3.3);

- explain qualitatively the factors affecting the emf induced in a coil when there is relative motion between the coil and a permanent magnet and when there is a change of current in a primary coil linked with it (3.4);

- understand and use the terms *magnetic flux density B*, *flux* Φ, and *magnetic flux linkage NΦ* (3.3, 3.4);

- recognise and use the expression $E = -\mathrm{d}(N\Phi)/\mathrm{d}t$, and explain how it is a consequence of Faraday's and Lenz's Laws (3.4);

- describe the operation of an ideal transformer and recall and use the relationship $N_\mathrm{s}/N_\mathrm{p} = V_\mathrm{s}/V_\mathrm{p}$ (3.5);

- recognise digital signals and describe how they can be used in situations incorporating feedback and control (4.1);

- recall and use the expression $C = Q/V$ (4.2);

- recall and explain the effect that a change of resistance or capacitance has in timing circuits (4.2);

- recall that the growth and decay curves for resistor–capacitor circuits are exponential, and know the significance of the time constant RC (4.2);

- recognise and use the expression $Q = Q_0 \mathrm{e}^{-t/RC}$, and derive and use related expressions, for exponential discharge in RC circuits (4.2).

* Numbers indicate the section(s) that relate to each achievement.

Answers

1   Electrically insulated blocks are twin lengths of rail separated from the rest of the rail by an electrically insulating material.

2   A solenoid with current in it becomes an electromagnet whose magnetic field is very similar to that produced by a simple bar magnet.

3   Track circuiting is said to be fail-safe because if something short-circuits the track, or if the relay power supply fails, the signal is automatically set to red.·

4   Leaves on the line or a coating of rust may prevent proper contact between a train's wheels and the track. If this occurs, the low-resistance path required to cause a short-circuit and activate the 'danger' lights may not be present, i.e. a train could go undetected. (Rusty rails are a particular problem because as trains get lighter with modern materials and engines get smoother, coatings of rust may not be removed by the passage of trains. To combat this, a device called a Track Circuit Actuator has been developed to break down the rust electrically.)

5 (a)   Theoretically, we have the technology to bring trains to a halt extremely rapidly. If we did this, however, the inertia of unrestrained passengers would keep them moving forward (think about Newton's first law) and they would undergo dangerous collisions with structures within the train. (See part 5 *Structure and safety*.)

  (b)   Freight trains can operate in smaller envelopes as their speeds are lower and they therefore have smaller braking distances.

  (c)   Smaller envelopes mean more trains can fit on a particular section of track, and so more trains can pass along the track in a particular time interval.

6 (a)   Without the additional resistors in parallel with the relay, circuit resistance $R = 15\,\Omega$.

$$I = \frac{V}{R} = \frac{6\,\text{V}}{15\,\Omega} = 0.4\,\text{A}.$$

pd across relay $= \dfrac{5\,\Omega}{15\,\Omega} \times 6\,\text{V}$. (The circuit can be treated as a potential divider.)

  (b) (i)   Now there are four $5\,\Omega$ resistors in parallel, which have a net resistance R_{par} given by

$$\frac{1}{R_{par}} = \frac{1}{5\,\Omega} + \frac{1}{5\,\Omega} + \frac{1}{5\,\Omega} + \frac{1}{5\,\Omega}$$

so $\quad R_{par} = \dfrac{5\,\Omega}{4} = 1.25\,\Omega$

This resistance is in series with the $10\,\Omega$ resistor so the circuit resistance is now reduced to $11.25\,\Omega$. (The circuit resistance decreases whatever the value of R_1, R_2 and R_3.)

(ii) $I = \dfrac{V}{R} = \dfrac{6\,\text{V}}{11.25\,\Omega} = 0.53\,\text{A}$ (to 2 sig. fig.)

(iii) As you can treat the circuit like a potential divider, the pd across the relay (and the additional resistors) is given by

$$V = \left(\frac{1.25\,\Omega}{11.25\,\Omega}\right) \times 6\,\text{V} = 0.67\,\text{V} \text{ (to 2 sig. fig.)}$$

(Whatever the additional resistors, the pd will always be reduced.)

(iv) Current in relay, $I = \dfrac{V}{R} = \dfrac{0.67\,\text{V}}{5\,\Omega} = 0.13\,\text{A}$ (2 sig. fig.)

(v) The relay current will be reduced (whatever the size of the additional resistors in parallel) and the magnetic field in the solenoid might not be large enough to operate the switch.

7 (a)   First, find the combined resistance, R_c, of ballast and relay – they are in parallel.

$$\frac{1}{R_c} = \frac{1}{50\,\Omega} + \frac{1}{8\,\Omega} = 0.145\,\Omega^{-1}$$

$$R_c = \frac{1}{0.145\,\Omega^{-1}} = 6.9\,\Omega$$

Now use the potential divider formula to get resistance, R:

$$\frac{R_c}{R + R_c} \times 15\,\text{V} = 6\,\text{V}$$

$$R_c \times 15 = 6 \times (R + R_c) = 6R + 6R_c$$
$$6R = 9R_c$$

$$R = \frac{9R_c}{6} = 9 \times \frac{6.9\,\Omega}{6} = 10.35\,\Omega$$

  (b)   Through relay, $I_{relay} = \dfrac{V}{R} = \dfrac{6\,\text{V}}{8\,\Omega} = 0.75\,\text{A}$

  (c)   Current through variable resistor $= I_{ballast} + I_{relay}$

Through ballast, $I_{ballast} = \dfrac{V}{R} = \dfrac{6\,\text{V}}{50\,\Omega} = 0.12\,\text{A}$

So through variable resistor,
$I = 0.12\,\text{A} + 0.75\,\text{A} = 0.87\,\text{A}.$

8 (a)   0.5 V as they are in parallel.
  (b)   Cell voltage – track voltage $= 2\,\text{V} - 0.5\,\text{V} = 1.5\,\text{V}$
  (c)   The voltmeter was recording as the 'lorry' rolled along the track. At different points, different conditions of contact between wheels and track gave different readings.
  (d)   The voltage decreases with increasing load.
  (e)   The resistance from track to track must decrease (to make the combined resistance of L, B and R smaller).

(f) The resistance decreases as the contact between the lorry's wheels and the track gets better. This 'contact resistance' is the most important factor in the resistance of a vehicle between two tracks.

(g) If a train is too light, it may not make a good enough contact with the rails. This could prevent it from causing the pd across the relay to fall below the 'drop-off' voltage and the train may go undetected.

9 (a) Using $F = ma$, $a = \dfrac{F}{m}$

$$a = \frac{400 \times 10^3\,\text{N}}{750 \times 10^3\,\text{kg}} = 0.53\,\text{m s}^{-2}$$

(b) Power = work done per second, $P = Fv$
$P = 400 \times 10^3\,\text{N} \times 10\,\text{m s}^{-1} = 4 \times 10^6\,\text{W} = 4\,\text{MW}$

10 N s or kg m s^{-1}. The units are interchangeable (see equation 2).

11 (a) $\Delta p = 50\,000\,\text{kg} \times (+40\,\text{m s}^{-1})$
$\quad - 50\,000\,\text{kg} \times (+20\,\text{m s}^{-1})$
$\quad = 1.00 \times 10^6\,\text{kg m s}^{-1}$

(b) $\Delta p = 50\,000\,\text{kg} \times (-20\,\text{m s}^{-1})$
$\quad - 50\,000\,\text{kg} \times (+20\,\text{m s}^{-1})$
$\quad = -2.0 \times 10^6\,\text{kg m s}^{-1}$

(c) $\Delta p = 50\,000\,\text{kg} \times 0\,\text{m s}^{-1} - 50\,000\,\text{kg} \times (+20\,\text{m s}^{-1})$
$\quad = -1.00 \times 10^6\,\text{kg m s}^{-1}$

12 (a) $\Delta p = (1200\,\text{kg} \times 25\,\text{m s}^{-1} - 1200 \times 0\,\text{m s}^{-1})$
$\quad = 30 \times 10^3\,\text{kg m s}^{-1}$

(b) $F = \dfrac{\Delta p}{\Delta t}$

$$F = \frac{30 \times 10^3\,\text{kg m s}^{-1}}{10\,\text{s}}$$

$F = 3\,\text{kN}$ in direction of the motion

(c) $\Delta s = \dfrac{1}{2}(u + v)\Delta t$

$s = 0.5(0\,\text{m s}^{-1} + 25\,\text{m s}^{-1}) \times 10\,\text{s} = 125\,\text{m}$

(d) $P = \dfrac{\text{work}}{\text{time}} = \dfrac{\text{force} \times \text{distance}}{\text{time}}$

$$P = \frac{(3000\,\text{N} \times 125\,\text{m})}{10\,\text{s}}$$

$= 3.75 \times 10^4\,\text{W} = 37.5\,\text{kW}$

13 Although the mass for the power unit to pull is so much greater it would be very uncomfortable to leave a station at the acceleration quoted for a car. Trains contain passengers who expect to be able to walk about.

14 (a) $F = \dfrac{\Delta(mv)}{\Delta t}$

$F = (750 \times 10^3\,\text{kg} \times 83\,\text{m s}^{-1} - 750 \times 10^3\,\text{kg}$
$\quad \times 44\,\text{m s}^{-1}) \div (14 \times 60\,\text{s})$
$\quad = 35\,\text{kN}$

(b) To produce the same acceleration with only one third the mass requires a tractive force one third of that found in (a).

(c) It takes the same size force to change speed from $83\,\text{m s}^{-1}$ to $44\,\text{m s}^{-1}$ over the same length of time, but it now acts in the opposite direction to the direction of travel.

(d) To produce the same resultant force, the tractive force provided by the engines must increase by 40 kN to 75 kN in the case of *Eurostar* and 52 kN for the lighter train.

15 (a) Using $F = \dfrac{\Delta p}{\Delta t}$

(i) $F = 2\,400\,000\,\text{kg} \times \dfrac{44\,\text{m s}^{-1}}{60\,\text{s}} = 1\,760\,000\,\text{N}$
$\quad = 1.8\,\text{MN}$ opposed to the direction of travel.

(ii) The same method gives $F = 550\,\text{kN}$ for *Eurostar*.

(b) $F = (750\,000\,\text{kg} \times 83\,\text{m s}^{-1} - 750\,000 \times 0\,\text{m s}^{-1}) \div 180\,\text{s}$
$\quad = 35\,000\,\text{N} = 350\,\text{kN}$ opposite to the direction of travel.

(c) Far larger forces are needed to stop these trains quickly than it does to get them going, because the time interval is shorter.

16 (a) Equation (3): $\Delta s = \dfrac{mu^2}{2F}$

$\Delta s = 2100 \times 10^3\,\text{kg} \times (40\,\text{m s}^{-1})^2 \div (2 \times 1.2 \times 10^6\,\text{N})$
$\quad = 1400\,\text{m}$

(b) $F = \dfrac{mu^2}{2\Delta s}$

$= 750 \times 10^3\,\text{kg} \times (80\,\text{m s}^{-1})^2 \div (2 \times 1500\,\text{m})$
$= 1.6\,\text{MN}.$

(c) At high speeds the drag will help to slow down the trains but 40 kN is small compared to the meganewton braking forces. As speed decreases, so will the drag force. Both answers will thus be smaller than calculated in (a) and (b), but only slightly.

17 (a) Now equation (1) is again the best one to use:

$\Delta t = \dfrac{\Delta p}{F}$

$= 750 \times 10^3\,\text{kg} \times 80\,\text{m s}^{-1} \div (1.6 \times 10^6\,\text{N})$
$= 37.5\,\text{s}$

(b) $a = (80 - 0)\,\text{m s}^{-1} \div 37.5\,\text{s} = 2.1\,\text{m s}^{-2}$

18 (a) (i) Momentum doubles (mv to $2mv$). (ii) Kinetic energy is four times greater: $0.5\,mv^2 \to 0.5\,m(2v)^2$

(b) Both quantities are in the ratio 2:1. For the more massive train, momentum doubles (mv to $2mv$) and kinetic energy is also doubled $0.5\,mv^2 \to 0.5 \times 2m(v)^2$

19 (a) Net force is found using
$F = ma = 2.40 \times 10^6\,\text{kg} \times 0.13\,\text{m s}^{-2} = 312\,\text{kN}$
force = 40 kN, so to produce the required resultant, we need a tractive force $T = 352\,\text{kN}$

(b) Resolving along the slope, with T representing tractive force and W the weight of the train:

$$T = W \sin\theta = mg\sin\theta$$
$$= \frac{2.40 \times 10^6 \, \text{kg} \times 9.8 \, \text{N kg}^{-1} \times 1}{90} = 261 \, \text{kN}$$

(c) Total tractive force required $= 352 \, \text{kN} + 261 \, \text{kN}$
$$= 613 \, \text{kN}$$

(d) $\Delta t = \dfrac{\Delta p}{F}$

where F is the net accelerating force, i.e. $F = 312 \, \text{kN}$ (from (a)).

$$\frac{\Delta t = 2.40 \times 10^6 \, \text{kg} \times 44 \, \text{m s}^{-1}}{312\,000 \, \text{N}}$$
$$= 338 \, \text{s} = 5 \, \text{min} \, 38 \, \text{s}$$

(e) (i) From (a) and (b), net force along slope is
$$F = 400 \, \text{kN} - 261 \, \text{kN} - 40 \, \text{kN} = 99 \, \text{kN}$$
$$a = \frac{F}{m} = 99 \times 10^3 \, \text{N} \div 2.40 \times 10^6 \, \text{kg} = 0.041 \, \text{m s}^{-2}$$

(ii) $\Delta t = \dfrac{\Delta v}{a} = \dfrac{(v - u)}{a}$
$$= \frac{44 \, \text{m s}^{-1}}{0.041 \, \text{m s}^{-2}}$$
$$= 1073 \, \text{s} = 17 \, \text{min} \, 53 \, \text{s}$$

(iii) $\Delta s = \dfrac{\Delta E_k}{F} = \dfrac{0.5 \times 2.40 \times 10^6 \, \text{kg} \times (44 \, \text{m s}^{-1})^2}{99 \times 10^3 \, \text{N}}$
$$= 2.35 \times 10^4 \, \text{m} = 23.5 \, \text{km}.$$

20 (a) One possible approach is to note that acceleration due to gravity is a vector, and so can be resolved as shown in Figure 65.

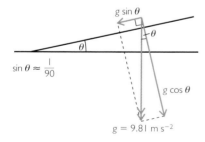

$\sin\theta \approx \dfrac{1}{90}$

$g = 9.81 \, \text{m s}^{-2}$

Figure 65 *Diagram for the answer to question 20*

Along the slope, $u = 44 \, \text{m s}^{-1}$, $v = 0 \, \text{m s}^{-1}$,
$$a = 9.8 \times (\tfrac{1}{90}) \, \text{m s}^{-2}$$
$$v^2 = u^2 + 2as$$
$$s = \frac{(v^2 - u^2)}{2a}$$
$$= \frac{(-44 \, \text{m s}^{-1})^2}{2 \times (-9.8 \times (\tfrac{1}{90})) \, \text{m s}^{-2}}$$
$$= 8.89 \times 10^3 \, \text{m} \approx 9 \, \text{km, i.e. not far enough to get out.}$$

(We have chosen the positive direction to be the direction of travel, i.e. up the slope.)

(b) The net force along the slope $=$ drag $+$ component of weight acting along slope. This has magnitude
$$F = D + W\sin\theta$$
which is related to the acceleration by $F = ma$

So $a = \dfrac{F}{m} = \dfrac{D}{m} + g\sin\theta$

$$= \frac{30 \times 10^3 \, \text{N}}{2400 \times 10^3 \, \text{kg}} + \frac{9.8 \, \text{m s}^{-2}}{90}$$
$$= 0.121 \, \text{m s}^{-2}$$

Taking the positive direction to be up the slope,
$$a = -0.121 \, \text{m s}^{-2}$$
Using the same method as in question 19
$$s = \frac{(v^2 - u^2)}{2a}$$
$$= \frac{(-44 \, \text{m s}^{-1})^2}{2 \times (-0.121) \, \text{m s}^{-2}}$$
$$= 8.0 \, \text{km}$$

21 (a) downwards, (b) out of the page, (c) to the right.

22 (a) $F = 2\,\text{T} \times 4\,\text{A} \times 10 \times 10^{-3} \, \text{m} = 0.08 \, \text{N}$

(b) $F = 0 \, \text{N}$

(c) $F = 2\,\text{T} \times 4\,\text{A} \times 10 \times 10^{-3} \, \text{m} \times \sin 30° = 0.04 \, \text{N}$

23 The electromagnetic force must be equal in size (but opposite in direction) to the weight of the rider.
$$BI\ell = mg$$
$$B = \frac{mg}{I\ell}$$
$$= \frac{15 \times 10^{-3} \, \text{kg} \times 9.8 \, \text{N kg}^{-1}}{5.0 \, \text{A} \times 100 \times 10^{-3} \, \text{m}}$$
$$= 0.3 \, \text{N A}^{-1} \, \text{m}^1 = 0.3 \, \text{T}$$

24 The missing ingredient is the number of turns, n. The force is increased for every extra turn in the coil. This gives $F = nBI\ell$ for the force on each side of the coil. These are some plausible estimates: suppose we have current between 10 and 100 A, B between 0.1 and 1 T, length of coil is limited by space, say 2 m, n depends on thickness of wire (too thin and the resistance is too high for the high currents we need, but thicker means fewer turns fit on coil) – let's say 1000 turns.

These values give

$$F \approx 1000 \times 1 \, \text{T} \times 100 \, \text{A} \times 2 \, \text{m} = 2 \times 10^5 \, \text{N}$$

This is half our target. Each side of the coil will experience this force. Provided one of these forces can be made to act in the opposite direction (e.g. using levers or gears), then a net force of $4 \times 10^5 \, \text{N}$ can be achieved.

25 The SI units of the right-hand side are $Wb\,s^{-1}$.
$1\,Wb\,s^{-1} = 1\,N\,A^{-1}\,m\,s^{-1}$
But $1\,N\,m = 1\,J$, and $1\,A\,s = 1\,C$ (because
$1\,A = 1\,C\,s^{-1}$), so $1\,Wb\,s^{-1} = 1\,J\,C^{-1}$ and
$1\,J\,C^{-1} = 1\,V$ – which is the SI unit for emf as required
for the left-hand side.

26 Using equation (6b), with $\Delta\Phi = 50 \times 10\,Wb$,
$\Delta t = 2.0\,s$:
$$\mathscr{E} = \frac{50 \times 10\,Wb}{2.0\,s} = 250\,V$$

27 Using equation (6e), with $\Delta A = 0.03\,m^2$, $\Delta t = 0.2\,s$,
$B = 2\,T$ and $N = 10$:
$$\mathscr{E} = \frac{10 \times 2\,T \times 0.03\,m^2}{0.2\,s} = 3\,V$$

28 The changing current produces a changing magnetic
field. A radio receiver is sensitive to the changing fields
that make up electromagnetic waves, so will also
respond to the changing field produced by a current
and hence may produce an audible signal.

29 As the field has a vertical component, any horizontal
conducting path on the aeroplane will have an induced
emf across it during flight. If flying due north, this will be
from right to left (east to west) across wings and
fuselage. (Check this with the right-hand rule looking
down on the plane.) There will be no emf along the
length of the fuselage as this is not 'cutting' across the
field. The induced emf is a potential danger as it could
interfere with control systems within the plane.

30 (a) The induced emf will be away from you – into the page.
   (b) Use equation (7) with $B = 4 \times 10^{-5}\,T$, $v = 60\,m\,s^{-1}$,
   $\ell = 4\,m$ (the height is irrelevant)
   $\mathscr{E} = 4 \times 10^{-5}\,T \times 4\,m \times 60\,m\,s^{-1} = 9.6\,mV$

31 (a) Magnetic fields extend across space so no contact is
   required.
   (b) No, it depends on motion for its effect so would not
   work when at rest.

32 The disc should have low electrical resistance, i.e. it
should be thick, have a large diameter, and be made
of good conducting material.

33 Vary the distance of the magnet from the disc. Alter the
strength of the magnet (only possible if the system uses
an electromagnet).

34 (a) The electricity supply to the coils is switched off. The
   motor no longer drives the wheels round. The reverse
   happens – the momentum in the wheels keep the coils
   rotating in the magnetic field and so inducing a current,
   i.e. acting as a generator.

(b) Either the current is switched to pass through
resistances which heat up readily or the current is
passed back into the supply system available along the
rail track. The third rail is the British method. On the
continent it would be to the overhead supply line.

35 From equation (8), $N_s = N_p \times \left(\frac{V_s}{V_p}\right) = \frac{N_p V_s}{V_p}$. The
motors always require $V_s = 1500\,V$, and we always
have $N_p = 1000$, so $N_p V_s = 1.5 \times 10^6\,V$.

France: $N_s = \dfrac{1.5 \times 10^6\,V}{25 \times 10^3\,V} = 60$

Belgium: $N_s = \dfrac{1.5 \times 10^6\,V}{3000\,V} = 500$

36 (a) Equation (8): $\dfrac{N_p}{N_s} = \dfrac{V_p}{V_s} = \dfrac{750\,V}{1500\,V} = 0.5$

   (b) Assuming that input power = output power = $1200\,kW$,
   $$I_p = \frac{P}{V_p} = \frac{1200 \times 10^3\,W}{750\,V} = 1600\,A.$$

37 (a) The alternating magnetic field induces eddy currents
   within the iron nail. These currents heat the iron.
   (b) The layers of glue have high electrical resistance and so
   inhibit the circulation of eddy currents. This reduces the
   heating of the core. In a transformer, eddy-current heating
   of the core is one factor that would reduce the efficiency.

38 The tunnel lining would act like a giant solenoid. Any
electric train, with very strong motor magnets, would set
up an induced current in it, which would be directed to
push back on the train like a brake. More energy is then
required to drive the train into the tunnel, i.e. increased
fuel costs – a potentially expensive mistake.

39 Only the vertical component of B contributes to the
emf. Using equation (7),
$$\mathscr{E} = 4.1 \times 10^{-5}\,T \times 47\,m \times 268\,m\,s^{-1} = 0.516\,V$$

40 (a) $\Phi = BA\cos\theta$
   $B = 3.5 \times 10^{-6}\,T$, $\theta = 45°$,
   $A = 5.0 \times 10^{-2}\,m \times 8.0 \times 10^{-2}\,m = 4.0 \times 10^{-3}\,m^2$
   $\Phi = 3.5 \times 10^{-6}\,T \times 4.0 \times 10^{-3}\,m^2 \times \cos 45°$
   $\quad = 9.9 \times 10^{-9}\,Wb$
   (b) Flux linkage $= N\Phi$
   $\quad = 100 \times 9.9 \times 10^{-9}\,Wb = 9.9 \times 10^{-7}\,Wb$
   (c) Use equation (6), with $\Delta\Phi = 9.9 \times 10^{-7}\,Wb$,
   $\Delta t = 1.0 \times 10^{-4}\,s$
   $$\mathscr{E} = \frac{9.9 \times 10^{-7}\,Wb}{1.0 \times 10^{-4}\,s} = 9.9 \times 10^{-3}\,V = 9.9\,mV.$$

41 (a) From equation (14), fraction of charge left $= \dfrac{Q}{Q_0} = e^{-t/RC}$
   $RC = 250 \times 10^3\,\Omega \times 100 \times 10^{-6}\,F = 25\,\Omega F$
   $\dfrac{t}{RC} = \dfrac{20}{25} = 0.8$
   $e^{-t/RC} = 0.45$ (2 sig. fig.)

(b) From equation (11), initial charge $Q_0 = CV_0$
= $100 \times 10^{-6}\,F \times 10\,V = 10^{-3}\,C$
After 20 s, $Q_0 = 0.45$ and $Q = 4.5 \times 10^{-4}\,C$

42 (a) In equation (13b), the left-hand side has units of charge ÷ charge, i.e. it is dimensionless. The right-hand side, $\dfrac{\Delta t}{RC}$, must also be dimensionless. As $\dfrac{\Delta t}{RC}$ has dimensions of time (SI units of second), then so must RC.

(b) If $t = RC$, then $\dfrac{V}{V_0} = e^{-RC/RC} = e^{-1}$

$= \dfrac{1}{e} = \dfrac{1}{2.718} = 0.37$ to 2 d.p.

43 (a) From equation (13), $\dfrac{Q}{Q_0} = e^{-3} \approx 0.05 = 5\%$.

(b) Similarly, $\dfrac{Q}{Q_0} = e^{-5} \approx 0.0067 \approx 0.7\%$.

Strictly mathematically speaking, the charge never actually reaches zero, but more than 99% of the initial charge will have been released from a discharging capacitor after 5 time constants. Depending on how precisely one can detect this small amount of remaining charge, one can say that the capacitor is 'fully discharged' for all practical purposes.

44 (a) 6 V
(b) $t = RC = 1 \times 10^5\,\Omega \times 47 \times 10^{-6}\,F = 4.7\,s$
(c) From equation (15), $V = V_0 e^{-t/RC}$

$\dfrac{t}{RC} = \dfrac{5\,s}{4.7\,s} = 1.06$, $V_0 = 6\,V$

$V = 6\,V \times e^{-1.06} = 2.07\,V\ (\approx 2\,V)$

45 (a) When a train is occupying the block, there is a connection across XY. This instantly charges the capacitor and also makes the NOT gate input high. The NOT gate output is therefore low, or close to zero volts, allowing the red LED to light. When the train leaves the block, the capacitor discharges and the pd across it gradually falls. Hence, the input voltage to the NOT gate also falls. When this voltage drops below 1.5 V, it is read as low and the NOT gate output goes high, close to 6 V. This allows the green LED to light, thus indicating all clear.

(b) We need to show that the capacitor voltage falls to 1.5 V when $t = 10\,s$. At this time, $\dfrac{t}{RC} = \dfrac{10\,s}{7.2\,s} = 1.39$.

From equation (15), $V = 6\,V \times e^{-1.39} = 1.5\,V$ as required.

(c) $RC = 1000 \times 10^3\,\Omega \times 10 \times 10^{-6}\,F = 10\,s$. This is a little longer than the required τ of 7.2 s, so discharge will be slower, which gives a delay that is longer than the required 10 s.

46 Using equation (17) with $m_1 = 5\,t$ (wagon), $m_2 = 41\,t$ (Eurostar loco), $u_2 = 0\,m\,s^{-1}$ and $v_1 = v_2 = v = 5\,m\,s^{-1}$, we have $m_2u_2 = 0$ and so $m_1u_1 = (m_1 + m_2)v$

$u_1 = \dfrac{(m_1 + m_2)v}{m_1}$

$= \dfrac{(46t \times 5\,m\,s^{-1})}{5t} = 46\,m\,s^{-1}$

(this is over 100 mph!)

(Notice that we have kept all masses in tonnes. You could convert to kilograms but the factors of 1000 would cancel at the final stage.)

47 Using equation (17) and taking left-to-right as positive $m_1 = 90\,t$, $m_2 = 20\,t$ (as in question 46, we have kept masses in tonnes) $u_1 = +50\,m\,s^{-1}$, $u_2 = -30\,m\,s^{-1}$, $v_1 = +30\,m\,s^{-1}$ Momentum beforehand $= m_1u_1 + m_2u_2$ $= 90t \times 50\,m\,s^{-1} - 20t \times 30\,m\,s^{-1} = 3900\,t\,m\,s^{-1}$ Momentum afterwards $= m_1v_1 + m_2v_2$ $= 90t \times 30\,m\,s^{-1} + m_2v_2$ $= 2700\,t\,m\,s^{-1} + m_2v_2$ Since momentum must be conserved $m_2v_2 = 3900\,t\,m\,s^{-1} - 2700\,t\,m\,s^{-1} = 1200\,t\,m\,s^{-1}$

$v_2 = \dfrac{1200\,t\,m\,s^{-1}}{20\,t} = 60\,m\,s^{-1}$.

Notice that the final answer gives v_2 in the correct units (the tonnes cancel) and because the number is positive we know the coach must be moving from left to right.

48 Air plus balloon initially have no velocity and so no momentum. The air is held inside at high pressure and so once released the air moves out at high speed. To conserve momentum the balloon must move in the opposite direction with a momentum equal to that of the air.

49 (a) See Figure 66.

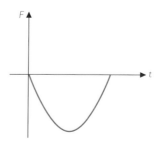

Figure 66 *The answer to question 49*

(b) The area gives the impulse and hence the change in momentum.

(c) A straight line parallel to the time axis (since the force has to be constant).

50 It lengthens the time of the impact. The required change in momentum to stop the ball can be achieved by either a large force for a short time (painful) or by a smaller force for a longer time (comfortable).

51 (a) Using equation (2): $F = \dfrac{\Delta(mv)}{\Delta t}$. In a time interval

$\Delta t = 1$ s, 70 kg strikes the wall and its horizontal velocity decreases from 30 m s^{-1} to zero so

$$\Delta(mv) = 70\,\text{kg} \times 30\,\text{m s}^{-1} = 2100\,\text{kg m s}^{-1}$$

and so $F = 2100$ N in the opposite direction to the water's motion.

(b) The force exerted on the wall is also 2100 N, but in the opposite direction, i.e. outwards.

52 D
Force is equal to rate of momentum change (see question 51). The air mass is moving twice as quickly so twice the mass hits the train per second. Twice the mass moving at twice the velocity has four times as much momentum, so the force will increase fourfold.

53 (a) Using $\Delta W = F\Delta s$ and $F = ma$:

$$F = \frac{\Delta W}{\Delta s}, \quad a = \frac{F}{m} = \frac{\Delta W}{m\Delta s}$$

$$= \frac{1 \times 10^6\,\text{J}}{(1\,\text{m} \times 24 \times 10^3\,\text{kg})} = 41.7\,\text{m s}^{-2} \approx 4 \times g.$$

This is a very large acceleration, so would be very uncomfortable to experience.

(b) Using the same method as in (a), $a = 1.3$ m s^{-2} (which is much more comfortable but still a real jolt).

54 (a) $E_k = \dfrac{1}{2}mv^2$

$$= 0.5 \times 750 \times 10^3\,\text{kg} \times (83\,\text{m s}^{-1})^2 = 2.58 \times 10^9\,\text{J}$$
$$\Delta E_{\text{grav}} = mg\Delta h$$
$$= 750 \times 10^3\,\text{kg} \times 9.8\,\text{N kg}^{-1} \times 318\,\text{m}$$
$$= 2.34 \times 10^9\,\text{J}$$

so there is *more* than enough energy to reach the top of the Eiffel Tower.

(b) The track would need to curve upwards, enabling the train to 'coast' to a great height – and it would need to be engineered so as to reduce frictional energy losses almost to zero.

55 From question 46, with $m_1 = 5$ t (wagon), $m_2 = 41$ t (*Eurostar* loco), $u_1 = 46$ m s^{-1}, $u_2 = 0$ m s^{-1} and $v_1 = v_2 = v = 5$ m s^{-1},

before collision, total $E_k = \dfrac{1}{2}m_1u_1^2 + \dfrac{1}{2}m_2u_2^2$

$$= 0.5 \times 5 \times 10^3\,\text{kg} \times (46\,\text{m s}^{-1})^2 = 5.3 \times 10^6\,\text{J}$$

after collision, total $E_k = \dfrac{1}{2}(m_1 + m_2)v^2$

$$= 0.5 \times 46 \times 10^3\,\text{kg} \times (5\,\text{m s}^{-1})^2 = 5.8 \times 10^5\,\text{J}.$$

This collision is *not* elastic, since kinetic energy is not conserved.

From question 47, with $m_1 = 90$ t, $m_2 = 20$ t
$u_1 = +50$ m s^{-1}, $u_2 = -30$ m s^{-1},
$v_1 = +30$ m s^{-1}, $v_2 = 60$ m s^{-1}
before, $E_k = 0.5 \times 90 \times 10^3\,\text{kg} \times (50\,\text{m s}^{-1})^2$
$\qquad\qquad + 0.5 \times 20 \times 10^3\,\text{kg} \times (30\,\text{m s}^{-1})^2$
$\qquad\quad = 1.215 \times 10^8\,\text{J}$
after, $E_k = 0.5 \times 90 \times 10^3\,\text{kg} \times (30\,\text{m s}^{-1})^2$
$\qquad\qquad + 0.5 \times 20 \times 10^3\,\text{kg} \times (60\,\text{m s}^{-1})^2$
$\qquad\quad = 7.65 \times 10^7\,\text{J}$

Again, this is not an elastic collision since there is a net loss of kinetic energy.

56 (a) Suppose the system is initially at rest, i.e. momentum is zero. If a rivet, mass $m_1 = 50$ g, is fired with a velocity $v_1 = 20$ m s^{-1}, then the trolley-plus-man, total mass $m_2 = 400$ kg, must acquire a velocity v_2 where $m_1v_1 + m_2v_2 = 0$ (because the total momentum must still be zero).

$$v_2 = \frac{-m_1v_1}{m_2} = \frac{0.050\,\text{kg} \times 20\,\text{m s}^{-1}}{400\,\text{kg}}$$
$$= -2.5 \times 10^{-3}\,\text{m s}^{-1}$$

i.e. the trolley-plus-man moves at 2.5 mm s^{-1} in the opposite direction to the rivet.

(b) One way to approach this problem is to find the force on the trolley-plus-man, using $F = \dfrac{\Delta p}{\Delta t}$.

With $\Delta t = 1$s, $\dfrac{\Delta p}{\Delta t} = \dfrac{2 \times 400\,\text{kg} \times 2.5 \times 10^{-3}\,\text{m s}^{-1}}{1\,\text{s}}$

$$= 2\,\text{kg m s}^{-2} = 2\,\text{N}$$

(Or use the momentum change of two rivets to get the same result.)

Acceleration of trolley, $a = \dfrac{2\,\text{N}}{400\,\text{kg}} = 0.0050\,\text{m s}^{-2}$

$v = u + at$, with $t = 60$ s
$u = 0$ m s^{-1}, $v = 0.0050$ m s$^{-2} \times 60$ s $= 0.30$ m s^{-1}.
(Or use the same method as in (a), with $m_1 = 2 \times 60 \times 0.050$ kg.)

(c) For rivets, in 1 minute
$\Delta E_k = 0.5 \times 2 \times 60 \times 0.050\,\text{kg} \times (20\,\text{m s}^{-1})^2 = 1200\,\text{J}$
For trolley-plus-man, in 1 minute
$\Delta E_k = 0.5 \times 400\,\text{kg} \times (0.30\,\text{m s}^{-1})^2 = 18\,\text{J}$

(d) No chance! The train takes only 500 s to reach the man's original position. By this time, his speed is only 2.5 m s^{-1} (using the same method as in (b)) and he will still be very close to the on-rushing train.

(By plotting s–t graphs for the train and for the trolley, perhaps using a spreadsheet, you could find the time for the train to catch up with the trolley.)

THE MEDIUM IS THE MESSAGE

Figure 1 *Airbus A340 flight deck*

Why a unit called The Medium is the Message?

The world today depends on communications – speaking to someone, sending a letter or an e-mail, hearing the news on the radio or television, or transferring data from and to the Stock Exchange or a bank.

Electricity and magnetism first played their part in communication when the idea of telegraphy was put forward in 1820 by the French physicist André Ampère (1775–1836). Early versions involved switching electromagnets so that needles pointed to particular characters. By 1843 Samuel Morse (1791–1872) had invented his famous code, enabling the much faster transmission of messages. In 1878 Alexander Bell (1847–1922), the Scottish-born American scientist, invented the telephone. Radio followed a little later with Marconi sending a Morse code signal across the Atlantic Ocean in 1901 and with the first speech transmission by Reginald Fessenden in 1906. Television was established in 1925.

Since then electronic developments have come thick and fast with facsimile (fax) machines, the sending of signals through fibre optic cables, displaying information on liquid crystal displays and other devices, and connections between computers via the Internet. The world seems to want to communicate faster and more often, and progress in physics has helped this come about; the telecommunications industry is one of the major employers of physicists.

While we tend to think of communications in terms of messages and images sent between people, communication can involve any transmission, reception and display of information. In order to illustrate and explore a range of modern techniques, in this unit we focus on the measurement and communication of information within an aircraft (Figure 1).

Overview of physics principles and techniques

In this unit you will learn how sensors based on potentiometers are used to monitor the position of wing flaps, etc., how the output from sensors is sampled and encoded into modulated signals, and how the technique of multiplexing allows more than one signal to be sent along a single fibre optic cable. You will also explore how a signal is attenuated as it travels along such a cable.

Next you will explore the operation of a CCD (charge-coupled device), which uses the physics of charge, voltage and capacitance to produce and display two-dimensional images. Finally you will look at the physics behind other instrument displays: cathode-ray tubes, light-emitting diodes and liquid crystal displays, where electric and magnetic fields play a key part.

In this unit you will extend your knowledge of

- signals from *The Sound of Music* and *Transport on Track*;

- using graphs from *Higher, Faster, Stronger* and *Digging Up the Past*;

- charge and potential difference from *Technology in Space* and *Digging Up the Past*;

- the behaviour of light from *The Sound of Music* and *Good Enough to Eat*;

- capacitors and exponential changes from *Transport on Track*.

In other units you will do more work on

- electric and magnetic fields in *Probing the Heart of Matter*;

- electromagnetic radiation in *Reach for the Stars*.

▌ *Control and safety in the air*

Control of powered flight is attributed to the two bicycle manufacturers from Dayton, Ohio, USA – the brothers Orville and Wilbur Wright. In the first flights of their biplane 'The Flyer', Orville was able to exert control on movable wing tips, move the rudder and wing flaps, all by movements of his body. The first flight, in 1903, lasted twelve seconds. In 1911 the Wright Brothers' Model A (Figure 2) had wing warping, rudder and elevator control wires operated by the pilot.

Figure 2 *Wilbur Wright at the controls of a Model A*

Until the 1970s, with the exception of experimental aircraft, control of an aircraft's flying surfaces (Figure 3) was through mechanical linkages, though with connections generally made with rods, gears and hydraulics rather than with wires. Most motor vehicles today still use mechanical linkages. For example, in most cars a foot on the brake pedal produces a force on a piston that pushes against incompressible brake fluid in a pipe; this force is transmitted by the fluid to push another piston at the far end of the pipe, which in turn pushes the brake pads into contact with the wheels. Similarly, a turn of the steering produces movement of a rack and pinion gear system through which the wheels are changed in direction, and information about the speed of a car may be transferred via a rotating cable linking the wheels to the speedometer.

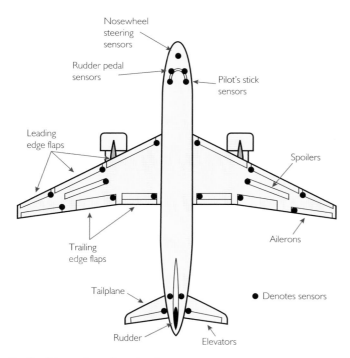

Figure 3 *The flying surfaces of an aircraft*

These days both motor vehicles and aircraft are becoming more computer controlled and on-board sensors relay electronic information to those computers. Flying an aircraft, be it a civil airliner or a military fighter, requires the collection of lots of data, often at very frequent intervals. The position of the aircraft, its heading (direction of travel), its altitude, orientation (pitch, yaw and roll), its airspeed, the position of the various flight control surfaces, the engine thrust, coolant temperatures, cabin pressure ... and so much more – all need to be sensed, transmitted, processed and, where necessary, displayed in order that the pilot can take the required actions.

1.1 *Avionics*

Avionics – an aircraft's electronic control, sensing and display systems – nowadays accounts for at least ten per cent of the cost of a new aircraft. This high initial expenditure reduces running costs, allowing just two pilots to operate the flight deck where previously a flight engineer was also needed to check the vast array of instruments. Computer-based instrument displays have brought many instruments together into a smaller space and any malfunction can be instantly highlighted and brought to the attention of the pilot (see Figure 1).

In a modern avionics system, information is sensed electronically and signals are sent along metal or fibre optic cables – known as fly-by-wire and fly-by-light, respectively. The control mechanisms and linkages are less bulky, and mechanical devices are needed only to move the control surfaces, lower the wheels and so on.

Such systems produce great savings in weight and volume compared with mechanical systems, 5:1 at least. Using a technique known as **multiplexing**, several signals can be combined and sent down the same cable, thus reducing the weight still further.

There are other advantages as, being linked through computers, the actions of the pilot can be moderated within safe and comfortable boundaries. For example, passengers do not appreciate the nose being tipped up at angles greater than 25° or tipped down through more than 10°, or being banked over at more than 45°.

Lots of redundancy is built into the system, with sensors usually being connected to computers in parallel by four independent channels. The computers compare signals with one another and act on the 'majority vote' if there is a discrepancy.

You might be concerned about computers running aircraft, and might remember the failure of the Ariane 5 rocket on its maiden flight in 1996 (Figure 4). The subsequent Inquiry Board suggested that one of the main problems was in transferring software from Ariane 4 without changing all the anticipated sensor readings in line with the new and more powerful rocket. Because of this human error, the system was unable to interpret the readings it sensed correctly, and acted as though something was wrong. The control software for aircraft has to satisfy certain standards, much as you saw for the HACCP (Hazard and Critical Control Points) system for food safety in the unit *Good Enough to Eat*. Aircraft software is subjected to many checks and has 60–70% redundancy built in so that failures can be accommodated.

Figure 4 *Debris raining down after self-destruct of Ar-501 (Ariane 5)*

Fly-by-wire or fly-by-light?

Communications along screened electrical and fibre optic cables, respectively, with computer control, are now commonly known as fly-by-wire (FBW) and fly-by-light (FBL) technology.

FBW was first introduced on an airliner by Airbus Industrie, a European multinational consortium owned by Aerospatiale of France, British Aerospace of Great Britain, CASA of Spain and Daimler-Benz Aerospace of Germany, with Italy's Alenia, Fokker in the Netherlands and Belairbus in Belgium acting as associate risk-takers on special projects (see Figure 5). The four owning companies have responsibility for constructing different parts of the aircraft before they are finally assembled by Aerospatiale. The consortium was put together in 1970 and by 1998 had taken over three thousand orders for aircraft and delivered over eighteen hundred to world markets.

Since the A320 (Figure 6) went into service as the first FBW airliner in April 1988, some 700 Airbus Industrie aircraft of similar type have covered seven million flying hours without major mishap caused by the system. The catastrophe rate for a fleet of 3000 such aircraft averaging 3000 hours per year is estimated at one in a hundred years. Lightning strikes on an Airbus 320 and an A330-300

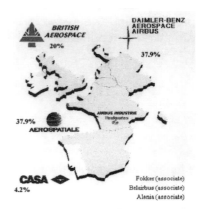

Figure 5 *Airbus Industrie map of owners*

(Figure 7) have resulted in visible damage to the aircraft skin but have left the avionics systems unaffected.

Fly-by-light (FBL) relies on exactly the same type of system except that now all the sensors are optically rather than electronically or electrically based, with fibre optic cable providing the communications links. Such a system will further reduce weight and provide links that are immune to electromagnetic interference that might occur in lightning storms or overflying high-power radio and radar transmitters. With a military aircraft it would also provide immunity from the electromagnetic pulse (EMP) that is emitted in a nuclear explosion and which would otherwise interfere with or even destroy any on-board electronics. Such systems are being developed by NASA and they have performed tests on an F-18 fighter with FBL control and are planning tests on a Boeing 757. The Skyship 600 airship has had FBL controls since 1988.

In the military context both FBL and FBW enable an aircraft to be far more manoeuvrable than those with conventional controls. The airframe can be turned and twisted at high speed and yet can be safely controlled through the fast responses of its on-board computer system. The Eurofighter 2000 (Typhoon) is a fly-by-wire aircraft.

Figure 6 *Airbus A319, A320 and A321 aircraft*

Figure 7 *Lightning damage on an A330*

ACTIVITY I   **Building an Airbus**

Look at the Airbus web page <http://www.airbus.com/> to get an overview of the operation of such a large company. Identify some of the problems that such an organisation has to overcome in designing and making aircraft co-operatively. Factors might include (i) fitting it all together, (ii) languages, (iii) finance and (iv) harmony and agreement.

Drawing on what you have read in this unit so far, make brief notes on the following:

In a mechanical control system for an aircraft, what problems would be associated with long pipes, lots of fluid and quite a large mass and volume of equipment? How does the reduction of weight and staff increase an airline's profit?

Outline some of the safety advantages of FBW and FBL technology.

1.2 *Sensing the situation*

On an aircraft, there are many different transducers or sensors, i.e. devices that produce an electrical signal that varies in response to changes in some other physical factor. Some are used to sense pressure, which, indirectly, provides a measure of airspeed. More complex are the gyros and accelerometers that sense the attitude and position of the aircraft, and optical pyrometers that provide information on the engine temperature. Somewhat simpler transducers sense the position of control surfaces (see Figure 3), the pilot's stick or control column, or the angle of the nosewheel. How might this be achieved?

The potentiometer

A simple but commonly used position sensor depends on the rotary **potentiometer** or **potential divider**. Figure 8 shows a linear potentiometer with a resistive element of uniform thickness, width and resistivity. As you saw in the AS unit *Digging Up the Past*, the potential difference between the sliding contact and a fixed end depends on the position of the sliding contact.

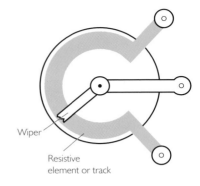

Figure 8 *Insides of a linear potentiometer*

ACTIVITY **2** | **Sensing position**

Discuss how a potentiometer, attached to a model flap, aileron or nosewheel, could be arranged to give a voltage output that depends on their position.

Then use a potentiometer attached to a model aircraft part to show how the voltage output varies with angular position (see Figure 9).

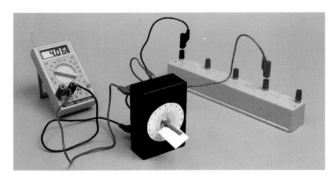

Figure 9 *Model flap attached to a potentiometer*

In Activity 2 you should have found that the variation of voltage output with angle was fairly linear. In practice this variation will be affected by the resistance of the device that is measuring the voltage output. If there is time, you might be able to explore this further in Activity 3.

ACTIVITY **3** | **What if the voltmeter's resistance is low?**

Investigate the effect of taking the potentiometer output to a low-resistance voltmeter. See how a voltage follower or buffer amplifier can help deal with the problem that arises.

The voltage output from the position sensor needs to be transmitted to the computers that are managing the aircraft's flight. This could be achieved by simply having long wires connected, via an appropriate interface or link, to the computers. However, long wires produce large voltage drops and so what started at 5 V might end up at only 2 V, with a consequent faulty interpretation of position. So other means of communicating information are needed that do not get degraded *en route* – these will be considered in part 2 of this unit.

QUESTION

1 Why is a large voltage drop associated with a current in a long cable?

1.3 Summing up part 1

This part of the unit has explained why FBW and FBL are useful technologies for aerospace, how they have increased safety, and how a potentiometer can be used as a position sensor. This has involved some revision of work from the AS units *Technology in Space* and *Digging Up the Past*. Use Activity 4 and question 2 to check your progress and understanding.

ACTIVITY 4 | **Summing up part I**

Look back through your work and make sure you know the meaning of each of the terms printed in bold type in the section.

At the end of this unit, you will be asked to produce a 'handbook' for airline passengers outlining the principles behind FBL and FBW, and explaining how they can enhance safety. You might like to start gathering information for this now.

QUESTION

2 Assume that the voltmeter in Figure 10 has an infinite resistance. State the readings in each case. (In (c), the contact is at the mid point on the potentiometer.)

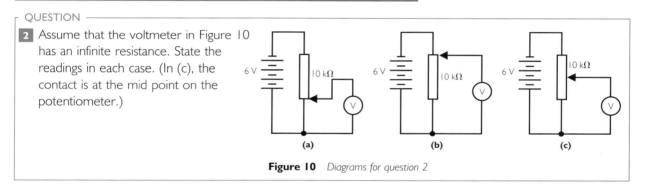

Figure 10 *Diagrams for question 2*

---

2 Sending and receiving information

As was indicated at the end of part 1, a direct electrical connection is not a good way to transfer information from a sensor to a computer. In practice, the information is usually conveyed by an electromagnetic wave that is either broadcast through the air or, more commonly, sent along a cable. The varying voltage output from a sensor is combined with a much higher frequency signal known as a **carrier wave**. This process is known as **modulation** and can be done in various ways. We will be looking at just three: AM or **amplitude modulation**, FM or **frequency modulation** and PCM or **pulse code modulation**. Exactly the same techniques can be used in radio broadcasting (Figure 11), only now the varying electrical signal is the voltage output from a microphone that mimics the vibrations produced by a sound wave.

Figure 11 *The dial of a radio set*

2.1 Amplitude and frequency modulation

Amplitude modulation is a relatively simple type of modulation and is used for many radio broadcasts. The desired information – the voltage output from a microphone or sensor – is combined with a high-frequency carrier voltage. The **superposition** of these two waves results in a signal that has the same frequency as the initial carrier and an amplitude that varies (see Figure 12).

Study note

You might wish to look back at the AS unit *The Sound of Music*, where superposition was introduced.

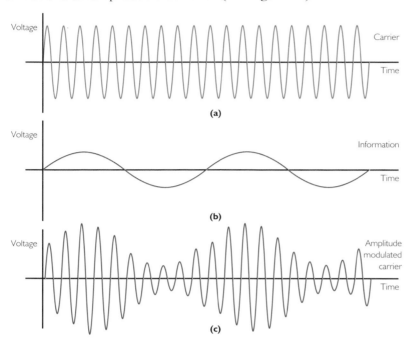

Figure 12   *Amplitude modulation: (a) carrier wave, (b) information, (c) resulting signal*

The carrier wave can be a radio wave, but it can also be light, as you may see in Activity 5. On reception the carrier trace has to be removed from the signal to leave the original information – this part of the process is known as **demodulation.**

AM transmission is relatively cheap but it does suffer from **noise** (unwanted electrical signals such as those produced by electric lawnmowers, drills, etc.) and from fading, which can come about when signals reach the receiver by two or more different routes (e.g. by taking different paths through the atmosphere, or by reflecting off buildings or aircraft as well as travelling directly to the receiver).

ACTIVITY 5   **Amplitude modulation**

Set up two signal generators to show amplitude modulation.

With the Philip Harris Fibre Optic kit, see how the model flap's output voltage modulates light from a light-emitting diode (LED). Then, after transmission down an optical fibre, see how the demodulated light can indicate the model flap's output voltage, and hence its position. This is what happens in 'fly-by-light'.

Activity 5 demonstrates an analogue system and, although it works, it would not be adopted in modern aircraft. Instead, a pulse code modulated system is used – see section 2.2.

Frequency modulation is also a technique used for radio broadcasts. Now the *frequency* of the carrier wave is varied according to the variation of voltage of the information signal. Where the information signal's voltage is high and positive the frequency is raised, and vice versa (see Figure 13). At the receiver the FM carrier wave needs to be demodulated in order to recover just the information signal. FM modulated transmission is more expensive than AM but is far less affected by noise.

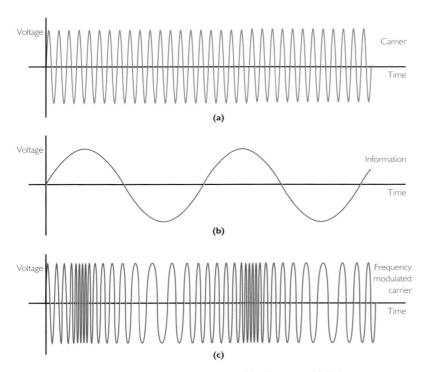

Figure 13 *Frequency modulation: (a) carrier wave, (b) information, (c) FM carrier*

ACTIVITY 6 **Frequency modulation**

Set up two signal generators, or alternative equipment, to show frequency modulation.

Although FM is less vulnerable to noise, it still allows information to be degraded in transmission. Both AM and FM use **analogue** signals, i.e. voltages that vary continuously. When an analogue signal is received, there is no reliable way to tell whether it has been altered, nor of correcting for any alterations. For more reliable transmission of information, **digital** signals are used – see the AS unit *The Sound of Music* and section 2.2 of this unit.

QUESTIONS

3 What is the advantage of transmitting a sound-modulated radio signal rather than just the sound wave itself?

4 Explain how the combination of two signals can produce fading.

5 How will 'noise' from an amplitude-varying signal affect (**a**) an AM system and (**b**) an FM system? Explain.

6 Outline the difference between an analogue and a digital signal.

2.2   *Pulse code modulation*

Pulse code modulation (PCM) is the process by which a continuously varying voltage signal is represented as a series of numbers. This involves measuring (sampling) the varying voltage at regular intervals, and expressing each measurement as a number in binary code. Each number is then transmitted as a sequence of on/off pulses. Even if the signal is degraded so that the 'high' and 'low' voltages are not exactly as they were when transmitted, the signal can still be decoded accurately at the receiver since each pulse need only be somewhere above or below a cut-off voltage and it will still be interpreted correctly as 'high' or 'low'.

There are other advantages, too. First, digital signals can be fed direct to computers, since they operate on such signals anyway. Second, it is possible to include a 'check' in the transmission. A simple check would be to add up all the signals in a given number of samples, and send an additional number that represented that sum; at the receiver, the 'check' number would be compared with the sum of received samples.

There are two aspects of PCM that need to be considered. First, what should be the time interval between samples? And second, with what precision should each voltage sample be measured? We will consider each in turn.

Pulse amplitude modulation and sampling

The first stage of the process is pulse amplitude modulation (PAM) in which the signal is sampled at regular intervals to produce a sequence of voltage pulses as shown in Figure 14.

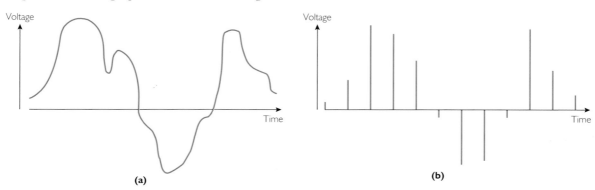

(a)   **(b)**

Figure 14   *Pulse amplitude modulation: (a) original trace and (b) sampled trace*

The sampling has to be done at a rate greater than twice that of the highest frequency present in the signal. Activity 7 illustrates the effect of sampling at too low a rate.

Study note

In *The Sound of Music* you saw that most sounds contain sinusoidal sound waves with a range of frequencies.

ACTIVITY 7 | **Name that tune**

Listen to the effect of sampling music at various frequencies.

As well as the problems illustrated in Activity 7, there is another problem produced by sampling at too low a frequency. This is called aliasing, and is illustrated in Activity 8.

ACTIVITY 8 | **What is the frequency?**

Place a card with slits cut into it (the sampler) over pictures of waveforms with various frequencies. By 'joining the dots', sketch what the reconstructed waveform appears to be in each case, and try to decide on its frequency. The spurious frequencies (i.e. those that appear to be there but were not present in the original waveform) are called aliases.

QUESTIONS

7 A person with 'perfect' hearing can hear sounds over a frequency range of about 10 Hz to 20 kHz. Explain why music CDs use a sampling rate of 44 kHz.

8 How might aliasing create a problem when trying to communicate information?

Quantisation

The next stage is for an analogue to digital (A-D) converter (see section 2.3) to code each sample. To do this the whole voltage range of the signal is split into a number of discrete levels called **quantum levels** and the process is called **quantisation**.

The words 'quantum' and 'quantisation' are used when a physical quantity can only take certain distinct values and cannot vary continuously. The same words are used, for example, to describe the energy levels of an electron bound in an atom – as you saw in *The Sound of Music*, such an electron can only have certain energies, i.e. its energy levels are quantised. The branch of physics known as quantum mechanics deals with quantisation on an atomic scale, where the size of the steps is determined by nature. In the case of PCM, however, the step size is a matter of human choice, so in discussing PCM we are *not* getting into quantum mechanics.

When the voltage falls within a level it is given the value of that level. In Figure 15(a) samples 7 and 8 have a quantum level of 2 and signals 3, 4 and 10 a quantum level of 8. In Figure 15(b), each level is represented by a four-**bit** (**bi**nary dig**it**) code; 2 is binary 0010 and 8 is binary 1000.

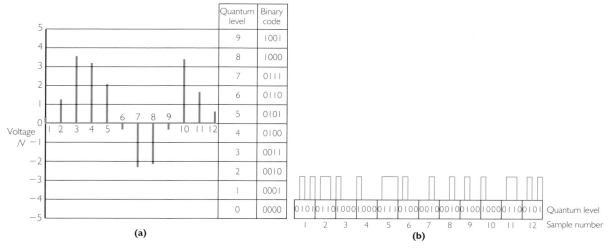

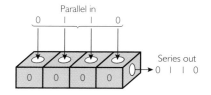

Figure 15 *Each voltage sample is assigned a quantum level (a), which is coded as a series of pulses representing binary numbers (b)*

Each binary digit appears at the output of the analogue to digital converter at the same time. These digits then have to be arranged in order one behind the other to allow them to travel down a single cable as a series of on/off signals or flashes of light. This is achieved, as shown in Figure 16, with a device called a parallel in–series out shift register. In an aircraft, these codes can now be fed into the computers to indicate the positions of the control surfaces and so on.

As you can see from Figure 15, each quantum level corresponds to a range of voltages, so the information will be distorted somewhat; this effect is known as quantising distortion.

Low-amplitude signals are more seriously affected by quantising distortion than signals of larger amplitude, because the 'rounding' introduced in sampling a low amplitude is a greater fraction of its actual value. Rather than dividing the voltage range into equal steps, it is common to arrange the quantum levels as shown in Figure 17. This process, known as **companding** (from **com**pressing and ex**panding**), is particularly useful when dealing with the transmission of speech, where for much of the time the output has low amplitude. At the other end of the communications link the process has to be reversed to reproduce the speech correctly. Special integrated circuits deal with the tasks of companding and decompanding.

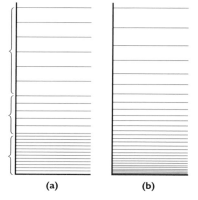

Figure 16 *Parallel in–series out shift register*

Figure 17 *Arrangements of quantum levels used in companding: (a) three bands, with the same spacing of levels within each band, and (b) continuous variation in band spacing*

QUESTIONS

9 What would be the effect on quantising distortion of splitting the same voltage range into a greater number of equal quantum levels?

10 Figure 15 shows a four-bit output (0000, 0001, 0010, etc.). The highest four-bit output is 1111. What is the greatest number of quantum levels that a four-bit output could provide? (Do not forget quantum level 0.)

11 It is usual in avionics to have information transmitted in 16-bit code. How many quantum levels would this provide?

12 Explain how companding can reduce distortion of a speech signal.

2.3 Converting the signals

Pulse code modulation involves the conversion of analogue signals into digital ones. When digital signals are received, it is sometimes necessary to convert them back to analogue. For example, the output from a digital broadcast needs to produce an analogue sound wave; in an aircraft analogue signals might be required to drive mechanical devices. We will look at each type of conversion in turn.

Analogue to digital (A-D) conversion

Converting an analogue signal to a digital one is quite a complicated process, but it is solved cheaply today with purpose-built integrated circuits. Figures 18 and 19 show the principles behind one type of **A-D converter**.

Initially a ramp voltage (really a series of steps – see Figure 18) is generated at a regular rate, and the number of steps counted. The input voltage to the A-D converter is then compared with the ramp voltage using an integrated circuit device called a comparator. When the input voltage just exceeds the ramp voltage the counting of the steps stops. The number of steps, which is proportional to the size of the input voltage, is recorded by a binary counter which then provides the digital output (see Figure 19). A parallel in–series out shift register is then used to arrange the bits one after the other ready to send down the cable (see Figure 16).

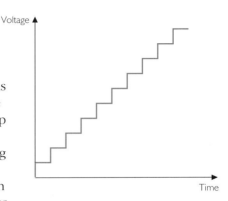

Figure 18   *Ramp voltage*

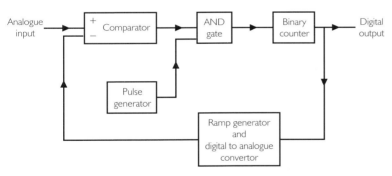

Figure 19   *Block diagram of ramp A-D converter*

This simple technique is not commonly used as the conversion time depends on the input voltage. With a high input voltage a lot of steps will have to be gone through before the counting stops, and in that time the signal might have changed considerably.

Another faster technique initially compares the input voltage with half the maximum voltage it can deal with. If the input is higher it then generates a higher voltage and compares that. If it is lower it generates a lower voltage and compares that, and so on. Eventually the input is neither higher nor lower than the one being compared, so the input voltage is known. Conversion still takes time, but usually less than with the previous method. This method is known as conversion by successive approximation and is rather like the technique used by contestants on 'The Price is Right' trying to home in on the correct price of a mystery item.

Digital to analogue (D-A) conversion

Conversion from a digital to an analogue signal will give you an opportunity to revisit some ideas about resistance and potential difference from the AS units *Technology in Space* and *Digging Up the Past*.

Using an op-amp

One type of digital to analogue (D-A) converter uses an **operational amplifier** (commonly called an op-amp) and some resistors. An op-amp has two input connections, marked − and +. These are called the 'inverting' and 'non-inverting' inputs, respectively, and are marked on the circuit symbol shown in Figure 20.

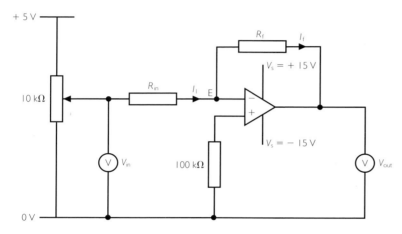

Figure 20   *An op-amp with a single connection to the inverting input*

An op-amp is designed to have two important properties. First, the potential difference between the + and − input connections is extremely small – essentially zero. Second, the current through the op-amp itself is always extremely small (a few nanoamperes or less; $1\,\text{nA} = 1 \times 10^{-9}\,\text{A}$), so it, too, is essentially zero.

In D-A conversion, the non-inverting input is connected via a fixed resistor to the 0 V line, and is then essentially ignored; it is the inverting input that plays a key role in processing the signals. D-A conversion involves several input resistors connected in parallel to the inverting input, each with a different voltage across it. But to begin with we will look at a simpler arrangement with just one input resistor, as shown in Figure 20.

In the circuit of Figure 20, R_f is known as the feedback resistor and R_{in} the input resistor. The input voltage, V_{in}, is connected across R_{in}, and V_{out} is the output voltage. Since the pd between the two inputs is zero, and the non-inverting input is connected to 0 V, the inverting input is also at a potential of 0 V – it is known as a virtual earth. As there is essentially no current through the op-amp, the current must be the same throughout R_{in} and R_f. We can therefore draw a simplified partial circuit diagram for just these two resistors, as in Figure 21.

Study note

The idea of potential at a point was discussed in the AS unit *Digging Up the Past*.

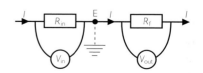

Figure 21   *Single input resistor and feedback resistor connected to an op-amp*

Since the current, I, is the same in both resistors, we can write

$$I = \frac{V_{out}}{R_f} = \frac{V_{in}}{R_{in}} \qquad (1)$$

However, as point E is at zero potential, if V_{in} is positive then V_{out} will have to be negative. So we need to take care with signs, and write

$$V_{out} = -\frac{R_f}{R_{in}} \times V_{in} \qquad (2)$$

You can think of the resistors in Figure 21 as being like a seesaw; as the input voltage is made larger and more positive (V_{in} 'goes up'), the output also becomes larger, but in the negative sense (V_{out} 'goes down'). The ratio of V_{out} to V_{in} depends on the ratio of the resistors, rather as the ratio of displacements of the ends of a seesaw depends on the ratio of the lengths either side of the pivot.

ACTIVITY 9 **Using an op-amp**

Using either an electronic circuit board, or a simulator such as *Crocodile Clips*, explore the behaviour of an op-amp with a single input resistor. Does it behave as predicted by equation (2)?

Then explore the behaviour when there are two parallel input voltages and the input and feedback resistors are all equal, as shown in Figure 22.

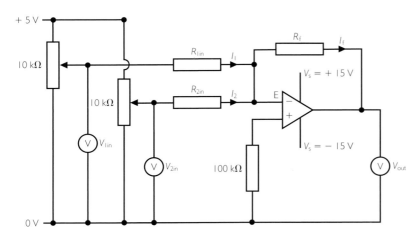

Figure 22 *An op-amp with two parallel connections to the inverting input*

In Activity 9, you should have found that an op-amp with two parallel inputs, with all the resistors the same, just adds the two input voltages to produce an (inverted) output voltage. The partial circuit diagram in Figure 23 helps explain how this comes about.

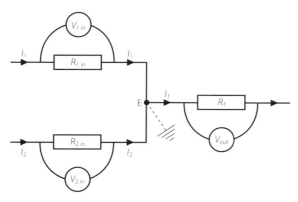

Figure 23 *Two input resistors and a feedback resistor connected to an op-amp*

As there is no current in the op-amp, we can write

$$I_f = I_1 + I_2 \tag{3}$$

Remembering that point E is at $0\,V$, and taking care with signs, we can therefore write

$$-\frac{V_{out}}{R_f} = \frac{V_{1\,in}}{R_{1\,in}} + \frac{V_{2\,in}}{R_{2\,in}} \tag{4}$$

and so when all three resistors are equal, V_{out} is the sum of the two input voltages, but with a negative sign.

D-A conversion with an op-amp

A **D-A converter** needs to add together a set of voltage pulses that represent a binary number, and produce a single output voltage. The 'high' and 'low' pulses (1s or 0s) represent the 'ones', 'twos', fours', etc., as the binary number is read from right to left. Figure 24 shows an op-amp used to add together such a set of pulses that have first been through a series in–parallel out shift register so that they all reach the op-amp together. Each pulse forms an input voltage across one of the input resistors. In this case, the input resistors must produce a weighted sum – for example, the pulse representing the 'fours' must contribute four times as much as the pulse representing the 'ones' – so now the input resistors must all be different. As question 13 illustrates, the input resistors must be in the ratio 1: 2: 4: 8 and so on.

QUESTIONS

13 **(a)** Write down an expression for I_f in terms of the input currents I_1, I_2, I_3 and I_4 in Figure 24.

(b) By substituting $I_f = -\dfrac{V_{out}}{R_f}$ $I_1 = \dfrac{V_{1\,in}}{R_1}$, etc. in your answer to part (a), write an expression that involves all the voltages and resistances in the circuit.

(c) If $R_4 = 8R_f$, $R_3 = 4R_f$, $R_2 = 2R_f$ and $R_1 = R_f$, write an expression for V_{out} in terms of $V_{1\,in}$, $V_{2\,in}$, $V_{3\,in}$ and $V_{4\,in}$ only.

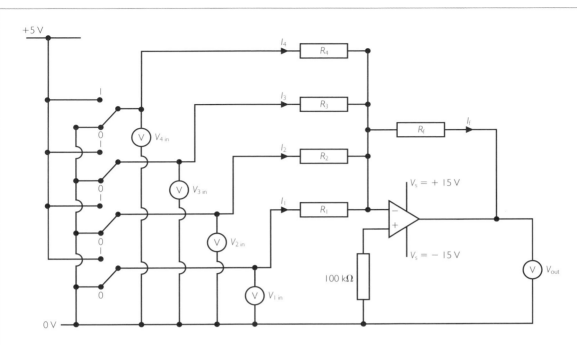

Figure 24   *A four-input binary weighted op-amp*

(**d**) In this example, which input voltage represents the 'ones' and which represents the 'eights' in a four-bit binary number?

14 In a D-A converter the input voltage represents binary 0 or binary 1. Consider the set-up in Figure 24 where binary 1 is 5 V and binary 0 is 0 V.

(**a**) What output voltage would result from the following inputs:
(**i**) 1111, (**ii**) 1000, (**iii**) 0001, (**iv**) 0000?

(**b**) (**i**) What is the smallest voltage difference that this four-bit device can deal with?

(**ii**) If you wished to be able to deal with much smaller changes of voltage, what would you have to do?

15 You might prefer to have an output voltage that is positive. How can you use a second op-amp to achieve this without changing the size of the final output voltage?

Activities 10 and 11 allow you to explore the behaviour of a D-A converter and a series in–parallel out (SIPO) shift register. Rather than the arrangement shown in Figure 24, most D-A converters use an arrangement known as an R-2R ladder network of resistors, which is more compact (see Figure 25). You can also explore this in Activity 10.

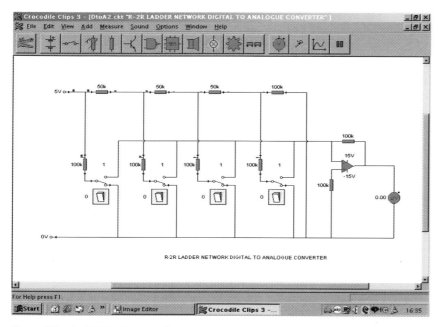

Figure 25 *An R-2R ladder network*

D-A conversion with an op-amp

Use *Crocodile Clips* to illustrate the behaviour of D-A converters similar to those shown in Figures 24 and 25.

A SIPO shift register

Use *Crocodile Clips* to illustrate the behaviour of a SIPO shift register as shown in Figure 26.

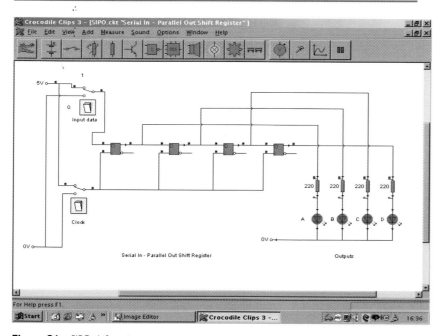

Figure 26 *SIPO shift register*

2.4 *Multiplexing*

It is important in an aircraft to keep both the weight and volume of components to a minimum. Rather than having a separate strand of cable from each sensor to each actuator, it is possible to send many separate signals down one cable by the technique known as **multiplexing.**

A common method of multiplexing, used in telephone networks, on aircraft and in computer data transfer, is **time division multiplexing** (TDM). Figure 27 shows the principles behind this technique.

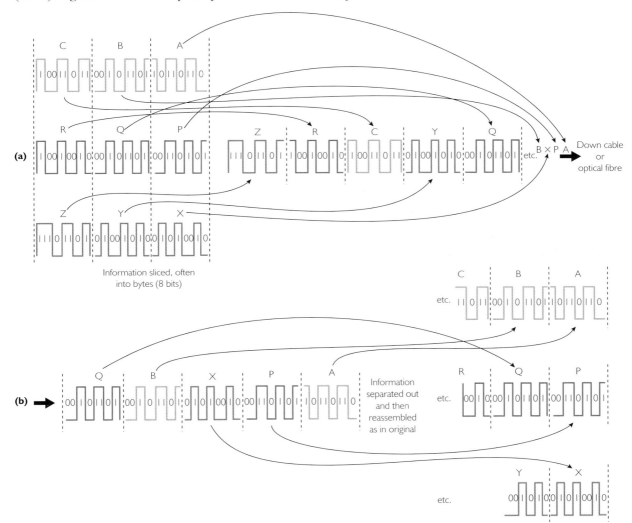

Figure 27 *Time division multiplexing system: (a) multiplexer and (b) demultiplexer*

Each set of input data is sampled and sliced up into equal time sections. Sections from each are then assembled in order, one behind the other, and sent down the one cable. At the other end the sections are extracted in order and reassembled to give the same number of data outputs as there were inputs. The device that does the initial splitting and assembly is known as a **multiplexer** (MUX) and that at the other end as a **demultiplexer** (DEMUX). They are effectively very fast switches.

In Activity 12, you can use a model to illustrate TDM. In this set-up, the multiplexer and demultiplexer units have so-called analogue switches built into them. These switches are electronically operated on-off switches (the name 'analogue' is perhaps a bit confusing, since they can only be on or off). The same type of switch was used in the sampler in Activity 7.

The arrangement is shown in Figure 28(a). As the analogue switch in the multiplexer connects the signal from the Red switch through, it automatically stops that from the Green switch, and vice versa. At the demultiplexer the same type of analogue switch is used to divert the signals to the Red and/or Green LEDs. A crucial element is getting the analogue switches to operate in phase with each other and this is brought about in this model system by using ac from the mains.

A different arrangement is shown in Figure 28(b). Here, encoding and decoding 'chips' (integrated circuits) sense which switches are closed, send the information along a fibre link, and decode the information at the far end. Other more sophisticated methods are employed in commercial TDM.

(a)

(b)

Figure 28 *Models to illustrate TDM: (a) controlled by the mains frequency and (b) encoding and decoding*

ACTIVITY 12 **Multiplexing**

Use the model communications systems shown in Figure 28 to illustrate TDM

For the transmission of analogue signals **frequency division multiplexing** is used. The basis of this technique is shown in Figure 29; here three signals are modulated onto a carrier wave to produce signals in the range 12–16 kHz, 16–20 kHz and 20–24 kHz. They are then transmitted together on the same cable. At the other end they are separated out by band-pass filters and demodulated to recover the original signals. A band-pass filter severely reduces the intensity of signals above and below its operating range.

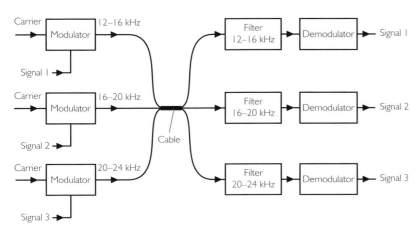

Figure 29   *Frequency division multiplexing*

QUESTIONS

16 A time division multiplexed optical fibre system transmitting at a rate of 10^9 bits s^{-1} has a number of sensors to be connected to it. If each sensor needs to transmit at a rate of 10^3 bits s^{-1}, what is the greatest number of sensors that can be connected?

17 If a frequency division multiplexed system had eight sensors connected to it, each requiring a bandwidth of 10 kHz, what would have to be the overall bandwidth of the system?

ACTIVITY 13 **All down one cable**

Design an article like those in Dorling Kindersley's 'The Way Things Work' CD, to show how the two types of multiplexing allow thousands of signals to all travel together down one cable. You might like to design this with a computer graphics package or even make it into a web page with one of the web page design packages, though a paper drawn version would still be very adequate.

2.5 *Digital sensors*

You may have wondered if there are sensors that have a digital output and so do not require the use of an A-D converter. They are indeed available and most are of the type that sense position and rely on a coded strip or disc. They are commonly used in robotics to sense the position of robotic arms.

Figure 30 shows how a three-bit digital sensor works. Radiation from light- or infrared-emitting diodes (LEDs and IREDs) shines on to the strip or disc from one side, with three phototransistor detectors directly opposite them on the other. Where the strip or disc has a clear section the radiation passes through and where it is opaque the radiation is stopped. Figure 31 shows how a digital sensor could be used to sense the position of an aircraft's nosewheel.

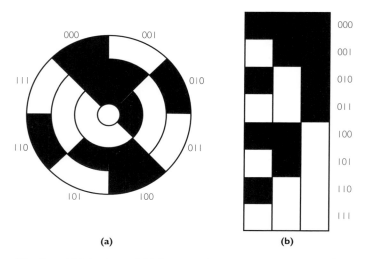

(a)   **(b)**

Figure 30   *Three-bit (a) rotary and (b) linear encoders*

Figure 31   *Digital sensor on model nosewheel*

Activity 14 uses a simple optical sensor with two types of encoding strips: a binary encoder as shown in Figure 30, and another that uses the Gray code which, as you will see, avoids the problem of having all the bits changing at once. Activity 15 shows how the output from the Gray code strip can be converted into binary code.

ACTIVITY 14 **Digital optical sensor**

Connect a digital sensor to its power supply and see how movement of its encoding discs or strips affects the lighting of the LEDs that display which bits are high (lit) or low (unlit).

ACTIVITY 15 **Gray code to binary converter**

Devise and draw a circuit diagram that shows how two Exclusive OR (XOR) logic gates can be connected so that a three-bit binary code output results from a three-bit Gray code input.

QUESTIONS

18 Outline the principle of an optical encoding disc and how it enables position to be indicated in a digital form.

2.6 Summing up part 2

This part of the unit introduced the techniques of modulation and outlined the advantages and disadvantages of three forms of modulation. You also saw how sampling, quantising and companding are involved in pulse code modulation. We then concentrated on digital signals and the ways in which they are processed in communications systems. You saw the principle of a simple A-D converter before exploring how an op-amp can be used as the basis of a D-A converter, and then had a brief introduction to the idea of multiplexing. Finally there was a brief account of digital sensors.

Use Activities 16 and 17 and questions 19 and 20 to help you check your progress.

ACTIVITY 16 **Summing up part 2**

Look back through your work and make sure you know the meaning of each term printed in bold.

ACTIVITY 17 **How it works: the R-2R D-A converter**

Suppose that a student in your group had been absent when you discussed the R-2R ladder network D-A converter. Write a short account that will help this student to understand how it works.

---

3 *In transmission*

In this part of the unit, we consider a signal in transit along a cable. In a fly-by-wire system, signals are transmitted down coaxial cables. A number of the Airbus Industrie civil aircraft – A319, A320, A321, A330, A340 and the Eurofighter 2000 – have such systems. The air balloon Skyship 600 and other prototype aircraft have fly-by-light systems that use fibre optic cables to carry infrared or visible light signals. Figures 32 and 33 show the structures and relative sizes of these cables. We will concentrate on fibre optic cables.

Figure 32   *Coaxial cable (left) and a bundle of optical fibre (right)*

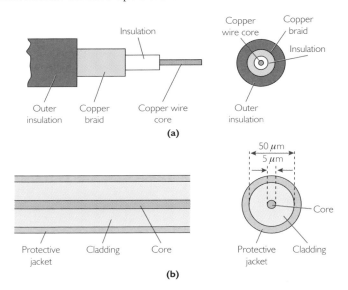

Insulation

Copper wire core
Copper braid
Insulation

Outer insulation
Copper braid
Copper wire core
Outer insulation

(a)

50 μm
5 μm

Core

Protective jacket
Cladding
Core
Protective jacket
Cladding

(b)

Figure 33   *The structure of (a) coaxial cable and (b) fibre optic cable*

3.1 Dispersion in fibre optic cables

In fibre optic cables the signal travels inside a thin transparent fibre, meeting the surface at an angle of incidence greater than the critical angle. It therefore undergoes total internal reflection and is confined to the interior of the fibre. Figure 34 shows this for a fibre made of a single material. The radiation is reflected at the surface, i.e. $i = r$ in Figure 34, and if the angle of incidence, i, is greater than the critical angle, C, then total internal reflection takes place. C depends on the refractive index, μ, between the fibre and its surroundings:

$$\mu = \frac{1}{\sin C} \qquad (5)$$

Path of radiation

Fibre

Figure 34   *Radiation undergoes total internal reflection within an optical fibre*

Study note

You might wish to refer back to your work in the AS units *The Sound of Music* and *Good Enough to Eat* for a reminder of these ideas.

Unfortunately a pulse of radiation (light or infrared) entering a simple fibre is not just directed one way. It spreads sideways and results in many rays travelling by different routes down the fibre (Figure 35). This **dispersion** (spreading) means that a signal that starts as a sharp pulse is smeared out after travelling along the fibre. Because the refractive index is the same throughout the fibre, the speed of propagation of the light through it is the same regardless of route. Hence ray C in Figure 35 takes the least time and A the most. The result is that a sharp pulse gets spread out. The longer the fibre, the worse things get. This effect is known as **multipath dispersion.** The net effect is shown in Figure 36.

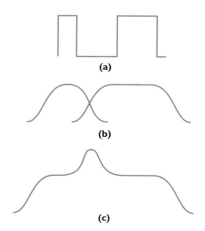

(a)

(b)

(c)

Figure 36 *(a) Original pulses, (b) after dispersion and (c) combined effect*

Figure 35 *Rays travelling different routes in a fibre*

C

A B

Multipath dispersion can be reduced somewhat by limiting the range of angles of incidence that result in total internal reflection. This can be achieved by surrounding the core fibre with a **cladding** material whose refractive index is slightly smaller than that of the core to produce a **stepped index** fibre. Activity 18 illustrates how this works.

ACTIVITY 18 **Multipath dispersion**

Draw accurate diagrams to show how rays of light travel along (a) an optical fibre of refractive index $\mu_1 = 1.6$ surrounded by air and (b) the same fibre clad with material whose refractive index is $\mu_2 = 1.4$. Compare the ranges of angles of incidence that result in total internal reflection in each case.

Even a clad fibre, though, is subject to multipath dispersion. To reduce the dispersion further, **graded index** or **multimode** fibres were developed in which the refractive index changes gradually across the fibre in such a way that the middle of the fibre has a greater refractive index than its edges (see Figure 37). Then the ray travelling down the centre will have a lower speed of travel than that taking the zig-zag longer path. With careful grading it is possible to get the rays to meet at the end to within $1\,\text{ns}\,\text{km}^{-1}$. This is the type of fibre used in prototype aircraft.

The most recent development has been what is called single or **monomode** fibres in which the rays can only pass down the centre of the fibre. You might then think that no dispersion would occur as all the rays would have travelled the same path in the

Figure 37 *Paths of rays within a graded index fibre*

same time. This would be so if the light was of a single wavelength, but even laser light has a small spread of wavelengths – 1 to 2 nm or less. The refractive index of a material varies with wavelength, which causes the small spread of wavelengths to arrive at different times due to their different speeds. The result is again a slight spreading of the pulse.

QUESTIONS

21 Outline the ways in which optical fibres and radiation sources have been developed to reduce dispersion.

22 On aircraft cable lengths are typically less than 100 m. If the dispersion is 1 ns km^{-1}, and the pulse rate is 10^9 s^{-1}, explain whether dispersion is likely to be a major problem.

3.2 Attenuation

Both coaxial and fibre optic systems have their advantages and drawbacks, and **attenuation** (loss of intensity) occurs in both. Attenuation in metal cables occurs where there is a transfer of energy from the signal to the cable due in part to its resistance and leakage through the insulation. The fibre cannot in practice be completely transparent, and some of the signal is absorbed by the material through which it passes. The attenuation in an optical fibre is modelled in Activity 19 using a jelly 'fibre' that absorbs strongly in the infrared region (see Figure 38). This activity also demonstrates a mathematical way of describing the attenuation.

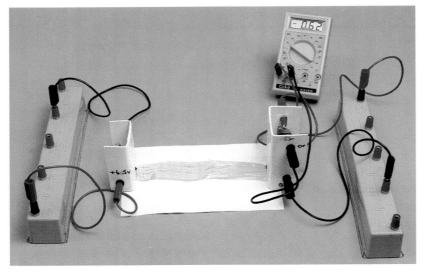

Figure 38 *The jelly fibre*

ACTIVITY 19 **The jelly fibre**

Using an infrared emitting diode as the source and an infrared-sensitive phototransistor as the detector, investigate attenuation in a glass fibre modelled with jelly.

Figure 39 shows some typical results from Activity 19. As you should have found, the intensity (as measured by the voltage) always changes by the same fraction when the length is changed in equal steps. For example, in Figure 39, a length of $x = 7\,\text{cm}$ reduces the voltage to half its initial value (V falls from 1.0 V to 0.5 V), after a further 7 cm the voltage has halved again ($x = 14\,\text{cm}$, $V = 0.25\,\text{V}$), and after another 7 cm it has halved yet again ($x = 21\,\text{cm}$, $V = 0.125\,\text{V}$).

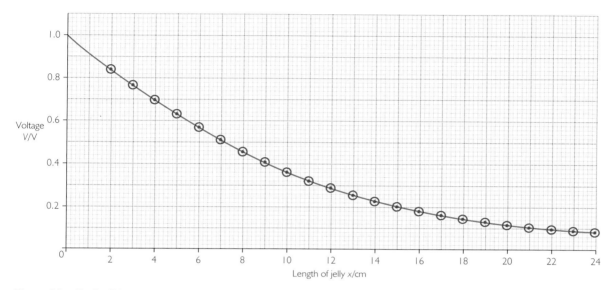

Figure 39 *Graph of V against x for a jelly fibre*

Exponential change

The attenuation of radiation intensity in a fibre is one example of an **exponential** change. Exponential changes are characterised by the 'equal steps resulting in equal fractional changes' pattern. In the case of capacitor discharge, the steps are time intervals, whereas here they are equal changes in length.

Mathematically, the exponential change in intensity with distance can be described by the equation

$$I = I_0 \, e^{-\mu x} \tag{6}$$

where I_0 is the intensity of radiation that enters the jelly, I the intensity after it has travelled a distance x, and e is the exponential number: $e \approx 2.718$. μ is the **absorption coefficient** which describes how rapidly the intensity is attenuated with distance – if μ is large, then $e^{-\mu x}$ rapidly becomes small as x is increased, i.e. the radiation is strongly attenuated.

After a distance $x = 1/\mu$, the intensity will fall to $1/e$ of its initial value ($\mu x = 1$, and so $I = I_0 \, e^{-1}$). The value of μ can therefore be found from a graph such as that in Figure 39 – find the distance over which I falls to $1/e$ of its initial value, and then find the reciprocal of that distance. This reasoning also tells us the units of

μ – if x is expressed in m, then μ has units m^{-1}, and if x is in cm, then μ is in cm^{-1}.

Many, but by no means all, naturally occurring changes are exponential. How can you tell whether a change is exponential? One way is to see whether it fits the 'equal steps resulting in equal fractional changes' pattern – but this can be time-consuming, and if there are large experimental uncertainties is hard to decide where to draw a best-fit curve. A neater way is to plot a **log–linear graph**. Taking the log of both sides of equation (6) gives

$$\log(I) = \log(I_0) - \mu x \log(e) \qquad (7)$$

Equation (7) describes a relationship of the form $y = mx + c$; $\log(I_0)$, μ and $\log(e)$ are all constants. If $\log(I)$ is plotted on the y-axis and x on the x-axis, then the graph is a straight line as shown in Figure 40. This gives another way to test whether a change is exponential – a log-linear graph produces a straight line. This is usually quicker than looking for the 'equal steps, equal fractions' pattern, and it is often easier to tell whether points lie close to a straight line than it is to draw a best-fit curve through points with error bars.

Study note

If you are familiar with calculus, you can show that the 'equal steps resulting in equal fractional changes' pattern will always be described by an equation such as equation (6).

Study note

A log–linear graph is so called because the y-axis has a logarithmic scale whereas the x-axis is linear.

Maths reference

Using log graphs
See Maths note 8.7

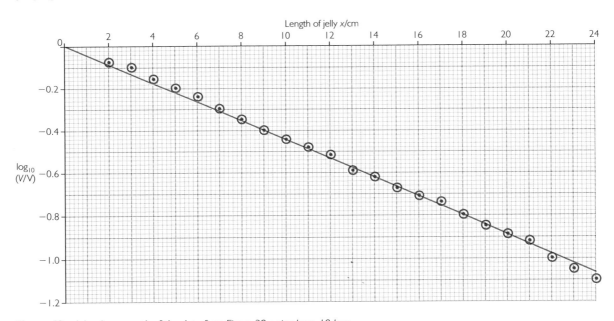

Figure 40 *A log–linear graph of the data from Figure 39, using base 10 logs*

If you use so-called natural logarithms (logs to base e, $\log_e$) then equation (7) becomes

$$\log_e(I) = \log_e(I_0) - \mu x \qquad (8)$$

because $\log_e(e) = 1$. A graph of $\log_e(I)$ against x is a straight line with gradient $-\mu$. Figure 41 shows a plot of the same data in Figures 39 and 40, using logs to base e. From the triangle drawn, the gradient of this graph is -0.1, so the absorption coefficient in this case is approximately 0.1 cm^{-1}.

Maths reference

Logs to base e
See Maths note 8.5

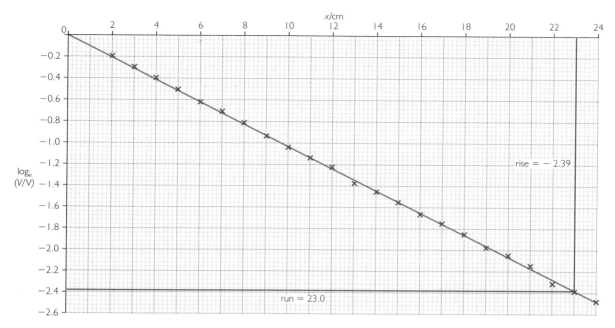

Figure 41 *A logarithmic graph of the data from Figure 39, using natural logs (logs to base e)*

The fibre optic cables used in communications have *much* smaller absorption coefficients than a jelly fibre – absorption coefficients are typically about $10^{-5}\,\mathrm{m}^{-1}$ or less. On board an aircraft, any attenuation is negligible. However, for long-distance communications attenuation can still be a problem, and so it is important to reduce it as much as possible. One way in which attenuation can be reduced is by careful choice of fibre material and wavelength of radiation. As shown in Figure 42, attenuation can depend markedly on wavelength.

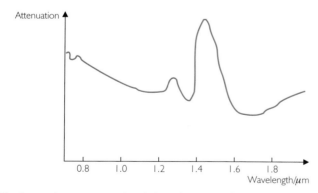

Figure 42 *Attenuation against wavelength for a glass optical fibre*

QUESTIONS

23 An optical fibre has an absorption coefficient $\mu = 2.0 \times 10^{-6}\,\mathrm{m}^{-1}$.

(**a**) Over what distance will the intensity of a signal fall to $1/e$ of its initial value?

(**b**) What will be the intensity of the signal, expressed as a fraction of its initial value, after it has travelled $100\,\mathrm{km}$ along the cable?

3.3 Summing up part 3

This part of the unit looked in detail at the degrading or attenuation of signals due to dispersion and absorption. Attenuation in a jelly fibre illustrated an exponential change, and showed how logarithmic graphs can help analyse such changes. Use Activity 20 and questions 24 and 25 to help you check your progress.

ACTIVITY **20** **Summing up part 3**

Look back through your work and check that you know the meaning of all the terms highlighted in bold.

QUESTIONS

24 In a certain optical fibre, the intensity of the signal falls to half its initial value after travelling 50 km. What is the absorption coefficient of the material expressed in units of m^{-1}?

25 To minimise attenuation, what would be the best wavelength to use for sending signals along the fibre in Figure 42?

4 Making an image

In part 2 of this unit, we were concerned with measurements (e.g. of position) that could each be expressed as a single number or as a sequence of numbers that changed with time. Sometimes, however, a two-dimensional picture is required, which can be encoded electronically and transmitted in exactly the same way as a single measurement. In some aircraft, there are devices that give a pilot 'night vision' by first producing an infrared image of the surroundings and then displaying the image visually in a helmet-mounted display (Figure 43) – the image is projected into the pilot's field of vision, giving him or her a realistic picture of the view ahead. Other examples of communicating two-dimensional images will probably be more familiar – TV pictures, for example.

Figure 43 *A helmet-mounted display*

4.1 Charge-coupled devices

This part of the unit is about one particular device, the CCD (charge-coupled device), which is used to obtain two-dimensional images. CCDs are used to obtain the images for helmet-mounted displays, and are also in common use in video cameras – they are also replacing photographic plates for recording astronomical images obtained by telescopes.

A CCD is a small 'chip' made of layers of semiconductor material. It is typically about 2 cm by 2 cm, made up of about 1000 by 1000 tiny light- or infrared-sensitive pixels (from 'picture element') (see Figure 44). When a photon is absorbed by a pixel, a photoelectron is released from the semiconductor – this is rather similar to what

Figure 44 *A CCD 'chip'*

happens in the photovoltaic cells that you used in the AS unit *Technology in Space*, and in the photoelectric effect that you met in the AS unit *Digging Up the Past*. However, in this case, the released electron remains trapped within the pixel. As more photons are absorbed, more electrons are released. If an image is projected on to a CCD (e.g. through a system of lenses) then charge builds up in each pixel according to the number of photons that have reached it, thus recording the image.

In order to 'read' a CCD image, the electrons are electrically shuffled along the CCD step by step in a sort of 'bucket brigade', producing a small pulse of current as each 'package' reaches the edge. The size of each pulse can be detected and encoded to produce a digital signal, and the signals can then be processed and transmitted in just the same way as those that represent single measurements.

If the image is bright, then only a very short exposure time is needed – the CCD images that give a pilot 'night vision' are produced so rapidly that there is no noticeable time delay. However, if a CCD is being used in an astronomical telescope to build up a image of a very faint galaxy, that takes much longer. Figure 45 shows some CCD images taken with various exposure times. You can see that the image gradually builds up as more and more photons arrive (if your school or college has a telescope and CCD imager, you might be able to see this for yourself).

Each pixel in a CCD behaves rather like a tiny solar cell attached to a **capacitor** – a device that stores electric charge. The simplest type of capacitor consists of two parallel conducting plates separated by an air gap. When a capacitor becomes charged, electrons simply redistribute themselves between the plates, making one positive and one negative. There is no net charge added to the device (see Figure 46). Most practical capacitors (Figure 47) consist of thin layers of conducting material separated by thin layers of electrical insulation and fitted into a compact space, thus concealing the layered structure.

Study note

Encoding and decoding are discussed in part 2 of this unit.

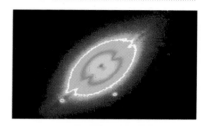

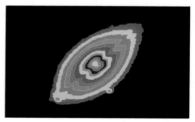

Figure 45 *CCD images taken through a telescope with various exposure times*

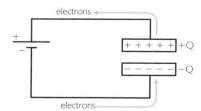

Figure 46 *Charging a capacitor*

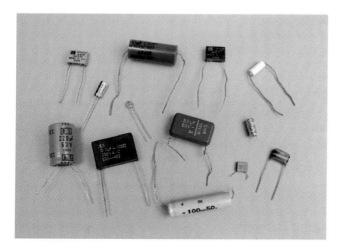

Figure 47 *Various types of capacitor*

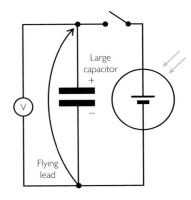

Model CCD imager

Use an array of capacitors and solar cells, each connected as in Figure 48, to model the behaviour of a CCD imager.

In Activity 21 you probably took it on trust that the voltage across a capacitor is proportional to the charge it stores. You can explore this in more detail in Activity 22.

ACTIVITY 22 **Spooning charge on to a capacitor**

Transfer measured amounts of charge on to a capacitor and observe how the voltage across the capacitor changes.

Figure 48 *Circuit of model CCD pixel*

In Activity 22 you will have found that equal additions of charge raised the voltage across the capacitor by equal amounts. In other words, $Q \propto V$. The constant of proportionality, C, is the **capacitance** of the device.

$$Q = CV \qquad \text{or} \qquad C = \frac{Q}{V} \tag{9}$$

The SI unit of capacitance is the farad, F, where $1\,\text{F} = 1\,\text{C}\,\text{V}^{-1}$. Most practical capacitors are rated in microfarads, μF ($1\,\mu\text{F} = 1 \times 10^{-6}\,\text{F}$) or picofarads, pF ($1\,\text{pF} = 1 \times 10^{-12}\,\text{F}$); the ones you used in Activity 21 were unusual in being rated at about $1\,\text{F}$ – they were 'memory back-up' capacitors for use in computers.

Study note

If you have studied the unit *Transport on Track* you will have met capacitance there.

QUESTIONS

26 A typical MOS (metal oxide semiconductor) capacitor in a CCD imager has a capacitance of 1 pF and can store a charge of $Q \approx 0.16\,\text{pC}$.

(**a**) How many electrons would have to be collected by the MOS capacitor to give it a charge of $0.16\,\text{pC}$? (Electron charge $e = 1.6 \times 10^{-19}\,\text{C}$.)

(**b**) What will be the voltage across such a capacitor when it is charged to this extent?

27 The capacitors used in the model CCD imager were rated at about 1 F. If the highest voltage the solar cells can provide is 0.45 V, what is the maximum charge that one of these capacitors could have stored?

28 If a solar cell provides an average current of 50 mA at 0.45 V to a 1 F capacitor, calculate how long it is before it reaches its maximum charge for that voltage. (The current actually varies as the capacitor charges, as you may recall if you have studied the unit *Transport on Track*.)

CCD readout

In order to extract information from the array, each packet of charge has to be moved to an output system (like the voltmeter in the model in Activity 21) and measured. Each package of charge is moved to a separate read-out register. To enable this to be done, the CCD is designed so that each tiny light-sensitive capacitor is separated from its neighbour by another capacitor that remains unaffected by light. One complete step in the read-out for one pixel is shown in Figure 49. First a temporary voltage is applied to the 'empty' capacitor so that charge spreads into it. The first capacitor's voltage is then reduced to zero leaving all the charge on the adjacent one.

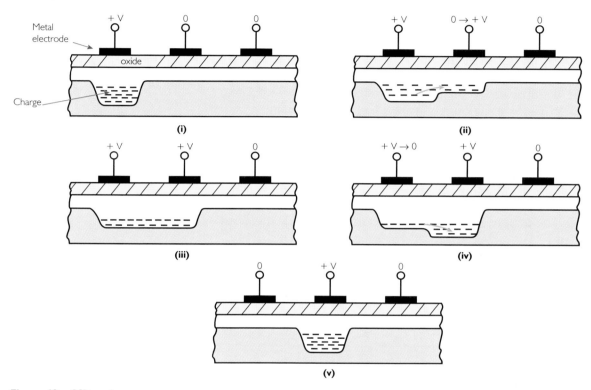

Figure 49   *CCD read-out*

This process is repeated until each capacitor's initial charge gets to an output sensor where the voltage across the capacitor is finally measured. All of this is done with the aid of a computer, which controls the application of the voltages, and an A-D converter, which encodes each measured voltage in order to determine how bright an image it should display on each point on a screen.

4.2 *Energy and capacitors*

Capacitors are not just stores of charge. The storage of charge also involves storing energy. In Activity 23 you will see how the stored energy is related to the capacitor voltage.

ACTIVITY 23 **How many bulbs will it light?**

By charging a 10 000 μF capacitor to different voltages and discharging into various numbers of small light bulbs, suggest a relationship between capacitor voltage and the energy it stores.

In Activity 23, you should have found that 3 V provided enough energy to light one bulb with a moderately bright flash, doubling the voltage to 6 V provided enough energy to light four bulbs, and tripling the voltage enabled nine times as many bulbs to be lit. This suggests that the stored energy is proportional to the square of the capacitor voltage. The following argument shows why this is indeed the case.

We already know that charge stored is proportional to the voltage to which the capacitor has been charged. A graph of voltage, V, against charge, Q, will therefore be a straight line through the origin, as in Figure 50.

Think now of a very small amount of extra charge δQ that has been placed on the capacitor, so small that the voltage across the capacitor remains at V. The small amount of work done, δW, is given by

$$\delta W = V \times \delta Q \tag{10}$$

which is the shaded area in Figure 50.

To charge the capacitor from zero to V would require the addition of lots of extra tiny amounts of charge δQ, each of which would need work done equal to the area of another tiny strip on the graph. The total energy transferred would be given by the areas of all the tiny strips added together, i.e. the area under the graph. Since the graph is a straight line, we can write

$$W = \frac{1}{2}QV \tag{11}$$

where W is the total work done when the capacitor is charged to a potential difference V. Since energy is conserved, this must also be the energy stored in the capacitor and which is recovered when it discharges.

Combining equations (9) and (11) we get:

$$W = \frac{1}{2}CV^2 \tag{12}$$

and

$$W = \frac{1}{2}\frac{Q^2}{C} \tag{13}$$

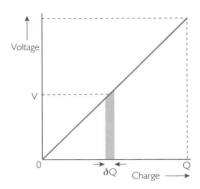

Figure 50   *Graph of voltage, V, against charge, Q, for a capacitor*

Study note

Remember in the AS unit *Technology in Space* you saw that $W = QV$.

QUESTIONS

29 How much energy is stored in a $10\,000\,\mu F$ capacitor when it is charged to: (**a**) 3 V, (**b**) 6 V, (**c**) 9 V?

4.3 Summing up part 4

This part of the unit has shown you how a CCD responds to incident radiation, building up a pattern of charge that represent the brightness of an image, and has involved some aspects of the physics of capacitors.

ACTIVITY **24** **Summing up part 4**

Look back through your work and make sure you know the meaning of each term printed in bold.

5 *On display*

A pilot needs to be able to see clearly how an aircraft is functioning, and so the display of information is a crucial aspect of avionics. Various techniques have been developed to improve the quality of such displays so that they can be easily seen and interpreted. Many of these techniques are not specific to avionics, however, and are to be found in many other types of communication system.

Modern airliners like the A340 and the Eurofighter 2000 have arrays of instruments giving details of speed, heading, altitude, position ... and a myriad of other pieces of information (see Figures 51 and 52). Some displays only appear on screen when required.

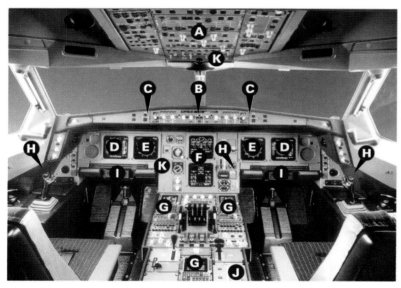

A OVERHEAD PANEL
System panels used more frequently are in lower part, centre row for engine related systems, flow scheme from bottom to top. Push-button controls, dark cockpit philosophy

B FLIGHT CONTROL UNIT (FCU)
Engages autopilot and autothrust. Selection of modes HEADING, SPEED, MACH, ALTITUDE, VERTICAL SPEED, LOC, APPROACH

C EFIS CONTROL PANEL
Select modes, ranges and options of Electronic Flight Instruments System, BARO:STD selection, master warning, master caution, autoland warning and sidestick priority lights

D PRIMARY FLIGHT DISPLAY (PFD)
Engage status of Flight Director, autopilot and autothrust. Flight Mode Annunciation. Indication of ATTITUDE, AIRSPEED, ALTITUDE, VERTICAL SPEED, HEADING, ILS-DEVIATION, MARKER, RADIO ALTITUDE

E NAVIGATION DISPLAY (ND)

F ELECTRONIC CENTRALISED AIRCRAFT MONITORING SYSTEM - ECAM
UPPER DISPLAY UNIT (DU)
Engine primary indication, fuel quantity, slats/flaps position, warning/caution/memo message
LOWER DISPLAY UNIT (DU)
Aircraft system synoptics, status of systems

G MULTI-PURPOSE CONTROL DISPLAY UNIT (MCDU)
Controls the Flight Management System (FMS) and the Central Fault and Display System (CFDS)

H SIDESTICK

I PULL-OUT WORKING TABLE
In stowed position - Footrest pedals right and left

J FULL-SIZE PRINTER

K STAND-BY INSTRUMENTS
Attitude, altitude, speed, DDRMI, compass

Figure 51 *Instrument displays in the A340*

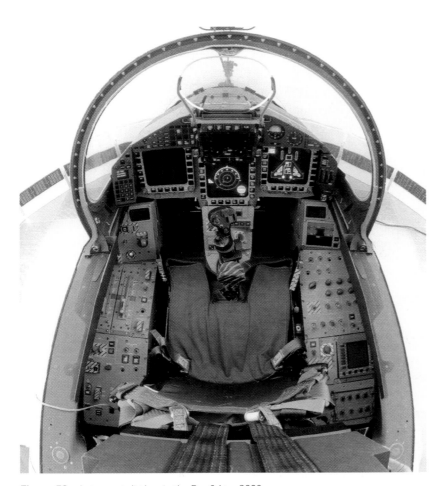

Figure 52 *Instrument displays in the Eurofighter 2000*

Originally, virtually all the instruments were needle dial displays, much like the analogue electrical meters and pressure gauges (see Figure 53) you probably met earlier in your science and technology education.

(a)

(b)

Figure 53 *Needle-type (a) electrical meter and (b) pressure gauge*

Displays in modern aircraft are of three types. In head-down displays (HDDs) the viewer has to look directly at the instrument – it might well be a case of looking down, but could also be upwards or sideways. Head-up displays (HUDs) project an image directly in front of the viewer to combine with the view of the environment (see Figure 54). Helmet-mounted displays (HMDs) are essentially HUDs provided direct to an image-forming system attached to the aviator's helmet (see Figure 43). If you have studied part 4 of the unit, you will already have come across one of the key elements of a helmet-mounted display – the CCD imager. The display moves with the head.

Figure 54 *Head-up display*

In this part of the unit we will concentrate on head-down displays; making these into head-up or helmet-mounted displays simply essentially involves optical projection of the image, which lies outside the scope of this unit. We will deal in turn with three types of display – the light-emitting diode (LED), the liquid crystal display (LCD) and the cathode-ray tube (CRT).

5.1 Light-emitting diode displays

You will have almost certainly met visible LEDs as 'power on' indicators on a hi-fi or video, but they have much wider usage. On aircraft single LEDs tend to be used for warnings, engine monitoring, as on/off indicators in programmable switches, and in small matrix displays. Much larger screen displays can also be made using a million or so small LEDs. By grouping the LEDS in sets of red, green and blue mounted close together a full colour image can be produced by adjusting the brightness of each LED appropriately. To make a moving image, each LED is switched on or off by a computer at the correct time to produce the picture. Switching times can be quite short – in the nanosecond (10^{-9} s) region.

Activity 25 involves an exploration of LEDS, and includes some revision of ideas about charge and voltage that you met in the AS unit *Technology in Space*, and about photons and energy levels that you met in the AS units *The Sound of Music* and *Digging Up the Past*.

ACTIVITY **25** **Illuminating LEDs**

Using LEDs of at least two different colours, find the voltage that will just light each one, and suggest an explanation for your results.

Measure the power required to light each LED.

In Activity 25 you should have found that different coloured LEDS required different voltages to make them light. For an explanation, think back to what you have already learned about electronic energies. In a semiconductor light-emitting diode, charge carriers are accelerated across a gap between energy bands, which results in a photon being emitted whose energy is equal to the size of the energy gap. The voltage that is *just* big enough to light the diode corresponds to charge carriers *just* crossing the gap. If a particle with charge q is accelerated through a potential difference ΔV, then it acquires energy ΔE where

$$\Delta E = q\Delta V \tag{14}$$

If this energy is then radiated as a photon, then the frequency f and wavelength λ of the radiation are related to the energy via the expressions

$$\Delta E = hf = \frac{hc}{\lambda} \tag{15}$$

where c is the speed of light in a vacuum and h is the Planck constant.

The following data will be needed when you tackle questions 30 and 31:

electron charge, $e = 1.60 \times 10^{-19}$ C

$1\,\text{eV} = 1.60 \times 10^{-19}$ J

Planck constant, $h = 6.63 \times 10^{-34}$ J s

speed of light in vacuum, $c = 3.00 \times 10^8 \, \text{m s}^{-1}$.

QUESTIONS

30 The bandgaps for compounds of indium and antimony can be as small as 0.18 eV and those of gallium and nitrogen up to 3.4 eV. Calculate the wavelength of the radiations given off by LEDs with each of those bandgaps.

31 What bandgap energies would be needed to produce visible LEDs emitting light over the range 400 nm to 600 nm? Express your answer in joules and in eV.

32 (**a**) A standard red LED was found to be passing a current of 15 mA when there was a pd of 2.15 V across it. What power was it drawing from the supply?

(**b**) An infrared-emitting diode, operating at a voltage of 1.3 V, passed a current of 100 mA. What power was it drawing from the supply?

(**c**) If you need 10^6 LEDs to produce a screen display, estimate the power required.

5.2 *Liquid crystal displays*

Liquid crystal displays (LCDs) are a fairly recent development but their manufacture is now a multi-billion pound industry and LCDs are used in watches, calculators, on cookers, video-recorders, televisions, computer monitors and so on – and in aircraft cockpits.

A **liquid crystal** is a liquid in which the molecules arrange themselves in some sort of ordered pattern. Although we tend to think of molecules in liquids being completely randomly distributed, many liquids are in fact liquid crystals – these include DNA, RNA, soaps and detergents, and even the brain is about 70% liquid crystal. Liquid crystal display technology has its origins in the 1970s, when George Gray of Hull University made the first stable synthetic liquid crystals known as nematic alkylcyanobiphenyls, which have the important characteristic that their optical properties can be controlled electrically.

A so-called nematic liquid crystal consists of long thin molecules (the Greek word *nematos* means thread-like) that tend to arrange themselves with their long axes parallel to each other, as shown in Figure 55. This comes about because the molecules are **polar** – that is, their charge is neutral overall but not evenly distributed, so one end is slightly positive and the other slightly negative, forming an **electric dipole** (Figure 56). They line up because the positive end of one molecule attracts the negative end of another.

The LCDs in use today are of a type known as twisted nematic (TN) or super twisted nematic (STN). A TN display consists of a thin layer of nematic liquid crystal between two glass plates whose surfaces have been coated with a very thin conducting layer and treated with a rubbed polymer layer that has the effect of creating small parallel grooves. The molecules prefer to lie along, rather than across, the grooves. The glass plates are oriented with one set of grooves running at right angles to the other, which introduces a 90° twist in the molecular arrangement as shown in Figure 57(a). (In an STN display, there is a twist of 270°.) This 'sandwich' is mounted between two pieces of polarising filter set in the 'crossed' position.

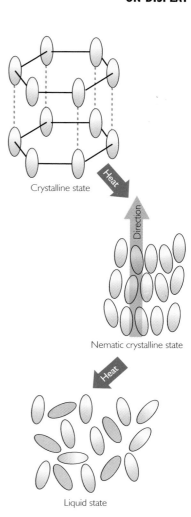

Figure 55 *Molecules in a nematic liquid crystal*

Figure 56 *An electric dipole*

Study note

You met polarised light and polarising filters in the AS unit *Good Enough to Eat*.

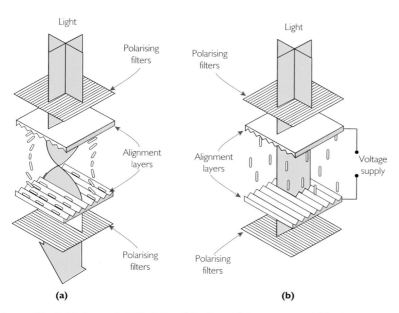

Figure 57 *Twisted nematic LCD display: (a) voltage off, transparent and (b) voltage on, opaque*

The light emerging through the first filter is polarised, and as it travels through the liquid crystal the twisted line of dipoles guides its plane of polarisation so that it rotates through 90° and can emerge through the second filter – the 'sandwich' is transparent. But if a potential difference is applied across the liquid crystal, the molecules are forced to line up end-to-end between the plates as shown in Figure 57(b). There is no longer any rotation of the plane of polarised light, so the light cannot emerge through the second filter and the 'sandwich' is opaque.

To make a display, the thin conducting coating is applied in a suitable pattern (e.g. line segments to make up numbers), each connected to a separate small electrode that can be controlled by a digital on/off signal. Colours can be obtained by placing coloured filters in front of the display and shining white light through it. TV screens, computer monitors and various instruments can be made from arrays of many thousands of individual LCDs.

Electric field

To explain how the molecules are aligned by the applied potential difference, it is useful to introduce the idea of an **electric field**, which is defined as a region in which a charged object experiences a force. The **electric field strength**, E, is defined as the force experienced by a charge of 1 coulomb, in other words, the force per unit charge. If a charge q experiences a force of magnitude F, then the magnitude of field strength is

$$E = \frac{F}{q} \qquad (16)$$

The SI units of electric field strength are $N\,C^{-1}$. As force is a vector, electric field is also a vector – i.e. it has direction as well as magnitude. The **direction of an electric field** is defined as that of the force experienced by a positive charge. An electric field can be represented diagramatically by drawing **electric field lines**, which show the direction in which a free positive charge would move.

It is quite difficult to measure electric field strength by directly measuring the force on a charged object, mainly because in most practical cases the force is quite small. However, there is an alternative way of thinking about electric fields, which both provides an easier way to measure E and also gives some insight into the type of field that is present in an LCD.

Figure 58 shows an arrangement for producing an electric field between two parallel conducting plates, separated by a distance Δx and with a potential difference ΔV applied between them.

If an electric dipole (such as polar molecule) is placed in such a field, then the positive and negative ends will experience forces in opposite directions, i.e. there will be a couple and the dipole will twist round until it is aligned with the field direction as shown in Figure 59.

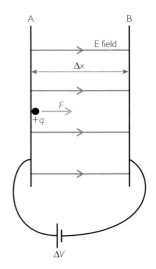

Figure 58   *An electric field between two parallel plates*

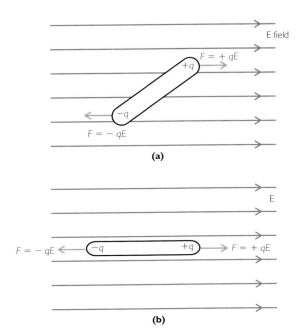

Figure 59 *A dipole in an electric field experiences a couple (a) and so turns until it is aligned with the field direction (b) and there is no longer a couple*

Now think of placing a single small positive charge, q, on plate A in Figure 58. As A is connected to the positive terminal of the power supply, the charged particle will move straight across the gap to plate B – the field direction is straight across from A to B as shown by the field lines in Figure 58. As the particle moves through the potential difference ΔV between the plates, it will gain energy ΔW, where

$$\Delta W = q\Delta V \tag{17}$$

Another way to look to the same situation is to say that there is a force of magnitude F acting on the particle. As the particle crosses the gap, width Δx, this force does work ΔW, where

$$\Delta W = F\Delta x \tag{18}$$

As equations (17) and (18) are just two ways of describing the same thing, we can write

$$F\Delta x = q\Delta V \tag{19}$$

As the electric field strength is defined as the force per unit charge, we can rearrange equation (19) to get its magnitude

$$E = \frac{F}{q} = \frac{\Delta V}{\Delta x} \tag{20}$$

In other words, the field strength is equal to the potential gradient – the rate at which the potential changes with distance across the gap. As field strength is a vector, we should really be careful with signs. The field is directed from A to B, which is the direction in which the potential is decreasing from positive to zero – that is, the potential gradient is negative. We can therefore write equation (20) as

$$E = \frac{-\Delta V}{\Delta x} \tag{20a}$$

Equation (20) provides an alternative way to define and measure electric field strength, and also gives its alternative SI unit: $V\,m^{-1}$.

Figure 60 shows a piece of apparatus that can be used to measure field strength – a double flame probe. There are two tiny flames at the tips of two fine metal tubes (which are connected to a gas supply). A flame produces some ionisation in the air, and the ions move until there is no potential difference between the flame and its immediate surroundings. The two fine tubes are connected to the cap and case of an electroscope, where the deflection of the leaf depends on the potential difference between the cap and the case. The electric field strength close to the tips of the fine tubes can then be found from a measurement of the potential difference indicated by the electroscope and the physical separation of the tips.

Figure 60 *Using a double flame probe to explore an electric field*

ACTIVITY 26 **Probing the field**

Use a double flame probe to investigate the size and direction of the electric field between parallel plates and in some other arrangements.

Further investigations

Measure the capacitance of various arrangements of metal plates, including some where they are not parallel.

QUESTIONS

33 Show that the SI units $N\,C^{-1}$ and $V\,m^{-1}$ are exactly equivalent.

34 (**a**) If the voltage between two parallel plates is 1 kV and they are separated by 0.1 m, what is the magnitude of the electric field strength between them? Give your answer in both possible SI units.

(**b**) How large a force would this electric field exert on a charge of $3\,\mu C$?

35 An LCD operating at a voltage of 2.5 V passed a current of 140 pA ($1\,pA = 1 \times 10^{-12}\,A$). What power was it drawing from the supply?

36 An LCD in a pocket calculator is operated by a 1.5 V power supply.

(**a**) If the conducting layers in the display are separated by $10\,\mu m$, what is the strength of the electric field within the display?

(**b**) What would be the magnitude of the force experienced by a free electron within this field? (Electron charge $e = 1.60 \times 10^{-19}\,C$.)

ACTIVITY **27** **Comparing LCD and LED displays**

Compare the voltages and powers required to operate an LCD and an LED 7-segment display.

Further **investigations**

Measure and compare the response times of LEDs and LCDs.

5.3 Cathode-ray tube

The oldest type of electronic display is the cathode-ray tube (CRT). These are still very widely used in TVs, oscilloscopes and computer monitors, and form the basis for many of the displays used in avionics.

Figure 61 shows one type of cathode-ray tube, known as a Perrin tube after its designer Jean Baptiste Perrin (1870–1942), and Figure 62 shows a CRT from a television. Inside each tube there is an **electron gun** in which electrons are released from a negative electrode (a cathode), and accelerated in an electric field between the cathode and anode (positive electrode). The resulting stream of high-energy electrons hits a phosphor screen, causing it to glow. (Originally the electron beam was called a 'cathode ray' before people knew what it consisted of.) There must be a vacuum inside the tube, otherwise air molecules would scatter the electron beam. Around the outside of the tube are deflection coils – current in these coils produces a magnetic field that deflects the electron beam.

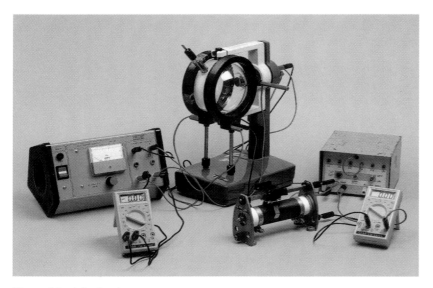

Figure 61   *A Perrin tube*

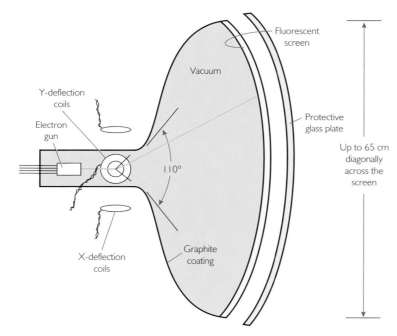

Figure 62   *A CRT used in a television*

ACTIVITY **28** **The Perrin tube**

Use a Perrin tube to explore the operation of a cathode-ray tube. Adjust the tube so as to produce a 20 mm deflection of the spot on the screen.

We will now look in more detail at the operation of each part of a CRT and see how it contributes to the formation of an image.

Electron gun

Figure 63 shows details of an electron gun. The filament, F, is heated by an electric current and, by a process known as **thermionic emission**, electrons that have enough energy escape from the filament's surface much as water evaporates from a puddle of rain. These electrons and the radiant energy from the filament heat up a nickel cathode (C) coated with a mixture of barium and strontium oxides, which results in the thermionic emission of a large number of electrons from the cathode. A potential difference (often called the gun voltage) between the cathode C and anodes A_1 and A_2 produces an electric field that accelerates the electrons. A_1 is either a hollow cylinder or a disc with a hole in it and focuses the electrons into a narrow beam. A_2 is usually a cylinder with a disc with a hole in at the screen end through which the accelerated electrons pass on their way to the screen. Most guns also incorporate a grid (G), which is negative with respect to the cathode and so controls the overall rate at which electrons pass through the whole system.

The electrons hit the phosphor screen and are brought to rest. Their kinetic energy is transferred to the atoms and molecules in the phosphor screen coating, which become excited and then lose energy by emitting photons.

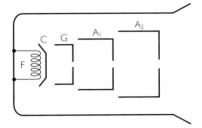

Figure 63 *Electron gun*

QUESTIONS

37 (**a**) If an electron is accelerated by a gun voltage of 5000 V, how much energy does it acquire?

(**b**) What is the electron's (**i**) kinetic energy and (**ii**) speed when it emerges from the gun?

(**c**) How would the presence of air in the CRT affect your answer to (**b**)?

(Electron charge, $e = 1.6 \times 10^{-19}$ C. Electron mass, $m = 9.11 \times 10^{-31}$ kg.)

38 Explain how each of the following would affect the brightness of the spot on the screen:

(**a**) increasing the potential of anode A_2;

(**b**) increasing the voltage across the filament;

(**c**) making the grid more negative with respect to the cathode.

Deflecting the beam

To produce an image, the beam is swept rapidly across the screen in a scanning pattern (Figure 64). As you saw in Activity 28, the deflection is produced by current-carrying coils.

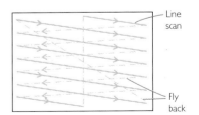

Figure 64 *Line scanning to build up an image*

You may have wondered why an electron beam is deflected in a magnetic field. If you have studied the unit *Transport on Track* you will know that a current-carrying wire in a magnetic field experiences a force at right angles to the wire and to the field direction. The magnitude of this force, F, is given by

$$F = BI\ell \sin \theta \qquad (21)$$

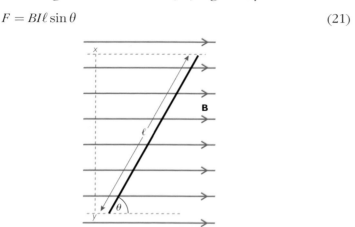

Figure 65   *A current-carrying wire in a magnetic field*

where B is the **magnetic flux density**, I the current, ℓ the length of the wire and θ the angle between the wire and the field direction (see Figure 65). The direction of the force is given by **Fleming's left-hand rule** (Figure 66): where the first finger points along the direction of the magnetic field, and the second finger along the direction of the (conventional) current, the thumb points in the direction of the resulting motion, i.e. the direction of the force.

This force arises because of the motion of the charged particles in the magnetic field – so electrons that are not confined to a wire will still experience a force when they move in a magnetic field. The size of the force can be related directly to the electrons' speed. So what about the force on an electron, or indeed any other charge carrier? To deal with this we need to peer inside our current-carrying conductor (as in Figure 67) and consider the charge carriers that are drifting along at an average speed v.

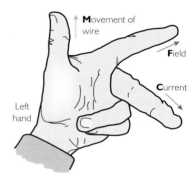

Figure 66   *Fleming's left-hand rule*

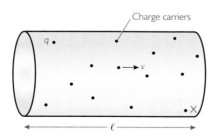

Figure 67   *Charged particles in a conductor*

If each charge carrier has a charge q, and all n charge carriers in this section of conductor pass point X in a time t, then a total charge nq passes point X in that time, and we can write

$$I = \frac{nq}{t} \qquad (22)$$

Substituting for I in equation (21) we have

$$F = B \times \left(\frac{nq}{t}\right) \times \ell \sin \theta = Bnq \times \left(\frac{\ell}{t}\right) \sin \theta \qquad (23)$$

Since the particles are moving at speed v, and the last particle to move past X must have travelled a distance ℓ in time t, we can also write

$$\ell = vt \qquad (24)$$

and so equation (23) becomes

$$F = Bnqv \sin \theta \qquad (25)$$

But this is the force on all n particles. The magnitude of the force on a *single* particle is given by

$$F = Bqv \sin \theta \qquad (26)$$

The direction of the force is still given by Fleming's left-hand rule. But beware – the direction of conventional current is that of the apparent movement of *positive* charge, i.e. in the opposite direction to the movement of electrons.

Study note

The direction of conventional current is that in which positive charge appears to move, i.e. from the positive to the negative terminal of a power supply. Electrons, having negative charge, move in the opposite direction.

QUESTIONS

39 What is the magnitude of the force that acts on an electron moving at a speed of $8.0 \times 10^7 \mathrm{~m~s^{-1}}$ at right angles to a field whose magnetic flux density is $0.10 \mathrm{~T}$? (Electron charge $e = 1.6 \times 10^{-19} \mathrm{~C}$.)

40 In Activity 28, you saw that Helmholtz coils placed either side of a CRT deflected the beam vertically. What can you deduce from this about the direction of the magnetic field produced by the coils?

Helmholtz coils are named after their inventor, German scientist Hermann Helmholtz (1821–1894). They are rather special, being designed to produce a fairly uniform field in the region between them. This is achieved by having their centres separated by a distance equal to their radius (Figure 68). The magnitude, B, of the magnetic flux density thus produced can be calculated using the following expression:

$$B = \frac{8\mu_0 nI}{5r\sqrt{5}} \qquad (27)$$

where I is the coil current, r the radius and separation of the coils, n the number of turns on each coil, and μ_0 is the constant known as the permeability of a vacuum. $\mu_0 = 4\pi \times 10^{-7} \mathrm{~NA^{-2}}$.

In a CRT used to produce a display (e.g. on a TV screen, Figure 69), the coils are mounted close to the electron gun, and they are not in fact Helmholtz coils. As you can see in Figure 62, two sets of coils are used – this is in order to scan the beam in two dimensions and build up an image. The coils and the current they carry must be designed to produce a deflection that matches the screen size. In Activity 28, you found the field that would deflect a

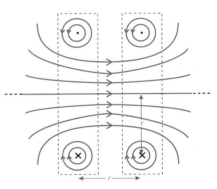

Figure 68 *Magnetic field produced by Helmholtz coils ⊗ indicates current flowing into page ⊙ indicates current flowing out of page*

Figure 69 *TV screen*

particular electron beam through 20 mm, as would be required for a screen 40 mm from top to bottom. To produce a larger image, e.g. on a wide-screen TV, a larger field would be needed.

ACTIVITY 29 **Scanning the screen**

Explain how the magnetic field must change – in both direction and magnitude – in order to produce the line scanning shown in Figure 64.

The image on the screen

To produce a monochrome (single-coloured) image, all that is required is that signals fed to the gun control the brightness of the spot as it is swept across the screen. There are various ways to produce a coloured image. The system most commonly used in aircraft display is the shadow mask type shown in Figure 70.

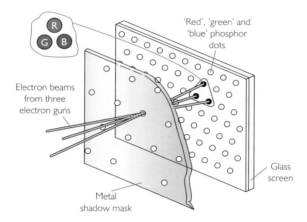

Figure 70 *Shadow mask CRT display*

This system has three electron guns, each accelerating electrons through voltages of around 25 kV. The three electron beams are moved across and down the screen by the magnetic fields provided by the deflection coils. In doing so each beam passes through the shadow mask (a metal plate with holes in) to hit the red, green and blue phosphor dots, respectively, on the screen. Equal exciting of each phosphor would cause white light to be emitted from the screen. Exciting just the blue and green phosphors equally would give cyan, the red and green equally would give yellow, and the red and blue equally would give magenta. Any colour, and its intensity, can be controlled by the speed and number of electrons hitting the combination of phosphors. These, and the position on the screen, are controlled by the signals fed to the electron gun and the deflecting coils by a computer. Television often uses the same type of tube but the images are controlled by signals put out by the broadcasters.

Various other versions of CRT exist, such as the Beam Index tube, which has just a single electron gun that scans over tiny vertical red, green and blue phosphor stripes. Panasonic have designed what is known as a Field Emission Display, which has over ten thousand electron guns, each targeting its electrons on a tiny portion of the screen.

As you will know from your own television, cathode-ray tubes produce good colour, brightness and definition. Their problem is power ratings, which are in the range 500 W and above, which would be undesirable on a military fighter aircraft such as the Eurofighter 2000 (Figure 71).

Figure 71 *Eurofighter 2000*

QUESTIONS

41 Why might having a lot of CRT displays prove a disadvantage on a military fighter?

5.4 Summing up part 5

In this part of the unit you have looked at instrument displays: cathode-ray tubes, light-emitting diodes and liquid crystal displays, and the physics behind them. Magnetic and electric fields played their part and you saw how to calculate and measure these. Use Activity 30 to check your progress and understanding before tackling Activity 31.

ACTIVITY **30** **Summing up part 5**

Look back through your work and check that you know the meaning of all the terms printed in bold.

ACTIVITY **31** **What else is going on?**

There are several other types of display: electroluminescent, plasma, vacuum fluorescent and light-emitting polymer. Search the Internet for information on some of these. Try the following sites:

Cambridge Display Technology <http://www.cdtltd.co.uk>

Centre for Display Technology and Manufacturing – University of Michigan
<http://dtm.eecs.umich.edu/define.html>

Prepare a brief report on the various types of display technology now available or currently being researched.

6 Message received

6.1 Delivering the message

Your brief flight through avionics, signalling and display is now at an end. You have covered many aspects of modern communications technology, all of which are very widely used and not restricted to aircraft. Since this has been a unit about communications, Activity 32 asks you to review and consolidate your progress by communicating what you have learned.

ACTIVITY **32** **Fly-by-wire/light handbook**

Many passengers, or indeed pilots, may be concerned at the technology used on modern aircraft. Produce an illustrated pamphlet that introduces people to the avionic systems used in fly-by-wire or fly-by-light, and outline how safety is enhanced by such systems.

6.2 *Questions on the whole unit*

QUESTIONS

42 (**a**) Plasmas (ionised gases) have been studied using the fast discharge of banks of capacitors to deliver a burst of energy. If a bank of capacitors totalling $100\,\mu F$ was to be charged to $50\,kV$ and then discharged into the plasma in $1\,ms$, what mean power would be delivered?

(**b**) A $100\,\mu F$ capacitor is charged up to just $10\,V$ and the energy stored then discharged into a thermally insulated coil of wire of very low resistance. The temperature rise of the coil is recorded by a very sensitive thermometer as $0.005°\,C$. What rise in temperature would you expect if this same capacitor was charged to $20\,V$ and then discharged into the same coil?

43 In 1982 the first pocket-sized television went on sale. It was the Sinclair Microvision flat-screen TV from Sinclair Research Ltd (Figure 72). It had a cathode-ray tube measuring only $10\,cm \times 5\,cm \times 2\,cm$ and, compared with a normal size tube of that time, was much brighter and drew far less power from the supply.

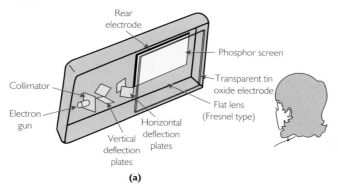

(**a**)

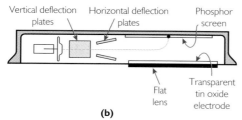

(**b**)

Figure 72 *The Sinclair Microvision cathode-ray tube: (a) front view and (b) view from above*

The tube consisted of an electron gun, collimator (to produce a narrow electron beam), vertical and horizontal deflection plates, a phosphor screen mounted on the rear electrode, a transparent front electrode and a flat lens (a so-called Fresnel lens like those used on overhead projectors). The electron beam was fired in from the side of the screen.

The electric field between the deflection plates and another between the front tin oxide electrode and the rear electrode caused the electrons to be deflected towards the phosphor screen. The viewer looked through the flat lens at the screen at the back of the tube.

(**a**) (**i**)   What must have been the direction of the electric field between the front tin oxide and rear electrodes?

(**ii**)   The potential difference between these electrodes was 800 V and the separation between them 14 mm. What was the electric field strength between these electrodes?

(**iii**)   Calculate the force on an electron in this electric field. (Electron charge $e = 1.60 \times 10^{-19}$ C.)

(**b**) The electrons were produced in a conventional electron gun by the process of thermionic emission.

(**i**)   If fewer electrons were required to be given off each second, what would have to be done to the filament?

(**ii**)   What effect would this have on the screen image?

(**iii**)   If the accelerating voltage of the electron gun was increased, what effect would this now have on the image on the screen?

(**c**) The phosphor screen was mounted on a metal plate. What was the advantage of this over the more usual glass?

(**d**) This television operated from a 6 V lithium battery with a current of approximately 0.08 A.

(**i**)   What was the power drawn from the supply?

(**ii**)   The battery was rated at approximately 1.2 A h (ampere-hours). For how long could you have watched this television before the battery was discharged?

(**e**) Why do modern pocket televisions and portable computers have LED or LCD displays rather than a CRT?

44 In 1897 Sir Joseph John Thomson (1856–1940), who believed that cathode rays consisted of a stream of charged particles, devised an experiment with which to measure their specific charge, i.e. the charge per unit mass. Thomson's result confirmed that the 'rays' were indeed streams of the particles we now call electrons; their specific charge is usually written as e/m.

Thomson's apparatus is shown in Figure 73. Electrons were accelerated into the electric field between the parallel metal plates and deflected downwards from the initial straight-through path. A magnetic field was then applied across the tube deflecting the electron beam back upwards, so nullifying the original deflection.

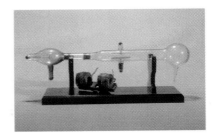

Figure 73   *J J Thomson's apparatus*

(a) (i) If the separation between the plates was 2.0 cm and the potential difference across the plates 2000 V, calculate the electric field, E, produced.

(ii) If the charge on the electron is given the symbol e, write an expression for the magnitude of the force, F_{el}, on an electron in this electric field.

(b) A magnetic field of flux density $B = 3.125 \times 10^{-3}$ T is applied that brings the electron beam back up to the straight-through line. If v is the speed of these electrons, write an expression for the magnitude of the force, F_{mag}, on these electrons due to this magnetic field.

(c) (i) From your answers to (a) and (b), obtain an expression for the electrons' speed, v, in terms of E and B.

(ii) Use your previous answers to obtain a numerical value for v.

(d) (i) If V is the accelerating potential difference, write an expression for the energy transferred to each electron as it is accelerated by the electron gun.

(ii) Assuming that all the energy transferred by the gun is used to increase the electron's kinetic energy, write an expression relating an electron's kinetic energy to the accelerating voltage.

(e) (i) Use your previous answers to obtain an expression for e/m in terms of E, B and V.

(ii) The electrons in this apparatus had been accelerated through a potential difference of 3000 V. Calculate a value for e/m.

6.3 Achievements

Now you have studied this unit you should be able to:

- understand and use the terms *companding*, *quantisation* and *sampling* (2.2)*;

- recall some advantages and limitations of digital and analogue transmission systems (2.1, 2.2, 2.3, 2.4);

- understand the term *modulation* and be able to outline the principles of *amplitude modulation* (AM), *frequency modulation* (FM) and *pulse code modulation* (PCM) (2.1, 2.2);

- explain the principles of how waveforms are encoded and decoded and the need for a sampling rate greater than twice the frequency of the signal being sampled (2.1, 2.2);

- explain the principles of *frequency division multiplexing* (FDM) and *time division multiplexing* (TDM) and why such techniques are needed (2.4);

- recall some advantages and disadvantages of optical fibre and coaxial cables (1.1, 3.1, 3.2);

- explain the effect of *dispersion* in an optical fibre and know how this can be reduced with both graded index and single mode fibres (3.1);

- recognise and use the expression $I = I_0 e^{-\mu x}$ as applied to attenuation losses (3.2);

- plot data on a log-linear graph and hence determine whether they change exponentially (3.2);

- recall and use the expression $C = Q/V$ (4.1, 4.2);

- recognise and use the expression $W = QV/2$ for the energy stored by a capacitor, derive the expression from the area under a graph of charge stored against potential difference, and derive and use related expressions, e.g. $W = CV^2/2$ (4.2);

- explain what is meant by an *electric field* and recognise and use the expression electric field strength $E = F/Q$ (5.2);

- recall that applying a potential difference to two parallel plates produces a uniform electric field in the central region between them, and recognise and use the expression $E = V/d$ (5.2);

- understand and use the term *magnetic flux density* (5.3);

- recognise and use the expression $F = Bqv \sin \theta$ (5.3);

- recall that electrons are released in the process of thermionic emission and explain how they can be accelerated by electric and magnetic fields. (5.3)

*Numbers indicate the section(s) that relate to each achievement.

Answers

1   Think of the expression $V = IR$. If the cables have any resistance (R), then any current (I) must also be associated with a potential difference (V) between the ends.

2   (i) $0\,V$, (ii) $6\,V$, (iii) $3\,V$

3   A radio signal can be readily detected over a much greater distance than a sound wave.

4   If two signals arrive at the receiver with a phase difference of $180°$ (π radians) then they will superpose destructively and the resulting signal will have very low, or zero, amplitude.

5   (a) The noise will affect the modulated signal making it vary in amplitude according to the level of the noise. On demodulation the noise will be reproduced.
    (b) Small changes in amplitude will have little effect on the frequency change in an FM signal and so, on demodulation, the noise is reproduced to a lesser extent.

6   An analogue signal can vary over a continuous range. A digital signal just has two levels – usually expressed as 'on', 'high' or 1 and 'off', 'low' or 0.

7   The sampling frequency must be at least twice the highest audible frequency, hence a frequency of $44\,kHz$ gives an acceptable reproduction of the original sound. Sampling at a much higher frequency would be pointless, as human ears could not detect the improvement.

8   The true transmitted frequency would not be recovered. Only its aliases would be detected by the receiver.

9   The voltage would be more finely sampled so the distortion would be lessened.

10   There are $2^4 = 16$ levels.

11   There are $2^{16} = 65\,536$ levels.

12   In order to retain the refinement of speech, at low amplitude the number of levels needs to be high with the spacings between them small. This reduces quantisation distortion at those levels.

13   (a) $I_f = I_1 + I_2 + I_3 + I_4$

    (b) $\dfrac{V_{out}}{R_f} = -\left(\dfrac{V_{1\,in}}{R_1} + \dfrac{V_{2in}}{R_2} + \dfrac{V_{3in}}{R_3} + \dfrac{V_{4in}}{R_4}\right)$

    (See equation 4.)

    (c) $\dfrac{V_{out}}{R_f} = -\left(\dfrac{V_{1\,in}}{R_f} + \dfrac{V_{2in}}{2R_f} + \dfrac{V_{3in}}{4R_f} + \dfrac{V_{4in}}{8R_f}\right)$

    cancelling R_f throughout:

    $$V_{out} = -\left(V_{in} + \dfrac{V_{2in}}{2} + \dfrac{V_{3in}}{4} + \dfrac{V_{4in}}{8}\right)$$

(d) $V_{1\,in}$ must represent the 'eights' and V_{4in} the 'ones', as $V_{1\,in}$ contributes eight times as much to the sum that makes V_{out}.

14 (a) It can be helpful to rewrite the answer to question 13(c) as

    $$V_{out} = -\left(V_{in} + \dfrac{V_{2in}}{2} + \dfrac{V_{3in}}{4} + \dfrac{V_{4in}}{8}\right) \times 5\,V$$

    where each V_{in} is either 0 or 1.

    (i) $V_{out} = -\left(1 + \dfrac{1}{2} + \dfrac{1}{4} + \dfrac{1}{8}\right) \times 5\,V$

    $\quad = -\left(\dfrac{15}{8}\right) \times 5\,V = -9.375\,V$

    (ii) $V_{out} = -\left(1 + \dfrac{0}{2} + \dfrac{0}{4} + \dfrac{0}{8}\right) \times 5\,V = -5\,V$

    (iii) $V_{out} = -\left(0 + \dfrac{0}{2} + \dfrac{0}{4} + \dfrac{1}{8}\right) \times 5\,V$

    $\quad = -\dfrac{5\,V}{8} = -0.625\,V$

    (iv) $V_{out} = 0\,V$

    (b) (i) $0.625\,V$ (ii) Add more inputs with successively larger resistors.

15   Make V_{out} the input to a second op-amp that has $R_f = R_{in}$ – this will simply invert the voltage without changing its size.

16   If the system can manage 10^9 bits s^{-1} and each sensor transmits at 10^3 bits s^{-1}, then $\dfrac{10^9}{10^3}$ or 10^6 sensors could be connected.

17   The bandwidth must be $8 \times 10\,kHz = 80\,kHz$.

18   Radiation can either pass through a transparent sector or be absorbed by a black sector of the encoding disc. Each combination of transparent and black sectors is unique to a particular position and so, when the LEDs are lit (bit 1/high) or not lit (bit 0/low) the position is identifiable.

19   (a) The information signal makes the carrier wave vary in amplitude to match its variation in amplitude.
    (b) The information signal makes the carrier wave vary in frequency to match its variation in amplitude.
    (c) The information signal is first sampled at regular intervals to provide a pulse amplitude modulated trace. This is then analysed by an A-D converter, which splits the samples into a range of voltages or quantum levels and then converts each into a binary code.

20   The high-frequency components of the signal will be lost, and so the reconstructed signal will not be a good copy of the original. There may be aliasing.

21 Graded index fibres were produced so that rays following different paths met to within 1 ns km^{-1}. Monomode fibres have also been made in which the rays only pass down the centre of the fibre and so no path differences can occur.

A narrow wavelength band source is needed so that the spread due to the variation in wavelength is lessened.

22 Over a path of 100 m, a pulse will be spread by 0.1 ns. Each pulse has a length of 1 ns, so a spread of 0.1 ns would only make a slight difference to the pulse length and dispersion will not be a major problem.

23 (a) $I_x = \dfrac{I_0}{e}$ when

$$x = \frac{1}{\mu} = \frac{1}{(2.0 \times 10^{-6}\,\text{m}^{-1})} = 5.0 \times 10^5\,\text{m}\,(=500\,\text{km}).$$

(b) From equation (6), $\dfrac{I}{I_0} = e^{-\mu x}$. When $x = 1.0 \times 10^5$ m,

$\mu x = 2.0 \times 10^{-6}\,\text{m}^{-1} \times 1.0 \times 10^5\,\text{m} = 0.20$.

$\dfrac{I}{I_0} = e^{-0.2} = 0.82$, i.e. the intensity has fallen to 0.82 times its initial value.

24 From equation (6) or equation (8), we have

$$\log_e\left(\frac{I}{I_0}\right) = -\mu x.$$

Putting $I = \dfrac{I_0}{2}$, $\log_e\left(\dfrac{1}{2}\right) = -\mu x$, i.e. $-0.693 = -\mu x$

With $x = 50$ km $= 5.0 \times 10^4$ m,

$$\mu = \frac{0.693}{5.0 \times 10^4\,\text{m}} = 1.4 \times 10^{-5}\,\text{m}^{-1}.$$

25 Around 1.7 μm would be best. The range 1.6–1.8 μm gives the lowest attenuation.

26 (a) Number of electrons $= \dfrac{Q}{e} = \dfrac{0.16 \times 10^{-12}\,\text{C}}{1.60 \times 10^{-19}\,\text{C}}$

$= 10^6$ electrons.

(b) From equation (9), $V = \dfrac{Q}{C} = \dfrac{0.16 \times 10^{-12}\,\text{C}}{1 \times 10^{-12}\,\text{F}}$

$= 0.16$ V.

27 From equation (9), $Q = CV = 1\,\text{F} \times 0.45\,\text{V} = 0.45\,\text{C}$

28 From question 27, $Q = 0.45$ C.
Current $I = 50$ mA $= 50 \times 10^{-3}\,\text{C s}^{-1}$.

Time to charge $= \dfrac{0.45\,\text{C}}{50 \times 10^{-3}\,\text{C s}^{-1}} = 9\,\text{s}$.

29 The most convenient expression is equation (12):

$$W = \frac{1}{2}CV^2$$

Substituting values:

(a) $W = \dfrac{1}{2}\,10^4 \times 10^{-6}\,\text{F} \times (3\,\text{V})^2 = 4.5 \times 10^{-2}\,\text{J}$.

For parts (b) and (c) you can multiply the answer to (a) by 4 and then by 9, since W is proportional to V^2. This gives

(b) $W = 4 \times 4.5 \times 10^{-2}\,\text{J} = 0.18\,\text{J}$.

(c) $W = 9 \times 4.5 \times 10^{-2}\,\text{J} = 0.405\,\text{J}$.

30 From equation (15): $\lambda = \dfrac{hc}{\Delta E}$

indium/antimony:

$$\lambda = \frac{(6.63 \times 10^{-34}\,\text{J s} \times 3.00 \times 10^8\,\text{ms}^{-1})}{(0.18 \times 1.60 \times 10^{-19}\,\text{J})}$$

$= 6.91 \times 10^{-6}$ m.

gallium/nitrogen:

$$\lambda = \frac{(6.63 \times 10^{-34}\,\text{J s} \times 3.00 \times 10^8\,\text{ms}^{-1})}{(3.4 \times 1.60 \times 10^{-19}\,\text{J})}$$

$= 3.66 \times 10^{-7}$ m.

31 Using equation (15): $\Delta E = \dfrac{hc}{\lambda}$

$\lambda = 400$ nm,

$$\Delta E = \frac{6.63 \times 10^{-34}\,\text{J s} \times 3.00 \times 10^8\,\text{m s}^{-1}}{400 \times 10^{-9}\,\text{m}}$$

$= 5.0 \times 10^{-19}$ J

$= \dfrac{5.0 \times 10^{-19}}{1.60 \times 10^{-19}\,\text{eV}} = 3.1$ eV.

Similarly for $\lambda = 600$ nm,
$\Delta E = 3.3 \times 10^{-19}\,\text{J} = 2.1$ eV.

32 (a) $P = VI = 2.15\,\text{V} \times 15 \times 10^{-3}\,\text{A} = 3.23 \times 10^{-2}\,\text{W}$.

(b) $P = VI = 1.3\,\text{V} \times 100 \times 10^{-3}\,\text{A} = 0.13\,\text{W}$.

(c) Taking the answer to (a) to be typical of visible LEDs, 10^6 of them would have a rating of $10^6 \times 3 \times 10^{-2}\,\text{W} = 3 \times 10^4\,\text{W} = 30\,\text{kW}$.

33 $1\,\text{V} = 1\,\text{J C}^{-1}$, so and $1\,\text{J} = 1\,\text{N m}$,

so

$1\,\text{V m}^{-1} = 1\,\text{J C}^{-1}\,\text{m}^{-1} = 1\,\text{N m C}^{-1}\,\text{m}^{-1} = 1\,\text{N C}^{-1}$.

Maths reference

Derived units

See Maths note 2.3

34 (a) From equation (20),

$$E = \frac{1 \times 10^3\,\text{V}}{0.1\,\text{m}} = 1 \times 10^4\,\text{V m}^{-1} = 1 \times 10^4\,\text{N C}^{-1}.$$

(b) From equation (16),
$F = qE = 3 \times 10^{-6}\,\text{C} \times 1 \times 10^4\,\text{N C}^{-1} = 3 \times 10^{-2}\,\text{N}$.

35 $P = IV = 140 \times 10^{-12}\,\text{A} \times 2.5\,\text{V} = 3.5 \times 10^{-10}\,\text{W}$
$(= 0.35\,\text{nW})$.

36 (a) From equation (20),

$$E = \frac{1.5\,V}{10 \times 10^{-6}\,m}$$

$$= 1.5 \times 10^5\,V\,m^{-1} = 1.5 \times 10^5\,N\,C^{-1}.$$

(b) From equation (16),

$$F = eE = 1.6 \times 10^{-19}\,C \times 1.5 \times 10^5\,N\,C^{-1}.$$

$$= 2.4 \times 10^{-14}\,N.$$

37 (a) Using equation (17), $\Delta W = q\Delta V$, energy transferred to electron

$$= 1.6 \times 10^{-19}\,C \times 5000\,V = 8.0 \times 10^{-16}\,J.$$

(b) (i) Assuming that the kinetic energy gained by the electron is equal to the energy transferred by the electric field in the gun, $E_k = 8.0 \times 10^{-16}\,J$.

(ii) $E_k = \frac{1}{2}mv^2$, and so

$$v = \sqrt{\left(\frac{2E_k}{m}\right)}$$

$$= \sqrt{\left(\frac{2 \times 8.0 \times 10^{-16}\,J}{9.11 \times 10^{-31}\,kg}\right)}$$

$$= 4.19 \times 10^7\,m\,s^{-1}.$$

(c) Electrons would collide with air molecules, transferring energy to them, so the electrons' kinetic energy would be greatly reduced. (They would also be scattered and the beam would not remain focused.)

38 (a) The spot would be brighter as the kinetic energy of each electron would be increased, so each electron would transfer more energy to the phosphor screen,

(b) The spot would be brighter as more electrons would be produced by thermionic emission, more would be accelerated, and so there would be a greater overall rate of energy transfer to the phosphor.

(c) The spot would be less bright as the electrons would be decelerated to some extent by the grid.

39 From equation (26) with $\theta = 90°$, $\sin\theta = 1$,

$$F = 0.10\,T \times 1.60 \times 10^{-19}\,C \times 8.0 \times 10^7\,m\,s^{-1}$$

$$= 1.3 \times 10^{-12}\,N$$

40 From Fleming's left-hand rule, the field must be horizontal and directed across the tube along a line through the centres of the two circular coils.

41 They would take a lot of power that might otherwise be used for manoeuvring. Also, the screens become heated by the bombardment of high-energy electrons, so might provide an enhanced target for heat-seeking missiles.

PROBING THE HEART OF MATTER

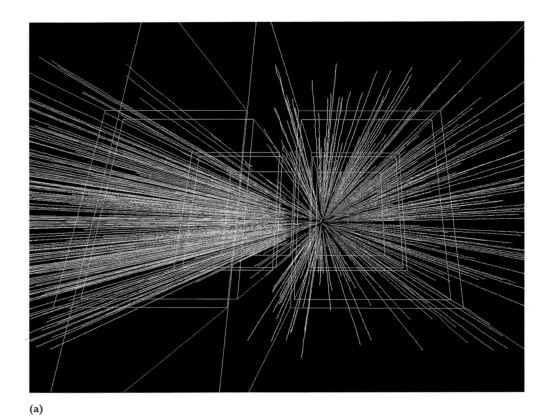

(a)

(b)

Figure 1 *(a) Particle tracks produced from a quark–gluon plasma, (b) Computer-generated model of a quark–gluon plasma*

Why a unit called Probing the Heart of Matter?

Science has followed a long quest to probe the structure of matter in an attempt to discover what we are all made of. In recent years this story has taken a new twist. Two different strands of physics have come together to provide a picture of how the fundamental structure of matter and the Universe itself are linked.

In the 1970s, theoreticians working on the physics of fundamental particles developed theories that were far ahead of the experimental physicists' means to test them out, so they started searching for new ways of seeing if their theories made sense. At the same time, physicists working on the relatively new subject of cosmology (the study of how the Universe came into being) discovered that they needed to understand particle physics in order to chart the very early history of the Universe.

The particle physicists realised that one way to test their theories was to see if they made sensible predictions about the way in which the early Universe evolved. This helped the cosmologists to solve some of their most difficult problems regarding the development of the Universe after the Big Bang. As a consequence physicists think that they have a fairly complete theory telling them how the Universe evolved from 10^{-35} seconds after the Big Bang right up to the present day.

The theory is very well supported by experimental results, but it is not without its problems. You may have read about the latest developments in this field in newspapers and science magazines, or you may have seen television documentaries on the subject. For example, in February 2000 scientists at CERN (the European particle physics lab) announced that they had created a type of matter called quark–gluon plasma (Figure 1) thought to have existed in the very early Universe. It is a subject that is alive with new possibilities and many of the most able young physicists starting their research careers choose to work in this exciting field. In this unit you will study some of the ideas that underpin this theory. You will also see where some of the problems lie and the work that is being done, by experimenters and theoreticians, to try to produce solutions. In doing so, you will be introduced to some aspects of modern particle physics and will also study the physics of circular motion and particle acceleration that underlies many of the experiments.

Overview of physics principles and techniques

You will begin by looking at the Big Bang theory of the creation of the Universe and how it manages to take us from a short time after the creation event right up to the present day. Along the way, some of the physics of fundamental particles will be introduced together with some key ideas about conservation laws and forces. Next you will look at the use of beams of particles to probe matter, which will involve learning about electrostatic and magnetic forces and about circular motion. In the final part of the unit you will see some of the most important results that these devices have produced. In the course of the unit, you will also carry out several activities that involve communication and IT skills: researching information and discussing and communicating what you have found.

In this unit you will extend your knowledge of

- momentum from *Transport on Track*;
- kinetic energy and work from *Higher, Faster, Stronger* and *Transport on Track*;
- wave–particle duality from *The Sound of Music* and *Digging Up the Past*;
- force fields from *Good Enough to Eat*, *Digging Up the Past* and *The Medium is the Message*;
- vectors from *Higher, Faster, Stronger* and *Transport on Track*;
- using graphs from *Higher, Faster, Stronger*, *Digging Up the Past* and *The Medium is the Message*.

Elsewhere you will do more work on

- motion in a circle in *Reach for the Stars*;
- kinetic energy and work in *Reach for the Stars*;
- inverse-square law fields in *Reach for the Stars*.

▌ *In the beginning*

1.1 Very large and very small

You will have read in the Introduction about the **Big Bang theory** of the origin of the Universe. The idea is that at some time in the past, roughly 15 000 million years ago, the Universe came into being. All of the matter and energy in the observable Universe, which is now spread out to the furthest distance we can see (about 10^{20} km), was compressed into a space much smaller than an atom. From that tiny, super-dense state at the instant of creation, the Universe grew. As it expanded, it cooled, and matter clumped together to form galaxies, stars and planets. The evidence for this model of the history of the Universe comes from observations of the light from distant galaxies.

Study note

You will learn more about the evolution of the Universe in the unit *Reach for the Stars*.

ACTIVITY I   **The expanding Universe**

What ideas do you already have, from GCSE science and from general reading, about the history of the Universe? Share your ideas with a partner, and then with the rest of your class. Here are some phrases that may help you to recall what you have studied or read about previously:

- galaxies moving apart
- red shifts
- distant galaxies – looking into the past
- the age of the Universe

You know that we think of matter as being made up of atoms – the building blocks of the chemical elements (see Figure 2). But atoms are not the smallest, most basic particles of matter, and not all matter is made up of atoms. For example, there is a beam of electrons inside most television sets (when they are producing a picture); electrons are matter, and they are much smaller than atoms.

Figure 2 *Model of a DNA molecule showing the atoms from which it is made*

ACTIVITY **2** | **The particles of matter**

In the next part of this unit, you will go on to learn about the current picture which physicists have developed of the sub-atomic particles of matter. What ideas do you already have about particles? Share your ideas with a partner, and then with the rest of the class. Here are some phrases which may help you to recall what you have studied or read about previously:

- atoms, nuclei and electrons
- quarks
- particle accelerators – atom smashers
- radioactivity, fission and fusion

---

2 *Theories of Everything*

One of the things that scientists like to do is to develop theories. They want their theories to account for as many different observations as possible. For example, Newton developed a theory of gravity. He managed to come up with a theory that explained how things fall on the Earth, and how the Moon orbits the Earth. Until then, people felt that there must be one set of laws for what happens on Earth, and another for what happens in the heavens. So Newton's theory was a dramatic advance, unifying two previous separate realms of ideas.

Today, we know much more about the laws of physics, especially about the particles of which matter is made and the forces that act between them. Physicists would like to come up with a single theory that could explain everything we know about these things, and they call this a 'theory of everything'. It's perhaps a rather arrogant idea. Such a theory won't explain everything such as evolution, human consciousness, poetry or love. But such a theory would still be a remarkable achievement, and in this part of the unit you will learn something about how physicists have made progress towards this end during the last few decades.

2.1 *Ideas in cosmology*

Late on 6 December 1979, Alan Guth (Figure 3), then a researcher at SLAC (the Stanford Linear Accelerator Centre in California), sat down to start some work. He was accustomed to working late at night, once his young son had gone to bed, as he could concentrate better.

He had been working on a paper about the early Universe with some colleagues and had decided to check to see if their ideas had any influence on the way the Universe expanded at about 10^{-35} seconds after the Big Bang. Guth had been doing such calculations for some time and the work that night was quite routine. The results he discovered were *not* routine, however. They were to change thinking about cosmology completely.

Not yet realising the full implications of what he had done, Guth cycled into the lab the next morning. In his book *The Inflationary Universe*, Guth records that he set a personal best time of nine minutes 32 seconds on that ride. Arriving at his office he opened his notebook, wrote

Figure 3 *Alan Guth*

SPECTACULAR REALIZATION

at the top of one of the pages and set out to refine the rough work that he had done the night before. Guth records that he cannot find any other instance in his notes where he has used a double box to emphasise a point.

At the time Guth was coming to the end of his period of employment at SLAC and was looking to find another job. He decided to take the risk of not immediately setting down his new ideas in a published paper. Instead he travelled round several research centres in America presenting his ideas in a seminar and seeing if he could impress people enough to offer him a job. The risk paid off. At one conference he was given 10 minutes to explain his theory to the attending physicists. Part way through his presentation Murray Gell-Mann, a Nobel Prize winner and important character in this unit, jumped up and shouted, 'You've solved the most important problem in cosmology!' On the Monday after, Guth took the plunge and rang MIT (the Massachusetts Institute of Technology) asking if they were interested in offering him a job. Twenty-four hours later he was offered an assistant professorship.

What Guth had done was to apply some of the very latest ideas in particle physics to the Universe shortly after the Big Bang. Particle physicists had started working on **Grand Unified Theories** (GUTs), which brought the fundamental forces that act between fundamental particles together into one theory. Unfortunately, these theories cannot be directly checked by experiments. The effects that they predict can only be seen if the particles involved have very high energies – much higher than could be produced in experiments. However, particles with high enough energies would have existed early in the history of the Universe when all matter and energy were compressed into a tiny space, so GUTs should have something to say about what was going on at the time. What Guth's calculations told him was that, instead of expanding at a relatively gradual rate, as everyone had assumed, the Universe must have exploded in size at a gigantic rate for a short period of time. So fast would be this expansion that in a time interval of 10^{-35} seconds, the Universe would become 10^{50} times bigger. This is like magnifying a proton to the current size of the visible Universe in less time that it takes for a light ray to travel from one side of a proton to another. Guth named this effect **inflation**, and it has become a central part of our thinking about the early history of the Universe.

2.2   *Building blocks*

You probably picture an atom as being like a miniature solar system, with a nucleus made up of protons and neutrons, surrounded by orbiting electrons. This is the picture that scientists developed in the early decades of the 20th century, and for many purposes it is still a very useful model. Electrons, protons and neutrons were at first thought to be **fundamental particles**, i.e. particles that cannot be divided into smaller constituents. However, it was inevitable that physicists would question whether, just as the atom was found to be divisible, these particles too could be subdivided (Figure 4).

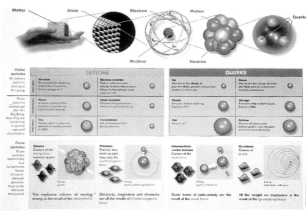

Figure 4   *The constituents of matter*

Later in this unit, you will learn something of how this question was investigated. In the meantime, we will look at some of the results of these investigations.

The **standard model of particle physics**, which is currently our best theory of how the Universe works, identifies 12 fundamental particles from which all matter is made and four fundamental forces that govern reactions between the particles.

The 12 fundamental particles divide into two distinct groups according to their properties. There are:

- 6 types of **quark**, the particles of which protons and neutrons (and some other particles) are made. The name 'quark' was coined by Murray Gell-Mann;

- 6 types of **lepton**, including the electron. The name 'lepton' comes from Greek and means 'light'; leptons have very small masses.

Although electrons are thought to be truly fundamental, physicists have shown that protons and neutrons are not – each is made up of three quarks.

The particles are generally grouped into three **generations** – so-called because there is some 'family' resemblance between particles of one generation and another (*not* because one group precedes another). Table 1 lists the names (which are often slightly weird), symbols and some properties of the quarks. All three quarks in a horizontal row have the same electrical charge, shown in units of the proton charge *e*. There are also three generations of lepton (Table 2). In each generation, one of the leptons is a neutrino. Many of the names in Tables 1 and 2 will be new to you. Probably the only familiar one is the electron. As this unit progresses you will start to see how the others fit into our description of the Universe. Do not get worried if you feel that you are not entirely sure what these particles are. This was the problem that faced physicists as they started to discover them!

1st generation	2nd generation	3rd generation	Charge
up, u	charm, c	top, t	$+2/3\ e$
down, d	strange, s	bottom, b	$-1/3\ e$

Table 1 *Quarks*

1st generation	2nd generation	3rd generation	Charge
electron, e	muon, μ	tau, τ	$-1e$
electron-neutrino, v_e	muon-neutrino, v_μ	tau-neutrino, v_τ	0

Table 2 *Leptons*

Table 3 shows where leptons are found in nature. We cannot provide a similar table for quarks, because it is believed that quarks always occur bound together in twos or threes, never separately.

electron	found in atoms
	important in electrical currents
	produced in beta radioactivity
muon	produced in large numbers in the upper atmosphere by 'cosmic rays'
tau	so far only seen in lab experiments
electron-neutrino	produced in beta radioactivity
	produced in large numbers by atomic reactors
	produced in huge numbers by the nuclear reactions in the Sun
muon-neutrino	produced by atomic reactors
	produced in upper atmosphere by cosmic rays
	produced in the Sun by nuclear reactions
tau-neutrino	so far only seen in lab experiments

Table 3 *Leptons in nature*

It is worth mentioning something about the masses of the fundamental particles.

- The top quark is the heaviest (most massive) of all fundamental particles. Its mass is almost 200 times the mass of a proton. That makes it much heavier than many molecules, such as a water molecule, H_2O.

- An electron has a mass roughly 1/2000 times that of a proton.

- The mass of an electron-neutrino is either zero or very tiny indeed, much less than a millionth of the mass of a proton. For many years it was suggested that these weird particles (which appear during beta decay of a radioactive material) have absolutely no mass at all. There is a possibility that the mass is not quite zero – but so far the uncertainty in experimental measurements is comparable to any mass that the neutrino might have.

ACTIVITY 3 | **Charge and no charge**

A proton is made up of three quarks: two up quarks and a down (written uud). A neutron is also made of three quarks, a different combination of up and down quarks.

- Show that the charge of a proton is correctly given by adding the charges of two up quarks and one down quark.

- What combination of up and down quarks make up a neutron?

A proton is made of two up quarks and a down (uud); a neutron is an up and two downs (udd). All other possible collections of three quarks also correspond to particles, although all of them apart from the proton (which has the lowest mass) are unstable. This means that they will decay into other (less massive) particles. That is why they are unfamiliar to you. Particles such as the Δ^+ (pronounced 'delta plus' and made from three up quarks, uuu) and the Δ^- ('delta minus', ddd) typically last about 10^{-25} seconds before they decay so they are not seen in the everyday world. We only understand their properties to the extent that we do because we have been able to make and study them in experiments. However, in the early moments after the Big Bang such particles were much more common than they are now, so our attempts to discover their properties also help us to understand the early Universe.

2.3 *Fundamental forces and interactions*

Physicists have identified four **fundamental forces** that operate in nature. Two of these, gravity and the electromagnetic force, will be familiar to you from your studies in physics so far. By a fundamental force we mean a force that cannot be explained in terms of another force acting. For example, the force of friction is not a fundamental force as it is caused by the electrostatic forces between atoms as one object rubs against another. The four fundamental forces are shown in Table 4.

Study note

The electromagnetic force combines both magnetic and electrostatic effects; if you have studied the unit *Transport on Track*, you will have seen that these effects are closely interconnected.

Force	Range	Relative strength	Acts between ...
gravity	No limit	10^{-34}	all objects
electromagnetic	No limit	10	charged objects
strong force	10^{-15} m	10^3	quarks
weak force	10^{-18} m	10^{-10}	fundamental particles

Table 4 *The four fundamental forces of nature*

Range and strength

The **range** of a force is the maximum distance by which two objects can be separated and still feel the force acting. The **relative strength** of the force is a way of comparing how big an influence each force would have on the same pair of objects. The relative strengths quoted correspond roughly to the force in newtons between two protons separated by 10^{-15} m.

The so-called strong and weak forces have not come into your study of physics before as they only act over very short distances – smaller than the diameter of a nucleus. For this reason physicists did not discover them until they started to experiment with nuclei.

As this unit progresses you will start to get a feel for the properties of the strong and weak forces. For the moment, just think of them as new forces that we do not see in our everyday life as their size is so small at the sort of distances we deal with (though as you can see from Table 4, over small enough distances even the weak force is not as weak as gravity). You would not worry about the force of gravity pulling you towards the Moon as you cross the road because it is so small; likewise when we hit a tennis ball the strong and weak forces do not influence its motion.

ACTIVITY 4   **Forces – fundamental or not?**

Make a list of the forces you have come across in physics so far – Figure 5 illustrates several examples. Divide them into two categories – contact forces, which require two objects to be touching each other for the force to exist (such as friction), and force fields, which do not require contact (such as gravity). Try to explain each of the forces you have listed in terms of a fundamental force from Table 4. Which category of force do you think is the more fundamental – force fields or contact forces?

Binding particles together

Not all of the fundamental forces act on each of the fundamental particles. For example, the main difference between quarks and leptons is that quarks experience the strong force but leptons do not. As you can see from Table 4, between two quarks the strong force would completely dominate over the weak force. In fact the strong force is so strong that it pulls quarks together into groups from which they can never be separated. These groups are essentially particles in their own right, called **hadrons** (see Figure 6). As far as we can tell, quarks are never found on their own. They are always bound together into hadrons.

The strong force allows only two types of quark combination to exist. One type, the **baryon**, is always composed of three quarks. The most familiar examples of such a combination are the particles that are found in the nucleus – the proton and neutron. The second type of hadron is the **meson**. Mesons are made of just two quarks bound together (actually a quark and an antiquark – see section 2.4).

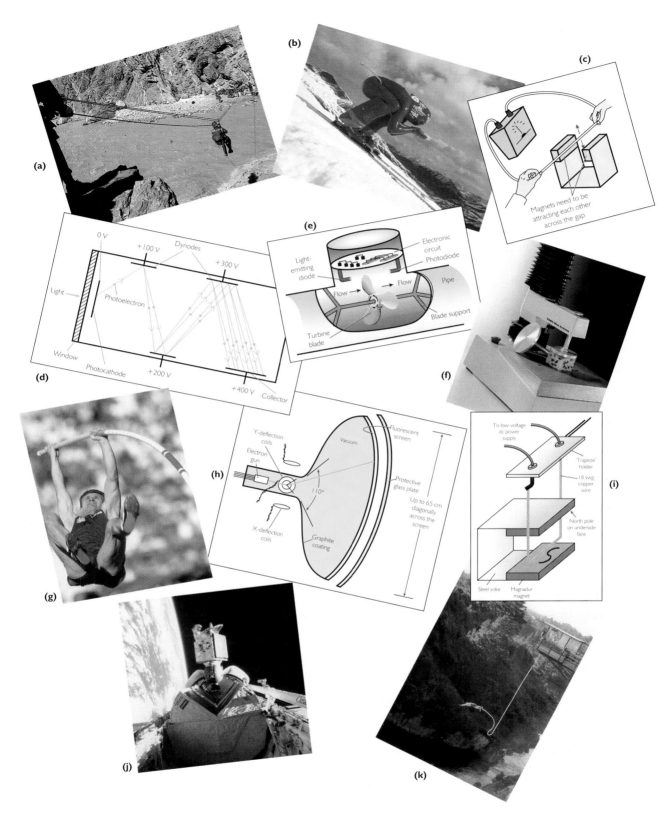

Figure 5 *Forces in action: (a) Tyrolean traverse; (b) speed skier; (c) demonstration of electromagnetic induction moving a wire in a magnetic field; (d) a photomultiplier; (e) a light-gate flowmeter; (f) compression testing of a cake; (g) pole vaulting; (h) a CRT used in television; (i) demonstrating the direction of an electromagnetic force; (j) communications satellite; (k) bungee jumping*

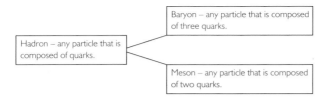

Figure 6 *Two types of hadron*

QUESTIONS

1 In each of (**a**) to (**e**), say which of the fundamental forces is or are involved:

(**a**) two quarks are held together to make a meson;
(**b**) the Earth is held in its orbit around the Sun;
(**c**) a compass needle points north;
(**d**) protons and neutrons are close together in an atomic nucleus;
(**e**) an electron-neutrino is absorbed by an atomic nucleus.

Changing the nature of particles

The action of the weak force is to cause particles to change from one type into another. For example, if an electron e^- happens to fly near to a muon-neutrino v_μ, then the weak force acting between them can turn the particles into a muon μ^- and an electron-neutrino v_e. We would write this down as a **reaction equation** in the following way:

$$e^- + v_\mu \longrightarrow \mu^- + v_e$$

The charges of the electron and muon are shown by the superscripts, which give charge in multiples of the proton charge. By looking at the charges of the particles involved, you can see that, in this reaction, charge is conserved:

$$-1e + 0 \longrightarrow -1e + 0$$

The total charge on each side of the reaction equation is always the same. Charge is *always* conserved.

ACTIVITY 5 | **Equations and conservation**

Write a reaction equation to represent the following event:

- A muon reacts with an electron-neutrino to form an electron and a muon-neutrino.

Show that charge is conserved in this reaction.

2.4 Antimatter

Modern particle physics has generally used huge experiments involving multiple millions of pounds and hundreds of scientists and engineers from many institutions around the globe. However, particle physicists are aware that their access to funds may be drying up. In 1993, the proposed giant American collider (the Superconducting Supercollider) was cancelled due to spiralling costs ($11 billion). More recently, hard bargaining between the member states has led to a phased reduction in the budget for CERN, the European particle physics lab at Geneva.

Aside from the arguments as to the rights and wrongs of public money supporting research into fundamental physics, the interesting effect of this change in financial fortunes is the rise of the smaller, clever experiment using a few people and some bits and pieces left over from previous experiments. Just such an experiment announced its first results at CERN in September 1995 (Figure 7). PS210 may not sound very glamorous, but it may well turn out to be one of the more important pieces of research carried out in the last 20 years of the 20th century. PS210 was the first experiment to produce atoms of antihydrogen. Physicists have known about the existence of **antimatter** since the **positron** (the antimatter version of the electron – see below) was discovered in 1932. Since then antimatter versions of all the fundamental particles have been discovered. Antimatter has become standard stuff used in experiments. Indeed, CERN sent a 'bottle' of antiprotons to the Expo 92 exhibition in Spain (a magnetic bottle). However, a complete antiatom had never before been made.

There is nothing in the laws of physics to suggest that a positron in orbit around an antiproton will not be as stable as a familiar hydrogen atom (an electron in orbit around a proton). The problem is what happens when this hydrogen antiatom meets a hydrogen atom – the two annihilate one another, leaving only a flash of gamma rays. Physicists believe that matter and antimatter behave in exactly the same manner in most circumstances. But, as always, physicists like to check such things just in case they happen to be wrong. PS210 was designed to produce and detect such antiatoms as a first step to confirming their properties.

Figure 7   *The CERN experiment that produced antihydrogen*

ACTIVITY 6   **Making antiatoms**

Read about the PS210 experiment and write a summary of 80–100 words, explaining what was done and why it was significant.

The first thing to understand about antimatter is that it is not very special stuff. Despite what you may have read in science fiction, it does not have antigravity properties or anything weird like that. For every type of particle of matter that exists, there is a type of particle of antimatter with the same mass but with opposite electrical charge (if it is electrically charged). Thus as well as there being electrons in the Universe, there are also objects called antielectrons, also known as positrons. These have the same mass as the electron, but they have a positive charge identical in size to that of a proton. For every quark that we mentioned earlier there is an antiquark; for every lepton, there is an antilepton. These are shown in Tables 5 and 6. Each antiparticle is represented by the same symbol as its corresponding particle, with a bar above it – except for the positron, which has its own symbol, e^+.

Study note

The $\bar{\mu}$ and $\bar{\tau}$ are also sometimes written μ^+ and τ^+, respectively.

1st generation	2nd generation	3rd generation	Charge
$\bar{u}$	$\bar{c}$	$\bar{t}$	$-2/3\,e$
$\bar{d}$	$\bar{s}$	$\bar{b}$	$+1/3\,e$

Table 5 *Antiquarks*

1st generation	2nd generation	3rd generation	Charge
$\bar{e}$ or e^+	$\bar{\mu}$	$\bar{\tau}$	$+1\,e$
electron-antineutrino $\bar{v}_e$	muon-antineutrino $\bar{v}_\mu$	tau-antineutrino $\bar{v}_\tau$	0

Table 6 *Antileptons*

You will no doubt have noticed the similarities between the patterns of the lepton and quark families. Each has six members in three generations. The particles' masses increase as you move up the generations. The model is said to have **symmetry**. When this model was first proposed by Murray Gell-Mann (Figure 8), there was no experimental evidence for the top and bottom quarks. He suggested that they must exist, because of this symmetry. The bottom quark was identified in 1977, a great vindication of his theory. The top quark was eventually found in 1994, in an experiment at Fermilab in the USA.

Figure 8 *Murray Gell-Mann*

Mesons

In section 2.3, we discussed the action of the strong force on quarks and said that it is so strong that it binds them together into particles. One such grouping combines three quarks together (such as in the proton and neutron) to form a baryon. We also mentioned another possible combination; a quark can bind to an antiquark to make a meson. An example of such a quark–antiquark pairing is a u quark with a $\bar{d}$ antiquark, $u\bar{d}$. Such an object would have a charge equal to the sum of the two quark charges:

$$u \text{ charge} = +\frac{2}{3}\,e$$

$$\bar{d} \text{ charge} = +\frac{1}{3}\,e$$

$$\text{total charge} = +1\,e$$

Any pairing is possible. Table 7 shows the possibilities if we just take the lightest quarks, the up and the down.

Quarks	Total charge	Name of bound particle	Symbol
$u\bar{u}$	0	pi zero	π^0
$d\bar{d}$	0	pi zero	π^0
$u\bar{d}$	$+1\,e$	pi plus	π^+
$d\bar{u}$	$-1\,e$	pi minus	π^-

Table 7 *Combining up and down quarks to make pions*

All these combinations correspond to one of a family of three particles called pi-mesons or **pions** (notice that there are two ways to make a pi zero meson). Pions are the lightest of the meson family of particles and are very commonly produced in particle physics experiments. They are also produced high in the Earth's atmosphere when cosmic rays (high-energy protons) from the Sun and beyond the solar system hit the nuclei of atoms in the atmosphere.

Figure 9 shows a schematic diagram of a typical shower of particles produced by a single cosmic ray particle, together with some of the detectors and observations used to study the effects of cosmic rays. N is used to represent a light nucleus. Notice that the shower contains many muons, neutrinos and positrons as well as pions.

ACTIVITY 7   **Making mesons**

All mesons are made up of a quark and an antiquark.

- A phi meson (ϕ) is made of a strange quark and a strange antiquark. What will be its charge?
- Four types of K meson are possible: $u\bar{s}$, $\bar{u}s$, $d\bar{s}$ and $\bar{d}s$. Which of these is/are neutral?

Playing with fire

It is very difficult to experiment with antimatter. If an antimatter particle comes into contact with a matter particle of the same type (e.g. an electron and a positron or a proton and an antiproton), then they will react with each other and turn into electromagnetic radiation (usually gamma-ray photons). This is called an **annihilation reaction**. The amount of energy released in a single reaction of this sort is tiny and poses no safety risk – the problem is keeping the antimatter particles away from the matter particles for long enough to experiment on them. (Remember, any equipment used will be made of matter particles.) Here is the equation that represents an electron and an antielectron (positron) annihilating:

$$e^- + e^+ \longrightarrow \text{electromagnetic radiation}$$

The reverse can also occur:

$$\text{electromagnetic radiation} \longrightarrow e^- + e^+$$

Figure 9 shows such reactions occurring naturally in the atmosphere as a result of cosmic ray bombardment. A wiggly line labelled γ (gamma) represents a photon of electromagnetic radiation. Physicists can exploit these reactions to create new particles to study. The idea is to take a beam of matter particles (say electrons) and a beam of antimatter particles (positrons in this case) and accelerate them to very high energy. The beams are then allowed to collide with one another. This process sounds simple, but steering the beams is actually a highly complex affair.

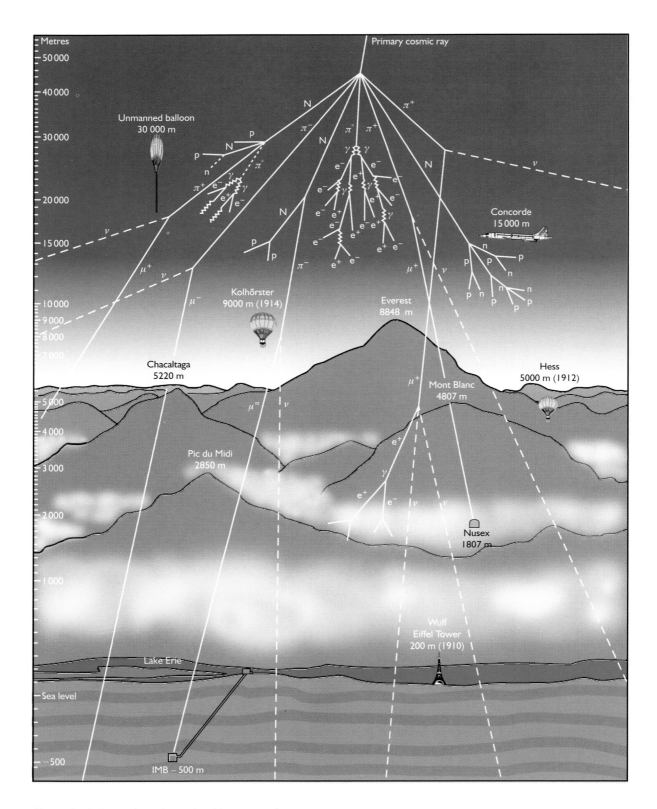

Figure 9 *A shower of particles produced by cosmic radiation*

When the matter and antimatter come within range of each other, they annihilate, producing a burst of electromagnetic radiation that will rapidly materialise into new particles, perhaps ones that have never been seen before. Here are three equations that show possible reactions:

$$e^- + e^+ \longrightarrow \text{electromagnetic radiation} \longrightarrow \mu^- + \mu^+$$

$$e^- + e^+ \longrightarrow \text{electromagnetic radiation} \longrightarrow \tau^- + \tau^+$$

$$e^- + e^+ \longrightarrow \text{electromagnetic radiation} \longrightarrow u + \bar{u}$$

In the first reaction, two mu leptons are produced. In the second, two tau leptons are produced – this is how the tau was discovered. In the third, two quarks are produced; they cannot exist freely like this, but bind together to form a pion (see Table 7).

Study note

You will find out more about steering beams in part 4 of this unit.

QUESTIONS

2 Write an equation to show what happens when a mu lepton annihilates with its antiparticle.

3 Some mesons are made from a quark bound to its own antiquark. Explain why such a meson has no electric charge.

Mass from energy

It is surprising to find that particles of matter can disappear, leaving only energy. It is also surprising to find that particles can appear where before there was only energy. This sounds as if the laws of conservation of energy and mass are both being broken, and in a sense that's true. When a particle and an antiparticle collide and annihilate one another, their mass disappears and we are left with photons of electromagnetic radiation. If mass m disappears and energy E appears, then these two are related by Einstein's equation

$$E = mc^2 \tag{1}$$

where c is the speed of light in a vacuum (also called 'free space'). Similarly, when a particle–antiparticle pair are created out of energy, we can use the same expression to deduce the possible mass that might be created. To produce particles 'out of nothing', the photons of electromagnetic radiation must have a great deal of energy; the more massive the particles produced, the greater the energy of the photons.

Equation (1) has a more general application. If ever the mass of particles changes by an amount Δm, there is a corresponding change in the amount of energy ΔE, and these two are related by:

$$\Delta E = c^2 \Delta m \tag{1a}$$

QUESTIONS

4 Explain why electron and positron beams must be accelerated to high energies in order to produce particles such as tau leptons, which are more massive than electrons.

5 Using equation (1), calculate the energy equivalent to the mass of a proton.

6 An electron–positron pair can be created from a single photon, if it is energetic enough. Any excess energy is shared equally between the two particles, as kinetic energy.

(**a**) What energy of photon is required to create an electron–positron pair?

(**b**) A photon of energy 2×10^{-13} J disappears, and an electron–positron pair is created. Calculate the kinetic energies of the electron and the positron.

Data for questions 4 to 6:
mass of positron = mass of electron, $m_e = 9.11 \times 10^{-31}$ kg
mass of proton, $m_p = 1.67 \times 10^{-27}$ kg
speed of light in vacuum $c = 3.00 \times 10^8$ m s^{-1}

Antimatter space fuel?

It has often been suggested that antimatter might be the answer to providing fuel for future space missions. The idea is that a spacecraft would be accelerated by a rocket in which matter and antimatter annihilated one another. This would power it so that it could flash across the galaxy, just like the Starship Enterprise, at speeds approaching the speed of light (Figure 10). Scientists estimate that just 20 kg of antimatter would do the job. The problem is making the stuff, and containing it. Physicists at the CERN lab are now planning to produce antimatter in very small quantities. According to project leader Dr Rolf Landua, 'At our proposed rate of production, it would take billions of years to manufacture enough antimatter to make a bomb or drive a spaceship' (*The Observer*, 7 February 1999). So antimatter drives are still some way off.

Figure 10 *Starship Enterprise*

2.5 History of the Universe

We started this part of the unit by discussing the Big Bang and the idea of an expanding Universe. You may have felt that we followed a bit of a diversion by considering the current view of the fundamental particles and forces that govern the Universe. Now we need to bring these two topics together.

As the Universe expands, it cools down; energy and matter are spread more thinly, and temperature is related to the concentration of energy. Out in space, it's cold. The COBE satellite (Cosmic Background Explorer, Figure 11) measured the temperature out there to be about 2.7 K. (Stars are of course much hotter, so is some of the gas between them. The 2.7 K refers to the temperature of 'empty space' where there is essentially no matter, just radiation.) Matter is very thinly spread – on average, less than one proton per cubic metre.

Figure 11 *The Cosmic Background Explorer*

When the Universe was much younger than it is today, the energy was concentrated in a smaller volume, and so the temperature was much higher. At high temperatures, the particles of matter have much higher energies, and they rush around, colliding and interacting. (These are the conditions that physicists try to reproduce in their giant accelerators.) These temperatures are too high for atoms and molecules to exist – they knock one another into their constituent parts.

So the history of the Universe can be summarised as:

- In its early stages: small, hot, dense; matter in the form of quarks, hadrons, leptons.

- Today: vast, cold, matter spread thinly; matter in the form of atoms and molecules.

Using a log–log graph

Figure 12 shows in more detail how the temperature of the Universe has changed with time. Here you can see the different phases that the Universe has gone through since the end of the inflationary phase. Notice that *both* scales are logarithmic. This is necessary in order to show the great ranges of these quantities.

Study note

You met logarithmic scales in the AS unit *Digging Up the Past*.

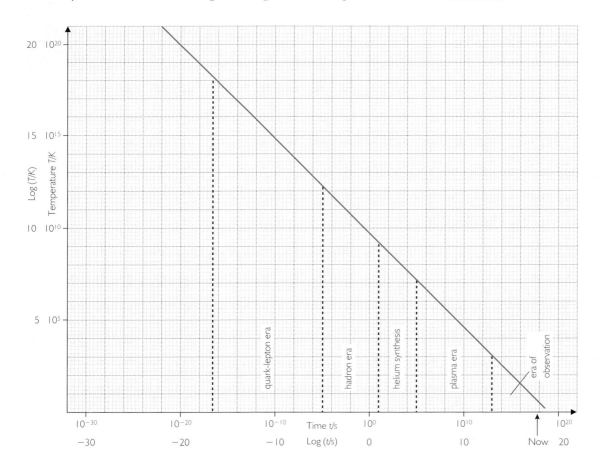

Figure 12 *The temperature of the Universe falls with time*

The shape of the graph has been worked out from theoretical calculations that predict a relationship between temperature and time:

$$T = \frac{k}{\sqrt{t}} = kt^{-1/2} \qquad (2)$$

where T is the absolute temperature (i.e. in kelvin), t the time since the Big Bang, and k is a constant. Equation (2) is an example of a **power-law relationship** – where one variable (T in this case) is directly proportional to another variable (t) raised to a power or **exponent** (here, the exponent is $-1/2$).

When numbers related by a power law are plotted in a log–log graph (i.e. one where *both* axes are logarithmic), then the resulting graph is a straight line. We can illustrate this by taking logs of equation (2):

$$\log(T) = \log(k) + \log(t^{-1/2})$$

$$\log(T) = \log(k) - \frac{1}{2}\log(t) \qquad (3)$$

Plotting $\log(T)$ on the y-axis against $\log(t)$ on the x-axis gives a graph of the type $y = mx + c$, where the gradient, m, is equal to the exponent.

Study note

Figure 12 is an example of a log–log graph. Both scales are logarithmic.

Maths reference

Index notation and powers of ten
See Maths note 1.1

Powers that are not whole numbers
See Maths note 1.5

Gradient of a linear graph
See Maths note 5.3

Logs and powers
See Maths note 8.4

Log scales
See Maths note 8.6

Using logarithmic graphs
See Maths note 8.7

ACTIVITY 8   **The universal story**

Use Figure 12 to find out the following information.

- How many seconds is it now since the origin of the Universe?
- At what time did the 'hadron era' start? What was the temperature at that time?
- According to the graph, what is the temperature (of 'space') now?

Find the gradient of the graph in Figure 12 and check that the graph is described by equations (2) and (3).

Use Figure 12 to find the value of the constant k in equations (2) and (3), and use equation (2) to deduce its SI units.

Step by step history

Now we can look in more detail at the different periods in the history of the Universe, as shown in Figure 12. Physicists like to divide the history of the Universe up into distinct periods depending on what was happening at the time.

After inflation

We will start just after the end of the period of inflation, 10^{-35} s after the origin of the Universe. At this time, the particles of matter and antimatter that were in the Universe had been scattered over vast distances. If nothing had happened to fill the Universe again then matter would now be very scarce indeed. Certainly life could never have evolved, as it is difficult to see how stars could ever form in such a 'thin' Universe. However, at the end of the inflation period the Universe was topped up with matter and antimatter by the decay of particles called 'Higgs particles'. These are very important in the theory of the Universe and particle physics in general. Unfortunately they have never been seen in our experiments. New experiments are being constructed now which should be able to detect the Higgs – if they don't, a lot of people are going to have to do some very hard thinking!

In summer of the year 2000, scientists at CERN announced results that gave some evidence for the detection of Higgs particles. In an attempt to gather more evidence, their experiment continued for some weeks after it had been scheduled to close. At the time of writing (autumn 2000) no more conclusive results have yet been announced.

After inflation had stopped, the Universe was filled with matter, antimatter and radiation again. You may think that nothing important has therefore happened, but that is not true. The amount of new matter and antimatter that appeared seems to be just enough to slow the Universe down to a gentle expansion – its gravity stops it from expanding so fast that stars and galaxies would never get the chance to form. But with much more matter, the Universe would have collapsed under its own gravity back to a 'big crunch' long ago. Inflation seems to have been just what was needed to get the right amount of matter into the Universe.

Soon after inflation ended, most of the antimatter in the Universe disappeared. This is a very interesting puzzle that has had physicists thinking for decades. Where did the antimatter go? You may ask how we know that it vanished at all. The answer is simple – we are here! (see Figure 13). Everything that we touch is made of matter (even the Moon – we know because people have walked on it). In reactions such as those you saw in section 2.4, matter and antimatter are created and destroyed in equal amounts. But to account for the predominance of matter, antimatter must in fact decay more rapidly than matter, so physicists are having to think how their ideas might need to be modified or even overturned completely.

Figure 13 *The Earth, and the living creatures that inhabit it, are made from matter*

Quark–gluon plasma

10^{-18}–10^{-12} seconds after Big Bang no hadrons existed. The Universe was composed of a soup of quarks, leptons and various particles involved with the four fundamental forces (see Figure 1). As the Universe expanded, so the average distance between the quarks got bigger until at the end of this period in history they started to group into the hadrons that we find now.

The hadron era

Hardly surprisingly the next period, 10^{-12} seconds to 3 minutes after Big Bang, is called the hadron era. As well as leptons, the Universe is now full of hadrons – mostly protons and neutrons. Various reactions are going on and the numbers of protons and neutrons are being kept in balance. However, the protons and neutrons are not able to join together to make nuclei as the electromagnetic radiation in the Universe is hot enough (has enough energy) to break them apart again straight away. As the end of this era drew near, the radiation had cooled down enough to let hadrons start to combine.

Nucleosynthesis

Three to 13 minutes after the Big Bang, nuclei start to form. Protons and neutrons come together to make deuterium, an isotope of hydrogen. Deuterium nuclei come together to make helium nuclei. As this process takes place all the free neutrons are effectively swept up into nuclei. A detailed calculation shows that at the end of nucleosynthesis the Universe had about 78% hydrogen and 22% helium (measured by mass), which is almost exactly what we see now.

Study note

A very similar nuclear process goes on in the Sun now – you will learn more about this in the unit *Reach for the Stars*.

Plasma era

For the next 3000 years, the Universe is basically made up of leptons (especially electrons), electromagnetic radiation, helium nuclei and protons. The electrons cannot stick to the nuclei to make atoms as the energy in the radiation is great enough to blast them away again. The Universe is effectively an ionised gas – what physicists call a **plasma**.

After about 3000 years the temperature has dropped (the radiation is less energetic) to such an extent that electrons that do stick to nuclei can stay there. This is a very important step in the history of the Universe. Until now the electromagnetic force has been very important as all the objects in the Universe were charged. After the loose charges have been stuck together and the Universe has become neutral, gravity becomes the most important of the fundamental forces.

Towards the present

After the plasma era, stars and galaxies form, planets revolve in orbit about some stars (Figure 14). One planet (that we know of) takes the radical step of evolving life. After some time, one complex form of life starts to wonder about the Universe it lives in. And that's where you come in . . .

Figure 14 *The planets of the solar system*

2.6 Summing up part 2

In this part of the unit you have learned about two important areas of physics:

● cosmology – the way the Universe has evolved since the Big Bang;

● particle physics – the standard model of the fundamental particles and the forces which act between them.

You have also seen how these two areas, which might at first seem unrelated, are in fact intimately connected.

ACTIVITY **9** **Summing up part 2**

Look back at your notes on Activities 1 and 2 in part 1 of this unit. How might you respond to these activities, now that you know a lot more about cosmology and particle physics?

QUESTIONS

7 (**a**) What two particles are represented by e^+ and e^-?

(**b**) What difference is there between them?

(**c**) What happens when these two particles meet?

8 Why was Murray Gell-Mann able to predict the existence of the top and bottom quarks, even though there was no experimental evidence for their existence? What could he have predicted about their charges and masses?

9 For each of the particles in the list below, say whether it is a hadron, meson, baryon, quark or lepton (it may fall into more than one category).

proton   pion   electron   charm   neutron
antielectron   electron-neutrino   up

3 *Towards the standard model*

The standard model of particle physics, with its 12 fundamental particles and four fundamental forces, has been very successful. As we have seen in part 2, it has allowed physicists to link their picture of the tiniest particles to their picture of the history of the whole Universe – particle physics has been united with cosmology. This has been one of the great achievements of physics in the second half of the 20th century. But the standard model hasn't always been with us. In this part of the unit, we will look at what went before.

3.1 The discovery of the atomic nucleus

In the 19th century, most scientists came to accept that matter is made of atoms, although they never expected to see one. The idea of atoms allowed scientists to explain all sorts of things – the molecular kinetic theory, for example, in which the behaviour of gases was explained in terms of the movement of the particles that make up a gas; and much of chemistry depends on our understanding of the ways in which atoms arrange and rearrange themselves. It was thought that atoms were indivisible, the fundamental building blocks of matter. Then came two discoveries that changed all that:

- In 1896, Henri Becquerel discovered radioactivity. Atoms of some elements, including uranium and radium, were capable of giving out smaller particles. Atoms were not indivisible.

- In 1897, Joseph (J J) Thomson discovered the electron. These were tiny particles, much lighter than atoms, that could be emitted by many different metals; this suggested that they must be more fundamental than atoms.

Thomson devised a model of the atom, based on his discovery of the negatively charged electron. He suggested that each atom was made up of thousands of electrons, spinning in such a way that they stuck together to form a neutral atom. This was not a very successful model. You have probably come across two other models of the atom, the plum-pudding model and the nuclear model, like a miniature solar system. These are shown in Figure 15.

Study note

Z (the atomic number) represents the number of protons in the nucleus.

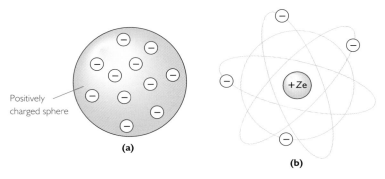

Positively charged sphere

(a)

(b)

Figure 15   *(a) The plum-pudding model and (b) the nuclear model*

ACTIVITY 10 **Model atoms**

Discuss the two models shown in Figure 15, and J J Thomson's all-electron model. Here are some points to consider:

- How are the positive and negative electric charges arranged in each model?
- What can you say about the attraction and repulsion between electric charges in each model?
- What do we mean by the term 'model' here?

The discovery of radioactivity was important not just because it showed that atoms could fall apart; it also became a useful research tool. The radiation produced by radioactive substances could be used as a probe to find out more about matter on the scale of individual atoms. Someone who made profound use of this tool was Ernest Rutherford.

Figure 16 shows the apparatus used by Rutherford's co-workers Geiger and Marsden to investigate the scattering of alpha radiation by a thin foil of gold. It was Rutherford who suggested the experiment and who interpreted the results. The source of radiation R is a thin-walled glass tube containing purified radium. The gold foil F is less than a thousandth of a millimetre thick. The tube T is used to pump the air out of the chamber. Radiation passing through the foil hits the scintillator S and produces a flash of light. The flashes are counted by the experimenter looking through the microscope M.

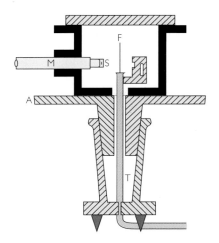

Figure 16   *Geiger and Marsden's apparatus*

With the microscope aimed directly at the source of radiation, Geiger and Marsden saw frequent flashes of light, showing that most of the alpha particles passed straight through the gold foil. When they moved the microscope round through a small angle, they found that the number of flashes became much less. Relatively few alpha particles were deflected by the foil. This was what they had anticipated. However, when they moved the microscope round through large angles, they were surprised to find that they could still see some flashes even when the microscope was on the same side of the foil as the source. A very few alpha particles were being reflected back from the gold foil towards their original source. It was this 'back-scattering' that Rutherford had to explain.

Rutherford explains back-scattering

To understand how alpha particles are scattered by gold foil, we need to know something about electrostatic forces. Alpha particles are positively charged, so they are repelled by other positive charges and attracted by negative charges. Rutherford pictured an alpha particle as a tiny, positively charged bullet moving at high speed. If it encountered a gold 'plum-pudding atom', it would be deflected slightly as the positive and negative charges of the atom pushed and pulled the alpha particle. But because the positive charge of the pudding is spread out, and the electrons are very light, it would not be deflected very much.

To explain the back-scattering of alpha particles, Rutherford had to come up with the nuclear model of the atom. He suggested that all of the atom's positive charge, together with most of its mass, was concentrated at the centre of the atom in a tiny nucleus. The electrons orbited around this nucleus. Figure 17 shows how Rutherford's model explained Geiger and Marsden's results.

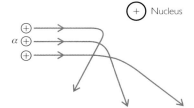

Figure 17 *Alpha particles are deflected as they pass close to a nucleus*

- An alpha particle passing through the edge of an atom is barely affected, because the electrons it encounters are very light (their mass is tiny compared to the alpha particle).

- An alpha particle passing close to the nucleus will be deflected, because it is repelled by the positive charge of the nucleus. The degree of deflection depends on how closely it approaches the nucleus of a gold atom.

- An alpha particle scoring a direct hit on the nucleus is repelled back in the direction which it came.

Rutherford realised that the nucleus of the atom must be very tiny compared to the whole atom – this explains why most alpha particles whiz straight through without ever coming close to a nucleus.

Geiger and Marsden measured the numbers of alpha particles scattered through different angles, and Rutherford produced a mathematical model that was able to explain the pattern of their results. His model also predicted the results that would be obtained if the alpha particles had different energy, and if foils of different thickness, and made from different metals, were used. Geiger and Marsden carried out a series of experiments to test Rutherford's model – and every time the results were as predicted. This was enough to convince most physicists that the nuclear model of the atom was correct. Table 8 shows some results obtained using gold foils of different thickness.

Thickness of gold foil $t/10^{-6}$m	Number N of scintillations per minute
0.23	21.9
0.46	38.4
1.07	84.3
1.70	121.5
1.89	145.0

Table 8 *Some of Geiger and Marsden's results*

ACTIVITY 11 A model for Rutherford scattering

Use a model such as the one shown in Figure 18 to investigate Rutherford scattering. A marble runs down a ramp, and then past a plastic or metal 'hill'. The closer it gets to the hill, the more it is deflected.

Figure 18 *A model to represent the scattering of an alpha particle by a nucleus*

ACTIVITY 12 Analysing the results

By drawing suitable graphs using the data from Table 8, find a mathematical relationship between N, the number of scintillations per minute, and t, the thickness of the foil.

QUESTIONS

10 Alpha radiation is easily absorbed. An alpha particle has a range of about 5 cm in air, because it collides with innumerable molecules of the air and loses its energy. Alpha particles travel even shorter distances through solid materials, because they are much denser than air. Use these ideas to explain some of the features of the design of Geiger and Marsden's apparatus.

11 Geiger and Marsden tested Rutherford's model using thicker gold foils. Would this make it more or less likely that an alpha particle would score a direct hit on a gold nucleus? How would you expect their results to change?

12 Geiger and Marsden used thin sheets of mica to slow down the alpha particles, so that they would not pass so rapidly through the gold foil. How would you expect their results to change?

13 Silver atoms are the same size as gold atoms, but their nuclei are smaller and have lower charge. Geiger and Marsden tried silver foil instead of gold. What do you think they observed?

Charge repelling charge

Rutherford used his model to say something about the size of the nucleus of the gold atom. To see how he did this, think about an alpha particle that approaches the nucleus of a gold atom head-on, as shown in Figure 19. As the alpha particle approaches, it begins to feel the repulsion of the gold nucleus. (The two positive charges repel one another.) The repulsive force slows it down. The closer the alpha particle gets, the greater the force, and so the greater its deceleration. Eventually it comes instantaneously to a halt, and then starts to move back towards where it came from. You can compare this motion with that of a ball thrown up in the air. The ball moves fast as it leaves your hand; it gradually slows as it rises in the air; it stops instantaneously, and then it accelerates downwards. In this case, the force is caused by the gravitational attraction between the ball and the Earth; for the alpha particle, the force is the electrostatic repulsion.

If we can find out how close the alpha particle gets to the gold nucleus, that could give us an idea of how big the nucleus is. To do this, Rutherford needed to know about the law that describes the electrostatic force between two charged particles. He was able to show that the alpha particles reached within about 10^{-14} m of the centre of the atom. (This is the distance shown as d in Figure 19.) So, although he could not say how big the nucleus was, he could deduce that its diameter must be no greater than about 10^{-13} m. That's no more than a thousandth of the diameter of the atom – today we know that it's even smaller, about 10^{-15} m across. In the next section we will go on to look at the law that allowed Rutherford to make his estimate.

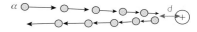

Figure 19 *A fast-moving alpha particle slows down as it approaches a gold nucleus, until it goes into reverse*

3.2 *Electrical forces*

No doubt you have carried out some simple experiments on static electricity. If you rub a balloon on your jumper, it becomes charged and you can do interesting things with it – stick it to the wall, for example. Here you are making use of the attractive force between opposite charges. Suppose the balloon gains a positive charge when you rub it. It will then attract negative charges in the wall, and the two stick together.

If you rub two balloons so that they both become positively charged, you can observe the repulsive force between like charges (charges with the same sign). Hang the balloons side by side and they repel one another, as shown in Figure 20.

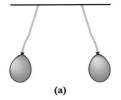

Figure 20 *(a) Like charges repel one another (b) unlike charges attract one another*

The fact that there are two types of electric charge, and the rules of attraction and repulsion, were known in the 18th century. Today we understand that a balloon becomes charged when you rub it because electrons are transferred from one object to another. If electrons are transferred from the balloon to your jumper, the balloon will become positively charged because it has lost electrons, which are negatively charged.

The French physicist Charles Coulomb (1736–1806) went beyond these simple rules of attraction and repulsion. He wanted to know more about the nature of the force, and in particular how the force between two charged objects depended on their separation. He used balls of pith, because pith is a good insulating material which retains an electric charge long enough for measurements to be made. Today we might use expanded polystyrene. Figure 21 shows two charged balls suspended so that they repel one another. This is a clever arrangement because, provided we know the weight of each ball, we can determine the force between them.

Note that Figure 21 is symmetrical. Each ball feels a horizontal electrostatic force of magnitude F, because it is repelled by the charge of the other ball. The pair of electrostatic forces are an example of **Newton's third law of motion:**

- they are equal in magnitude and opposite in direction;

- they act on different bodies (the two balls);

- they are the same type of force (electrostatic).

Now let's look at the forces acting on just one of the balls, as shown in the vector diagram in Figure 22. There are three forces:

>   the ball's weight mg;
>
>   the electrostatic force F;
>
>   the tension of the string T.

The easiest of these to measure is the weight mg. We can use this, along with the angle θ, to find the electrostatic force F. The ball is stationary, i.e. it is in equilibrium, so we know that the forces are balanced. The weight mg downwards is balanced by the vertical component of the tension T acting upwards:

$$mg = T \cos \theta \tag{4}$$

The electrostatic force F to the right is balanced by the horizontal component of the tension T acting to the left:

$$F = T \sin \theta \tag{5}$$

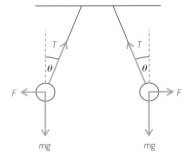

Figure 21 *Two identical charged balls suspended by insulating threads*

Study note

This consideration of forces uses several ideas that you met in the AS unit *Higher, Faster, Stronger.*

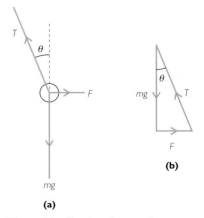

Figure 22 *The three forces acting on one of the balls shown in Figure 21*

We can eliminate T from these equations by dividing equation (5) by equation (4):

$$\frac{F}{mg} = \frac{T \sin \theta}{T \cos \theta} = \tan \theta \qquad (6)$$

Rearranging gives:

$$F = mg \tan \theta \qquad (6a)$$

So if we can measure mg and the angle θ, we can calculate F. Alternatively, you could measure F from a scale drawing of Figure 22.

QUESTIONS

14 Figure 21 shows two charged balls repelling one another. Sketch diagrams to show how the situation would change (**a**) if the balls had more charge; (**b**) if the balls had less charge.

15 Sketch two charged balls hanging close to one another, one having twice as much positive charge as the other. (Hint: remember Newton's third law!)

16 Calculate the electrostatic force on each of the balls shown in Figure 23, using data from the diagram.

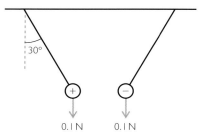

Figure 23 *Diagram for question 16*

Coulomb's law

Coulomb investigated the force between two charged spheres. Two spheres with charges Q_1 and Q_2 are separated by a distance r; note that r is measured from the centre of one sphere to the centre of the other (Figure 24). It is not surprising to find that the force depends on the size of each of the two charges, and that the force decreases as the spheres are moved apart. Coulomb found that the force is proportional to each of the charges:

$$F \propto Q_1 \quad \text{and} \quad F \propto Q_2 \qquad (7)$$

and that the force is inversely proportional to the square of the distance r between the two charges – the force obeys an **inverse square law**:

$$F \propto \frac{1}{r^2} \qquad (8)$$

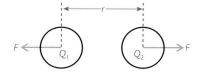

Figure 24 *Defining quantities: the force between two charged spheres*

These relationships can be combined:

$$F \propto \frac{Q_1 Q_2}{r^2}$$

$$F = \frac{k Q_1 Q_2}{r^2} \tag{9}$$

where k is a constant of proportionality. Equation (9) represents **Coulomb's law** of electrostatic force. In SI units, with F in newtons, r in metres and Q in coulombs:

$$k = 9.0 \times 10^9 \, \text{N m}^2 \, \text{C}^{-2}$$

The constant k is sometimes written in a different form as

$$k = \frac{1}{4\pi\varepsilon_0}$$

where the quantity ε_0 is known as the **permittivity of free space** and has the value $8.854 \times 10^{-12} \, \text{F m}^{-1}$ (farads per metre). Coulomb's law is written as

$$F = \frac{1}{4\pi\varepsilon_0} \frac{Q_1 Q_2}{r^2} \tag{9a}$$

Coulomb's law tells us about one of the four fundamental forces of nature, part of the standard model. One remarkable feature of this law is that, while Coulomb found out about it by making measurements on charged pith balls in his laboratory, it applies equally to the charged particles of the subatomic world – protons, electrons and the other members of the subatomic menagerie.

Study note

If you have studied either of the units *Transport on Track* or *The Medium is the Message*, you will have met the farad as a unit of capacitance. $1 \, \text{F} = 1 \, \text{C V}^{-1}$.

QUESTIONS

17 Show that the units of k and ε_0 are consistent with one another, i.e. that the units F m^{-1} and $(\text{N m}^2 \, \text{C}^{-2})^{-1}$ are equivalent.

18 Calculate the force that acts between two charges, each of $10 \, \text{nC}$, separated by a distance of $5 \, \text{cm}$.

19 The average separation of a proton and an electron in a hydrogen atom is about $0.037 \, \text{nm}$.

(**a**) Calculate the force each exerts on the other.

(**b**) Draw a diagram to show the directions in which these forces act. ($e = 1.60 \times 10^{-19} \, \text{C}$, $k = 9.0 \times 10^9 \, \text{N m}^2 \, \text{C}^{-2}$)

ACTIVITY **13** **Exploring Coulomb's law**

Explore the inverse square relationship of the force between two charged objects. This requires care, as well as dry atmospheric conditions.

Force, work and energy

Now that we know an expression for the electrostatic force between two charged particles, we can go back to Rutherford's problem. How close can an alpha particle get to the nucleus of a gold atom?

Figure 25 shows, in graphical form, how the force depends on distance of the alpha particle from the gold nucleus. As an alpha particle ($Q_1 = +2e$) speeds directly towards a gold nucleus ($Q_2 = +79e$), it feels a force that is at first small, but which increases more and more rapidly. When the values are plotted on a logarithmic graph, the gradient is -2, showing that there is an inverse square relationship between F and r. The force slows the alpha particle until it stops, goes into reverse, and accelerates back towards where it came from.

As the alpha particle approaches the nucleus, it loses kinetic energy and gains electrostatic potential energy; the repulsive force does work. At the point of closest approach, in a head-on encounter, the kinetic energy is zero; all of the initial kinetic energy has been transformed to potential energy. This is similar to the situations that you met in the AS unit *Higher, Faster, Stronger*, where a vertically launched projectile gains gravitational potential energy at the expense of its kinetic energy, and where a bungee jumper loses kinetic and gravitational potential energy as the cord gains elastic potential energy.

The work done on the alpha particle as it approaches to a distance r_0 is represented by the shaded area under the graph in Figure 25. The alpha particle stops and goes into reverse when the area is equal to its initial kinetic energy. Knowing the initial kinetic energy of the alpha particles, Rutherford was able to calculate how closely they must have approached the nucleus.

Using calculus, it is possible to show that, as an alpha particle approaches from a very large distance to a distance r, the increase in electrostatic potential energy, ΔE, is given by

$$\Delta E = \frac{kQ_1Q_2}{r} \tag{10}$$

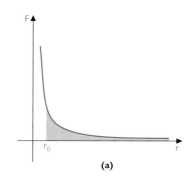

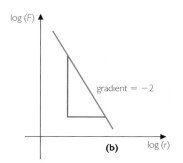

Figure 25 (a) The force F between an alpha particle and a gold nucleus changes with their separation r. (b) The same values plotted on a logarithmic graph

---

QUESTIONS

20 Sketch and explain how the graphs shown in Figure 25 would change if the nucleus used was that of a copper atom, containing 29 protons.

21 Alpha particles typically have a kinetic energy of 8.0×10^{-13} J. If such an alpha particle travelled directly towards a gold nucleus ($Q_2 = +79e$), what would be its distance of closest approach? ($e = 1.60 \times 10^{-19}$ C, $k = 9.0 \times 10^9$ N m^2 C^{-2})

3.3 Force fields

Coulomb's law is an example of an inverse square law, so-called because the force decreases in inverse proportion to the square of the distance between the two charged spheres. At twice the distance, the force drops to one quarter its previous value, at three times the distance the force drops to one ninth its previous value – and so on.

Figure 26 shows one way of thinking of this inverse square law. The influence of a charged sphere spreads out into the space around it, represented by the radial straight lines. The lines get further apart as they spread out, showing that the force gets weaker with distance. At twice the distance the lines are spread out over four times the area, showing that the force is a quarter of the strength. This is an inverse square relationship – doubling the distance gives a quarter of the force.

The lines shown in Figure 26 are called **field lines** or **lines of force**. As you will have seen in the unit *The Medium is the Message*, an **electric field** is defined as a region in which a charged object experiences a force, and the **electric field strength**, E, is defined as the force experienced by a charge of 1 coulomb. If a charge q experiences a force of magnitude F, then the magnitude of field strength is

$$E = \frac{F}{q} \tag{11}$$

The **direction of an electric field** is defined as that of the force experienced by a positive charge. An electric field can be represented diagramatically by drawing **electric field lines**, which tell us two things about the electric field near a charged object:

- the strength of the field (closer together means stronger);

- the direction of the field (a small positive charge will feel a force in the direction of the arrow – note that the arrows go from positive to negative charge).

Figure 27 shows how field lines can be used to represent the electric field in a variety of situations. Notice that we can still say that a field exists around an isolated charged sphere (Figure 27c), even if it is not exerting a force on another charged object. The field lines show us that there would be a force if we placed another charged object nearby.

To find out about the field strength at point X, a distance r from the charge Q, we place a small test charge q at X (see Figure 28). Outside a charged sphere, we have to measure r from the centre of the sphere. The force F on q is given by Coulomb's law, from equations (9) and (11):

$$F = \frac{kQq}{r^2}$$

and electric field strength E is then

$$E = \frac{kQ}{r^2} \tag{12}$$

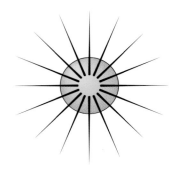

Figure 26   *A field of force surrounds a charged sphere*

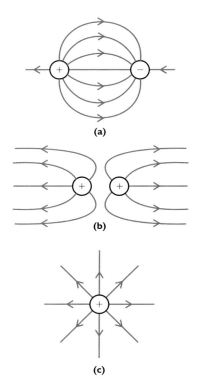

Figure 27   *Electric fields around (a) two charged spheres with opposite charges, (b) two charged spheres with like charges, and (c) an isolated positively charged sphere*

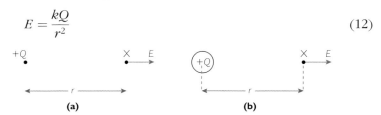

Figure 28   *Calculating the electric field strength near (a) a point charge Q and (b) a charged sphere*

ACTIVITY 14 **Probing the field**

Use a double flame probe to investigate the size and direction of the electric field around a charged sphere.

QUESTIONS

22 Draw a diagram to show the field lines around an isolated negatively-charged sphere. Explain why your diagram is different from Figure 27(c).

23 Copy the diagram of Figure 27(a). Mark and label a point where the electric field is strong, and another point where the field is weak. Draw arrows to show the electrostatic forces acting on the two spheres. Repeat for Figure 27(b).

24 Calculate the electric field strength at a point where a charge of 20 mC feels a force of 10 N.

25 An electron, charge $e = 1.60 \times 10^{-19}$ C, passes between two charged plates; the electric field strength between the plates is 2000 N C^{-1}. What force acts on the electron? If its mass is 9.11×10^{-31} kg, what is its acceleration?

26 What is the electric field strength at a distance of 1.0×10^{-13} m from a gold nucleus (charge $= +79e$)? (10^{-13} m is the approximate distance of closest approach for an alpha particle.) ($e = 1.60 \times 10^{-19}$ C, $k = 9.0 \times 10^9$ N m^2 C^{-2})

3.4 Collisions

Rutherford used collisions to probe the structure of atoms. Since then, particle physicists have used collisions as one of their main ways to deduce the nature of subatomic particles.

A gold nucleus is much more massive than an alpha particle – about 50 times as massive. So in Rutherford's experiments, a small particle was colliding with a much bigger one that remained more or less at rest. If there is less of a difference in the masses, the 'target' particle is set in motion; this is what happens in most particle physics experiments. The diagram in Figure 29 shows what happens when an alpha particle collides with a much smaller nucleus – that of a helium atom.

The diagram in Figure 29 was made using a cloud chamber, a device that can show up the tracks of charged subatomic particles. In this case, the cloud chamber was filled with helium gas, and a source of alpha radiation was then inserted. The tracks of alpha particles appear as straight lines extending out from the source. One alpha particle has hit a helium nucleus, and the two particles have gone off at right angles to each other.

The nucleus of a helium atom consists of two protons and two neutrons, so it is identical to an alpha particle. You can investigate a collision between two identical particles using pucks containing

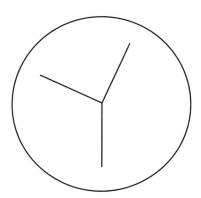

Figure 29 *A collision between an alpha particle and a helium nucleus*

dry ice, so that they glide on a layer of carbon dioxide gas. When a moving puck collides with an identical, stationary puck they move off at 90° to one another, as shown in Figure 30, just like the alpha particle tracks in Figure 29.

Momentum and energy in collisions

By analysing the tracks left in particle detectors, particle physicists can make deductions about the mass and energy of subatomic particles. In order to do this, they use some fundamental physical laws – the conservation of momentum and of energy.

In the unit *Transport on Track*, you explored one-dimensional collisions and met the vector quantity, *mass × velocity* known as **momentum** (which is usually given the symbol p, and has SI units kg m s^{-1}). You saw that, in a collision (or an explosion), momentum is always conserved – that is, the total momentum of the interacting objects is unchanged. We can now generalise this to all collisions. As momentum is a vector, we can draw a vector diagram to represent the momentum of the objects before and after they collide. Figure 31 shows such a diagram drawn from a multiflash photo such as that shown in Figure 30; the speed was deduced from the spacing of the images in the multiflash photographs. You can see that the vector sum of momenta afterwards is equal to the momentum of the single moving puck before the collision. Momentum is conserved in *all* collisions.

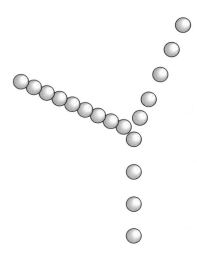

Figure 30 *Diagram drawn from a multiflash photo of a collision between two identical pucks*

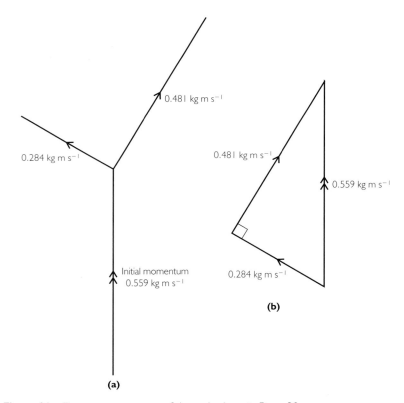

0.481 kg m s⁻¹

0.284 kg m s⁻¹

0.481 kg m s⁻¹

0.559 kg m s⁻¹

Initial momentum
0.559 kg m s⁻¹

0.284 kg m s⁻¹

(a)

(b)

Figure 31 *The momentum vectors of the pucks shown in Figure 30*

As you saw in the unit *Transport on Track*, an **elastic collision** is one in which kinetic energy is conserved. By analysing the momentum and energy in a collision, particle physicists can make deductions about the nature of the particles involved and the interactions between them. You will illustrate some aspects of this in Activities 15 and 16. For these activities, it is useful to be able to relate kinetic energy directly to momentum without needing first to find the speeds of the moving objects.

An object of mass m moving at speed v has momentum of magnitude p given by

$$p = mv \tag{13}$$

and that the same object's kinetic energy, E_k, is given by

$$E_k = \frac{1}{2}mv^2 \tag{14}$$

To express E_k in terms of p, square equation (13):

$$p^2 = m^2 v^2$$

then divide both sides by $2m$:

$$\frac{p^2}{2m} = \frac{m^2 v^2}{2m} = \frac{mv^2}{2}$$

and so we have

$$E_k = \frac{p^2}{2m} \tag{15}$$

It turns out that a non-relativistic *elastic* collision between a moving and a stationary object of *equal mass* always results in the two moving at right angles to each other. Analysis of Figure 31 illustrates why this is the case. Since momentum is conserved, we can write the vector sum

$$\mathbf{p} = \mathbf{p}_1 + \mathbf{p}_2 \tag{16}$$

Since both particles have the same mass, m, conservation of kinetic energy gives

$$\frac{p^2}{2m} = \frac{p_1^2}{2m} + \frac{p_2^2}{2m} \tag{17}$$

Multiplying equation (17) by $2m$ leads to a relationship between the magnitudes of the vectors (in other words, between the lengths of the sides of the triangle):

$$p^2 = p_1^2 + p_2^2 \tag{18}$$

Equation (18) is Pythagoras's relationship between the sides of a *right-angled* triangle – so the angle θ must be 90°, i.e. in this particular case the particles must move at right angles to one another after they collide.

In Activities 15 and 16, you will explore collisions that give rise to different angles between the tracks.

Study note

In fact equations (13)–(15) only apply to objects moving at speeds much less than that of light. They are appropriate for analysing collisions such as those in Activities 15 and 16, but in particle physics experiments, the particles travel very close to the speed of light and so the equations of **special relativity** are needed.

Study note

In the special case of a head-on collision, the moving particle comes to rest and the other moves off along the same direction as the original.

ACTIVITY **15**   **Nuclear dodgems**

Use frictionless pucks to model collisions between subatomic particles. Explore what happens when a moving puck collides with a stationary puck whose mass is the same as, greater than, or less than its own. If possible, record the collisions as multiflash photographs.

ACTIVITY **16**   **Accounting for momentum and energy**

By making measurements on multiflash photographs such as that in Figure 30 or your own from Activity 15, draw vector diagrams to represent momentum before and after the collision and also investigate how the kinetic energy changes.

QUESTIONS

27 Estimate your own mass, and the fastest speed at which you can run. Use equations (13) and (14) to calculate your momentum and kinetic energy. Confirm that your answers are related by equation (15).

28 Calculate the kinetic energy of an alpha particle (mass 6.7×10^{-27} kg) whose momentum is 5.0×10^{-20} kg m s^{-1}.

29 Many particle collisions result in the creation of new particles, for example when an electron and positron collide and interact to produce a muon/antimuon pair. Muons have greater mass than electrons.

   (**a**) Would momentum be conserved in such a collision?

   (**b**) Would such a collision be elastic? If not, would the total kinetic energy increase or decrease?

30 Particles with no electric charge (such as neutrons and neutrinos) leave no tracks in particle detectors. How might particle physicists deduce the presence of such particles from a record of tracks left by charged particles before and after a collision?

3.5 *Particle diffraction*

Rutherford's alpha particle scattering experiment, carried out in 1908, showed how the underlying structure of matter could be investigated by firing a beam of charged particles at the matter and looking at the pattern that the particles formed after they had interacted with the matter. This is the basic approach used in much of particle physics, an approach that was developed and extended throughout the 20th century. In section 3.4, we analysed the results of such experiments in terms of collisions. In this section we see how ideas about diffraction and wave–particle duality can be brought to bear on such experiments.

In the AS unit *Digging Up the Past*, you saw how diffraction of X-rays enables archaeologists to probe the structure of materials. In *Spare Part Surgery* you saw that electron beams, too, behave like waves and can be diffracted; electron diffraction is used to investigate the structure of certain materials – polymers, for example – on an atomic scale. Electron diffraction is also used to probe matter on an even smaller scale – electron beams are used to measure the size of nuclei and to reveal the presence of quarks within protons. After a brief review of diffraction in Activity 17, this section looks in more detail at electron diffraction and you will see how it comes about that electron beams can be used to probe matter on such a minute scale.

ACTIVITY **17** **Diffraction of light**

Observe what happens when light is diffracted by:

- a grating of parallel lines;
- a regular grid of crossed lines;
- a random array of fine dust particles.

Explore the effects of changing the separation of the lines and the wavelength of the light.

Most TV sets incorporate a cathode-ray tube – a vacuum tube in which a beam of electrons can be produced. As you saw in the AS unit *Spare Part Surgery*, such a beam can be used to investigate the structure of matter. Figure 32 shows apparatus that you can use in the laboratory to demonstrate electron diffraction by graphite, and Figure 33 shows the pattern produced on the screen with such apparatus when polycrystalline graphite is placed in the electron beam. With a single crystal the pattern is an array of dots,

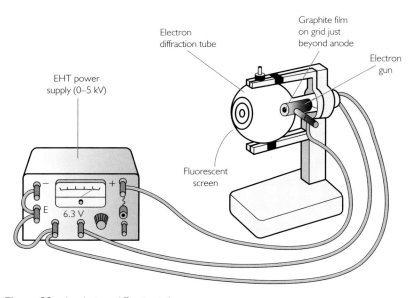

Figure 32 *An electron diffraction tube*

like the pattern you get if you shine a laser beam through crossed diffraction gratings. Just as laser light is diffracted by the grating, so the beam of electrons is diffracted by the regular array of atoms that make up the graphite crystal. The photograph in Figure 33 shows what happens when a beam of electrons shines through a piece of polycrystalline graphite. (It's difficult to obtain a single crystal.) This material is made of many tiny crystals, all at different orientations. Because of this, the spots of the diffraction pattern are smeared out into rings.

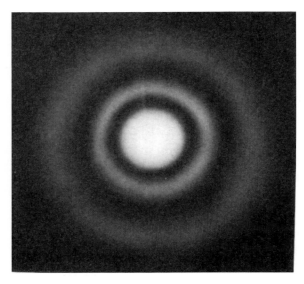

Figure 33 *A diffraction pattern produced when an electron beam passes through polycrystalline graphite*

Wave–particle duality

Diffraction is something that happens to waves. When waves pass through a narrow gap, they spread out. The bright spots you see in the laser-light diffraction pattern are formed when many waves arrive at the same point in step with one another.

The fact that electrons can be diffracted tells us something striking about electrons: sometimes they seem to behave as particles, sometimes as waves. When they are moving freely as a beam, and when they strike the screen at the end of the tube, they behave as particles. When they pass between the atoms of a crystal of graphite, they behave like waves. This double behaviour is not like anything we experience on the macroscopic scale of things, but it is a phenomenon we have to come to terms with when considering the behaviour of matter and energy on the microscopic scale.

The rule is that sometimes we have to use wave ideas to explain our observations, and sometimes particle ideas. We can't say that under certain circumstances electrons are waves; they are neither waves nor particles, and all we can do is use our ideas of waves or particles to explain their behaviour as best we can. What we need is a way of translating back and forth between the two ways of describing electrons. In the AS unit *Spare Part Surgery*, you met this 'translation' – it is the de Broglie equation

$$\lambda = \frac{h}{p} \tag{19}$$

where p is the electron's momentum and λ is its wavelength (more correctly, its **de Broglie wavelength**, after Louis de Broglie who found this relationship). The quantity h is the Planck constant:

$$h = 6.63 \times 10^{-34}\,\text{J s}$$

Equation (19) thus allows us to translate from a particle property (momentum) to a wave property (wavelength). Figure 34 shows a logarithmic graph relating λ to p. Notice that the gradient of the graph is negative (because the two quantities vary in inverse proportion). The gradient is -1 (because $\lambda \propto p^{-1}$).

In Activity 17 of this unit and in the AS unit *Digging Up the Past* you saw that, in order to analyse the structure of a material using a diffraction technique, the wavelength of the radiation should be comparable with the separation of the diffracting objects. So probing matter on a subatomic scale requires a shorter wavelength than that used to investigate structure on the scale of whole atoms or molecules. In Activity 18, you will explore how the de Broglie wavelength of electrons can be controlled. You will need to draw on ideas about charge and voltage that you met in earlier units (e.g. *Technology in Space*).

The electron beam is produced in an electron gun (Figure 35). Electrons are first released from a heated cathode by thermionic emission, and then accelerated by a high voltage applied between cathode and anode. They pass through a hole in the anode and then travel at constant speed as they pass through the diffracting object (a graphite crystal, for example) and then strike the fluorescent screen.

So long as there is no other energy transfer taking place, the kinetic energy, E_k, acquired by an electron as it is accelerated in the gun is given by

$$E_k = eV \tag{20}$$

where e is the electron's charge and V the potential difference between cathode and anode. Provided the electron's speed does not approach the speed of light, we can use the non-relativistic equations (15), (19) and (20) to derive an expression for the de Broglie wavelength. From equations (15) and (20):

$$p = \sqrt{(2mE_k)} = \sqrt{(2meV)}$$

and so, using equation (19):

$$\lambda = \frac{h}{p} = \frac{h}{\sqrt{(2meV)}} \tag{21}$$

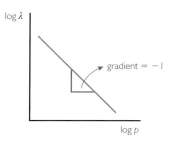

Figure 34   *A log–log graph of de Broglie wavelength λ and momentum p for an electron*

Maths reference

Using logarithmic graphs
See Maths note 8.7

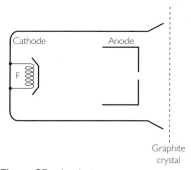

Figure 35   *An electron gun*

ACTIVITY 18 **Diffraction of electrons**

Use apparatus such as that shown in Figure 32 to explore electron diffraction and the relationship between de Broglie wavelength and accelerating voltage.

QUESTIONS

31 Calculate the kinetic energy, the speed and the momentum of an electron which is accelerated through a pd of 500 V.
(Electron mass $m_e = 9.11 \times 10^{-31}$ kg; electron charge $e = 1.60 \times 10^{-19}$ C)

32 What pd is required to accelerate an electron to a speed of 1.0×10^6 m s^{-1}?

33 As electrons are accelerated from the cathode to the anode of an electron beam tube, does their de Broglie wavelength increase or decrease?

34 If the cathode–anode voltage is increased in an electron beam tube, does the de Broglie wavelength of the electrons in the beam increase or decrease?

35 Calculate the de Broglie wavelength of an electron moving at 1.0×10^6 m s^{-1}. (Electron mass $m_e = 9.11 \times 10^{-31}$ kg; Planck constant $h = 6.63 \times 10^{-34}$ J s)

36 Calculate the momentum of an electron whose de Broglie wavelength is 3.0×10^{-10} m.

37 Estimate your own mass and your speed when walking. Find the order of magnitude of your own de Broglie wavelength, and hence explain why you do not notice the wave-like aspect of your nature – for example, you are not noticeably diffracted when walking through a metre-wide doorway.

Faster electrons

When electrons are diffracted as they pass through a graphite crystal, they are interacting with the electrons of the carbon atoms that make up the graphite. Electrons can be used to look at the nuclei of atoms, too, but if they are to be diffracted by something as small as an atomic nucleus, they must have a very short wavelength, similar to the dimensions of the nucleus itself.

Since atomic nuclei are of the order of 10^{-15} m in diameter, we need electrons whose wavelength is of this order too. To achieve this, the electrons must be accelerated through many millions of volts.

At this point, we need to be aware of the limitations of some of the equations used earlier. In particular, consider what happens if we try to calculate the speed of an electron that has been accelerated through 100 MV ($= 1.00 \times 10^8$ V).

$$E_k = eV = 1.60 \times 10^{-19} \, C \times 1.00 \times 10^8 \, V$$
$$= 1.60 \times 10^{-11} \, J$$

(no problem here)

assuming $E_k = \dfrac{1}{2}\,mv^2$,

$$v = \sqrt{\dfrac{2E_k}{m}}$$

$$= \sqrt{\left(\dfrac{2 \times 1.60 \times 10^{-11}\ \text{J}}{9.11 \times 10^{-31}\ \text{kg}}\right)}$$

$$= 5.9 \times 10^9\ \text{m s}^{-1}$$

This is greater than the speed of light ($c = 3.00 \times 10^8\ \text{m s}^{-1}$), which is impossible (according to the theory of relativity). For speeds approaching the speed of light we need to use a different expression for the particle's energy, derived from relativity. Particles that are moving at speeds that are greater than, say, $0.1c$ are described as relativistic, and some of the relationships between quantities such as velocity, kinetic energy and momentum have to be revised. In particular, we can no longer calculate a particle's kinetic energy using $E_k = \dfrac{1}{2}\,mv^2$.

Diffraction patterns

Figure 33 shows the diffraction pattern of electrons that have been diffracted by polycrystalline graphite. You saw a similar pattern in Activity 17 when light is diffracted by tiny dust particles. There is a bright central spot, surrounded by rings of decreasing brightness. The graph in Figure 36 shows how the brightness varies across the centre of this diffraction pattern. The central hump of the graph corresponds to the bright central spot; then there is a dip where the pattern is dark, then a lower peak for the first bright ring, and so on.

The diffraction pattern can change in two ways: the electrons' de Broglie wavelength can be changed, as can the size of the particles that are causing the diffraction. We will concentrate on the size of the particles. With smaller and smaller particles, the diffraction rings get wider and wider. So measuring the diameter of the rings can tell us about the size of the tiny particles that are doing the diffracting.

Figure 37 shows what happens when high-energy electrons are diffracted by samples of carbon and oxygen. The de Broglie wavelength of the electrons is similar to the diameter of the nuclei, so the electrons are strongly diffracted. In this case, the results don't appear as a set of rings on a screen. Instead, the detector is moved round to different positions to measure the intensity of the diffracted electrons. The result is a graph of intensity against angle. You can see the similarity in shape between these graphs and the graph for the diffraction of light (Figure 36). In Figure 37(a) there is a central peak, then a minimum at an angle of about $50°$, and then a smaller peak. From this, the diameter of the carbon nuclei can be determined.

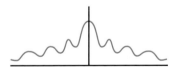

Figure 36 *A graph showing how the brightness varies along the diameter of the pattern produced when light is diffracted by a random array of fine particles.*

ACTIVITY **19** **Interpreting electron diffraction patterns**

Use the electron diffraction patterns shown in Figure 37 to
determine the diameters of carbon and oxygen nuclei.

'Seeing' protons

The smallest, lightest of all atoms is the hydrogen atom. Its nucleus
is a single proton. In the 1950s, experiments were done using
electron diffraction with liquid hydrogen as the target. With
electrons accelerated though nearly 1000 MV (10^9 V), Robert
Hofstadter of Stanford University in California was able to estimate
the diameter of the proton as 5.6×10^{-15} m. This result gained him
the Nobel Prize for Physics in 1961.

As far as Hofstadter could tell, a proton was simply a single
particle, not much different from a rather fuzzy billiard ball. The
electrons he used interacted with the protons via the Coulomb force
– their charges interacted. Hofstadter could find no evidence that the
proton was anything other than a sphere of charge.

Today, as we have seen in part 2 of this unit, our picture of
protons is rather different. High-energy electron accelerators have
been used to probe right inside protons, and this has shown that
the charge inside a proton is not uniformly distributed; each
proton is made of three quarks tightly bound together. This three-
fold structure was revealed by 'deep inelastic scattering'
experiments in the late 1980s in which beams of high-energy
electrons were fired at protons, rather as Rutherford had fired
alpha particles at gold foil many years previously.

ACTIVITY **20** **Deep inelastic scattering**

Write a paragraph to explain why very high-energy electrons were
needed to reveal the quarks which make up a proton. Include the
following terms:

energy   wavelength   diffraction

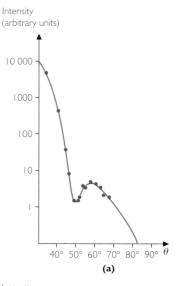

(a)

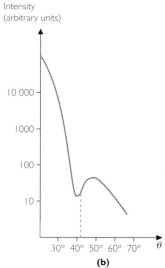

(b)

Figure 37 *Electron diffraction patterns
for (a) carbon nuclei and (b) oxygen nuclei*

3.6 Summing up part 3

In this part of the unit, you have seen that the story of our
understanding of the particles that make up matter has developed
rapidly during the 20th century. This has been achieved by probing
matter with increasingly energetic particles – electrons, alpha
particles and others. The electrons used in deep inelastic scattering
experiments had energies equivalent to being accelerated through
tens or hundreds of billions of volts. In part 4, we will go on to see
how such high energies can be achieved.

You have looked at the development of our understanding of the
structure of matter, starting from Rutherford's alpha particle
scattering experiment – an understanding of electrostatic forces,
developed in the 19th century, helped to make this possible. You
have seen how the conservation of momentum (a fundamental law

of physics) is brought into the analysis of collisions, and how a knowledge of the wave-like nature of electrons (and other particles) explains their usefulness as a tool for probing the heart of matter.

ACTIVITY 21 | Summing up part 3

During the course of the 20th century, experiments using a variety of subatomic 'probes' were carried out to investigate the structure of atoms, and to find out about other aspects of the fundamental nature of matter. Draw a timeline to show this, giving dates and brief descriptions of the experiments, along with any other details you wish to include. Include as many as possible of the terms printed in bold – and make sure you know their meanings. Refer back to part 2 for information about some other experiments that you might show on your timeline.

4 *Particle beams and accelerators*

In this part of the unit, you will find out how charged particles are accelerated to high energies, so that they can be used in experiments to recreate the conditions in the early stages of the history of the Universe.

4.1 *Big experiments*

CERN is the European centre for nuclear research. It sits between the Alps and the Jura mountains, near Geneva in Switzerland. It's a great place to work if you're a particle physicist and you enjoy skiing. The photograph in Figure 38 shows an aerial view of CERN, with the positions of the underground tunnels marked. The main particle accelerator is circular in shape. It is so large – 8.6 km across – that it extends under the border into France.

Figure 38 *The CERN lab near Geneva*

Once reason for building this vast particle physics laboratory was political. During the Second World War, scientists had been fighting each other, competing to develop the nuclear bomb. After the war, it was hoped that a European centre could be built so that scientists from different countries could work together for non-military research. The Conseil Européen pour la Recherche Nucléaire (its original name) was established in 1952. It was the first international organisation that Germany joined after the war. Currently, CERN attracts more than 300 PhD students each year. Along with these students are post-doctoral workers, professors and full-time staff.

ACTIVITY 22 Physics in conflict

Discuss the following in small groups. You may find that you have opinions, but need to look up information to back up your arguments.

- Is it ever right for politics to interfere with scientific research?
- Are there any examples from the 20th century where politics has played a part in the development of physics research?
- Do the developments of physics ever affect political decisions? Try to use some contemporary examples.

People and ideas

Physicists like to develop theories that are simple. To simplify, they are currently trying to come up with one theory that can explain the four fundamental forces (electromagnetic, weak, strong and gravitational) in terms of a single theory – rather as, in the 19th century, electrostatics and magnetism were unified through the theory of electromagnetism. In the 1960s, the electromagnetic and weak forces were unified in this way. This theory then predicted the existence of so-called W and Z boson particles. These particles have a lot of mass. This led teams of scientists to try to accelerate particles to high energies, collide them and try to create the Z and W particles. In 1983, Italian physicist Carlo Rubbia headed a team of 100 physicists at CERN that detected these particles. This helped to confirm the electroweak unified theory. Carlo Rubbia and his colleague Simon van de Meer got the Nobel prize for this work.

If you ever visit CERN, you will see people from many different countries. Because particle physics research involves using expensive machines, single universities and research institutes rarely do research in isolation. Organisations collaborate not just within one country, but internationally. If you look at scientific papers written today, they list all the scientists who have contributed to the project, and in particle physics this may mean scores of names (Figure 39).

Someone once joked that broken English, not English, is the international language at CERN. In the cafeteria, you can hear

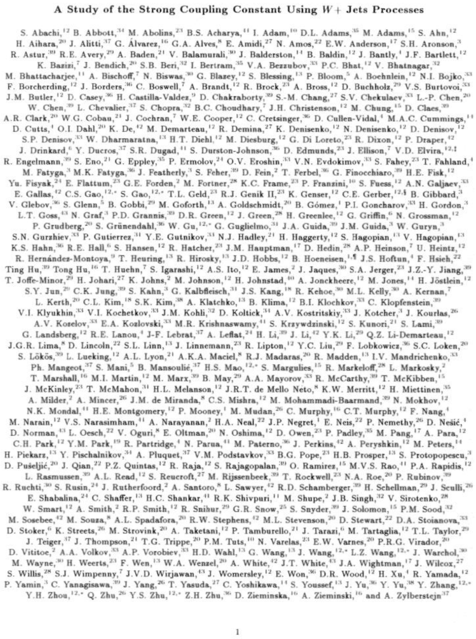
A Study of the Strong Coupling Constant Using $W+$ Jets Processes

S. Abachi,[12] B. Abbott,[34] M. Abolins,[23] B.S. Acharya,[11] I. Adam,[10] D.L. Adams,[35] M. Adams,[15] S. Ahn,[12]
H. Aihara,[20] J. Alitti,[37] G. Álvarez,[16] G.A. Alves,[8] E. Amidi,[27] N. Amos,[22] E.W. Anderson,[17] S.H. Aronson,[3]
R. Astur,[39] R.E. Avery,[29] A. Baden,[21] V. Balamurali,[30] J. Balderston,[14] B. Baldin,[12] J. Bantly,[4] J.F. Bartlett,[12]
K. Bazizi,[7] J. Bendich,[20] S.B. Beri,[32] I. Bertram,[35] V.A. Bezzubov,[33] P.C. Bhat,[12] V. Bhatnagar,[32]
M. Bhattacharjee,[11] A. Bischoff,[7] N. Biswas,[30] G. Blazey,[12] S. Blessing,[13] P. Bloom,[5] A. Boehnlein,[12] N.I. Bojko,[33]
F. Borcherding,[12] J. Borders,[36] C. Boswell,[7] A. Brandt,[12] R. Brock,[23] A. Bross,[12] D. Buchholz,[29] V.S. Burtovoi,[33]
J.M. Butler,[12] D. Casey,[36] H. Castilla-Valdez,[9] D. Chakraborty,[39] S.-M. Chang,[27] S.V. Chekulaev,[33] L.-P. Chen,[20]
W. Chen,[39] L. Chevalier,[37] S. Chopra,[32] B.C. Choudhary,[7] J.H. Christenson,[12] M. Chung,[15] D. Claes,[39]
A.R. Clark,[20] W.G. Cobau,[21] J. Cochran,[7] W.E. Cooper,[12] C. Cretsinger,[36] D. Cullen-Vidal,[4] M.A.C. Cummings,[11]
D. Cutts,[4] O.I. Dahl,[20] K. De,[42] M. Demarteau,[12] R. Demina,[27] K. Denisenko,[12] N. Denisenko,[12] D. Denisov,[12]
S.P. Denisov,[33] W. Dharmaratna,[13] H.T. Diehl,[12] M. Diesburg,[12] G. Di Loreto,[23] R. Dixon,[12] P. Draper,[42]
J. Drinkard,[6] Y. Ducros,[37] S.R. Dugad,[11] S. Durston-Johnson,[36] D. Edmunds,[23] J. Ellison,[7] V.D. Elvira,[12,‡]
R. Engelmann,[39] S. Eno,[21] G. Eppley,[35] P. Ermolov,[24] O.V. Eroshin,[33] V.N. Evdokimov,[33] S. Fahey,[23] T. Fahland,[4]
M. Fatyga,[3] M.K. Fatyga,[36] J. Featherly,[3] S. Feher,[39] D. Fein,[2] T. Ferbel,[36] G. Finocchiaro,[39] H.E. Fisk,[12]
Yu. Fisyak,[24] E. Flattum,[23] G.E. Forden,[2] M. Fortner,[28] K.C. Frame,[23] P. Franzini,[10] S. Fuess,[12] A.N. Galjaev,[33]
E. Gallas,[42] C.S. Gao,[12,*] S. Gao,[12,*] T.L. Geld,[23] R.J. Genik II,[23] K. Genser,[12] C.E. Gerber,[12,§] B. Gibbard,[3]
V. Glebov,[36] S. Glenn,[5] B. Gobbi,[29] M. Goforth,[13] A. Goldschmidt,[20] B. Gómez,[1] P.I. Goncharov,[33] H. Gordon,[3]
L.T. Goss,[43] N. Graf,[3] P.D. Grannis,[39] D.R. Green,[12] J. Green,[28] H. Greenlee,[12] G. Griffin,[6] N. Grossman,[12]
P. Grudberg,[20] S. Grünendahl,[36] W. Gu,[12,*] G. Guglielmo,[31] J.A. Guida,[39] J.M. Guida,[3] W. Guryn,[3]
S.N. Gurzhiev,[33] P. Gutierrez,[31] Y.E. Gutnikov,[33] N.J. Hadley,[21] H. Haggerty,[12] S. Hagopian,[13] V. Hagopian,[13]
K.S. Hahn,[36] R.E. Hall,[6] S. Hansen,[12] R. Hatcher,[23] J.M. Hauptman,[17] D. Hedin,[28] A.P. Heinson,[7] U. Heintz,[12]
R. Hernández-Montoya,[9] T. Heuring,[13] R. Hirosky,[13] J.D. Hobbs,[12] B. Hoeneisen,[1,¶] J.S. Hoftun,[4] F. Hsieh,[22]
Ting Hu,[39] Tong Hu,[16] T. Huehn,[7] S. Igarashi,[12] A.S. Ito,[12] E. James,[2] J. Jaques,[30] S.A. Jerger,[23] J.Z.-Y. Jiang,[39]
T. Joffe-Minor,[29] H. Johari,[27] K. Johns,[2] M. Johnson,[12] H. Johnstad,[40] A. Jonckheere,[12] M. Jones,[14] H. Jöstlein,[12]
S.Y. Jun,[29] C.K. Jung,[39] S. Kahn,[3] G. Kalbfleisch,[31] J.S. Kang,[18] R. Kehoe,[30] M.L. Kelly,[30] A. Kernan,[7]
L. Kerth,[20] C.L. Kim,[18] S.K. Kim,[38] A. Klatchko,[13] B. Klima,[12] B.I. Klochkov,[33] C. Klopfenstein,[39]
V.I. Klyukhin,[33] V.I. Kochetkov,[33] J.M. Kohli,[32] D. Koltick,[34] A.V. Kostritskiy,[33] J. Kotcher,[3] J. Kourlas,[26]
A.V. Kozelov,[33] E.A. Kozlovski,[33] M.R. Krishnaswamy,[11] S. Krzywdzinski,[12] S. Kunori,[21] S. Lami,[39]
G. Landsberg,[12] R.E. Lanou,[4] J-F. Lebrat,[37] A. Leflat,[24] H. Li,[39] J. Li,[42] Y.K. Li,[29] Q.Z. Li-Demarteau,[12]
J.G.R. Lima,[8] D. Lincoln,[22] S.L. Linn,[13] J. Linnemann,[23] R. Lipton,[12] Y.C. Liu,[29] F. Lobkowicz,[36] S.C. Loken,[20]
S. Lökös,[39] L. Lueking,[12] A.L. Lyon,[21] A.K.A. Maciel,[8] R.J. Madaras,[20] R. Madden,[13] I.V. Mandrichenko,[33]
Ph. Mangeot,[37] S. Mani,[5] B. Mansoulié,[37] H.S. Mao,[12,*] S. Margulies,[15] R. Markeloff,[28] L. Markosky,[2]
T. Marshall,[16] M.I. Martin,[12] M. Marx,[39] B. May,[29] A.A. Mayorov,[33] R. McCarthy,[39] T. McKibben,[15]
J. McKinley,[23] T. McMahon,[31] H.L. Melanson,[12] J.R.T. de Mello Neto,[8] K.W. Merritt,[12] H. Miettinen,[35]
A. Milder,[2] A. Mincer,[26] J.M. de Miranda,[8] C.S. Mishra,[12] M. Mohammadi-Baarmand,[39] N. Mokhov,[12]
N.K. Mondal,[11] H.E. Montgomery,[12] P. Mooney,[1] M. Mudan,[26] C. Murphy,[16] C.T. Murphy,[12] F. Nang,[4]
M. Narain,[12] V.S. Narasimham,[11] A. Narayanan,[2] H.A. Neal,[22] J.P. Negret,[1] E. Neis,[22] P. Nemethy,[26] D. Nešić,[4]
D. Norman,[43] L. Oesch,[22] V. Oguri,[8] E. Oltman,[20] N. Oshima,[12] D. Owen,[23] P. Padley,[35] M. Pang,[17] A. Para,[12]
C.H. Park,[12] Y.M. Park,[19] R. Partridge,[4] N. Parua,[41] M. Paterno,[36] J. Perkins,[42] A. Peryshkin,[12] M. Peters,[14]
H. Piekarz,[13] Y. Pischalnikov,[34] A. Pluquet,[37] V.M. Podstavkov,[33] B.G. Pope,[23] H.B. Prosper,[13] S. Protopopescu,[3]
D. Pušeljić,[20] J. Qian,[22] P.Z. Quintas,[12] R. Raja,[12] S. Rajagopalan,[39] O. Ramirez,[15] M.V.S. Rao,[41] P.A. Rapidis,[12]
L. Rasmussen,[39] A.L. Read,[12] S. Reucroft,[27] M. Rijssenbeek,[39] T. Rockwell,[23] N.A. Roe,[20] P. Rubinov,[39]
R. Ruchti,[30] S. Rusin,[24] J. Rutherfoord,[2] A. Santoro,[8] L. Sawyer,[42] R.D. Schamberger,[39] H. Schellman,[29] J. Sculli,[26]
E. Shabalina,[24] C. Shaffer,[13] H.C. Shankar,[41] R.K. Shivpuri,[11] M. Shupe,[2] J.B. Singh,[32] V. Sirotenko,[28]
W. Smart,[12] A. Smith,[2] R.P. Smith,[12] R. Snihur,[29] G.R. Snow,[25] S. Snyder,[39] J. Solomon,[15] P.M. Sood,[32]
M. Sosebee,[42] M. Souza,[8] A.L. Spadafora,[20] R.W. Stephens,[42] M.L. Stevenson,[20] D. Stewart,[22] D.A. Stoianova,[33]
D. Stoker,[6] K. Streets,[26] M. Strovink,[20] A. Taketani,[12] P. Tamburello,[21] J. Tarazi,[6] M. Tartaglia,[12] T.L. Taylor,[29]
J. Teiger,[37] J. Thompson,[21] T.G. Trippe,[20] P.M. Tuts,[10] N. Varelas,[23] E.W. Varnes,[20] P.R.G. Virador,[20]
D. Vititoe,[2] A.A. Volkov,[33] A.P. Vorobiev,[33] H.D. Wahl,[13] G. Wang,[13] J. Wang,[12,*] L.Z. Wang,[12,*] J. Warchol,[30]
M. Wayne,[30] H. Weerts,[23] F. Wen,[13] W.A. Wenzel,[20] A. White,[42] J.T. White,[43] J.A. Wightman,[17] J. Wilcox,[27]
S. Willis,[28] S.J. Wimpenny,[7] J.V.D. Wirjawan,[43] J. Womersley,[12] E. Won,[36] D.R. Wood,[12] H. Xu,[4] R. Yamada,[12]
P. Yamin,[3] C. Yanagisawa,[39] J. Yang,[26] T. Yasuda,[27] C. Yoshikawa,[11] S. Youssef,[13] J. Yu,[36] Y. Yu,[38] Y. Zhang,[12,*]
Y.H. Zhou,[12,*] Q. Zhu,[26] Y.S. Zhu,[12,*] Z.H. Zhu,[36] D. Zieminska,[16] A. Zieminski,[16] and A. Zylberstejn[37]

1

Figure 39 *Particle physics research involves collaboration between physicists of many different nationalities* physicists arguing about the meaning of the results that they have just analysed. Much of this work involves mathematical modelling, computer programming and careful, detailed discussion. All of the skills that they learn and practise are transferable to other disciplines. Most young physicists do not remain in physics after their PhDs at CERN. Some of them go on to work in the City as merchant bankers, stockbrokers, managers, etc. In these jobs they are using many of the same skills that they needed in their scientific research.

Over the years, it became increasingly important to be able to send data from CERN back to their home universities overseas very quickly to help speed up analysis by their teams of scientists. The World Wide Web was established by scientists at CERN to help them communicate with each other across different continents as well as countries.

Helenka Przysiezniak completed a masters degree in Canada as a theoretician in astrophysics and decided to do her PhD in particle physics at CERN. In the *Times Higher Education Supplement*, 24 April 1998, she described the impromptu debates that happen in corridors, in the cafeteria and in offices at CERN:

(a)

> It sounds like you're having a big argument, but actually you're just discussing things. You want to prove that something is right if you believe in it. That's just how it works when you're discussing the 'truth'. You can't survive as a physicist unless you have a bit of ego.

Przysiezniak went on to suggest that physicists tend to be just as passionate about their other interests – many are accomplished musicians and concerts are frequently held at CERN. The mountains and lakes around CERN attract physicists who are keen skiers, mountaineers and sailors (Figure 40).

(b)

Figure 40   *(a) Lake Geneva (b) Mont Blanc*

ACTIVITY **23** | **Particle physics today**

Use the Internet to find out some up-to-date information about current and planned particle physics experiments.

With a small group of students, discuss your opinions on the way modern particle physics research is organised and funded.

4.2 Achieving high energy

In the 1960s as particle physics developed there grew a demand for higher and higher energy accelerators. Partly this demand was fuelled by the desire of the engineer and practical physicist to see what could be built and discovered at higher energies. At the same time, theoreticians wanted experiments that could test the predictions of the standard model of fundamental particles and forces. The theory predicted the existence of quarks; it also suggested that there were other much more massive particles. To discover these particles required bigger accelerators capable of delivering more energy.

Particle physics is often known as High Energy Physics (HEP). As you have seen in parts 2 and 3, there are three main reasons why high energies are used by particle physicists:

- if you want a positively charged particle to get closer to a nucleus of an atom, a lot of energy must be supplied;

- the more energy that can be given to particles, the shorter their wavelength and the smaller the detail that can be investigated using them as a probe;

- colliding particles together, the energy is re-distributed, producing new particles. The higher the collision energy, the larger the mass of particles that can be produced.

As theory predicted different particles, this drove the advancement of the technology – more energetic machines were needed. Sometimes unexpected results were found and this led to refinements in the theory, which sometimes needed even higher energies in order to be tested.

You have already used particle accelerators that operate on essentially the same principle as those used in particle physics research. In the electron gun that forms part of any cathode-ray tube, electrons are accelerated in an electric field, produced by applying a potential difference between the cathode and anode. In such a tube used in a TV set, or in demonstrating electron beams in the laboratory, electrons are accelerated through a few thousand volts at most. In particle physics experiments, much higher energies are required. This has several consequences. One is that the required energies cannot be achieved all in one go; accelerators have to be designed that 'kick' the particles many times over, increasing their energy each time. Another consequence is that the equations of classical physics break down at speeds close to that of light, and to describe and predict the behaviour of such energetic particles, the equations of special relativity must be used. The second of these is related to some of the units that particle physicists use, and that you are likely to come across in your reading about particle physics.

Relativistic effects

In section 3.5, you saw that, according to classical physics, an electron accelerated through 100 MV would travel faster than light. This is actually impossible, and the incorrect prediction arose because we used inappropriate equations. In particle physics accelerators, electrons (and other charged particles, such as protons and positrons) are accelerated through potential differences of several gigavolts ($1 \text{ GV} = 10^9 \text{ V}$) or even teravolts ($1 \text{ TV} = 10^{12} \text{ V}$).

Accelerators give particles energy. When particles are accelerated, they go faster, but they can never reach the speed of light. Einstein was able to show that any particle that has mass when at rest can never be accelerated to the speed of light. Even if we keep giving the particle energy when it is close to the speed of light, its speed will keep increasing but it will never reach that elusive 3×10^8 m s^{-1}. The reason for this is that the particle's mass keeps increasing, the more energy it is given. (You might guess this from the famous equation $E = mc^2$. The energy you give the particle reappears as mass.) So the particle becomes more and more massive, and more and more difficult to accelerate. That's why, unless you can find a loophole in Einstein's theory of relativity, faster-than-light travel will remain in the realm of science fiction.

In 1964, Bertozzi conducted an experiment to find the speeds of electrons accelerated by electric fields. Figure 41 shows Bertozzi's apparatus. The electrons were effectively accelerated through potential differences up to 15 MV. The 'time-of-flight' of the electrons between the two detectors was measured using an oscilloscope, enabling their speeds to be found. To check that their energies were as expected, the electrons were allowed to strike a target, which heated up. Bertozzi measured their speeds and found that the electrons did not exceed the speed of light and that the relationship between their speed and energy was as predicted by Einstein.

Study note

This uses the same ideas about heating and specific heat capacity that you met in the AS unit *Technology in Space*.

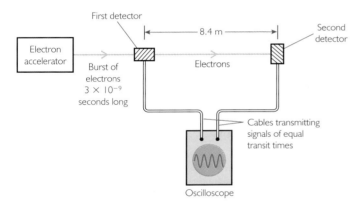

Figure 41   *Bertozzi's apparatus*

ACTIVITY **24**   **The universal speed limit**

By analysing some of Bertozzi's results, demonstrate that electrons behave as Einstein predicted and do not obey the equations of classical physics when they reach high energies.

Units

When a particle has been accelerated to a very high energy, it is more useful to talk about its energy than its speed – its speed is in any case very nearly the speed of light, regardless of any additional energy it acquires, and if you want to know what a particle can do (e.g. create new particles in a collision) then its energy is the most important thing to know. For this reason, particle physicists nearly always use a system of units that relates directly to particle energies.

When talking about the energy of an electron (or other subatomic particle), it's rather awkward to work in joules, with all those negative powers of ten. Instead, we often state its energy in units of electronvolts (eV).

The kinetic energy of an electron accelerated through 1 V is 1 electronvolt (1 eV).

magnitude of electron charge, $e = 1.60 \times 10^{-19}$ C, so

$$1 \text{ eV} = 1.60 \times 10^{-19} \text{ J}$$

Study note

You met eV in the AS unit *Digging Up The Past*

The most energetic accelerators can produce particles with energies in the giga-electronvolt (GeV) or even tera-electronvolt (TeV) range. Remember that the electron-volt is a unit of energy, not of voltage. It can be used for any particle, not just electrons – and they do not have to be electrically accelerated.

Particle physicists commonly express mass in units that, at first, look a little odd but do in fact make their life simpler. In part 2 you met Einstein's equation:

$$E = mc^2 \qquad \text{(equation 1)}$$

We can use this to find the energy associated with a particle when it is at rest – the energy that would be liberated if its entire **rest mass** were to dematerialise or, equivalently, the energy needed to create the particle 'from nothing'. This energy, E_0, is called the particle's **rest-mass energy** (or, sometimes, just its rest energy). An example shows how this leads to new (non-SI) units for mass.

An electron at rest has mass $m_0 = 9.11 \times 10^{-31}$ kg. Its energy equivalent is

$$E_0 = 9.11 \times 10^{-31} \text{ kg} \times (3.00 \times 10^8 \text{m s}^{-1})^2$$

$$= 8.199 \times 10^{-14} \text{ J} = 5.12 \times 10^5 \text{ eV} = 0.512 \text{ MeV}$$

We can express the mass in terms of its energy equivalent, again using equation (1):

$$m_0 = \frac{E_0}{c^2} = 0.512 \text{ MeV}/c^2$$

Rather than putting in numbers and doing any calculations, particle physicists leave this expression just as it is! The mass of the electron is now expressed in the rather odd-looking units of MeV/c^2.

Now imagine the electron has been accelerated so that its total energy is 1 GeV. Its mass is still given by equation (1), where E is its total energy (rest energy and kinetic energy combined – though now its kinetic energy vastly exceeds its rest energy).

$$m = \frac{E}{c^2} = 1 \text{ GeV}/c^2$$

Without needing to convert back to kg, you can see that the mass equivalent to the electron's total energy is now about two thousand times its rest mass (as $1 \text{ GeV} = 10^3 \text{ MeV}$).

Now suppose this 1 GeV electron were to collide head-on with a positron that had also been accelerated to 1 GeV. Given that a muon has rest mass 0.106 GeV/c^2, would the collision be able to produce a muon–antimuon pair? We can see straight away that it would be possible to produce *many* such pairs, as the energy of the electron and positron greatly exceeds the energy associated with a muon and an antimuon at rest.

So by expressing particle masses in units of MeV/c^2 or GeV/c^2, particle physicists can tell whether there is enough energy in a given collision to produce a given particle, without having to do any arithmetic at all.

QUESTIONS

38 A proton has rest mass $m_0 = 1.67 \times 10^{-27}$ kg.

   (**a**) What is its rest energy (**i**) in J, (**ii**) in GeV?

   (**b**) What is its rest mass expressed in units of GeV/c^2?

39 A pi-zero meson has a rest mass of 0.14 GeV/c^2. How many such particles could, in principle, be produced in a collision between an electron and a positron, each with energy 1 GeV?

40 Suppose an electron is accelerated so that its total energy is 20 GeV. Express the mass equivalent of this energy in units of GeV/c^2.

Designing accelerators

In 1928, a Norwegian, Rolf Wideroe, invented the **linear accelerator** (LINAC). A LINAC accelerates charged particles to very high energies without the need for high voltages. Instead of being accelerated once, charged particles travel along a series of tubes separated by gaps, and are given voltage kicks at each gap.

In a LINAC there is a series of tubular electrodes (see Figure 42). These are connected to an alternating voltage supply, so that the voltage of each electrode switches back and forth between positive and negative. The aim is that the particle should emerge from the end of one tube and find that the next tube attracts it.

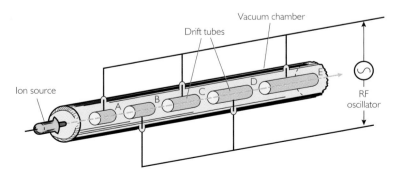

Figure 42 *The construction of a linear accelerator*

A proton leaves the ion source when electrode A is negative. It accelerates towards A, then travels at a steady speed inside the tube. While it is inside the electrode, the voltage switches so that A is positive and B is negative. Now, when the proton enters the gap between A and B, it accelerates towards B. When it is inside B, again the voltage is switched so that on exiting, B is positive and C is negative.

Each time, the same magnitude of voltage V is used and so the energy of the particle is built up in steps. After n electrode gaps, the proton's kinetic energy is equal to $n \times e \times V$.

An alternating voltage is used, so it can easily be stepped up using transformers. The frequency of the oscillating voltage is 'radio frequency' (i.e. a few MHz) and is kept constant. What does this mean for the design of the electrode drift tube tubes? They need to get longer as the proton gains speed so that the time to move between gaps is constant.

However, to achieve very high energies, very long accelerators are needed. The longest linear accelerator is at Stanford, California (Figure 43). The Stanford Linear Accelerator (SLAC) is 3 km long and can produce 20 GeV–50 GeV electrons. This has been used to smash electrons into protons and neutrons to help probe their structure. It was using this accelerator that physicists managed to show that protons and neutrons have a substructure of three quarks (see section 3.5).

LINACs have the advantage that high voltages are not required. The main limitation of a LINAC, however, is that each accelerating section is only used once, and so to achieve higher energies the machines must be made longer and so are more expensive.

Although LINACs are still the most common type of accelerator, another type of accelerator was conceived that could achieve higher energies – a circular accelerator, in which charged particles went round and round. The same accelerating sections could be used again and again, giving the particles more energy each time they came around. In this way, not only could the energy of a particle be increased, but two particles (oppositely charged) could be accelerated in opposite directions around the circle and then made to collide – increasing the total energy of interactions further.

The first circular accelerator was the **cyclotron**, invented by the American Ernest Lawrence in 1929. He used the idea (developed by Wideroe for the linear accelerators) of accelerating charged particles in a gap between electrodes, then allowing them to drift to the next gap. But rather than let the particles drift to the next gap along a straight line, requiring more electrodes, he used a magnetic field to bring the particles round in a circle to be accelerated through the same gap every half-turn. Figure 44 shows a simplified illustration of the cyclotron.

The electrodes were two hollow semi-circular pieces of metal – called 'dees' because of their shape – inside which the particles orbited. In 1931 Lawrence achieved a proton energy of 80 keV with a cyclotron 11 cm in diameter. The following year he achieved 1 MeV with a 26-cm diameter instrument. To reach energies much beyond 25 MeV, a new type of cyclotron had to be developed. As

Figure 43 *The Stanford Linear Accelerator*

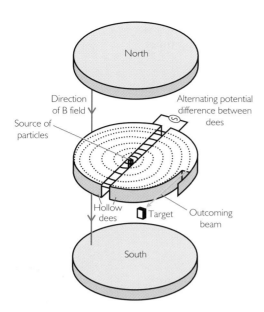

Figure 44 *The principle of the first cyclotron*

they reach higher kinetic energies, the particles' mass increases, which means that they take longer to complete each orbit. In a synchrocyclotron the frequency of the accelerating voltage is reduced as the kinetic energy of the particle increases – the accelerating 'kicks' are synchronised with the particles' orbital motion. To reach still higher energies, the design has to be modified again, and in modern large accelerators such as those at CERN, the particles are steered around in a path of constant radius as their energy is increased.

4.3 Circular motion

To see how particles can be steered in a circular path, we need to consider circular motion in general and also to see how charged particles behave in magnetic fields. These two aspects of particle accelerators are the subjects of this section.

Circular motion: finding the force

How can an object be made to travel in a circular path at constant speed? In the absence of any net force, a moving object continues along a straight line at constant velocity, as described by **Newton's first law of motion**. To produce circular motion, then, a net force must be acting. An object in circular motion is constantly changing its direction – in other words, it is accelerating in the sense that its velocity is changing, but the change is one of direction not of speed.

A few examples will help to identify the forces that produce motion in a circle. Imagine that you are the hammer-thrower shown in Figure 45. The hammer is massive. You have to whirl it around so that it builds up speed before you release it. If your grip isn't strong enough, the hammer will fly off before you mean to let go. To keep the hammer moving round, you need to keep pulling on it. You can feel the hammer pulling on you outwards as you pull it inwards. So an *inwards* force is needed to keep the hammer moving along its circular path.

Figure 45 *Throwing the hammer*

As a second example, consider the motion of the Moon or an artificial satellite around the Earth (Figure 46). (The motion is not quite circular, but it is very nearly so.) What forces are acting on a satellite as it orbits? There is no air resistance slowing the satellite down, as space is essentially a vacuum. The only force is the gravitational attraction between the Earth and the satellite. If this is the only force acting on the satellite, then it must be the force causing the satellite to accelerate as it orbits. The force is directed towards the Earth – towards the centre of the circle. In fact, for any object to move in a circle, a force towards the centre of the circle is required.

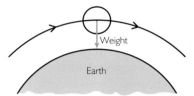

Figure 46 *A satellite orbiting the Earth*

Centripetal, not centrifugal

Any force that acts towards the centre of a circle is described as a **centripetal force**. The word 'centripetal' means 'directed towards the centre' or 'centre-seeking'.

Because of our experience of circular motion, we can believe that such motion involves a force acting radially outwards from the centre of a circle – a centrifugal ('centre-fleeing') force. When you are in a car that is turning a bend quickly, you feel thrown outwards, away from the centre of the circle. But there is no force actually pushing you outwards. The illusion arises because you are experiencing your motion relative to the car. Seen relative to a car cornering, you may seem to be moving outwards, but relative to the ground, you are actually trying to continue in a straight line – just as Newton's first law states. You will continue to move in a straight line until a resultant force acts on you that provides enough centripetal force to move you in the same circle as the car. This is normally provided by a seat-belt and friction from the seat, or by the side of the car if you're not belted up.

Table 9 lists some further examples of circular motion, with the name of the force (or forces) that act as the centripetal force in each case. In Activities 25 and 26, you explore two more examples of circular motion.

Example of circular motion	Inward force
The Earth orbiting the Sun	The gravitational attraction between the Sun and Earth
A car rounding a bend on a flat road	The frictional force of the road on the tyres
A plane turning in a horizontal circle	The lift force on the plane's tilted wings
A car rounding a bend on a banked track (Figure 47)	The normal reaction of the road (and friction)

Table 9 *Some examples of circular motion*

Figure 47 *A car rounding a bend on a banked track*

ACTIVITY 25 Whirling a bung

Take a rubber bung and tie it to one end of a piece of string about 1.5 m long. Find a suitable safe space and whirl the bung at a controlled speed in a horizontal circle around your head, initially with a radius of about 1 m. You can feel a force on your hand through the string as the bung whirls round. The string is pulling outwards on you because you are pulling inwards on the string.

List the forces that are acting on the bung as it moves and describe the direction it acts on the bung. Which of these forces is affecting the horizontal motion of the bung?

Investigate qualitatively how different factors affect the size of the force on your hand from the string. You could start by changing the radius of the circle, or by using bungs of different mass. How do they affect the size of the force? What else affects the size of the force?

In the unit *The Medium is the Message*, you saw that a charged particle moving in a magnetic field experiences a force at right angles to its direction of motion. This is just the sort of force that is required to produce motion in a circle. In Activity 26, you can see how a magnetic field can be used to steer an electron beam into a circular path as required in a particle accelerator.

ACTIVITY 26 **Electrons in orbit**

Use a fine-beam tube (Figure 48) to observe electrons moving in circular paths under the influence of a magnetic field.

Figure 48 *A fine-beam tube*

We will return to magnetic fields and particle accelerators later. In order to understand the situation properly, we must first take a more precise look at circular motion.

Describing circular motion

If we want to analyse motion in a circle, it is useful to be able to describe the position of a body around a circle, and how fast it is moving. Figure 49 shows how we do this.

The important quantities are as follows:

- The **radius** of the circle, r, which has SI units of metres, m.

- The object's **angular displacement**, $\Delta\theta$. This is the angle through which the object has moved, relative to some fixed position. Although degrees are most commonly used to measure angles, they are not the SI unit. The unit used for angle (or angular displacement) is the radian, rad.

- The object's speed, v, with SI units m s^{-1}. Notice that the speed is directed along the tangent to the circle.

- The **angular velocity**, ω (omega). Measured in rad s^{-1}. The relationship between angular velocity and angular displacement is similar to that between linear velocity and linear displacement:

$$\omega = \frac{\Delta\theta}{\Delta t} \tag{22}$$

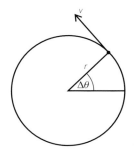

Figure 49 *Defining quantities in circular motion*

Study note

You met radians in the AS unit *The Sound of Music* and used them to describe the phase of waves.

Maths reference

Degrees and radians
See Maths note 6.1

We will consider angular velocity in a little more detail. The rate at which many devices turn in a circle or spin is measured by counting how many revolutions they complete in a certain time. The most common everyday unit is 'revolutions per minute' (rpm). Most car engines rotate at between 2000 rpm and 3000 rpm in normal operation. A compact disc rotates at between 200 rpm and 500 rpm (depending on which part of the disc is being read).

In order to have consistent units, we do not measure angular velocity in rpm. Instead, ω is measured in radians per second. For example, if a wheel is rotating at a constant rate of 1 revolution per second, it turns through 2π rad (360°) every second. Its angular velocity, $\omega = 2\pi$ rad s^{-1}.

Worked example

Q A compact disc is rotating at 300 rpm. How many revolutions does it complete every second? What is its angular velocity?

A The disc completes $\frac{300}{60} = 5$ revs per second $= 5\,\text{s}^{-1}$

In each revolution, the compact disc turns through 2π rad.

So its angular velocity

$$\omega = 5\text{s}^{-1} \times 2\pi\,\text{rad} = 10\pi\,\text{rad s}^{-1} = 31.4\,\text{rad s}^{-1}$$

Another important quantity associated with circular motion is the **period** (symbol T), which is the time for one complete revolution. The angular velocity and the period are related:

$$\omega = \frac{2\pi}{T} \quad \text{or} \quad T = \frac{2\pi}{\omega} \tag{23}$$

For example, if a body in circular motion has a period $T = 0.5\,\text{s}$, it completes two revolutions every second, so the angle it turns through every second is 4π rad. Thus, $\omega = 4\pi\,\text{rad s}^{-1}$.

Speed and angular velocity

Picture two athletes jogging around a circular running track, side by side. The athlete in the outside lane has to run slightly faster than the athlete in the inside lane in order to complete a lap in the same time. Both athletes have the same angular velocity ω, but the one whose track has a greater radius r has to run with a greater speed v. How are these three quantities (v, ω and r) related?

In one complete circuit, the athlete runs a distance $2\pi r$. The time taken to run around 2π radians with angular velocity ω is $T = 2\pi/\omega$. So the athlete's speed is given by

$$v = \frac{\Delta s}{\Delta t} = 2\pi r \times \frac{\omega}{2\pi} = \omega r$$

Hence

$$v = \omega r \tag{24}$$

Worked example

Q Turbine-generators in a power station rotate at 3000 rpm. The longest blades in a turbine are about 1.5 m long. Calculate the linear speed of the rotor tip.

A First, calculate the angular velocity ω:

$$\omega = \frac{3000}{60}\,\text{rev s}^{-1} = 50\,\text{rev s}^{-1} = 50 \times 2\pi\,\text{rad s}^{-1} = 314\,\text{rad s}^{-1}$$

Now calculate the speed of the tip:

$$v = \omega r = 314\,\text{rad s}^{-1} \times 1.5\,\text{m} = 471\,\text{m s}^{-1}$$

(The rotor tip is moving faster than the speed of sound in air.)

41 A car engine is rotating at 3000 rpm.

   (**a**) How many revolutions does it complete in 1 second?

   (**b**) What is its angular velocity?

   (**c**) What is the period of its motion?

42 A CD has an angular velocity of 30 rad s^{-1}.

   (**a**) How many revolutions does it complete in 1 second?

   (**b**) What is the period of its motion?

43 A positron is travelling around the circular accelerator at CERN. Its speed is close to the speed of light ($c = 3.00 \times 10^8$ m s^{-1}). The accelerator's diameter is 8.6 km. Calculate the positron's angular velocity.

44 A spinning roundabout of radius 2 m has a period $T = 1.25$ s.

   (**a**) What is the angular velocity of the roundabout?

   (**b**) (**i**) What is the speed of a boy sitting on the edge of the roundabout?

   (**ii**) If the boy moves halfway to the centre of the roundabout, what is his speed there?

   (**iii**) If he then moves to the centre of the roundabout, what is his speed there?

45 A garden strimmer cuts grass with a fast rotating piece of cord. The cord is 15 cm long and the strimmer spins at 100 revs per second.

   (**a**) What is the angular velocity of the cord?

   (**b**) What is the speed of the tip of the cord as it spins?

46 The head of a golf club has a speed of approximately 30 m s^{-1} when it strikes a ball. Estimate the angular velocity of a golf club at this point of a golf swing.

Centripetal acceleration

We will now return to the idea that an object moving in a circle at constant speed is accelerating. Picture a car travelling at a steady speed around a bend in the road. Although its speed is constant, its direction is changing all the time, so its velocity is not constant. Figure 50 shows that the car's velocity is changing all the time as it moves around the bend. If its velocity changes, it must be accelerating, even though its speed is constant. Our car is moving at a constant speed, but it is not moving in a straight line. It is constantly changing direction.

In Figure 50, you can see that the change in velocity of the car, as it moves a short distance around the bend, is directed towards the centre of the circle. It is a **centripetal acceleration**, produced by the centripetal force that we identified earlier. We can derive an equation for this acceleration, with the help of Figure 51.

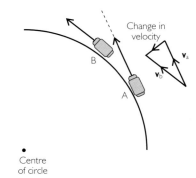

Figure 50 *A car moving at constant speed around a bend*

The object shown in Figure 51(a) moves at a steady speed v from A to B in time Δt. It moves through angle $\Delta\theta$, so its angular velocity ω is

$$\omega = \frac{\Delta\theta}{\Delta t} \qquad \text{(equation 22)}$$

In this time, its velocity changes direction, as shown. Its velocity vector also moves through angle $\Delta\theta$.

Figure 51(b) shows how we work out the object's change in velocity. We draw a vector triangle; the short third side is the change in velocity Δv. From this triangle *provided $\Delta\theta$ is small* (and using the definition of an angle in radians) we can write

$$\Delta v = \Delta\theta \times v$$

Dividing both sides by Δt gives

$$\frac{\Delta v}{\Delta t} = \left(\frac{\Delta\theta}{\Delta t}\right) \times v$$

But

$$\frac{\Delta v}{\Delta t} = a \quad \text{and} \quad \frac{\Delta\theta}{\Delta t} = \omega$$

so we have

$$a = \omega v$$

Now, if we substitute $\omega = \dfrac{v}{r}$, we get a useful expression for the centripetal acceleration

$$a = \frac{v^2}{r} \qquad (25)$$

and if we substitute $v = \omega r$ we get another useful expression

$$a = r\omega^2 \qquad (26)$$

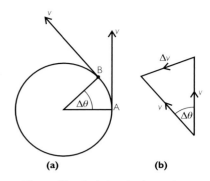

(a)   **(b)**

Figure 51 *Analysing circular motion*

Maths reference
....
Degrees and radians
The small angle approximations
See Maths notes 6.1 and 6.6
....

QUESTION

47 Go back to questions 43–46 and calculate the centripetal acceleration in each case.

Centripetal force again

We can now work out what force is needed to make an object move in a circle, because we have two expressions for centripetal acceleration. Using the familiar relationship $F = ma$, we can simply multiply equations (25) and (26) by the object's mass m to find the centripetal force:

$$F = \frac{mv^2}{r} \qquad (27)$$

and

$$F = mr\omega^2 \qquad (28)$$

QUESTIONS

48 You are cycling along, and decide to turn off to the left.

(**a**) Which requires a greater sideways force, turning sharply left or following a more gentle path?

(**b**) If you were travelling faster, would you need a bigger or smaller sideways force?

49 What force is required to keep a 5 kg object moving at 10 m s^{-1} in a circle of radius 2 m?

50 What force is required to keep a 1 kg object moving with angular velocity 10 rad s^{-1} in a circle of radius 10 m?

51 A man's competition hammer has a mass of 7.26 kg. The length of the hammer chain is 1.2 m and the length of the man's arms is 0.9 m. Before throwing, the man whirls the hammer round his head in a horizontal circle a few times. The average period for each revolution is 0.75 s.

(**a**) What is the average angular velocity of the hammer?

(**b**) What is the average tension required in the hammer chain if it is horizontal?

52 A girl of mass 35 kg is swinging on a tyre of mass 10 kg attached to a tree branch by a rope of length 6 m.

(**a**) What is the weight of the tyre and the girl? (Use $g = 9.81$ N kg^{-1})

(**b**) If her speed at the bottom of the swing is 4 m s^{-1}, what centripetal force is required at this point by the tyre and the girl?

(**c**) Use your answers to (**a**) and (**b**) to calculate the tension in the rope at this point. Remember that the resultant force on the child and tyre must equal the value of the centripetal force and act in the right direction.

53 A car rounding a bend requires a centripetal force of 2 kN. This is provided by friction between the tyres and the road.

(**a**) If the same car at the same speed rounds another bend of twice the radius, what centripetal force is required?

(**b**) If the same car rounds the original bend at twice the original speed, what centripetal force is required?

4.4 Steering charged particles

Now we can return to thinking about making charged particles move in circular orbits; you will recall that this is how we can avoid the problem of making very long linear accelerators. In Activity 26 you saw how a magnetic field can steer a beam of electrons into a circular path.

In the unit *The Medium is the Message*, you saw that a particle of charge q moving at speed v in a magnetic field of flux density B will experience a force of magnitude

$$F = Bqv \sin \theta \qquad (29)$$

where θ is the angle between the directions of the particle's motion and the magnetic field.

Fleming's left-hand rule (Figure 52) tells us how the directions of the magnetic field, the current and the force are related; the force always acts at right angles to the other two. But take care! Recall that for moving electrons, whose charge is negative, the conventional direction of current is in the *opposite* direction to the motion of the charges.

Figure 53 shows what happens when a positive charge $+q$ enters a region where there is a magnetic field; the crosses indicate that the flux is directed into the page. The direction of the current is left-to-right. From the left-hand rule, the force on the charge is directed upwards, at right angles to the motion of the charge. This force will alter the direction of motion of the charge (but will not affect its speed). Even when the direction of motion is changed, the force will still be at right angles to it. Because the force is always perpendicular to the motion, it will produce a circular path. The effect of the magnetic field on the charge is providing a centripetal force that enables the charge to move in a circle.

In a circular particle accelerator or in a fine-beam tube, the magnetic force provides the centripetal force needed to keep the electrons moving in a circle. The field is applied at right angles to the direction of motion, $(\theta = 90°, \sin \theta = 1)$, so from $ma = F$ we have:

$$\frac{mv^2}{r} = Bqv$$

Now we can rearrange this to deduce an expression for the radius of the particle's orbit:

$$r = \frac{mv}{Bq} \qquad (30)$$

Substituting p for the momentum mv of the particle, we can write this expression as:

$$r = \frac{p}{Bq} \qquad (30a)$$

So, the greater the momentum of a particle, the greater the radius of its path in a given field; put another way, the stronger the field needed to keep it in a given orbit.

ISIS, at the Rutherford Appleton Laboratory outside Oxford in the UK, is the most intense source of pulsed neutrons in the world (Figure 54). The beams of particles it produces are used to study the properties of solid materials. H⁻ ions are produced with an energy of 665 keV and accelerated to 70 MeV in a linear accelerator, before being stripped of their electrons to leave a beam of protons. These are accelerated to 800 MeV in a 52-m diameter synchrotron. Instead of using a fixed magnetic field strength and allowing the radius of orbit to increase, as in a cyclotron or a synchro-cyclotron, particles in a synchrotron orbit at a fixed radius and the magnetic field is varied to provide the correct centripetal force as the particles accelerate. The ions then knock neutrons out of a target material. In a head-on collision the ion comes to rest and a neutron moves off with exactly the same velocity.

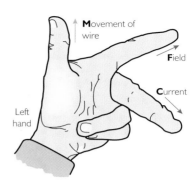

Figure 52 *Fleming's left-hand rule*

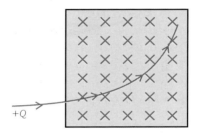

Figure 53 *A positively charged particle moving in a magnetic field*

Study note

Equation 30(a) has the advantage that it applies equally to relativistic and non-relativistic particles.

Study note

H⁻ ions are hydrogen atoms with an extra electron.

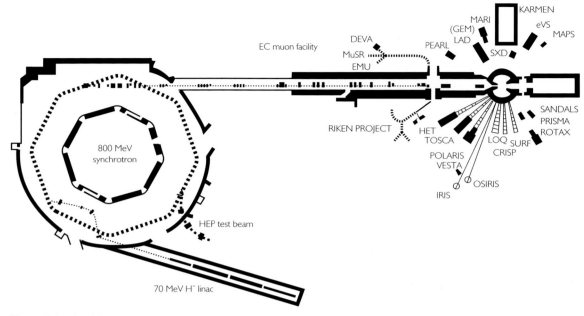

Figure 54 *The ISIS accelerator*

ACTIVITY **27** **The fine-beam tube**

Use a fine-beam tube to explore how the accelerating voltage and the magnetic field affect the radius of the electrons' path.

QUESTIONS

54 Redraw Figure 53, showing how the situation would change if the charge shown was negative.

55 Beta particles, produced in radioactive decay, are fast-moving electrons. If a narrow beam of beta radiation from a source is passed into a magnetic field, it curves around and spreads out. What does this tell you about the energies of the beta particles?

56 An electron is travelling at 1% of the speed of light ($c = 3.00 \times 10^8\,\mathrm{m\,s^{-1}}$). If a magnetic field $B = 0.2\,\mathrm{T}$ is applied at right angles to its motion, what radius of path will result? (Electron mass $m_e = 9.11 \times 10^{-31}\,\mathrm{kg}$; electron charge $e = 1.60 \times 10^{-19}\,\mathrm{C}$)

57 Electrons in a fine-beam tube are accelerated through a pd of 2.5 kV. A magnetic field of 1 T is applied at right angles to the electron beam. (Electron mass $m_e = 9.11 \times 10^{-31}\,\mathrm{kg}$; electron charge $e = 1.60 \times 10^{-19}\,\mathrm{C}$)

(**a**) What is the speed of the electrons as they leave the electron gun? (Ignore relativistic effects.)

(**b**) What force is exerted on each electron because of the magnetic field? Describe the direction of the force.

(**c**) What acceleration will the electrons have as a result of this force? Does their speed increase?

(**d**) What will be the radius of the path that the electrons follow?

4.5 Summing up part 4

In this part of the unit, you have seen how an understanding of the way in which charged particles behave in electric and magnetic fields can be used to accelerate particles to high energies. High-energy particles are needed to recreate the conditions of the early Universe, on a small scale.

ACTIVITY 28 | **Accelerator energy**

STOP PRESS ... In May 1998, the LEP accelerator at CERN reached 189 GeV and was edging towards 200 GeV, which was scheduled for 1999.

Find out the latest from CERN and other accelerator labs by checking their websites.

Using CD-ROMs, the Internet or your library, find out how the energy available from different particle accelerators has increased as the technology has developed. In doing this, you may read about many types of accelerator: linacs, cyclotrons, synchro-cyclotrons, etc. For each accelerator, state briefly the type of particles it accelerates, how it accelerates them, how it directs its particle beam, and the energies it can achieve.

All energies should be quoted in electronvolts. (Some accelerators, such as the Tevatron, are named after the energy that they can reach.)

Tracking particles

To finish this part of the unit, you will see how what you have learned about circular motion and about electric and magnetic fields is applied to another aspect of particle physics – that of studying the results of collisions between particles.

In many particle physics experiments, such as those carried out in the LEP (large electron-positron) collider at CERN, beams of particles are steered so that they collide at particular locations. In the LEP tunnel, there are four such collision points, and each is surrounded by a vast detector to record the resulting debris. Figure 55(a) shows the LEP detector known as Aleph. Other detectors have a slightly different arrangement of layers, but they all have a similar overall design. Figure 55(b) shows a typical cross-section through a typical detector. There are several things to notice: the detector's vast size, its layered construction, and the presence of a large iron cylinder.

The different layers are designed each to be sensitive to different types of particle, and each works in a slightly different way. But in each layer, passage of a charged particle is detected by the ionisation it produces in the low-density gas that fills the detector. To detect ionisation, most modern detectors use so-called multiwire chambers or drift chambers. A multiwire chamber consists of an array of fine wires, with potential differences applied between them. When ions are created in the detector, the electric fields between the wires sweep the ions on to the wires, and the

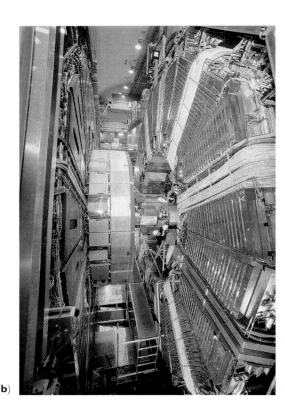

(a)

(b)

Figure 55 *(a) The Aleph detector and (b) the structure of Aleph*

resulting small pulse of current is recorded electronically (rather as a Geiger tube records the ionisation produced by the passage of an alpha or beta particle). The record of current pulses provides a record of a particle's passage through the chamber. A drift chamber works in a very similar way, except that it measures the time taken for ions to drift towards the nearest wire, enabling a more accurate record to be built up.

A detector such as Aleph or ATLAS (Figure 56) incorporates some layers whose function is to measure the energy deposited – these are the calorimeters shown in Figure 55. Such measurements provide information about the energy of the particles produced in a collision, but that on its own is not enough for particle physicists to unravel what went on.

As well as using electric fields to detect ionisation, detectors such as Aleph and ATLAS use magnetic fields to obtain information about particles. A strong magnetic field is applied along the axis of the detector. The layer of iron is important in maintaining this field, and in order to make the field as strong as possible, superconducting magnets are sometimes used. The colliding particles travel in the same direction as the field, so their paths are not affected, but charged particles produced in a collision are likely to be travelling across the field and so they are forced into curved paths. The sign of their charge can be deduced from the direction of curvature of their tracks, and further measurements enable their momentum to be found.

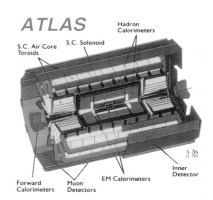

Figure 56 *The ATLAS detector, to be used with CERN's new large hadron collider (LHC)*

ACTIVITY **29** **Particle tracks**

Many particle physics websites include examples of particle tracks. To find out how such records are analysed, visit the Manchester University website:

http://h2.ph.man.ac.uk/~wyatt/events/home.html

ACTIVITY **30** **Track and field events**

Write a short account of how electric and magnetic fields are used in particle detectors. Include an explanation of how momentum could be measured from a particle track (refer back to section 4.3).

5 *On target*

5.1 *Big ideas*

This unit has looked at some of the most profound ideas in physics: the nature of the Universe, the fundamental particles of nature, the forces which act between them. Along the way, you have learnt about circular motion, and the way charged particles behave in electric and magnetic fields. Use the following activity to remind yourself how these ideas fit together.

ACTIVITY **31** **Unification**

Copy the words below on to separate, small pieces of paper. With a partner, discuss the ideas that link groups of words. (Move the pieces of paper around to show how they can be grouped together.)

Now, on a single sheet of paper, draw a concept map to show your thoughts. Write the words on the paper, and add arrows showing connections between them. Annotate the arrows to explain the connections.

fundamental particles	quarks	electrons
leptons	gravitation	electromagnetism
nuclear forces	magnetic fields	electric fields
electric charge	moving charges	circular motion
angular velocity	centripetal force	the Big Bang
particle accelerators	high-energy particles	the Universe

5.2 *Questions on the whole unit*

You will need the following information when you answer questions 58 to 60:

permittivity of free space $\varepsilon_0 = 8.85 \times 10^{-12}\,\mathrm{F\,m^{-1}}$

electron charge, $e = 1.60 \times 10^{-19}\,\mathrm{C}$

electron mass, $m_e = 9.11 \times 10^{-31}\,\mathrm{kg}$

proton mass, $m_p = 1.67 \times 10^{-27}\,\mathrm{kg}$

speed of light in vacuum, $c = 3.00 \times 10^8\,\mathrm{m\,s^{-1}}$

58 We can picture an antiatom of 'antihydrogen' as a positron (an antielectron) in a circular orbit around antiproton. The average separation of the two particles in the antiatom is 0.037 nm.

(**a**) What force holds the positron in its orbit? Sketch a diagram of the antiatom. Draw an arrow to show the force acting on the positron.

(**b**) Explain why a force is needed to keep the positron in its orbit.

(**c**) Calculate the force exerted on the positron by the antiproton, and the force exerted on the antiproton by the positron.

(**d**) How many times per second does the positron orbit the antiproton?

59 In an experiment to investigate the annihilation of particles, beams of high-energy electrons and positrons are produced, and then caused to collide with one another. In one collision, a 500 keV electron collides head-on with a 500 keV positron. The two particles annihilate one another, and two photons of electromagnetic energy are produced.

(**a**) What is the combined momentum of the two particles, just before they collide?

(**b**) What is the energy of a 500 keV electron, in joules?

(**c**) What is the combined energy of the two photons, in joules?

60 This question is about the acceleration of protons in the Proton Synchrotron (PS) at CERN (see Figure 57). Table 10 lists some data about the PS and the Super Proton Synchrotron (SPS), also at CERN.

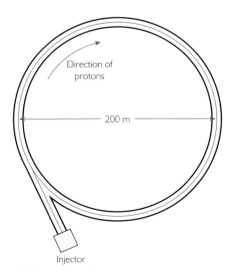

Figure 57 *The CERN proton synchrotron*

	PS	SPS
diameter of ring	200 m	2.2 km
circumference of ring	528 m	
no. of accelerating points	14	
average accelerating voltage	4 kV	
proton energy at injection	50 MeV	
final energy of proton	28 GeV	
final momentum of proton	1.7×10^{-17} kg m s^{-1}	
final speed of proton	almost 3×10^8 m s^{-1}	almost 3×10^8 m s^{-1}

Table 10 *Data for question 60*

Particle accelerators are used to increase the energy of charged particles such as protons and electrons. The accelerated particles are made to collide with other particles on a 'target' in order to investigate the structure of matter. Subatomic particles created in these collisions can be studied.

One type of particle accelerator is the synchrotron. In this machine a magnetic field causes charged particles to move in a circular path. The particles are accelerated to higher energies by an electric field. As their momentum increases, the magnetic flux density is increased to keep them travelling in a path of constant radius.

(**a**) Ignoring relativistic effects, show that:

(**i**) The speed of a proton at injection into the PS is about 1×10^8 m s^{-1}.

(**ii**) A proton takes about 6 μs to travel round the ring at this speed.

(**iii**) The momentum of a proton at injection is about 1.6×10^{-19} kg m s^{-1}.

(**b**) The accelerator ring is a pipe maintained at very low pressure. It is 'filled' with protons by injecting a proton current of 100 mA for 6 μs.

(**i**) Calculate the number of protons injected.

(**ii**) Explain why the interior of the ring must be maintained at very low pressure.

(**c**) Before the protons are accelerated, an electric field is used to group the protons in the ring into a number of bunches. The bunches are then accelerated as they pass through the acceleration points, which are spaced equally around the ring. An acceleration point is essentially a pair of electrodes between which an alternating voltage is applied.

(**i**) Explain why an *alternating* voltage is needed.

The proton bunches pass through an acceleration point when the potential difference between its electrodes is about 4 kV.

(**ii**) By how much does the energy of one proton increase in one revolution? (Give your answer in eV.)

(iii) Estimate the number of times a proton must travel round the ring in order to reach its final energy.

(iv) Explain briefly why *linear* accelerators are not used to accelerate protons to this final energy.

(d) (i) Show that the magnetic flux density B required to maintain a proton in a circular path of radius r is proportional to its momentum p.

(ii) Estimate the magnetic flux density needed to maintain 50 MeV protons within the PS.

(iii) Explain why the frequency of the alternating voltage must change as the protons are accelerated to higher energies.

(e) Estimate:

(i) by what factor the magnetic field must be increased during the acceleration:

(ii) by what factor the mass of the proton increases during acceleration.

Protons from the PS can be injected into the SPS for further acceleration in the PS.

(iii) Explain why the magnetic field in the SPS is increased as protons are accelerated, but the frequency of the accelerating voltage is kept almost constant.

5.3 *Achievements*

Now you have studied this unit you should be able to:

- write and interpret equations using standard nuclear notation and standard particle symbols (e.g. π^+, e^-) (2.2, 2.3)*;

- recall that in the standard quark–lepton model each particle has a corresponding antiparticle, that *baryons* (e.g. neutrons and protons) are made from three quarks and *mesons* (e.g. pions) from a quark and an antiquark and that the symmetry of the model predicted the top and bottom quark (2.3, 2.4);

- recognise and use the expression $\Delta E = c^2 \Delta m$ in situations involving the creation and annihilation of particles (2.4);

- plot data on a logarithmic graph and hence decide whether data obey a power law and, if they do, determine the exponent (2.5);

- describe how large-angle alpha particle scattering gives evidence for a nuclear atom (3.1);

- recall and use the expression $F = kQ_1Q_2/r^2$, where $k = 1/4\pi\varepsilon_0$ (3.2, 3.3);

- derive and use the expression $E = kQ/r^2$ for the electric field due to a point charge (3.3);

- derive and use the expression $E_k = p^2/2m$ for the kinetic energy of a (non-relativistic) particle (3.4);

- recall how to calculate the momentum of (non-relativistic) particles and be able to apply the principle of conservation of linear momentum to problems in one and two dimensions (3.4);

- recall and use the fact that charge, energy and momentum are always conserved in interactions between particles (2.3, 2.4, 3.4);

- combine any number of coplanar vectors at any angle to each other by drawing (3.4);

- recognise and use the expression $\lambda = h/p$ for the de Broglie wavelength (3.5);

- explain why high energies are required to break particles into their constituents and to see fine structure (3.5);

- be aware of relativistic effects and know that these need to be taken into account at speeds near that of light (use of relativistic equations *not* required) (3.5);

- use the non-SI units MeV and GeV (energy), and MeV/c^2 and GeV/c^2 (mass), and convert between these and SI units (4.2);

- express angular displacement in radians and in degrees and be able to convert between those units (4.3);

* Numbers indicate the section(s) that relate to each achievement.

- understand the concept of *angular velocity*, and recognise and use the relationships $v = \omega r$ and $T = 2\pi/\omega$ (4.3);

- recall and use the expression for centripetal force $F = mv^2/r$ (4.3);

- derive and use the expressions for centripetal acceleration $a = v^2/r$ and $a = r\omega^2$ (4.3);

- recognise and use the expression $r = p/Bq$ for a charged particle in a magnetic field (4.4);

- explain the role of electric fields in particle accelerators and detectors (4.2, 4.5);

- explain the role of magnetic fields in particle accelerators and detectors (4.4, 4.5).

Answers

1 (a) Strong; (b) gravity; (c) electromagnetic; (d) strong and electromagnetic; (e) weak.

2 $\mu^+ + \mu^- \longrightarrow$ electromagnetic radiation.

3 A quark and its antiquark have equal but opposite charges, so they cancel out.

4 Creating the mass of the tau leptons requires much more than the energy equivalent of an electron–positron pair at rest; additional energy must be supplied in the form of kinetic energy of the colliding particles.

5 $E = mc^2 = 1.67 \times 10^{-27}\,\text{kg} \times (3.00 \times 10^8\,\text{m s}^{-1})^2$
   $= 1.50 \times 10^{-10}\,\text{J}.$

6 (a) $E = mc^2$
      $= 2 \times 9.11 \times 10^{-31}\,\text{kg} \times (3.00 \times 10^8\,\text{m s}^{-1})^2$
      $= 1.64 \times 10^{-13}\,\text{J}.$

   (b) Energy 'left over' $= 2.00 \times 10^{-13}\,\text{J} - 1.64 \times 10^{-13}\,\text{J}$
       $= 0.36 \times 10^{-13}\,\text{J}.$

   This is shared equally between the two particles, so the kinetic energy of each is $0.18 \times 10^{-13}\,\text{J}\,(1.8 \times 10^{-14}\,\text{J}).$

7 (a) Electron and positron (antielectron).

   (b) They have opposite charges.

   (c) They annihilate, leaving a photon of electromagnetic radiation.

8 He guessed they showed the same pattern as the leptons, i.e. six quarks in three generations of two each – they had the same symmetry. He could predict their charges, and that their masses were much greater than those of the other quarks.

9 hadrons: proton, neutron, pion;

   meson: pion;

   baryons: proton, neutron;

   quarks: charm, up;

   leptons: electron, antielectron, electron-neutrino.

10 In Figure 16, to avoid the absorption of alpha particles: air is pumped out through tube T; source R and detector S are close to foil F; foil F is thin.

11 Direct hits are more likely, so more alpha particles will be back-scattered.

12 Slower alpha particles wouldn't whiz straight past so easily, so more would be scattered through bigger angles.

13 There is less chance of a direct hit, and the force is weaker, so fewer alpha particles will be back-scattered.

14 See Figure 58.

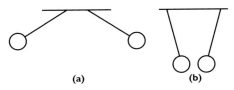

Figure 58   *The answer to question 14*

15 See Figure 59

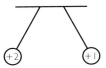

Figure 59   *Answer to question 15*

16 Figure 60 shows the forces acting on one ball (not to scale).

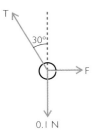

Figure 60   *Diagram for the answer to question 16*

Resolving horizontally: $F = T \sin 30°$
Resolving vertically: $W = T \cos 30°$
Dividing one equation by the other and cancelling T:
$F/W = \tan 30°$
so $F = 0.10\,\text{N} \times \tan 30° = 0.058\,\text{N}$

17 $1\,\text{F} = 1\,\text{C V}^{-1}$, and $1\,\text{V} = 1\,\text{J C}^{-1}$, so $1\,\text{F} = 1\,\text{C}^2\,\text{J}^{-1}$.
   $1\,\text{J} = 1\,\text{N m}$, so $1\,\text{F} = 1\,\text{C}^2\,\text{N}^{-1}\,\text{m}^{-1}$
   Hence $1\,\text{F m}^{-1} = 1\,\text{C}^2\,\text{N}^{-1}\,\text{m}^{-2} = (1\,\text{N m}^2\,\text{C}^{-2})^{-1}$ as required.

18 $F = \left(\dfrac{1}{4\pi\varepsilon_0}\right)\dfrac{Q_1 Q_2}{r^2}$

   $= \dfrac{9.0 \times 10^9\,\text{N m}^2\,\text{C}^{-2} \times (10^{-8}\,\text{C})^2}{(0.05\,\text{m})^2}$

   $= 3.6 \times 10^{-4}\,\text{N}.$

19 (a) $F = \left(\dfrac{1}{4\pi\varepsilon_0}\right)\dfrac{Q_1 Q_2}{r^2}$

      $= \dfrac{9.0 \times 10^9\,\text{N m}^2\,\text{C}^{-2} \times (1.60 \times 10^{-19}\,\text{C})^2}{(0.037 \times 10^{-9}\,\text{m})^2}$

      $= 1.68 \times 10^{-7}\,\text{N}.$

(b) See Figure 61.

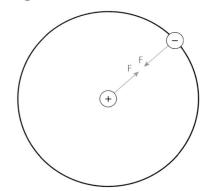

Figure 61 *The answer to question 19(b)*

20 The nuclear charge is smaller, so the force is weaker at a given distance (about one third of that with gold). As shown in Figure 62, the graph plotted on a linear scale is scaled down by a factor of about 3, and the log graph is *shifted* downwards.

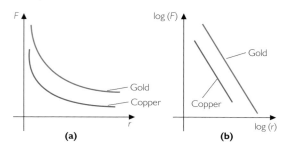

Figure 62 *The answer to question 20*

21 Initial $E_k = \Delta E = \dfrac{kQ_1 Q_2}{r}$ (equation 10), so

$r = \dfrac{kQ_1 Q_2}{E_k}$

$= \dfrac{9.0 \times 10^9\,\mathrm{N\,m^2\,C^{-2}} \times (79 \times 1.60 \times 10^{-19}\,\mathrm{C}) \times (2 \times 1.60 \times 10^{-19}\,\mathrm{C})}{(8.0 \times 10^{-13}\,\mathrm{J})}$

$= 4.6 \times 10^{-14}\,\mathrm{m}$.

22 Lines of force go *towards* a negatively charged sphere. See Figure 63.

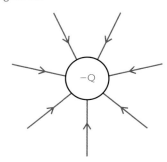

Figure 63 *The answer to question 22*

23 See Figure 64.

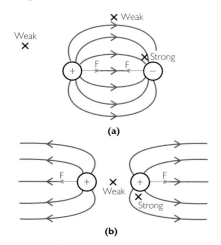

(a)

(b)

Figure 64 *The answers to question 23*

24 $E = \dfrac{F}{q} = \dfrac{10\,\mathrm{N}}{20 \times 10^{-3}\,\mathrm{C}} = 500\,\mathrm{N\,C^{-1}}$.

25 $F = Eq = 2000\,\mathrm{N\,C^{-1}} \times 1.6 \times 10^{-19}\,\mathrm{C} = 3.2 \times 10^{-16}\,\mathrm{N}$

Acceleration $a = \dfrac{F}{m} = \dfrac{3.2 \times 10^{-16}\,\mathrm{N}}{9.11 \times 10^{-31}\,\mathrm{kg}}$

$= 3.5 \times 10^{14}\,\mathrm{m\,s^{-2}}$.

(Note that this is more than a million million times the acceleration due to gravity.)

26 $E = \dfrac{kQ}{r^2}$

$= \dfrac{9.0 \times 10^9\,\mathrm{N\,m^2\,C^{-2}} \times (79 \times 1.6 \times 10^{-19}\,\mathrm{C})}{(1 \times 10^{-13}\,\mathrm{m})^2}$

$= 1.1 \times 10^{19}\,\mathrm{N\,C^{-1}}$.

27 For someone of mass 60 kg capable of running at $10\,\mathrm{m\,s^{-1}}$ (close to the world record for the 100 m sprint!):

$p = mv = 60\,\mathrm{kg} \times 10\,\mathrm{m\,s^{-1}} = 600\,\mathrm{kg\,m\,s^{-1}}$

$E_k = \dfrac{1}{2}mv^2 = \dfrac{1}{2} \times 60\,\mathrm{kg} \times (10\,\mathrm{m\,s^{-1}})^2 = 3000\,\mathrm{J}$

$\dfrac{p^2}{2m} = \dfrac{(600\,\mathrm{kg\,m\,s^{-1}})^2}{2 \times 60\,\mathrm{kg}} = 3000\,\mathrm{J}$.

28 $E_k = \dfrac{p^2}{2m}$

$= \dfrac{(5.0 \times 10^{-20}\,\mathrm{kg\,m\,s^{-1}})^2}{2 \times 6.7 \times 10^{-27}\,\mathrm{kg}}$

$= 1.9 \times 10^{-13}\,\mathrm{J}$.

29 (a) Momentum would be conserved – it is *always* conserved in any interaction.

(b) It is *not* elastic. Some of the initial kinetic energy would provide the additional mass of the muons (see section 2.4 of this unit) so there would be an overall decrease in the kinetic energy.

30 They would measure the momentum before and after the collision (you will see in part 4 how this can be done). Any discrepancy can be accounted for in terms of the momentum of 'unseen' particles.

31 $E_k = eV = 1.60 \times 10^{-19}\,C \times 500\,V = 8.00 \times 10^{-17}\,J$

$p = \sqrt{(2meV)} = 1.21 \times 10^{-23}\,kg\,m\,s^{-1}$

$v = \dfrac{p}{m} = \dfrac{1.21 \times 10^{-23}\,kg\,m\,s^{-1}}{9.11 \times 10^{-31}\,kg}$

$\quad = 1.33 \times 10^7\,m\,s^{-1}.$

32 $E_k = \dfrac{1}{2}mv^2 = \dfrac{1}{2} \times 9.11 \times 10^{-31}\,kg \times (10^6\,m\,s^{-1})^2$

$\quad = 4.55 \times 10^{-19}\,J$

$V = \dfrac{E_k}{e} = \dfrac{4.55 \times 10^{-19}\,J}{1.60 \times 10^{-19}\,C} = 2.84\,V.$

33 Greater kinetic energy means greater momentum and hence shorter wavelength.

34 Greater voltage means greater kinetic energy and momentum, so shorter wavelength.

35 De Broglie wavelength $\lambda = \dfrac{h}{p}$

$\quad = \dfrac{6.63 \times 10^{-34}\,J\,s}{9.1 \times 10^{-31}\,kg \times 10^6\,m\,s^{-1}}$

$\quad = 7.3 \times 10^{-10}\,m.$

(This wavelength is comparable to the spacing of atoms in a solid.)

36 $p = \dfrac{h}{\lambda} = \dfrac{6.63 \times 10^{-34}\,J\,s}{3.0 \times 10^{-10}\,m}$

$\quad = 2.21 \times 10^{-24}\,kg\,m\,s^{-1}.$

37 For a person of mass 60 kg walking at $1\,m\,s^{-1}$:

$p = 60\,kg\,m\,s^{-1}$

$\lambda = \dfrac{h}{p} = \dfrac{6.63 \times 10^{-34}\,J\,s}{60\,kg\,m\,s^{-1}} \approx 10^{-35}\,m.$

This wavelength is *extremely* small. You would only notice diffraction effects when passing through an aperture of comparable size – which is about 35 orders of magnitude smaller than your own physical size. A doorway is some 35 orders of magnitude too large, so any diffraction effects are unobservable.

38 (a) $E_0 = m_0 c^2$

$\quad = 1.67 \times 10^{-27}\,kg \times (3.00 \times 10^8\,m\,s^{-1})^2$

$\quad = 1.50 \times 10^{-10}\,J$

$\quad = 9.39 \times 10^8\,eV = 0.939\,GeV.$

(b) $m_0 = \dfrac{0.939\,GeV}{c^2}.$

39 Total energy available $= 2\,GeV$. Energy needed to create a single pi-zero at rest is $0.14\,GeV$.

$2/0.14 = 14.28$

So at most 14 pi-zeros could be created. (This assumes the pi-zeros are created at rest, and that no other particles are created. In practice, neither of those assumptions is likely to be correct.)

40 $m = 20\,GeV/c^2.$

41 (a) $\dfrac{3000\,rpm}{60\,s} = 50\,s^{-1}.$

(b) Angular velocity $\omega = 2\pi \times 50\,s^{-1} = 314\,rad\,s^{-1}.$

(c) Period $T = \dfrac{1}{50\,s^{-1}} = 0.02\,s.$

42 (a) Number of revolutions per second $= \dfrac{30}{2\pi} = 4.8.$

(b) Period $T = \dfrac{1}{4.8\,s^{-1}} = 0.21\,s.$

43 Radius of accelerator $r = 4300\,m.$

Angular velocity $\omega = \dfrac{v}{r} = \dfrac{3.00 \times 10^8\,m\,s^{-1}}{4300\,m}$

$\quad = 6.98 \times 10^4\,rad\,s^{-1}.$

44 (a) Angular velocity $\omega = \dfrac{2\pi}{T} = \dfrac{2\pi}{1.25\,s} = 5.0\,rad\,s^{-1}.$

(b) (i) Speed $v = \omega r = 5.0\,rad\,s^{-1} \times 2\,m = 10\,m\,s^{-1}.$

(ii) Speed is halved, i.e. $5\,m\,s^{-1}.$

(iii) Speed $= 0\,m\,s^{-1}.$

45 (a) Angular velocity $\omega = 100 \times 2\pi\,rad\,s^{-1}$

$\quad = 628\,rad\,s^{-1}.$

(b) Speed $v = \omega r = 628\,rad\,s^{-1} \times 0.15\,m = 94.2\,m\,s^{-1}.$

46 Radius $r \approx$ distance from shoulder to ground $\approx 1.5\,m$, say.

Angular velocity $= \omega = \dfrac{v}{r} = \dfrac{30\,m\,s^{-1}}{1.5\,m} = 20\,rad\,s^{-1}.$

47 From question 43: $a = \dfrac{v^2}{r} = \dfrac{(3.00 \times 10^8\,m\,s^{-1})^2}{4300\,m}$

$\quad = 2.1 \times 10^{13}\,m\,s^{-2}.$

From question 44: $a = \dfrac{v^2}{r} = \dfrac{(10\,m\,s^{-1})^2}{2\,m} = 50\,m\,s^{-2}.$

From question 45:

$a = \dfrac{v^2}{r} = \dfrac{(94.2\,m\,s^{-1})^2}{0.15\,m} = 5.9 \times 10^4\,m\,s^{-1}.$

From question 46: $a = \dfrac{v^2}{r} = \dfrac{(30\,m\,s^{-1})^2}{1.5\,m} = 600\,m\,s^{-2}.$

48 (a) Turning sharply.

(b) A bigger force is needed.

49 $F = \dfrac{mv^2}{r} = \dfrac{5 \text{ kg} \times (10 \text{ m s}^{-1})^2}{2 \text{ m}} = 250 \text{ N}.$

50 $F = mr\omega^2 = 1 \text{ kg} \times (10 \text{ rad s}^{-1})^2 \times 10 \text{ m} = 1000 \text{ N}.$

51 (a) $\omega = \dfrac{2\pi}{T} = \dfrac{2\pi}{0.75 \text{ s}} = 8.4 \text{ rad s}^{-1}.$

   (b) $F = mr\omega^2 = 7.26 \text{ kg} \times (8.4 \text{ rad s}^{-1})^2 \times 2.1 \text{ m} = 1075 \text{ N}.$

52 (a) $W = mg = 45 \text{ kg} \times 9.81 \text{ N kg}^{-1} = 442 \text{ N}.$

   (b) $F = \dfrac{mv^2}{r} = \dfrac{45 \text{ kg} \times (4 \text{ m s}^{-1})^2}{6 \text{ m}} = 120 \text{ N}.$

   (c) Tension in rope $= 442 \text{ N} + 120 \text{ N} = 562 \text{ N}.$

   (The rope must support the weight of the child + tyre, *and* supply the centripetal force.)

53 (a) $F \propto \dfrac{1}{r}$, so twice the radius requires half the force, i.e. 1 kN.

   (b) $F \propto v^2$, so twice the speed requires four times the force, i.e. 8 kN.

54 See Figure 65.

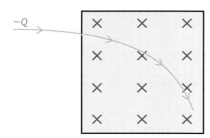

Figure 65 *The answer to question 54*

55 The electrons do not all have the same momentum (or, therefore, the same kinetic energy). Inspection of equation (30) tells us that the most energetic electrons will curve least.

56 $r = \dfrac{mv}{Bq}$

   $= \dfrac{9.11 \times 10^{-31} \text{ kg} \times 0.01 \times 3.00 \times 10^{8} \text{ m s}^{-1}}{0.2 \text{ T} \times 1.60 \times 10^{-19} \text{ C}}$

   $= 8.5 \times 10^{-5} \text{ m}.$

57 (a) $v = \sqrt{\left(\dfrac{2eV}{m}\right)}$

   $= \sqrt{\left(\dfrac{2 \times 1.60 \times 10^{-19} \text{ C} \times 2500 \text{ V}}{9.11 \times 10^{-31} \text{ kg}}\right)}$

   $= 2.96 \times 10^{7} \text{ m s}^{-1}.$

   (b) $F = Bqv = 1 \text{ T} \times 1.6 \times 10^{-19} \text{ C} \times 2.96 \times 10^{7} \text{ m s}^{-1}$
   $= 4.7 \times 10^{-12} \text{ N}.$

   (c) $a = \dfrac{F}{m} = \dfrac{4.7 \times 10^{-12} \text{ N}}{9.11 \times 10^{-31} \text{ kg}}$

   $= 5.2 \times 10^{18} \text{ m s}^{-2}.$

   The electrons change direction but not speed.

   (d) $r = \dfrac{mv}{Bq} = 1.68 \times 10^{-4} \text{ m}.$

   or use $a = \dfrac{v^2}{r}$

   $r = \dfrac{v^2}{a} = 1.68 \times 10^{-4} \text{ m}$

BUILD OR BUST?

Figure 1 *A major earthquake devastated the Japanese city of Kobe in 1995*

Why a unit called Build or Bust?

It is difficult to imagine the feeling of being in an earthquake – the terror as whole buildings collapse around you without warning, like a pack of cards, and the ground beneath your feet just opens up. Figure 1 shows the devastation that an earthquake can bring.

An earthquake consists of shock waves travelling through the Earth. Physicists can study these waves and discover a great deal about the structure and origin of the Earth and how it is evolving. An understanding of waves also enables us to design buildings and create materials that will withstand most earthquakes – and to locate valuable deposits of oil. And knowledge of how waves propagate can be used to enhance our lives – for example by creating the best possible experience of music or by cutting down the disturbance of noisy neighbours and passing traffic.

Overview of physics principles and techniques

In this unit you will continue your study of the physics of waves and materials. Much of the work will build on and extend ideas you have met in previous units but you will also study the type of oscillation known as simple harmonic motion and consider why objects vibrate most at certain frequencies (resonance) and what that means for building design. Simple harmonic motion underlies most studies of waves and vibrations, and is the most important topic in this unit. You will also see how the principle of superposition can be used to enhance the quality of life for employees and people in their homes by protecting them from noise.

In this unit you will extend your knowledge of

- travelling waves from *The Sound of Music* and *Spare Part Surgery*;

- superposition and standing waves from *The Sound of Music*;

- refraction and reflection from *The Sound of Music, Good Enough to Eat* and *Spare Part Surgery*;

- bulk properties of solids from *Good Enough to Eat* and *Spare Part Surgery*.

You will do more work on

- waves in *Reach for the Stars*.

▮ *Earthquakes*

1.1 Shaking the Earth

Earthquakes – the wrath of the Gods?

Earthquakes are killers in modern cities: 6000 people died in the earthquake in Kobe in 1995. In cities that are at high risk of earthquakes, such as Kobe or San Francisco, the major concerns are to predict accurately when an earthquake will occur, so that people can leave, and to build so that the buildings, bridges and roads will not collapse. A lot of effort has been put into predicting earthquakes but with little success. Building earthquake-resistant cities makes prediction less important and has been more successful. In Kobe (Figure 1) one building was able to withstand the earthquake while all those around were completely destroyed. If we specify that we want a building to be 'earthquake proof', how do engineers meet that specification?

In Bronze Age Crete the Minoans revered the bull (Figure 2) as the incarnation of Poseidon, in his role as god of earthquakes. There is even evidence of human sacrifice, with the remains of a youth found on an altar, his body having been drained of blood to offer to the gods. This failed to avert the earthquake: the bodies of the priests, the sacrificial knife and the vessel for containing the victim's blood were all found where they were crushed by the falling masonry as the earthquake shook the Earth.

Figure 2 *A Minoan bull statue*

We now know that the Earth is not solid and it is constantly moving and changing. Figure 3 shows the Earth's structure. The central solid core is made of iron and nickel and is held at immensely high temperature and pressure. The liquid core of molten iron and nickel surrounding this is continuously moving in convection currents and there are also convection currents in the mantle, which is soft and liquid in places. The Earth's crust is relatively thin (only a few kilometres in places) and is made of a number of continental and oceanic plates that float on the mantle. It is the movement of these plates that causes earthquakes.

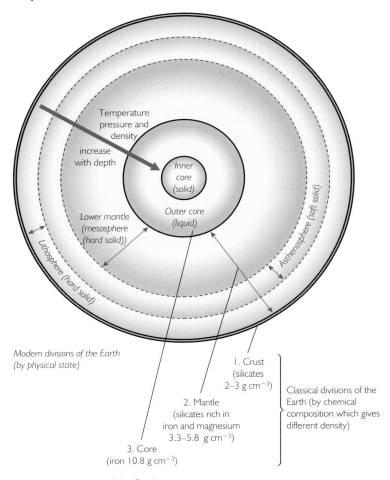

Temperature
pressure and
density

increase
with depth

Inner
core
(solid)

Lower mantle
(mesosphere
(hard solid))

Outer core
(liquid)

Lithosphere (hard solid)

Asthenosphere (soft solid)

Modern divisions of the Earth
(by physical state)

1. Crust
(silicates
$2-3$ g cm^{-3})

Classical divisions of the
Earth (by chemical
composition which gives
different density)

2. Mantle
(silicates rich in
iron and magnesium
$3.3-5.8$ g cm^{-3})

3. Core
(iron 10.8 g cm^{-3})

Figure 3 *The structure of the Earth*

As the plates are forced slowly towards, or past, one another, the forces increase and the strain gradually builds up until the plates suddenly move: an earthquake. Seismic waves (shock waves), spread out and travel all round the world. As rocks settle after the earthquake there are smaller aftershocks. Seismologists study how earthquake waves travel in order to establish more about the Earth and even use the information to locate oil and gas deposits.

Figure 4 shows the edges (margins) of the plates. At so-called constructive margins the plates are spreading or diverging, and new oceanic crust forms mid-ocean ridges with volcanoes. There are two types of destructive margin: subduction zones, where the oceanic crust moves towards the lighter continental crust, sinks and is destroyed; and collision zones, where two continental crusts collide and are forced up into mountains. At conservative margins, two plates move sideways past each other, and land is neither formed nor destroyed.

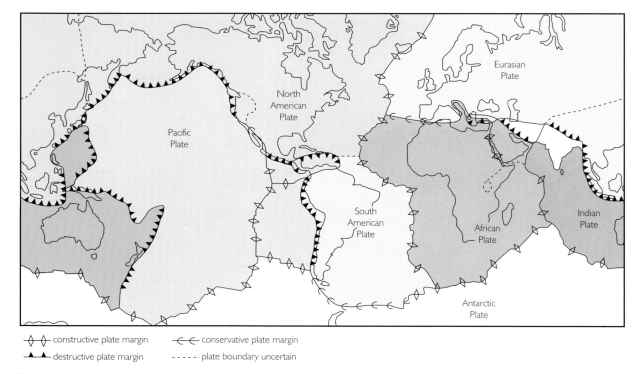

constructive plate margin   conservative plate margin
destructive plate margin   - - - - - plate boundary uncertain

Figure 4 *The plate margins of the Earth*

ACTIVITY I   **Earthquakes on the Internet**

Use the Internet to find out more about one or more of the following topics.

- What was the largest earthquake recorded in Britain? Roughly how many earthquakes occur in Britain each year?

- How are instruments designed to detect and measure earthquakes? What principles of physics are involved?

- How do engineers and architects choose materials, and use principles of physics, when designing earthquake-resistant buildings?

1.2 Seismology

Did the Earth move for you?

The study of earthquakes – seismology – increases our knowledge of the Earth and enables engineers to design earthquake-resistant cities. Earthquakes originate below the surface of the Earth at a point called the focus, or hypocentre, while the point on the Earth's surface directly above the earthquake is known as the epicentre. The seismic waves spread out from the focus in all directions (see Figure 5).

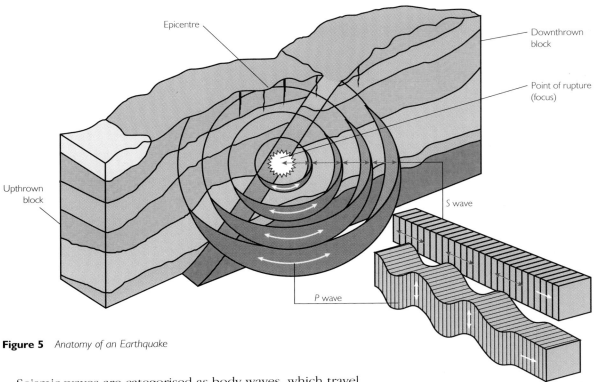

Figure 5 *Anatomy of an Earthquake*

Seismic waves are categorised as body waves, which travel through the whole body of the Earth, and surface waves, which travel only through the crust. It is the surface waves that cause the most damage.

There are two types of body waves, called primary waves (P waves) and secondary waves (S waves). They typically have frequencies of a few hertz.

P waves are **longitudinal waves** and can travel through the whole Earth, including the molten core. They travel through the rocks as a series of compressions and rarefactions. They are called primary waves because they travel faster than the S waves and arrive first at seismic monitoring stations.

S waves (sometimes also known as shear waves or shake waves) are **transverse waves** and cannot travel through the liquid parts of the Earth. The particles oscillate in a direction that is perpendicular to the direction of wave travel, so there is a shearing movement in the rock. As the longitudinal P waves travel out from the focus they cause these secondary transverse S waves to travel outwards at 90°, as shown in Figure 6. The delay between the arrival of the P and S waves can be used to calculate the distance of the station from the earthquake.

There are also two types of surface waves, named Rayleigh (R) waves and Love (Q) waves after the scientists who studied them. (see Figure 7). Surface or L waves only occur in the Earth's crust, when one boundary of the material in which the wave is travelling is a free boundary. They have longer wavelengths and lower frequencies than body waves (typically 0.1 Hz or less) and the displacement is largest at the surface, decreasing exponentially with the depth.

Study note

You have met longitudinal and transverse waves before, notably in the AS unit *The Sound of Music*.

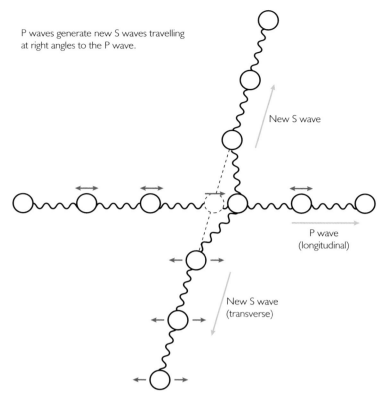

P waves generate new S waves travelling at right angles to the P wave.

New S wave

P wave (longitudinal)

New S wave (transverse)

Figure 6 *Body waves*

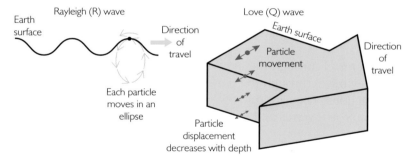

Rayleigh (R) wave

Earth surface

Direction of travel

Each particle moves in an ellipse

Love (Q) wave

Earth surface

Particle movement

Direction of travel

Particle displacement decreases with depth

Figure 7 *Surface waves*

Love or Q waves are transverse (or shear) waves where there is a strong horizontal displacement at right angles to the direction of travel. These waves are like water waves that have been turned on their side, through 90°.

Rayleigh or R waves are transverse waves, similar to water waves, where there is a strong vertical movement at right angles to the direction of travel. The particles that are being displaced have what is known as retrograde elliptical motion. This means that they are moving in the opposite direction to the wave at the crest. The path of each particle moved by the wave is an ellipse. Rayleigh waves travel more slowly than S or P waves.

ACTIVITY **2** **Revision of waves**

On a set of plain post cards, generate a set of 'Key Facts' revision cards that summarise what you have previously learned about waves. Include definitions of key terms such as longitudinal, wavelength, phase and so on.

ACTIVITY **3** **Revision of material properties**

Earthquakes result from the exposure of rocks to compressive stresses in three dimensions. Generate a concept map that summarises everything you need to know about Young modulus including the definitions of terms such as stress and strain. Find out what is meant by **bulk modulus** and **shear modulus** and include these terms in your concept map.

QUESTIONS

1 If the speed of waves in the Earth's crust is about $6.5 \, \text{km s}^{-1}$, estimate how long it would take for seismic waves to travel through the crust to reach the opposite side of the world. (Radius of Earth $= 6.378 \times 10^6 \, \text{m}$)

2 A quartz wire 10 cm long and $6 \, \mu\text{m}$ in diameter is used to suspend a small metal sphere of mass 2 g.

(**a**) Calculate the extension of the wire

(**b**) What is the maximum mass that can be suspended from the wire? (Use $g = 9.81 \, \text{N kg}^{-1}$. Data for quartz: Young modulus $E = 73.1 \, \text{GN m}^{-2}$; tensile strength $= 1000 \, \text{MN m}^{-2}$)

3 Table 1 shows the speeds of seismic waves in materials commonly found in and on the Earth.

Material	Elastic modulus/ $10^9 \, \text{N m}^{-2}$		Density/ $10^3 \, \text{kg m}^{-3}$	Speed of seismic waves/$10^3 \, \text{m s}^{-1}$	
	Bulk	**Shear**		**P waves**	**S waves**
air at 273 K	1.0×10^{-4}	0.0	1.0×10^{-3}	0.3	0.0
water at 298 K	2.2	0.0	1.0	1.4	0.0
ice	3.0	4.9	0.92	3.2	2.3
shale	8.8	17	2.4	3.6	2.6
sandstone	24	17	2.5	4.3	2.6
salt	24	18	2.2	4.7	2.9
limestone	38	22	2.7	5.0	2.9
quartz	33	39	2.7	5.7	3.8
granite	88	22	2.6	6.7	2.9
peridotite	1.4×10^2	58	3.3	8.1	4.2

Table 1   *Wave speeds, densities and elastic moduli for various materials*

(**a**) From the data in Table 1, suggest, qualitatively, how elastic modulus will affect wave speed. (Does increasing the modulus increase or decrease the wave speed for a given density?)

(**b**) Suggest how density affects wave speed.

Journey to the centre of the Earth

In recent years the study of earthquakes has provided us with a great deal of information about the Earth. It is now apparent that the Earth is made of many layers that have different characteristics, so that seismic waves have different speeds when travelling through these layers (Figure 8).

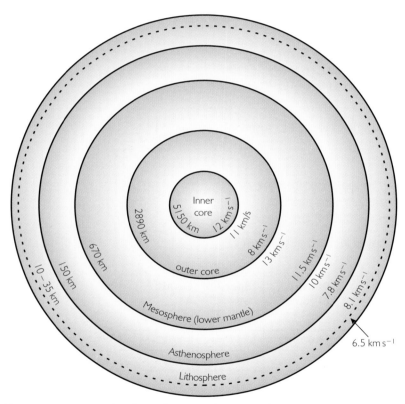

(**a**) The layered structure of the Earth – P wave velocities in km s⁻¹

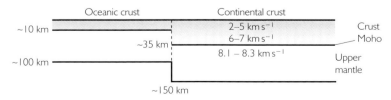

(**b**) Lithosphere in more detail – P wave velocities in km s⁻¹

Figure 8 *The layered structure of the Earth*

The lithosphere is made of rigid plates that consist of three layers: the crust, the Moho and the upper mantle. The crust has P wave velocities about 2 to $5 \, km \, s^{-1}$ for sedimentary rocks and about $6 \, km \, s^{-1}$ for igneous rocks. The Moho (short for Mohorovicic discontinuity) separates the crust from the mantle, and is about 10 km down under the oceans and 20 to 70 km down under continents; here P wave velocities increase to about $8 \, km \, s^{-1}$. The upper mantle extends down to 100 or 200 km.

The asthenosphere is a soft plastic solid. Some of it may be partially melted. Because of this the P and S waves have lower velocities, about 7 to $8 \, km \, s^{-1}$, gradually increasing to about $10 \, km \, s^{-1}$ with depth.

The mesosphere is a more rigid solid than the asthenosphere because the pressure at this depth is so great. The P and S wave velocities suddenly increase at the boundary and then slowly increase further with depth.

The outer core transmits no S waves, which results in a shadow zone (see Figure 9a). This tells us that the outer core is a fluid. There is also a P wave shadow zone (Figure 9b) due to the sudden change in velocity. The inner core is assumed to be solid since some weak P waves arrive on the other side of the Earth sooner than expected.

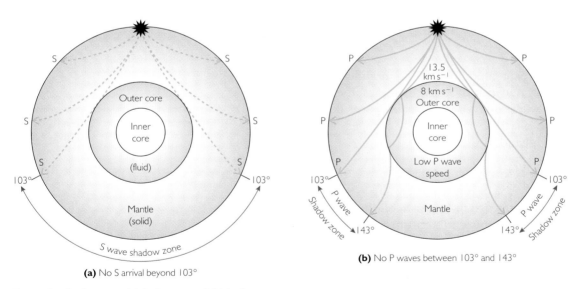

(a) No S arrival beyond 103°

(b) No P waves between 103° and 143°

Figure 9 *Shadow zones (a) for S waves and (b) for P waves*

The layered structure of the Earth has been deduced from measurements of seismic waves together with a knowledge of the waves' speeds in different types of rock. But what properties of a material will determine the speed of waves within it? Question 3 showed that density cannot be the only factor and Activity 3 gave a hint concerning elastic moduli. As Activity 4 demonstrates, the density and elastic modulus together determine the wave speed.

ACTIVITY **4** **Modelling earthquake waves**

Use the apparatus shown in Figure 10 to explore transverse and longitudinal waves. Investigate how the wave speed is affected by (i) adding mass to the trolleys (increasing the density) and (ii) adding more springs in parallel (increasing the stiffness).

(Notice that you are modelling waves in one dimension, whereas earthquake waves travel in three dimensions.)

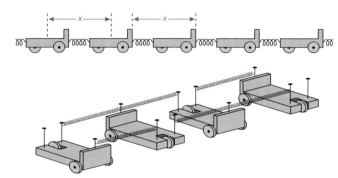

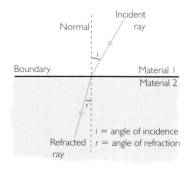

Figure 10 *Modelling earthquake waves*

As you will see in section 2.3 of this unit, the speed, v, of longitudinal waves is given by

$$v = \sqrt{\frac{E}{\rho}} \tag{1}$$

where E is the elastic modulus (Young modulus) and ρ the density.

At a boundary between different materials, the wave speed changes – the waves are refracted. If the waves do not meet the boundary head-on, their direction also changes. The speeds and directions are related by Snell's law

$$\frac{\sin i}{\sin r} = \frac{v_1}{v_2} = {}_1\mu_2 \tag{2}$$

where ${}_1\mu_2$ is the refractive index between the two materials, and i and r are the angles between the normal to the boundary and the incident and refracted wave directions, respectively (Figure 11).

Study note

For shear waves, E is replaced by the shear modulus.

Study note

You have met examples of refraction before, in the AS units *The Sound of Music* and *Spare Part Surgery*, and in the A2 unit *The Medium is the Message*. You may wish to look back at this earlier work as you tackle questions 4–7.

Normal | Incident ray

Boundary | Material 1 / Material 2

i = angle of incidence
r = angle of refraction

Refracted ray

Figure 11 *Refraction of waves at a boundary*

QUESTIONS

4 At the Moho there is a sudden increase in the velocity of seismic waves. Draw a ray diagram to show what happens to a wave when it crosses a boundary and its velocity increases. What is this phenomenon called? Also draw a wavefront diagram to show how the change in wavelength results in the change in direction of travel.

5 Figure 12 shows the paths of several waves that have been formed by a controlled explosion. The waves are detected by several monitoring stations.

(**a**) Describe what has happened to each wave to cause it to travel in the path shown.

(**b**) Explain how information from the monitoring stations could be used to find out about the structure of the Earth below the stations.

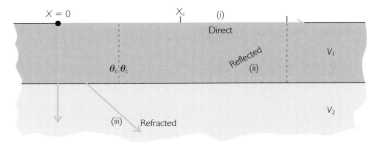

Figure 12 *Waves from a controlled explosion*

6 A P wave crosses the boundary from the mesosphere into the outer core at an angle of incidence $i = 30°$. Using information from Figure 8 calculate a value for the refractive index between the two layers and hence calculate the angle of refraction.

7 (**a**) The waves paths shown in Figure 9 are curved. What does this imply for the way that wave speed changes with depth in a given material?

(**b**) Deep within the Earth, the pressure is very high so materials are highly compressed. What effect will this have on the density of a given material?

(**c**) In view of your answers to parts (**a**) and (**b**), what can you deduce about the way that elastic modulus varies with depth (and hence with pressure)?

Seismology in action

Mike Evans is an Oil and Gas Exploration Geophysicist who graduated with a degree in Geological Geophysics from the University of Reading and now manages an E&P (Exploration & Prospection) consultancy, Focus Exploration.

> It can be very exciting as it's a high-risk game with companies committing millions of pounds to sink a well, often based primarily on your interpretation of seismic data.

Geophysics plays an important role in locating oil and gas deposits and deciding the best place to sink a well. The most important geophysical tool is the seismic method, which is a three-stage process requiring plenty of communication between each stage. The first stage is the seismic acquisition where acoustic waves generated at the surface are sent into the Earth. As the waves travel through the different rock types they are variably reflected, refracted and transmitted at each rock boundary. Hydrophones and geophones placed in arrays at the surface are used to pick up the reflected waves, building up a mass of data covering the whole area. Data processing is the next stage, where analysts use computers to produce a representation of the sub-surface – seismic profiles (2D seismic) or a seismic volume (3D seismic).

Mike works at the third stage, as a seismic interpreter. He has to use his interpretative experience and knowledge of geology to develop an understanding of the present-day geometries of rocks in the sub-surface, and their structural history. He's looking for evidence of mature hydrocarbon source rocks and structural or stratigraphic features where oil or gas may be trapped.

It's satisfying when all the bits of the jigsaw come together, and we're fortunate that our search for oil takes us all over the world from the remotest jungles of the Far East to downtown Los Angeles.

Seismometers

Earthquakes have long been the subject of human study. Figure 13 shows an early Chinese seismometer. Inside the large jar is a pendulum. An earthquake starts the pendulum swinging and rods inside move and open a dragon's mouth so that the ball falls into the mouth of one of the frogs, thus indicating the direction of the earthquake.

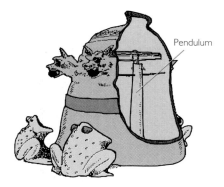

Pendulum

Figure 13   *An early Chinese seismometer*

Close to the epicentre, ground movements can be quite large. But at large distances the movements are very small. Modern seismometers are instruments that are able to detect very small movements from earthquakes thousands of kilometres away.

In the 1960s seismometers like the one in Figure 14 began to be used. This one records vertical movements. It has a heavy mass inside, which is mounted on springs. The instrument is bolted firmly to the ground. When the ground moves the instrument moves with it, but the mass will 'try' to stay in its original position due to inertia. A coil inside the mass will register changes in the magnetic field and an electrical signal showing the movement between the mass and the instrument can be used to operate a chart recorder or an oscilloscope, producing a record known as a seismogram. Seismic monitoring stations usually have three seismometers to measure oscillations in three directions at right angles to each other.

Figure 14 *A modern seismometer*

ACTIVITY 5 Seismic waves

Use a computer simulation to study the propagation of seismic waves. Relevant software can be downloaded free over the Internet:

http://www.geol/binghampton.edu/faculty/jones/

The software allows you to recreate the effects of some actual earthquakes, and to speed up or slow down the waves as they travel through the Earth. Note how the different types of waves disperse (separate out) as they travel through the Earth and are detected at various earthquake-monitoring stations (Figure 15).

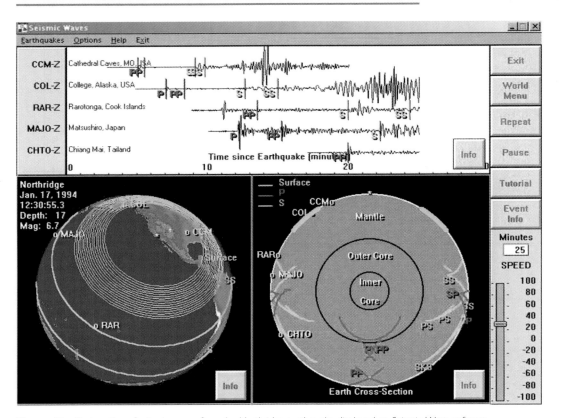

Figure 15 *Propagation of seismic waves from the Northridge earthquake displayed on Seismic Wave software.*

ACTIVITY **6** **Seismograms**

Figure 16 shows seismograms received at three monitoring stations for the same earthquake. The arrival of the P wavefront and the S wavefront have been marked, and also the arrival of the surface waves.

Write a short report on the wave traces. Your report should answer the following questions:

● How does the amplitude of the surface movement vary between the three stations?

● What do the different amplitudes suggest about the location of the earthquake's epicentre?

● What you notice about the time difference between the P wave arrival and the S wave arrival at each station? What will determine this time difference?

Use an atlas and a globe to find the locations of the stations. Use your observations of the seismograms and Figure 4 to make some suggestions about the possible location of the epicentre of the earthquake.

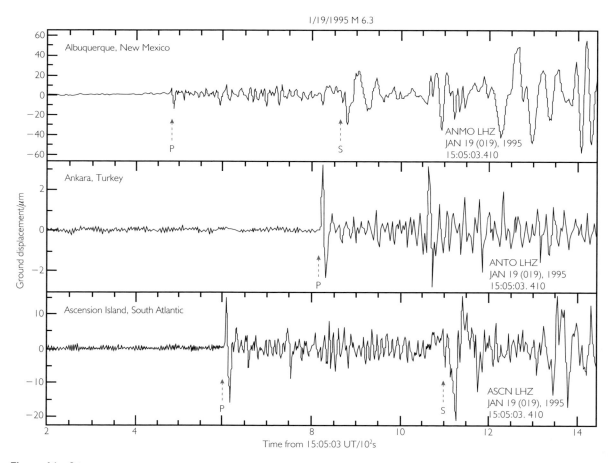

Figure 16 *Seismograms*

Earthquake scales

There are two scales commonly used to characterise the strength of an earthquake. They are summarised in Table 2.

Magnitude (Richter scale)	Intensity (Mercalli scale)	Effects
0.0 to 1.9	1	Recorded by instruments
2.0 to 2.9	2	Felt by very sensitive people. Suspended objects swing slightly.
3.0 to 3.9	3	Felt by some people. Vibration like a heavy vehicle
4.0 to 4.9	4 to 5	Felt by most people. Hanging objects swing. Dishes and windows rattle and may break.
5.0 to 5.9	6	People frightened. Chimneys topple, furniture moves.
6.0 to 6.9	7 to 9	Buildings may suffer substantial damage.
7.0 to 7.9	10 to 11	Few buildings remain standing. Large landslides and fissures.
8.0 to 8.9	12	Complete devastation. Ground waves.

Table 2   *The Richter and Mercalli scales for earthquakes*

The Richter scale

Ground movements in an earthquake can be as large as several metres, but movements of only a few μm can be detected with modern instruments. With such a wide range of values, a linear scale would be inconvenient. The Richter scale, devised in 1935, is a logarithmic scale that is based on the amplitude of the P waves. On this scale, earthquakes are given a magnitude, defined such that a magnitude 3 earthquake has movements ten times that of a magnitude 2 earthquake, and so on. The greater the distance from the epicentre the less the ground will move, so the scale must take into account the distance from the epicentre. The scale is defined so that the ground movement 100 km from a magnitude 3 earthquake is 1.0 mm; at the same distance, a magnitude 7 earthquake would produce movement of 10 m ($10 \text{ m} = 10^4 \times 1.0 \text{ mm}$).

Once the distance has been allowed for, each earthquake can be described in terms of a single magnitude. The largest recorded earthquake, with a magnitude of 8.9, occurred in Chile in 1960. There are two to three hundred earthquakes a year in the British Isles. The largest recorded was in 1931 and its epicentre was off the coast; it measured 6.1 on the Richter scale. In April 1990 there was a magnitude 5.2 earthquake in Britain.

Study note

The software for Activity 5 includes information about the magnitudes of earthquakes measured on the Richter scale.

Study note

You might like to look back at your work on logarithmic scales in *The Medium is the Message*, and at section 8 of the Maths Notes.

The Mercalli scale

The Mercalli scale uses the effects at the surface, as seen by people there at the time, to define 'intensity'. Like the Beaufort scale for wind conditions, it is empirical – in other words, it is defined initially in terms of observable effects. Intensity will vary according to distance from the epicentre and the type of ground you are standing on. The Mercalli scale ranges from 1, which is detected by instruments, but not felt by people except in special circumstances, to 12, where there is almost total destruction, objects are thrown in the air, and waves are seen on the Earth's surface.

ACTIVITY 7 | **Earthquake data**

Use sources such as the Princeton University Earth Physics Project at

http://lasker.princeton.edu/pepp.shtml

to research a number of earthquakes and plot them on the Richter scale (log scale). Plot them according to the magnitude of the Earth movement resulting from each one (mm scale). You will find that the linear scale has to be so big that it will not fit around the room – a logarithmic scale is more convenient

Maths reference
....
Using log scales
See Maths note 8.6
....

QUESTION
8 What was the ground displacement 100 km from the magnitude 5.2 earthquake recorded in Britain?

1.3 Summing up part 1

This part of the unit has been mainly revision of earlier work. You have reviewed some key ideas about waves, and have seen how the layered structure of the Earth affects the passage of seismic waves. You have also seen how logarithmic scales are used to describe earthquakes. Use the following activities to check your knowledge and understanding of waves in materials and of log scales.

ACTIVITY 8 | **Exam howlers**

In an exam, the question 'Why do P and S waves follow curved paths?' produced the following answers:

(i) because the Earth spins and causes the waves to spin to the surface.

(ii) because the waves are affected by the gravity of the core.

(iii) because the magnetic core repels the seismic waves because they are of opposite charge.

(iv) because the waves cannot travel through a vacuum.

For each one discuss and explain why the answer is not correct. Then give the correct explanation in answer to the question.

ACTIVITY 9 **Virtual earthquake**

Visit the website at

http://vcourseware3.calstatela.edu.VirtualEarthquake/
VQuakeIntro.html

Set off a virtual earthquake. Locate your earthquake and find its
magnitude on the Richter scale.

2 *Shaken not stirred*

Earthquakes are not the only cause of major building collapse. In
1940 the famous Tacoma Narrows Bridge in the USA (Figure 17)
finally shook itself to bits. For many months previously the fact that
it would sway and twist violently when the wind blew up the river
drew people from miles around to drive up and down this natural
'fairground' ride. In fact all buildings will sway if the wind is blowing
at the right speed but taller ones are more impressive – the Empire
State Building sways with a frequency of $\frac{1}{8}$ Hz when the wind blows
while the old Severn Bridge vibrates at $\frac{1}{7}$ Hz. Exactly how these
wind-induced oscillations get started is quite complicated and
depends on the complex pattern of air flow round a shaped beam.

Figure 17 *The Tacoma Narrows Bridge*

In this part of the unit, you will see how oscillations affect
buildings and other structures – the oscillations may be produced
by earthquakes, but there are other possible sources, too. You will
also see how one common type of oscillation can be analysed
mathematically.

2.1 Forced oscillations

Resonance rings a bell

Every structure has at least one **natural frequency** where it will sway, swing or vibrate most easily and goes into violent oscillation with a large amplitude when driven at this frequency. This phenomenon is called **resonance**, and engineers have to consider this very seriously when designing everything from skyscrapers to cars. A seated human body resonates at around 5 Hz. Car designers must ensure that the car body doesn't vibrate at this frequency, otherwise passengers would be shaken up quite badly by the end of the journey – regardless of the driving abilities of the driver. Examples of resonance include a wine glass 'humming' and then shattering when vibrated by a pure note (although this is very difficult to do with modern glasses, as they are made to be much stronger); a flag flapping audibly; and parts of vehicles that suddenly start vibrating as the revs increase and then stop as the revs climb higher.

Resonance occurs when a structure is driven or forced to vibrate at its natural frequency and consequently absorbs maximum energy from the driving source. It is possible to drive structures to vibrate at other frequencies but their response will be much less impressive (they vibrate with much smaller amplitude as much less energy is transferred). Activities 10, 11 and 12 illustrate resonance.

ACTIVITY 10 **Wind-induced oscillations**

Explore the oscillations of a simple structure such as that shown in Figure 18. The structure is a horizontal beam of semicircular cross-section suspended between four springs. (A rectangular strip would do, provided it is fairly thin compared with its width.) The air from a fan or blower is directed on to it and as the air speed is varied the beam leaps into violent vertical oscillations at a particular air speed. (Are there any other ways – 'modes' – in which you can see the structure vibrating, apart from those in a vertical plane?)

As an extension, devise some means of measuring air speed and measure the amplitude of vibrations produced at different speeds. Explore the effect of using different beams.

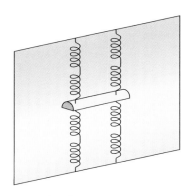

Figure 18 *Exploring wind-induced oscillations*

ACTIVITY **11** **Barton's pendulums**

Barton's pendulums are a set of pendulums of different lengths all attached to the same horizontal piece of string. One (the driver) is heavier than the rest (see Figure 19). Predict and then observe what happens when you set the driver pendulum in motion.

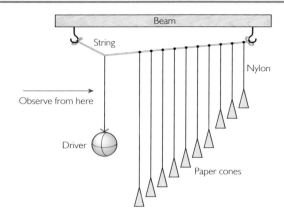

Figure 19 *Barton's pendulums*

ACTIVITY **12** **Coupled pendulums**

Set up two identical pendulums suspended from the same horizontal piece of string as in Figure 20. Predict what you will see happen if you set one swinging and wait.

As an extension, investigate whether the time of transfer of energy from one pendulum to the other and back depends on the separation of the pendulums.

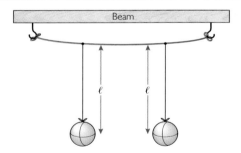

Figure 20 *Coupled pendulums*

Activities 10, 11 and 12 show just how easy it is to set something oscillating at its natural frequency compared with other frequencies. In Activity 11 you will have seen that the pendulums first begin to oscillate with what appear to be their natural frequencies, but these **transient** oscillations die away and the pendulums settle down to oscillating with the same frequency as the driver, though with different amplitudes and phases. Activities 11 and 12 also show how the phases of the driver and driven oscillators are related. Perhaps surprisingly, there is a phase difference of a quarter of a cycle – the two oscillators are said to be **in quadrature**.

Marching soldiers will be told to 'break step' when going over a bridge just in case the rhythm of their marching matches the natural frequency of the bridge and sets it vibrating, and anyone can set a rope bridge swinging by timing their bounces just right (see Figure 21). In the year 2000, London's new millennium footbridge (Figure 22) was found to sway alarmingly as people walked on it, and the motion was amplified by the way in which people adjusted the way they walked in an attempt to keep their balance. Shortly after its opening, the bridge was closed for further investigation and modification by engineers and architects.

Figure 21 *Break step when walking over a light suspension bridge!*

Figure 22 *The Millennium Bridge*

Many major engineering disasters have been attributed to resonance – bridges, buildings and turbine blades in marine and aeroengines. What is interesting, though, is that, with the notable exception of the Millennium Bridge, it is difficult to find recent examples of such failures – are we getting better at design? It does seem that experiment, together with theoretical and computer analysis, is increasing engineers' understanding of oscillations and resonance and that is feeding into better design practice. However, complacency could be disastrous; the problems with the Millennium Bridge occurred despite thorough testing and computer modelling. Engineers have to establish the natural frequencies of any structure they propose to build to ensure that it won't be set into violent oscillation, especially if it is in an earthquake zone. Studying how energy is transferred in waves and how structures oscillate is an important part of this.

Seismometers

In Activity 13 you will explore resonance further and see how it comes into play when designing a seismometer.

A seismometer is an example of a forced oscillator, where a system capable of undergoing free oscillations is driven from the outside by some external force which itself oscillates at a frequency called the **driver frequency** f_d. For a seismometer the earthquake itself constitutes the driver. There is a further slight complication in that an earthquake is unlikely to have a single frequency: there will be a spectrum of frequencies. However, in the simple model that you are going to use, it will be assumed that an earthquake can be modelled by a single frequency.

A simple seismometer consists of a mass hanging vertically on a spring (Figure 23). The top of the spring is driven by a vibrator at fixed amplitude from a variable-frequency generator. The generator/vibrator combination simulate a variable-frequency earthquake. The design has the two essential ingredients for an oscillation to occur – mass and stiffness. How likely is it in practice that the mass will stay still and not oscillate? One way of re-stating that the mass should be large in a 'good' seismometer is to say that the natural frequency should be low – but what does 'low' mean? What can we compare it with?

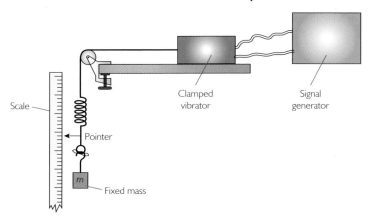

Figure 23   *A simple seismometer*

ACTIVITY 13 **Make and market a seismometer**

Make and test a simple seismometer as shown in Figure 23.

When you have made and tested your instrument, imagine that you represent a company that markets seismometers. Prepare a sales presentation to convince a client that your instrument has features that will make it work well.

It's not all bad news...

Vibrations can cause damage, but an interesting recent development, at the moment only at the laboratory stage, is that vibrations can reduce stress in steel and give stronger welds – leading to safer structures. Specimens of steel strip (formed by rolling steel slabs) are vibrated in a cantilever mode (i.e. held at one end) over a period of a few minutes. Portable X-ray diffraction equipment can measure the residual stress that the rolling process introduces into the steel. Both for strips and for simple welded structures it was found that the residual stresses were significantly reduced after vibration treatment; importantly, this reduction seems to be permanent.

Vibrations and resonance in machinery

Rotating machinery, particularly if it is slightly out of balance, can set up vibrations in neighbouring components or parts of itself. The driving frequency in some of these examples may be the frequency of rotation of the engine, or possibly of the wheels. It is clearly important to know what rates of rotation are involved if resonance is to be avoided.

Vibration effects on people

In order to protect passengers from excessive noise and vibration, it is important that large out-of-balance forces in a car engine are not transmitted to the vehicle body. Scientists study the effects of vibration on the human body and can then predict levels of passenger comfort or the degree of interference with activities or level of concentration. They can even predict the likelihood of motion sickness.

Vibration and vomiting

The motion sickness dose value (MSDV) predicts the probability of vomiting based on the frequency and magnitude of vertical vibrations and the time of exposure.

$$\text{MSDV} = a_{\text{rms}} \sqrt{t}$$

Here a_{rms} is the frequency-weighted acceleration reflecting the greatest sensitivity to vibrations in the range 0.125–0.25 Hz, and t is the time of exposure. The percentage of unadapted adults expected to vomit is $\frac{1}{3}$MSDV. These relationships have been derived from experiments in which up to 70% of subjects vomited during exposures lasting between 20 minutes and 6 hours.

Vibration control – the Porsche story

The Porsche 944 (Figure 24) is unusual in that its 2.5 litre engine is one of the world's largest four-cylinder engines but it is as quiet and smooth as a six-cylinder engine. This is chiefly due to the two counter-rotating balance shafts that eliminate the out-of-balance forces (trying to move the engine up and down) characteristic of large four-cylinder engines. This means the engine runs with a

Figure 24   *The Porsche 944*

minimum of vibration throughout its entire power range but has all the advantages of a four-cylinder engine, namely low friction losses, less weight and greater efficiency.

It is by no means easy to smooth out these vibrations, but it is essential because otherwise the engine feels rough and the car is noisy as the vibrations reach the body shell and create unpleasant body booms.

The counterbalance shafts have off-set weights, are positioned at the side of the engine at different heights and rotate at twice the engine speed. This arrangement helps cancel out the gas forces that occur upon ignition (every half-revolution) and thrust the pistons sideways, creating a moment about the engine's centre of gravity. The rotation of the balance shafts produce a counteracting torque every firing stroke.

Vibration-induced white finger

A well known occupational hazard is vibration-induced white finger (VWF), in which the sufferer experiences intermittent whitening of the ends of the fingers due to reduced blood flow as a result of the vibrations experienced in the use of machinery. In severe cases amputation is the only treatment.

ACTIVITY 14 **Further examples of resonance**

Discuss, or make notes on, the following questions.

- Machinery is normally operated at speeds well above any possible resonances. What problems might be presented, though, when the machinery is started up or shut down? (This can be a particular problem for ships with a very long transmission shaft from engine to propeller.) What instructions might you give to an operator?

- What does a garage always do – and charge for – when a tyre is changed and why?

2.2 A useful type of oscillation

To ensure that the effects of resonance are controlled, engineers must understand the fundamentals of vibration. Vibrations and any kind of motion that repeats itself, such as a simple pendulum or a mass bouncing on a spring, are described as a **harmonic motion**. There is a particular form of harmonic motion, called **simple harmonic motion** (SHM), which has the very important properties that:

- the period (or frequency) is independent of the **amplitude** (maximum displacement) of the motion; and

- the force is always directed towards the central point of the oscillation; if displacement is positive the force is negative, and vice versa. Mathematically this can be expressed as

$$F = -kx \qquad\qquad (3)$$

where F and x are the magnitudes of the force and displacement respectively, and k is a constant.

The second property means that the force – and hence the acceleration – must be zero as the system passes through its central position. This is therefore an **equilibrium position**, the one to which the system gradually returns as the oscillations die away. Because of this change in direction of force either side of equilibrium, it is usually called the **restoring force** and is provided by the **'stiffness'** (k) of the system. It is the momentum of the system that makes it continue on past its equilibrium position

---

ACTIVITY 15 **Oscillation circus**

Observe a variety of oscillating systems and decide whether each exhibits simple harmonic motion. Try to identify what provides the inertia and what provides the stiffness of the system. Some systems require detailed measurements, while others simply require observation.

As Activity 16 shows, there is a connection between simple harmonic motion and motion in a circle. This provides us with a useful way to analyse SHM mathematically.

ACTIVITY 16 **Circular motion and SHM**

Observe the shadow of a mass undergoing SHM on the end of a spring alongside the shadow of a ball rotating in a vertical circle, as in Figure 25.

Hold your arms out in front of you with index fingers pointing forwards and level with each other. Set your left hand counter-clockwise at a steady speed and move your right hand vertically so that your index fingers stay at the same horizontal level. While your left hand executes a circle the right is executing SHM.

You have just demonstrated that SHM and circular motion are closely related. Make sure you are familiar with the terms angular velocity, period, centripetal force and acceleration and the relationships between them. Also make sure you are familiar with angular displacements expressed in radians.

Study note

Look back at your work on circular motion in *Probing the Heart of Matter*.

Maths reference

Trigonometry and angular measurements
See *Maths notes 6*

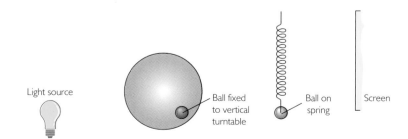

Light source   Ball fixed to vertical turntable   Ball on spring   Screen

Figure 25 *Shadows of SHM and circular motion*

Analysing SHM

Figure 26 shows an object, mass m, moving with angular velocity ω (measured in radians per second) in a circle of radius A. As was demonstrated in Activity 16, its 'shadow' cast on the x-axis performs simple harmonic motion; to describe its motion we need expressions for the x component of displacement, velocity and so on.

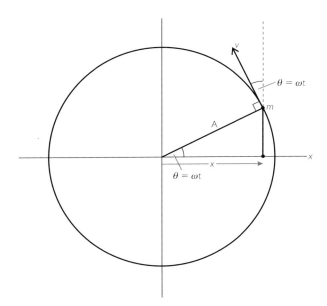

Figure 26 *SHM as a projection of circular motion*

The amplitude of the oscillating motion is A. For an angular displacement of ωt the horizontal displacement is

$$x = A \cos \omega t \qquad (4)$$

The maximum displacement is when $\cos \omega t = \pm 1$, i.e. $x_{max} = \pm A$.

In circular motion velocity is given by

$$v = A\omega \qquad (5)$$

at an angle ωt to the vertical. Here we need the horizontal component:

$$v_x = -A\omega \sin \omega t \qquad (6)$$

The negative sign shows that the mass is moving in the negative direction, i.e. back towards its equilibrium position. The speed (magnitude of velocity) is greatest when $\sin \omega t = \pm 1$, i.e. $v_{max} = A\omega$.

For the circular motion, the force acting on m always has magnitude

$$F = \frac{mv^2}{A} = m\omega^2 A \qquad (7)$$

and is directed towards the centre (it is a *centripetal* force). The x component is thus

$$F_x = -m\omega^2 A \cos \omega t \qquad (8)$$

Study note

In *Probing the Heart of Matter* you saw that $F = \dfrac{mv^2}{r}$, where r is the radius of the circle. Here $r = A$.

Comparing equations (4) and (8), we have

$$F_x = -m\omega^2 x \tag{9}$$

Since m and ω are both constants, equation (9) is equivalent to equation (3) and describes a key property of SHM – the restoring force is proportional to displacement. Equation (9) is often expressed in terms of the acceleration:

$$a_x = \frac{F_x}{m}$$

and so

$$a_x = -\omega^2 A \cos \omega t \tag{10}$$

i.e.

$$a_x = -\omega^2 x \tag{11}$$

Figure 27 shows graphs of the variation of displacement, velocity and acceleration with time for a simple harmonic oscillator. We have dropped the subscript x because we are now dealing with motion in just one dimension.

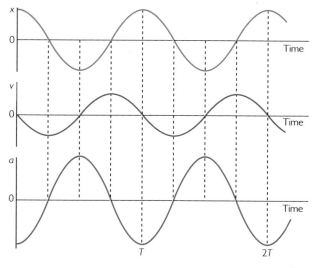

Figure 27   *Graphs of (a) x versus t (b) v versus t and (c) a versus t for an object executing SHM*

The circular motion also enables us to deduce the period, T, of the SHM. The time to make one complete oscillation (there and back) is the same as the period of the circular motion, i.e.

$$T = \frac{2\pi}{\omega} \tag{12}$$

Notice that the period T is independent of the amplitude, A – the other key property of SHM. We can also write an expression for frequency:

$$f = \frac{1}{T} = \frac{\omega}{2\pi} \tag{13}$$

Study note

You met equation 12 in connection with circular motion in section 4.3 of *Build or Bust.*

Springy oscillations

Use equations (3) to (13), and the worked example below, to predict the frequency of a mass oscillating on various combinations of springs (Figure 28a). Then compare your predictions with experimental measurements of frequency.

Produce a time-trace for the apparatus shown in Figure 28(b) (or similar) and compare the results with the theoretical equations (4), (6) and (12).

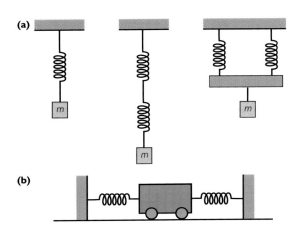

Figure 28 *Apparatus for Activity 17*

A useful recipe

The above theoretical treatment of SHM provides a very useful 'recipe' for analysing the motion of an oscillator. Simply carry out the following steps:

1 Is the restoring force proportional to displacement? If so, then the motion is simple harmonic. (If it is not, the motion is *not* SHM and you cannot proceed with this recipe.)

2 Since restoring force is proportional to displacement, then acceleration must also be proportional to displacement. Find the constant that relates displacement to acceleration. Sometimes it is easy to find this constant directly; sometimes it is easier to find the relationship between displacement and restoring force and then divide by mass.

3 The constant you have found in step 2 is equal to ω^2 in equation (11). Find its square root. You now know the value of ω for your oscillator.

4 Using your value of ω, you can now work out the period of the oscillation using equation (12). If you know the amplitude, you can also find the displacement, velocity and acceleration at any given time using equations (4), (6) and (11).

Worked examples

$\mathbb{Q}$ A mass $m = 0.1\,\text{kg}$ oscillates on the end of a spring that obeys Hooke's law and has a stiffness $k = 50\,\text{N}\,\text{m}^{-1}$. Is the motion simple harmonic? If so, what is its period?

$\mathbb{A}$ Since the spring obeys Hooke's law $F = -kx$, and so the motion *must* be SHM.

$$a = -\frac{kx}{m} = -\left(\frac{k}{m}\right)x$$

so

$$\omega^2 = \frac{k}{m}$$

and

$$\omega = \sqrt{\frac{k}{m}} = \sqrt{(50\,\text{N}\,\text{m}^{-1}/0.1\,\text{kg})} = 22.36\,\text{s}^{-1}$$

$T = 2\pi/\omega = 0.28\,\text{s}$ (to 2 sig. fig.).

Study note

Notice the units. Since $1\,\text{N} = 1\,\text{kg}\,\text{m}\,\text{s}^{-2}$, the SI units of $\sqrt{(k/m)}$ reduce to s^{-1}, giving appropriate SI units for T.

$\mathbb{Q}$ (Harder!) Suppose the mass in the previous question is displaced by 3.0 cm from its equilibrium position and then released. (a) What is its maximum speed? (b) What are its displacement and velocity after 0.05 s?

$\mathbb{A}$ We need to use equations (4) and (6), and so we need to know values of A and ωt. Since 3.0 cm is the maximum displacement, the amplitude $A = 3.0\,\text{cm}$.

(a) By inspection of equation (6), speed is maximum when $\sin \omega t$ is greatest, i.e. when $\sin \omega t = 1$, hence

$$v_{max} = A\omega = 3.0\,\text{cm} \times 22.36\,\text{s}^{-1} = 67\,\text{cm}\,\text{s}^{-1} \text{ (2 sig. fig.)}$$

(b) After 0.05 s, $\omega t = 0.05\,\text{s} \times 22.36\,\text{s}^{-1} = 1.118$.

Since ω can be interpreted as an angular velocity in radians per second, ωt can be interpreted as an angle expressed in radians.

$$\cos \omega t = \cos 1.118 = 0.1834$$

From equation (4):

$$x = A \cos \omega t = 3.0\,\text{cm} \times 0.1834 = 0.55\,\text{cm} \text{ (2 sig. fig.)}$$

$$\sin \omega t = \sin 1.118 = 0.8992$$

From equation (6):

$$v = -A\omega \sin \omega t = -3.0\,\text{cm} \times 22.36\,\text{s}^{-1} \times 0.8992$$
$$= -60\,\text{cm}\,\text{s}^{-1} \text{ (2 sig. fig.)}$$

Study note

Remember to switch your calculator into 'radian' mode.

Study note

The positive sign tells us that the mass is still on the positive side of the equilibrium position, as is expected after a little less than one quarter of a complete there-and-back oscillation.

Study note

Notice that v is negative; the mass has not yet reached the equilibrium position but is travelling towards it. It has almost reached its maximum speed, which it will reach after exactly one quarter of a cycle as it passes though the equilibrium position.

QUESTIONS

9 An object supported by a 'Hooke's law' spring oscillates with SHM and has $A = 0.30$ m and $\omega = 5.0\,\text{s}^{-1}$.

(**a**) What are (**i**) its maximum speed and (**ii**) the frequency of the oscillations?

(**b**) The object has mass 0.40 kg. What is the stiffness of the spring?

(**c**) After 0.20 seconds, what are (**i**) the displacement and (**ii**) the acceleration?

10 (**a**) An ultrasonic oscillator has a frequency of 50 kHz and amplitude of 2×10^{-6} m. What are the maximum values of speed and acceleration?

(**b**) Expressing the acceleration as a multiple of $g\,(= 9.81\,\text{m s}^{-2})$, do you think the value has any implications for the mechanical strength of the oscillating part?

(**c**) Gallstones in the body can often be broken up by irradiating them with ultrasonic vibrations. Why is increasing the frequency more effective than increasing the amplitude in this operation?

11 Figure 29 shows a simple pendulum of length ℓ displaced through a small angle θ.

(**a**) Show that, (**i**) provided θ is small, acceleration is proportional to displacement, with $\omega^2 = \dfrac{g}{\ell}$, and hence show (**ii**) that the pendulum has a period $T = 2\pi\sqrt{\dfrac{\ell}{g}}$.

(Hint: use the small angle approximation for angles in radians.)

(**b**) What is the length of a 1 Hz pendulum? (Use $g = 9.81\,\text{m s}^{-2}$.)

Maths reference
....
The small angle approximations
See Maths note 6.6
....

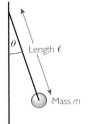

θ Length ℓ

Mass m

Figure 29   *A simple pendulum*

ACTIVITY **18**   **Virtual pendulum**

Use a computer simulation of a pendulum to explore factors affecting its oscillation.

Energy in SHM

The previous analysis can be extended to consider the energy of a simple harmonic oscillator. The general principles can be illustrated by considering a mass oscillating horizontally on the end of a light

Hooke's law spring, resting on a frictionless surface (Figure 30) – the only energies that change are the kinetic energy of the mass and the potential energy due to the stretched spring.

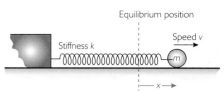

Figure 30   *A 'simple' simple harmonic oscillator*

At maximum displacement from equilibrium, the mass is momentarily at rest and the stretched (or compressed) spring has maximum potential energy. As the mass passes through its equilibrium position it has its greatest speed and hence its greatest kinetic energy, but the potential energy is momentarily zero. At all other positions, the system has both kinetic and potential energy.

The kinetic energy, E_k, of the mass, m, is related to its speed, v, by the familiar expression:

$$E_k = \tfrac{1}{2} mv^2 \tag{14}$$

By squaring equation (6) to obtain an expression for v^2 for the oscillator, we can get an expression showing how kinetic energy of the oscillating mass varies with time:

$$E_k = \tfrac{1}{2} mA^2\omega^2 \sin^2\omega t \tag{15}$$

The (elastic) potential energy E_p stored in the stretched spring with stiffness k is given by

$$E_p = \tfrac{1}{2} kx^2 \tag{16}$$

By squaring equation (4) to get an expression for x^2, we can see how the potential energy of the spring changes with time:

$$E_p = \tfrac{1}{2} kA^2 \cos^2\omega t \tag{17}$$

Figure 31 shows graphs of kinetic and potential energy plotted against time.

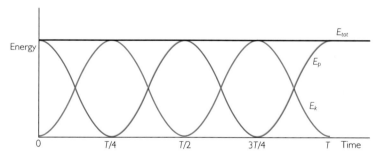

Figure 31   *The time variation of E_k and E_p for a mass oscillating on a spring*

The relationship between equations (15) and (17) becomes more apparent if we note that $\omega^2 = \dfrac{k}{m}$, and so equation (15) becomes

$$E_k = \tfrac{1}{2} kA^2 \sin^2\omega t \tag{18}$$

The total energy, E_{tot}, of the system is found by adding equations (17) and (18):

$$E_{tot} = E_p + E_k$$
$$E_{tot} = \tfrac{1}{2} kA^2(\cos^2\omega t + \sin^2\omega t)$$
$$E_{tot} = \tfrac{1}{2} kA^2 \tag{19}$$

because $\cos^2\omega t + \sin^2\omega t = 1$, irrespective of the value of ωt. In other words, the **total energy of a simple harmonic oscillator** is constant. This is true for *all* SHM systems, not just for the simple one we have chosen to study.

The energies can also be expressed in terms of m and ω rather than k and A, in which case equation (19) becomes

$$E_{\text{tot}} = \tfrac{1}{2}\, m\, \omega^2\, A^2 \qquad\qquad (20)$$

QUESTIONS

12 Calculate the total energies of (**a**) the oscillator considered in the worked example on page 222 and (**b**) the oscillator in question 9. In each case, show that equations (19) and (20) give the same answer.

13 (**a**) A spring of stiffness $1.0 \times 10^2\,\mathrm{N\,m^{-1}}$ is stretched by $0.15\,\mathrm{m}$. What is its elastic potential energy?

(**b**) It is used (at this stretch) to catapult a small missile of mass $2.0\,\mathrm{g}$. At what speed does the missile leave the catapult? What assumption did you have to make?

(**c**) Using appropriate symbols k, x and m (mass of missile), turn the reasoning of (**b**) into a general theoretical argument to produce an algebraic expression for the launch velocity v. Show that the launch velocity is proportional to the initial stretch.

(**d**) Without completely re-working the problem, find the launch velocity of (**i**) the same missile for an initial extension of $0.05\,\mathrm{m}$ and (**ii**) a missile twice as massive launched using the original extension of $0.15\,\mathrm{m}$.

2.3   *Earthquake waves revisited*

Knowing something about SHM, we can now return to the question of waves in a solid material. As you saw in Activity 4, a longitudinal wave in a solid can be modelled with a row of trolleys as in Figure 32. Each trolley (or atom in a solid) is held to its neighbours by springy connections, so you can consider each one as an oscillator like that in Activity 17. We can use the equations of SHM to deduce the speed of a compression wave along the row of oscillators.

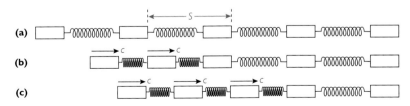

Figure 32   *A compression pulse travels along a row of oscillators*

Imagine pushing the oscillator at the end of the row. The spring joining it to its neighbour becomes compressed, exerting a force on the next oscillator and setting it in motion so that it passes on the force to its neighbour – and so a compression pulse travels along the row with a time lag between one oscillator and the next. If s is the distance from one oscillator to the next and τ the time interval, then the wave travels at speed v where

$$v = \frac{s}{\tau} \tag{21}$$

If you assume that each successive oscillator is affected only when its neighbour has reached its maximum displacement, then the time taken for the pulse to be 'handed on' will be one quarter of a cycle. In fact, the time interval is rather shorter – only $\frac{1}{2\pi}$ of a cycle:

$$\tau = \frac{T}{2\pi} \tag{22}$$

Since we know that, for an oscillator mass m held by springs of stiffness k,

$$T = 2\pi\sqrt{\frac{m}{k}} \tag{23}$$

we now have an expression for the speed at which the pulse travels along the row:

$$\tau = \sqrt{\frac{m}{k}}$$

so

$$v = s\sqrt{\frac{k}{m}} \tag{24}$$

Study note

See Activity 17 and the worked example on page 222

ACTIVITY 19   **The speed of a pulse along a row of trolleys**

Set up a row of trolleys like that in Figure 32. By moving the whole row (without compressing the springs) arrange for the end trolley to crash into a solid obstacle (e.g. a wall). Observe that, when the end trolley hits the wall, a compression pulse travels along to the free end, where it is reflected as a rarefaction pulse that travels back towards the wall. When this reflected pulse reaches the wall, the trolleys bounce back, losing contact with the wall. So the end trolley remains in contact with the wall for the time that it takes for a pulse to travel along the row and back again.

Use this observation to measure the there-and-back travel time and hence to deduce the speed of the pulse. Compare your result with the speed calculated using equation (24).

Waves in a solid

The arrangement in Figure 32 can be thought of as modelling a row of atoms, and we can use equation (24) to deduce the speed of longitudinal waves in a solid. Figure 33 shows a three-dimensional model of a solid in which atoms are held by spring bonds that, for small extensions and compressions, obeys Hooke's law.

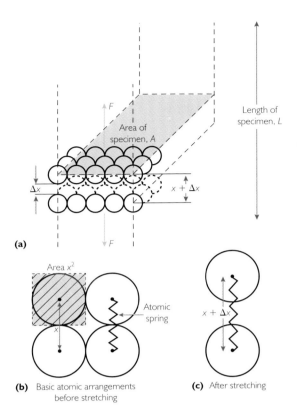

Figure 33 *A three-dimensional model of a solid*

For each bond we can write:

$$\Delta f = k \Delta x \qquad (25)$$

where Δf is the force and Δx is the resultant extension. k is the stiffness of each bond. We can relate this interatomic k to the Young modulus of the metal.

Each atom in Figure 33 occupies an area x^2. If the cross-sectional area of the sample is A, then the number of atoms in the layer is $\dfrac{A}{x^2}$ – and this is the number of springs being stretched. Hence the total force F is given by

$$F = \frac{Ak\Delta x}{x^2} \qquad (26)$$

which leads to an expression for stress:

$$\sigma = \frac{k\Delta x}{x^2} \qquad (27)$$

We can also write down an expression for strain:

$$\varepsilon = \frac{\Delta x}{x} \qquad (28)$$

Combining equations (27) and (28) leads to an expression for the Young modulus:

$$E = \frac{k}{x} \qquad (29)$$

Putting $s = x$ and $k = Ex$ in equation (24) we get a new expression for the wave speed:

$$v = x\sqrt{\frac{Ex}{m}} = \sqrt{\frac{Ex^3}{m}} \qquad (30)$$

But as x^3 is the volume occupied by each atom, then the density is

$$\rho = \frac{m}{x^3}$$

hence we can write the equation that you met in part 1 of this unit:

$$v = \sqrt{\frac{E}{\rho}} \qquad \text{(equation 1)}$$

Although we assumed a square arrangement of atoms, equation (1) applies to longitudinal waves in any solid, regardless of the way its atoms are arranged.

ACTIVITY **20** **Wave speed in a solid**

Use the arrangement shown in Figure 34, or similar, to measure the speed of a longitudinal wave in a steel or aluminium rod. The principle is the same as that used in Activity 19 – the rod behaves like the row of trolleys and so the contact time between rod and hammer is equal to the there-and-back travel time for a longitudinal pulse.

Compare your result with the speed calculated using equation (1) and the data given below.

Aluminium: $E = 7.0 \times 10^{10}\,\mathrm{N\,m^{-2}}$, $\rho = 2.7 \times 10^3\,\mathrm{kg\,m^{-3}}$.
Steel: $E = 2.0 \times 10^{11}\,\mathrm{N\,m^{-2}}$, $\rho = 7.8 \times 10^3\,\mathrm{kg\,m^{-3}}$.

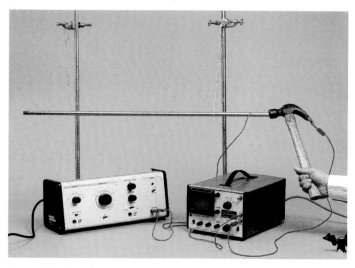

Figure 34 *Apparatus for Activity 20*

Table 1 (in part 1 of the unit) lists data for density and the speed of P waves in various materials. Seismologists use such data, derived from calculations and laboratory measurements, to help them to interpret observations of seismic waves and hence to make deductions about the internal structure of the Earth. As you will see in part 3 of this unit, a knowledge of wave speeds in materials also helps engineers to design buildings that are safe and comfortable for the occupants, and machines that are safe to operate.

QUESTIONS

14 Figure 35 shows some results obtained in Activity 20. On the screen trace shown in Figure 35 the contact time between a metal bar and the hammer that hit it was estimated at 347 μs. The bar was 0.70 m long. What was the speed of longitudinal waves in the bar?

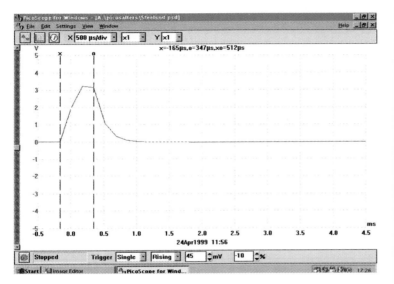

Figure 35 *Results from Activity 20*

15 Table 3 lists the speed of longitudinal waves in various common materials along with their densities.

(**a**) Without doing any calculations, what can you say about the Young modulus of oak compared with that of pine, and the Young moduli of metals compared with those of wood?

(**b**) Calculate the Young moduli of (**i**) pine and (**ii**) copper.

Material	Density ρ/kg m^{-3}	Wave speed v/m s^{-1}
pine	500	3313
oak	700	3837
aluminium	2698	5100
steel	7800	5060
copper	8933	3650
lead	11 343	1230

Table 3 *Densities and longitudinal wave speeds for various materials*

2.4 *Build it better – Summing up part 2*

The physics that you have studied in this part of the unit is the physics that enables an engineer to design a building for an earthquake zone. You have seen how an oscillator can be driven to oscillate by an external force, and that if the frequency of the driving force matches the oscillator's natural frequency, then resonance occurs and oscillations build up to large amplitude. You then went on to study and analyse simple harmonic motion – a type of motion that occurs in many natural and man-made systems and which underlies many more complex oscillatory motions.

Figure 36 shows a model structure being tested on an earthquake table in an engineering laboratory. As the 'Earth' shakes, the building vibrates. It is the engineer's task to ensure that the amplitude of the vibrations remains fairly small, and also to choose materials that will withstand deformation. In Activity 21, you will apply your knowledge of resonance and simple harmonic motion to the matter of limiting the vibrations. (In part 3 you will return to the question of deformation.)

Figure 36 *Testing a model structure on an earthquake table*

ACTIVITY **21** | **Earthquakes in the laboratory**

Make some simple model building structures (Figure 37). By assuming that each model vibrates like a mass on a spring, calculate its natural frequency of vibration. Test each model by vibrating it on an earthquake table.

As you work though this activity, take the opportunity to look back through part 2 of the unit and make sure you understand the meaning of the key terms printed in bold.

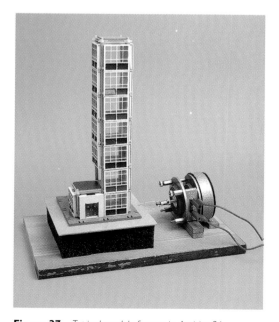

Figure 37 *Typical models for use in Activity 21*

ACTIVITY **22** **Resonance of a vibrating blade**

Explore the resonance of a thin metal blade vibrated by a vibration generator (Figure 38). As is often the case with vibrating machinery, you can only observe the blur of the oscillation.

Then construct and test a vibrating-blade rotation meter (tachometer).

 Safety
When dealing with an off-balance motor ensure that all parts are firmly fixed together, and that you are not making observations in the plane of rotation.

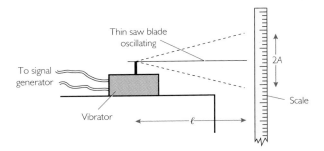

Figure 38 *Vibrating a metal blade*

Further investigations

If violently shaken, a jelly can be made to split apart. Use an earthquake table to explore the response of jellies to various vibrations.

QUESTIONS

16 The natural frequency of a building can be dramatically reduced (to remove it from typical earthquake frequencies) by mounting the whole building on rubber bearings. The building then really does oscillate as a single mass without bending.

(**a**) A 40 tonne model has a natural frequency of horizontal oscillations of 0.60 Hz when mounted on rubber. What is the horizontal stiffness of the bearings? (1 tonne = 1000 kg)

(**b**) The same model has a vertical natural frequency of 10 Hz.
(**i**) Using the fact that frequency squared is proportional to stiffness, use your answer to (**a**) to find the vertical stiffness of the bearings. (**ii**) Through what distance will the weight of the model compress the bearings? (Use $g = 9.81 \, \text{N kg}^{-1}$.)

(**c**) On the model *without* rubber bearings the maximum acceleration at 3rd floor level was measured to be $12 \, \text{m s}^{-2}$ at a frequency of 3.0 Hz. (**i**) What is the displacement amplitude? (**ii**) The building can be thought of as bending on a fixed base (like your model in Activity 21). If the model is one-third linear scale, what would be the amplitude of oscillation of the real building? Would you find this alarming?

17 The model in question 16 is built to a one-third linear scale, using the materials that would be used to construct the actual building.

(a) What would be the mass of the actual building?

(b) What would have to happen to the stiffness of the real rubber bearings compared with that of the model ones if the natural frequency of horizontal oscillation were to stay the same?

(c) Why are vertical earthquake oscillations likely to cause less damage than horizontal ones?

18 Figure 39 shows a pendulum made up of a spring of natural length $\ell = 0.40$ m attached to a string (which doesn't stretch significantly) of length $L = 0.20$ m. A mass is hung on the spring, which stretches it by 0.20 m. (In your answer use $g = 9.81 \, \mathrm{m\,s^{-2}}$.)

(a) What is the frequency of the 'springy' oscillation?

(b) What is the frequency of the pendulum oscillations – the sideways swinging of the whole arrangement? (Hint: refer to question 11.)

(c) What is the ratio of these two frequencies? How could you have written down the ratio straight away?

(d) When this arrangement is set oscillating as a pendulum it starts to 'go wild'. Suggest how your answer to (c) might help to explain this. If you have a moment it is worth setting this up and playing with it – it has some interesting properties. The actual values are not important – just adjust L for any mass and spring until you get the ratio of lengths you need: you will know when you're there.

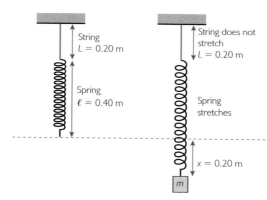

Figure 39 *A complex pendulum*

3 *Design for living*

In this part of the unit, you will use and extend what you have learned about vibrations and resonance, and see how buildings (and machines) can be designed to withstand vibrations. Whether the vibrations are the results of earthquakes or something else, the principles are the same.

3.1 Damping the motion

'The wheels on the bus go round and round ...' but they also go up and down every time they hit a bump in the road. Passengers expect a smooth ride so shock absorbers perform an essential task – they absorb the energy of the vibration and stop the car body from bouncing up and down long after the bump has been passed.

This is an example of **damping**. The energy of the oscillation is dissipated as heat in oil as pistons are made to move up and down in it. Some modern cars now include 'active suspension systems' whereby the 'bump' is sensed and a restoring force actively applied to stop the wheel pushing the car body up. Whatever the system, all oscillations are damped – a pendulum swinging in the air stops after a while because its energy is dissipated into the air (warming it up slightly). Make the same pendulum swing in syrup and ... that's damping to an extreme. There are many cases where damping is the best way of reducing the effects of oscillations – for example the thirteenth harmonic has to be damped out of notes on a piano otherwise it sounds awful.

ACTIVITY 23 **Damped oscillations**

Use a motion sensor to produce a displacement–time graph of a damped oscillator. Examine the results and see whether the amplitude decays exponentially with time.

Figure 40 shows typical results from Activity 23, showing how the amplitude of a damped oscillation dies away exponentially with time.

Study note

It is a common mistake to describe all growths and decays as exponential, but they're not.

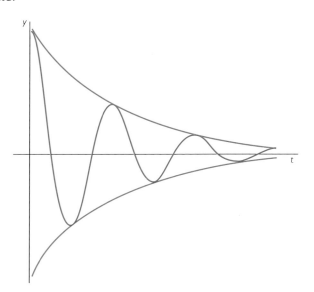

Figure 40 *The amplitude of damped oscillations decreases exponentially with time*

QUESTIONS

19 A tall tower-like model structure (like a radio mast) of mass 5.5×10^3 kg is being tested for its vibration characteristics to see if there is any risk of the actual tower being affected by earthquakes. It is initially given a static test by being pulled sideways by a steady force applied near the top. It is found that for the very small displacement possible the force obeys Hooke's law, a force of 1.0×10^5 N producing a deflection of 50 mm.

(**a**) At this deflection how much elastic potential energy is stored in the structure?

(**b**) The load is suddenly removed and the structure 'twangs' like a gigantic tuning fork. As an engineer involved in the test, you decide to make two drastic assumptions:

- damping may be ignored
- the kinetic energy of the tower as it passes through the central position can be represented by the motion of a point mass (equal to the tower mass) at the centre of mass of the tower moving with a speed v.

Using these assumptions, find the speed v.

(**c**) The dynamic test (the oscillation) now continues and the amplitude of the point of attachment is measured over five complete cycles. The results are listed in Table 4.

Cycle no., n	Amplitude, $A/10^{-3}$ m
0	50
1	36
2	26
3	19
4	13
5	10

Table 4 *Data for question 19*

What evidence is there that the damping is exponential – i.e. the amplitude decays exponentially with the number of cycles? State as many tests as you can for an exponential variation and apply one of these accurately.

(**d**) On a copy of Table 4, add a third column headed 'Stored energy at end of cycle' and fill in the values. The first entry should be your answer to (**a**).

(**e**) Compare the fractional decay in energy per cycle with the fractional decay in amplitude per cycle. Why do you think the energy decay rate is considerably greater?

(**f**) (**i**) What is the actual loss in energy in joules over the first cycle?
(**ii**) Assuming (again not quite correctly) that this damping loss takes place uniformly over the cycle, how much will have been lost over the first quarter cycle?

(**iii**) Use this value to re-calculate an answer to part (**b**) that takes account of damping.

(**g**) Assuming that the velocity found in (**b**) is not too different from the velocity of the point where the displacement was measured, what are (**i**) the average velocity over the first quarter cycle (remember it starts from rest), (**ii**) the time taken for this quarter cycle, (**iii**) the period, T, and (**iv**) the frequency, f? Does the frequency seem a sensible value? Does it relate to anything you know about earthquakes?

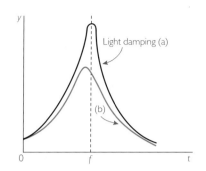

Figure 41 *Two frequency response curves (a) little damping (b) more damping*

Damping and resonance

Not only can damping make an oscillating system come to rest more quickly, it can also prevent it resonating quite so violently when driven at its natural frequency. A damped system will absorb energy and vibrate when driven (forced vibration) but, as you saw in Activities 10 and 12, the resonant vibrations will have a smaller amplitude and the increase in amplitude close to resonance will be 'spread' over a wider frequency range. See Figure 41.

Damping is therefore one way in which a building can be prevented from shaking itself to bits – even if the earthquake frequency happens to match the natural frequency of the building, it will not vibrate with such large amplitudes.

Components similar to the shock absorbers in cars, such as an oil-filled piston, can be incorporated into building design. The pistons move with the vibrations of the building, but are slowed by the oil. They absorb the energy of the seismic waves by converting it to heat. They have to be positioned in the building so that they link points that will move relative to each other during an earthquake (Figure 42(a)).

Other types of energy absorber may deform to absorb the energy, and will be replaced after the earthquake. For example, in the knee-bracing system shown in Figure 42(b) there is a large moment set up in links that deform, the energy is absorbed, and since the links are not structural the building is not affected. The links are replaced but the building is otherwise undamaged. Similarly, plastic hinges in the floors of buildings can allow movement without damage.

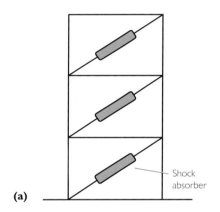

(**a**)

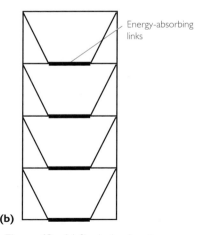

(**b**)

Figure 42 *(a) Shock absorbers in a building, (b) a knee-bracing system in a building*

3.2 *Other ways to reduce earthquake damage*

As well as avoiding resonance and incorporating some damping, there are other methods used by engineers to protect buildings and their occupants from vibrations. While the following information relates mainly to buildings and earthquakes, the same principles are used to prevent damage caused by vibrating machinery in factories and in vehicles.

Structural methods

Isolation

In this method the building is separated from the Earth in some way that prevents the vibrations being transmitted. In other words the structure is 'decoupled' from the ground. A very good example of such a structure is a ship. As water cannot transmit the horizontal components of the earthquake waves the ship will be unaffected.

Other possibilities include putting the building on rollers, or using a layer of sand, which would allow the building to slide. One type of construction uses sliders. If the structure can slide on the foundations, because of a low-friction interface, then the building will move and so will not suffer a shear force. But there can be problems with high winds causing movement. Also in an earthquake the building may move suddenly so that new vibrations caused by the sudden movement are set up in the structure. Connection of services such as gas, water and electricity would also be a problem. The movement could be in any direction, so the foundations on which the building moves would have to be large and extend in all directions. This could be reduced if the building were anchored with a weak link that would break when the force was large enough that the building needed to move or suffer damage.

Another type of isolation involves using bearings made mainly of rubber placed between the foundations and the building (Figure 43). Modern designs use steel and rubber laminated bearings that are strong enough to take the weight of the building (rubber alone would bulge outwards). The stiffness of the bearings is less than that of the ground and the building so the fundamental frequency of the whole structure is lower than that of the building on the ground, ensuring that an earthquake cannot set up vibrations at a resonance frequency.

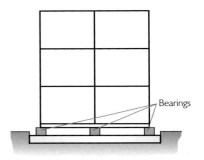

Figure 43 *A building mounted on bearings*

Active control

In this method, the idea is to have sensors measuring the movement and then using some feedback mechanism to move the building back to its equilibrium position. The principle is good but it is very difficult to realise in practice. The only buildings that have been tested are ones where the forces are due to the wind rather than to ground movement. Problems include: What happens if the sensors fail? How do you ensure they are reliable when needed? An earthquake may not happen for years after the building is completed.

Choice of materials

Every precaution must be taken to protect people from building collapse and the development of better building materials is one more weapon in the armoury.

Reinforced concrete design

Cracking is the main cause of failure. If important structural elements crack, the building may collapse. Reinforced concrete is concrete (which is strong in compression) containing steel bars or rods (which are strong in tension). If a concrete column has bars as shown in Figure 44 it will be strong if it is not moved, but in an earthquake the concrete will crack outside the steel links because there is nothing to hold it together. As it falls away the steel reinforcement is no longer held in position, so it can move and the column has lost its strength – often it will collapse. The links must be anchored to the centre of the column by concrete which is held in place by the links themselves (see Figure 45).

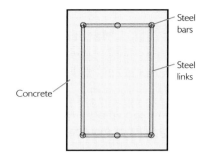

Figure 44 *Reinforced concrete for normal use*

Steel frames

Steel is a ductile material and will absorb energy while it is being deformed. In order to produce an earthquake-resistant building, the design must use this property. The design must ensure that there are no sections that are not ductile and that even in a major earthquake a brittle failure will not occur. Floors must always fail before columns so that a whole building will not collapse. There should be extra beams included so that the building will still stand if some fail. Figure 46 shows a braced steel frame design. There are some redundant parts of the structure. Buckling should occur first in the beams, and not in the diagonals or columns. This design includes energy-absorbing dampers.

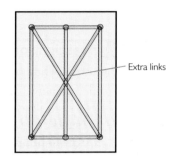

Figure 45 *Reinforced concrete for use in earthquake zones*

Polymers protecting people: a story of big vibrations

It's not only in earthquake zones that people suffer problems from the transmission of vibrations. Ever since the 1850s it has been recognised that the special properties of natural rubber enabled it to reduce the transmission of vibrations – and one man-made structure that is prone to vibrations is the bridge. Vibration problems occur both because of expansion and contraction of the bridge with changing temperature and because of passing road or rail traffic. It is not surprising, therefore, that as early as 1889 rubber was used to protect the railway viaduct in Melbourne, Australia, with a pad of rubber placed above each plinth to support the bridge deck and absorb impact and noise. In 1957 the Pelham Bridge in Lincoln became the first bridge in the UK to be built using a new type of rubber bearing. The bearing is made from alternating layers of steel and rubber that are securely bonded by chemical means during vulcanisation. This exhibits strength and stiffness in compression and softness in shear that easily absorbs vibration and movement in the bridge structure. Visitors to the parliament building in Wellington, New Zealand, are often shown the rubber bearings on which the building is mounted to protect it from earthquake damage.

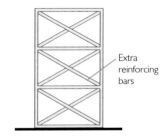

Figure 46 *A braced steel frame*

Often buildings in inner cities need to be protected from the low-frequency vibration caused by adjoining railways. In 1966 a new block of apartments, Albany Court, was built over St James Park Underground Station, London, and successfully used rubber bearings (the largest measuring only $60 \times 50 \times 28$ cm) to protect it from the ground-borne vibrations from the underground trains. There are now several hundred buildings using similar technology in London alone.

ACTIVITY **24** **Materials**

In the AS units *Good Enough to Eat* and *Spare Part Surgery*, you explored ductile and brittle materials. In a small group, discuss the following questions:

How would a structure behave in an earthquake if it were made entirely from materials that were (**i**) elastic, (**ii**) brittle, (**iii**) ductile?

What property is needed for earthquake-resistant building materials? How do you think reinforced concrete could be made so that it had this property?

Further **investigations**

Explore the use of vibration isolation within a hi-fi system.

3.3 Summing up part 3

This short part of the unit has been mainly revision. You have revisited the notion of damping and seen how damping affects resonance. You have seen various ways in which engineers design buildings to withstand earthquakes, and have related building design to your previous knowledge of materials.

Activity 25 draws on the work of this part of the unit, and also involves looking back at parts 1 and 2.

ACTIVITY **25** **Build a leisure centre**

A city in an earthquake-prone area requires a leisure centre that includes a cinema, bowling alley, swimming pool, gym and a supermarket. How would you design the centre to be earthquake resistant up to magnitude 6 on the Richter scale?

---

4 Vibration, noise and sound

In this part of the unit, attention turns from earthquakes to another source of vibrations – sound.

4.1 Sound sense

Neighbours from hell

There is evidence that people are becoming more concerned about noise; even homes with reasonably good sound insulation may not cope with modern stereos and other items that make life comfortable. We all make noise, but what is pleasurable noise to one person can be intolerable to another and destroy their quality of life (Figure 47).

Figure 47   *Neighbours from hell*

So what can you do if you really are faced with 'the neighbours from hell'? Obviously the first move should be to have a quiet word with them as they just may not have realised that they were disturbing you. Serious disputes with neighbours are best avoided as they can turn out to be acrimonious and very costly.

If, however, a quiet word doesn't help, your next move is to contact the Environmental Health Officer (EHO) at your Local Authority. The council has a duty to investigate your complaint and must take action if they are convinced that a 'statutory nuisance' exists – that the noise stops you from enjoying your property or is affecting your health.

You will need to prove that the noise is a statutory nuisance. You will be asked to keep a 'noise record sheet' over a period of at least 3 weeks and letters from other neighbours can be used to back up your complaint. If the council has noise-monitoring equipment, that may be left at your premises to collect evidence.

Although the volume of the sound, measured in decibels (dB), is important, there are other factors that are taken into account such as timing, frequency and the total number of hours for which the noise occurs.

At this point a letter will be sent to the person allegedly causing the complaint asking them to cooperate so that further action is not necessary.

If the action is to be taken further the EHO will make a maximum of three visits to witness the problem. If the EHO is convinced that a statutory nuisance exists then he or she will serve a noise abatement notice preventing your neighbour from continuing to make the noise or restricting it to certain times or days. If your neighbour does not comply the EHO could take them to court where they can be fined up to £2000 with a further £50 for each day on which the nuisance occurs after conviction.

Instead of involving the EHO you could apply direct to your local magistrate (sheriff court in Scotland) for a nuisance order which, if granted, will impose the same restrictions as the abatement order. Legal Aid is not available for nuisance cases but should you win the case you will be entitled to make a claim in court for costs. However, if your case does not succeed you will be liable for the defendant's costs.

The Noise Act 1996 gives EHOs additional powers to deal with loud noise from domestic premises at night, such as a riotous party. Offenders are liable to £100 on-the-spot fines and local authorities can confiscate noise-making equipment, such as a hi-fi, with the owner required to pay a fine and storage costs for its return.

Under the Environmental Protection Act EHOs can enter premises and disconnect a burglar alarm that keeps going off, and EHOs and police have the power to deactivate a car alarm if attempts to contact the owner have failed. Complaints about noisy neighbours are increasing. The most common causes are (in decreasing order):

- barking dogs and other animals
- doors banging
- loud hi-fi or TV
- shouting
- children
- cars and motorbikes
- DIY
- vacuum cleaners.

Environmental health officer

Justin Smith is an Environmental Health Officer with Wokingham Borough Council who tries to solve the problem of environmental noise pollution as part of his job.

With 10 GCSEs and A-levels in Chemistry, Biology and Sociology, Justin took a four-year sandwich degree in Environmental Health at King's College London. The degree is accredited by the Chartered Institute for Environmental Health (CIEH), who ensure that the course and the experience gained on the one-year work placement are sufficiently rigorous. Entry onto these degree courses typically requires one of your A-levels to be a science. Alternatively there are two-year MSc courses for those with different degree qualifications.

Justin is now a Graduate Member of the CIEH and a fully qualified Environmental Health Officer with a Certificate of Registration of the EHORB (Environmental Health Officers' Registration Board), which is the qualification recognised by employers and the government allowing the holder to practise as an EHO in the United Kingdom. To become a full member of the CIEH he will have to have at least two years' work experience and pass the CIEH professional examinations. He talked to us about his work.

> The job is very varied as all the cases are different and there's no one standing over you saying – 'Do that' – it all depends on what comes through on the phone. One day you're knocking on a door to say 'Turn down that noise', the next you're camped out in the middle of a new housing development taking noise readings.
>
> One of the good things about the job is that you get out and meet people and help them directly. You can see they're grateful as you're dealing with individual problems. You don't just deal with complaints about noise though. There's food safety, like a case of a mouse in a bottle of orange juice that the commercials team had recently.

Other areas that EHOs have to deal with are health and safety at work, pollution such as emissions from factories, reducing traffic pollution, and housing standards, especially in rented housing.

> We're working with The University of Reading at the moment to set up a 'Landlord Accreditation Scheme'. This will ensure minimum standards for student accommodation in the private sector. We also deal with licensing – not pubs, but public entertainment licences, animal welfare establishments such as kennels and pet shops, and body piercing and 'adult shops'.
>
> It certainly is varied. It takes a bit of a legal mind to understand the law and regulations for all of these areas, and it needs a bit of diplomacy to deal with the general public and sort out problems.

What exactly is noise?

The philosopher Bishop Berkeley posed the question 'If a tree falls in a forest and there's no one there to hear, does it still make a noise?'

Noise is perhaps best defined as unwanted sound. Sound is generated by vibrations that travel to the ear via some medium, typically air, at some finite speed. As you saw in the AS unit *The Sound of Music,* sound waves are mechanical, longitudinal, travelling waves. They transmit energy. The **intensity** or **energy flux** of a sound wave is defined as the rate at which energy crosses unit area; intensity has SI units of $W\,m^{-2}$.

The amplitude of a sound wave can be measured as a pressure, which has SI units of Pa. The human ear is sufficiently sensitive to notice a pressure change of 2×10^{-5} Pa (normal air pressure is about

Study note

This same definition is used for light and other radiation in the units *Technology in Space* and *Reach for the Stars.*

10^5 Pa). This corresponds to air molecules moving by less than 10^{-10} m, that is less than the diameter of an air molecule. The greater the amplitude of the wave, the greater the intensity of the sound. Just as the energy of an oscillator is proportional to the square of the amplitude (as you saw in part 2 of this unit), so is the intensity of a sound wave proportional to the square of its amplitude:

$$I \propto A^2 \tag{31}$$

The quietest audible sound corresponds to a sound intensity of about 10^{-12} W m^{-2}, whereas a thunderclap could be around 1 W m^{-2} (20 Pa) and a normal conversation around 10^{-6} W m^{-2} (2×10^{-2} Pa).

Intensity is not quite the same as our perception of the loudness of the sound, as our ears are more sensitive to some frequencies than others. Most people will perceive sounds of a few kHz as louder than other frequencies even though they may be receiving the same intensity of sound at their ears. Sound loudness (or, strictly speaking, sound pressure level) is typically measured on the decibel scale (dB) and the scale can be weighted so that the varying sensitivity of the ear is taken into account in the dB(A) scale. Table 5 lists some sounds with their rating on the dB scale.

Sound	Intensity/W m^{-2}	Pressure/Pa	Rating on dB scale
quietest audible sound	10^{-12}	2.0×10^{-5}	0 dB
ambient background in recording studio	10^{-10}	2.0×10^{-4}	20 dB
refrigerator humming at 2 m	10^{-8}	2.0×10^{-3}	40 dB
boiling kettle at 0.5 m	10^{-7}	6.3×10^{-3}	50 dB
normal conversation	10^{-6}	2.0×10^{-2}	60 dB
vacuum cleaner at 3 m	10^{-5}	6.3×10^{-2}	70 dB
heavy goods vehicle heard from pavement	10^{-3}	6.3×10^{-1}	90 dB
power lawn mower at operator's ear	10^{-3}	6.3×10^{-1}	90 dB
pneumatic drill at 5 m	10^{-2}	2.0×10^{0}	100 dB
thunderclap	1	2.0×10^{1}	120 dB
disco, 1 m in front of speaker	1	2.0×10^{1}	120 dB
pain threshold for continuous sound	10	6.3×10^{1}	130 dB
aircraft engine	10^{2}	2.0×10^{2}	140 dB
rifle	10^{5}	6.3×10^{3}	170 dB
Saturn rocket	10^{8}	2.0×10^{5}	200 dB

Table 5 *The dB scale for sounds*

Notice that, like the Richter scale, the dB scale is logarithmic, i.e. from 0 dB to 20 dB the sound intensity increases by a factor of 100, which is registered as 20 on the dB scale or 2 on the Bel scale ($100 = 10^2$). An increase of 10 dB will be perceived as a doubling of the loudness of the sound even though it's an increase of ten times the intensity.

ACTIVITY **26** **How loud does it sound?**

Connect a signal generator to a loudspeaker and monitor the amplitude via a cathode-ray oscilloscope (CRO). Turn the signal generator through a range of frequencies and, ensuring that the amplitude remains constant, make subjective judgements as to the range of frequencies over which you perceive the sound to be loudest. Then try also to produce a doubling of the *perceived* loudness of the sound and work out, from the CRO, the corresponding increase in sound intensity.

The dangers of noise pollution

Different types of people react to noise in different ways as it gets louder (Figure 48). Prolonged exposure to high levels of noise or exposure to peaks of noise of a very high level can cause hearing damage. There is a statutory requirement for employers to protect their workers from such exposure under the Noise at Work Regulations.

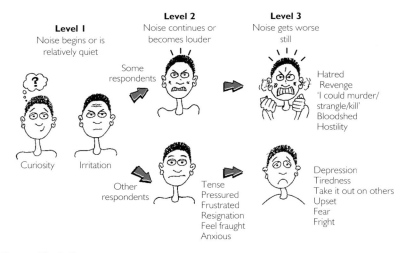

Figure 48 *Different responses to noise*

At work continuous noise levels above 90 dB pose a risk to hearing and employers must, by law, provide personal ear protection. For noise levels above 85 dB workers must be educated to understand the potential risk and employers must provide ear protection if requested.

Ear protectors typically reduce noise levels by 10 dB (i.e. they reduce the intensity by a factor of 10 and halve the perceived loudness). If provided, it is essential that ear protectors are worn at all times, as leaving them off for 10% of the time increases the energy received at the ear by a factor of ten and thus cancels out the benefit of wearing them for the rest of the time.

After exposure to loud noises you may have experienced a dullness in your hearing due to fatigue of the sensitive hair cells in your inner ear. Prolonged exposure leads to permanent hearing loss due to atrophy of the sensitive hair cell. You may experience a ringing in your ears (tinnitus), which is again due to temporary damage done to your ears, though the precise cause of the ringing sensation is not yet understood by scientists.

However, noise need not be loud to disturb activities such as conversation, relaxation or sleep and can cause emotional effects such as annoyance and tension. Research into people's psychological response to environmental noise has influenced the legislation, regulations, codes of practice and guidance from government departments that provide the framework for the control of environmental noise affecting people in their homes.

Psychoacoustic researchers claim to have found evidence of community noise exposure resulting in hypertension (high blood pressure), heart attack, low birthweight babies and psychiatric problems. The most convincing research results suggest that aircraft noise can reduce scholastic achievement.

ACTIVITY 27 **Noise survey**

Using a sound-pressure-level meter, undertake an Environmental Pollution Survey measuring the sound around a motorway, ringroad, factory, building site or similar location in which you can determine the way in which sounds 'drop off' with distance and the effects of mounds, barriers, fences or trees, etc. in absorbing the sound.

You could supplement your measurements by interviewing people who live or work in the locations you have surveyed.

Consider sharing your data with other schools or colleges via e-mail. This is particularly useful if you do not have a suitable site for your own investigation nearby.

QUESTIONS

20 Everyone's hearing becomes less sensitive with age, but exposure to loud noise makes the problem worse. On the graphs in Figure 49, a hearing level of 0 dB represents 'perfect' hearing. If someone's hearing level is −20 dB, a 60 dB sound seems only as loud to them as a 40 dB sound would seem to someone with no hearing loss. As 0 dB represents the faintest sound that can be detected by someone with perfect hearing, someone with a relative hearing level of −20 dB can only hear sounds louder than 20 dB.

(a) At age 40, what is the faintest sound at 2 kHz that can be heard by a person who has had prolonged exposure to 105 dB noise?

(b) What is the faintest 2 kHz sound the same person can hear at age 65?

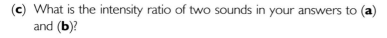

(**c**) What is the intensity ratio of two sounds in your answers to (**a**) and (**b**)?

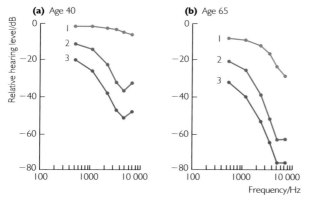

Figure 49 *Audiograms for people of different ages and noise exposures: (1) after no noise exposure; (2) after prolonged exposure to 96 dB; and (3) after prolonged exposure to 105 dB*

4.2 Sound control

Prevention, they say, is better than cure. Although it's not always possible to prevent noise entirely, the best way forward is to devise ways of reducing the effects of noise through sound insulation and through other means of control. In this section you will see how physics principles are exploited in the cause of noise control. You will also see how the science of acoustics is used to enhance our experience of sounds that we actually want to hear – in a concert hall, for example.

ACTIVITY 28 **Noise on the net**

Use the Internet to find out about the science of noise control. In particular, note the ways in which physics plays a part in this aspect of engineering.

A question and answer guide to acoustics, including sources of further information, is available at the Acoustical Society of America website

http://asa.aip.org/

Some potential architectural solutions to noise pollution are produced by Wylie Architects website

http://www.wylie-associates.com

Barriers and insulation

The planning system plays a major role in reducing noise at source; noise is often a consideration in determining the acceptability of planning applications. Similarly when the Highways Authority publishes details of proposed new roads the public has the right to object on any grounds, including noise, as a doubling of vehicle flow rate results in a 3 dB increase in noise levels. Barriers are often used around major roads to screen the noise. The problem here is that diffraction occurs over the barrier, which together with reflections from hard ground can result in reinforcement of the sound in some places. A second barrier parallel to the first can eliminate these interference effects.

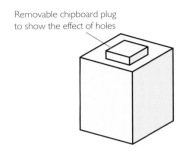

Removable chipboard plug to show the effect of holes

ACTIVITY 29 Sound insulation

Using a buzzer in a box (Figure 50) investigate a range of factors that might reduce the sound experienced outside the box. Try covering the walls with different insulating material, and try isolating the buzzer by supporting it in various ways.

NB Look at the spectrum of sound transmitted (compared with that emitted) as well as the intensity of sound. If it is available, the CD-ROM *Multimedia Sound* could be used to help your analysis.

As an extension, consider the effect of different thicknesses of material and the effect of holes in the box.

Alternatively a double glazing unit could be built into one face of the box and an investigation made of the effect of different gaps between the two sheets of glass on sound insulation.

Try to explain your results in terms of the properties of the materials you have used for insulation or isolation.

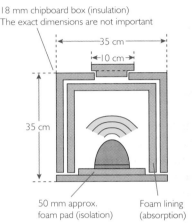

18 mm chipboard box (insulation)
The exact dimensions are not important

35 cm

10 cm

35 cm

50 mm approx. foam pad (isolation)

Foam lining (absorption)

Figure 50 *A buzzer in a box*

Designing for low-noise environments

Noise control engineers seek to design and construct economical and effective partitions for noise reduction. So far the main way of reducing noise pollution considered here has been by absorption of the airborne sound using porous or fibrous materials. This is very effective as the sound energy simply dissipates as heat.

A sound wave imparts additional kinetic energy to air molecules. Within a porous or fibrous material, the large surface area ensures that air molecules collide frequently with the material. If the material deforms plastically, the collisions are inelastic; energy is transferred to the material and causes a small amount of heating. The air molecules thus lose kinetic energy. In other words, the sound wave is absorbed rather than being reflected from the material or transmitted through it.

But sometimes a radio or TV in a ground floor room of one house can be heard in the upstairs bedroom of a neighbouring house because the wall itself is set into vibration by the sound waves. Vibration set up in the separating wall at ground level can even travel up the separating wall, then radiate into the upper floor rooms. This is known as 'flanking transmission'. It can occur when rooms adjoin either horizontally or vertically and often provides a serious addition to sound passing by the obvious path through the common wall or floor (Figure 51).

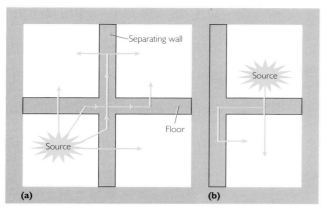 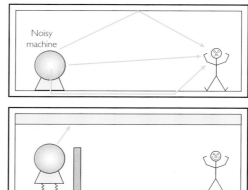

Figure 51 *Noise transmission through a building*

To insulate against flanking transmission of sound, walls and barriers need to have sufficient mass so that it is more difficult to set them into vibration. A single leaf barrier results in a 5 to 6 dB reduction in sound transmission per doubling of its mass. But this is expensive and may be inappropriate in such constructions as aircraft cockpits or TV studio partitions. A double (or even triple) leaf wall with flexible leaves can provide satisfactory insulation with much less mass than is needed in a single leaf wall because of the insulating properties of the air or other material between the leaves.

Rubber roads reduce noise

This development was reported *The Sunday Times*, 13 September 1998.

> What one action can both reduce the amount of non-biodegradable rubber waste and cut noise pollution from roads? Answer: Grinding up old car tyres and mixing the granules with the traditional aggregate and bitumen used to surface roads. 'Most traffic noise is due to tyres on roads and everyone knows that rubber absorbs vibration so this is the obvious step,' said Brian Hicks, business manager of road recycling at Colas, who are pioneering this technique. 'Results show that we can reduce traffic noise by 70%, which is great news for residents near the M3 who complain about the noise even though noise barriers have been put up.'

ACTIVITY **30** **Neighbourhood noise**

Either

design an information leaflet persuading people to be 'good neighbours' and explaining how sound can often transmit to unexpected places and how problems might be avoided by effective reduction of sound transmission,

Or

prepare a presentation that defends the location of a motorway, ringroad or factory on the basis of proposed sound reduction methods to be put in place.

Active noise control

When noise is a problem within a confined space (inside a building or a vehicle) then some ingenious engineering can reduce the problem. The trick of so-called **active noise control** is to exploit the superposition of waves, which you met in the AS unit *The Sound of Music*.

Noise control in a tractor cab

The following article is adapted from *Snippets* Winter 1987/8, which was produced with the help of AFRC Institute of Engineering Research (now part of Cranfield University).

Figure 52   *Tractor with cab*

At present, to protect tractor drivers from excessive noise, noise isolation enclosures are fitted to agricultural tractor cabs (Figure 52). When all the windows are closed the driver is effectively cut off from the outside world and modern tractor cabs can achieve levels as low as one tenth of the legal noise limit. However, the driver really needs to hear some external sounds, in particular those telling him about machinery performance, malfunctions and other warnings.

Now the possibility of using active noise control (ANC) techniques in tractor cabs is being investigated. An ANC system is one in which noise reduction is achieved by the introduction of additional noise. Sound field cancellation occurs because an exact replica of the waveform of an existing sound is generated but with its phase exactly opposite to the existing wave phase so that destructive interference occurs specifically in the area around the driver's head. This begs the question 'Where does all the energy go?' Of course, local areas of cancellation are balanced by other areas of reinforcement.

A system has been built that cancels noise at the driver's ears by feeding back antiphase signals to microphones mounted inside open back headphones. This system has achieved an average noise reduction of about 60%. A final version would use multiple speakers mounted inside the cab rather than headphones.

Advantages are that such a system would allow for cheap, open-structure cab designs and while steady engine noise would be cancelled, the driver could still hear unusual, changing noises outside the cab.

GEC Marconi-Avionics (now part of BAe systems) has developed an ANC system for aircraft to cut down the noise from turbine blades in the frequency range 50–500 Hz. Control microphone assemblies and loudspeaker assemblies are located in the aircraft trim. The system is controlled by a digital signal processor that generates a cancelling sound with amplitude and envelope matching the noise but phased shifted by 180°. Typical results of this can be seen in Figure 53. Active noise control has already been successfully applied to the exhaust from a diesel-driven tug boat, to lorry and motorcycle exhausts, to gas turbine exhausts, to ventilation duct noise and to cars and even refrigerator noise.

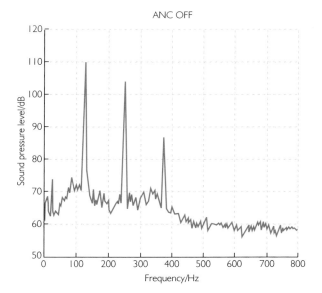

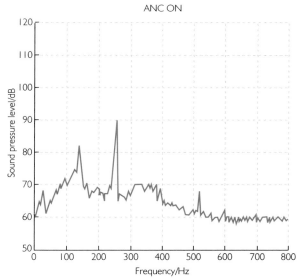

Figure 53 *Demonstrating the effects of active noise control*

Cancelling the noise

In a small group, discuss and answer the following questions referring to the article above. Include diagrams where they will clarify your answer.

1 Explain what is meant by the phrase 'an exact replica wave ... but with its phase exactly opposite to the existing wave phase'.

2 Explain how the superposition of two such waves results in noise cancellation. Where does the missing energy go?

3 Such a technique is often referred to as **negative feedback**. Explain the term negative feedback.

4 How is it envisaged that the system would operate?

5 Why is an ANC system not 100% effective?

Active noise control

It is possible to simulate (partially) an ANC system using two speakers connected to the same signal generator.

Place the speakers a couple of metres apart in the lab and walk across the room in front of them. Notice the regular variation of sound intensity as you move. Explain what you hear.

Place speakers in a box with a listening port where one would expect to find destructive interference. Note the effect of changing frequency on the production of destructive interference.

Magic walls

Scientists at Southampton's Institute of Sound and Vibration Research have taken up the challenge of developing an ANC system for use in homes. Bass notes from rock music are very effective in making walls vibrate like giant loudspeakers and disturb the neighbours. The researchers hope to cancel out the repetitive bass sounds by active control. The technology will use small strategically placed microphones to pick up the noise and loudspeakers to broadcast mirror images of the bass notes back into the room as antiphase signals. The antiphase sound waves will neutralise the neighbours' music so that just a faint rumble is heard. This is not simple interference, as that would merely result in large noise reduction in some locations at the expense of increased noise at other locations. The goal is to excite vibrations in the walls themselves that are equal in amplitude but opposite in phase to the primary source.

The system will be controlled by a microprocessor. The researchers are at present studying the acoustics of typical residential rooms in houses so that they can feed the information into a mathematical model. If the mathematical model suggests the technology will work in a room, the team will proceed with a prototype active control system. This is the first time that ANC technology has been applied to buildings.

Magic wallpaper

Going further down the same line of reasoning, it should be possible to create 'sound-cancelling wallpaper'. When a sound wave hits the wallpaper the wallpaper vibrates. This vibration could be picked up by a sensor that converts it to a tiny electric current. A microprocessor or simple electric circuit would then convert this current into its mirror image, which is then fed back to the wallpaper. The wallpaper vibrates in response to this signal and generates a sound wave that cancels the first. This idea is similar to the active suspension systems in cars and the active control of building vibration mentioned in part 3.

Smart materials

'Magic wallpaper' was reported in *Prism PRI* Issue 3 Autumn 1997. The same issue described some other interesting new materials that are being developed for vibration control.

- Skis made of a particular ceramic material can detect vibration as the skier passes over uneven snow. The mechanical energy is converted into electrical energy; this is dumped in the electrical circuit and thus reduces the vibrations. See the 'Active Control eXperts' website

    http://www.acx.com/cool_smartski.html

    and the company's work on shock absorbers for mountain bikes at

    http://www.acx.com/cool_smartshock.html

- 'Smart' baseball bats damp the vibrations produced by contact with a ball. See

  http://www.acx.com/cool_smartbat.html

- Embedding shape memory metals into a structure can change the structure's stiffness simply by the application of a voltage. The metal responds by taking up a particular shape that it has previously been 'trained' to adopt and this counteracts any vibration.

- Vibration in lightweight structures such as aircraft can be controlled by 'smart' piezoceramic crystals bonded to them. The crystals are actuated by an applied voltage and expand or contract accordingly, which will either induce or counteract bending.

Acoustics in concert halls

Sound is not always a problem. The following article, adapted from *Physics World* May 1997, described how principles of physics can be used to enhance our experience of listening to speech and music.

The most important characteristic of any concert hall must be the sound it delivers to the listener yet the Boston Symphony Hall (Figure 54), which opened in 1900, was the first to be designed with the science of acoustics in mind. It is now recognised as one of the best concert halls in the world.

For any performance the sound pulse that travels directly to the listener arrives first and has the largest amplitude. However, it is followed by several discrete reflections and their arrival times, amplitudes and directions of arrival depend on the geometry of the room. Sounds continue to arrive for some time and the total reverberation time is defined as the total time taken for the total sound amplitude to decrease by 60 dB (a factor of 10^6 in intensity). Wallice Sabine from Harvard University was first to discover the precise relationship between reverberation time and the sound absorption qualities and volume of the room. (He found that a human body absorbs sound equivalent to 1 square metre of open window. Based on his work, concert hall seats are upholstered so that they simulate the sound absorption of people so that the size of audience does not make much difference to the acoustics of the hall.)

Figure 54 *The Boston Symphony Hall*

The optimum reverberation time for any hall will depend on whether the source of sound is to be music, speech or some other type of performance. Speech requires much shorter reverberation times than music, for example, and high levels of reverberation time will cause successive sounds to blend into each other and, in extreme cases the music or speech can sound 'muddy'.

We now know that there is more to concert hall acoustics than simply achieving the correct reverberation time. Studies

Concert hall sounds in the laboratory

It is very difficult for people to compare the sound quality of two different concert halls because such intrinsically subjective judgements can be influenced by many different factors. Laboratory tests using simulated sound fields can help the listeners to reach more reliable judgements. This is because the sound field can be switched almost instantly, allowing a more precise comparison of different acoustic conditions.

There are two main ways of simulating sound fields in the lab, and both have their advantages and limitations. One method is to surround the listener with an array of loudspeakers. Each loudspeaker reproduces a different signal, and each signal contains one or more discrete reflections plus a reverberant decay. The amplitude, time of arrival and frequency content of each component in the signal can be precisely controlled using a variety of digital signal-processing devices. Changes to the sound field can be made almost instantaneously, allowing different sound fields to be compared. This type of experiment is performed in an "anechoic chamber", which has walls that absorb as much sound as possible (figure *a*). The simulated sound fields are not corrupted by reflections in the test room.

This method has the advantage that each parameter of the sound field can be precisely controlled, which allows researchers to assess the effect of varying a single acoustical parameter while the others are kept constant. Moreover, listeners are able to turn their heads, enabling them to more naturally consider how the direction of arrival might affect the sound. The main problem is that the realism of the reproduced sound fields is limited by the number of loudspeakers and independent signal channels that are used.

The other simulation method provides more realistic sound fields. This approach is based on "binaural simulation", which tries to recreate the same sounds at both ears of the listener as would be heard in a concert hall. This is achieved using an artificial head with two microphones fitted in the ears. The impulse response – the sound field created by a short burst of sound – is then recorded by both microphones and the responses are combined to give the binaural impulse response.

The binaural impulse response is measured at various positions in a concert hall. These responses are convolved with music that has been recorded in an anechoic room to simulate the sound of the music at different positions in the concert hall. The binaural impulse responses can also be edited to some extent, allowing the effects of certain acoustical parameters to be investigated.

The resulting sound fields can be reproduced through headphones or loudspeakers, although headphones can make it more difficult to identify the direction of the source of the sound. For example, sounds often appear to be located inside the listener's head, and sounds that originate in front of the listener can seem to come from behind.

Loudspeakers overcome this problem but introduce two new challenges. First, an anechoic chamber is needed to prevent the sound fields from becoming corrupted. Second, loudspeakers produce acoustic cross-talk: the left ear can hear sounds intended for the right ear and vice versa. Both of these problems can be overcome by using a loudspeaker configuration proposed by one of us (GS). In this set up the loudspeakers are placed close to the listener, avoiding the need for an anechoic room, and mechanical barriers are used to reduce cross-talk (figure *b*).

The key advantage of binaural simulation is that more realistic sound fields, as recorded in concert halls, can be generated. Its main drawback is that the control a researcher can have over the sound fields is more limited. The ideal solution is therefore to use both methods to explore fully the subjective effects of various acoustic measures. □

a

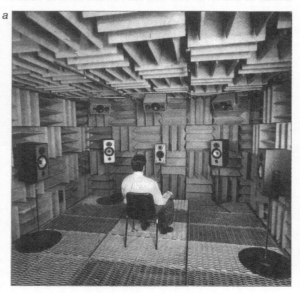

b

Figure 55 *Concert hall acoustic sounds in the laboratory*

in the 1950s showed that 'early reflections' are highly significant for sound quality.

Listeners combine the direct sound together with all the energy in the 50–80 ms after its arrival. Early reflections effectively reinforce the direct sound and therefore increase the clarity and definition of the room's acoustics.

The direction and time of arrival of specific reflections are determined by the geometry of the room. Most early concert halls, such as the Boston Symphony Hall, tend to be rectangular, but fan-shaped halls have gained in popularity because more people sit closer to the stage. In a rectangular hall the 'early reflections' tend to come from the side walls whereas in a fan-shaped hall they will come from the ceiling.

Michael Barron, then of Southampton University, found that the early reflections coming from the side walls increase a listener's sense of spaciousness. This increased sense of spaciousness provides two desirable effects: a stronger impression of being in an indoor space and an apparent widening of the source. It was soon accepted that strong early reflections from the side walls are a vital component in concert hall design and many designers incorporated large side-wall reflectors into new concert halls, which thereby allowed then to consider many new shapes.

During the 1990s Masayuki Morimoto at Kobe University in Japan found that the reason why there is an apparent widening of the source if early lateral reflections are stronger is because our hearing tends to combine these early reflections with the direct sound, and this gives a certain ambiguity to the position of the source.

Morimoto has also found that the listener can feel surrounded by the sound – now known as listener envelopment – if strong lateral reflections arrive at later times. This corroborates evidence that an increased sense of spaciousness was related to longer reverberation times because longer reverberation times would tend to correlate with increased reverberate (late-arriving) sound coming from the sides of the room. It would therefore seem that late-arriving lateral reflections could be more important than early reflections for generating a sense of spaciousness in concert halls.

Adequate spatial impression is essential for a concert hall to sound good. While modern design trends have encouraged strong early lateral reflections we now know that strong late-arriving lateral reflections are just as important. Strong early reflections cause an apparent widening of the source while strong late reflections improve the sense of listener envelopment.

The importance of late lateral reflections has implications beyond the design of concert halls. Developers of home entertainment systems are beginning to recognise that late lateral reflections are needed to recreate the concert-hall feeling of being immersed in sound. CD-quality 'surround sound' will be an integral part of digital high-definition television systems and this should allow both components of spatial impression to be improved in the home.

ACTIVITY 33 **Concert hall acoustics**

Figure 55, on p. 252 reproduces a short article from *Physics World* that accompanied the previous passage. Read the article and answer the following questions

1   What is the advantage of using laboratory-based sound field to test the subjective judgement of sound quality?

2   What is an anechoic chamber?

3   Describe briefly the two different ways of simulating sound field in a lab.

4   What are the advantages of each of these two techniques?

5   What are the disadvantages of the two techniques?

Further investigations

Reverberation time is typically measured as the time for a gun shot (or other sharp sound such as a hand clap) to die away to inaudibility. Investigate the reverberation times of different rooms e.g. hall, gym, rooms in house. Consider altering what is in the room (furniture, furnishings, people) to see how reverberation times change. If it is available, you could use the *Multimedia Sound* CD-ROM to produce graphs of the sound as it dies away.

Look at the advertising claims for 'surround sound' home entertainment systems and decide whether they are valid and based on good science.

4.3   *Summing up part 4*

This part of the unit has mainly involved revision of work from earlier in the unit and from elsewhere in the course. You have met another example of a logarithmic scale (the dB scale) and seen how an understanding of sound and vibrations, and a knowledge of properties of materials, can be applied to problems of noise control and concert-hall acoustics.

ACTIVITY 34 **Selling ANC systems**

Design a promotional leaflet to sell active noise control wallpaper. Explain in scientific terms how the system will work and consider the legal problems of disputes with neighbours, etc., as a reason for customers to buy it.

21 Double glazed windows consist of two glass sheets separated by a layer of air. The double glazing specification uses a code based on the thicknesses of the glass and the gap. For example, two panes of glass with thickness 6.0 mm, separated by an air gap of 12 mm, would be specified as 6-12-6 double glazing. Table 6 shows how sound insulation varies with frequency for two types of double glazing and a single pane of glass of 6.0 mm. The sound insulation, S, is measured in dB:

$$S = -10 \log_{10} \left(\frac{I_0}{I} \right) \text{ dB}$$

where I_0 is the intensity when there is no insulation and I the intensity when the insulation is in place. Higher values of S represent more noise reduction but a change of less than 3 dB is not detectable by the human ear.

Frequency, f/Hz	Sound insulation, S/dB		
	6-12-6 double glazing	6-200-6 double glazing	single pane 6 mm thick
100	21	32	22
125	27	35	22
160	27	38	23
200	23	40	24
250	25	42	25
315	28	43	26
400	29	45	27
500	31	46	29
630	32	47	30
800	33	48	31
1000	34	49	31

Table 6   *Insulation by windows*

(**a**) Plot a graph to show how sound insulation varies with frequency for 6-200-6 double glazing.

(**b**) On a TV advertisement for double glazing the effectiveness of the sound insulation was demonstrated by using machinery that produced noise at about 1 kHz. Comment on whether the demonstration could be misleading for a potential customer who wishes to insulate against the low-frequency rumbling noise of traffic.

(c) Figure 56 shows the variation with frequency of the sound insulation provided by a 6 mm thickness of glass.

  (i) From Figure 56 read off the value of sound insulation for a frequency of 350 Hz.

  (ii) Calculate the ratio $\left(\dfrac{I}{I_0}\right)$ produced by 6 mm glass for a frequency of 350 Hz.

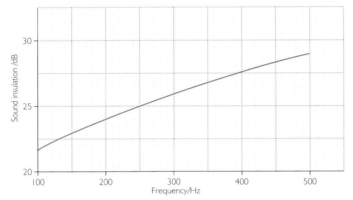

Figure 56 *Diagram for question 21*

5 *Rebuilding*

5.1 *Building up knowledge*

Having finished this unit you are now quite close to the end of your course. In this unit, you have revisited some earlier work on waves and material properties, and have also used ideas about forces and motion.

ACTIVITY 35 **Building on firm foundations**

Take time to have a thorough look at all the work you have done in this unit, and at all the related work in other parts of the course.

  Go back to Activities 2 and 3 from part 1 of this unit and extend your summaries so that they include the new things you have learned.

ACTIVITY 36 **Why SHM?**

Imagine you are designing a course of study for engineers. Write the prospectus entry that will persuade them that studying SHM will be of value to their future careers. Outline briefly what they will cover in each section and explain:

- why it is important to understand the fundamentals of SHM
- why it is important to know a building's natural frequency
- whether a large structure is likely to have a high or low natural frequency
- what could excite a building at low frequencies
- why is it useful to know about damping.

Bouncy castle

Many principles of physics can be illustrated through everyday situations and events. In a 'bouncy castle', a large pillow is kept inflated by means of an air pump while small children bounce around on it. This illustrates many aspects of the physics of oscillations and materials that you have covered in this unit, as well as principles from earlier in the course (such as forces and energy).

Imagine you have been asked to write an illustrated article for a newspaper or magazine about the physics of a bouncy castle. Draft a set of headings and notes, with diagrams, equations and order-of-magnitude calculations, showing some of the things that you could include in the article. Include clear statements of principles of physics and show how they are relevant to a bouncy castle.

5.2 Questions on the whole unit

QUESTIONS

22 An earthquake occurs at a point X on the surface of the Earth, shown in Figure 57. Draw the ray paths to show how the P waves and the S waves would travel within the Earth if (**a**) the Earth were completely liquid, (**b**) the Earth were completely solid, and (**c**) the Earth were solid with a liquid core starting halfway to the centre.

23 Domestic washing machines often incorporate washing, rinsing, spinning and drying. This question is about the spinning.

(**a**) The inner drum of the machine into which the clothes are placed has quite large holes in it. Explain carefully how, when the clothes are being spin-dried, the water gets from the clothes and out through the holes.

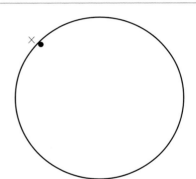

Figure 57 *Diagram for question 22*

(**b**) One of the spin speeds in one model of washing machine was listed as 1000 rpm (rpm stands for revolutions per minute).
 (**i**) What is this spin speed in radians per second?
 (**ii**) If the radius of the spinning drum is 12.5 cm, what would be the highest centripetal force that could be exerted on a wet sweatshirt of mass $m = 0.5\,\text{kg}$?

(**c**) If clothes are unevenly distributed in the machine, it vibrates slightly as it rotates. The outer drum within which the spinning drum rotates is attached to the rest of the framework of the washing machine by springs (Figure 58). What is the purpose of these springs?

(**d**) For each spring, the spring constant $k \approx 200\,\text{N}\,\text{m}^{-1}$. In use, the loading on each spring is effectively 5 kg. Explain, with the aid of a calculation, what is likely to happen when an unevenly loaded machine begins to spin the clothes.

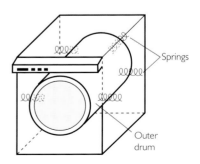

Figure 58 *Schematic diagram of a washing machine*

24 A very accurate method for monitoring the density of a liquid in many industrial processes involves filling a hollow U-tube with the liquid and then measuring the period of natural oscillations by making it resonate to an external variable frequency oscillator. (The arrangement is rather like a hollow tuning fork.) The period of oscillation T is given by

$$T = 2\pi\sqrt{\left(\frac{m + \rho V}{c}\right)}$$

where m is the mass of the empty tube of volume V, c is the elastic stiffness of the tube and ρ is the density of the liquid filling the tube.

For a particular tube, $m = 15 \times 10^{-3}$ kg and $V = 2.2 \times 10^{-6}$ m^3.

(a) The evacuated tube has a natural frequency of 800 Hz. What is the value of c, the elastic stiffness of the tube?

(b) The expression for T can be re-written as

$$T^2 = A\rho + B$$

What are (i) the algebraic expressions for A and B and (ii) their numerical values and SI units?

(c) A manufacturer of an instrument using this technique quotes only numerical values of A and B for calibration. Assuming frequencies are measured in Hz, why do you not need to ask the manufacturer what units are being used for B but you do for A?

(d) What is the frequency of oscillation when the tube is filled with a liquid of density 1.2×10^3 kg m^{-3}?

(e) A calibration graph is drawn of T^2 (y-axis) against density ρ.
(i) Express the gradient and intercept in terms of A and B.
(ii) Sketch the graph and explain the significance of the point where it crosses the y-axis.

(f) Explain how you could use the calibration graph to find ρ from a measurement of the resonant frequency of the tube.

5.3 *Achievements*

Now you have studied this unit you should be able to:

- recognise and use the expression for the speed of longitudinal waves in a solid $v = \sqrt{(E/\rho)}$ (where E is the Young modulus) (1.2, 2.3)*;

- recall that the condition for simple harmonic motion is $F = -kx$ and hence identify situations in which simple harmonic motion will occur (2.2);

- recognise and use the expressions $a = -\omega^2 x$ and $a = -A\omega^2 \cos \omega t$, $x = A \cos \omega t$, and $T = 2\pi/\omega$, as applied to a simple harmonic oscillator (2.2);

- recall that the total energy of an undamped simple harmonic system remains constant and recognise and use expressions for kinetic, potential and total energy of an oscillator (2.2);

- distinguish between free, damped and forced oscillations (3.1);

- recall how the amplitude of a forced oscillation changes at and around the natural frequency of a system and describe, qualitatively, how damping affects resonance (3.1);

- explain how damping and the plastic deformation of ductile materials reduce the amplitude of oscillation (3.1, 3.2);

- recall that the intensity of a sound wave is directly proportional to the square of its amplitude (4.1);

- explain why good absorbers of sound tend to be made of porous materials made up of small fibres or cells surrounded by air (4.2);

- explain how negative feedback and the principle of superposition are used to bring about active noise control (4.2).

*Numbers indicate the section(s) that relate to each achievement.

Answers

1   Distance $= 0.5 \times$ circumference $= \pi r$

$$time = \frac{distance}{speed} = \frac{\pi \times 6.378 \times 10^6 \, m}{6.5 \times 10^3 \, ms^{-1}}$$

$$= 3083 \, s$$

$$= 51 \text{ minutes (to the nearest minute)}.$$

(In fact the waves also travel through the Earth as well as around the surface, so they will arrive sooner than this. The waves in the crust will also gradually get smaller as energy is transferred to other forms, so in practice these surface waves will have little effect on the far side of the Earth.)

2   (a) Stress, $\sigma = \dfrac{force}{area} = \dfrac{F}{A}$

Strain $\varepsilon = \dfrac{extension}{original \ length} = \dfrac{x}{\ell}$

$$E = \frac{\sigma}{\varepsilon}$$

and so $\varepsilon = \dfrac{F/A}{E}$, hence

$$x = \frac{F\ell}{AE} = \frac{2 \times 10^{-3} \, kg \times 9.81 \, N \, kg^{-1} \times 10 \times 10^{-2} \, m}{\pi \times (3 \times 10^{-6} \, m)^2 \times 73.1 \times 10^9 \, N \, m^{-2}}$$

$$= 0.95 \times 10^{-3} \, m = 0.95 \, mm.$$

(b) Maximum mass, $m = $ tensile strength $\times \dfrac{A}{g}$

$$= \frac{1000 \times 10^6 \, N \, m^{-2} \times \pi \times (3 \times 10^{-6} \, m)^2}{9.81 \, N \, kg^{-1}}$$

$$= 2.9 \times 10^{-3} \, kg = 2.9 \, g.$$

3   (a) Increasing the elastic modulus appears to increases the wave speed. You can deduce this from various numbers in Table 1, e.g. a shear modulus of zero corresponds to a wave speed of zero; shale and sandstone have similar densities but the one with the larger bulk modulus has the larger P-wave speed.

(b) Increasing density appears to reduce the speed. For example sandstone and salt have the same bulk modulus; salt is less dense and has a higher wave speed.

4   The phenomenon is called refraction. The rays bend away from the normal and the wavelength increases. See Figure 59.

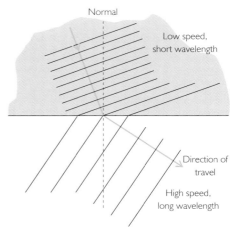

Figure 59 *The answer to question 4*

5   (a) (i) has travelled directly, (ii) has met the interface at an angle greater than the critical angle and undergone total internal reflection, and (iii) has been refracted into a deeper layer.

(b) The time of arrival of the waves will give information about the paths taken and so the depth of the Moho (or other boundaries between layers) can be found.

6   Refractive index, $\mu = \dfrac{v_1}{v_2}$

$$= \frac{velocity \ in \ mesosphere}{velocity \ in \ outer \ core}$$

From Figure 8, $\mu = \dfrac{13 \, km \, s^{-1}}{8 \, km \, s^{-1}} = 1.625$

Snell's law: $\mu = \dfrac{\sin i}{\sin r}$

$$\sin r = \frac{\sin i}{\mu} = \frac{\sin 30°}{1.625} = 0.3077$$

$$r = 17.9°$$

7   (a) The speed must increase with depth – the waves follow paths similar to that in Figure 3, only they curve gradually rather than changing direction abruptly.

(b) Density will increase with depth.

(c) On its own, an increase in density will produce a *reduction* in wave speed (see equation 1). To bring about an increase in speed the elastic modulus must also increase with depth, and the increase must outstrip the increase in density.

8   From the definition of the Richter scale, an earthquake of magnitude m has a displacement $x = 10^m \times 1.0 \, \mu m$. With $m = 5.2$,
$x = 10^{5.2} \times 1.0 \, \mu m = 1.58 \times 10^5 \times 10^{-6} \, m$
$= 0.158 \, m.$

9 (a) (i) From equation (6), max. speed occurs when $\sin \omega t = 1$, i.e.
$v = A\omega = 0.30\,\text{m} \times 5.0\,\text{s}^{-1} = 1.5\,\text{m s}^{-1}$.

(ii) $f = \dfrac{1}{T} = \dfrac{\omega}{2\pi} = \dfrac{5.0\,\text{s}^{-1}}{2\pi} = 0.80\,\text{Hz}$ (2 sig. fig).

(b) $\omega^2 = \dfrac{k}{m}$ so $k = m\omega^2 = 4.0\,\text{kg} \times (5.0\,\text{s}^{-1})^2 = 10\,\text{kg s}^{-2}$
$= 10\,\text{N m}^{-1}$.

(c) When $t = 0.20\,\text{s}$, $\omega t = 1\,\text{rad}$.
(i) $x = A\cos(1\,\text{rad}) = 0.16\,\text{m}$.
(ii) $a = -\omega^2 x = -(5.0\,\text{s}^{-1})^2 \times 0.16 = 4.0\,\text{m s}^{-2}$.

10 (a) (i) $v_{\text{max}} = A\omega$ (from equation 6) and $\omega = 2\pi f$ (from equation 13) so
$v_{\text{max}} = 2\pi f A = 2\pi \times 50 \times 10^3\,\text{s}^{-1} \times 10^{-6}\,\text{m} = 0.6\,\text{m s}^{-1}$

(ii) From equation (11), $a_{\text{max}} = \omega^2 A$
$= (2\pi \times 50 \times 10^3\,\text{s}^{-1})^2 \times 2 \times 10^{-6}\,\text{m} = 2 \times 10^5\,\text{m s}^{-2}$

(b) $a \approx 2 \times 10^4\,g$. The peak force will be 20 000 times the weight of an oscillating part – so the material needs to withstand a high stress.

(c) Since $a_{\text{max}} = \omega^2 A = (2\pi f)^2 A$, the acceleration (and hence the internal stresses) is proportional to frequency squared.

11 (a) (i) From Figure 60, there is an unbalanced force of magnitude $F_x = mg\sin\theta$ acting on the mass along the direction marked x. If θ is small, $\sin\theta \approx \theta$ in radians $\approx \dfrac{x}{\ell}$. Hence $F_x \approx \dfrac{mgx}{\ell}$ when θ is small. There is therefore a restoring force that is proportional to displacement, i.e. the resulting motion is SHM. Since $a = \dfrac{F}{m}$, along the direction x we have $a_x = \dfrac{gx}{\ell}$. From equation (11), $\omega^2 = \dfrac{a}{x}$ so we can identify $\omega^2 = \dfrac{g}{\ell}$.

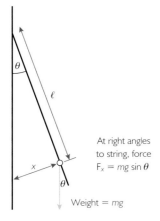

At right angles to string, force $F_x = mg\sin\theta$

Weight $= mg$

Figure 60 *Diagram for the answer to question 11(a)*

(ii) From equation (12), $T = \dfrac{2\pi}{\omega} = 2\pi\sqrt{\dfrac{\ell}{g}}$

(b) For $f = 1\,\text{Hz}$, $T = 1\,\text{s}$. From the answer above,
$\ell = \dfrac{gT}{4\pi^2} = \dfrac{9.81\,\text{m s}^{-2} \times 1\,\text{s}}{4\pi^2} = 0.25\,\text{m}$.

12 (a) From worked example,
$k = 50\,\text{N m}^{-1}$, $A = 3.0 \times 10^{-2}\,\text{m}$.
$E_{\text{tot}} = \tfrac{1}{2}kA^2$
$= \tfrac{1}{2} \times 50\,\text{N m}^{-1} \times (3.0 \times 10^{-2}\,\text{m})^2$
$= 2.25 \times 10^{-2}\,\text{J}$.
$m = 0.1\,\text{kg}$, $\omega = 22.36\,\text{s}^{-1}$
$E_{\text{tot}} = \tfrac{1}{2}m\,\omega^2 A^2$
$= \tfrac{1}{2} \times 0.1\,\text{kg} \times (22.36\,\text{s})^2 \times (3.0 \times 10^{-2}\,\text{m})^2$
$= 2.25 \times 10^{-2}\,\text{J}$.

(b) From question 9, $k = 10\,\text{N m}^{-1}$, $A = 0.30\,\text{m}$, $m = 4.0\,\text{kg}$, $\omega = 5.0\,\text{s}^{-1}$.
$E_{\text{tot}} = \tfrac{1}{2}kA^2 = \tfrac{1}{2} \times 10\,\text{N m}^{-1} \times (0.30\,\text{m})^2 = 0.45\,\text{J}$
$E_{\text{tot}} = \tfrac{1}{2}m\omega^2 A^2 = \tfrac{1}{2}4.0\,\text{kg} \times (5.0\,\text{s}^{-1}) \times (0.30\,\text{m})^2$
$= 0.45\,\text{J}$.

13 (a) $E_p = \tfrac{1}{2}k\,x^2 = \tfrac{1}{2} \times 1.0 \times 10^2\,\text{N m}^{-2} \times (0.15\,\text{m})^2 = 1.1\,\text{J}$

(b) Assuming that the energy transfer to the missile is 100% efficient, i.e. that E_k gained $= E_p$ lost by catapult:
$\tfrac{1}{2}m\,v^2 = 1.1\,\text{J}$
$v = \sqrt{\left(\dfrac{2 \times 1.1\,\text{J}}{2.0 \times 10^{-3}\,\text{kg}}\right)} = 34\,\text{m s}^{-1}$.

(c) $\tfrac{1}{2}m\,v^2 = \tfrac{1}{2}k\,x^2$ so $v = x\sqrt{\dfrac{k}{m}}$.

(d) (i) Since $v \propto x$, the speed is one-third that in (b), i.e. $11\,\text{m s}^{-1}$

(ii) $v \propto \dfrac{1}{\sqrt{m}}$ so multiplying m by a factor of two will lead to
v being divided by $\sqrt{2}$, i.e. $v = \dfrac{34\,\text{m s}^{-1}}{\sqrt{2}} = 24\,\text{m s}^{-1}$.

14 Speed $= \dfrac{2 \times \text{length of bar}}{\text{time taken}} = \dfrac{1.40\,\text{m}}{(347 \times 10^{-6}\,\text{s})}$
$= 4.03 \times 10^3\,\text{ms}^{-1}$.

15 (a) The Young modulus of oak must be significantly greater than that of pine – despite oak having a higher density, it also has a higher wave speed. Similarly, metals in general have higher Young moduli than woods – their wave speeds are higher despite their higher densities.

(b) From equation (1), $E = \rho v^2$.
(i) Pine: $E = 500\,\text{kg m}^{-3} \times (3313\,\text{m s}^{-1})^2$
$= 5.49 \times 10^9\,\text{N m}^{-2}$.
(ii) Copper: $E = 8933\,\text{kg m}^{-3} \times (3650\,\text{m s}^{-1})^2$
$= 1.19 \times 10^{11}\,\text{N m}^{-2}$.

16 (a) From section 2.2, $f = \frac{1}{2\pi}\sqrt{\frac{k}{m}}$ so

$k_{horiz} = m \times (2\pi f) = 40 \times 10^3\,kg \times (2\pi \times 0.60\,Hz)^2$
$= 5.7 \times 10^5\,N\,m^{-1}$.

(b) (i) $k \propto f$, so
$k_{vert} = k_{horiz} \times \left(\frac{10\,Hz}{0.60\,Hz}\right)^2 = 1.6 \times 10^8\,N\,m^{-1}$

(ii) Compression $\Delta h = \frac{F}{k}$. $F = mg$, so

$\Delta h = \frac{40 \times 10^3\,kg \times 9.81\,N\,kg^{-1}}{1.6 \times 10^8\,N\,m^{-1}}$
$= 2.5 \times 10^{-3}\,m$ (2.5 mm).

(c) (i) Use equation (12): $a = -\omega^2 x$, where $\omega = 2\pi f$.

$x = \frac{a}{(2\pi f)^2}$ (dropping the minus as we are only
interested in size, not direction)

$x = \frac{12\,m\,s^{-2}}{(2\pi \times 3.0\,Hz)^2} = 3.4 \times 10^{-2}\,m$

(ii) If the amplitude scales up by a factor 3, then it will
be 0.1 m – which would be alarming.

17 (a) Linear dimensions are all multiplied by 3, so volume
(and hence mass) will be multiplied by 27.
Actual mass = 27×40 tonne = 1080 t.

(b) As f depends on the ratio $\frac{k}{m}$, stiffness would also have to
be multiplied by 27.

(c) Horizontal oscillations will increase in amplitude as you
go up the building, but the vertical amplitude will remain
more or less constant with height. Any building is under
vertical compression because of its weight (largest stress
at the bottom); with vertical oscillations the acceleration
will increase and decrease this compressive stress, but
will be unlikely to put materials under tension (when
they are more likely to fail).

18 (a) We need to find $f = \frac{1}{T}$, where $T = 2\pi\sqrt{\frac{m}{k}}$. The

suspended mass is unknown – but it is not needed. Let
the mass be m and its weight mg.
Force extending spring $F = mg$.
Extension $x = 0.20\,m$.
So $k = \frac{F}{x} = \frac{mg}{x}$

Hence $\frac{m}{k} = \frac{x}{g}$ and we have $T = 2\pi\sqrt{\frac{x}{g}}$

$f_{spring} = \frac{1}{2\pi} \times \sqrt{\frac{g}{x}} = \frac{1}{2\pi} \times \sqrt{\frac{9.81\,m\,s^{-2}}{0.20\,m}} = 1.1\,Hz$.

(b) The overall length $\ell = 0.80\,m$. From question 11,

$T = 2\pi\sqrt{\frac{\ell}{g}}$.

$f_{pend} = \frac{1}{2\pi} \times \sqrt{\frac{g}{\ell}} = \frac{1}{2\pi} \times \sqrt{\frac{9.81\,m\,s^{-2}}{0.80\,m}} = 0.56\,Hz$.

(c) $\frac{f_{spring}}{f_{pend}} = 2 : 1$

Both frequencies are proportional to $\frac{1}{\sqrt{length}}$. The

lengths are in a ratio 4 : 1 so the frequencies must be in
the ratio $\sqrt{4} : \sqrt{1}$, i.e. 2 : 1.

(d) There are two spring oscillations to every pendulum
oscillation. Starting off a spring oscillation can gradually
set off a pendulum oscillation so that one complete
spring cycle takes place in half a pendulum cycle. The
system gradually switches from one kind of oscillation to
the other – and then back again. It can be thought of as
a kind of resonance, but where the frequencies are in
the ratio 2 : 1 and it is not clear which is the driving
system and which the driven.

19 (a) Use $E_p = \frac{1}{2}Fx$
$= \frac{1}{2} \times 1.0 \times 10^5\,N \times 50 \times 10^{-3}\,m = 2.5 \times 10^3\,J$.

(b) Assuming that $E_p = E_k = \frac{1}{2}mv^2$,

$v = \sqrt{\frac{2E_p}{m}} = \sqrt{\frac{2 \times 2.5 \times 10^3\,J}{5.5 \times 10^5\,kg}} = 0.95\,m\,s^{-1}$.

(c) The decay is exponential. You could use any of the
following tests: constant half-life; equal fractions (of A) in
equal times; a graph of $\log(A)$ against n is linear.

(d) See Table 7.

Cycle no., n	Amplitude A/ 10^{-3} m	Stored energy at end of cycle/J
0	50	2500
1	36	1300
2	26	680
3	19	360
4	13	170
5	10	100

Table 7 *The answer to question 19(d)*

(e) Fractions lost are: energy, 0.48; amplitude, 0.28.
The energy decreases by a larger fraction because
energy is proportional to the square of the amplitude
(e.g. if amplitude halves, energy falls to one-quarter of
its initial value).

(f) (i) 1200 J,

(ii) 300 J over $\frac{1}{4}$ cycle

(iii) The kinetic energy as the tower passes through its
mid point is thus $2.2 \times 10^3\,J$. Using the same method
as in (a), this gives $v = 0.89\,m\,s^{-1}$.

(g) (i) $v_{av} = \dfrac{0.89\,\text{m s}^{-1}}{2} = 0.45\,\text{m s}^{-1}$

(ii) Displacement $x = 50 \times 10^{-3}\,\text{m}$, so

$\dfrac{T}{4} = \dfrac{x}{v_{av}} = \dfrac{50 \times 10^{-3}\,\text{m}}{0.45\,\text{m s}^{-1}} = 0.11\,\text{s}$

(iii) $T = 0.44\,\text{s}$

(iv) $f = \dfrac{1}{T} = \dfrac{1}{0.44\,\text{s}} = 2.3\,\text{Hz}$

You could probably imagine a tower oscillating at around this frequency – it is not implausible and it is within the range of earthquake frequencies.

20 (a) 40 dB

(b) 60 dB

(c) From Table 5, an increase of 20 dB corresponds to a change of intensity of $10^2\,\text{W m}^{-2}$, so the ratio is 100.

21 (a) See Figure 61.

(b) From part (a) and from Table 6, insulation seems to be better at higher frequencies, so insulation from low-frequency traffic noise would be less good than that demonstrated with noise at 1 kHz.

(c) (i) At 350 Hz, $S \approx 26.7\,\text{dB}$

(ii) Rearranging the expression for S $\left(\text{and taking care with signs – remember that } \log\left(\dfrac{a}{b}\right) = -\log\left(\dfrac{b}{a}\right)\right)$:

$S = -10 \log_{10}\left(\dfrac{I_0}{I}\right)$

$\log\left(\dfrac{I}{I_0}\right) = \dfrac{+S}{10} = 2.67$

$\dfrac{I}{I_0} = 10^{2.67} = \text{antilog}_{10}(2.67) = 468.$

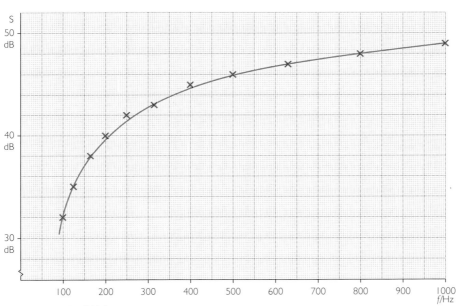

Figure 61   *The answer to question 21(a)*

REACH FOR THE STARS

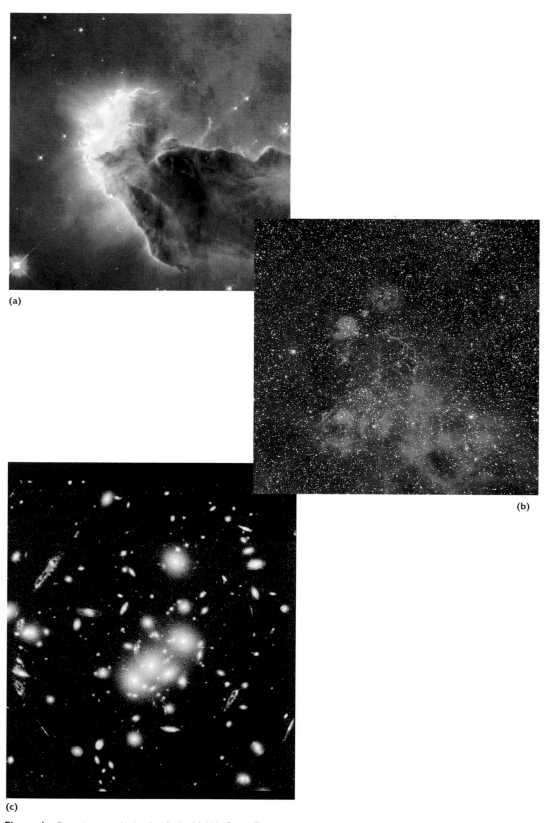

(a)

(b)

(c)

Figure I *Some images obtained with the Hubble Space Telescope in the late 1990s: (a) the Eagle nebula, a region where stars are forming; (b) a supernova remnant, the exploded remains of a 'dead' star; (c) some of the most distant galaxies yet observed*

Why a unit called Reach for the Stars?

Ever since humans with modern brains have walked the planet, they've been doing cosmology – asking themselves questions about their ultimate origins: how the world came into being, and what will happen to it – but it's only in the 20th century AD that science has been able to tackle such questions. And the pace of discovery has been astounding. Half-way through the 20th century, the physicist Hermann Bondi said: 'there are only two-and-a-half facts in cosmology'. Now we have experimental and observational evidence (Figure 1) to support our own myths of creation. And we can even begin to speculate on almost unimaginable questions like the existence of other universes.

This unit will show how physics has helped modern day cosmologists unlock some of the secrets of the Universe and its origins: What makes stars shine? Do black holes exist? Is the Universe infinite?

Overview of physics principles and techniques

In this unit, you will study several areas of physics that relate to astronomy and cosmology. You will learn about the behaviour of light that enables astronomers to interpret observations of distant objects, the nuclear reactions that power the stars, the use of radioactivity to date rocks that make up our planet, the ideas about molecules that help us to understand how stars form, and about the gravitational forces that keep stars and planets in their orbits and will determine the ultimate fate of the Universe. This unit will also give you several opportunities to look back over your work from previous units and to review your knowledge and understanding.

In this unit you will extend your knowledge of

- motion in a circle from *Probing the Heart of Matter*;

- energy and work from *Higher, Faster, Stronger*, and from *Transport on Track* and *Probing the Heart of Matter*;

- radiation from *Technology in Space* and *The Medium is the Message*;

- radioactivity and nuclear reactions from *Digging Up the Past* and *Probing the Heart of Matter*;

- waves from *The Sound of Music, Spare Part Surgery* and *Build or Bust?*

- inverse square law fields from *Probing the Heart of Matter*.

1 In the beginning

1.1 Big questions

As the following two passages show, **cosmology** (the study of the Universe) is an ancient science, which today is still probing some of the deepest questions about the origins and future of the Universe.

AD 1200, India

As he watched from the rock beside the River Indus, the sky shifted through a kaleidoscope of colours, from blood red, to rich velvet, to inky black. Then, out of the darkness popped a single white dot. Soon the whole sky was studded with bright points of light, twinkling at him.

On such occasions, Vishnor's mind was full of mysterious questions: How did all of this get here? His friends were no help, they just laughed at him. So, as in all matters of wisdom, he turned to one of the great Indian legends for an answer:

> Some foolish men declare that a Creator made the world. The doctrine that the world was created is ill-advised, and should be rejected. If God created the world, where was He before creation? How could God have made the world without any raw material? If you say He made this first, and then the world, you are faced with an endless regression. Know that the world is uncreated, as time itself is, without beginning and end.

Extract from *The Mahapurana the Great Legend*

AD 1999, Yorkshire, England

One kilometre below the Earth's surface, and David Davidge was sweating more than ever. He was making his way through the mine tunnel, towards the experiment control room. The air was a roasting 50 °C, and the bare rock felt hot to the touch. Not really an obvious place for a group of physicists to go looking for clues to the fate of the Universe.

'Could we really find those strange, elusive particles, known only as **dark matter**?' he mused. 'The consequences were mind-blowing. We might actually know what would happen to the whole Universe in the distant future. Would it go on forever? Or collapse again in a titanic fireball, like the one that created it?'

Certainly down here, the team had a good chance of detecting the particles. All other radiation should get absorbed by the rocks above him. But dark matter was so hard to pick up. The particles – whatever they were – hardly interacted with a damn thing. They passed through virtually anything, as though it weren't there. And instruments that were sensitive enough to detect dark matter were still beyond current technology. But as everyone said, just give it a few more years ...

David Davidge is a 2nd year PhD student at Imperial College, London. He talked about his work.

> People think you have to be a genius to work in an area like mine. It's not true. You just gradually learn to think in certain ways. If you'd told me 10 years ago I would be doing this now, I wouldn't have believed you.
>
> What first got me excited about cosmology was reading books like Stephen Hawking's *A Brief History of Time*. The Universe sounded such a bizarre, alien place. I wanted to understand it, to get closer to the truth. As I studied physics through school and university, I felt I was getting closer, towards the limit of what was known. Then I opted to do astronomy and cosmology in my last year. The concepts were making sense to me now.
>
> Getting onto the dark matter project happened by chance. It seems such an important area of research, and I thought I could help. I love the work. It can be frustrating working on such a long, difficult project, but every so often there's a breakthrough, and then it makes me think we can do it.

You will find out more about the search for dark matter later in the unit. You will also learn about other aspects of astronomy and cosmology, as illustrated in Figures 1(c) and 2. These pictures show how modern instruments are helping to probe the mysteries of the

Figure 2 *Hubble Space Telescope (HST) image of a possible planet*

Universe. To the naked eye, the picture in Figure 1(c) would be a faint speck of light, probably too faint to see. The Hubble telescope reveals that it is a cluster of galaxies, made of hundreds of galaxies, each containing perhaps hundreds of billions of stars. Figure 2 shows what might be a possible planet outside our solar system. The planet is the faint object in the lower left. If there are other planets, then perhaps life exists elsewhere in the Universe.

Study note

Note that in scientific usage a billion is defined to be 10^9 – an 'American' billion.

2 *Our nearest star*

2.1 *The Sun*

Worked example

Q Which is the star nearest to Earth?

A No, it's not Proxima Centauri, a faint star in the constellation Centaurus and second closest to Earth. The answer is the Sun.

An old joke, but it is still easy to trick people with this question. Because the Sun looks so different from anything else in the sky we sometimes forget that it is really a star. In fact the Sun is a very ordinary, average-sized typical star. Compared with the billions of other stars in the Universe there is nothing special about it – but it is very much closer to Earth.

Proxima Centauri is a distance of 4.24 light years from Earth. A **light year** is the distance light travels in a vacuum in one year. The average distance between the Earth and the Sun is 1.50×10^{11} m.

ACTIVITY 1 **Into the Sun**

Use the Internet to research some information about the Sun. In particular, look for information about space missions and telescopes that are studying physics processes and conditions in the Sun.

Study note

This activity should help remind you about aspects of the AS unit *Technology in Space*, and help you to look ahead to later sections of this unit.

QUESTIONS

1 (a) How long does it take light to travel from the Sun to Earth, given that light travels at $3.00 \times 10^8 \, \text{m s}^{-1}$?

(b) Calculate the distance to the Sun in light years, given that 1 year $= 3.16 \times 10^7$ s.

(c) Calculate the ratio $\dfrac{d_{pc}}{d_{sun}}$, where

d_{pc} = distance from Earth to Proxima Centauri
d_{sun} = distance from Earth to the Sun

Then express your answer as an order of magnitude – that is, state the nearest power of ten ($10, \ldots 10^4, 10^5, 10^6, \ldots$).

Because the Sun is so close to Earth it is the star we are best placed to study, and so our detailed study of stars begins here. But first a word of caution before you start any activities involving the Sun. Many of the early scientists who studied the Sun lost their sight by staring directly at the Sun.

There are various ways to image the Sun safely; these will be explained in the activities later in this unit.

Brightness and distance

The reason that the Sun appears so much brighter than the other stars is because it is so much closer. As you move closer to the source of any radiation the radiation becomes more intense. This is because the radiation is spreading out in all directions, so the amount that will land on you will become less as you move away. As you blow up a balloon the rubber gets thinner and thinner – the radiation gets weaker and weaker in the same way. Figure 3 shows that if you double the distance from a star, then the area over which the radiation is spread is multiplied by four; if you multiply the distance by three, then the area is multiplied by nine.

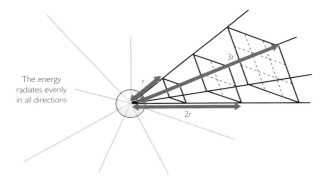

The energy radiates evenly in all directions

Figure 3   *Radiation spreads out as it travels*

Figure 3 shows that the **energy flux, *F*** or **intensity, *I*** of the radiation must obey an **inverse square law**.

An inverse square law is one in which two quantities (say x and y) are related by an equation of the type

$$y = \frac{\text{constant}}{x^2}$$

Energy flux is the rate at which energy is transferred across unit area square-on to the light beam. Energy flux is not quite the same as observed brightness, since the brightness we observe depends only on the visible component of the radiation, whereas energy flux refers to the whole electromagnetic spectrum. Think of this page. If you increase the radiation hitting the page it will appear to be more brightly lit, won't it? It will if the increased radiation is in the visible spectrum. But we have to remember that most of the electromagnetic spectrum is invisible to us. For example, if the page was illuminated with X-rays we wouldn't detect them with our eyes, even though the actual radiant energy flux might be quite large.

Study note

You met the idea of energy flux in the AS unit *Technology in Space*.

The **luminosity**, **L**, of a radiation source (such as a star) is defined as the rate at which the source radiates energy – the total energy it loses every second. The SI unit of luminosity is the watt. You may like to think of luminosity as being a measure of how bright a star really is, as opposed to how bright it appears from Earth.

Energy flux is related to luminosity – the brighter a star, the greater the energy flux at a given distance. F is proportional to L. However, we must allow for the distance, d, to the star. Figure 4 shows a star at the centre of an imaginary sphere of radius d.

The radiation emitted from the star in one second will spread out so that it is shared evenly over the surface of the sphere. Travelling at a steady speed, if it is not absorbed or scattered *en route*, the radiation will pass through the imaginary sphere in one second in such a way that

$$\text{flux} = \frac{\text{total energy emitted from source per second}}{\text{surface area of sphere}}$$

$$F = \frac{L}{4\pi d^2} \tag{1}$$

Equation (1) is important. It expresses the inverse square law for energy flux, and enables us to calculate the luminosity of a star if we can measure its radiant energy flux at Earth and its distance.

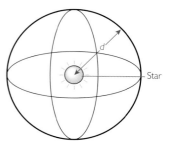

Figure 4   *Radiation from a star*

QUESTIONS

2 The Sun is the main source of energy for all of the planets in the solar system. By calculating the radiant flux energy at a planet we can begin to have some idea of the environmental conditions on that planet. Table 1 shows the distance to the Sun from various planets.

Planet	Distance from Sun/10^9 m
Mercury	57.9
Venus	108.2
Earth	149.6
Mars	227.9
Pluto	5900

Table 1   *Distances to planets from the Sun*

(**a**) For each planet in Table 1, calculate the ratio $F_{\text{planet}}/F_{\text{Earth}}$, where F_{Earth} is the energy flux at Earth and F_{planet} is the energy flux at the planet in question. (Hint, use equation (1). You don't need to know the Sun's luminosity L because when you calculate the ratio it cancels.)

(**b**) How will the radiant energy flux from the Sun affect the temperature on each planet?

(**c**) What other factors do you think might affect the temperature on the surface of a planet?

3 In the 17th century Christiaan Huygens (Figure 5) worked out the approximate distance to the star Sirius by the 'faintness means farness' principle. He made a small hole in the blackened window of a dark room and adjusted the opening until the beam of sunlight appeared to match the brightness of the star as he remembered it. He then measured the diameter of his hole (D_a) and the apparent diameter of the Sun (D_s) as it appeared at the window. He found that the hole had a diameter $D_s/26\,644$. Since the brightness of the beam, depends on the area of the light beam he then reasoned that

$$\frac{F_{Sir}}{F_{Sun}} = \frac{\text{area of aperture}}{\text{apparent area of Sun}} = \frac{1}{(26\,644)^2}$$

(**a**) Huygens assumed that Sirius and the Sun were equally luminous. Use his assumption and equation (1) to calculate, as he did, the ratio of distances from the Earth, d_{Sir}/d_{Sun}

(**b**) In question 1 you calculated the distance to the Sun as 1.58×10^{-5} light years. Given that Sirius's true distance is about 8 light years, calculate the real ratio d_{Sir}/d_{Sun}.

(**c**) Compare your answers from parts (**a**) and (**b**). At a time when no-one had any idea how far it was to the stars, Huygens's work was brilliant, but not above criticism. Suggest an explanation for his result being so far out, and criticise his experimental technique.

Figure 5 *Christiaan Huygens*

Luminosity and temperature

As was clear from the answer to question 3, stars do not all have the same luminosity. One factor that affects luminosity is the star's size; a large star will emit more radiation from its surface than a small star. But the other key factor is temperature. As you will see in Activity 2, temperature affects both the luminosity and the colour of a radiation source. Because stars other than the Sun are so far away and faint it can be difficult to see that they are coloured. It is much easier to see their colours using binoculars or using a

Figure 6 *A 'true colour' photograph of part of the sky above the South Pole*

telescope to gather more light (or by looking at photographs such as Figure 6). However, most people can see the differences in colour when they look carefully at some of the brighter stars. In part 3 of this unit you will be looking at the constellation Orion. Even with the naked eye it is possible to see that Betelgeuse, one of the brightest stars in the constellation, has a red colour, whereas Sirius is blue-white.

In Activity 2 you will see that as objects get hotter they go from emitting invisible (infrared) radiation to emitting red, orange, yellow and white light; the hotter the whiter. Also as the body gets hotter the intensity of the radiation increases; the hotter the brighter. You might argue that red objects are not necessarily red hot – an object, such as a pillar box, will appear red if it is illuminated because it reflects red light. But a red hot object glows red in the dark because of the light that it emits. This radiation given off from a body because of its temperature (which is determined by the thermal motion of its constituent atoms and molecules) is called **black body radiation**. A body does not have to be black to emit black body radiation – the term distinguishes bodies that are emitting radiation because they are hot from those that are coloured by dyes and paints. A perfectly black body will glow orange, red or white if you get it hot enough.

Figure 7 shows how the distribution of radiation (in other words, the **spectrum**) emitted from a black body varies as the body's temperature rises. The curves all have the same sort of shape but, as you observed in Activity 2, the intensity of the radiation increases dramatically as the temperature rises. Notice, too, that the position of the maximum shifts to shorter wavelengths.

Study note

In section 3.3 you will see how molecular motion is related to temperature.

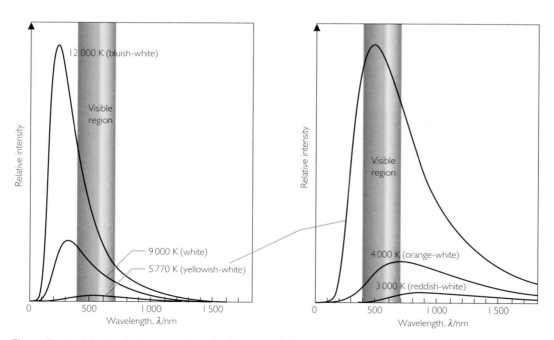

Figure 7 *Black body radiation curves. Note the different vertical scales*

ACTIVITY 2   Colour, luminosity and temperature

Switch on an electric heater or a laboratory radiant heater in a dimly lit room and observe the change in its appearance as it gets hotter. Notice in particular the changes in colour and in brightness.

What is happening? Discuss your observations with other students. There is a transfer of energy to the heating element, so it gets hotter. But why do we see what we do? And why does the element eventually stop getting hotter, even though energy is still being transferred to it at roughly the same rate?

Compare the colour and brightness of the electric heater with some hotter objects: e.g. a candle flame, a tungsten filament in a light bulb and the Sun. Use Figure 7 to help you estimate very roughly the temperature of these objects. (Remember not to look directly at the Sun.)

QUESTIONS

4 Predict the colour of (**a**) a very hot star that has a surface temperature of 10 000 K; (**b**) a giant star with a surface temperature of about 2700 K

5 You will be learning about different types of stars in part 3. But based on their names alone, put the following types of star in order of increasing temperature: red giant, white dwarf, brown dwarf.

Luminosity, flux and distance

Equation (1) describes how the radiant energy flux from a source depends on the distance to the source and its luminosity. If we know (or assume) the luminosity of a star and measure its energy flux, then we can calculate its distance – or, knowing the distance, we can calculate its luminosity. As you will see in part 3, it is quite easy to deduce a star's luminosity from its visual appearance, and so equation (1) underlies most methods of determining stellar distances.

A very simple way to measure the radiant energy flux, using an oil spot on a piece of paper, was devised by Robert Bunsen (1811–1899) in the middle of the 19th century. Ordinary paper becomes extremely translucent when it is made greasy, so it is easily lit from behind. If a piece of paper is held in front of a lamp, any oil spots show up brightly. However, if the paper is also being lit from the observer's side, the ordinary white paper is bright. Bunsen made the assumption that if the oil spot and the paper in such a situation appeared to be of equal brightness, then the radiant energy flux falling on the front and the back of the paper were equal.

In Activity 4 you will use Bunsen's method to find the Sun's luminosity. The essence of the experiment is very simple. You need a clear sunny day to carry it out. A piece of paper, dotted with oil, is held between a lamp and an observer. The lamp illuminates the oil from below while the Sun illuminates the paper from above (see Figure 8). The distance between the paper and the lamp is adjusted until the paper and the oil spot appear equally bright.

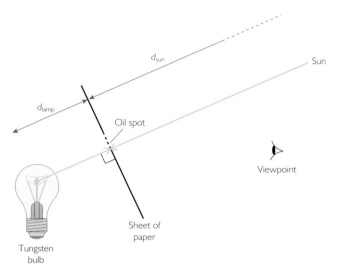

Figure 8 *Bunsen's method of measuring luminosity*

We know that

$$F_{\text{Sun}} = F_{\text{lamp}}$$

where F refers to the radiant energy flux on the paper. From equation (1):

$$\frac{L_{\text{Sun}}}{4\pi d^2{}_{\text{Sun}}} = \frac{L_{\text{lamp}}}{4\pi d^2{}_{\text{lamp}}}$$

which can be rearranged to find L_{Sun} if the other quantities are known.

ACTIVITY **3**   **The distance to the Sun**

In Activity 4, you need to use a known value of the distance to the Sun in order to measure its luminosity. With a partner, discuss how you think this distance might have been measured.

ACTIVITY **4**   **The Sun's luminosity**

Using Bunsen's method, determine the Sun's luminosity. You will need to know the distance to the Sun: $d_{\text{Sun}} = 1.50 \times 10^{11}$ m.

Your measurement will be subject to experimental uncertainty, and your calculation of luminosity is based on several assumptions. Try to think what these assumptions are, and suggest how you might correct for them.

Size and distance

It is difficult to imagine the vastness of the Sun. We know that it is much further away than the Moon, but appears to be just about the same size as we observe it from Earth – in other words it has a very similar **angular diameter**. The Moon is at a distance of about 3.85×10^8 m from Earth. The Sun is approximately 400 times further away than the Moon – but it is much bigger. Figure 9 shows how angular diameter is defined; the ratio of actual diameter to distance defines the angle α, measured in radians, that the object subtends at the observer. Angular diameters and angular separations are used quite a lot by astronomers, since they can be measured directly, unlike true sizes and separations.

$$\alpha/\text{radians} = \frac{D}{d} \qquad (2)$$

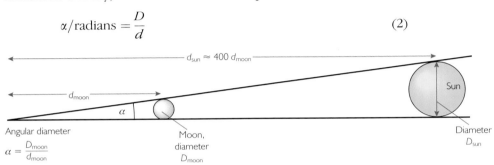

Angular diameter

$\alpha = \dfrac{D_{moon}}{d_{moon}}$

Moon, diameter D_{moon}

$d_{sun} \approx 400\, d_{moon}$

Sun

Diameter D_{sun}

Figure 9 *The Sun and Moon have similar angular diameters*

Unlike the Earth, the Sun doesn't have a solid surface. When we talk about the 'surface' of the Sun we usually mean the edge of the ball of light we see. This is the photosphere – a layer of extremely hot gases that emit most of the Sun's electromagnetic radiation. The photosphere has a diameter of 1.4×10^9 m. The Sun's outer atmosphere, the corona, extends out into space sometimes by more than twice the radius of the photosphere, and the flares that erupt from the surface of the Sun arch in loops bigger than the Earth (Figure 10). We can only observe the solar corona during a total eclipse, when light from the photosphere is blocked by the Moon.

It is relatively easy to measure the angular diameter of the Sun's photosphere. In Activity 5, you do this using a pinhole camera. It works best with a big camera so that the image of the Sun can be measured accurately.

Maths reference

Degrees and radians
See Maths note 6.1
The small angle approximations
See Maths note 6.6
Angular units
See Maths note 6.7

(a)

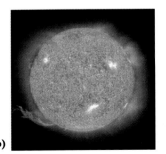

(b)

Figure 10 *(a) The solar corona, showing the inner streamer belt along the Sun's equator. The field of view in this coronagraph encompasses 8.4 million kilometres of the inner heliosphere. (b) A solar flare arches above the photosphere.*

ACTIVITY 5 **Measuring the Sun and Moon**

Use a large pinhole camera to measure the angular size of the Sun as shown in Figure 11 and use an 'eclipse' method to measure the angular diameter of the Moon (Figure 12). Compare your two results.

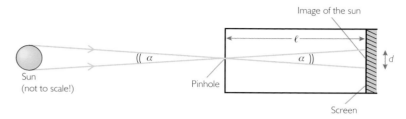

Figure 11 *Measuring the angular diameter of the Sun*

Figure 12 *Measuring the angular diameter of the Moon*

QUESTIONS

For these questions, you will need to use information from the paragraphs above.

6 Calculate the approximate angular diameters, in radians, of the Sun and Moon as observed from Earth.

7 The Earth has a radius of about 6.4×10^3 km. Calculate the volumes of the Earth and Sun. To the nearest order of magnitude, how many Earth volumes would fit into the Sun?

8 According to 'Windows on the Universe' (http://www.windows. engin.umich.edu/Windows2.html) each square centimetre of solar surface emits as much light as a 6000 W lamp. Check this claim by calculation.
(Use $L_{Sun} = 3.84 \times 10^{26}$ W.)

2.2 How old is the solar system?

According to the Bible, and most other creation stories, the first thing that God made was the Sun. Without the Sun there can be no life as we know it. The Sun was worshipped by many civilisations (Figure 13). The Chinese appointed special astronomers to predict the times of eclipses. This meant that when the eclipse occurred the people were ready to make lots of noise and frighten off the dragon they believed was attacking the Sun. The job of forecasting eclipses was felt to be so crucial that when two astronomers failed in their duty, and an eclipse occurred without warning, the astronomers were executed. Feelings ran high about the Sun in western Europe, too. When Galileo first observed spots on the 'immaculate' Sun the church leaders were so shocked that they questioned Galileo's sanity rather than entertain the possibility that the Sun could be 'blemished'.

Human beings have always been interested in where we came from, and where we are going. All civilisations and cultures have stories that explain our place in the history of the world, and the Universe. Because the Sun is so obviously crucial to our life, there has always been a great deal of speculation and thought concerning the age of the Sun (Figure 14). We can't imagine that life began before the Sun shone on the Earth, and we know that if the Sun ceases to shine, life as we know it will come to an end.

Figure 13 *A Mayan Sun temple*

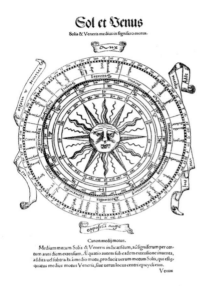

Figure 14 *Mediaeval picture of the Sun*

ACTIVITY 6   **The Sun in history**

Use the Internet to find out what your ancestors may have been told about the Sun. The Stanford Solar Center website contains a wealth of information about the Sun's folklore of many cultures:

http://solar-center.stanford.edu/folklore/folklore.html

Some 19th century theologians worked out the date of creation by counting back the generations to Adam and Eve (if the Bible is taken literally, Adam and Eve were created in the same week as the Sun). This made the Sun around 10 000 years old. However, during the 19th century more and more scientists became convinced that life on Earth developed from extremely simple organisms by the process of evolution. The idea of evolution is now well established – we can observe changes in populations of insects as environmental conditions change. But these changes are very small, and they occur slowly over many generations. If we assume that in the past evolution changed species at the same slow pace we can see that life on Earth must be much more than 10 000 years old. It must have taken millions of years to develop the complex organisms we observe on Earth today if life began as simple replicating molecules. If the Sun had to shine to begin life, the Sun must be older.

Geologists nowadays can determine the relative ages of rocks back to about 600 million years before the present. (During this time many shelly fossils first appear in sedimentary rocks.) If the development of life depends on the Sun, then the Sun must be more than 600 million years old.

In 1796 the French scientist Pierre Simon Laplace suggested that the whole solar system formed from one large rotating cloud of gas and dust, now known as the solar nebula. Most of the material contracted to form the Sun, but other fragments condensed ultimately to form the planets (Figure 15). Since Laplace proposed his idea, powerful telescopes have allowed us to observe discs of matter surrounding young stars, making the solar nebula theory widely accepted. (Figure 2 showed the next stage on – a possible planet.) This gives us another possibility for dating the Sun – if we can find some of the rocks that condensed while the Sun was forming, and if we can date them, then we can date the Sun.

Figure 15 *Artist's impression of the formation of the Sun and planets*

Isotopes

If we want to find out where a rock has come from we might study the minerals, the fossils or the basic elements present in the rock. However, we may need to look more closely to find out the **isotopes** of the elements present. Isotopes of an element are atoms that are chemically identical, but have different masses. They contain exactly the same number of protons in the nucleus of the atom. Neutral isotopes must therefore contain the same number of electrons, so they have the same chemical properties. Isotopes differ only in the number of neutrons in the nucleus of the atoms, hence they have very slightly different masses. Only using special equipment, which measures the mass of individual atoms (a mass spectrometer), can we tell isotopes apart. By analysing the atoms in a rock according to mass we can determine the relative proportions of each isotope in the rock. This gives us a clue to the origin of the rock.

When we refer to different isotopes of an element we add the **nucleon number** to the name of the element. The nucleon number is the total number of protons and neutrons in the nucleus of the atom. (Protons and neutrons are collectively known as **nucleons**.) For example, oxygen exists on the Earth as several stable isotopes: oxygen-16, oxygen-17 and oxygen-18. Chemically identical, all these isotopes have eight protons in their nuclei; they each have a **proton number** 8 (the proton number is also known as the **atomic number**). Oxygen-16, or $^{16}_{8}O$ as it is written, contains 16 nucleons of which eight are protons; this means that there are $16 - 8 = 8$ neutrons in the nucleus. Similarly, $^{17}_{8}O$ contains nine neutrons, and $^{18}_{8}O$ contains ten neutrons (see Figure 16). Table 2 (on p. 282) lists the symbols for chemical elements and their proton numbers. Note that hydrogen, $^{1}_{1}H$, is simply a proton, and so it is sometimes represented by the symbol p.

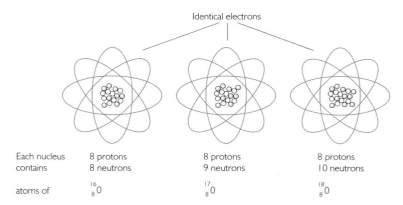

| Each nucleus contains | 8 protons 8 neutrons | 8 protons 9 neutrons | 8 protons 10 neutrons |
| atoms of | $^{16}_{8}O$ | $^{17}_{8}O$ | $^{18}_{8}O$ |

Figure 16 *Schematic representations of oxygen isotopes*

Since masses of atoms and nuclei are sometimes expressed as multiples of the proton mass, and since protons and neutrons have virtually the same mass, the nucleon number is also called the **mass number**.

By measuring the oxygen isotope compositions in different rocks we find that rocks, the atmosphere and the water on the Earth have oxygen isotope compositions that tell us that they formed from the same kind of original material.

What about rocks that were not formed on the Earth? Meteorites are simply extraterrestrial lumps of rock that land on Earth. They may be made of rock, metal, or a mixture of both. For dating the solar system the most important meteorites to study are those known as carbonaceous chondrites (Figure 17). These meteorites have chemical compositions very similar to that of the Sun, leading us to suspect that they have the composition of the solar nebula. Carbonaceous chondrites are relatively unaltered by processes that have affected other planetary matter. Their oxygen isotope compositions are very different from those measured on materials from Earth. We can thus be certain that they formed in a different part of the solar nebula.

Study note

You might recall some of these ideas from GCSE or from the AS unit *Digging Up the Past*.

Proton number	Name	Chemical symbol	Proton number	Name	Chemical symbol
1	hydrogen	H	54	xenon	Xe
2	helium	He	55	caesium	Cs
3	lithium	Li	56	barium	Ba
4	beryllium	Be	57	lanthanum	La
5	boron	B	58	cerium	Ce
6	carbon	C	59	praseodymium	Pr
7	nitrogen	N	60	neodymium	Nd
8	oxygen	O	61	promethium	Pm
9	fluorine	F	62	samarium	Sm
10	neon	Ne	63	europium	Eu
11	sodium	Na	64	gadolinium	Gd
12	magnesium	Mg	65	terbium	Tb
13	aluminium	Al	66	dysprosium	Dy
14	silicon	Si	67	holmium	Ho
15	phosphorus	P	68	erbium	Er
16	sulfur	S	69	thulium	Tm
17	chlorine	Cl	70	ytterbium	Yb
18	argon	Ar	71	lutetium	Lu
19	potassium	K	72	hafnium	Hf
20	calcium	Ca	73	tantalum	Ta
21	scandium	Sc	74	tungsten	W
22	titanium	Ti	75	rhenium	Re
23	vanadium	V	76	osmium	Os
24	chromium	Cr	77	iridium	Ir
25	manganese	Mn	78	platinum	Pt
26	iron	Fe	79	gold	Au
27	cobalt	Co	80	mercury	Hg
28	nickel	Ni	81	thallium	Tl
29	copper	Cu	82	lead	Pb
30	zinc	Zn	83	bismuth	Bi
31	gallium	Ga	84	polonium	Po
32	germanium	Ge	85	astatine	At
33	arsenic	As	86	radon	Rn
34	selenium	Se	87	francium	Fr
35	bromine	Br	88	radium	Ra
36	krypton	Kr	89	actinium	Ac
37	rubidium	Rb	90	thorium	Th
38	strontium	Sr	91	protoactinium	Pa
39	yttrium	Y	92	uranium	U
40	zirconium	Zr	93	neptunium	Np
41	niobium	Nb	94	plutonium	Pu
42	molybdenum	Mo	95	americium	Am
43	technetium	Tc	96	curium	Cm
44	ruthenium	Ru	97	berkelium	Bk
45	rhodium	Rh	98	californium	Cf
46	palladium	Pd	99	einsteinium	Es
47	silver	Ag	100	fermium	Fm
48	cadmium	Cd	101	mendelevium	Md
49	indium	In	102	nobelium	No
50	tin	Sn	103	lawrencium	Lr
51	antimony	Sb	104	unnilquadium	Unq
52	tellurium	Te	105	unnilpentium	Unp
53	iodine				

Table 2   *The chemical elements, their symbols and their proton numbers*

Figure 17 *A layer from a larger carbonaceous chondrite meteorite seen under a microscope*

Radioactive decay

Not all isotopes of an element are stable. Take carbon, for example. Much of the material that makes up your body is based on chains of carbon atoms, the vast majority of which are stable, carbon-12, atoms. However, an unstable version of carbon, carbon-14, which is chemically identical to carbon-12, also forms a tiny percentage of the carbon in your body.

How are carbon-12 and carbon-14 different? Both contain six protons, but carbon-14 contains two extra neutrons compared with carbon-12. This makes its nucleus unstable. There are too many neutrons for the nucleus to stay together for ever, and it will rearrange itself to become more stable. The nucleus converts a neutron into a proton plus an electron, flinging out the electron from the nucleus at high speed, accompanied by an antineutrino. This changes the nucleus into that of another element – one that has one more proton and one less neutron than the original carbon-14 nucleus. This is the element with a proton number $6 + 1$, i.e. it is nitrogen, $^{14}_{7}N$ (Figure 18). Using the convention that an electron has a proton number of -1 (i.e. its charge is equal and opposite to the proton's), we can write this reaction using symbols:

$$^{14}_{6}C \rightarrow \, ^{14}_{7}N + \, ^{0}_{-1}e^{-} + \bar{\nu}_e$$

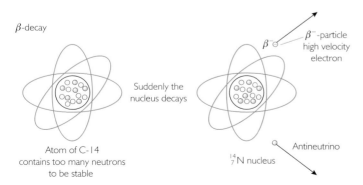

β-decay

Suddenly the nucleus decays

β^{-}-particle
high velocity
electron

β^{-}

$^{14}_{7}N$ nucleus

Antineutrino

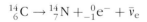

Atom of C-14
contains too many neutrons
to be stable

Figure 18 *Radioactive β^{-} decay of carbon-14*

The atom changes from one element to another. For example, when carbon-14 decays it becomes nitrogen, with all the usual chemical properties of nitrogen and none of the properties of carbon. Notice that the total electric charge (proton number) is unchanged by the reaction (you can check this by adding up the subscripts on the right- and left-hand sides). The electrons that orbit the nucleus of the decaying atoms are disturbed during the decay, then settle back into orbit around the new, **daughter nucleus**. The total nucleon number is also unchanged, as shown by the superscripts on the right- and left-hand sides.

The high-speed electron ejected from the nucleus is known as a beta-minus particle (β^-), and the whole reaction is one example of the process called **beta-minus decay** (or often simply beta decay). The high-speed electron travels at almost the speed of light, and has enough energy to ionise atoms it encounters, knocking out some of their electrons. The release of energy that accompanies radioactive decay is vast compared with energies involved in chemical reactions.

The decay of carbon-14 is of enormous scientific interest because it allows us to date plant- or animal-derived materials. Living plants absorb carbon-14 from the air. Once they die the carbon-14 concentration falls as the carbon-14 decays. By measuring the carbon-14 concentrations we can estimate the age of organic matter.

Beta-minus decay is one type of **radioactive decay**, a general name for processes in which nuclei rearrange themselves to become more stable by emitting a particle that has high enough energy to cause ionisation.

There is also a process known as **beta-plus decay**, which involves the emission of a positron and a neutrino while a proton in the nucleus turns into a neutron. The positron is symbolised $_{+1}^{0}e$; perhaps confusingly, it has a proton number of +1 because it has a positive charge, but the nucleon number of 0 shows that it is definitely not a proton – it is not a nucleon. The same result is produced if one of the orbiting electrons is captured by the nucleus and combines with a proton to produce a neutron.

A carbon-14 nucleus is unstable because it contains too many neutrons. Many more massive nuclei are unstable because they contain too many protons. Such nuclei become more stable by **alpha decay** in which they emit an alpha particle (α), which consists of two neutrons and two protons (and is identical to a helium nucleus). Uranium-238 is one example of an alpha emitter. The equation for the alpha decay of uranium-238 is

$$_{92}^{238}\text{U} \rightarrow {}_{90}^{234}\text{Th} + {}_{2}^{4}\text{He}$$

See Figure 19. Again, notice that the total electric charge and nucleon number are each conserved.

Study note

You used charge conservation in the unit *Probing the Heart of Matter*.

Study note

You read about carbon-14 and other dating techniques in the AS unit *Digging Up the Past*.

Study note

You met the positron, neutrinos and antineutrinos, and their symbols, in the unit *Probing the Heart of Matter*.

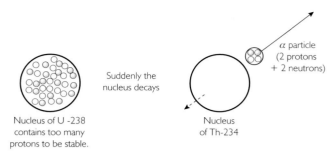

Figure 19 *Radioactive alpha decay of uranium-238*

The third main type of radioactive decay is **gamma decay**, in which a nucleus becomes more stable by emitting a photon of gamma radiation. Gamma radiation is very high energy electromagnetic radiation. In common with all electromagnetic radiation it travels at a speed of 3.00×10^8 m s^{-1} in a vacuum. Gamma radiation has a very short wavelength (about 10^{-14} m or less); each photon carries a large amount of energy and is very penetrating. In gamma decay, there is no change to the proton number or neutron number, just a loss of energy from the nucleus. Gamma emissions usually accompany alpha or beta decay, because these decays often produce a new nucleus which is in an excited state.

Alpha, beta and gamma emissions all cause ionisation of air and other materials through which they pass. This ionisation can be very dangerous to life. If the atoms of a living organism become ionised, electrons are disturbed and chemical bonds are disrupted. Biochemistry, the chemistry of life, depends on precise chemical reactions. Ionisation can cause things to go badly wrong. Large doses of radiation cause death very quickly but even tiny doses can damage the DNA in replicating cells so that the cells cannot replicate correctly and become cancerous. We are always surrounded by very low level radiation from naturally occurring rocks and cosmic rays, but we should avoid any unnecessary extra exposure to ionising radiations. Pay particular attention to the safety instructions when carrying out experiments involving radioactivity.

ACTIVITY **7** **Properties of α, β and γ radiation**

Investigate the properties of α, β and γ radiation using sealed lab sources. They can all be detected with a suitably adjusted Geiger–Müller (GM) tube with a scaler/ratemeter. Use paper, aluminium foils of different thicknesses and lead of different thicknesses to investigate how easy it is to stop each type of radiation. Send a stream of α, β and γ radiation through a strong magnetic field and observe any deflection.

  Safety
Before attempting this activity, make sure that you know the safety precautions you must follow when using radioactive materials.

Cloud chambers are designed to show the tracks of ionising radiation (Figure 20). Rather like miniature versions of the vapour trails we see in the sky when jets fly high overhead, the tracks form as droplets condense in a supersaturated vapour. Radioactive emissions ionise air and this causes the vapour to condense, so the vapour trails show the particles' tracks.

Figure 20 *Tracks in a cloud chamber*

ACTIVITY 8 Using a cloud chamber

Set up the cloud chamber according to the manufacturer's instructions. Take care to observe correct radiation protection procedures. Using information from Activity 7 (Table A7.1 on the Activity Sheet), decide which type of radiation will produce the thickest tracks.

Watch the tracks appear and answer the following questions.

- Can you predict where or when a track will form?
- Are all the tracks the same length?

QUESTIONS

9 Carbon dating, by measuring carbon-14 concentrations, is a valuable tool in archaeology. Why couldn't it be used to date the Earth or the Sun?

10 The core of the Earth is heated by the energy released by the radioactive decay of naturally occurring isotopes. The most significant of these are uranium-235, uranium-238, thorium-232 and potassium-40. For each of these isotopes write its abbreviated symbol, including the nucleon and proton numbers, and state the number of neutrons in the nucleus.

> **11** One of the radioactive decay processes commonly used for dating rocks is the decay of $^{87}_{37}$Rb to form $^{87}_{38}$Sr. What type of decay has occurred? Write a full, balanced equation to show the decay process.
>
> **12** What is the difference between a helium atom and an alpha particle?

Time to go

The minerals we find in rocks originally crystallised when the rock was molten. Like all crystals, minerals crystallise with a fairly precise chemical formula. However, if some of the atoms in the mineral are radioactive isotopes, they will, in time, decay. Chemical analysis of old rocks may reveal elements that could not have been present in the original crystal: they must have formed as daughter products by radioactive decay. By measuring the relative proportions of parent and daughter nuclei we can find out how much time has passed since the mineral first crystallised. This method of dating rocks depends on our understanding how rapidly a sample of radioactive material will decay.

As you will see in Activity 9, the activity of a radioactive sample changes exponentially with time. If some quantity, N, decreases exponentially with time, t, then the change of N with time is described by equations of the form

Study note
You met exponential changes in the units *Transport on Track* and *The Medium is the Message*.

$$\frac{dN}{dt} = -\lambda N \qquad (3)$$

and (equivalently)

$$N = N_0\, e^{-\lambda t} \qquad (4)$$

where λ is a constant – a **decay constant** in this case – and N_0 the value of N when $t = 0$. A graph of N against t shows N changing by equal fractions in equal time intervals, and a graph of $\log(N)$ against t is a straight line.

Another way of looking at the rate of change of N, dN/dt, is to realise that it is the number of disintegrations per unit time (e.g. per second, or per minute) and is hence also the number of alphas, betas or gammas emitted per unit time, which can be measured quite easily using a GM tube or similar instrument. The number of disintegrations per unit time is the **activity**, A, of a sample:

$$A = \frac{dN}{dt} \qquad (5)$$

The SI unit of activity is the becquerel, Bq. One becquerel is one disintegration per second.

Since the number of unstable nuclei decays exponentially, so does the activity – with the same decay constant. If you are familiar with calculus, you can show this by differentiating equation (4):

$$A = \frac{dN}{dt} = -\lambda N_0\, e^{-\lambda t}$$

and then using equation (3) to substitute an expression for A_0, i.e. the activity when $t = 0$

$$A = A_0\, e^{-\lambda t} \qquad (6)$$

Another way to see this is by analogy with the decay of charge and current when a capacitor discharges through a resistor. The stored charge, Q, decays exponentially and so does the current I, where $I = \dfrac{dQ}{dt}$.

Study note

You studied the exponential discharge of capacitors in the unit *The Medium is the Message*.

The decay of a radioactive isotope is usually described in terms of its **half-life** – that is, the time for the number of nuclei of that isotope to halve. Some isotopes are very unstable and have short half-lives (a few seconds or even less), whereas more stable isotopes have much longer half-lives – perhaps millions of years.

The half-life is related to the decay constant. From the definition of half-life, when $N = \dfrac{N_0}{2}$, $t = t_{1/2}$. Putting these values into equation (4) we have

$$\frac{N_0}{2} = N_0\, e^{-\lambda t_{1/2}}$$

Dividing by N_0 and taking the reciprocal of both sides:

$$2 = e^{\lambda t_{1/2}}$$

Taking natural logs of both sides:

$$\log_e (2) = \lambda t_{1/2}$$

$$t_{1/2} = \frac{\log_e (2)}{\lambda} \qquad (7)$$

Note that $t_{1/2}$ can be expressed in any unit of time – e.g. seconds, minutes or years, and the corresponding units for λ are then s^{-1}, min^{-1} or yr^{-1}.

Maths reference

Using log graphs
See Maths note 8.7
Exponential changes
See Maths note 9.1
Exponential functions
See Maths note 9.2
Exponentials and logs
See Maths note 9.3

ACTIVITY 9 **Measuring half-life**

Following your school or college's safety procedures carefully, measure the half-life of a short-lived radioactive isotope. Plot a suitable graph showing how the activity of the sample changes with time, and hence show that the decay is indeed exponential.

Why is radioactive decay exponential?

A radioactive nucleus is an unstable nucleus that could decay at any moment. The chance that it will decay at a given moment is governed by the laws of probability. If you toss a coin you know that there is a 50% chance of it coming up heads each time, and that within a few tosses it almost certainly *will* come up heads. If you roll a die there is a one in six chance of a given number coming up. Atoms of radioactive isotopes behave in rather the same way: in any one second there is a certain probability that the isotopes will decay. Some isotopes are extremely unstable, so there is a high probability that in one second a nucleus will decay. Some isotopes are relatively stable, so any given nucleus is very unlikely to decay in any one second. Activity 10 uses a model to demonstrate how the number of radioactive nuclei varies with time.

ACTIVITY 10 **Modelling radioactive decay**

Use dice, coins or a computer model to simulate the random decay of radioactive nuclei. Plot a graph showing how the number of remaining 'nuclei' changes with time.

In Activity 10 you will have seen that the number of 'nuclei', ΔN, decaying in a given time interval, Δt, is proportional to the number of nuclei, N, remaining in the sample. Expressing this mathematically for a very small time interval (effectively 'at an instant'):

$$\frac{\mathrm{d}N}{\mathrm{d}t} \propto N$$

This is one of the characteristic equations of exponential decay (equation 3). The fact that radioactive decay *is* exponential indicates that the decay of individual nuclei really is governed by probability. This is quite a disturbing (and interesting!) idea. After all, in most situations that you meet in physics, something either definitely happens or definitely does not; on an atomic scale things look rather different. It is also interesting that, even though the decay of each nucleus happens by chance, we can still make very definite predictions and measurements of the behaviour of a large number of nuclei – the half-life of a sample, for example.

Dating

Radiometric dating of rocks (or of archaeological artefacts) essentially involves knowing, or assuming, the amount of an isotope of known half-life initially present in the sample, measuring the amount present now, and hence calculating the time elapsed since the sample was formed. The following examples illustrate the principle, and also show how the units of $t_{1/2}$ and λ are interrelated.

Worked example

Q Uranium-238 ($^{238}_{92}$U) decays by alpha emission to form thorium-234 ($^{234}_{90}$Th). The decay constant for this process is 1.54×10^{-10} yr^{-1}.

(a) If you had 1.00 tonne of pure uranium-238, how long will it take before the activity of the uranium-238 has halved?

(b) How much would you expect to remain 1.00 billion years later (i.e. after 1.00×10^9 yr)?

(c) How long would it take for the mass of uranium-238 to decrease to 0.80 tonne?

A (a) The time to halve (i.e. the half-life) does not depend on the initial activity. Using equation (5):

$$t_{1/2} = \frac{\log_e (2)}{\lambda}$$

$$= \frac{\log_e (2)}{1.54 \times 10^{-10}\, \text{yr}^{-1}} = 4.5 \times 10^9\, \text{yr}$$

(b) Here we need to use equation (4) with $t = 1.00 \times 10^9$ yr.

$$\lambda t = 1.54 \times 10^{-10}\, \text{yr}^{-1} \times 1.00 \times 10^9\, \text{yr} = 0.154$$

(Note that the quantity λt has no units.)

$e^{-\lambda t} = 0.857$, and so $N = 0.857 N_0$, and there will be 0.857 tonne of uranium-238 remaining.

(c) Now we need equation (4) with $N = 0.80 N_0$:

$$0.80 N_0 = N_0\, e^{-\lambda t}$$

so $0.80 = e^{-\lambda t}$

Taking natural logs of both sides

$$\log_e (0.80) = -\lambda t$$

$$t = \frac{\log_e (0.80)}{-\lambda} = \frac{\log_e (0.80)}{-1.54 \times 10^{-10}\, \text{yr}^{-1}}$$

$$= 1.45 \times 10^9\, \text{yr}.$$

Table 3 shows a slightly different way of relating the age of a sample to its half-life. The 'amount' could be either the mass or the number of nuclei.

No. of half-lives elapsed	Amount of parent isotope remaining		
0	100%		
1	50%	1/2	$1/2^1$
2	25%	1/4	$1/2^2$
3	12.5%	1/8	$1/2^3$

Table 3 *Half-life and age*

QUESTIONS

13 Study Table 3 and write a mathematical expression relating the number of half-lives that have elapsed to the amount of parent isotope remaining.

When we are dating rocks we need to study isotopes with relatively long half-lives if they are still to be detectable today. Table 4 shows some of the isotopes commonly used for dating rocks by geologists. NB the daughter products listed for ^{238}U and ^{235}U are not the immediate products but are the stable products produced by a series of decay reactions. The stated half-lives and decay constants refer to the complete series of decays.

Parent isotope	Daughter isotope	Half-life, $t_{1/2}/10^6$ yr	Decay constant, $\lambda/10^{-10}$ yr^{-1}
$^{238}_{92}$U	$^{206}_{82}$Pb		1.552
$^{235}_{92}$U	$^{207}_{82}$Pb	704	
$^{40}_{19}$K	See question 24		5.810
$^{87}_{37}$Rb	$^{87}_{38}$Sr	48 800	

Table 4 *Some isotopes commonly used for dating rocks*

If a sample initially contained none of the daughter isotope, then dating is straightforward. Figure 21 shows how the amounts of ^{235}U and ^{207}Pb change with time in a rock that initially contained no ^{207}Pb. If we measure the current proportions of ^{235}U and ^{207}Pb we can calculate the time since the sample crystallised. The proportions of ^{235}U and ^{207}Pb are equal after one half-life, and as time goes on the proportion of lead increases.

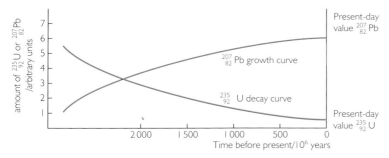

Figure 21 *The proportions of ^{235}U and ^{207}Pb change with time*

Radiometric dating techniques typically assign ages of over 4 billion years to many Earth rocks. By comparing the ^{87}Rb and ^{87}Sr ratios in zircon crystals (Figure 22) found in ancient rocks in Australia, the rocks have been dated as 4200 million years old. Some deep sea sediments give results that suggest they are even older. Using similar techniques the oldest Moon rocks and meteorites have been shown to be about 4600 million years old. If we accept the solar nebula theory of the formation of the solar system, it is fair to give the Sun a similar age.

Figure 22 *Zircon crystals*

QUESTIONS

In answering these questions, you will need to refer to Table 4 and to information in the text

14 Calculate the missing decay constants and half-lives needed to complete Table 4.

15 Using the answer to question 14, calculate the proportion of ^{87}Rb you would expect to find remaining in a sample that is analysed 24 400 million years after it crystallised.

16 A grain of mineral, which contained uranium but was assumed to have contained no lead when it crystallised, was found to have 15 times as much $^{207}_{82}$Pb as $^{235}_{92}$U. How old is it?

17 Some recently discovered meteorites are believed to have come from Mars – the pockets of gas trapped in the rock closely match that of the Martian atmosphere. The crystallisation ages of these rocks (the time since they crystallised) are found to be 0.2–1.3 billion years.

   (**a**) If we are to assume that Mars formed from the solar nebula at the same time as Earth, what crystallisation age would we expect from these rocks?

   (**b**) Mars has many extinct volcanoes, some very high. Suggest a way in which the meteorites got to Earth.

   (**c**) If Mars formed at the same time as Earth, how might we explain the younger crystallisation ages of the Martian meteorites?

2.3 *What fuels the Sun?*

The active Sun

Until the invention of telescopes people thought that the Sun was a globe of pure fire and light. Galileo shook the world when he discovered imperfections – dark spots – on the Sun (Figure 23). In the 18th and 19th centuries most scientists believed that the Sun had a cool, dark interior surrounded by a burning shell: sunspots were explained as either mountains of cool material poking out of the burning clouds, or holes in the burning clouds.

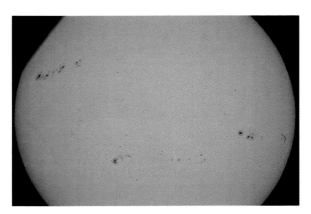

Figure 23 *Sunspots*

We now know that sunspots are relatively cool regions of the photosphere, and are related to large-scale upheavals in the photosphere that involve the Sun's magnetic field and prevent hot material reaching the photosphere. The amount of this so-called solar activity, and the numbers of sunspots, vary regularly with time and follow an approximately 11-year cycle.

ACTIVITY **11** **Sunspots**

By projecting an image of the Sun on to a screen, study and record the positions of sunspots and hence demonstrate the Sun's rotation.

Use the Internet to find images of the Sun produced at solar observatories.

Compare your images of the Sun with images obtained in quiet and active periods of the sunspot cycle. Where are we now in the cycle?

In the 19th century the technique of spectroscopy was developed. This allowed a chemical analysis of distant objects by analysing their light. It was soon discovered that the Sun emitted the continuous spectrum of an intensely hot body, but that there were dark lines in the spectrum where light had been absorbed by elements in a cooler outer atmosphere beyond the photosphere (Figure 24). These are named Fraunhofer lines after the German physicist who first recorded them.

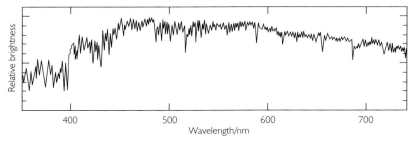

Figure 24 *The solar spectrum: a graphical record*

By shining continuous spectra through vaporised materials in the laboratory and comparing them with the spectra of the Sun, the German scientist Kirchhoff was able to detect many elements in the outer atmospheres of the Sun: sodium, calcium, magnesium, iron, he even discovered new elements that were only later detected on Earth. Kirchhoff worked with Robert Bunsen and Henry Roscoe (Figure 25). Figure 26 shows the first spectroscopes made by Bunsen for the lab work.

Figure 25 *Kirchhoff, Bunsen and Roscoe*

ACTIVITY 12 The Sun's spectrum

Use a spectroscope to observe the solar spectrum in sunlight reflected from a matt white surface or from clouds. Do not point a spectroscope directly at the Sun. Alternatively use a spectrometer fitted with a diffraction grating. You should be able to see the full 'rainbow' of colours, plus the Fraunhofer lines.

Figure 26 *Bunsen's spectroscope*

Solar power

In December 1838 Sir John Herschel, an English astronomer, was visiting South Africa. At noon, while the Sun was almost directly overhead (12° north), he used the Sun's rays to heat a carefully measured amount of water for 10 minutes. By measuring the rise in temperature of the water he calculated the energy received by the Earth from the Sun, and hence he was able to calculate the total power output of the Sun.

QUESTION

18 We currently believe the luminosity of the Sun to be about 3.84×10^{26} W. In 1838 the unit of power was the horse: 1 horsepower (hp) = 746 W. A steam engine with a 1000 hp engine would have seemed incredibly powerful. What is the approximate luminosity of the Sun in horsepower?

It was soon shown that such a vast energy output from the Sun was difficult to explain. Scientists began to wonder where such energy came from and in 1842 Julius Robert Mayer proposed the law of conservation of energy. Scientists realised that the energy from the Sun must be being transformed from another form of energy. But what kind of fuel could sustain such a power output?

As far as 19th-century scientists knew, the richest source of energy was coal, so the idea was proposed that the Sun was a huge piece of coal. However, if the Sun consisted of anthracite (a type of coal), a layer of 20 feet in thickness would have to be burned every hour to account for the energy released by the Sun. This would have consumed the whole of the Sun in less than 5000 years, and no-one then believed the solar system to be younger than that.

Mayer's idea was that the kinetic energy of meteorites falling into the Sun would provide the energy for the observed output of radiation. But this would have increased the mass of the Sun and changed the orbits of planets. In 1854 Hermann von Helmholtz, a German physicist, came up with a more successful theory. He proposed that the Sun contracted and condensed, and as it did so it became hotter – so hot that it could have been radiating at its current rate for 22 million years and still have another 17 million years before it cooled. In the mid-19th century this seemed plausible, but as geologists and palaeontologists became more precise in their estimates of the time for life on Earth (then 100–250 million years) the theory lost credibility.

Nuclear fusion

With the discovery of radioactivity and the nuclear atom at the beginning of the 20th century, physicists and astronomers began to realise that the source of the Sun's energy could more realistically be explained by nuclear energy of some kind. In 1919 Rutherford showed that it was possible to change one element into another by bombarding them with very rapidly moving particles and in a classic book of 1926 Sir Arthur Eddington proposed that the Sun's energy might be accounted for by the combination of hydrogen nuclei to form helium. We now believe that he was correct – the **fusion** of nuclei releases huge amounts of energy, and can fully explain why the Sun is still shining billions of years after it formed.

To understand why nuclear fusion can release energy, it can be helpful to carry out a 'thought experiment'. Imagine assembling a nucleus from its constituent protons and neutrons (which in practice would be extremely difficult to achieve). As these nucleons become very close together, they are attracted to one another by the strong nuclear force, and as they are drawn together and become more tightly bound they lose 'nuclear potential energy', rather like an object falling towards Earth loses gravitational potential energy. Making the lightest nuclei in this way only releases a relatively small amount of energy, but as more massive nuclei are formed, the amount of energy released per nucleon increases, up to the formation of iron and nickel (proton numbers 56 and 57), which are the most tightly bound of all nuclei. Figure 27 shows the energy that would be released per nucleon if each nucleus were to be created in this way. (Notice that the energy is measured in MeV per nucleon. $1\,\text{MeV} = 1.6 \times 10^{-13}\,\text{J}$.)

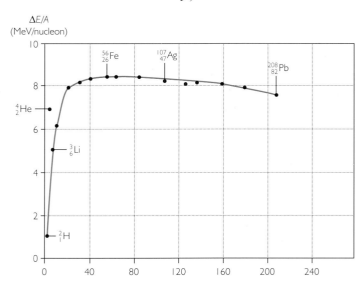

Figure 27 *Energy released in the formation of nuclei from separate nucleons*

The energy released when a nucleus is formed is called the nuclear **binding energy**. Remember that binding nucleons together involves a release of energy. One way to think of the binding energy is that it is the energy that you would need to supply in order to separate a nucleus into its nucleons – perhaps 'unbinding energy' would be a better term.

When two light nuclei react to produce a more massive nucleus, additional energy is released. In the thought experiment, you can picture this as pulling apart each reacting nucleus into its separate nucleons and then reassembling them to make a single, larger nucleus – this involves a net release of energy.

The Sun is composed mostly of hydrogen with some helium. Figure 27 shows that if hydrogen nuclei fuse to form helium, there is a release of several MeV per nucleon. The release of energy manifests itself mainly in the emission of high-energy (gamma ray) photons and neutrinos. While a few MeV might not be a very large amount of energy on its own, remember that this is the energy released per nucleon. In just 1 g of hydrogen there would be about 6×10^{23} nuclei, and so the energy released by the fusion of 1 g of hydrogen would be many billions of joules – far more than the energy involved in any chemical reaction using a similar amount of material.

It would be nice if we could control a nuclear fusion reaction on the Earth to generate electricity, because hydrogen (in water, H_2O) is plentiful, and there would be no polluting waste products. Unfortunately, to get the hydrogen nuclei to fuse requires them to be moving close together at high speeds. This is because of their positive charge; unless they are moving very fast, the electrostatic repulsion ensures that they never become close enough to react. Also, to give the hydrogen nuclei a good chance of colliding with one another, the density, too, needs to be high.

It is very difficult to produce the huge temperatures and densities required for fusion on Earth, but the core (centre) of a star (such as the Sun), with the enormous pressure due to the weight of overlying material, is able to reach a temperature of over 10^7 K, high enough to sustain hydrogen fusion. Such high temperatures can be produced in laboratories on Earth (Figure 28), but it is difficult to maintain them for very long and there is the additional problem of controlling a very hot hydrogen plasma (ionised gas), since it would vaporise the walls of any solid container.

The precise details of the fusion reactions that occur in a star depend on its temperature and pressure. It was only as recently as 1938 that the details of the nuclear reactions were worked out. Hans Bethe and Charles Critchfield showed that in the Sun it is a proton–proton chain reaction (known as the ppI chain) that releases energy. The chain has several stages, and the overall effect is:

$$4{}^{1}_{1}\mathrm{H} \rightarrow {}^{4}_{2}\mathrm{He} + 2\,\mathrm{e}^{+} + 2\nu_{e} + 2\gamma$$

The two positrons annihilate with two electrons to produce more gamma photons

$$2\mathrm{e}^{+} + 2\mathrm{e}^{-} \rightarrow 4\gamma$$

Figure 28 *The Joint European Torus (JET), where research into nuclear fusion is carried out*

In stars like the Sun, the core temperature and pressure are just high enough to sustain the reaction, so it actually proceeds quite slowly. Since its formation about 5 billion years ago, the Sun has converted only about half the hydrogen in its core, so it will be able to go on shining for about another 5 billion years.

Nuclear fission

Very massive nuclei can also release energy. By breaking up into smaller nuclei in a process called nuclear **fission**, they become more stable. Fission plays no part in supplying the energy output of stars, but it is worth mentioning for completeness. Some unstable massive nuclei can decay by splitting into two less massive nuclei, usually accompanied by a few neutrons. For example, an isotope of fermium can decay into xenon and palladium, like this:

$$^{256}_{100}\text{Fm} \rightarrow {}^{140}_{54}\text{Xe} + {}^{112}_{46}\text{Pd} + 4{}^{1}_{0}\text{n}$$

As you can see from Figure 27, such a reaction involves a release of energy – the two lighter nuclei are more tightly bound than the initial nucleus. Spontaneous fission reactions such as this are rare, and tend to occur only in nuclei (such as $^{256}_{100}\text{Fm}$) that are produced artificially rather than occurring in nature. However, as with fusion, the energy released per reacting particle is vast, far outstripping that in chemical reactions, and since the mid 20th century people have sought to exploit this energy in nuclear reactors for generating electricity and in nuclear bombs. In both of these, a commonly used reaction is the fission of uranium-235. If a nucleus of ^{235}U absorbs an extra neutron, it becomes unstable and undergoes fission in reactions such as:

$$^{235}_{92}\text{U} + {}^{1}_{0}\text{n} \rightarrow {}^{236}_{92}\text{U} \rightarrow {}^{141}_{56}\text{Ba} + {}^{92}_{36}\text{Kr} + 3{}^{1}_{0}\text{n}$$

If the neutrons are absorbed by three further nuclei of ^{235}U, then they too will undergo fission, releasing further neutrons … and so on. Provided the neutrons neither escape from the sample nor get absorbed by other nuclei that cannot undergo fission, then the reaction is self-sustaining. In a nuclear reactor (Figure 29), the presence of other materials ensures that there are just enough surviving neutrons to sustain the reaction at a steady rate. But in a nuclear bomb, once the reaction is triggered to start, most of the neutrons go on to produce fission of another ^{235}U nucleus, leading to a runaway reaction – an explosion that causes huge damage not only because of the vast energy released, but also because of the ejection of highly radioactive materials into the surroundings (Figure 30).

Mass and energy

So much energy is released in a nuclear reaction that we can measure the associated loss of mass. Mass and energy are interrelated by Einstein's equation:

$$\Delta E = c^2 \Delta m \tag{8}$$

Figure 29   *A nuclear power station*

Figure 30   *Explosion of a nuclear bomb*

Study note

You met the relationship between matter and energy in the unit *Probing the Heart of Matter*.

where ΔE is the energy released, c is the speed of light in a vacuum ($3.00 \times 10^8 \, \mathrm{m\,s^{-1}}$) and Δm is the loss of mass, often called the **mass deficit** or **mass defect** when associated with nuclear reactions. In a spontaneous reaction, energy is always emitted and the total mass of the products is always less than that of the reactants. An example using nuclear fission illustrates this.

Worked example

Q Using data from Table 5, calculate the mass deficit when a nucleus of ^{235}U absorbs a neutron and undergoes fission into ^{141}Ba and ^{92}Kr, and hence calculate the energy released.

Particle	Mass/1.661×10^{-27} kg
$^{1}_{0}\mathrm{n}$	1.008 665
$^{235}_{92}\mathrm{U}$	235.043 93
$^{92}_{36}\mathrm{Kr}$	91.926 25
$^{141}_{56}\mathrm{Ba}$	140.914 34

Table 5   *Particles involved in a fission reaction of uranium-235*

A Initial mass $= (1.008\,665 + 235.043\,93) \times 1.661 \times 10^{-27}\,\mathrm{kg}$

$$= 236.0526 \times 1.661 \times 10^{-27}\,\mathrm{kg}$$

Final mass $= (91.926\,25 + 140.914\,34 + 3 \times 1.008\,665)$

$$\times 1.661 \times 10^{-27}\,\mathrm{kg}$$

$$= 235.8666 \times 1.661 \times 10^{-27}\,\mathrm{kg}$$

$\Delta m = (236.0526 - 235.8666) \times 1.661 \times 10^{-27}\,\mathrm{kg}$

$$= 0.1860 \times 1.661 \times 10^{-27}\,\mathrm{kg} = 3.090 \times 10^{-28}\,\mathrm{kg}$$

$\Delta E = c^2 \Delta m$

$$= (3.00 \times 10^8 \, \mathrm{m\,s^{-1}})^2 \times 3.090 \times 10^{-28}\,\mathrm{kg} = 2.78 \times 10^{-11}\,\mathrm{J}.$$

Study note

We have calculated the actual values of initial and final mass, but you could reduce the arithmetic by doing the calculation all in one stage, and noticing that, for this purpose, one neutron could be removed from each side. We have not carried out the multiplication by the factor of 1.661×10^{-27} before the final stage since the masses are quoted to a greater precision than this factor and we do not wish to introduce rounding errors at an intermediate stage.

QUESTIONS

19 The Sun has a mass of 1.99×10^{30} kg and is emitting energy at a rate of 3.84×10^{26} W.

(**a**) How much energy will the Sun emit in 1000 years? (1 year $\approx 3 \times 10^7$ s)

(**b**) (**i**) If this energy were converted back into mass, how much mass would that be?
(**ii**) What percentage of the Sun's mass is this?

(**c**) What percentage of its mass will the Sun lose over its lifetime (roughly 10^{10} years)?

20 (**a**) Write an equation that shows the overall effect of the pp1 chain including the electron–positron annihilations. Include sub- and superscripts to show that both charge and nucleon number are conserved.

(b) Use the data in Table 6 to calculate the mass deficit associated with the production of one nucleus of $^4_2$He in the pp1 fusion chain.

(c) How much energy is therefore released when one nucleus of $^4_2$He is produced?

(d) How many hydrogen nuclei must be consumed per second in order to maintain the Sun's luminosity of 3.84×10^{26} W?

(e) The Sun's mass is 1.99×10^{30} kg. Given that when it formed from the solar nebula about 75% of its mass was hydrogen, and that about 15% of this hydrogen will eventually be converted to helium, estimate the Sun's lifetime. Express your answer in years. (1 year $\approx 3 \times 10^7$ s)

Particle	Mass/10^{-27} kg
$^4_2$He	6.645
$^1_1$H	1.673
e^+	9.110×10^{-4}
e^-	9.110×10^{-4}
ν	0.000

Table 6   *Particles involved in the pp1 chain*

21 Without doing any calculations, sketch a graph showing how the mass per nucleon (i.e. mass of nucleus divided by nucleon number) will vary with atomic number.

2.4 Summing up part 2

In this part of the unit, there have been two main strands of physics. One is chiefly geometry, involving angular size and the inverse square relationship between flux and distance for a point source; and the other is nuclear physics – radioactive decay, fusion, fission and binding energy. You also saw how the radiation emitted by a body depends on its temperature.

ACTIVITY 13 **Understanding the Sun**

Use the information from this part of the unit to make a timeline showing how our knowledge and understanding of the Sun have developed. If you have time, use library resources and the Internet to supplement the information given.

ACTIVITY 14 **Summing up part 2**

Spend some time looking through your work on this part of the unit, making sure you understand all the terms highlighted in bold.

22 The planet Jupiter orbits the Sun at a distance of 7.78×10^{11} m and has a radius of 7.14×10^7 m. It is composed mainly of hydrogen and helium, but it is believed that its central core has a similar composition to the rocks of the Earth. The outer parts of Jupiter are at a temperature of about 130 K, which is slightly higher than that which is calculated on the basis of its absorption of solar energy alone, suggesting that there is some internal heat source. The Earth is 1.49×10^{11} m from the Sun.

(**a**) (**i**) Calculate the maximum and minimum angular diameter, in radians, of Jupiter when observed from the Earth.
(**ii**) Express the smaller value as a percentage of the larger one.

(**b**) Calculate the ratio $F_{Jupiter}/F_{Earth}$, where F is the solar energy flux at each planet. Express the ratio as a percentage.

(**c**) In which part of the electromagnetic spectrum would you expect to receive radiation emitted by Jupiter?

(**d**) Suggest a possible mechanism by which Jupiter might be heated internally.

23 The radioactive sources used for demonstrations in schools and colleges have long half-lives. Suggest a reason why it is desirable to use such sources for this purpose.

24 To answer this question you will need to refer to Tables 2, 4 and 6.

(**a**) The isotope $^{40}_{19}K$ is used in dating rocks. It decays to form a stable isotope of argon gas, which becomes trapped in the rock. Write a balanced equation for the decay of ^{40}K to argon, and hence deduce nucleon number of the daughter isotope and the type of decay that might be involved. (Hint: there are two possibilities.)

(**b**) A geophysicist finds that a certain rock sample contains 0.5 μg of ^{40}K and 3.3 μg of ^{40}Ar. Assuming that the rock initially contained no argon, and that all the argon produced has remained trapped in the rock, calculate the age of the sample.

(**c**) Calculate the approximate number of ^{40}K nuclei in the sample and hence calculate the activity due to their decay. Express your answer in suitable units. (1 yr $\approx 3 \times 10^7$ s)

3 *Stars*

In part 2 of this unit you studied the nature of our own Sun, its structure and the way in which it generates the heat and light that keeps us in comfort here on Earth. What we have seen is a snapshot view of our local star, which is how it appears to us over a very limited portion of its immense lifespan.

Now we will broaden the discussion of one star at a particular moment of its life to include the formation and evolution of stars in general. You will see how simple physical ideas and calculations can help us to understand the physical and evolutionary processes in stars.

For many centuries, the stars were seen as unchanging points of light, fixed in position for eternity, and astronomers had little concept of their nature. In the early part of the 19th century it was thought unlikely that it would be possible to find anything out about the structure and composition of stars. Within a few years, however, the science of spectroscopy had been developed and the first spectra of stars had been obtained. It turned out that the light from the stars contained a wealth of scientific information that would help astronomers to unravel their hidden secrets.

At the same time, astronomers such as Sir William Herschel, with access to new and powerful telescopes, were beginning to make new detailed maps of the heavens that would eventually result in the understanding of the structure of our galaxy; you will learn more about this in part 4.

3.1 *Studying the stars*

How far are the stars?

As the Earth rotates on its axis we see the stars move across the sky, as is demonstrated in Activity 15. Figure 31 also reveals the stars' apparent motion.

Figure 31 *A long-exposure photograph of the night sky*

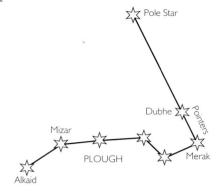

Figure 32 *Finding Polaris*

ACTIVITY 15 Star watch

On a clear night, find the major constellation known as the Plough. Figure 32 shows you how to find Polaris, the Pole Star, using two of the stars in the Plough.

Draw a circle on a sheet of A4 paper and put the Pole Star in the centre. Observe the position of the Plough and draw it onto your diagram. Do the same thing every hour for, say, 3 hours.

Note how the Plough changes its position relative to the Pole Star and the horizon over the 3-hour period. Find the approximate angle through which the Plough rotates in 1 hour and relate this to the length of the day.

An important thing to note from Activity 15 is that although the stars appear to move across the sky as the Earth rotates, the relative motion of the stars, that is the motion of one star with respect to another, seems to be zero. Another way of saying this is that the star patterns or constellations are fixed. One might expect that, as the Earth moves around its orbit, the nearer stars would move relative to the more distant background stars in much the same way nearby objects move more rapidly across the field of view compared to more distant objects, e.g. as one drives down a motorway. The effect is called **parallax**.

Since there was no observable stellar parallax, some of Newton's contemporaries in the 17th century assumed that stars were infinitely distant and the observation even led some astronomers to doubt the **heliocentric** (Sun-centred) model of the Universe that had been proposed by Copernicus in the 16th century. However, as you saw in part 2, Huygens used the inverse square law (equation 1) to estimate the distance to Sirius; Isaac Newton, too, devised ways to estimate stellar distances based on the same law.

Astronomical instruments became accurate enough to detect the parallax of nearby stars in 1838, when Frederick Bessel detected the parallax motion of 61 Cygni, and F. Struve detected that of the star Vega (this star is mentioned in the film 'Contact'). Figure 33 shows the idea.

On 1 January star X appears in position A against the distant background stars but by 1 June, six months later, it appears in position B. The parallax angle, α, is defined as half the total angular motion, so the star appears to have moved through an angle of 2α in six months (due *only* to the orbital motion of the Earth). Knowing the distance from Earth to Sun, r, we can calculate the distance, d, to the star:

$$d = r/\alpha \qquad (9)$$

where α, the parallax angle, is in radians. This equation relies on α being small. In practice, for stars, it always is; the nearest star to the Sun is Alpha Centauri, which has a parallax less than 1".

Parallax measurements give rise to the unit of distance commonly used by professional astronomers, the **parsec**, pc, which is short for *par*allax *sec*ond. One parsec is defined as the distance of an object that would have a parallax of one arcsecond when observed from Earth. 1 pc $= 3.09 \times 10^{16}$ m $= 3.26$ light years.

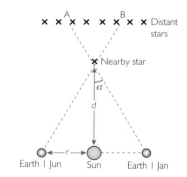

Figure 33 *Stellar parallax*

Study note

The angle α in equation (9) must be in radians, as in equation (2).

Study note

The angle of 1" (1 arcsec) is $1°/3600$.

Maths reference

Angular units
See Maths note 6.7

Measuring the distances to stars and galaxies may not seem the most interesting of activities for an astronomer but its importance cannot be overestimated. The main reason for this is that it allows astronomers to determine the scale of the Universe, which in turn has a bearing on its past and future. Another important reason for knowing the distances to stars is that the fundamental physical properties of the stars can be found. This is essential for the study of stellar evolution.

So important is it to obtain accurate stellar parallaxes that the European Space Agency (ESA) designed and launched a special satellite called Hipparcos (High Precision Parallax Collecting Satellite), in August 1989, with the aim of measuring parallaxes to an unprecedented degree of accuracy (Figure 34). The name honours the Greek astronomer Hipparchus (190–120 BC), who first measured the parallax of the Moon. The data from this satellite has already allowed astronomers to refine their estimates of distances to many nearby familiar objects such as the Pleiades star cluster. You can learn more about Hipparcos and the implications of its findings at

> http://astro.estec.esa.nl/SA-general/Projects/Hipparcos/
> hipparcos.html

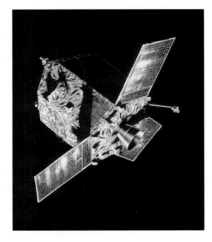

Figure 34   *The Hipparcos satellite*

QUESTIONS

Data: Earth–Sun distance, $r = 1.49 \times 10^{11}$ m; speed of light, $c = 3.00 \times 10^8$ m s^{-1}; 1 year $= 3.1536 \times 10^7$ s; 1 rad $= 2.06 \times 10^5$ arcsec; 1 parsec $= 3.1 \times 10^{16}$ m.

25 (**a**) The star Alpha Centauri is 4.351 light years from the solar system. Calculate its parallax in radians and in arcsec.

(**b**) Use the definition of the parsec to confirm that it has the value quoted above.

26 The smallest parallax Hipparcos can measure is 0.002". Determine the distance of the furthest star that Hipparcos can measure accurately. Express your answer in metres, in light years and in parsecs.

How hot are the stars?

In Activity 2, 'Colour, luminosity and temperature', you saw that the radiation emitted by a black body depends on its temperature – the hotter the body, the brighter and whiter it appears, as summarised in Figure 7. The fact that the distribution of radiation over different wavelengths depends on the temperature enables astronomers to measure the surface temperatures of stars just by analysing the radiation they receive.

Colours of the stars

On a clear winter's night, find the constellation Orion and identify the stars Betelgeuse and Rigel as shown in Figure 35. Give your eyes about 10 minutes to adapt to the darkness and then you should be able to see a distinct difference in the colours of these stars. Which of these two stars is the hotter?

When we view stars in the night sky their light is weak and our eyes do not respond to colour well in these conditions. Some people will inevitably find it difficult to discern the colours of different stars. You will see the colours more clearly if you use binoculars. You could try to take a series of colour photographs of Orion with different exposure times, which should bring out the colour difference.

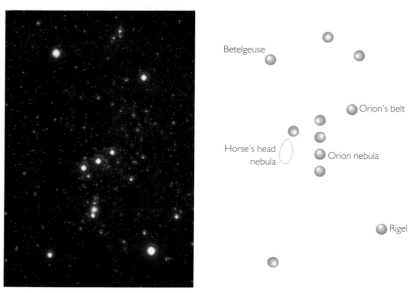

Figure 35 *Orion: (a) colour photograph, (b) the brightest stars in the constellation*

Astronomers classify stars according to their surface temperature, as shown in Table 7. The spectral type indicates the temperature range, and was originally based on the appearance of absorption lines in stellar spectra. The way in which the spectra of stars can be systematically arranged was mainly developed by an American astronomer, Annie Jump Cannon (1863–1941) (Figure 36). She classified the spectra of about 200 000 stars, a monumental task requiring great skill and dedication.

Figure 36 *Annie Jump Cannon*

Surface temperature/K	Colour	Spectral type
> 30 000	blue	O
11 000–30 000	bluish-white	B
7500–11 000	bluish-white	A
6000–7500	white	F
5000–6000	yellow-white	G
3500–6000	yellow-orange	K
< 3500	red	M

Table 7 *Spectral classification of stars*

We will not go into detail about the spectral type of a star, but when reading other texts you may find it useful to know that when astronomers talk about an O-type star they mean a star with a temperature in excess of 30 000 K. As you will see in part 4, such stars are much more massive and brighter than our Sun, but live short lives. On the other hand, the M-type stars glow a dull red because their surface temperature is low. The Sun is a type G star with a yellowish-white colour. Astronomers sometimes use a rather ridiculous (but memorable) mnemonic for the sequence of letters: Oh Be A Fine Girl (or Guy), Kiss Me.

How bright are the stars?

As we observe them in the sky, stars have a range of brightness. One reason why some stars appear brighter than others is simply that they are closer to us. Another reason is that some stars are more luminous than others. As you saw in part 2, the energy flux, F, we receive is proportional to the luminosity, L, of a star and is inversely proportional to the square of its distance, d:

$$F = \frac{L}{4\pi d^2} \qquad \text{(equation 1)}$$

There are other reasons, too, for differences in observed brightness: the radiation from some stars might have been absorbed or scattered more than others *en route* to us, and the proportion of radiation in the visible part of the electromagnetic spectrum also varies between stars.

QUESTIONS

27 Table 8 lists the distances of some stars and the flux we receive from them. Assuming that the flux refers to the complete wavelength range, and that no radiation is absorbed or scattered *en route*, complete the table.

Star	Distance, d/m	Flux, F/W m^{-2}	Luminosity, L/W
Sirius	8.22×10^{16}	1.17×10^{-7}	
Rigel	2.38×10^{18}	5.37×10^{-7}	
Betelgeuse	6.18×10^{18}	1.11×10^{-8}	
Proxima Centauri	4.11×10^{16}	1.09×10^{-11}	
Sun	1.49×10^{11}		3.83×10^{26}

Table 8 *Star data for question 27*

Of the stars listed in Table 8 the one that appears brightest to us is the one that produces the greatest energy flux at the Earth – the Sun, by a long way – and the one that seems faintest is Proxima Centauri. From the answer to question 27 we can see that the Sun is actually much less luminous than some of the other stars listed, and that although Sirius appears brighter than Betelgeuse in the night sky it actually is much less luminous.

If astronomers wish to compare stars with one another, they can do one of two things. One is to measure their distances and thus calculate their luminosities as you did in question 27. Alternatively they can study stars that they believe all to be at similar distances from Earth.

In the early years of the 20th century, American astronomer Henry Norris Russell (1877–1957) (Figure 37a) took the first approach. He studied stars that were close enough for their parallaxes to be measured, and looked for a relationship between stellar luminosity and colour (i.e. their surface temperature). Around the same time, Danish astronomer Ejnar Hertzsprung (1873–1967) (Figure 37b) looked at stars that were grouped closely together in clusters (see Figure 38). He reasoned that stars found clustered closely together must be all at the same distance, hence their fluxes would be a good indication of the relative luminosities, so he looked for a relationship between colour and flux.

Both Hertzsprung and Russell constructed graphs that were essentially plots of luminosity (or flux) against temperature for the stars they observed. This type of diagram is called a **Hertzsprung–Russell diagram** (or HR diagram) and was of tremendous importance in helping astronomers to understand stars; it is still very widely used as a way of displaying and analysing stellar data.

Figure 39 shows the axes for a Hertzsprung–Russell diagram. Notice that the luminosities are expressed in units of the Sun's luminosity, L_{Sun}, rather than watts, as this more convenient than dealing with the huge numbers involved in stellar luminosity. The range of luminosities is large, from about $10^{-4} L_{Sun}$ to about $10^6 L_{Sun}$. To cope with this range of values, a logarithmic scale is used. Although the range of surface temperatures is not as large it is still convenient to use a logarithmic scale. A very odd thing about the temperature axis (horizontal axis) is that it goes backwards. The high temperatures are plotted on the left of the axis and the low temperatures are on the right. Both Hertzsprung and Russell chose to put the blue-white stars on the left, and the convention remains today.

(a)

(b)

Figure 37 *(a) Henry Norris Russell, (b) Ejnar Hertzsprung*

Figure 38 *A cluster of stars*

Maths reference

Using log scales
See Maths note 8.7

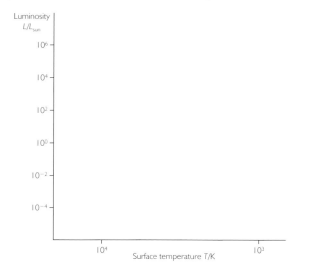

Figure 39 *Axes for a Hertzsprung–Russell diagram*

In other texts, you might come across HR diagrams plotted with other quantities. On the *y*-axis you might find 'absolute magnitude', which is related to the logarithm of luminosity, or 'apparent magnitude', which is related to the logarithm of flux. On the *x*-axis, you might find spectral type, which is, as you know, related to temperature, or 'colour index', which is also related to temperature. However, we will stick with luminosity and temperature.

ACTIVITY 17 A Hertzsprung–Russell diagram

Use logarithmic graph paper and a table of stellar luminosities and temperatures to construct a Hertzsprung–Russell diagram for a large number of stars. Include the Sun on your diagram.
Comment on any groupings of stars that are apparent from your graph.

From the HR diagram you plotted in Activity 17, three distinct groups of stars can be identified. The main group, containing the greatest number of stars and running roughly diagonally across the diagram from top left to bottom right, is called the **main sequence**. Most of the stars we see in the night sky are in this band. A second group of stars inhabits the top right of the HR diagram. These stars are cool but also very luminous; they must be very large in order to emit such large amounts of radiation from their surface. These are the **red giant** stars. A third group is found at the bottom left of the HR diagram. These are the **white dwarf** stars. Despite being very hot they have low luminosity, so must be small. Because they are so faint, white dwarf stars are hard to find – there are no such stars visible with the naked eye from Earth – and it is likely that the data you used in Activity 17 included few, if any, white dwarfs.

Once the patterns apparent in the HR diagram became known, astronomers found they had a powerful tool. For example, it enabled them to estimate stellar distances from measurements of flux and temperature, as you will see in question 28.

In sections 3.3 and 3.4 we shall see how the HR diagram can help us to understand the evolution of stars and we will see how these three regions of the HR diagram are linked together to give a coherent account of the birth, life and death of a star. But it is not easy to piece together the life history of a star from a 'snapshot' picture of a large number of stars at a particular point in time, as question 29 indicates.

QUESTIONS

28 There are subtle differences in the line spectra of stars that have the same temperature but different luminosities, so it is possible to distinguish a main sequence star from, say, a red giant with the same surface temperature.

Suppose an astronomer observes a star at unknown distance, whose spectrum indicates that it belongs on the main sequence. Outline how the distance to such a star might be measured – say what measurements need to be made, what quantities need to be deduced (and how) and explain how the distance would then be calculated.

29 (a) (i) Describe in words how luminosity varies with temperature for stars on the main sequence.

(ii) Suggest a possible mathematical relationship between L and T for stars on the main sequence.

(b) Is it possible to say anything about the size of stars on the main sequence? For example, how might a hot, highly luminous star at one end of the main sequence compare in size with a star at the other end?

(c) What, if anything, can be said about the masses of the stars on the main sequence?

(d) Does the HR diagram give any clues about the way stars form, or the way they change with age? If so, what?

3.2 Stars in motion

In section 3.1 you saw how astronomers can use the radiation they receive from stars to deduce the stars' temperatures and distances. Now we will turn our attention to another line of enquiry – how do stars and other bodies influence one another's motion, and what does that enable us to deduce about their properties?

Before the discoveries of Isaac Newton (1642–1727), it must have seemed impossible to say anything meaningful about the masses of distant stars or even the Sun. However, Newton made fundamental breakthroughs in the science of gravitational physics that now enable astronomers to make these calculations as a matter of routine.

Arguably, Newton's greatest scientific work was called *Philosophiae Naturalis Principia Mathematica*, or in English, *The Mathematical Principles of Natural Philosophy* (Figure 40). Often referred to as simply the *Principia*, this book is regarded by many as the greatest feat of intellectual endeavour ever achieved. It was published in 1687 and contains a complete description of the laws of mechanics and gravitation, explaining the orbital motion of the planets and how the tides of the sea are generated – among many other things. These laws, discovered by Newton, are still used every day by scientists some 300 years after their formulation. They enable spacecraft to be launched to distant planets, and provide the means to measure the masses of stars and galaxies.

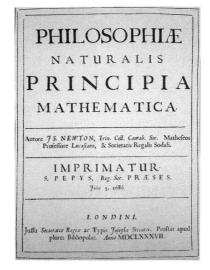

Figure 40 *Newton's Principia*

Universal gravitation

You probably know the famous tale of the falling apple. A descendant of the apple tree from which it fell can be seen today, in the garden of Woolsthorpe Manor in Lincolnshire, Newton's childhood home (Figure 41). The important thing about this story is that it inspired the concept of **universal gravitation**. The word 'universal' means what it says. Newton's great insight was to realise there is an attractive force of gravity between *all* masses, no matter where they are in the Universe – previously, it had been thought that the motion of objects on Earth was governed by rules quite different from those that applied to 'heavenly bodies'.

Newton argued that the force of gravity exerted by a body on another must be proportional to its mass. He also argued that the force exerted by a body of mass m_1 on one with mass m_2 must be equal in size to that exerted by the second on the first. From this it follows that the magnitude, F_{grav}, of the gravitational force must be proportional to the product $m_1 m_2$:

$$F_{grav} \propto m_1 m_2$$

By studying the motion of the Moon in its orbit about Earth, Newton was also able to deduce how F_{grav} depends on the separation of the objects. He did this by realising that the gravitational force between Earth and Moon must be responsible for the centripetal force needed to maintain the Moon's near-circular motion. By an ingenious mathematical argument, he was able to show that the Earth–Moon force must diminish with distance according to an inverse square law, i.e.

$$F_{grav} \propto \frac{m_1 m_2}{r^2}$$

where r is the distance between the *centres* of the two masses (Figure 42). To make this relationship into an equation, we need a constant of proportionality. This is called the gravitational constant and given the symbol G. The full mathematical expression of Newtons' law of universal gravitation is therefore

$$F_{grav} = \frac{G m_1 m_2}{r^2} \qquad (10)$$

Figure 41   *Woolsthorpe Manor*

Study note

This is an example of Newton's third law of motion, which you met in the AS unit *Higher, Faster, Stronger*.

Figure 42   *Two masses, m_1 and m_2, separated by a distance r*

QUESTION

30 Use equation (10) to deduce the SI units of G.

Measuring G experimentally is difficult, mainly because the gravitational force is very small unless at least one of the masses is very large. In principle it is possible to deduce G from measuring the force between two large bodies such as the Earth and Moon, but in practice this is difficult since determining the masses of such bodies relies on knowing G in the first place, as you will see shortly. However, it is possible to set up delicate laboratory experiments to measure the forces between quite small masses, and these yield a value of $G = 6.67\ 10^{-11}\ \text{N m}^2\ \text{kg}^{-2}$. In Activity 18 you will get a feel for the sizes of some gravitational forces.

ACTIVITY 18 **Universal gravity**

Table 9 lists some objects, their masses and separations. Use a spreadsheet to calculate the magnitude of the gravitational force between each pair listed, and hence complete Table 9.

Objects	m_1/kg	m_2/kg	r/m	F_{grav}/N
Moon in orbit around Earth	7.35×10^{22}	5.98×10^{24}	3.85×10^8	
Earth in orbit around Sun	5.98×10^{24}	1.99×10^{30}	1.49×10^{11}	
Moon and Sun	7.35×10^{22}	1.99×10^{30}	1.49×10^{11}	
Person on surface of Earth	60.0	5.98×10^{24}	6.38×10^6	
Person on surface of Moon	60.0	7.35×10^{22}	1.74×10^6	
Person at Sun's photosphere(!)	60.0	1.99×10^{30}	6.96×10^8	
Two people standing together	60.0	60.0	1.00	
Electron in orbit around proton	9.11×10^{-31}	1.67×10^{-27}	5.3×10^{-12}	

Table 9 *Data for Activity 18. The mass m_1 is that of the first object listed in each pair*

Gravitational field

Gravitational field strength, g, is defined as the gravitational force per unit mass. Close to the Earth's surface, $g = 9.8\ \text{N kg}^{-1}$. The gravitational force on an object, i.e. its weight, W, is related to is mass, m, via the gravitational field strength:

$$W = F_{grav} = mg \qquad (11)$$

Electric field, is defined as a region in which a charged object experiences an electrostatic force. The direction of an electric field is defined to be that of the force acting on a positive charge, and the strength, E, of an electric field is defined as the force per unit charge. The electrostatic force, F_{elec}, on a charged particle is related to its charge, q, via the electric field strength:

$$F_{elec} = qE \qquad (12)$$

There is a marked similarity between equations (11) and (12). You have probably also noticed the similarity between the mathematical expression of Newton's law of gravitational and Coulomb's law of electrostatic force

$$F_{elec} = \frac{kQ_1Q_2}{r^2} \qquad (13)$$

Study note

You met gravitational field strength in the AS unit *Higher, Faster, Stronger*.

Study note

You met electric fields strength in the units *The Medium is the Message* and *Probing the Heart of Matter*.

Study note

Coulomb's law was introduced in the unit *Probing the Heart of Matter*.

From this relationship we can drive an expression for the field strength at a distance r from a point charge Q:

$$E = \frac{kQ}{r^2} \tag{14}$$

Similarly, we can use the definition of gravitational field strength to derive an expression for the gravitational field due to a point mass. Imagine placing a small mass m at a distance r from the centre of a mass M. The gravitational force acting on m is given by

$$F_{grav} = \frac{GmM}{r^2} \tag{equation 10}$$

and the gravitational field strength g is then

$$g = \frac{GM}{r^2} \tag{15}$$

Like force, gravitational field is a vector, and its direction is the same as that of the gravitational force. Just as we represented electric fields by drawing field lines, we can draw lines of gravitational field. Figure 43 shows the gravitational field around a planet (or any spherical mass). The field is represented by arrows, each arrow representing the direction and magnitude of the force on a 1 kg mass placed at the notched end of the arrow. Notice that the field is spherically symmetric, which means that the field strength is dependent only on the radial distance from the mass and not on direction. Also notice that the length of the arrows decreases with increasing distance from the mass. This indicates that the field strength decreases with radial distance, according to the inverse square law.

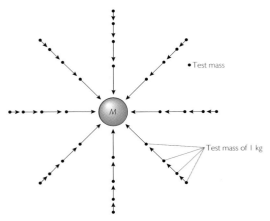

Figure 43   *Gravitational field lines around a planet*

ACTIVITY 19   **Compare and contrast**

As you have seen, there are many similarities between electrical and gravitational forces and fields, but there are also some important differences. Complete a copy of Table 10 to summarise key features of these two types of force. You may need to refer back to work from earlier parts of the course, and you may wish to add further rows to your table.

	Gravitational	Electrical
Force acts on . . .	all matter	
Direction of force	always attractive	
Force law between two objects formulated by . . .		Charles Coulomb 1736–1806
Equation for force law between two objects		$F = kQ_1Q_2/r^2$
SI units of constant in above equation		
Field strength	$g =$	$E = F/q$
SI units of field strength		
Direction of field around isolated object	towards object	
Change in potential energy in uniform field	$\Delta E_{grav} = mg\Delta h$	

Table 10 *Electrical and gravitational forces*

QUESTIONS

31 (**a**) Calculate the gravitational field strength at the surface of Mars, which has a mass of 6.42×10^{23} kg and a radius of 3.39×10^6 m.

(**b**) Calculate your own weight on the surface of Mars.

32 Assuming that a planet with radius r has uniform density, ρ, show that the gravitational field strength at its surface is given by

$$g = \frac{4\pi r \rho G}{3}$$

(Hint: the volume, V, of a sphere of radius r is $\dfrac{4\pi r^3}{3}$)

Orbits

Newton's law of gravitation is, as we have already stated, universal. This means that it applies anywhere in the Universe and gives the gravitational force between any two masses, be they atoms or stars. The law is particularly useful for determining the masses of stars and planets. This method is of great importance in astronomy, since it is the only means by which such masses can be directly measured.

Figure 44 shows two objects attracting one another gravitationally and moving in orbit. If the mass of one object is very much greater than the other, it remains essentially at rest while the less massive object orbits around it (Figure 44a). If the two are comparable in mass, they both move as shown in Figure 44(b), where point X (their centre of mass) remains at rest and the two masses orbit so that they are always on opposite sides of X. The two objects might be a planet and one of its moons, a star and a planet, or two stars

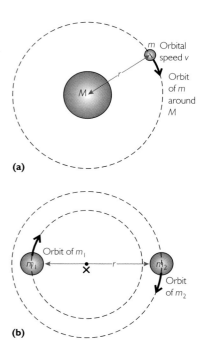

(a)

(b)

Figure 44 *Two objects in orbit: (a) $M \gg m$, (b) $m_1 \sim m_2$*

– in which case they are called a binary pair of stars or, more often, the two together are called a **binary star**. It may surprise you to learn that many stars are either binary pairs or members of multiple star systems whereas our Sun, as a single star, is in a minority. Imagine what it would be like to live in a binary star system. What would happen to night and day?

To see how mass can be measured, consider the situation in Figure 44(a), where the small mass, m, is moving in a circle, radius r, at speed v. There must be a centripetal force, F, acting to keep m moving in a circle, where

$$F = \frac{mv^2}{r} \tag{16}$$

Here, the force must be provided by the gravitational attraction, F_{grav}, between the two masses:

$$F_{grav} = \frac{GMm}{r^2} \tag{equation 10}$$

Identifying the two forces as one and the same:

$$\frac{GMm}{r^2} \equiv \frac{mv^2}{r}$$

Cancelling m and r and rearranging gives:

$$M = \frac{v^2 r}{G} \tag{17}$$

It is often useful to rewrite equation (17) in terms of the period T (the time for one orbit) where

$$v = \frac{2\pi r}{T}$$

and so

$$M = \left(\frac{2\pi r}{T}\right)^2 \times \frac{r}{G} = \frac{4\pi^2 r^3}{T^2 G} \tag{18}$$

Equation (18) tells us that to measure the mass of the central object we need to know the radius of the orbit of its companion and the period of the orbit. It can be used to determine the masses of planets by observing the orbits of their moons, or the Sun's mass from measurements of the orbit of planets. Note that the mass, m, of the orbiting object does not feature in equation (18) – we do not need to know m, nor can m be found using this method.

Analysis of the situation in Figure 44(b) is more complicated, but it yields the same expression, where M is now the total mass of the pair of objects ($M = m_1 + m_2$). (This analysis also yields expressions that enable the two masses to be determined separately.) So, to measure the mass of a star it must have an observable gravitational effect on another object, usually another star. The masses of isolated stars must be deduced by other means.

Study note

You met centripetal force and circular motion in the unit *Probing the Heart of Matter*.

ACTIVITY 20 **In orbit**

Use the gravity applet

http://users.ox.ac.uk/~pemb0499/gravity.html

to explore the motion of objects under an inverse square law force.

Sketch (or describe) the paths of the orbiter when it passes close to, and far away from, the central object.

By trial and error, find an orbit that keeps the orbiter on screen for as long as possible. Sketch the orbit, and identify objects that orbit the Sun in similar paths.

Binary stars

Studying binary stars and measuring the periods and separations is the job of the observational astronomer. It is possible for us to observe some binaries directly and to see both stars in the eyepiece of the telescope, but mostly they are 'unresolved' – that is, they appear as a single star, even with the most powerful telescopes available. So how do astronomers know that they are looking at a binary star?

Unresolved binaries give themselves away in two ways. First, if the orbital plane of the binary system is in our line of sight, then one star will at some stage eclipse the other. When this happens there will be a change in the brightness of the star just as when the Moon eclipses the Sun. Figure 45 shows the effect. The graph (known as a light curve) shows the variation in observed brightness as the small bright star passes behind, and later in front of, the larger star.

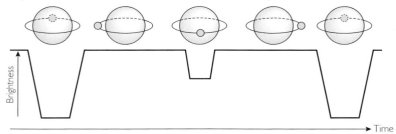

Figure 45 *The light curve of an eclipsing binary star*

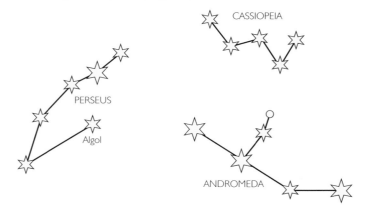

Figure 46 *Algol in the constellation of Perseus, which is close to Andromeda and Cassiopeia*

The bright star Algol, in the constellation of Perseus, is an eclipsing binary (see Figure 46). It is most easily observed in the autumn night sky. For most of the time it is about as bright as Polaris, the Pole star, but every $2\frac{1}{2}$ days it fades noticeably over about 4 hours. It stays dim for about 20 minutes, then takes another four hours to return to its normal brightness. Algol's behaviour was first explained by a young astronomer, John Goodricke of York (1764–1786) (Figure 47). A sculpture representing the two stars of Algol stands outside the college named after Goodricke at York University (Figure 48).

Figure 47   *John Goodricke*

The second way that an astronomer knows that a star is a binary is to observe the spectrum of the star. Consider again the smaller star in Figure 45. As it moves towards or away from us, the lines in its observed spectrum will be Doppler shifted. As the star recedes the lines will be shifted to longer wavelengths, and as it approaches they will be shifted to shorter wavelengths. You met the **Doppler effect** in the AS unit *Spare Part Surgery*, and used an expression for the shift in frequency:

Figure 48   *The Algol sculpture at Goodricke College*

$$\frac{\Delta f}{f} \approx \frac{u}{v} \tag{19}$$

where u is the speed of the source or detector, v is the wave speed and $\Delta f = f_{em} - f_{rec}$, where em and rec refer to the emitted and received frequencies. The expression applies only when $u \ll v$. In the case of binary stars, $v = c$ (the speed of light) and it is still true that $u \ll c$ (u is the speed of the star along our line of sight). When studying spectra it is more convenient to measure wavelength, λ, than frequency, and the appropriate expression is then:

$$\frac{\Delta \lambda}{\lambda_{em}} \approx \frac{u}{c} \tag{20}$$

where

$$\Delta \lambda = \lambda_{rec} - \lambda_{em} \tag{21}$$

So, using equation (20), it is quite straightforward to measure the orbital speed (symbol u or v). Orbital period, T, can be deduced simply from seeing how the amount of Doppler shift changes with time, and thus all the information is available for determining the separation r and hence the mass M.

Masses of stars

In the middle decades of the 20th century, measurement of large numbers of stellar masses provided astronomers with further clues to the nature and evolution of stars. One important finding was that the masses of main sequence stars are strongly linked to their temperature and luminosity. Main sequence stars with the same luminosity and temperature also have the same mass. The most luminous main sequence stars are also the most massive, with masses up to about 20 times that of the Sun. The faintest main sequence stars, on the other hand, have masses less than half the Sun's mass.

The measurement of mass provide very good reasons for believing that main sequence stars do *not* change their luminosity and temperature, since to do so they would need to change their mass by a considerable amount – it would be very difficult to see how they could do this. The main sequence, then, does *not* represent a star's evolution, even though its name tends to suggest otherwise.

In sections 3.3 to 3.5 you will see how the 'story' of star formation and evolution has been developed to explain the features of the HR diagram that you saw in section 3.1.

QUESTIONS

33 (**a**) From the graph in Figure 45, decide which of the two stars has the brighter surface and explain how you reached your decision.

(**b**) Label a copy of Figure 45 to show the orbital period.

34 (**a**) Sketch the light curve of a binary pair of stars, of equal sizes and luminosities, in a circular orbit viewed edge-on. Mark the orbital period on your sketch.

(**b**) How would the light curve be affected if the orbit were elliptical, as in Figure 49?

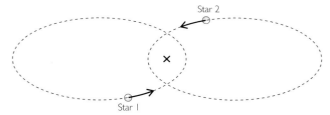

Figure 49   *A binary pair of stars with elliptical orbits*

35 Use the wave equation, $v = f\lambda$, to derive equation (20) from equation (19). (Hint: near the end you will need to use the fact that $\lambda_{rec} \approx \lambda_{em}$.)

36 In February 1987, astronomers observed a huge stellar explosion (a supernova) in a nearby galaxy. About 6 months later, they measured the wavelength of a spectral line of helium as being $1.070\,\mu m$, whereas in the laboratory this line has a wavelength $1.083\,\mu m$.

Were the gases from the explosion approaching or receding, and how fast were they moving? Express your answer as a fraction of the speed of light, c, and in $km\,s^{-1}$. ($c = 3.00 \times 10^8\,m\,s^{-1}$)

37 Analysis of the spectrum of an eclipsing, spectroscopic binary of period $T = 8.6$ years shows that the maximum Doppler shift of a hydrogen absorption line with $\lambda_{em} = 656.28\,nm$ is $0.041\,nm$.

Assume the system consists of a small star in orbit about a much more massive companion. Calculate the radius of the small star's orbit (assuming it to be circular) and hence determine the mass of the large star. ($c = 3.00 \times 10^8\,m\,s^{-1}$; 1 year $= 3.16 \times 10^7\,s$; $G = 6.67 \times 10^{-11}\,N\,m^2\,kg^{-2}$)

3.3 Star formation

We have seen how some of the properties of stars are measured and calculated – we now turn to the evolution of stars; how they are born, live and die. This is a story of real scientific endeavour and achievement. Until the early part of the 20th century, it was thought to be impossible to find out anything about the nature of stars and how they evolved, but since then, astronomers, physicists and mathematicians have made great progress in this area, to the extent that we can now describe the life story of a star with some degree of confidence. In this section, we will follow some aspects of this story, from the gas clouds that are the stellar nurseries, and in section 3.4 we will continue the story to the final stages of the lives of stars.

What lies between the stars? You might think 'empty space', but that would not be quite true. Within our galaxy, the space between the stars is filled with gas and dust (minute solid particles). By our own everyday standards, this **interstellar material** is very tenuous (i.e. has very low density), but we can still detect it. Figure 50 shows the Orion nebula – visible to the naked eye as a fuzzy patch of light in Orion (see Figure 35). This and photographs of other **nebulae** (a general term for 'fuzzy objects' or clouds) show that between the stars there are huge clouds of hot gas, many light years across, that emit their own light, and cool, darker regions that show their presence by blocking out the light from more distant stars. And in between the visible clouds, there is gas that is too cold, or too tenuous, for us to detect with visible light.

Figure 50 *The Orion nebula*

The bright stars embedded in the Orion nebula are believed to have formed quite recently, so the nebula is a site of star formation. But how can a tenuous cloud of gas give rise to the conditions of very high density and temperature needed for the nuclear fusion reactions that power stars? Understanding what is involved requires some knowledge of gravitation (from section 3.2) and of the behaviour of gases.

In the 17th century, scientists such as Robert Boyle first investigated the physical properties of gases. They did experiments on the relationships between the pressure, volume and temperature of gases. We can repeat their pioneering experiments fairly easily in a modern physics laboratory.

ACTIVITY 21 Experiments on gases

Use the apparatus shown in Figure 51 to measure the volume of the gas trapped in the glass tube as the pressure is *slowly* increased. (The pressure must be slowly increased, otherwise the temperature of the gas will also increase.)

Use a spreadsheet to plot pressure against volume. Suggest a simple mathematical form for the relationship between these two variables and use the spreadsheet to test your idea.

If apparatus is available, also investigate the relationships between pressure and temperature at constant volume, and between volume and temperature at constant pressure.

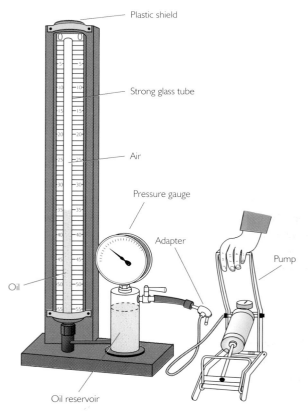

Figure 51 *Apparatus for demonstrating the change of volume with pressure of a gas*

The graphs in Figure 52 are based on experiments such as those in Activity 21, and show the relationships between pressure, p, volume, V, and temperature, T, for a fixed mass of gas as each variable in turn is held constant.

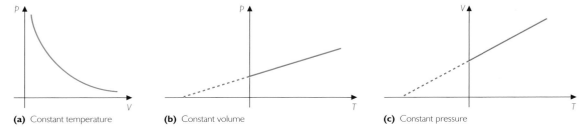

(a) Constant temperature   **(b)** Constant volume   **(c)** Constant pressure

Figure 52   *Temperature, volume and pressure graphs for a fixed mass of gas*

Temperature scales

Notice that the pressure–temperature graph and the volume–temperature graph are both straight lines. If extrapolated, both these lines meet the horizontal axis at a temperature of $-273\,°C$. You should realise that this could never be achieved in practice, since any real gas will liquefy and stop exerting a pressure well before zero temperature is reached, and it is impossible to imagine a gas with zero volume (what would happen to the molecules?). The extrapolation shows the behaviour of an **ideal gas** – one that does not liquefy, among other things. However, the theoretical idea can be put to good use in the definition of an **absolute temperature scale**. The **absolute zero** of temperature, zero kelvins ($0\,K$ – notice no degree symbol) is defined as the temperature at which the pressure of an ideal gas becomes zero. Absolute zero, $0\,K$, is equivalent to $-273\,°C$.

The other fixed point on the absolute temperature scale is the 'triple point of water', which is the unique temperature at which pure water, pure ice and water vapour can coexist; this is $0\,°C$. Thus we have:

$$\text{temperature in K} = \text{temperature in } °C + 273 \qquad (22)$$

We have emphasised the connection between the Celsius and Kelvin scales is that the gas laws use K as a measure of temperature, but everyday life uses $°C$ – you will need to convert between the two. Note, though, that the kelvin is the same size as the degree Celsius, so a temperature *change* ΔT has the same numerical value expressed in either scale.

Gas laws

Provided temperature is measured in kelvins, then the results shown in Figure 52 for a fixed mass of gas can be expressed as follows.

The **pressure law**: at constant volume, pressure is directly proportional to temperature:

$$p \propto T \qquad (23)$$

Charles's law: at constant pressure, volume is directly proportional to temperature:

$$V \propto T \tag{24}$$

Boyle's law: at constant temperature (in any units!) pressure is inversely proportional to volume:

$$p \propto \frac{1}{V} \tag{25}$$

Collectively, these three laws are known as the **gas laws**. These laws are empirical, that is, they are purely experimental – they tell us how ideal gases behave under a variety of conditions, but they do not tell us *why* they behave in this way. The gas laws can be combined in the form of a single equation:

$$\frac{pV}{T} = \text{constant}$$

This is called the **ideal gas equation** or the **equation of state for an ideal gas**. An ideal gas is defined as one that exactly obeys the gas laws. In reality, ideal gases do not exist – there is no gas that exactly obeys the gas laws, although if a gas is at a high enough temperature and low enough pressure to avoid liquefying then it will approximate to an ideal gas.

Experiment shows that the constant is proportional to the quantity of gas. This might give the impression that the 'constant' is not constant. But remember that the ideal gas equation applies to a *fixed mass* of gas and the 'constant' is only constant if the quantity of gas is fixed. If the mass of gas is changed, or the type of gas, then the constant also changes. A complete statement of the ideal gas equation is

$$pV = nRT \tag{26}$$

where n is the number of moles of the gas and R is the **universal gas constant**.

The mole (abbreviation, mol) is the SI unit of the amount of substance. The idea of 'amount of substance' may seem fairly vague but in fact it is precisely defined. A mole of material consists of a definite number of particles, called the **Avogadro number** N_A:

$$N_A = 6.02 \times 10^{23} \text{ particles}$$

Notice that the word 'particle' has been used rather than 'atom' or 'molecule'. In a monatomic material such as copper, sodium or argon, the particle would be an atom so that 1 mole of copper would consist of 6.02×10^{23} atoms, whereas for a substance that exists in molecular form, such as hydrogen (H_2), the particle would be a molecule of hydrogen. Thus a mole of hydrogen would contain 6.02×10^{23} molecules.

To calculate the number of moles in a given mass of substance we need to know the mass per mole of the substance. This is called its **molar mass** – molar masses are tabulated in chemistry data books. (You can also work out the molar mass by multiplying the mass of one particle (atom or molecule) by the Avogadro number.) The number of moles is the actual mass divided by the molar mass.

QUESTIONS

38 Show that pV has SI units of J, and hence show that the universal gas constant, R, has SI units $J\,mol^{-1}\,K^{-1}$.

39 The Sun can be modelled as a spherical ball of hydrogen atoms (molar mass $m = 1\,g\,mol^{-1}$) with a total mass $M = 2 \times 10^{30}$ kg and a radius $r = 7 \times 10^8$ m. If the temperature inside the Sun is $T = 1 \times 10^7$ K (i.e. high enough for fusion) what is the pressure? ($R = 8.31\,J\,mol^{-1}\,K^{-1}$. Assume the temperature and pressure are uniform throughout the Sun.)

Kinetic theory of gases

Two hundred years after the laws were discovered physicists began to develop the **molecular kinetic theory of gases**, which explains the behaviour of gases (including the ideal gas equation) in terms of the motion of their molecules.

The kinetic theory was developed mainly in the 19th century, principally by James Clerk Maxwell (Scottish physicist, 1831–1879) (Figure 53a) and subsequently by Ludwig Boltzmann (Austrian physicist, 1844–1906) (Figure 53b). Maxwell was a remarkable scientist. As well as the kinetic theory, he produced the theory of electromagnetism, which led to his prediction of electromagnetic waves.

The kinetic theory is based on the idea that all matter (solids, liquids and gases) is made of discrete particles (molecules or atoms) in a state of motion. To explain the gas laws using the kinetic theory a number of assumptions about the particles and their behaviour are made, namely that:

- particles in a gas collide frequently;

- a very large number of particles are present;

- the particles have negligible forces between them;

- the particles travel in straight lines between collisions and obey Newton's laws of motion;

- the volume of the particles themselves is negligible compared with the volume of their container;

- collisions between particles in a gas and walls of containers are perfectly elastic; and

- the time taken for collisions is negligible compared with the time between collisions.

These assumptions, along with ideas about force and momentum, lead to an equation that relates the pressure of a gas to the motion

(a)

(b)

Figure 53 (a) James Clerk Maxwell, (b) Ludwig Boltzmann

of its particles. To see how this works, consider the situation shown in Figure 54, which contains a gas of N particles, each of mass m, moving randomly. We will first fix attention on just one particle, moving at velocity $\mathbf{c}$, with components u, v and w in the x, y, and z directions, respectively – and imagine that all the other particles have been removed.

Study note

Notice the use of vector notation to describe the particle's motion.

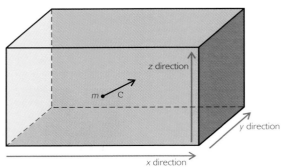

Figure 54   *A container of gas with one particle singled out for attention*

Suppose the particle collides elastically with the shaded face of the container. The x component, u, of its velocity will be reversed, and the other components unchanged. It therefore undergoes a change of momentum in the x direction, ΔP_x, where

Study note

Unfortunately lowercase letter p is conventionally used for both pressure and momentum. We will use uppercase P for momentum here to reduce confusion.

$$\Delta P_x = \text{final momentum} - \text{initial momentum}$$
$$= -(mu) - mu$$
$$= -2mu \tag{27}$$

The particle continues to bounce back and forth, colliding repeatedly with the shaded face of the box. Between successive collisions it travels a distance $2x$ (there and back), so the time interval, Δt, between collisions is

$$\Delta t = \frac{2x}{u} \tag{28}$$

The repeated bombardment of the face of the box produces a force on it. Since the force experienced by the particle is equal to the rate of change of its momentum, the force on the particle is

$$\frac{\Delta P_x}{\Delta t} = -\frac{-2mu}{(2x/u)} = -\frac{-mu^2}{x}$$

Then by Newton's third law, the (outward) force on the wall is

$$F_x = +\frac{mu^2}{x} \tag{29}$$

We add a suffix x because the force acts in the x direction.

The pressure exerted on the shaded face is

$$p_x = \frac{F_x}{yz} \tag{30}$$

because yz is the area of the face. Hence we have

$$p_x = \frac{mu^2}{xyz} = \frac{mu^2}{V} \tag{31}$$

where V is the volume of the container.

Study note

Alternatively, you can say that the number of collisions per second on the shaded end is $\dfrac{u}{2x}$, and so the total change of momentum per second is $\dfrac{u}{2x} \times 2mu$, which gives the same result.

Now think of all N particles in the container, each with its own velocity that can be resolved into components in the x, y and z directions. Each particle contributes to the pressure exerted on the shaded face, so that the total pressure on that face is

$$p_x = \frac{m}{V} \times (u_1^2 + u_1^2 + \ldots + u_N^2) \tag{32}$$

which we can write as

$$p_x = \frac{Nm\langle u^2 \rangle}{V} \tag{33a}$$

where $\langle u^2 \rangle$ is the mean value of u^2 for all the particles – see notes below.

However, there is nothing special about the x direction, so we could equally well have derived similar expressions by considering the other directions:

$$p_y = \frac{Nm\langle v^2 \rangle}{V} \tag{33b}$$

$$p_z = \frac{Nm\langle w^2 \rangle}{V} \tag{33c}$$

But the pressure, p, of a gas is the same in all directions, so we can drop the subscripts and write

$$3p = p_x + p_y + p_z = \frac{Nm}{V} \times (\langle u^2 \rangle + \langle v^2 \rangle + \langle w^2 \rangle) \tag{34}$$

At this stage we can also note that the velocity components for any one particle are related by

$$u^2 + v^2 + w^2 = c^2 \tag{35}$$

and so

$$(\langle u^2 + \langle v^2 \rangle + \langle w^2 \rangle) = \langle c^2 \rangle \tag{36}$$

where $\langle c^2 \rangle$ is the **mean square speed** of the particles (see below). Equation (34) then becomes

$$pV = \frac{Nm\langle c^2 \rangle}{3} \tag{37}$$

This equation relates properties that we can measure (p and V) to the motion of the particles, which we cannot see. It is also remarkably similar to the ideal gas equation:

$$pV = nRT \tag{equation 26}$$

which indicates that the kinetic theory can indeed explain the behaviour of gases. Using equations (26) and (37) together, we can produce many useful relationships that describe the behaviour of gases, as you will see below.

Study note

We use angle brackets $\langle$ and $\rangle$ to denote a mean value. Some texts use a bar over the averaged quantity: $\overline{c^2}$.)

Mean squares and r.m.s. speeds

In producing equations (33) and (37), we used the idea of a mean square speed. This is the mean value of c^2, averaged over all the particles, which is *not* the same thing as finding the mean speed and squaring it. The square root of the mean square speed, called the **root-mean-square speed** (or **r.m.s. speed**), $\sqrt{\langle c^2 \rangle}$, is a useful quantity when dealing with particles in a gas, since it is an 'average' speed that is directly related to the pressure exerted by the particles.

To find $\sqrt{\langle c^2 \rangle}$, you need to:

- square all the individual speeds
- sum all the squares
- divide by the total number of particles
- take the square root of the result.

The r.m.s. speed is in general not the same as the 'ordinary' mean speed. For example, suppose we have three particles with speed $200\,\mathrm{m\,s^{-1}}$, five with speed $300\,\mathrm{m\,s^{-1}}$ and one with speed $700\,\mathrm{m\,s^{-1}}$.

$$\sqrt{\frac{\langle c^2 \rangle}{(100\,\mathrm{m\,s^{-1}})}} = \sqrt{\left\{ \frac{3 \times 2^2 + 5 \times 3^2 + 1 \times 7^2}{9} \right\}}$$

$$\sqrt{\langle c^2 \rangle} = 343\,\mathrm{m\,s^{-1}}.$$

But the 'ordinary' average speed is $311\,\mathrm{m\,s^{-1}}$.

ACTIVITY 22 **Root mean squares**

Use a spreadsheet to explore root-mean-square speed.

Use the RAND() function to generate 100 different speeds. In one of the cells put the formula ' = RAND()*1000'. This will generate 100 different speeds between 0 and $1000\,\mathrm{m\,s^{-1}}$.

In the next column put 100 randomly chosen integers between 1 and 10. This represents the number of particles with that speed. To do this use the function ' = INT(RAND()*10)'.

Use these values to find the r.m.s. speed and the average speed of the molecules in the spreadsheet. Compare the two values.

Results based on the kinetic theory

The kinetic theory and the gas laws together provide a powerful tool in furthering our understanding of gases. By rewriting and combining equations (26) and (37) in various ways, we can make many deductions about the behaviour of gases and the particles of which they are made. Here we will derive just some of the many useful relationships. The fact that these all produce a self-consistent picture of gases, which ties in with experimental results, provides a good reason to believe that particles in real gases do behave more or less in the ways assumed by the kinetic theory.

First look again at equation (37). On the right-hand side the product Nm, the number of particles times the mass of a single particle, gives the total mass, M, of the gas in the container. Noting that

$$\frac{M}{V} = \rho$$

where ρ is the gas density, we can write equation (37) as

$$p = \frac{\rho \langle c^2 \rangle}{3} \tag{38}$$

So we now have an expression that relates the r.m.s. speed to properties of the gas itself, regardless of the volume present. Note that equation (38) does not require a gas of identical particles – it applies equally well to a mixture.

QUESTIONS

40 At atmospheric pressure (1×10^5 Pa) and room temperature, the density of air is about $1 \ \text{kg m}^{-3}$. What is the approximate r.m.s. speed of the air molecules?

41 In question 39 we modelled the Sun as a sphere of hydrogen atoms, total mass $M = 2 \times 10^{30}$ kg at a temperature $T = 1 \times 10^7$ K. *En route* to the answer, the number of moles of hydrogen atoms was found to be $n = 2 \times 10^{33}$ mol.

(**a**) Use equations (26) and (37) to derive an expression for the r.m.s. speed of the particles in terms of n, M, T and the gas constant R, and hence find the r.m.s. speed of the particles in this model of the Sun. ($R = 8.31 \ \text{J mol}^{-1} \ \text{K}^{-1}$) (Hint: the right-hand sides of equations (26) and (37) are both equal to pV.)

(**b**) The expression you derived in (**a**) was a bit clumsy, because it used the number of moles, n, which had been calculated (in question 39) using the total mass M – effectively, you multiplied by M (to find n) and then divided by it. Use the fact that $n = N/N_A$ to derive a new expression for $\langle c^2 \rangle$ which depends only on the mass, m, of each particle, R, N_A and T and not on the quantity of gas present.

42 In question 41(b) you produced an expression showing that the r.m.s. speed of particles depends only on their mass and temperature. Given that the mass of an oxygen molecule is 16 times that of a hydrogen molecule, at a given temperature, which molecules would have the greater r.m.s. speed, and by what factor?

In the answer to question 41(b) we produced this expression

$$\langle c^2 \rangle = \left(\frac{3RT}{mN_A} \right) \tag{39}$$

On the right-hand side there are two constants, and it is convenient to combine them to produce a single new constant, called the **Boltzmann constant**, k, where

$$k = \frac{R}{N_A} = 1.38 \times 10^{-23}\,\mathrm{J\,K^{-1}}$$

Equation (39) then becomes

$$\langle c^2 \rangle = \frac{3kT}{m} \tag{40}$$

By noticing that the average molecular kinetic energy is

$$\langle E_k \rangle = \frac{m\langle c^2 \rangle}{2} \tag{41}$$

we can also write

$$\frac{m\langle c^2 \rangle}{2} = \langle E_k \rangle = \frac{3kT}{2} \tag{42}$$

Notice that the average kinetic energy depends *only* on the temperature, and not on the mass of the particles. This gives us a way to interpret absolute zero in terms of the behaviour of particles in an ideal gas: it is the temperature at which they cease to move.

Here it is worth thinking a bit more about the speed and kinetic energy of particles at any temperature above 0 K. The particles have a range of kinetic energies and collide frequently. When they collide they exchange kinetic energy with one another, but total momentum and total kinetic energy are conserved. The way the total energy is shared between the particles depends *only* on the temperature, and the speeds found in a particular gas depend only on the temperature and the mass of the molecules (or particles) in the gas. At a particular instant some particles will have high kinetic energy and others will have only a low kinetic energy. The majority will have kinetic energy close to the average for that particular temperature. As the temperature increases the average kinetic energy will increase, as will the average speed of the particles. Figure 55 shows the number of atoms plotted on the vertical axis against the speed on the horizontal axis. A few particles have very small speeds and a few have very large speeds. The majority of the particles have intermediate speeds.

Study note

You studied similar collisions in the unit *Transport on Track*, only they involved much larger objects.

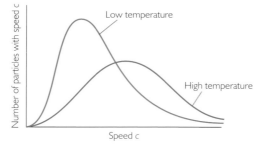

Figure 55 *Distributions of molecular speeds*

In an ideal gas, the particles do not interact with one another (except when they collide). But in a liquid or solid (and in a non-ideal gas) the particles exert forces on one another (in a solid, rather as if they were joined by springs). So the energy of the particles cannot be described in terms of kinetic energy alone –

their potential energy also varies – and so the **internal energy** of a collection of particles is now the total of their kinetic and potential energies. However, it is still the case that the interactions between particles ensure that the overall distribution of kinetic energy depends only on the temperature.

QUESTIONS

43 Use equation (40) to find the r.m.s. speed of hydrogen ions ($m = 1.67 \times 10^{-27}$ kg) at a temperature of 1×10^7 K. Compare the result with your answer to question 41(a).

44 Show that equation (26) can be rewritten as $pV = NkT$.

45 Table 11 contains some data on various types of interstellar gas. (You can see pictures of the examples mentioned in many astronomy books and CD-ROMs.)

(**a**) Find the r.m.s. speed of:
(**i**) hydrogen molecules ($m = 2 \times 1.67 \times 10^{-27}$ kg) in a typical molecular cloud.
(**ii**) hydrogen ions in a supernova remnant which has $T = 10^6$ K.
(Hint: there is a short cut to (**ii**) using your answer to question 43.)

(**b**) The number density of particles is the number per unit volume, equal to N/V.
(**i**) Use this information and the expression in question 44 to calculate the values missing from the 'pressure' column of Table 11.
(**ii**) Comment on the range of values in this column.

Type of ISM	Typical diameter/ light years	Typical number density of particles/ m^{-3}	Typical temperature/ K	Composition	Typical pressure/ 10^{-13} Pa	Example(s)
Molecular clouds (also called dense clouds)	0.3–60	10^{10}	30	H_2, He, small and large molecules	40	Horsehead nebula
Diffuse clouds	10–300	10^8	100	H_2, H, He, other atoms, diatomic molecules	1.4	(not detected in visible light)
Supernova remnants	up to 3000	10^5	10^6	H^+ or H, other atoms and/or ions		Crab nebula Vela nebula
Regions of ionised hydrogen	3–60	10^8	8000	H^+, He^+, other singly charged ions		Rosette nebula Carina nebula Lagoon nebula

Table 11   *Interstellar material (ISM)*

Making stars

Having established some important points about the behaviour of particles in gases, we now return to the question of star formation. The stars we see in the sky are hot and dense, and yet they form from interstellar material (ISM) that is very tenuous. As you can see from Table 11, the temperature in the hottest parts of the ISM is not quite high enough for hydrogen fusion (which needs over 10^7 K), but the main problem is the density and pressure. As you saw in question 39, the pressure inside the Sun is about 10^{14} Pa, while question 45 showed that in the ISM it is no more than about 10^{-11} Pa – a difference of some 25 orders of magnitude. The following passage explains how star formation happens. Read it carefully, then answer questions 46 to 48.

To form stars, an interstellar cloud must collapse under its own gravity to form a hot, dense concentration of matter. To see how this works, imagine a particle (e.g. a hydrogen atom or molecule) near the edge of an interstellar cloud (Figure 56). Newton's law of gravitation tells us that the particle will experience gravitational forces due to all the other matter around it. As there is a greater concentration of matter on one side of the particle, it accelerates towards the centre of the cloud. The same will be true of all particles near the edge of the cloud – they are all drawn gradually inwards and so after many thousands of years all the material will eventually become concentrated within a small volume.

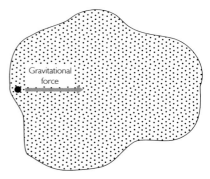

Figure 56 *A particle near the edge of an interstellar cloud*

But if that were all that happens, then all interstellar material would be clumped together in stars, rather than existing as tenuous gas. As we know from the success of the kinetic theory of gases, the particles in a gas are moving around at high speeds. If they are moving fast enough, they can escape from the cloud, rather as a rocket fired from Earth at high enough speed can travel out into space instead of falling back to the ground, and so the cloud will disperse rather than collapse.

Whether a cloud collapses under its own gravity to form stars, or disperses due to the motion of its particles, depends on the 'competition' between those two factors. A detailed analysis shows that only the coldest, densest regions of the ISM can collapse under their own gravity. But that then raises the problem of how such material can ever become hot enough for nuclear fusion to occur. It turns out that gravity and kinetic theory again play a part.

During the collapse of a cloud, particles can be thought of as gradually 'falling' towards the centre, rather like objects falling to Earth. As they fall, they accelerate. Put another way, they gain kinetic energy at the expense of gravitational potential energy. The increasing concentration of matter is enough to maintain the collapse, despite the increasing speed of the particles.

As you can see from pictures of interstellar clouds (such as the Orion nebula in Figure 50), they are not smooth and uniform. As a cloud collapses, it breaks up into fragments that continue to collapse separately.

By the time a fragment has collapsed into a small volume – several million years after the collapse first started – the particles are moving at very high speeds and are colliding with one another. As the temperature rises, the collisions become increasingly violent, so molecules are first disrupted into atoms, and then the electrons become dislodged from the atoms to make ions.

By the time the material has collapsed to the size of a star, it is a very dense plasma (an ionised gas) with a temperature of about 10^7 K. Now nuclear fusion begins to take place, and the release of energy halts the collapse. A star is born!

This is a nice story, but do we have any evidence to support it? The processes are all much too slow for us to observe them happening during our lifetime, but one key piece of evidence comes from infrared astronomy. We know that all objects emit radiation at wavelengths that depend on their surface temperature, and so we would expect to detect infrared radiation from fragments that were collapsing and getting hotter on the way to becoming stars. And this is what astronomers find when they turn infrared-sensitive telescopes to regions such as the Orion nebula – clusters of 'hot spots' that are just as we would expect to see if the cloud were in the process of collapsing, fragmenting and heating up (Figure 57).

Figure 57   *Infrared image of the Orion nebula*

QUESTIONS

In answering these questions, you will need to refer to Table 11 and to your work in section 3.2 as well as to the passage above.

46 In the following paragraphs, choose the correct word or phrase from each pair to make a correct summary of star formation.

Stars are formed by the collapse of a molecular cloud/region of ionised hydrogen. The particles in the cloud are far apart/close together. The force of gravitational/ electrostatic attraction pulls them all towards the edge/centre of the cloud. Each particle is falling inwards, like a ball falling towards the Earth. As the cloud collapses, the particles move more quickly/slowly, and they collide more frequently with one another, sharing their kinetic energy. The faster the particles move, the higher/lower the temperature of the gas. As the cloud collapses: its density increases/decreases; its pressure increases/ decreases; the particles' kinetic energy increases/decreases; and their gravitational potential energy increases/decreases.

The particles collide frequently and energetically so that they break up to form a hot plasma of fast moving/slow moving positively/negatively charged nuclei and electrons. When the temperature is high/low enough, the nuclei can approach one another so closely that nuclear fission/fusion can start.

47 Estimate the mass of a typical molecular cloud, assuming that it is made entirely of hydrogen molecules, H_2, and hence estimate the number of Sun-like stars that could form when such a cloud collapses. Quote your answer to the nearest order of magnitude. (Mass of H_2, $m = 3.34 \times 10^{-27}$ kg; mass of Sun, $M_{Sun} = 2 \times 10^{30}$ kg; 1 light year $= 9.46 \times 10^{15}$ m)

48 (**a**) Estimate (**i**) the acceleration of a hydrogen molecule at the edge of a typical molecular cloud (see question 47); (**ii**) the time it would take the molecule to reach the centre of the cloud if it started from rest, travelled in a straight line, and its acceleration did not change; (**iii**) the molecule's speed when it reached the centre; and (**iv**) the temperature of a gas or plasma where this was the r.m.s. speed of hydrogen molecules.

(**b**) Comment on your answer to (**a**)(**iv**).

($G = 6.67 \times 10^{-11}$ N m^2 kg^{-2}; 1 year $\approx 3 \times 10^7$ s; $k = 1.38 \times 10^{-23}$ J K^{-1})

ACTIVITY **23** **Star formation**

Scientists who wish to publicise their research findings often produce a poster for display and discussion at conferences. The most eye-catching of these is likely to have the most immediate impact.

Make a conference poster showing the main stages in star formation from an interstellar cloud to the arrival of the star onto the main sequence. Use sketches or photographs and add plenty of information, including details of density, temperature and pressure in the interstellar medium. Include any relevant equations and example calculations to make your poster as informative as possible.

3.4 Evolution and end points – Summing up part 3

This section continues the story of stars with an account of what happens after they are formed and, in doing so, reminds you of the physics that you have studied in sections 3.1 to 3.3 (and also some of the physics from part 2 of this unit). The questions and activities are intended to help you look back over your work.

ACTIVITY **24** **Summing up part 3**

Before going on to read more about stars, look back through your work in this part of the unit and make sure you understand the meaning of all the terms printed in bold.

A star on the main sequence

In section 3.3 you saw how a fragment of interstellar cloud could collapse under its own weight to form a small, dense ball of matter that was hot enough for nuclear fusion to begin. Once the star has settled down to a steady rate of fusion, its size, luminosity and temperature remain more or less constant until its supply of hydrogen fuel is exhausted. It has become a main sequence star. This stage of its life takes a long time, which is why we observe so many stars on the main sequence of a Hertzsprung–Russell diagram (see Figure 58), which is based on observations of a very large number of stars. The numbers give the masses of the stars in units of the Sun's mass, $M_{Sun} \approx 2 \times 10^{30}$ kg.

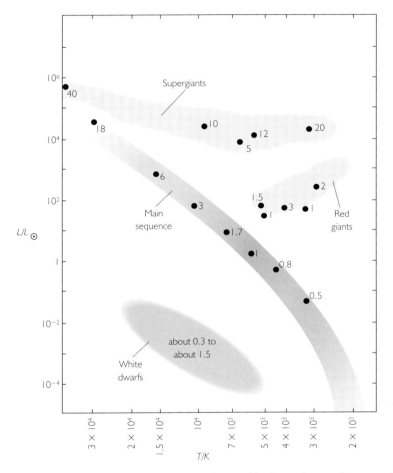

Figure 58 *Schematic Hertzsprung–Russell diagram. Numbers indicate stellar masses in multiples of the Sun's mass*

A star with the same mass as the Sun will remain on the main sequence for about 10^{10} years (see question 20 in section 2.3). The main sequence lifetime of a star depends on its mass and the rate at which it converts hydrogen to helium. Perhaps surprisingly, low-mass stars live for much longer than the Sun. A star of $0.5\,M_{Sun}$ has $L \approx 0.1\,L_{Sun}$. It has only half the amount of fuel but it is consuming it at one tenth the rate found in the Sun, so it will remain on the main sequence for five times as long – about 5×10^{10} years. The most massive stars are the shortest lived, because their nuclear reactions proceed more rapidly, giving them a very high luminosity, and so they exhaust their fuel supplies in a relatively short time. So if we observe any very luminous main sequence stars, we know they must have formed quite recently – only a few million years ago.

QUESTIONS

49 In two or three sentences, outline how the stars' masses in Figure 58 might have been determined.

50 Use Figure 58 to find the approximate luminosity of a star of mass $18\,M_{Sun}$. Assuming that all stars fuse the same fraction of their total mass while on the main sequence, estimate the main sequence lifetime of this star.

After the main sequence

As with the 'story' of star formation, astronomers have drawn on observations and on physics in order to piece together an account of what happens to a star after the hydrogen in its core has all undergone fusion to helium.

When hydrogen fusion ceases, the inner parts of the star cool down, which allows the star to collapse again under its own gravity. Just as happened when the star was forming, there is a gain of kinetic energy at the expense of gravitational potential energy, which leads to heating. Now the material surrounding the helium core becomes hot enough for hydrogen fusion to helium to begin, so inside the star there is now a cool(ish) shrinking core surrounded by a layer where nuclear fusion is releasing energy. The material surrounding this fusion layer expands enormously, cooling as it does so. If the star's mass is less than that of the Sun, or only a few times greater, it is now a red giant – a star with a cool exterior but very luminous because of its large size. A more massive star (say about five times the Sun's mass or more) becomes a **supergiant** – it is not only large but the exterior is still quite hot. Figure 58 shows where red giants and supergiants are located on an HR diagram.

As the core continues to shrink under its own gravity, the temperature rises. In stars at least as massive as the Sun, the core becomes hot enough for new fusion reactions to take place:

$$^{4}_{2}\text{He} + ^{4}_{2}\text{He} \rightarrow ^{8}_{4}\text{Be}$$

$$^{4}_{2}\text{He} + ^{8}_{4}\text{Be} \rightarrow ^{12}_{6}\text{C} + 2\gamma$$

(The beryllium nucleus is very unstable, and decays in less than a second if it does not immediately undergo fusion with another helium nucleus.)

In stars up to about twice the mass of the Sun, the onset of helium fusion causes great upheavals in the outer parts of the star. The upheavals can cause the outer parts of a star to pulsate in and out with periods of only a few days, and astronomers observe a variable star as its luminosity changes. The outermost layers are eventually thrown off to form an expanding shell of glowing gas called a **planetary nebula** (though it has absolutely nothing to do with planets). Figure 59 shows an example of such a shell – you can also see the star in its centre.

When the helium in the core has been converted to carbon, then the star again begins to collapse under its own weight and to heat up. In stars up to about the mass of the Sun, the temperature never gets high enough for any further fusion reactions that would stop the gravitational collapse, so the star gradually shrinks to become a white dwarf – a small, hot, dense star about the size of the Earth that will eventually cool and fade from view.

Figure 59 *The Helix nebula in Aquarius*

ACTIVITY **25** **End of the Sun**

Figure 60 summarises the evolution of a Sun-like star by tracing the changes in its luminosity and surface temperature from just before it joins the main sequence right up to its end as a white dwarf. Table 12 summarises the physical processes that take place at each stage. Use Figure 60 and the preceding text to help you complete the table – in the 'luminosity' column, state the nearest order of magnitude.

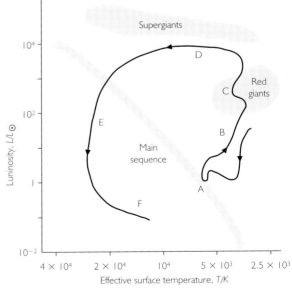

Figure 60 *The evolution of a Sun-like star*

Point on Figure 44	Stage	Physical process	Luminosity/L$_{Sun}$	Surface temperature/ K
	Evolution away from main sequence	Fusion of H continues		
		All fusion stops; slow cooling		
	Red giant			
		Outer layers thrown off leaving hot core		
	Variable star	Violent pulsations of outer layers		
	Main sequence			

Table 12 *The evolution of a Sun-like star*

The fate of massive stars

In stars more massive than the Sun, there is now a pattern that repeats itself:

- the star contracts
- loss of gravitational energy leads to heating
- new fusion reactions produce more massive nuclei
- reactions cease
- the star contracts

…and so it goes on. The successive stages of fusion each happen more and more rapidly, so a star can get through many stages of fusion in a much shorter time than it spends on the main sequence. Each stage of fusion can give rise to changes in the external appearance of the star: it may become a variable star as the outer parts repeatedly expand and shrink before being ejected to form a planetary nebula.

For stars with masses up to about eight times that of the Sun, the series of fusion reactions will eventually cease when the rise in temperature is not great enough to trigger the next stage. Figure 61 shows the interior of an eight solar mass star at the point when fusion stops.

More massive stars can continue with fusion until they produce iron nuclei in their cores (Figure 62), reaching a core temperature of about 4×10^9 K. The successive fusion episodes, leading to the creation of iron, have effectively kept the star stable. As the core has collapsed, the material in the core has started to burn, releasing energy that has kept gravity in check by providing the pressure to support the weight of the star. This feedback mechanism fails when the core is composed of iron because the fusion of iron nuclei to heavier nuclei is not possible. At this point the star consists of an iron core about as big as the Earth and a hydrogen envelope that may be as big as the orbit of Jupiter.

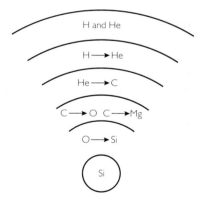

Figure 61 *Schematic cross-section through a star of 8M$_{Sun}$ after core fusion has ceased*

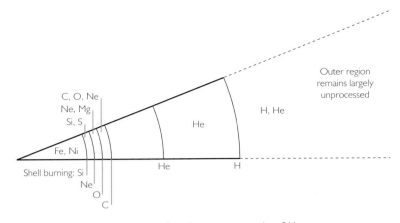

Figure 62 *Schematic cross-section through a star greater than 8M*$_{Sun}$

It has taken the star millions of years to reach this stage, but the next stage takes place with extraordinary rapidity. As fusion ceases, the core collapses. The temperature rises but instead of the production of heavier elements by nuclear fusion, the opposite happens. The collapse causes the temperature of the core to exceed 5 billion K. The gamma rays associated with this high temperature cause the iron atoms to break down into alpha particles. This reaction takes energy away from the core and the collapse continues to gather pace. The alpha particles themselves break down into protons and neutrons. The protons combine with electrons and the core is now nuclear matter (neutrons) with a density of about $4 \times 10^{17}\,\mathrm{kg\,m^{-3}}$. The core now ceases to collapse.

The hydrogen envelope falls onto the now rigid core. This material rises in temperature and pressure and creates a shock wave that travels outwards, blowing the star apart in just a few seconds in a tremendous explosion called a **supernova**. The explosion produces vast numbers of neutrons that can be absorbed by remaining heavy nuclei to form elements heavier than iron. (Note that this process of neutron capture is not nuclear fusion – it requires a source of energy, whereas fusion leads to a release of energy.) The entire star, apart from a tiny condensed core, is blown out into the interstellar medium as a rapidly expanding cloud of very hot gases called a **supernova remnant**. Figure 63 shows one of the most famous supernova remnants in our galaxy. The Crab nebula is the remains of a star that was seen to explode in AD 1054, and was so bright that it was visible in daytime despite being about 6000 light years away.

Supernovae are the source of nearly all the elements heavier than hydrogen and helium. The Big Bang that began the Universe created only hydrogen, helium and traces of some other light elements. Heavier elements are created by nuclear fusion in stars, but most remain locked in stellar cores as they cool. It is only through the violent supernova explosions that elements are scattered into the ISM. Here they cool down and might eventually condense to form another star, perhaps with planets in orbit around it, where carbon-based life (or perhaps some other life forms) can evolve.

Figure 63 *The Crab nebula*

ACTIVITY 26 **Fusion in stars**

'The more massive the star, the more massive the nuclei it can produce by fusion, but even the most massive stars cannot produce nuclei more massive than iron in this way.'

Write a paragraph explaining the physics behind this statement. Include the following terms: gravitational force, electrostatic force, binding energy, kinetic energy. Also include any other key terms from parts 2 and 3 of this unit that you think are relevant.

ACTIVITY 27 **SETI**

Imagine you are an astronomer involved in the SETI (Search for Extraterrestrial Intelligence) programme. You are bidding for time to use the Arecibo Radio Astronomy facility in Puerto Rico (Figure 64). Your aim is to try and pick up radio transmissions that might have been emitted by an alien civilisation on a planet orbiting another star. Prepare a bid to be given to the time-allocation committee that explains which type of stars you intend to observe and why.

You can find out more about SETI, planets and the possibility of life elsewhere in the Universe from the following websites:

http://setiathome.ssl.berkeley.edu

http://www.exoplanets.org

http://astrobiology.arc.nasa.gov/index.cfm

http://www.seti-inst.edu/

Figure 64 *The giant radio telescope at Arecibo*

51 Explain the physics behind the phrase 'gamma rays associated with this high temperature'.

52 (**a**) Making the rash assumption that the core of a highly evolved star behaves like an ideal gas, calculate (**i**) the mean kinetic energy and (**ii**) the r.m.s. speed of ^{56}Fe nuclei at a temperature of 5×10^9 K. (Mass of ^{56}Fe nucleus, $m = 9.3 \times 10^{-26}$ kg; $k = 1.38 \times 10^{-23}$ J K^{-1})

(**b**) Repeat for an electron in the star's core, and comment on your answer. (Electron mass $m_e = 9.1 \times 10^{-31}$ kg)

End points

After a massive star has blown itself up in a supernova explosion, most of its material is scattered into the interstellar medium leaving just the innermost core of the star. If this central object has less than about twice the mass of the Sun, it survives as a **neutron star**. This is an object made mainly of neutrons and with the density of nuclear matter. The entire mass is contained within a sphere about 10 km in diameter.

Neutron stars are small and emit little visible light, but some can be detected using radio telescopes. In 1967 Jocelyn Bell Burnell, who at the time was a research student at Cambridge, was the first to detect a neutron star – completely unintentionally. The star produced a rapid periodic radio pulse, so regular that at first the Cambridge astronomers thought that they had discovered extra-terrestrial intelligent life. The regular pulses led to this type of star being named a **pulsar**, and the regular pulses were explained as being due to a rapidly spinning neutron star.

If a star is rotating before it explodes (and all stars do rotate), then as the core collapses it will spin much more rapidly. This happens to any rotating object that becomes more compact. You can illustrate this by sitting on a swivel chair and spinning round slowly with your arms and legs outstretched; as you bring your limbs closer to your body, you can feel yourself spin faster. When a star's core shrinks to become a neutron star, it can be spinning with a period of less than a second. The collapse also concentrates the star's magnetic field, and the interaction of this very strong field and any charged particles in the vicinity gives rise to a narrow beam of radiation emerging from the star's magnetic poles. If the beam emerges at an angle to the rotation axis, then an observer in the path of the beam will detect a sharp 'flash' each time the beam sweeps past, rather like a lighthouse beam (see Figure 65). Many pulsars have now been observed, including one in the centre of the Crab nebula supernova remnant (shown in the right-hand part of Figure 63).

If the central core has more than about twice the mass of the Sun, then even neutrons are crushed by the strong gravitational forces. The object becomes unimaginably small and compact, and it has such a strong gravitational field that all nearby matter will inexorably be drawn into it; nothing can escape – not even light. It

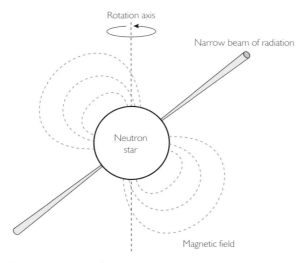

Rotation axis

Narrow beam of radiation

Neutron star

Magnetic field

Figure 65 *Schematic diagram of a pulsar*

is a **black hole**. It may surprise you to learn that the notion of black holes has been around since the middle of the 18th century when they were speculated upon by the Rev. John Michell, vicar of Thornhill near Barnsley in Yorkshire. Like many clergymen of his day, he had studied mathematics at Cambridge and was aware of the discoveries of Sir Isaac Newton. In his paper to the Royal Society in 1783 he said 'Let us now suppose the particles of light to be attracted (to a body) in the same manner as all other bodies which we are acquainted . . . all light emitted from such a body would be made to return towards it, by its own proper gravity.' (It is interesting that he thought of light as being made of particles, as did Isaac Newton. The use of waves to explain the behaviour of light came rather later.)

By their very nature black holes cannot be seen directly. However, astronomers have detected several objects called X-ray binaries. These are believed to be binary stars consisting of a black hole and an ordinary star, in which the intense gravity of the black hole is dragging material away from its companion. As this material spirals towards the black hole like water down a plughole, it is accelerated to high speed and so becomes very hot and emits X-rays (Figure 66).

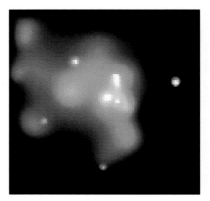

Figure 66 *X-rays detected from a (probable) black hole in the Andromeda galaxy*

QUESTIONS

53 **(a)** Calculate the densities of **(i)** a neutron star that has a radius of 5 km and mass of 4×10^{30} kg (i.e. twice the mass of the Sun) and **(ii)** a helium nucleus that has a radius of approximately 10^{-15} m and a mass 6.7×10^{-27} kg. **(iii)** Hence comment on the statement that a neutron star 'has the density of nuclear matter'.

(b) **(i)** Calculate the gravitational field strength at the surface of the neutron star in **(a)**.
(ii) To the nearest order of magnitude, express your answer as a multiple of the field strength at the Earth's surface.
($G = 6.67 \times 10^{-11}$ N m^2 kg^{-2}; $g_{Earth} = 9.8$ N kg^{-1})

54 Pulsars have been detected with periods of about a millisecond. The material at the surface of a spinning neutron star must experience a centripetal force strong enough to keep it in orbit, and the only force available is the star's own gravity. If the gravitational force is not strong enough, then the star will fly apart.

(**a**) Show that the minimum possible rotation period, T, of a star mass M and radius r is given by

$$T \geqslant \sqrt{\left(\frac{4\pi^2 r^3}{GM}\right)}$$

(**b**) Find the minimum possible rotation period for the neutron star in question 53 and hence say whether a 'millisecond pulsar' could reasonably be a rotating neutron star.

55 Theoretical physicists (and science-fiction writers) have speculated what might happen to space travellers who approached a black hole. As a person fell towards a black hole, they would suffer a process dubbed 'spaghettification', which this question illustrates.

Jo is very tall and she has a large head and large feet (see Figure 67). Her spacecraft has brought her close to a black hole of mass $M = 10^{26}$ kg.

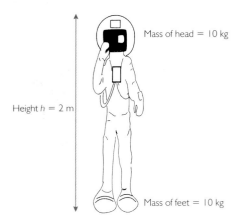

Mass of head = 10 kg

Height h = 2 m

Mass of feet = 10 kg

Figure 67 *Diagram for question 55*

(**a**) Calculate (**i**) the gravitational force on Jo's feet, which are exactly 50 km from the black hole, and (**ii**) the gravitational force on her head, which is exactly 2.0 m further from the black hole. (Keep at least five figures in each answer, even though you might not feel that this is justified.)

(**b**) Explain how these forces will affect Jo.

ACTIVITY **28** **Going out with a bang**

Produce a sequence of annotated cartoon sketches, based on the information above, to summarise the post-main sequence evolution of a massive star. Present your work as a series of overhead projection transparencies or use a computer presentation package such as PowerPoint.

---

4 *The story of our Universe*

In this final part of the unit, you will see how, since the early 20th century, scientists have been looking for answers to such incredible questions as: 'How did the Universe begin?' and 'How will it end?' You will see how some of these questions can be tackled using physics that you have been studying in parts 2 and 3 of the unit, and extend your knowledge and understanding of those areas of physics.

4.1 *Taking on the biggest question in science*

A telescope is a time machine

J. Silk, *A Short History of the Universe*

The birth of modern cosmology

The greatest scientist of the 20th century (Figure 68) hated school. But he was fascinated by science and maths, and read up on them at home. Disappointed about not getting a post as a lecturer, he left Germany, moved to Switzerland, and became an examiner of patents for scientific inventions. In his spare time, he came up with two major new theories that changed the whole face of physics in the 20th century. First, 'special relativity', which revolutionised the way we think about time. And then, general relativity, which changed the way we think about space.

But Albert Einstein (1879–1955) was a complex and tragic character. He was deeply concerned about human rights and freedom on the one hand, yet completely detached from everyday life on the other. He desperately needed affection, but could not maintain close relationships with his family. Despite his giant steps in physics, he died feeling a failure, because he hadn't managed to work out a complete theory of physics.

In 1917 he turned his attention to cosmology and tried to devise equations for how the whole Universe behaves. He didn't know much about astronomy, and had no experimental evidence on which to base his equations. Truly pioneering work. One of his ideas provided a foundation for cosmology in the future...

Einstein made the bold assumption that, on average, the Universe looks the same from any point and the same in all directions.

Figure 68 *The young Albert Einstein*

Matter, galaxies and clusters of galaxies are evenly scattered on a large scale. The Universe is 'homogeneous'. This is called the **cosmological principle**. Without the cosmological principle, the equations of cosmology would be just too hard to solve, and scientists would not have made the astonishing progress they achieved in the 20th century. Mercifully Einstein's assumption turns out to be true – the Universe does seem to be pretty much the same everywhere.

Study note

You will see some evidence for homogeneity in section 4.2.

Like virtually everyone in his day, Einstein believed that the Universe was unchanging, that it was the same now as it was when it was created. But he realised that the gravitational attraction of all the matter in the Universe would cause it to be drawn together (rather like the collapsing cloud idea that you met in section 3.3). He therefore included in his equations a term describing an unknown repulsive force that would ensure that the Universe would indeed continue to look the same for ever. He later called this 'the biggest blunder in my life', as Edwin Hubble made some observations that indicated that the Universe would not always stay the same.

Hubble and the galaxies

> I see beyond this island universe,
> Beyond our sun, and all those other suns
> That throng the Milky Way, far, far beyond,
> A thousand little wisps, faint nebulae.

> Alfred Noyes, *The Torch Bearers*

Edwin Hubble (1889–1953), a tall, athletic young American, had a tricky choice to make. He excelled in maths, astronomy and boxing. Would he take the chance of fighting the then world heavyweight champion he had been offered? Thankfully for the future of cosmology, he chose instead to come and study at Oxford University, England. But his discoveries had to wait until he'd served in the First World War. (He began as a private in the US army and ended the war a major.)

Eventually, at the age of 30, he began his famous work at the new 100-inch telescope at Mount Wilson, California (Figure 69). His first discovery was a special type of star within a faint misty patch of light known as the Andromeda nebula (Figure 70). Astronomers had puzzled over what these nebulae were for centuries. Hubble was able to measure the distance to the star accurately, and managed to show that the nebula was simply a congregation of stars – just like our Milky Way galaxy, but far beyond it. For the first time, we knew something about the real scale of the Universe. The basic units of matter in the Universe are galaxies, not stars. And if that was not enough, Hubble was soon to make sense of a phenomenon that was to change our whole conception of the Universe even more. This concerned the line spectra of distant galaxies.

As mentioned in part 2 of this unit, the spectrum of light from the Sun and other stars contains many narrow absorption lines, produced when atoms in the cool outer parts of the star absorb

Figure 69 *Edwin Hubble*

Figure 70 *The Andromeda nebula*

radiation at their own characteristic wavelengths. When astronomers began looking at the spectra of whole galaxies beyond our own, they found the same general pattern of absorption lines in the light from all the stars superimposed. But they also noticed something rather surprising. For all but the closest galaxies, the dark lines seemed to be shifted from their normal positions, towards longer wavelengths. Wouldn't you be surprised if you looked outside and saw a green sky, orange grass, and a red midday Sun? This phenomenon became known as **redshift**, because the lines were shifted towards the red (low-frequency, long-wavelength) end of the spectrum.

Redshift is defined as the ratio of the change in wavelength $\Delta\lambda$ as a fraction of the wavelength λ measured in the laboratory, and is usually given the symbol z. Provided the wavelength change is small, this is very nearly the same as the ratio of the change in frequency Δf to the 'lab' frequency f, and so

$$z = \frac{\Delta\lambda}{\lambda} \approx \frac{\Delta f}{f} \tag{43}$$

Figure 71 shows the spectra of three galaxies with different redshifts.

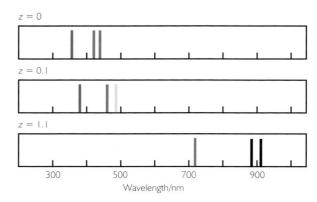

Figure 71 *The effect of redshift on wavelength*

You have met something like equation (43) before – in the AS unit *Spare Part Surgery* and in part 3 of this unit. There you saw that the Doppler shift was given by

$$\frac{\Delta\lambda}{\lambda} \approx \frac{\Delta f}{f} \approx \frac{v}{c} \qquad \text{(equations 19 and 20)}$$

provided $v \ll c$, where v is the speed of the source of the radiation and c the speed of light in a vacuum. In other words, the redshift is related to the speed of the source of radiation. We can combine these expressions and write

$$z = \frac{\Delta\lambda}{\lambda} \approx \frac{\Delta f}{f} \approx \frac{v}{c} \tag{44}$$

Using the largest telescope in the world Hubble was able to measure the redshifts and distances of 24 galaxies. He noticed that

Study note

Note that we, and other texts, also use u to represent the speed of the source.

the redshift was greater for more distant galaxies. He plotted his results on a graph of distance against 'recessional' speed. Figure 72 shows his results, taken from his paper published in 1929. Notice that the units of distance here is the parsec, pc (see section 3.1). Each black dot is an individual galaxy, and each circle is a group of galaxies. Figure 73 shows some more recent data. You can see the linear relationship extends to very distant galaxies – note the huge range of values plotted, making it necessary to use a logarithmic scale. The distance unit here is the megaparsec, Mpc. $1\,\text{Mpc} = 10^6\,\text{pc}$.

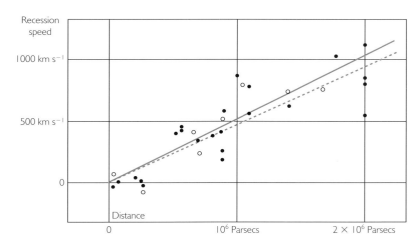

Figure 72 *Hubble's graph of recession speed versus distance*

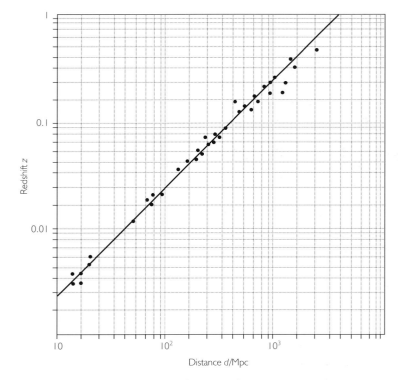

Figure 73 *A graph of more recent redshift–distance data*

Study note

Notice the log scales in Figure 74. Zero does not feature on the graph, since that would require an infinite length of graph paper.

ACTIVITY 29 **Redshift**

The CLEA software lets you experience some aspects of modern observational astronomy and provides you with some authentic data. Use the software to measure the redshifts of some galaxies and to relate the redshifts to their distances.

Hubble had found a simple link between distance, d, and redshift:

$$z \propto d$$

If $v \ll c$, then z is proportional to v so we can write

$$v \approx H_0 d \qquad (45)$$

where H_0 is called the **Hubble constant**. This is known as **Hubble's law**. Equation (44) can now be written as

$$z = \frac{H_0 d}{c} \qquad (46)$$

Hubble's constant can be found from the gradients of graphs such as those in Figures 72 and 73. It is usually quoted in units of $\mathrm{km\,s^{-1}}$ $\mathrm{Mpc^{-1}}$ (think of equation (45) with v in $\mathrm{km\,s^{-1}}$ and d in Mpc). It is difficult to determine accurately, because it relies on the accurate measurement of d for very distant galaxies, and current values range from about $50\,\mathrm{km\,s^{-1}}\,\mathrm{Mpc^{-1}}$ to about $100\,\mathrm{km\,s^{-1}}\,\mathrm{Mpc^{-1}}$.

Study note

The current 'favourite' value for H_0 is about $70\,\mathrm{km\,s^{-1}}\,\mathrm{Mpc^{-1}}$.

The expanding Universe

The most surprising thing about Hubble's discovery was its interpretation. It implied that the Universe was expanding! Activity 30 shows how Hubble's law implies an expanding Universe.

ACTIVITY 30 **The expanding rubber universe**

Cut a wide elastic band to make a strip of rubber. With a pen, make three marks at 1 cm intervals, labelled 1, 2 and 3. These represent galaxies.

Draw an observer (a small bug?) on one of the galaxies.

Stretch the rubber band to simulate the expansion of the Universe (Figure 74).

Measure how far the other galaxies have moved away from the observer, and so compare the recession speeds of the two galaxies.

Repeat with the observer on one of the other galaxies.

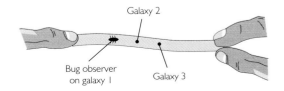

Figure 74 *Stretching the Universe*

Stretching the rubber band produces Hubble's law: speed is proportional to distance. Any uniformly stretching material would do the same. And the converse is true: if galaxies obey Hubble's law, you know that the 'material' that holds them – in this case the Universe – is uniformly stretching.

Hubble's observational evidence wasn't completely convincing. He had only been able to measure relatively nearby galaxies. It was a leap of faith to believe that Hubble's law applied to the rest of the galaxies in the Universe. But the leap turned out to be correct, as you can see from Figure 73. Hubble's law is now so well established that astronomers use it to estimate distances by measuring redshifts from galaxies that are too far away to have their distances measured by other methods.

In fact, Hubble's law had already been predicted. A Belgian physicist and priest, Georges Lemaître (Figure 75), had just written a theoretical paper that claimed that the Universe was expanding. The link that Hubble discovered followed directly from this. So, it seemed that Einstein's static view of the Universe had to be thrown away. The evidence pointed to a Universe that was expanding equally in all directions. Georges Lemaître is sometimes called the father of the Big Bang, as he predicted the expanding Universe before Hubble discovered it

Thinking about Activity 30 may help you to understand a fundamental fact about the Universe. The Universe is expanding not because the things in it (galaxies) are moving outwards, but because space itself is expanding. The rubber band is like the space in the Universe. When it expands, it carries the dots (representing galaxies) with it.

Try not to imagine the Big Bang as being like an ordinary explosion, where matter flies outwards *into* space in all directions. Instead, think of the Universe as a balloon, and imagine that the surface of the balloon contains every single thing in the Universe within it. So when the Universe expands, it's like blowing up the balloon. The Universe (or balloon) is not expanding into anything – it *is* everything. It's just that the surface of the balloon grows bigger. Or you can imagine that the expanding universe is like raisin bread rising in an oven. In the edible universe it is the expansion of the dough that moves the raisins apart (Figure 76). In the real Universe, it is the expansion of space that moves galaxies apart.

Figure 75 *Georges Lemaître*

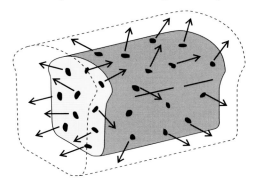

Figure 76 *Raisin bread being baked in an oven*

When astronomers explain why galaxies appear redshifted, they are careful *not* to say that it's because of the Doppler effect. Why? Because the Doppler effect is a change in observed wavelength owing to a moving source. In the case of galaxies, it is the expansion of space itself that causes the shift in wavelength; Figure 77 illustrates the difference. To mark the difference, the redshift of receding galaxies is properly called **cosmological redshift**. However, you can use the formula for the Doppler effect to calculate the cosmological redshift for receding galaxies, because the result of expanding space is that galaxies are speeding away from us.

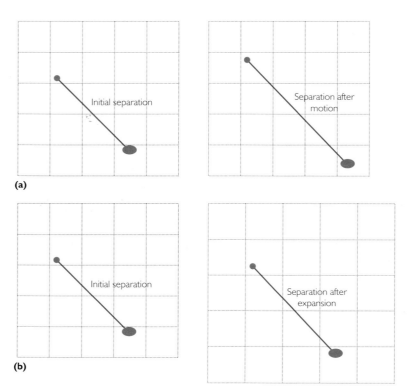

(a)

(b)

Figure 77 *Galaxies increasing their separation because of (a) motion through space; (b) the expansion of the Universe*

You might wonder why, if the Universe is expanding, the Earth is not getting further from the Sun. The expansion of the Universe only applies to sufficiently distant objects like galaxies. Particles that are relatively close together are much more affected by attractive forces, and stay together. For instance, the Sun and Earth are held together by gravity, and the particles in your body are kept in place by electrical forces.

> The Universe is an infinite sphere, the centre of which is everywhere, the circumference nowhere
>
> Pascal, *Pensées*

Activity 30 helps answer the question: is our galaxy at the centre of the expanding Universe? Whichever ink mark you measure from, you will see that speed is proportional to distance. Likewise, an intelligent being on a planet in another galaxy would see all other galaxies speeding away from them too.

It started with a bang

If we imagine travelling back in time, then galaxies would all be speeding towards each other, making the Universe a denser place in the past. If we continue going backwards, then we should reach a moment in time when the Universe was crammed together into a state of almost infinite density.

This reasoning suggests that the Universe began in a sort of explosion. It's hard to conceive of such a colossal event. The Universe began at infinite density and temperature, and all the matter and energy in the Universe today was released. Ever since then the matter and energy have been travelling outwards, thinning out and cooling. This is basically the **Big Bang** model of the origin of the Universe.

People sometimes ask what happened before the Big Bang. Strange as it may seem, there is no *before* the Big Bang. Time itself came into being at the moment of the Big Bang.

A useful website that addresses some frequently asked questions (FAQs) about cosmology is:

http://www.astro.ucla.edu/~wright/cosmology_faq.html

The Big Bang in fact follows logically from Einstein's theory of general relativity (and a few other assumptions). But it wasn't that long before an alternative theory appeared, as you will see in section 4.2.

QUESTIONS

56 Hubble's law holds from any viewpoint in the Universe. Explain why this supports the cosmological principle.

57 Explain the difference between Doppler redshift and cosmological redshift.

4.2 Was there a Big Bang?

In November 1996, *Focus* magazine published an article about an imagined punch-up between two well-known cosmologists (Figure 78).

Big Bang punch up
The Big Bang is a load of old balderdash

Vs

The Big Bang is the way it all started

In the red corner: that old bruiser Professor Sir Fred Hoyle, arch-enemy of the Big Bang theory of the origin of the Universe, who describes it as 'a form of religious fundamentalism'.

Figure 78   *Adapted from* Focus *magazine, November 1996*

In the blue corner: the urbane Astronomer Royal, Professor Sir Martin Rees, and just about every other astronomer in the world.

It may seem like an uneven contest, but that is failing to take into account the legendary prowess of Sir Fred, the greatest living scientist never to win a Nobel Prize. Together with some redoubtable companions around the world, he has consistently argued that the Big Bang theory is total and utter scientific codswallop and presented a welter of evidence to back his claims, from stars seemingly older than the Universe to galaxies separated by unfeasibly huge distances being joined by 'impossible' arcs of gas and dust.

And then there are all those riddles such as what came 'before the Big Bang'. Sir Fred's answer is simple; the Big Bang never happened. Instead, he and his followers claim that the Universe exists in a 'steady state', which never had a beginning, but is kept topped up with fresh matter bursting into our Universe at the centres of galaxies.

For those in the blue corner with Sir Martin Rees, the knock-out punch is obvious . . .

Big Bang or steady state?

Fred Hoyle and colleagues devised their steady state theory in the 1950s. Oddly enough, the idea for the steady state theory came to Hoyle after seeing a film. The fact the film ended with everything returning to how it was at the beginning started him wondering whether the Universe could be like that too (with the expansion of the Universe compensated by extra matter forming within it).

For a while, the steady state theory presented a real challenge to the Big Bang explanation. It explained the expanding Universe by proposing that new matter is continually created in space, compensating for the spreading apart of individual galaxies. In this way, the Universe maintained its steady state.

So what makes us think that the Universe did begin with a bang? The two theories make different predictions about what the Universe looked like a long time ago. One way to find this out is simply to look far out into space. As light travels with a finite speed, we observe distant galaxies as they were a long time ago, not as they are now.

The steady state theory predicts that distant places in the Universe should look just the same as nearby places. However, the Big Bang theory predicts that distant places should be denser, since in the early Universe the same amount of matter occupied a smaller space.

In the mid 1950s, the British astronomer Sir Martin Ryle and colleagues tried to settle the debate using a radio telescope to look at nearby and at distant galaxies. They found that galaxies further away were much more concentrated than those near to us. This observation did not match the prediction of a steady state Universe.

Fred Hoyle was on the ropes, struck by a theory that he had originally named the 'Big Bang', as a term of abuse. But despite the evidence, the controversy continued. It was in the late 1960s that the Big Bang struck the knock-out punch.

Knock-out punch

The Big Bang theory made another specific prediction. The birth of the Universe must have produced colossal numbers of extremely high-energy photons from energetic collisions between subatomic particles. Some radiation would have been absorbed, but not all. What happened to it? Shouldn't we be able to see it today?

In the 1950s Russian-American physicist George Gamow and colleagues realised that today's Universe should be bathed in **cosmic background radiation**, the remnant of the heat of creation, greatly cooled by the expansion of the Universe. (Remember, it was the whole Universe itself which emitted it, not just one part of it.) The radiation from the Big Bang has been travelling for about 15 billion years. The expansion of the Universe has literally stretched the waves, increasing the wavelength and reducing the energy of the photons (Figure 79). Gamow predicted that the peak wavelength of that radiation should now be in the microwave part of the spectrum, corresponding to the energy emitted by an object at approximately 3 K – just three degrees above absolute zero. Scientists thought the radiation would be very difficult to detect – it would require extremely sensitive microwave equipment.

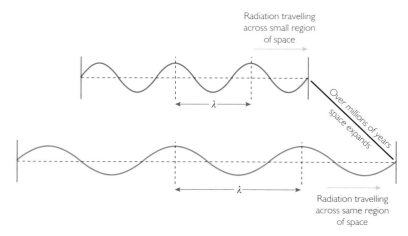

Radiation travelling across small region of space

Over millions of years space expands

Radiation travelling across same region of space

Figure 79 *The wavelength of cosmic background radiation increases as space expands*

However, in 1965, two American radio engineers, Arno Penzias and Robert Wilson (Figure 80), were testing a new horn-shaped microwave antenna. They had found an annoying constant hiss of static, which for months they thought was black body radiation from pigeon droppings. But try as they might, they couldn't get rid of it. Later they realised they had discovered the cosmic background radiation. It was like finding a smoking gun – direct evidence that the Universe started off incredibly hot and dense. The steady state theory practically vanished overnight. The discovery of cosmic background radiation also supported the cosmological principle. The intensity of the microwaves was the same in all directions.

Figure 80 *Arno Penzias (foreground) and Robert Wilson*

Later measurements (including those by the Cosmic Background Explorer satellite in the 1980s) have confirmed that the spectrum closely matches that of a black body at a temperature of 2.7 K (see Figure 81 and compare it with Figure 7 in part 2).

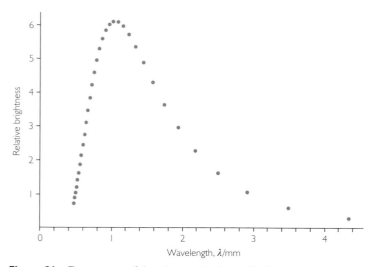

Figure 81 *The spectrum of the microwave background radiation*

A third line of evidence for the Big Bang is its successful prediction of the amount of helium in the Universe. Large amounts were produced in the first few minute of the Big Bang (see section 4.3). The model predicts that about 23% of the matter in the early Universe was helium. Indeed, astronomers have been able to measure the proportion of helium in some of the oldest objects in the Universe – and they've found that it lies between 23% and 24%.

QUESTIONS

58 Explain why the finding of the cosmic background radiation proved fatal to the steady state theory.

59 What will happen to the spectrum of the cosmic background radiation if the Universe expands forever?

ACTIVITY **31** **Cosmology chat show**

Imagine a chat show where the two guests are Sir Martin Rees and Sir Fred Hoyle. Each comes on in turn, answers questions from the host about their theory, and then there is a chance for them to 'discuss' together. In a small group write and act out the script for the show – or improvise what you think they might say.

How old is the Universe?

The Big Bang may have neatly disposed of its rival theory, but it still had to contend with problems of its own (Figure 82).

The Big Bang theory allows scientists to find the age of the Universe. By knowing how fast the Universe has been expanding, they can work out how long it must have taken to get to its current state. The Universe is believed to be between about 10 and 20 billion years old – scientists are still not in agreement.

An old Universe (nearer 20 billion years) is fine. The problem arises if the age as predicted by the Big Bang turns out to be nearer 10 billion years, as some recent measurements by the Hubble Space Telescope have suggested. For astronomers have detected galaxies whose ages have been reliably measured to be 15–17 billion years old (by another method). It doesn't make any sense to say that a galaxy is older than the Universe. So is there something wrong with the Big Bang? Or is it simply difficult to get an accurate result for the age of the Universe? Let's now look at how cosmologists estimate the Universe's age.

The low-redshift approximation of Hubble's law gives us a simple way to estimate the age of the Universe.

$$v = H_0 d \qquad \text{(equation 45)}$$

Suppose a galaxy has been travelling at speed v for a time t since the Big Bang. The distance it has travelled is given by:

$$d = v t$$

"THIS GALAXY SEEMS TO HAVE BEEN CREATED BEFORE THE BIG BANG, AND IT'S COMING TOWARD US. WE MAY HAVE TO RE-THINK SOME OF OUR OLD THEORIES."

Figure 82   *The Big Bang theory has some problems*

where t is the age of the Universe. Substituting for d from equation (45) gives:

$$\frac{v}{H_0} = v\,t$$

so

$$t = \frac{1}{H_0} \tag{47}$$

With H_0 expressed in its normal units of $\text{km s}^{-1}\,\text{Mpc}^{-1}$, its relation to the age of the Universe is not obvious. The following example shows how to deal with the units.

Worked example

Q If $H_0 = 50\,\text{km s}^{-1}\,\text{Mpc}^{-1}$, what does equation (47) imply is the age of the Universe?

A 1 Mpc $= 3.09 \times 10^{22}\,\text{m}$, so 1 $\text{Mpc}^{-1} = (3.09 \times 10^{22}\,\text{m})^{-1}$
In SI units,

Study note

As you will see in section 4.4, the expansion has not continued at a steady rate. But equation (47) still gives a good way to estimate the age of the Universe.

$$H_0 = \frac{50 \times 10^3 \, \text{m s}^{-1}}{(3.09 \times 10^{22} \, \text{m})} = 1.62 \times 10^{-18} \, \text{s}^{-1}.$$

Then $t = \dfrac{1}{H_0} = \left(\dfrac{1}{1.62 \times 10^{-18}} \right) \text{s} = 61.8 \times 10^{17} \, \text{s}$

1 year $= 3.16 \times 10^7$ s, so $t = 1.96 \times 10^{10}$ years (i.e. about 20 billion years)

One cause of the controversy over the age of the Universe is the large uncertainty in the Hubble constant – which is about a factor of 2. Why can't we know H_0 more precisely?

Determining H_0 relies on accurate measurements of distances to galaxies. Although astronomers can measure the distance to relatively nearby galaxies accurately, it's hard to get accurate measurements of distances of galaxies tens or hundreds of millions of light years away.

Most techniques for finding distances to galaxies and stars are based on the principle (covered in section 2.1) that when light radiates from a source, its flux decreases with distance. If you know the intrinsic luminosity of a star or galaxy and its flux you can work out how far away it is. To do this, we simply need types of object, known as 'standard candles', whose luminosity we already know or can reliably estimate (Figure 83). Easier said than done.

Figure 83   *Standard candles*

In the early 20th century, American astronomer Henrietta Swan Leavitt (Figure 84) found that certain variable stars, called Cepheid variables, which grow bright and then dim in a regular cycle (Figure 85), appear to be standard candles. Astronomers have a formula for determining their luminosity from their periods and can thus find their distance. But Cepheid variables are no use beyond about 30 million light years away because their flux becomes too low and they cannot be seen. For such vast distances, astronomers use supernova explosions – one particular type always seem to have the same peak luminosity – but these are rare and unpredictable events. Other methods are based on assuming that all galaxies of the same type are equally luminous. But the greater the distance, the more difficult it is to find standard candles, hence the uncertainties in the Hubble constant and the age of the Universe.

Figure 84 *Henrietta Swan Leavitt*

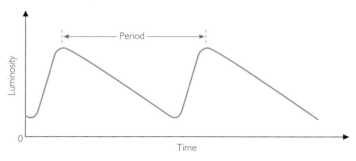

Figure 85 *The light curve of a Cepheid variable star*

The size of the Universe

The Universe is, presumably, infinitely big. If the Universe had an 'edge' then it would not be the same throughout – parts near the edge would appear different from parts near the centre, and the cosmological principle would not apply. Yet astronomers sometimes quote a size for the Universe. What can they mean?

We can only see a small fraction of the Universe. If light has only been travelling for up to 20 billion years (since the Big Bang) we can only see parts of the Universe up to 20 billion light years away. Light from more distant parts hasn't reached us yet. When people talk about the 'size' of the Universe they mean the size of the part we can observe, which is related to its age.

QUESTIONS

60 If $H_0 = 100 \, \text{km s}^{-1} \, \text{Mpc}^{-1}$, how old, approximately, is the Universe?

61 A low-redshift quasar is believed to be 350 Mpc from our galaxy. If $H_0 = 75 \, \text{km s}^{-1} \, \text{Mpc}^{-1}$, what are (**i**) the quasar's recessional speed in km s^{-1}, and (**ii**) its redshift, z?

4.3 *Riding through time*

A newspaper once conducted a poll of its readers, asking 'Scientists have managed to work out the physics for how the Universe behaves from 1 s after the Big Bang, until now. True or false?'

The majority of people thought 'false'. But in fact, we do have experimental evidence that backs up theories of the early Universe to within a second of the Big Bang. Not from telescopes, but from particle physics. A particle accelerator, by accelerating particles to close to the speed of light, can recreate the incredible temperatures of the birth of the Universe.

With the Big Bang model, and drawing on the results of particle physics experiments, we can take a ride through time, charting the history of the Universe from the first instant of creation. So put on your virtual reality headset for a ride through the early history of the Universe – Figure 86 shows what you would see.

QUESTIONS

62 **(a)** Explain why looking at the light from distant galaxies is like looking back in time.

(b) We can't see through telescopes anything that happened earlier than 300 000 years after the Big Bang. Why not?

ACTIVITY 32 | **Matter in the Universe**

Draw a diagram to show the stages by which fundamental particles in the early Universe became the large structures we see in the Universe today. Use the information in the 'ride' (Figure 86), and label each main stage with its temperature and its time from the Big Bang.

The 'ride through time' is also a 'ride' through some important areas of physics. The reactions between fundamental particles are like some of those that you met in the unit *Probing the Heart of Matter*, and the other key areas of physics are those that you studied in parts 2 and 3 of this unit: nuclear physics, kinetic theory and gravity. We will take a brief look at the role of each of these in turn.

Making nuclei

An important piece of evidence supporting the Big Bang theory is that it predicts the ratio of the mass of hydrogen to helium in the Universe exactly as scientists have measured it: 75% hydrogen, 25% helium. How were scientists able to make such a prediction?

According to the Big Bang model, the very early Universe was extremely hot and dense. Did you notice how in the virtual reality ride, as the temperature dropped, particles began to move more slowly? This illustrates the relationship between the temperature of a substance, and the kinetic energy of its particles, which you met in section 3.3.

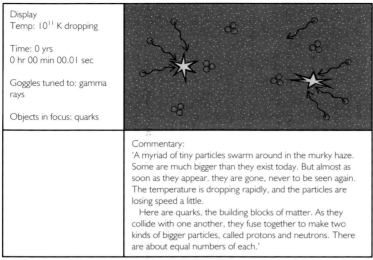

Display
Temp: 10^{11} K dropping

Time: 0 yrs
0 hr 00 min 00.01 sec

Goggles tuned to: gamma rays

Objects in focus: quarks

Commentary:
'A myriad of tiny particles swarm around in the murky haze. Some are much bigger than they exist today. But almost as soon as they appear, they are gone, never to be seen again. The temperature is dropping rapidly, and the particles are losing speed a little.

Here are quarks, the building blocks of matter. As they collide with one another, they fuse together to make two kinds of bigger particles, called protons and neutrons. There are about equal numbers of each.'

(a)

Display
Temp: 10^8 K dropping

Time: 0 yrs 0 hr 10 min

Goggles tuned to: X-rays

Objects in view: protons, neutrons nuclei of helium, and lithium

Commentary:
'It's still hazy. The newly created protons and neutrons will later go on to form atoms. But wait! The neutrons are disappearing – there's only one left for every 7 protons. Just in time, the particles are slowing down enough that when a neutron collides with a proton, they stick together, preventing more neutrons from disappearing. So we can see the first atomic nuclei.'

(b)

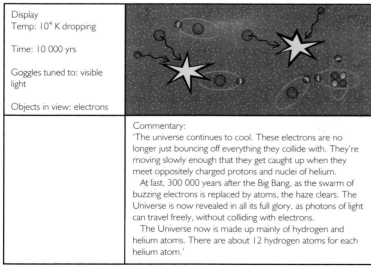

Display
Temp: 10^4 K dropping

Time: 10 000 yrs

Goggles tuned to: visible light

Objects in view: electrons

Commentary:
'The universe continues to cool. These electrons are no longer just bouncing off everything they collide with. They're moving slowly enough that they get caught up when they meet oppositely charged protons and nuclei of helium.

At last, 300 000 years after the Big Bang, as the swarm of buzzing electrons is replaced by atoms, the haze clears. The Universe is now revealed in all its full glory, as photons of light can travel freely, without colliding with electrons.

The Universe now is made up mainly of hydrogen and helium atoms. There are about 12 hydrogen atoms for each helium atom.'

(c)

Figure 86 *(a)–(c) Riding through time*

Display Temp: 10^4 K dropping Time: 10 000 yrs Goggles tuned to: microwave Objects in view: pink areas – hotter than average blue areas – colder than average	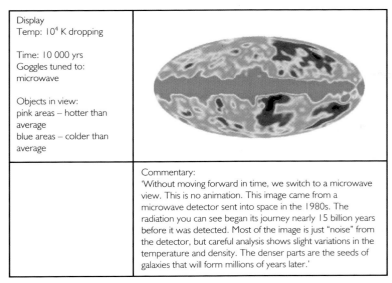
	Commentary: 'Without moving forward in time, we switch to a microwave view. This is no animation. This image came from a microwave detector sent into space in the 1980s. The radiation you can see began its journey nearly 15 billion years before it was detected. Most of the image is just "noise" from the detector, but careful analysis shows slight variations in the temperature and density. The denser parts are the seeds of galaxies that will form millions of years later.'

(d)

Display Temp: 1000 K dropping Time: 1 million yrs Goggles tuned to: visible Objects in view: dust, gas, clouds	
	Commentary: 'The Universe continues to cool and expand. Bits of dust and gas clump together, pulled by their gravity. The first structures start to appear in the Universe – big and small. As time goes on they grow.'

(e)

Display Temp: 100 K dropping Time: 30 million yrs Goggles tuned to: infrared Objects in view: galaxies, stars	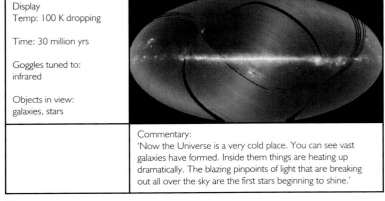
	Commentary: 'Now the Universe is a very cold place. You can see vast galaxies have formed. Inside them things are heating up dramatically. The blazing pinpoints of light that are breaking out all over the sky are the first stars beginning to shine.'

(f)

Figure 86 *(d)–(f) Riding through time*

Figure 87 shows how the temperature changed with time as the Universe expanded, calculated using the Big Bang model. Particle physicists can work out what reactions took place, and which particles could survive at each stage. At first, the Universe would consist of fundamental particles (quarks and leptons) and high-energy photons. As the temperature dropped, quarks could become bound into hadrons (e.g. protons and neutrons) without being shaken apart in violent collisions. Then, as the Universe cooled further, larger particles could begin to form in reactions like this:

$$\,^{1}_{0}n + \,^{1}_{1}H \rightarrow \,^{2}_{1}H + \gamma$$

forming the isotope $^{2}_{1}H$ known as 'heavy hydrogen' or deuterium; its nucleus $^{2}_{1}H$ is sometimes known as a deuteron. Fusion of $^{2}_{1}H$ and $^{1}_{1}H$ produces another hydrogen isotope, $^{3}_{1}H$, called tritium, and then a tritium and a deuterium nucleus can fuse to make a nucleus of helium $^{4}_{2}He$.

Study note

You met and analysed Figure 87 in the unit *Probing the Heart of Matter*.

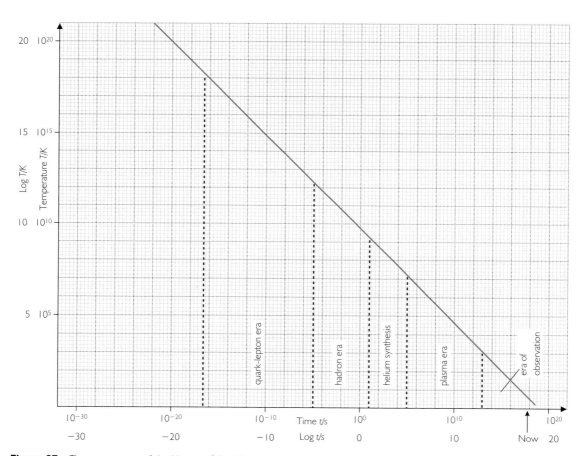

Figure 87 *The temperature of the Universe falls with time*

Detailed calculations show that there is time only to convert less than one twelfth of the protons into helium, and to produce minute amounts of lithium, before the Universe becomes too cold for further fusion to take place.

QUESTIONS

63 Write a balanced nuclear equation showing the fusion of $^3_1$H and $^2_1$H to make $^4_2$He. Which other particle must be produced in this reaction?

64 Calculate the mean kinetic energy and r.m.s. speed of helium nuclei when the temperature is 1.0×10^8 K. (Mass of ^{4}He nucleus $m = 6.68 \times 10^{-27}$ kg; $k = 1.38 \times 10^{-23}$ J K^{-1})

65 Given that the mass of a helium nucleus is four times that of a hydrogen nucleus, show that a ratio of 12 hydrogen atoms to one helium atom is consistent with a mass ratio of about 75% H to 25% He.

66 In stars, the production of helium is followed by further fusion to produce carbon. Explain why no carbon would have been produced in the early Universe.

Gravity takes over

Electric forces gave rise to atoms in the early Universe. Then, over large distances, gravity holds sway, and is the driving force of the evolution of the Universe. In the early Universe, the differences in density and temperature were tiny. But if there weren't differences, gravity would not have been able to clump matter together. Gravity pulls vast galaxies together. Gravity keeps planets orbiting their suns (Figure 88a). But with one little finger, you can overcome the gravitational pull from the whole Earth (Figure 88b).

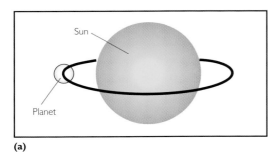

(a)

(b)

Figure 88   *(a) Gravity holds vast objects together but (b) it can easily be overcome*

Gravity is an incredibly weak force. Compare it with another familiar force: the electrostatic force, which is responsible for the force when any two objects are in contact, for friction, and for surface tension.

QUESTIONS

67 Compare the magnitudes of the electrostatic force and the gravitational force between two electrons.

Data: electron mass $m = 9.11 \times 10^{-31}$ kg

electron charge $e = -1.60 \times 10^{-19}$ C

$G = 6.67 \times 10^{-11}$ N m^2 kg^{-1}

$\varepsilon_0 = 8.85 \times 10^{-12}$ F m^{-1}

$k = \dfrac{1}{4\pi\varepsilon_0} = 8.99 \times 10^9$ N m^2 C^{-2}

Your answer to question 67 should show that the electric force between electrons is an incredible 10^{42} times stronger than gravity, regardless of the separation of the particles.

So why is gravity so important on a big scale? Matter tends to be made of pairs of oppositely charged particles whose charge cancels, leaving no net electrostatic force. And the amounts of matter in big structures like stars and galaxies is huge, so their gravitational effect is noticeable, causing atoms and molecules to gather together to form stars, holding stars together in galaxies and binding whole galaxies together into clusters (Figure 89).

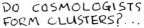

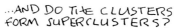

Figure 89 *Gravity causes clustering of matter*

ACTIVITY 33 **A matter of gravity**

Suppose that gravity were much stronger, say only about 10^{26} times weaker than the forces between charged particles. Discuss what consequences this might have for star formation and the evolution of life.

We've seen how the Big Bang can give us a glimpse of the ancient past. But it can also take us on a trip to the future, as you will see in section 4.4.

4.4 *Into the future*

One of the most embarrassing admissions which cosmologists and astronomers have to make is that they don't know what most of the mass of the Universe is made of.

Malcolm Longair, British astronomer

An open and shut case

What do cosmologists put bets on? Not horses or football matches. They're much more likely to be putting money on a number known as Ω. Why? Because, wrapped up in this single constant, is the fate of the Universe.

If $\Omega < 1$ the Universe will carry on expanding for ever, a so-called **open universe** (a fate sometimes described as a 'big chill' or a 'big yawn').

If $\Omega > 1$ the Universe will eventually stop expanding, contract, and end up in a **Big Crunch**. This is a **closed universe**.

You can see these possible futures illustrated in Figure 90. If the Universe is closed, then instead of ending after its collapse, it could begin a new expansion – a 'bounce'. In which case, maybe we are living in one of the bounces, and our Universe is actually much older than 10 to 20 billion years. However, scientists have found no plausible mechanism to produce these bounces and the theory is currently out of fashion.

Why should the Universe ever stop expanding? Because the gravity between all the matter is trying to pull it together, and slow the expansion. In fact the expansion of the Universe has been

Study note

The case of the critical Universe is discussed on page 365.

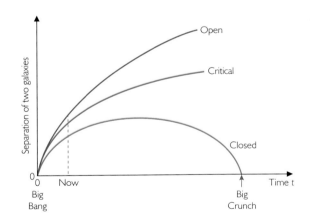

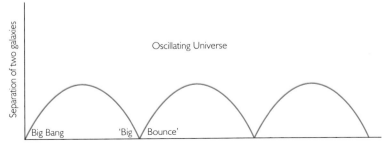

Figure 90 *Graphs showing open and closed universes*

slowing down ever since it started. Gravity and expansion are in direct competition. The winner dictates the fate of the Universe.

We can understand better the closed and open Universe, by imagining what happens to a rocket fired away from the Earth (Figure 91). The rocket in Figure 91(a) has been fired at fairly low velocity. As it climbs, it loses kinetic energy as it gains gravitational potential energy. Eventually, its kinetic energy will decrease to zero, and it then falls back to Earth. This is very much like what happens in a closed universe, where gravity wins (Figure 92). The rocket in Figure 91(b) has a higher velocity at launch. Even when it has reached a very great distance from Earth, it still has some kinetic energy and will keep on travelling out into space. This is like what happens in an open universe, where the expansion wins over gravity – or, more correctly, kinetic energy wins over gravitational potential energy.

The argument is very like the one that determines whether a cloud will collapse and form stars, or disperse owing to the motion of its particles. The main difference is that particles in a gas cloud are moving randomly, whereas galaxies are all moving apart from one another.

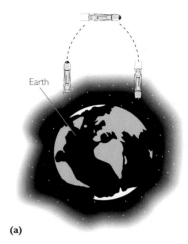

(a)

(b)

Figure 91 *A rocket launched from Earth (a) at low velocity and (b) at high velocity*

AS THE UNIVERSE CONTINUED TO CONTRACT...

Figure 92 *As the Universe continues to contract...*

What is the difference between an open and closed universe?
An open universe will carry on expanding forever. A closed universe
will one day (a long time in the future) stop expanding and start
contracting again.

*That's the future. Is there any difference between the two
now?*
Yes. They have a different shape. A closed universe has a limited
size. That doesn't mean, as you might think, that there is anything
outside it. It sort of bends around on itself, like the surface of a
sphere does, so if you could walk across the universe, you'd
eventually end up where you started. But it's very hard to picture
the shape of the universe; you need mathematics.

An open universe, on the other hand, has unlimited size. It
extends infinitely in all directions. It might be a bit confusing to
think something that's already infinite expanding even more. But all
it means is that the distance between any two galaxies is increasing.

*Do scientists know what will happen if the Universe did
collapse?*
Most of the time during the collapse, things will be pretty similar to
conditions during the expansion phase we're in now. Planets and
stars will be born, live and die. Similarly, galaxies will evolve and
black holes will form from big dying stars.

The main difference is that spectra from distant galaxies will be
blue-shifted (a cosmological blue shift), and the cosmic background
radiation will get slowly warmer and warmer (though too slowly for
people to notice).

Some people think that time will run backwards during collapse,
but we don't know that.

Later on, clusters of galaxies will start to merge, and the galaxies
they're made of will also combine. Stars in the galaxies will collide,
forming black holes, and other stars and planets will evaporate as
the temperature of space starts really hotting up.

Ultimately, the Universe may just end in the state it probably
began in, as a 'quantum vacuum' (where particles pop in and out of
existence). Or maybe it will bounce back into life again,
reincarnated. If this happens, it's likely that the familiar forces of
nature will be quite different, along with the particles that make up
atoms. So who knows what will happen.

*What if the Universe goes on expanding for ever? Isn't it
going to get a bit lonely?*
Quite true. One day (in about 10 000 billion years), all the stars will
eventually run out of fuel, and they'll stop shining. Then the
Universe will become dark, populated by planets and black dwarfs.
Its temperature will be just over absolute zero.

The Universe will shine its final brief dying light when remnant
galaxies get sucked into the black holes at their centres. Then
galaxies will lose their stars and planets, which will start wandering

around in almost complete loneliness. They'll be further apart than the whole of the observable Universe extends today. All they'll have for company will be some very old particles that have been wandering around since the Big Bang.

We're not too sure what happens after that. But frankly, whatever it is, it won't be very interesting.

QUESTIONS

68 Another way of saying the expansion of the Universe is slowing down, is that *the rate of change of expansion is decreasing*. Copy the graph for the open universe (Figure 90). By drawing tangents to the line, explain the statement in italics.

69 In section 4.2, Hubble's constant was used to estimate the age of the Universe, assuming a constant expansion. But the expansion is slowing down, so will the values estimated in section 4.2 be overestimates or underestimates?

ACTIVITY **34** **Back to the future?**

Plan a virtual reality 'ride into the future'. You could write your plan as a story, or produce a series of cartoons showing what the user will see at each stage, called a 'storyboard', to describe what the user will experience. You could add commentary and sound effects, too. Think about whether the 'rider' will be able to choose to experience an open or a closed universe, and how they will make that choice.

Big chill or big crunch?

> This is the way the world ends,
> This is the way the world ends,
> This is the way the world ends:
> Not with a bang but a whimper.

> T.S. Eliot, *The Hollow Men*

You might think that cosmologists are wasting their time betting on the fate of the Universe. Surely we can't know the result in advance. Wrong. The value of Ω, which determines the outcome, is already fixed. It's as though it were in a sealed envelope waiting to be opened.

Ω is a ratio of densities:

$$\Omega = \frac{\rho}{\rho_c} \tag{48}$$

where ρ is the actual average density of the Universe and ρ_c is called the **critical density**. If ρ is greater than this critical value (i.e. $\Omega > 1$), then there is enough mass in the Universe for gravity to defeat expansion, and the Universe to be closed. However, if $\rho < \rho_c$, the Universe is less dense than the critical value, expansion will win and the Universe will be open.

The way to calculate critical density is from the Hubble constant, since critical density is a measure of how much mass would be needed to halt the current expansion. Estimates of the critical density lie around $10^{-26}\,\text{kg}\,\text{m}^{-3}$. This is an extremely small value, and it is uncertain because of the difficulties of measuring the Hubble constant. From this value, the Universe must on average contain at least the mass of one poppy seed in each volume the size of the Earth, for gravity to win, collapsing the Universe in on itself one day. Does the Universe contain this density of matter?

Scientists have estimated ρ, the actual density of the Universe, by examining huge volumes of space and calculating the mass of stars and galaxies needed to produce the observed amount of light. They have also calculated the density by estimating how the motions of galaxies are affected by local concentrations of mass. Unfortunately, all these estimates depend on knowing the distances to the galaxies, and we have seen that this is hard to find accurately. But the highest estimates turn out to be only about $10^{-27}\,\text{kg}\,\text{m}^{-3}$, in which case

$$\Omega \approx \frac{10^{-26}\,\text{kg}\,\text{m}^{-3}}{10^{-27}\,\text{kg}\,\text{m}^{-3}} = 0.1$$

And many estimates of actual density and Ω are ten times lower. From these results, it looks as if the Universe is open, destined to end its days with matter spread ever wider, in a cold, lonely emptiness. But despite this, many cosmologists are betting on what seems an unlikely third way – that the density is exactly the critical value, making Ω precisely 1. This third possibility is called a **critical universe** (or, sometimes, a flat universe), as shown in Figure 90.

Why do many cosmologists think that gravity and expansion are so perfectly balanced? The evidence for Ω being 1 is partly that we know it's close to 1. It sounds absurd, but imagine the rocket again. This time it is launched with exactly the right vertical velocity just to keep on travelling away for ever. This critical velocity is called the **escape velocity**. If it launched with only slightly lower velocity, gravity would *soon* bring it back. Similarly, with slightly greater than escape velocity, you would *soon* know that it was going to escape easily. The longer time goes on the more the speed of the rocket would diverge from the critical value. What this means is, if you saw the rocket a *long* time later, still travelling with a speed just high enough to continue going for ever, it must have been launched with almost exactly the escape velocity.

Swapping the Universe for our rocket, seeing the value of Ω close to 1 means that it must have been almost exactly 1 at the Big Bang. Physicists have calculated that Ω would have to be only 1 part in 10^{59} away from the value of 1.

There is also reason to believe that a universe with $\Omega = 1$ is 'easy' to create, on the grounds of energy. Finding the Universe so close to critical today, means the kinetic energy and gravitational potential energies are closely balanced. The potential energies of all the matter in the Universe (due to being in a gravitational field) are negative. The positive kinetic energy balances exactly with the negative potential energy, making the total energy in the Universe zero. Some scientists have suggested that creating a universe with zero total energy is easier.

In the unit *Probing the Heart of Matter*, you read that physicist Alan Guth had a 'spectacular realisation' that led him to propose that the Universe had undergone a rapid 'inflation' about 10^{-35} seconds after the Big Bang. One consequence of this inflation is that the Universe would achieve a density exactly equal to the critical density.

But as far as observational evidence is concerned for $\Omega = 1$, the jury is still out.

The riddle of dark matter

Nobody ever said all matter radiated.

Vera Rubin, American astronomer

I hope the missing matter isn't there.

Jesse Greenstein, American astronomer

If the Universe is flat, there is a big problem. We can only see a few per cent of the matter needed to make $\Omega = 1$. The rest is lurking unseen, invisible to our telescopes. This hidden stuff is called **dark matter** (Figure 93). But just because we can't see it doesn't mean it isn't there. When you turn out the light in a room most objects disappear – only the luminous objects remain visible.

In fact we already know that dark matter exists. Though we can't see it, astronomers have measured its gravitational effect on galaxies and stars, and believe there must be at least ten times as much matter as that we can actually see.

Some of the strongest evidence comes from the rotation of galaxies. Just as you saw in part 3 that astronomers can determine the masses of stars from observing their effect on the orbits of planets or on one another, they can also determine the mass of a galaxy from the motions of stars near its edge. In the early 1970s, American astronomer Vera Rubin did just this for the Andromeda galaxy and some other spiral galaxies, and was surprised to find that the mass thus calculated was about ten times the mass of the stars and interstellar material needed to account for the output of radiation.

Other evidence comes from whole clusters of galaxies, in which the galaxies are seen to move around at random – rather like the kinetic theory model of particles in a gas. Some years before Rubin's work, Swiss-American astronomer Fritz Zwicky measured the random speeds of galaxies in clusters and calculated the mass that would need to be present in order to stop the clusters dispersing. (This is another example of the sort of argument that we used in part 3 when considering whether a gas cloud would disperse or collapse.) Here, too, there seemed to be about ten times as much mass in the clusters as could be accounted for by the radiating material.

(a)

(b)

Figure 93 *(a) Non-dark matter, (b) dark matter*

ACTIVITY **35** **Mass and motion**

Use computer simulations to explore:

- how the rotation of a galaxy is affected by the distribution of mass
- how the mass in a cluster of galaxies influences the galaxies' random velocities.

Both are Java programs that you can download from Dark Matter, Cosmology and Large Scale Structure of the Universe:

http://www.astro.queensu.ca/~dursi/dm-tutorial/dm0.html

The baffling question is: 'What is dark matter?' Simply, it is matter that we cannot detect by either its emission or its absorption of radiation (the dust that shows up as dark streaks on photographs of nebulae is *not*, technically speaking, 'dark matter', as we detect its absorption of starlight). There are two main possibilities:

- baryonic matter, made from baryons (protons and neutrons) and their accompanying electrons – in other words, ordinary everyday matter, in a form that renders it undetectable by the emission or absorption of radiation;
- non-baryonic matter – which could include all manner of exotic particles not yet detected.

Baryonic matter could be in the form of planets or dim stars. Earth-like planets aren't going to contribute a lot of mass to the Universe, but perhaps Jupiter-size planets could. Other candidates include brown dwarfs – these are failed stars that weren't quite massive enough to start fusion and become luminous. But we don't know. For all we know some dark matter could turn out to be bricks in space – they would be very hard to detect.

However, we know that not all the dark matter can be baryonic. The Big Bang theory makes a clear prediction for the total amount of ordinary, atom-forming matter in the Universe. It says there should only be enough baryonic matter to make $\Omega = 0.1$. If Ω really is 1, then the remaining 90% of the Universe has to be made of stranger forms of matter.

One possible candidate for non-baryonic dark matter is the neutrino. It is not yet established whether neutrinos have any mass at all, but there are so many neutrinos in the Universe that with even a very small mass they could together make a significant contribution to the total mass of the Universe.

Current research

One technique that might help solve the riddle of dark matter goes by the name of gravitational lensing. It's based on Einstein's theory of gravity (general relativity). Einstein realised that, as well as matter, light is affected by gravity. So a beam of light would curve as it passes a large concentration of matter.

Study note

Baryons were discussed in the unit *Probing the Heart of Matter*.

The technique is based on looking at the image of a very distant object, and seeing how it is altered by gravity. When light from a very distant galaxy (billions of light years away) makes the long journey to Earth, it is sometimes deflected on its journey to Earth by matter en route. The matter acts like a lens, distorting and splitting the image into two. About a dozen gravitational lenses have been discovered so far.

Figure 94 shows some examples of gravitational lensing. In Figure 94(a), the four images around the central one are all of the same galaxy, and in 94(b) the arc of light is an image of a galaxy that has been magnified and distorted. Figure 95 shows how a cluster of galaxies can produce gravitational lensing of light from a very distant object. Notice how the wavefronts and the rays behave as if they were passing through a converging lens. By studying images such as those in Figure 94, physicists can then reconstruct what the lens would be, its distribution in space, and, importantly, its total mass.

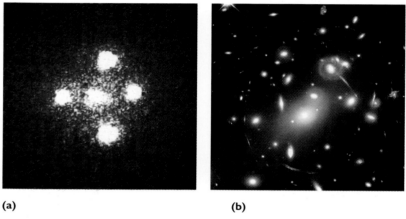

(a)   **(b)**

Figure 94   *Images produced by gravitational lensing*

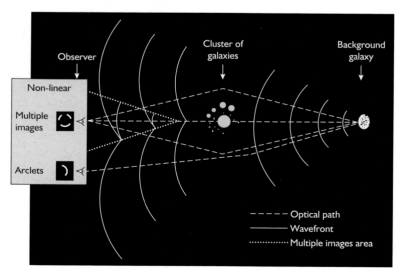

Figure 95   *Schematic diagram of gravitational lensing*

David Davidge and colleagues have been pursuing a very different approach, searching for the missing matter a kilometre underground in a Yorkshire potash mine, for a week at a time (Figure 96). They have set up an incredibly sensitive detector to pick up signals from one of the best candidates for dark matter. They are searching for WIMPs. Weakly Interacting Massive Particles are generally heavy particles (thousands of times the mass of a proton) that only interact weakly with other matter. Scientists know that WIMPs must exist, and some of the proposed types of WIMP have been given exotic names like neutralinos, axions and others. But, right now, scientists don't know what WIMPs there actually are. That's because they don't interact readily with anything. WIMPs can glide through the gaps between electrons and nuclei with ease, and could be streaming right through you as you read this. So this makes them nearly impossible to detect.

Figure 96 *You'll find physicists in some odd places*

However, David Davidge's team expects that there ought to be one WIMP passing through their experiment (called a WIMP event) every few days. You might think an event this rare would be easy to spot. But unfortunately, there are a million other events to confuse them, which are nothing to do with WIMPS. Which is why they've come down to the bottom of the mine (Figure 97), to shield the detector from all the noise.

David's team is one of several around the world, using different methods, but all in the race to find dark matter. And what a discovery it would make. You can check out their website to see if they've managed to find any WIMPs.

But maybe even finding dark matter won't be the end of the story. Some physicists now believe the fate of the Universe isn't wholly dependent on the value of Ω. It's possible that there is another number that affects whether the Universe expands forever or not. This is called the 'cosmological constant' and, if it exists, it means

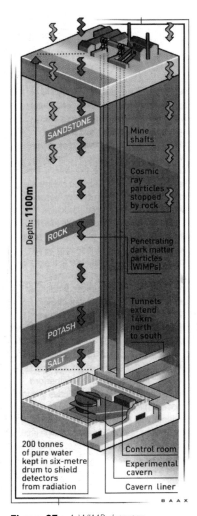

Depth: 1100m

SANDSTONE

Mine shafts

Cosmic ray particles stopped by rock

ROCK

Penetrating dark matter particles (WIMPs)

Tunnels extend 14km north to south

POTASH

SALT

200 tonnes of pure water kept in six-metre drum to shield detectors from radiation

Control room

Experimental cavern

Cavern liner

Figure 97 *A WIMP detector*

that a complete vacuum somehow exerts a pressure. This was the term in his equations that Einstein called his 'greatest blunder'. But now some physicists believe it may really exist. It could make the Universe flat, even if there is not much more matter than we can see. Maybe Albert Einstein will have the last laugh after all.

4.5 Summing up part 4

In this part of the unit you have read about some of the biggest questions currently being addressed by astronomers and cosmologists, and seen how they relate to the physics that you have studied in the whole of this unit and elsewhere in the course.

Activities 36 to 40 are intended to help you look back over this part of the unit. You will find further questions in part 5.

ACTIVITY 36 **Spot the mistakes**

Read the newspaper article in Figure 98. There are several scientific inaccuracies in the text. Can you spot them? Make a list and, for each one, write what you think the article should have said.

ACTIVITY 37 **The cosmologists**

Put yourself in the position of one of the great astronomers or cosmologists of the 20th century, giving a 5-minute presentation about your ideas at a scientific conference. You could choose one featured in this unit or one that you have researched yourself.

Do the presentation as a group. One person in the group could introduce the scientists, explaining to the audience, e.g. when the scientist worked, and a few details about their lives.

Include a brief account of your theory or experiment and say why it was important. To help you communicate your message, use props or audiovisuals (e.g. a clear diagram on an overhead projector). You can find further information from books or websites. Try these:

http://www.sofitec.lu/misc/einstein.htm

http://spaceboy.nasda.go.jp/note/note_e.html

http://www.absa.org.uk/Briefings/cosmology.htm

http://antwrp.gsfc.nasa.gov/diamond-jubilee/debate98.html

ACTIVITY 38 **In the beginning**

Read the poem by Primo Levi printed on p. 372, and answer the following questions

- Why do you think Levi calls the fireball 'solitary and eternal'?

- What does Primo Levi believe the fate of the Universe to be? How do you know?

- Explain (in terms a non-scientist would understand) how the 'thin echo' of the Big Bang 'resounds from the furthest reaches'.

This is the largest ever map of the universe and you are here (give or take a million miles or so…)

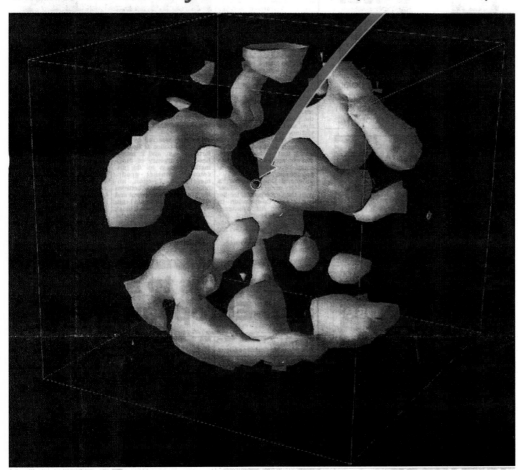

A new 3D map of space has convinced scientists that the heavens will go on expanding for ever, writes **Stuart Millar**

IT LOOKS like a diagram of human organs or a surreal collection of floating potatoes. But yesterday scientists were hailing the production of the largest ever map of the cosmos as a breakthrough akin to the discovery of a new continent.

Ten years in the making, the three-dimensional map charts 15,500 galaxies and covers an area so large that it would take 500 million years for a light shone on one side to reach the other.

Although it represents only about one ten-thousandth of the cosmos, the Anglo-German team of astronomical cartographers who compiled it believe they have finally charted a large enough region to offer a representative sample of the universe.

As a result, they have been able to come up with an encouraging answer to the most enduring scientific conundrum of them all. Using complex mathematical models based on the map, they have calculated that there is enough gravitational power in the cosmos to ensure that the universe will carry on expanding forever.

"This map would be an incredible achievement if all it did was chart the universe," Carlos Frenk, professor of astrophysics at Durham University and a member of the research team told the Guardian.

"But it is far more than that. It allows us to make a long-term forecast on the fundamental questions affecting our universe. If you can imagine how 15th century exploreres felt when they discovered the Americas, then it is something like that."

The map is unique not only in its scale but in the way it was compiled, using infra-red telescopes to push further into space and to remove the measurement problems caused by dust floating in the cosmos.

That allowed the galaxies to be plotted accurately and the distances between them measured, a task which alone took five years, under the supervision of Will Saunders, a Royal Society research fellow at Edinburgh University.

They were then charted in three dimensions, represented as superclusters — gigantic structures made of a clusters of galaxies. Our own, the Milky Way, lies somewhere in the centre, because all the measurements were taken from Earth.

"This is the only map that givens us a vision of the universe across the whole of the sky," said Prof Frenk.

But it is the spaces between the superclusters — the voids — which offer the most interesting findings.

Under the Big Bang theory it is gravity which has kept the universe expanding since the initial "quantum fluctuations" which created it. Scientists have already established that because the visible galaxies alone could not exert enough gravitational power to drive that expansion, the extra force must come from invisible "dark matter".

Giving the relative positions and sizes of the visible galaxies, the new map has offered researchers a way of calculating how much dark matter there is. Their conclusion is that there is enough to provide sufficient gravitational force for expansion to continue forever.

But can the findings be relied upon? Despite the experience of many of history's other great maps which turned out to be wildly inaccurate, Prof Frenk is convinced that the answer is yes.

"The amazing thing is that map will not be superceded for at least a generation," he said. "There is not another infra-red project planned in my lifetime, so we have produced the definitive work."

World views

Hereford Mappa Mundi, c.1290
Drawn by a cleric, Richard of Haldingham, as a medieval description of God's main creation rather than a literal guide. Jerusalem is dead centre and Paradise is at the top.

Claudius Ptolemaeus (Ptolemy), 1482
Based on geographical data compiled more than a millennium earlier by Ptolemy of Alexandria. Underestimated the length of a degree so much that Columbus though he had reached Japan rather than America.

Gerardus Mercator, 1569
A celebrated projection which set out to satisfy the navigators' demand for a chart on which his compass course would be laid down as a straight line. Continuing use by sailors ever since is testimony to its value.

Frederick De Wit, 1668
Marked progress in mapping regions furthest from Europe after the first Renaissance voyages. Included the partial Dutch discoveries of Australia and New Zealand but wrongly transformed California into an island.

Figure 98 *Spot the mistakes*

Ten billion years before now,
Brilliant, soaring in space and time.
There was a bath of flame, solitary and eternal,
Our common father and our executioner.
It exploded, and every change began.
Even now the thin echo of this one reverse catastrophe
Resounds from the furthest reaches.

> Primo Levi, 'In the Beginning'. From *Shema*, translated by
> Ruth Feldman and Brian Swann, Menard Press, 1976

ACTIVITY 39 Cosmology today

Use the Internet to find out more about modern cosmology research.
Table 13 lists some useful websites.

Imagine you are applying for a research job in cosmology. Prepare
an application and then take part in an 'interview' with other
students.

Address of website	Description
http://cfa-www.harvard.edu/seuforum/	Explores facts, questions and new research about the Big Bang.
http://space.gsfc.nasa.gov/astro/cobe	The COBE (Cosmic Background Explorer) website. COBE discovered the 'seeds of galaxies' in the early Universe.
http://map.gsfc.nasa.gov/html/web_site.html	An introduction to cosmology, with lots of FAQs (frequently asked questions).
http://map.gsfc.nasa.gov/	Microwave Anisotropy Probe website. It is hoped the probe will reveal more about early conditions in the Universe.
http://www.astro.ucla.edu/~wright/cosmolog.htm	Another cosmology FAQ, with an advanced cosmology tutorial.
http://imagine.gsfc.nasa.gov.does/homepage.html	Another advanced tutorial on cosmology.

Table 13 *Some cosmology websites*

ACTIVITY 40 Origins

Cosmology has come a long way since the ancient beliefs of
civilisations from Greece, Rome, China and India.

Summarise what you think are the main achievements of
cosmology that have furthered our understanding of the Universe
and its origins and future.

5 *Synthesis*

5.1 *Universal physics*

In this unit, you have studied three main areas of physics: nuclear
physics, gravitation and kinetic theory. You have also touched on
several areas of physics from elsewhere in the course, including
radiant energy flux, the Doppler effect, electrostatic force, and

energy conservation. You have used many of the key ideas on more than one part of the unit, and seen how they have helped, and are still helping, astronomers and cosmologists to find out more about stars, galaxies and the Universe itself.

ACTIVITY 41 | **Universal physics**

For each of the major areas of physics covered in this unit (nuclear physics, gravitation and kinetic theory) make a summary chart in the form of a concept map.

Use a separate 'Post-it' sticker for each key term, diagram or equation, and arrange the stickers on a large piece of paper, moving them around so as to make the connections between them as clear as possible. Then stick them down firmly, and add extra notes to emphasise the links between the points.

5.2 Questions on the whole unit

QUESTIONS

70 A keen UFO spotter claims to have seen a 'mysterious object, about as bright as the brightest stars – maybe a bit brighter – and moving'. A cynic remarks that it was probably an aeroplane.

An Airbus landing light has a power of 600 W. The brightest star in the night sky, Sirius, has a luminosity of 1.2×10^{28} W and is 8.3×10^{16} m from Earth. By carrying out a suitable order-of-magnitude calculation, decide whether an aeroplane light would typically be seen from a distance at which it could look about as bright as Sirius. Show the steps in your working, and state clearly any assumptions and approximations you have made.

71 Refer to Table 2 (p. 282) to help you answer this question.

(**a**) Complete the following reactions that take place in some giant stars:

(**i**) $^{4}_{2}H + ^{12}_{6}C \rightarrow \ldots + \gamma$

(**ii**) $^{1}_{0}n + ^{38}_{16}S \rightarrow ^{37}_{16}S \rightarrow ^{37}_{17}Cl + \ldots$

(**b**) In a supernova explosion, neutron absorption produces a long-lived isotope of indium, $^{115}_{49}In$. This can absorb another neutron before decaying to give ^{116}In, which is itself unstable, decaying by beta-minus decay into an isotope of tin (Sn). Write equations for these two reactions, starting with ^{115}In.

72 Nuclear power stations use nuclear fission to provide energy for electricity generation. When a nucleus of ^{235}U absorbs a neutron, it becomes unstable and undergoes fission, producing two lighter nuclei and some more neutrons. A typical reaction is:

$$^{235}_{92}U + ^{1}_{0}n \rightarrow ^{141}_{56}Ba + ^{92}_{36}Kr + \text{neutrons}$$

The neutrons released can produce more fission reactions if they are captured by further ^{235}U nuclei. A reactor in a power station contains neutron-absorbing materials designed so that the chain reaction proceeds at a steady rate. The energy released per unit mass of nuclear fuel is several orders of magnitude greater than that produced by burning chemical fuels such as oil or gas. After use, the spent fuel can be chemically treated to extract any useful materials. The remaining waste is highly radioactive.

(**a**) (**i**) How many neutrons are produced in the reaction above? Explain your reasoning.

(**ii**) Explain why a nuclear fission reaction releases energy.

(**b**) The uranium fuel used in reactors consists of a mixture of isotopes. $^{238}_{92}$U, the most common isotope, does not undergo fission when it absorbs a neutron. Instead, it continues to absorb neutrons and heavier nuclei are produced. These nuclei are radioactive, and contribute to the hazards associated with nuclear waste.

For example, $^{238}_{92}$U $+ \ ^{1}_{0}$n $\rightarrow \ ^{239}_{93}$Np $+ \ \beta^{-} + \ \bar{\nu}_{e}$

Further absorption reactions produce $^{239}_{94}$Pu (plutonium), one of several nuclei that are particularly hazardous both because of the radiation they emit and because of their complex biological effects if they enter the body. $^{239}_{94}$Pu has a half-life of 24 400 years and decays by alpha emission.

(**i**) What fraction of the $^{239}_{94}$Pu nuclei in a sample of waste will remain after 1000 years?

(**ii**) By what percentage will the activity due to $^{239}_{94}$Pu have decreased in this time?

(**iii**) If you started with a sample of pure $^{239}_{94}$Pu, the activity of the sample after 1000 years would in fact be greater than indicated by your answer above. Suggest a reason for this.

73 Geophysicists study volcanoes in order to understand how they work and to predict eruptions. In some types of volcano, magma (molten rock) from deep inside the Earth moves upwards through underground fractures (large cracks forming gaps in the solid rock) and emerges at the Earth's surface. As the fractures fill with magma the gravitational field at the surface changes, giving warning of an eruption.

To measure small changes in gravitational field strength, geophysicists use a gravimeter, which is essentially a very sensitive spring balance. The gravimeter so very sensitive that precise measurements of height need to be made at the same time as the gravity measurements.

Data: near Earth's surface $g = 9.8 \, \text{N kg}^{-1}$;
$G = 6.67 \times 10^{-11} \, \text{N m}^2 \, \text{kg}^{-2}$

(a) (i) What is meant by the term *gravitational field strength*?

(ii) If a piece of magma moves upwards towards the Earth's surface, filling a gap in the rocks, what would happen to the gravitational field strength at the surface?

(iii) One type of gravimeter used in volcanic studies can detect changes in gravitational field of one part in 100 million at the Earth's surface. What is the order of magnitude of the smallest change in gravitational field that it could detect?

(b) Calculate the strength of the gravitational field due to a cube of magma, density $4000 \, kg \, m^{-3}$, measuring 100 m along each side, with its centre of mass 1.5 km below the surface.

(c) Explain why it is necessary to measure the height when monitoring changes in gravitational field due to underground magma movements.

74 During 1996 and 1997 the Galileo spacecraft investigated the planet Jupiter and its moons. One such moon is Io. Measurements of Io's orbital motion enable Jupiter's mass to be determined.

(a) The radius of Io's orbit around Jupiter $r = 4.22 \times 10^8$ m and its period of rotation $T = 1.53 \times 10^5$ s. What is Io's orbital speed v?

(b) (i) Write down an expression in terms of Io's mass m_{Io} for the centripetal force F_{cent} needed to keep it in orbit.

(ii) Using m_{Ju} to denote Jupiter's mass, write down an expression for the gravitational force of attraction F_{grav} between Jupiter and Io.

(c) Using your answer to (b), obtain an expression for m_{Ju} in terms of v, G and r.

(d) Calculate a value for the mass of Jupiter.
($G = 6.67 \times 10^{-11} \, N \, m^2 \, kg^{-2}$)

75 (a) A galaxy is moving away from Earth at $4.58 \times 10^5 \, m \, s^{-1}$. It emits light at a frequency 6.00×10^{14} Hz. Calculate the observed frequency of this light on Earth. ($c = 3.00 \times 10^8 \, m \, s^{-1}$)

(b) Hydrogen atoms emit and absorb electromagnetic radiation with a wavelength of 21.2 cm. This '21 cm line' is used by radio astronomers to study the Doppler shifts of radiation from the ISM in rotating galaxies. The receivers must be tuned to precisely the right frequency.

(i) What is the emitted frequency of this radiation?

(ii) If the hydrogen in a galaxy is moving at $7370 \, km \, s^{-1}$ away from Earth, what is the difference between the observed frequency and the emitted frequency?

76 Our galaxy, the Milky Way, forms part of a group of galaxies. The light from our neighbour in the group, called Andromeda, is slightly blue shifted. Suggest a reason why it is not redshifted as other galaxies are.

77 Creationists claim that the Universe was created 6000 years ago. If this were true, calculate the value that the Hubble constant would have (**i**) in years^{-1}, (**ii**) in s^{-1}, (**iii**) in km s^{-1} Mpc^{-1} (assuming uniform expansion). (1 year = 3.16×10^7 s; 1 Mpc = 3.09×10^{22} m)

78 Figure 99 show the spectrum of light received from the quasar known as 3C273 (a quasar is an extremely luminous type of galaxy). The four peaks marked are hydrogen lines that have been shifted in wavelength. In a laboratory, these lines have wavelengths 410 nm, 434 nm, 486 nm and 656 nm.

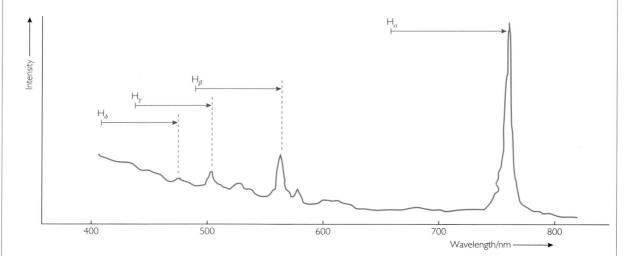

Figure 99   *The spectrum of 3C273*

(**a**) (**i**)   What is the name given to this shift in wavelength?
    (**ii**)   Without doing any calculations, what does the spectrum of 3C273 allow you deduce about its motion?

(**b**) Using any *one* of the lines marked in the diagram, calculate the speed of 3C273 relative to the Earth.

(**c**) Assuming that the Hubble constant $H_0 = 75$ km s^{-1} Mpc^{-1}, calculate the distance to 3C273. Express your answer in Mpc.

5.3 *Achievements*

Now you have studied this unit you should be able to:

- recognise and use the expression $F = \dfrac{L}{4\pi d^2}$ (2.1, 3.1)*;

- understand and use the terms *nucleon number* (*mass number*) and *proton number* (*atomic number*) (2.2);

- appreciate the spontaneous and random nature of nuclear decay (2.2);

- determine the half-lives of radioactive isotopes graphically and recognise and use the expressions for radioactive decay (2.2);

$$\frac{\mathrm{d}N}{\mathrm{d}t} = -\lambda N, \quad \lambda = \frac{\log_e 2}{t_{1/2}}, \quad \text{and} \quad N = N_0 e^{-\lambda t} \ (2.2);$$

- describe the processes of nuclear fusion and fission (2.3);

- explain the mechanism of nuclear fusion and the need for high densities of matter and high temperatures to bring it about and maintain it (2.3);

- understand the concept of *nuclear binding energy*, and recognise and use the expression $\Delta E = c^2 \Delta m$ (2.3);

- recognise and use a simple Hertzsprung–Russell diagram to relate luminosity and temperature for main sequence stars (3.1);

- recall and use the expression $F = \dfrac{Gm_1m_2}{r^2}$ (3.2);

- derive and use the expression $g = \dfrac{GM}{r^2}$ for the gravitational field due to a point mass (3.2);

- recall similarities and differences between electric and gravitational fields (3.2, 4.3);

- recall and use the expression $pV = nRT$ as the equation of state for an ideal gas (3.3);

- understand the concept of absolute zero, how the average kinetic energy of particles is related to the absolute temperature, and understand the concept of internal energy as the random distribution of potential and kinetic energy amongst particles (3.3);

- recognise and use the expression $\frac{1}{2}m \langle c^2 \rangle = \frac{3}{2}kT$ (3.2, 4.1, 4.2);

- recognise and use the expressions $z = \Delta\lambda/\lambda \approx \Delta f/f \approx v/c$ for a source of electromagnetic radiation moving relative to an observer and $z = H_0 d/c$ for objects at cosmological distances (3.2, 4.1, 4.2);

- be aware of the controversy over the age and ultimate fate of the Universe associated with the value of Hubble constant and the possible existence of dark matter (4.2, 4.3, 4.4).

*Numbers indicate the section(s) that relate to each achievement.

Answers

1   (a)   Time, $t = $ distance/speed so
$$t = \frac{1.50 \times 10^{11} \text{ m}}{3.00 \times 10^8 \text{ m s}^{-1}} = 500 \text{ s}.$$

   (b)   Distance to Sun $= 500$ light seconds
$$= \frac{500 \text{ s}}{3.16 \times 10^7 \text{ s yr}^{-1}}$$
$$= 1.58 \times 10^{-5} \text{ light years}.$$

   (c) $\dfrac{d_{pc}}{d_{sun}} = \dfrac{1.58 \times 10^{-4} \text{ light years}}{4.24 \text{ light years}}$
$$= 2.68 \times 10^5$$
To the nearest order of magnitude, the ratio is 10^5.

2   (a)   Using equation (1):
$$\frac{F_{\text{planet}}}{F_{\text{Earth}}} = \left(\frac{L}{4\pi d^2{}_{\text{planet}}}\right) \div \left(\frac{L}{4\pi d^2{}_{\text{Earth}}}\right)$$
$$= \left(\frac{d_{\text{Earth}}}{d_{\text{planet}}}\right)^2$$

For Mercury:
$$\frac{F_{\text{Mercury}}}{F_{\text{Earth}}} = \left(\frac{1.496 \times 10^9 \text{ m}}{57.9 \times 10^9 \text{ m}}\right)^2$$
$$= \left(\frac{149.6}{57.9}\right)^2 = 6.7$$
so $F_{\text{Mercury}} = 6.7 \, F_{\text{Earth}}$

Notice that the units of m and the factor 10^9 cancel in the final calculation. Using a similar approach for the other planets:
$$\frac{F_{\text{Venus}}}{F_{\text{Earth}}} = 1.91$$
$$\frac{F_{\text{Mars}}}{F_{\text{Earth}}} = 0.43$$
$$\frac{F_{\text{Pluto}}}{F_{\text{Earth}}} = 6.4 \times 10^{-4}$$

   (b)   In general we can expect that the planets with the higher radiant energy flux will be hotter than Earth and have brighter sunlight. Mars is cooler, and Pluto is only very dimly lit by the Sun and very cold.

   (c)   You might have thought of some of the following effects.

   The curvature of the planet reduces the incident energy flux near the poles. The planet's surface may reflect radiation back into space rather than absorbing it. Any atmosphere may trap heat radiation (the greenhouse effect); this causes Venus to be hotter than Mercury, even though it is further from the Sun. The atmosphere may also reflect or absorb radiation so the surface does not get so warm. Geothermal effects may warm up parts of the planet (volcanic activity, hot springs, etc.).

3   (a)   From equation (1), $d^2 = \dfrac{L}{4\pi F}$

   Assuming that Sirius and the Sun have the same luminosity, L, then
$$\frac{d_{\text{Sir}}}{d_{\text{Sun}}} = \left(\frac{L}{4\pi F_{\text{Sir}}}\right) \div \left(\frac{L}{4\pi F_{\text{Sun}}}\right) = \frac{F_{\text{Sun}}}{F_{\text{Sir}}}$$
   Using Huygens's measurements:
$$\frac{d^2{}_{\text{Sir}}}{d^2{}_{\text{Sun}}} = 26\,644^2$$
$$\frac{d_{\text{Sir}}}{d_{\text{Sun}}} = 26\,644$$

   (b)   True $\dfrac{d_{\text{Sir}}}{d_{\text{Sun}}} = \dfrac{8 \text{ light years}}{1.58 \times 10^{-5} \text{ light years}} = 5.06 \times 10^5$

   (c)   The ratio calculated by Huygens is too small by a factor of about 20. He was wrong to assume that Sirius has the same luminosity as the Sun; we now know that it is about 26 times more luminous. Also, his memory of the brightness of Sirius could not be very reliable, so the five significant figures he quotes for the ratio of diameters is incredibly optimistic.

4   (a)   Blue-white.
   (b)   Orange-red.

5   Brown dwarf (coolest), red giant, white dwarf (hottest).

6   We are told that the Sun is about 400 times further away than the Moon, and that the Sun and Moon have very similar angular diameters. We can therefore deduce that $d_{\text{Sun}} \approx 400 \, d_{\text{Moon}} \approx 400 \times 3.85 \times 10^8$ m.

From equation (2), $\alpha_{\text{Sun}} = \dfrac{D_{\text{Sun}}}{d_{\text{Sun}}}$
$$\approx \frac{1.4 \times 10^9 \text{ m}}{400 \times 3.85 \times 10^8 \text{ m}}$$
$$= 9 \times 10^{-3} \text{ radians}$$
We have already said (and used the fact) that $\alpha_{\text{sun}} = \alpha_{\text{Moon}}$, so, with no further calculation, $\alpha_{\text{Moon}} = 9 \times 10^{-3}$ radians.
(Alternatively, we could have started by saying $D_{\text{Moon}} = \dfrac{D_{\text{Sun}}}{400}$. This would give exactly the same answers.)

7   Volume of sphere, $V = \dfrac{4\pi r^3}{3}$
Volume of Earth, $V_{\text{Earth}} = \dfrac{4\pi \times (6.4 \times 10^6 \text{ m})^3}{3}$
$$= 1.1 \times 10^{21} \text{ m}^3$$
$$V_{\text{Sun}} = \frac{4\pi \times (7.0 \times 10^8 \text{ m})^3}{3} = 1.4 \times 10^{27} \text{ m}^3$$
$$\frac{V_{\text{Sun}}}{V_{\text{Earth}}} = \frac{1.4 \times 10^{27} \text{ m}^3}{1.1 \times 10^{21} \text{ m}^3} = 1.3 \times 10^6.$$

So in terms of volume, the Sun is about a million times bigger than the Earth.

8 Surface area of sphere, $A = 4\pi r^2$.

$A_{Sun} = 4\pi \times (7.0 \times 10^8 \text{ m})^2 = 6.16 \times 10^{18} \text{ m}^2$.

Power emitted from each m^2 of surface $= \dfrac{L_{Sun}}{A_{Sun}}$

$= \dfrac{3.84 \times 10^{26} \text{ W}}{6.16 \times 10^{18} \text{ m}^2} = 6.23 \times 10^7 \text{ W m}^{-2}$.

$1 \text{ m} = 1 \times 10^4 \text{ cm}^2$, so each cm^2 emits a power of 6.23×10^3 W, i.e. very close to the figure stated in the question.

9 We don't have any material that was alive when the Earth formed. Also, while carbon dating is good for dating objects from thousands up to millions of years old, in very ancient objects there would be too little carbon-14 to detect.

10 Uranium-235: $^{235}_{92}$U, contains 143 neutrons.

Uranium-238: $^{238}_{92}$U, 146 neutrons.

Thorium-232: $^{232}_{90}$Th, 142 neutrons.

Potassium-40: $^{40}_{19}$K, 21 neutrons.

11 This is β^- decay. $^{87}_{37}$Rb $\rightarrow$ $^{87}_{38}$Sr $+$ $^{0}_{-1}$e $+$ $\bar{\nu}_e$

12 An α particle is like a helium nucleus, with 2 protons and 2 neutrons. A helium atom also has 2 electrons in orbit about the nucleus.

13 If n half-lives have elapsed, then the amount of parent isotope is $(1/2^n) \times$ the initial amount. (Table 3 listed only whole-number values of n, but this rule works for n being any number.)

14 Using equation (7):

For ^{238}U, $t_{1/2} = \dfrac{\log_e(2)}{\lambda} = \dfrac{\log_e(2)}{1.552 \times 10^{-10} \text{ yr}^{-1}}$

$= 4.467 \times 10^9 \text{ yr} = 4467 \times 10^6 \text{ yr}$

Similarly, ^{40}K has $t_{1/2} = 1193 \times 10^6 \text{ yr}$

For ^{235}U, $\lambda = \dfrac{\log_e(2)}{t_{1/2}} = \dfrac{\log_e(2)}{(704 \times 10^6 \text{ yr})}$

$= 9.846 \times 10^{-10} \text{ yr}^{-1}$

Similarly, ^{87}Rb has $\lambda = 1.420 \times 10^{-11} \text{ yr}^{-1}$

$= 0.1420 \times 10^{-10} \text{ yr}^{-1}$

15 244 000 million years is half of the half-life, so $n = 0.5$, and the fraction remaining is $\dfrac{1}{2^{0.5}} = 0.71$ or 71%.

16 $\dfrac{1}{16}$ of the parent nuclei must have survived (and $\dfrac{15}{16}$ changed into lead), so the rock must be 4 half-lives old, i.e. its age must be 4×704 million years $= 2816$ million years.

17 (a) 4600 million years

(b) The meteorites could have formed in a volcanic explosion in which they were hurled at very high speed from the Martian surface (exceeding the escape velocity), eventually landing on Earth.

(c) The rocks from Mars are much younger than those formed on Earth, suggesting that they crystallised from molten rock long after Mars formed. This is consistent with their crystallising from the molten rock ejected from a volcano.

18 $\dfrac{3.84 \times 10 \text{ W}}{(746 \text{ W hp}^{-1})} \approx 5 \times 10^{23}$ hp.

19 (a) Total energy emitted in 1000 years,
$\Delta E = 3.84 \times 10^{26} \text{ J s}^{-1} \times 3 \times 10^{10} \text{ s} = 1.15 \times 10^{37}$ J

(b) (i) $\Delta m = \dfrac{\Delta E}{c^2} = \dfrac{1.15 \times 10^{37} \text{ J}}{(3.00 \times 10^8 \text{ m s}^{-1})^2}$

$= 1.28 \times 10^{20}$ kg

(ii) Using m to represent mass of Sun,

$\dfrac{\Delta m}{m} = \dfrac{1.28 \times 10^{20} \text{ kg}}{1.99 \times 10^{30} \text{ kg}} = 6.43 \times 10^{-11}$

$= 6.43 \times 10^{-9}$ %

(c) In 10^{10} years, the percentage mass loss will be $10^7 \times 6.43 \times 10^{-9}$ % $= 6.43 \times 10^{-2}$ %. (This is still a very small fraction of the Sun's mass.)

20 (a) 4^1_1H $+ 2^0_{-1}$e$^- \rightarrow ^4_2$He $+ 2\nu_e + 6\gamma$

(b) Initial mass $= 4 \times 1.673 \times 10^{-27} \text{ kg} + 2 \times 9.11 \times 10^{-31}$ kg
$= 6.694 \times 10^{-27}$ kg

Final mass $= 6.645 \times 10^{-27}$ kg

Mass deficit $\Delta m = 6.694 \times 10^{-27} \text{ kg} - 6.645 \times 10{-27} \text{ kg}$
$= 4.9 \times 10^{-29}$ kg.

(c) $\Delta E = c^2 \Delta m = (3.00 \times 10^8 \text{ m s}^{-1})^2 \times 4.9 \times 10^{-29}$ kg
$= 4.41 \times 10^{-12}$ J

(d) The Sun emits energy a rate of $= 3.84 \times 10^{26} \text{ J s}^{-1}$. To maintain this output, n nuclei of $^4_2$He produced must be produced per second, where

$n = \dfrac{3.84 \times 10^{26} \text{ J s}^{-1}}{4.41 \times 10^{-12} \text{ J}} = 8.71 \times 10^{37} \text{ s}^{-1}$

Each $^4_2$He is made from 4^1_1H, so the number of hydrogen nuclei consumed per second is
$4n = 48.71 \times 10^{37} = 3.48 \times 10^{38} \text{ s}^{-1}$

(e) There are various ways to tackle this part, which all give the same answer. Here is one way.

Initial mass of hydrogen in Sun $= 0.75 \times 1.99 \times 10^{30}$ kg
$= 1.49 \times 10^{30}$ kg.

Mass of hydrogen that will be converted to helium over the Sun's lifetime $= 0.15 \times 1.49 \times 10^{29}$ kg
$= 2.24 \times 10^{29}$ kg

No. of hydrogen nuclei contained in this mass
$= \dfrac{2.24 \times 10^{29} \text{ kg}}{(1.673 \times 10^{-27} \text{ kg})} = 1.34 \times 10^{56}$.

If hydrogen nuclei are consumed at a rate of $3.48 \times 10^{38} \text{ s}^{-1}$ then the time, t, for which the Sun can continue to emit energy is

$t = \dfrac{1.34 \times 10^{56}}{3.48 \times 10^{38} \text{ s}^{-1}} = 2.85 \times 10^{17}$ s

$\approx 1.3 \times 10^{10}$ years

21 See Figure 100. The curve is like an upside-down binding-energy curve (Figure 27). Think of the thought experiment in which nuclei are assembled for their constituent nucleons. In forming the most tightly bound nuclei, the nucleons lose the greatest amount of 'nuclear potential energy' – they lose energy therefore they also lose mass. You have also seen, in the worked example in the text and in question 20, that nuclei formed in fission and fusion reactions have less mass than the nuclei that initially took part in the reactions.

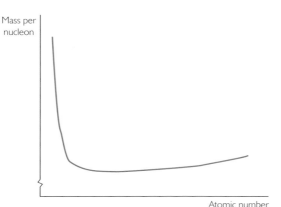

Figure 100 *The answer to question 21*

22 (a) (i) Diameter of Jupiter, $D = 2 \times 7.14 \times 10^7$ m
Maximum and minimum Earth–Jupiter separations:
$d_{max} = 7.78 \times 10^{11}$ m $+ 1.49 \times 10^{11}$ m
$\qquad = 9.27 \times 10^{11}$ m
$d_{min} = 7.78 \times 10^{11}$ m $- 1.49 \times 10^{11}$ m
$\qquad = 6.29 \times 10^{11}$ m
Using equation (2):
$$\alpha_{min} = \frac{D}{d_{max}} = \frac{2 \times 7.14 \times 10^7 \text{ m}}{9.27 \times 10^{11} \text{ m}}$$
$\qquad = 1.54 \times 10^{-4}$ radians
$$\alpha_{max} = \frac{D}{d_{min}} = \frac{2 \times 7.14 \times 10^7 \text{ m}}{6.29 \times 10^{11} \text{ m}}$$
$\qquad = 2.27 \times 10^{-4}$ radians

(ii) $\dfrac{\alpha_{min}}{\alpha_{max}} = \dfrac{1.54}{2.27} = 0.678 = 67.8\%$

(b) From equation (1)
$$\frac{F_{Jupiter}}{F_{Earth}} = \frac{L}{4\pi d^2{}_{Jupiter}} \div \frac{L}{4\pi d^2{}_{Earth}}$$
where d now represents distance from the Sun, and L is the Sun's luminosity. Therefore
$$\frac{F_{Jupiter}}{F_{Earth}} = \left(\frac{d_{Earth}}{d_{Jupiter}}\right)^2$$
$$= \left(\frac{1.49 \times 10^{11} \text{ m}}{7.78 \times 10^{11} \text{ m}}\right)^2 = 0.367 = 36.7\%.$$

(c) Referring to Figure 7, the radiation would peak at a wavelength very much longer than 1000 nm, so it would be in the infrared or microwave part of the spectrum. (You might be surprised that such a cold body emits radiation. All objects radiate, but we are usually unaware of the radiation from cold objects as it is weak and in a part of the spectrum that our bodies cannot sense.)

(d) Jupiter is probably heated by the energy released in radioactive decay processes similar to those that occur in the Earth's rocks. (You might have suggested fusion of hydrogen but this would only be possible at high temperatures so is unlikely because the outer parts of Jupiter, which contain hydrogen, are cold.)

23 The long half-life ensures that the activity of the source will not change much with time, so the source will not need to be replaced. Also, a long half-life means that the activity is relatively low, so the safety hazard is not so great as that associated with a more active, short-lived source.

24 (a) Argon has an atomic number 18. To conserve charge, any emitted particle must have a proton number of $+1$, i.e. it must therefore be a positron – this is an example of beta-plus decay. Since a positron has a nucleon number of zero, the argon isotope must have a nucleon number 40 – the same as the parent isotope. And just as beta-minus emission is accompanied by the emission of an antineutrino, beta-plus is accompanied by a neutrino. The reaction is thus:

$$^{40}_{19}\text{K} \rightarrow {}^{40}_{18}\text{Ar} + {}^{0}_{+1}\text{e} + \nu_e$$

Alternatively a captured electron could have joined with a proton in the nucleus to make a neutron. (This is in fact what happens.)

(b) One way to do this calculation is to use the same method as the worked example in section 2.2, using equation (4). The two isotopes have the same mass, so initial mass of argon is $m_0 = 3.8$ μg and the numbers of nuclei of each isotope are in proportion to their masses, i.e.

$$\frac{N}{N_0} = \frac{m}{m_0} = \frac{3.3 \mu g}{3.8 \mu g} = 0.868.$$

From Table 4, $\lambda = 5.810 \times 10^{-10}$ yr^{-1}.
$0.868 N_0 = N_0 e^{-\lambda t}$ so $0.868 = e^{-\lambda t}$
$\log_e(0.868) = -\lambda t$
$$t = \frac{\log_e(0.868)}{(-\lambda)} = \frac{\log_e(0.868)}{(-5.810 \times 10^{-10} \text{ yr}^{-1})}$$
$\qquad = 2.43 \times 10^8$ yr.

(Alternatively, using the method of question 13 and the half-life you calculated in question 14 gives the same answer.)

(c) Mass of ^{40}K nucleus ≈ 40 mass of proton (from Table 6)
$= 40 \times 1.673 \times 10^{-27} = 6.692 \times 10^{-26}$ kg
no. of ^{40}K nuclei, $N = \dfrac{5.0 \times 10^{-10} \text{ kg}}{6.692 \times 10^{-26} \text{ kg}}$
$\qquad = 7.5 \times 10^{15}$

From equations (4) and (5), activity $A = \dfrac{dN}{dt} = -\lambda N$

so $A = 7.5 \times 10^{15} \times 5.810 \times 10^{-10}\,\text{yr}^{-1}$

$= 4.3 \times 10^{6}\,\text{yr}^{-1} = \dfrac{4.3 \times 10^{6}\,\text{yr}^{-1}}{(3 \times 10^{7}\,\text{s}\,\text{yr}^{-1})}$

$\approx 0.14\,\text{s}^{-1} = 0.14\,\text{Bq}.$

25 (a) 1 light year $= 3.00 \times 10^{8}\,\text{m s}^{-1} \times 3.1536 \times 10^{7}\,\text{s}$

$= 9.46 \times 10^{15}\,\text{m}.$

$d = 4.351 \times 9.46 \times 10^{15}\,\text{m}$

$\alpha = \dfrac{r}{d} = \dfrac{1.49 \times 10^{11}\,\text{m}}{4.351 \times 9.46 \times 10^{15}\,\text{m}}$

$= 3.62 \times 10^{-6}\,\text{rad}$

$= 3.62 \times 10^{-6}\,\text{rad} \times 2.06 \times 10^{5}\,\text{arcsec rad}^{-1}$

$= 0.746''$

(b) If $\alpha = 1\,\text{arcsec} = \dfrac{1}{2.06 \times 10^{5}\,\text{rad}}$, then

$d = \dfrac{r}{\alpha} = 1.49 \times 10^{11}\,\text{m} \times 2.06 \times 10^{5}$

$= 3.1 \times 10^{16}\,\text{m}$, which is as stated.

26 $\quad \alpha = 0.002\,\text{arcsec} = \dfrac{0.002\,\text{arcsec}}{2.06 \times 10^{5}\,\text{arcsec rad}^{-1}}$

$= 9.71 \times 10^{-9}\,\text{rad}.$

From equation (9), $d = \dfrac{r}{\alpha}$

$= \dfrac{1.49 \times 10^{11}\,\text{m}}{9.71 \times 10^{-9}\,\text{rad}}$

$= 1.53 \times 10^{19}\,\text{m}$

From question 25, 1 light year $= 9.46 \times 10^{15}\,\text{m}$, so

$r = \dfrac{1.53 \times 10^{19}\,\text{m}}{9.46 \times 10^{15}\,\text{m lt yr}-1}$

$= 1.62 \times 10^{3}\,\text{light years}$

1 pc $= 3.1 \times 10^{16}\,\text{m}$ so

$r = \dfrac{1.53 \times 10^{19}\,\text{m}}{3.1 \times 10^{16}\,\text{m pc}-1} = 494\,\text{pc}$

27 Rearranging equation (1), $L = 4\pi d^{2} F$

For Sirius:

$L = 4\pi \times (8.22 \times 10^{16}\,\text{m})^{2} \times 1.17 \times 10^{-7}\,\text{W m}^{-2}$

$= 9.9 \times 10^{27}\,\text{W}$

Similarly for the other stars – see Table 14.

Star	Distance d/m	Flux $F/\text{W m}^{-2}$	Luminosity, L/W
Sirius	8.22×10^{16}	1.17×10^{-7}	9.9×10^{27}
Rigel	2.38×10^{18}	5.37×10^{-7}	3.9×10^{31}
Betelgeuse	6.18×10^{18}	1.11×10^{-8}	5.4×10^{30}
Proxima Centauri	4.11×10^{16}	1.09×10^{-11}	2.3×10^{23}
Sun	1.49×10^{11}	1.37×10^{3}	3.83×10^{26}

Table 14 *The answers to question 27*

28 You would need to determine the surface temperature from the star's spectrum. This would let you locate its position on the HR diagram (on the main sequence), from which you could read its luminosity, L. You would also need to measure its radiant energy flux, F, and then calculate its distance d using equation (1): $d = \sqrt{\left(\dfrac{L}{4\pi F}\right)}$.

29 (a) (i) The hotter the star, the greater its luminosity.

(ii) The main sequence is not quite a straight line, so L and T cannot be related by a simple power law. But if you draw a straight line going approximately through the main sequence, then you can see that an increase of a factor 10 in temperature (e.g. from 2500 K to 25 000 K) corresponds to an increase in luminosity of about a factor 10^{6} (from $10^{-2}\,L_{\text{Sun}}$ to $10^{4}\,L_{\text{Sun}}$), which suggest a relationship something like $L \propto T^{6}$.

Maths reference
....
Using log graphs
See Maths note 8.7
....

(b) It is difficult to be conclusive without more information. As you saw in Activity 2, increasing the surface temperature of an object increases its luminosity. We can also suppose that a large object is more luminous than a small one at the same temperature, since it has a greater surface area from which to radiate. All we can really say is that the most luminous main sequence stars cannot be significantly smaller than the least luminous ones, otherwise the effect of increasing temperature would be outweighed by the effect of decreasing size. (In fact, the hotter main sequence stars are larger than the cooler ones, and the differences in luminosity arise from the differences in temperature *and* in size.)

(c) As with the question about size, it is very difficult to say anything at all. Actually it is even more difficult, because size *can* be deduced from measurements of luminosity and temperature – but to deduce mass you would need to know a star's density, or else determine its mass by some completely independent means (which you will meet in section 3.3).

(d) Yet again, it is very difficult to say anything conclusive. One might be tempted to speculate that stars are cool and faint as they are formed and gradually heat up and become more luminous as a result of nuclear fusion in their interiors. Or perhaps they start off hot and luminous and gradually cool down. Similar suggestions were made when the HR diagram was first produced but they are entirely speculative and, we now believe, totally wrong.

Assuming that the stars are all at different stages in their evolution, the most we can say is that some combinations of luminosity and temperature must be more stable than others, indicating long-lasting phases in a star's life, since there are large numbers of stars on the main sequence, quite a few red giants, and some parts of the HR diagram that contain no stars.

30 Rearranging equation (10): $G = \dfrac{Fr^2}{m_1 m_2}$, so it has SI units $N\,m^2\,kg^{-2}$.

31 (a) Using equation (15) for Mars,
$$g = \frac{GM}{r^2}$$
$$= \frac{6.67 \times 10^{-11}\,N\,m^2\,kg^{-2} \times 6.42 \times 10^{23}\,kg}{(3.39 \times 10^6\,m)^2}$$
$$= 3.73\,N\,kg^{-1}.$$

(b) You need to multiply your mass (in kg) by the field strength, e.g. if your mass is 60.0 kg,
$$W = mg = 3.73\,N\,kg^{-1} \times 60.0\,kg = 224\,N.$$

32 Use equation (15), $g = \dfrac{GM}{r^2}$, and substitute for the mass M:
$$M = \rho V = \frac{4\pi r^3 \rho}{3} \text{ so}$$
$$g = \frac{4\pi r^3 \rho G}{3r^2} = \frac{4\pi r \rho G}{3}$$

33 (a) The smaller star must have a brighter surface, since when it passes behind its companion there is a large dip in the light curve, whereas when it blocks off light from the larger star the dip is smaller.

(b) The period is the time for one complete orbit, which could be shown as the time from the middle of one large dip in the light curve to the middle of the next large dip.

34 (a) See Figure 101(a). The received flux halves each time one star passes in front of the other.

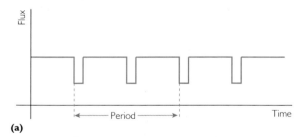

(a)

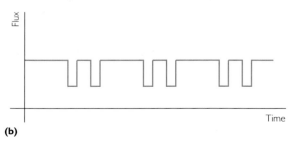

(b)

Figure 101 *The answer to question 34*

(b) See Figure 102(b)

35 Rewriting equation (19): $\dfrac{u}{c} \approx \dfrac{(f_{em} - f_{rec})}{f_{em}}$.

Substituting $f = \dfrac{c}{\lambda}$:
$$\frac{u}{c} \approx \left(\frac{c}{\lambda_{em}} - \frac{c}{\lambda_{rec}} \right) \times \frac{\lambda_{em}}{c}$$
On the right-hand side, cancel c and combine the terms inside the bracket:
$$\frac{u}{c} \approx \left\{ \frac{\lambda_{rec} - \lambda_{em}}{\lambda_{em}\lambda_{rec}} \right\} \times \lambda_{em}$$
Then cancel λ_{em} to get:
$$\frac{u}{c} \approx \left(\frac{\lambda_{rec} - \lambda_{em}}{\lambda_{rec}} \right)$$
and use $\lambda_{rec} \approx \lambda_{em}$ to get
$$\frac{u}{c} \approx \left(\frac{\lambda_{rec} - \lambda_{em}}{\lambda_{em}} \right)$$

36 The received wavelength is shorter than the emitted wavelength, so the gases were approaching. Using equations (20) and (21):
$$\frac{v}{c} = \frac{\Delta\lambda}{\lambda_{em}} = \left(\frac{\lambda_{rec} - \lambda_{em}}{\lambda_{em}} \right)$$
$$= \frac{(1.070\,\mu m - 1.083\,\mu m)}{1.083\,\mu m}$$
$$= -0.012$$
(The negative sign means the gases are approaching.)
$$v = 0.012\,c = 3.6 \times 10^3\,km\,s^{-1}$$

37 Using equation (20), $u = \dfrac{c\Delta\lambda}{\lambda_{em}}$
$$= \frac{3.00 \times 10^8\,m\,s^{-1} \times 0.041\,nm}{656.28\,nm}$$
$$= 1.87 \times 10^4\,m\,s^{-1}.$$
Assuming circular motion, $u = \dfrac{2\pi r}{T}$ so
$$r = \frac{uT}{2\pi} = \frac{1.87 \times 10^4\,m\,s^{-1} \times 8.6 \times 3.16 \times 10^7\,s}{2\pi}$$
$$= 8.1 \times 10^{11}\,m$$

Then using equation (17):
$$M = \frac{v^2 r}{G}$$
$$= \frac{(1.87 \times 10^4\,m\,s^{-1})^2 \times 8.1 \times 10^{11}\,m}{6.67 \times 10^{-11}\,N\,m^2\,kg^{-2}}$$
$$= 4.2 \times 10^{30}\,kg$$

(You would get the same answer if you used equation (18).)

38 $R = \dfrac{pV}{nT}$ so the units of R must be $\dfrac{(\text{units of } pV)}{\text{mol K}}$. Pressure has SI units of Pa, where $1\,Pa = 1\,N\,m^{-2}$. So pV has units $N\,m^{-2} \times m^3 = N\,m$, and $1\,N\,m = 1\,J$. Hence R has SI units $J\,mol^{-1}\,K^{-1}$.

39 From equation (26), $p = \dfrac{nRT}{V}$.

For a sphere, $V = \dfrac{4\pi r^3}{3}$, so $p = \dfrac{3nRT}{4\pi r^3}$

No. of moles, $n = \dfrac{M}{m}$

$$= \dfrac{2 \times 10^{30}\,\text{kg}}{1 \times 10^{-3}\,\text{kg mol}^{-1}} = 2 \times 10^{33}\,\text{mol}$$

$$p = \dfrac{3 \times 2 \times 10^{33}\,\text{mol} \times 8.31\,\text{J mol}^{-1}\,\text{K}^{-1} \times 1 \times 10^{7}\,\text{K}}{4\pi \times (7 \times 10^{8}\,\text{m})^{3}}$$

$$\approx 1 \times 10^{14}\,\text{Pa}.$$

40 From equation (38), $\langle c^2 \rangle = \dfrac{3p}{\rho}$, so $\sqrt{\langle c^2 \rangle} = \sqrt{\left(\dfrac{3p}{\rho}\right)}$

$$= \sqrt{\left(\dfrac{3 \times 10^{5}\,\text{Pa}}{1\,\text{kg m}^{-3}}\right)} \approx 500\,\text{m s}^{-1}.$$

41 (a) The right-hand sides of equations (26) and (37) must be equal, since they are both equal to pV, and hence

$\dfrac{Nm\langle c^2 \rangle}{3} = nRT$. Since $Nm = M$, $\langle c^2 \rangle = \dfrac{3nRT}{M}$, and so

$$\sqrt{\langle c^2 \rangle} = \sqrt{\left(\dfrac{3nRT}{M}\right)}$$

$$= \sqrt{\left(\dfrac{6 \times 10^{33}\,\text{mol} \times 8.31\,\text{J mol}^{-1}\,\text{K}^{-1} \times 1 \times 10^{7}\,\text{K}}{2 \times 10^{30}\,\text{kg}}\right)}$$

$$= 5 \times 10^{5}\,\text{m s}^{-1}.$$

(b) Starting from $\dfrac{Nm\langle c^2 \rangle}{3} = nRT$,

$$\dfrac{Nm\langle c^2 \rangle}{3} = \dfrac{NRT}{N_A}$$

Cancelling N and rearranging:

$$\langle c^2 \rangle = \dfrac{3RT}{mN_A}, \text{ and so}$$

$$\sqrt{\langle c^2 \rangle} = \sqrt{\left(\dfrac{3RT}{mN_A}\right)}$$

42 From the answer to question 41(b), $\sqrt{\langle c^2 \rangle} \propto \sqrt{\left(\dfrac{1}{m}\right)}$,

so the less massive molecules will be moving faster. Since

$\dfrac{m_{\text{ox}}}{m_{\text{hyd}}} = 16$, $\sqrt{\left(\dfrac{m_{\text{ox}}}{m_{\text{hyd}}}\right)} = 4$, and so the r.m.s. speed of hydrogen molecules will be four times that of oxygen molecules at the same temperature.

43 $\sqrt{\langle c^2 \rangle} = \sqrt{\left(\dfrac{3kT}{m}\right)}$

$$= \sqrt{\left(\dfrac{3 \times 1.38 \times 10^{-23}\,\text{J K}^{-1} \times 1 \times 10^{7}\,\text{K}}{1.67 \times 10^{-27}\,\text{kg}}\right)}$$

$$= 5 \times 10^{5}\,\text{m s}^{-1} \text{ (i.e. the same as in question 41(a)).}$$

44 One way is to write $n = \dfrac{N}{N_A}$ (see question 41(b)) and $R = N_A k$, hence $nR = Nk$ and so $pV = nRT = NkT$.

45 (a) (i) $\sqrt{\langle c^2 \rangle} = \sqrt{\left(\dfrac{3kT}{m}\right)}$

$$= \sqrt{\left(\dfrac{3 \times 1.38 \times 10^{-23}\,\text{J K}^{-1} \times 30\,\text{K}}{2 \times 1.67 \times 10^{-27}\,\text{kg}}\right)}$$

$$\approx 600\,\text{m s}^{-1}.$$

(ii) Since $c \propto \sqrt{T}$, and T is one-tenth that in question 43,

$$c = \dfrac{5 \times 10^{5}\,\text{m s}^{-1}}{\sqrt{10}} = 1.6 \times 10^{5}\,\text{m s}^{-1}.$$

(b) (i) Supernova remnant: $p = \left(\dfrac{N}{V}\right) \times kT$

$$= 10^{5}\,\text{m}^{-3} \times 1.38 \times 10^{-23}\,\text{J K}^{-1} \times 10^{6}\,\text{K}$$

$$\approx 1.4 \times 10^{-12}\,\text{Pa} = 14 \times 10^{-13}\,\text{Pa}$$

Similarly for ionised hydrogen region:

$$p = 10^{8}\,\text{m}^{-3} \times 1.38 \times 10^{-23}\,\text{J K}^{-1} \times 8000\,\text{K}$$

$$\approx 1.1 \times 10^{-11}\,\text{Pa} = 110 \times 10^{-13}\,\text{Pa}$$

(ii) Despite the huge differences in the temperatures and number densities in the ISM, it is remarkable that the pressure varies only by about two orders of magnitude.

46 Stars are formed by the collapse of a molecular cloud/~~region of ionised hydrogen~~. The particles in the cloud are far apart/~~close together~~. The force of gravitational/~~electrostatic~~ attraction pulls them all towards the ~~edge~~/centre of the cloud. Each particle is falling inwards, like a ball falling towards the Earth. As the cloud collapses, the particles move more quickly/~~slowly~~, and they collide more frequently with one another, sharing their kinetic energy. The faster the particles move, the higher/~~lower~~ the temperature of the gas. As the cloud collapses: its density increases/~~decreases~~; its pressure increases/~~decreases~~; the particles' kinetic energy increases/~~decreases~~; and their gravitational potential energy ~~increases~~/decreases.

The particles collide frequently and energetically so that they break up to form a hot plasma of fast moving/~~slow moving~~ positively/~~negatively~~ charged nuclei and electrons. When the temperature is high/~~low~~ enough, the nuclei can approach one another so closely that nuclear ~~fission~~/fusion can start.

47 Your answer will depend on what you have assumed for the size of the cloud. For a rough estimate, volume, $V \approx d^3$ where d is the diameter. If $d \approx 10$ light years $\sim 1 \times 10^{17}$ m, then $V \sim 10^{51}$ m^3. Such a cloud would contain roughly 10^{61} molecules of H_2, so its mass would be

$$M_{\text{cloud}} \approx 10^{61} \times 3.34 \times 10^{-27}\,\text{kg} \approx 3 \times 10^{34}\,\text{kg}$$

$$\dfrac{M_{\text{cloud}}}{M_{\text{Sun}}} \approx \dfrac{3 \times 10^{34}\,\text{kg}}{2 \times 10^{30}\,\text{kg}} \sim 10^{4} \text{ stars. (Some star clusters are found that do contain many thousand stars, so this is reasonable.)}$$

48 (a) (i) Since gravitational acceleration is equal to the field strength, use equation (15) $\left(g = \dfrac{GM}{r^2}\right)$ and your values from question 47. With our values,

$M = M_{cloud} = 3 \times 10^{34}$ kg, $r = \dfrac{d}{2} = 5 \times 10^{16}$ m, we get

$$g = \frac{6.67 \times 10^{-11}\,\text{N}\,\text{m}^2\,\text{kg}^{-2} \times 3 \times 10^{34}\,\text{kg}}{(5 \times 10^{16}\,\text{m})^2}$$

$\approx 8 \times 10^{-10}\,\text{m}\,\text{s}^{-2}$.

(ii) $s = ut + \dfrac{1}{2} a t^2$, with $u = 0$ and $s = r$,

$$t = \sqrt{\left(\frac{2r}{g}\right)} = \sqrt{\left(\frac{10^{17}\,\text{m}}{8 \times 10^{-10}\,\text{m}\,\text{s}^{-2}}\right)}$$

$\approx 1 \times 10^{13}\,\text{s} \approx 3 \times 10^5$ years.

(iii) $v = u + at$, $u = 0$ so

$v = gt \approx 8 \times 10^{-10}\,\text{m}\,\text{s}^{-2} \times 10^{13}\,\text{s} \approx 8000\,\text{m}\,\text{s}^{-1}$.

(iv) From equation (42), $T = \dfrac{m\langle c^2 \rangle}{3k}$

$$\approx \frac{3.34 \times 10^{-27}\,\text{kg} \times (8000\,\text{m}\,\text{s}^{-1})^2}{3 \times 1.38 \times 10^{-23}\,\text{J}\,\text{K}^{-1}}$$

$\approx 5000\,\text{K}$

(b) The temperature in (a) (iv) is not high enough for fusion. However, it does illustrate that gravitational collapse does lead to a substantial rise in temperature. In practice, the gravitational acceleration does *not* remain constant throughout the collapse – as the fragment shrinks to a smaller radius, the field strength at its surface increases, so particles will 'fall' with an ever-increasing acceleration, leading to a much greater temperature rise than estimated here.

49 Many stars are found in binary systems. Doppler shifts in the stars' spectral lines enable their orbital speeds and periods, and hence the sizes of the orbits, to be determined. The stellar mass can then be calculated using equations of gravitation.

50 Luminosity $\approx 7 \times 10^4\,L_{Sun}$ (note that the axis has a log scale). So time t on the main sequence would be

$$t \approx \frac{18 \times 10^{10}\,\text{years}}{7 \times 10^4} \approx 2.5 \times 10^6\,\text{years}$$

51 All bodies emit electromagnetic radiation that depends on their temperature. The higher the temperature, the shorter the wavelength at which most of the radiation is emitted. Gamma radiation is electromagnetic radiation at very short wavelengths, so is emitted by very hot bodies.

52 (a) From equation (42), $\langle E_k \rangle = \dfrac{3kT}{2} = \dfrac{m\langle c^2 \rangle}{2}$

(i) $\langle E_k \rangle = \dfrac{3 \times 1.38 \times 10^{-23}\,\text{J}\,\text{K}^{-1} \times 5 \times 10^9\,\text{K}}{2}$

$= 1 \times 10^{-13}\,\text{J}$

(ii) $\sqrt{\langle c^2 \rangle} = \sqrt{\left(\dfrac{3kT}{m}\right)}$

$$= \sqrt{\left(\frac{3 \times 1.38 \times 10^{-23}\,\text{J}\,\text{K}^{-1} \times 5 \times 10^9\,\text{K}}{9.3 \times 10^{-26}\,\text{kg}}\right)}$$

$= 1.5 \times 10^6\,\text{m}\,\text{s}^{-1}$.

(b) (i) $\langle E_k \rangle = 1 \times 10^{-13}\,\text{J}$

(i.e. the same as the iron nuclei, as the mean kinetic energy is independent of mass.)

(ii) $\sqrt{\langle c^2 \rangle} = \sqrt{\left(\dfrac{3kT}{m}\right)}$

$$= \sqrt{\left(\frac{3 \times 1.38 \times 10^{-23}\,\text{J}\,\text{K}^{-1} \times 5 \times 10^9\,\text{K}}{9.1 \times 10^{-31}\,\text{kg}}\right)}$$

$= 4.8 \times 10^8\,\text{m}\,\text{s}^{-1}$

This is greater than the speed of light, but no particle can travel this fast. (The material is so hot that electrons do travel close to the speed of light. To describe their behaviour properly we need the equations of special relativity instead of the 'classical' equations used here.)

53 (a) $\rho = \dfrac{M}{V}$, $V = \dfrac{4\pi r^3}{3}$, so $\rho = \dfrac{3M}{4\pi r^3}$.

(i) Neutron star: $\rho = \dfrac{3 \times 4 \times 10^{30}\,\text{kg}}{(4\pi \times (5 \times 10\,\text{m})^3)}$

$= 7.6 \times 10^{18}\,\text{kg}\,\text{m}^{-3}$.

(ii) He nucleus: $\rho = \dfrac{3 \times 6.7 \times 10^{-27}\,\text{kg}}{(4\pi \times (10^{-15}\,\text{m})^3)}$

$= 1.6 \times 10^{18}\,\text{kg}\,\text{m}^{-3}$.

(iii) The two densities are the same order of magnitude so the statement is justified.

(b) From equation (15), $g = \dfrac{GM}{r^2}$

$$= \frac{6.67 \times 10^{-11}\,\text{N}\,\text{m}^2\,\text{kg}^{-2} \times 4 \times 10^{30}\,\text{kg}}{(5 \times 10^3\,\text{m})^2}$$

$= 1.1 \times 10^{13}\,\text{N}\,\text{kg}^{-1} \approx 10^{13}\,g_{Earth}$

54 (a) Consider a particle mass m that is part of the star's surface at its equator, which moves in a circle of radius r. The gravitational force must be at least strong enough to provide the centripetal force so, from equations (10) and (16):

$\dfrac{GMm}{r^2} \geqslant \dfrac{mv^2}{r}$. We can cancel m and multiply by r, and

since $v = \dfrac{2\pi r}{T}$, we can write

$\dfrac{GM}{r} \geqslant \left(\dfrac{2\pi r}{T}\right)^2$, i.e. $\dfrac{GM}{r} \geqslant \dfrac{4\pi^2 r^2}{T^2}$ and hence

$$T \geqslant \sqrt{\left(\frac{4\pi^2 r^3}{GM}\right)}$$

(b) $T \geqslant \sqrt{\dfrac{(4\pi^2 \times (5 \times 10^3 \text{ m})^3}{(6.67 \times 10^{-11} \text{ N m}^2 \text{ kg}^{-2} \times 4 \times 10^{30} \text{ kg})}}$

$= 1.4 \times 10^{-4} \text{ s} \approx 0.1 \text{ ms}.$

So a period of a few ms would be reasonable, but a neutron star of this size and mass with a period less than 0.1 ms would have to spin so fast that it would fly apart.

55 (a) (i) Using equation (10), $F_{\text{feet}} = \dfrac{GMm}{r^2}$

$= \dfrac{6.67 \times 10^{11} \text{ N m}^2\text{kg}^{-2} \times 10^{26} \text{ kg} \times 10.0 \text{ kg}}{(5.0 \times 10^4 \text{ m})^2}$

$= 2.668\,0 \times 10^7 \text{ N}$

(ii) Similarly for the head with $r = 5.0002 \times 10^4$ m,

$F_{\text{head}} = 2.667\,8 \times 10^7 \text{ N}.$

(b) The difference between the forces is $0.000\,2 \times 10^7$ N $= 2 \times 10^3$ N. A difference of 2 kN will cause some serious stretching – imagine hanging by your hands with 200 kg suspended from your feet. Now you know why Jo is so tall.

56 The cosmological principle states that all large regions of space have the same properties. They should then be expanding at the same rate, which implies Hubble's Law holds everywhere.

57 Doppler shift is a change in wavelength (and frequency) resulting from movement of the source of waves away from the observer. Cosmological redshift is a similar change, but occurs as a result of space itself expanding.

58 The existence of the cosmic background radiation suggests the Universe was a hotter, denser place than it is now, whereas the steady state theory predicts the Universe has always been as it is now.

59 As the Universe expands, the peak wavelength of the radiation will become longer and longer and the temperature will move ever closer to absolute zero.

60 If H_0 has twice the value used in the worked example, then the age, t, will be half that calculated, i.e. about 10 billion years

61 (i) From equation (45),

$v = dH_0 = 350 \text{ Mpc} \times 75 \text{ km s}^{-1} \text{ Mpc}^{-1}$
$= 2.6 \times 10^4 \text{ km s}^{-1}$

(ii) As $v \ll c$ we can use equation (44): $z = \dfrac{v}{c}$

$= \dfrac{(2.6 \times 10^7 \text{ m s}^{-1})}{3.00 \times 10^8 \text{ m s}^{-1}} = 8.8 \times 10^{-2}$

(Equation (46) gives the same answer.)

62 (a) Light travels at finite speed. So light reaching us from a large distance has taken time to get here. We therefore see galaxies as they were when the light was emitted, not as they are right now.

(b) In the first 300 000 years after the Big Bang, light could not travel freely through the Universe. Photons were continuously colliding with other particles.

63 $^3_1\text{H} + ^2_1\text{H} \rightarrow ^4_2\text{He} + ^1_0\text{n}$

The neutron must be produced in order to conserve charge (proton number) and nucleon number.

64 Using equation (42), $\langle E_k \rangle = \dfrac{3kT}{2} = \dfrac{m\langle c^2 \rangle}{2}$

$\langle E_k \rangle = \dfrac{3 \times 1.38 \times 10^{-23} \text{ J K}^{-1} \times 1.0 \times 10^8 \text{ K}}{2}$

$= 2.1 \times 10^{-15} \text{ J}.$

$\sqrt{\langle c^2 \rangle} = \sqrt{\dfrac{3kT}{m}} = \sqrt{\left(\dfrac{2\langle E_k \rangle}{m}\right)}$

$= \sqrt{\left(\dfrac{2 \times 2.1 \times 10^{-15} \text{ J}}{6.68 \times 10^{-27} \text{ kg}}\right)}$

$= 7.8 \times 10^5 \text{ m s}^{-1}.$

65 If there are $12n$ hydrogen atoms (^1_1H) to n helium atoms (^4_2He), then

mass of H: mass of He $= 12 : 4 = 75\% : 25\%$

66 He nuclei carry more charge than H nuclei, so their mutual electrostatic repulsion is greater and hence they need to be moving with more kinetic energy in order to get close enough to fuse. Carbon carries an even higher nuclear charge than helium. Kinetic energy depends on temperature, so producing carbon requires a higher temperature than producing helium. In the expanding universe, unlike inside stars, temperature is falling so the next stage of fusion cannot take place.

67 From equations (10) and (13),

$\dfrac{F_e}{F_g} = \dfrac{ke^2}{Gm^2} = 4.16 \times 10^{42}.$

(Note that you do not need to know the separation r, since the magnitudes of both forces are proportional to $1/r^2$.)

68 See Figure 102. The tangents to the curve show that the slope, which represents the rate of expansion, is decreasing.

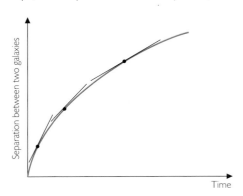

Figure 102 *The answer to question 68*

69   The actual age of the Universe will be less than estimated in section 4.2. As the Universe must have been expanding more rapidly in the past, it will have reached its present size in a shorter time than if the expansion had always been at the rate which is deduced from the present value of the Hubble constant. (In the very distant past, H_0 would have been larger, as the expansion was more rapid. Observations of *very* distant objects (quasars) show that they are indeed moving faster than is predicted by Hubble's law.)

Maths Notes

0 Signs and symbols

0.1 Equations and comparisons

In physics, we are often interested in whether two quantities are exactly equal, or almost equal, or whether one is greater than the other. Table 1 lists the signs used for expressing such relationships.

Symbol	Meaning	Notes
$=$	is equal to	
$\equiv$	is exactly the same as	used to emphasise the point that two expressions are two ways of writing exactly the same thing (as opposed to two different things being the same size)
$\neq$	is not equal to	
$\approx$	is approximately equal to	
$\sim$	is the same order of magnitude as	
$<$	is less than	the smaller quantity is written at the narrow end of the symbol
$>$	is greater than	
$\leqslant$	is less than or equal to	
$\geqslant$	is greater than or equal to	
$\ll$	is much less than	
$\gg$	is much greater than	

Table 1 *Signs for equations and comparisons*

Maths reference

Order of magnitude
See Maths note 7.4

0.2 The delta symbol

The symbol Δ (the capital Greek letter delta) is used to mean 'a small amount of' or 'a change in'. Notice that Δ does *not* represent a number, so resist the temptation to cancel Δ if it appears on the top and bottom of an expression.

For example, the symbol Δt represents a time interval and is often used when describing rates of flow or rates of change. For example, if an amount of charge ΔQ flows past a point in a time interval Δt, then the current I can be written

$$I = \frac{\Delta Q}{\Delta t}$$

The delta symbol is also used to denote an experimental uncertainty. For example, if a distance x is measured as 23 mm but could be out by 1 mm in either direction, then the uncertainty in the measurement is $\Delta x = 1$ mm. The measurement is written as $x \pm \Delta x$, i.e. 23 mm $\pm$ 1 mm.

▌ *Index notation*

An **index** (plural **indices**) or **power** is the superscript number which, when a positive whole number, means squared, cubed, etc. For example

$5^2 = 5 \times 5 = 25$

$7^3 = 7 \times 7 \times 7 = 147$

$0.6^4 = 0.6 \times 0.6 \times 0.6 \times 0.6 = 0.1296$

1.1 Index notation and powers of 10

Table 2 shows 'powers of 10'. The number in any row is found by dividing the number in the row above by 10.

$100\,000 =$	$10 \times 10 \times 10 \times 10 \times 10 =$	10^5
$10\,000 =$	$10 \times 10 \times 10 \times 10 =$	10^4
$1\,000 =$	$10 \times 10 \times 10 =$	10^3
$100 =$	$10 \times 10 =$	10^2
$10 =$	$10 =$	10^1
$1 =$	$1 =$	10^0
$0.1 =$	$\dfrac{1}{10} =$	10^{-1}
$0.01 =$	$\dfrac{1}{10 \times 10} = \dfrac{1}{10^2} =$	10^{-2}
$0.001 =$	$\dfrac{1}{10 \times 10 \times 10} = \dfrac{1}{10^3} =$	10^{-3}

Table 2 *Positive and negative powers of 10*

Extending the pattern gives a meaning to zero and negative indices. If you replace all the 10s in Table 2 by any other number that you choose, you should be able to convince yourself that

$$x^0 = 1 \qquad \text{for } any \text{ value of } x.$$

1.2 Standard form

To represent very large and very small numbers, we generally use **standard form**, also called **scientific notation**.

A number written in standard form consists of a number with a single digit (not zero) before the decimal point, multiplied by a power of 10.

Maths reference

Units and physical quantities
See Maths note 2.1

Large numbers

5 620 000 (five million six hundred and twenty thousand) becomes 5.62×10^6

407 300 (four hundred and seven thousand, three hundred) becomes 4.073×10^5.

Small numbers

$0.5680 = 5.680 \times 0.1 = 5.68 \times 10^{-1}$

$0.000\,702\,3 = 7.023 \times 0.0001 = 7.023 \times 10^{-4}$

1.3 Combining powers

Powers of the same number

When multiplying two numbers expressed as 'powers' of the same number, the powers add:

$$10^2 \times 10^3 = (10 \times 10) \times (10 \times 10 \times 10) = 10^5$$

i.e. $\quad 10^2 \times 10^3 = 10^{(2+3)}$

$$6^2 \times 6^2 = (6 \times 6) \times (6 \times 6) = 6^4$$

When dividing, the powers subtract

$$10^6 \div 10^2 = (10 \times 10 \times 10 \times 10 \times 10 \times 10) \div (10 \times 10) = 10^4$$

i.e. $\quad 10^6 \div 10^2 = 10^{(6-2)}$

The rules still work when negative powers are involved:

$$10^5 \times 10^{-2} = 10^5 \times \left(\frac{1}{10^2}\right) = 10^5 \div 10^2 = 10^3$$

i.e. $\quad 10^5 \times 10^{-2} = 10^{(5-2)}$

$$x^4 \times x^{-3} = x^{(4-3)} = x$$

$$4^3 \div 4^{-2} = 4^3 \div \left(\frac{1}{4^2}\right) = 4^3 \times 4^2 = 4^5$$

i.e. $\quad 4^3 \div 4^{-2} = 4^{(3--2)} = 4^{(3+2)}$

Maths reference

Reciprocals
See Maths note 3.3

Powers of different numbers

When dealing with a mixture of numbers of different type, collect together all numbers of the same type and combine their powers by adding or subtracting:

$$2 \times 10^4 \times 3 \times 10^5 = (2 \times 3) \times (10^4 \times 10^5) = 6 \times 10^9$$

$$1.38 \times 10^{-23} \times 2.3 \times 10^3 = 1.38 \times 2.3 \times 10^{(-23+3)}$$
$$= 3.174 \times 10^{-20}$$

$$3y^2 \times 7y^5 = 21y^7$$

$$5z^2 \times 3z^{-2} = 15z^0 = 15$$

1.4 Manipulating powers on a calculator

Powers of 10

Think of the EXP or EE key as 'times 10 to the power of'.

To enter 7.54×10^9: enter 7.54, press EXP and enter 9. (Notice that you do *not* type in 10 – if you do, you will multiply your number by 10, making it 10 times too big.)

Your calculator might use its own shorthand to display this number as 7.54 09, or 7.54^9, or 7.54 EE 9 (or similar). But you should always write it as 7.54×10^9.

Negative powers of 10

To enter a negative index, use the $\pm$ or $+/-$ key (not the 'minus' key, because that will subtract the next number from the one you have just entered).

To enter 1.38×10^{-23}: enter 1.38, press EXP, enter 23 and press $\pm$.

Squares, etc.

To square a number, use the x^2 key. For example, to work out 1.3^2, enter 1.3 and press x^2 to get 1.69.

Pressing x^2 again squares the answer, i.e. calculates your original number to the power of 4. Pressing x^2 three times altogether gives you your original number to the power of 8, and so on – each time you press x^2, you double the power.

Other powers

Use the y^x key to raise one number to the power of a second number. y is the first number you enter, and x the second.

To calculate 2.5^3: enter 2.5, press y^x, enter 3, press $=$.

Other negative powers

As with powers of 10, use the $\pm$ or $+/-$ key to enter negative numbers.

To calculate 2.5^{-3}: enter 2.5, press y^x, enter 3, press $\pm$, press $=$.

1.5 Powers that are not whole numbers

The square root of a number x can be written as $x^{\frac{1}{2}}$ or $x^{1/2}$:

$$x^{\frac{1}{2}} \times x^{\frac{1}{2}} = x^{(\frac{1}{2} + \frac{1}{2})} = x^1 = x$$

so $x^{\frac{1}{2}} = \sqrt{x}$.

Similarly, $x^{\frac{1}{3}} = \sqrt[3]{x}$ (the cube root of x); $x^{\frac{1}{4}} = \sqrt[4]{x}$ and so on.

Other fractional powers can also be interpreted in terms of roots, for example:

$$x^{\frac{3}{2}} = \sqrt{(x^3)} \text{ (the square root of } x\text{-cubed)}$$

$$= (\sqrt{x})^3 \text{ (the cube of the square root of } x\text{)}$$

and

$$x^{-\frac{1}{2}} = \frac{1}{x^{\frac{1}{2}}} = \frac{1}{\sqrt{x}}$$

Fractional powers can also be written using decimal numbers, for example:

$$x^{\frac{1}{2}} = x^{0.5}$$
$$x^{\frac{3}{2}} = x^{1.5}$$

Powers that are neither simple fractions nor whole numbers are less easy to interpret, but they still exist and can be calculated (e.g. using the y^x key of a calculator. For example:

$$10^{0.333} = 2.153$$
$$10^{0.6021} = 4.000$$
$$5.6^{\pi} = 224.1$$
$$9.34^{-0.83} = 0.1565$$

(All these answers are given to four significant figures.)

Maths reference
....
Significant figures
See Maths note 7.2
....

2 *Units*

The SI system of units (Système Internationale d'Unités) has been established by international agreement. In your study of physics you will use mainly SI units. The basic SI units are listed in Table 3. Notice that, when a unit is named after a person, the unit symbol has a capital but the name of the unit does not.

Quantity	SI unit	Notes
mass	kilogram, kg	
time	second, s	
length	metre, m	
electric current	ampere, A	used to define the unit of charge, the coulomb
temperature	kelvin, K	
luminous intensity	candela, cd	not used in this course, but included here for completeness
amount of substance	mole, mol	

Table 3   *The basic SI units*

2.1 *Units and physical quantities; graphs and tables*

A physical quantity consists of a number and a unit. Without the unit, the quantity is incomplete. When a symbol represents a physical quantity, it represents the *complete* quantity – units and all. For example, suppose v represents speed, and a particular speed is found to be $5\,\mathrm{m\,s^{-1}}$. You should write

$$v = 5\,\mathrm{m\,s^{-1}}$$

(not just $v = 5$ and not $v\,(\mathrm{m\,s^{-1}}) = 5$).

Units can be manipulated just like numbers and other symbols. When labelling axes of graphs, and when listing physical quantities in tables, it is conventional to divide each quantity by its unit to get a pure number.

For example, you can divide both sides of the expression for v above by $m\,s^{-1}$ and write

$$v/(m\,s^{-1}) = 5$$

If you were plotting values of v on a graph, or listing them in a table, you should label the graph axis, or the table column, as $v/m\,s^{-1}$.

Large and small numbers

Suppose you were dealing with speeds that were all several million metres per second:

$$v = 2 \times 10^6\,m\,s^{-1}, \quad v = 7 \times 10^6\,m\,s^{-1}, \text{ etc.}$$

To make the numbers more manageable, you could use the same rule as above to write $v/(10^6\,m\,s^{-1}) = 2$, etc., and label your graph and table as shown in Figure 1.

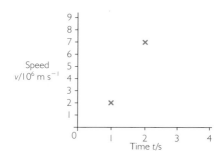

Figure 1 *Labelling graphs and tables*

2.2 *Manipulating units; index notation and units*

In calculations, the units should be manipulated as well as the numbers. This can help you keep track of what you are doing as well as being correct – so it is a good habit to get into.

Indices can be used with units and with algebraic symbols. For example,

$$4^{-1} = \frac{1}{4} = 0.25, \quad x^{-2} = \frac{1}{x^2}$$

Units such as coulombs per second, or joules per coulomb, can be written either as C/s and J/C or using index notation: $C\,s^{-1}$ and $J\,C^{-1}$. Similarly, metres per second, in calculations of unit of speed, can be written as m/s or $m\,s^{-1}$. Using the index notation helps prevent table headings and graph labels having too many oblique strokes. For example,

$$70\,m \div 20\,s = 3.5\,m\,s^{-1}$$

When multiplying numbers, units or symbols, collect together all those of the same type and add their indices. For example:

$$2\,C\,s^{-1} \times 4\,s = 8\,C$$

$$10\,m\,s^{-1} \div 5\,s = 2\,m\,s^{-2}$$

2.3 *Derived units*

Table 4 shows how SI units are combined to give units of various quantities. Some common combinations are given 'shorthand' names.

Quantity	Unit name	Symbol	Equivalent
speed			$\mathrm{m\,s^{-1}}$
acceleration			$\mathrm{m\,s^{-2}}$
force	newton	N	$1\,\mathrm{N} = 1\,\mathrm{kg\,m\,s^{-2}}$
gravitational field strength			$1\,\mathrm{N\,kg^{-1}} = 1\,\mathrm{m\,s^{-2}}$
energy, work	joule	J	$1\,\mathrm{J} = 1\,\mathrm{N\,m} = 1\,\mathrm{kg\,m^2\,s^{-2}}$
power	watt	W	$1\,\mathrm{W} = 1\,\mathrm{J\,s^{-1}}$ $(= 1\,\mathrm{kg\,m^2\,s^{-3}})$
frequency	hertz	Hz	$1\,\mathrm{Hz} = 1\,\mathrm{s^{-1}}$
electric charge	coulomb	C	$1\,\mathrm{C} = 1\,\mathrm{A\,s}$ $1\,\mathrm{A} = 1\,\mathrm{C\,s^{-1}}$
potential difference, emf	volt	V	$1\,\mathrm{V} = 1\,\mathrm{J\,C^{-1}}$ $(= 1\,\mathrm{kg\,m^2\,C^{-1}\,s^{-2}})$
electrical resistance	ohm	Ω	$1\,\Omega = 1\,\mathrm{V\,A^{-1}}$ $(= 1\,\mathrm{kg\,m^2\,C^{-2}\,s^{-1}})$

Table 4 *Some common derived SI units*

Study note

In writing units, the coulomb is often treated as if it were the basic unit rather than the ampere.

2.4 SI prefixes

When dealing with quantities that are large or small, we often use prefixes as an alternative to standard form. For example, a distance of 1.3×10^4 m could be written as 13 km, and a distance of 0.0037 m could be written as 3.7 mm. The official SI prefixes go up and down in steps of 10^3. Table 5 lists the SI prefixes that you are likely to encounter in your study of physics.

Prefix	Symbol	Equivalent in powers of 10
tera	T	10^{12}
giga	G	10^9
mega	M	10^6
kilo	k	10^3
centi	c	10^{-2}
milli	μ	10^{-3}
micro	m	10^{-6}
nano	n	10^{-9}
pico	p	10^{-12}
femto	f	10^{-15}

Table 5 *SI prefixes*

Study note

The centimetre is not officially an SI unit [because 'centi' (10^{-2}) does not fit the pattern] but is widely used.

When dealing with conversions involving prefixes, it is wise to write down each step using appropriate powers of 10, *and include the units at each stage.* For example, suppose light of a certain colour has a wavelength of 468 nm and you want to use standard form to write the wavelength in metres:

$$468\,\text{nm} = 468 \times 10^{-9}\,\text{m}$$
$$= 4.68 \times 10^2 \times 10^{-9}\,\text{m}$$
$$= 4.68 \times 10^{-7}\,\text{m}$$

Suppose the tension in a rope is $1.35 \times 10^5\,\text{N}$ and you want to express it in kN:

$$1\,\text{kN} = 10^3\,\text{N, so } 1\,\text{N} = \frac{1}{10^3}\,\text{kN} = 10^{-3}\,\text{kN}$$
$$1.35 \times 10^5\,\text{N} = 1.35 \times 10^5 \times 10^{-3}\,\text{kN}$$
$$= 1.35 \times 10^2\,\text{kN}$$
$$= 135\,\text{kN}$$

Suppose an electric current is $4.56 \times 10^{-4}\,\text{A}$ and you want to express it in μA:

$$1\,\mu A = 10^{-6}\,\text{A, so } 1\,\text{A} = \frac{1}{10^{-6}}\,\mu A = 10^6 \mu A$$
$$4.56 \times 10^{-4}\,\text{A} = 4.56 \times 10^{-4} \times 10^6\,\mu A$$
$$= 4.56 \times 10^2\,\mu A$$
$$= 456\,\mu A$$

2.5 Dimensions

The **dimensions** of a quantity show how it is related to the basic quantities listed in Table 3. Symbols M, L and T are used to represent the dimensions of mass, length and time.

For example, volume is calculated from length × breadth × height so has dimension of length^3 or L^3; speed is found from distance ÷ time so has dimensions of L/T or LT^{-1}. The dimensions of force are those of mass × acceleration: MLT^{-2}.

Square brackets are used to denote the dimensions of a quantity. For example

$$[\text{velocity}] = \text{LT}^{-1}$$
$$[\text{force}] = [\text{mass}] \times [\text{acceleration}] = \text{MLT}^{-2}$$

Dimensions are more fundamental than units. You might, for example, choose to express a speed in miles per hour rather than SI units of m s^{-1}, but the dimensions are still LT^{-1}, i.e. length (miles) ÷ time (hours).

Any equation must be dimensionally consistent, that is, the dimensions of the left-hand side must be the same as those of the right-hand side. This can help you check whether a particular equation is correct, and can also enable you to derive relationships between quantities.

3 *Arithmetic and algebra*

3.1 *Fractions, decimals and percentages*

A fraction is really a division sum, e.g.

$$\frac{4}{5} = 4 \div 5; \qquad \frac{7}{3} = 7 \div 3$$

You can express a fraction as a decimal number by doing the division on a calculator.

When fractions are multiplied together, you can often simplify the arithmetic by using the fact that the multiplication and division can be carried out in any order, e.g.

$$\frac{7}{5} \times \frac{3}{14} = \frac{7 \times 3}{5 \times 14}$$

and cancelling any common factors, e.g.

$$\frac{7 \times 3}{5 \times 14} = \frac{3}{5 \times 2} = \frac{3}{10} = 0.3$$

You can think of the **percentage** sign, %, as being made up of a 1, 0, 0 to remind you that it is a fraction of 100 parts. To calculate a percentage from a number expressed as a fraction or a decimal, you multiply by 100:

$$\frac{1}{2} = 0.5 \text{ and } 100 \times 0.5 = 50 \text{ so } \frac{1}{2} = 50\% \text{ (or 50/100)}$$

$$\frac{1}{4} = 0.25 \text{ and } 100 \times 0.25 = 25 \text{ so } \frac{1}{4} = 25\% \text{ (or 25/100)}$$

$$\frac{7}{8} = 0.875 \text{ and } 100 \times 0.875 = 87.5 \text{ so } \frac{7}{8} = 87.5\%$$

For example, if a solar array produces an output power of 600 W from an input power of 4 kW (4000 W), its efficiency is

$$\frac{600\,\text{W}}{4000\,\text{W}} = 0.15 = 15\%$$

To find a percentage of a quantity, you *multiply* the quantity by the percentage expressed as an ordinary fraction or decimal number. For example, to find 15% of 60 multiply 60 by 15/100 (or by 0.15)

$$\frac{15}{100} \times 60 = \frac{90}{10} = 9$$

or

$$0.15 \times 60 = 9$$

3.2 Brackets and common factors

To evaluate an expression such as

$$6(2 + 3 - 4 + 5), \quad \frac{12 + 8}{4} \quad \text{or} \quad I(R_1 + R_2 + R_3)$$

you usually first deal with the additions and subtractions inside the bracket and then multiply or divide the result by the number or symbol outside. Alternatively you can carry out several separate multiplications or divisions on each number or symbol inside the bracket in turn, then do the additions or subtractions. For example

either $\quad 6(2 + 3 - 4 + 5) = 6 \times 6 = 36$

or $\quad 6(2 + 3 - 4 + 5) = 12 + 18 - 24 + 30 = 36$

either $\quad \dfrac{12 + 8}{4} = \dfrac{20}{4} = 5$

or $\quad \dfrac{12 + 8}{4} = \dfrac{12}{4} + \dfrac{8}{4} = 3 + 2 = 5$

A calculation that involves several multiplications or divisions using the same number and then adding or subtracting the results can be simplified if it is rewritten using brackets with the **common factor** outside. For example

$$25 + 30 + 35 = 5(5 + 6 + 7)$$

$$3x + 3y + 3z = 3(x + y + z)$$

$$IR_1 + IR_2 + IR_3 = I(R_1 + R_2 + R_3)$$

$$\frac{7}{2} + \frac{3}{2} + \frac{6}{2} = \frac{(7 + 3 + 6)}{2}$$

$$\frac{a}{x} + \frac{b}{x} + \frac{c}{x} = \frac{a + b + c}{x}$$

3.3 Reciprocals

The value obtained by dividing 1 by a number is called the **reciprocal** of the number (reciprocals can be found using the $1/x$ key of a calculator). Finding the reciprocal of a reciprocal gets you back to the original number. For example:

$$\frac{1}{2} = 0.5, \quad \frac{1}{0.5} = 2$$

For a lens:

$$\text{power } P = \frac{1}{f}, \quad \text{focal length } f = \frac{1}{P}$$

Reciprocals are sometimes written using a negative index:

$$x^{-1} = \frac{1}{x}$$

To find the reciprocal of a fraction, simply turn it the other way up. For example:

$$\frac{1}{1/2} = \frac{2}{1} = 2$$

$$\frac{1}{2/3} = \frac{3}{2} = 1\frac{1}{2}$$

$$\left(\frac{3}{7}\right)^{-1} = \frac{7}{3}$$

This is not just an arbitrary rule. It makes sense if you think in terms of division sums. Consider the second example above. Question: 'How many times does $\frac{2}{3}$ go into 1?' Answer: 'one-and-a-half times.'

Adding and subtracting

One place where you need to add and subtract reciprocals is in calculations of resistors in parallel. To find the net resistance R of several resistors connected in parallel, you must first find the reciprocal of each resistor, then add the reciprocals together (to get $1/R$), then find the reciprocal of $1/R$ to get R.

For example, if $R_1 = 2.0\,\Omega$, $R_2 = 5.0\,\Omega$, $R_3 = 1.0\,\Omega$, then

$$\frac{1}{R_1} = \frac{1}{2}\Omega^{-1} = 0.50\,\Omega^{-1} \text{ (notice the unit of } 1/R)$$

$$\frac{1}{R_2} = 0.20\,\Omega^{-1},$$

$$\frac{1}{R_3} = 1.00\,\Omega^{-1}$$

(notice that $1/1 = 1$ – the number stays the same but the unit still changes). So

$$1/R = (0.50 + 0.20 + 1.00)\,\Omega^{-1} = 1.70\,\Omega^{-1}$$

$$R = \frac{1}{1.70}\Omega = 0.59\,\Omega$$

Notice that adding the reciprocals of two numbers is *not* the same as adding the two numbers and then finding the reciprocal of their sum.

Multiplying and dividing

Multiplying by the reciprocal of a number is the same as dividing by that number. For example

$$7 \times \frac{1}{2} = 7 \div 2 = 3.50$$

Dividing by the reciprocal of a number is the same as multiplying by that number. For example

$$4 \div \frac{1}{3} = 4 \times 3 = 12$$

$$9 \div \frac{3}{4} = 9 \times \frac{4}{3} = \frac{9 \times 4}{3} = 12$$

For a wave,

$$f = \frac{v}{\lambda}, \qquad \text{time period } T = \frac{1}{f} = \frac{1}{(v/\lambda)} = \frac{\lambda}{v}$$

We can simplify divisions involving fractions. For example:

$$\frac{3}{4} \div \frac{5}{4} = \frac{3}{4} \times \frac{4}{5} = \frac{3 \times 4}{4 \times 5} = \frac{3}{5} = 0.6$$

3.4 Algebra and elimination

If we have two different relationships that both involve some of the same things, we can combine them to produce a new equation. This allows us to avoid measuring, or calculating, something that is not already known – we can eliminate it (remove it) from the equations. For example, we can take an expression for electrical power

$$P = IV$$

and use the resistance equation

$$V = IR$$

to write IR instead of V:

$$P = I \times IR = I^2 R$$

This enables us to relate P directly to I and R without needing to know or calculate V. Similarly, if we want to eliminate I:

$$P = \frac{V}{R} \times V = \frac{V^2}{R}$$

3.5 Adding and subtracting fractions

You can of course add and subtract fractions on a calculator – you carry out several division sums and add or subtract the results. But for simple fractions it can often be quicker to do the sums 'by hand'.

The trick is to write the fractions so that they have the same denominator (the number underneath the fraction). Sometimes it is quite easy to spot how to do this. For example:

$$\frac{3}{4} + \frac{5}{6} = \frac{3 \times 3}{3 \times 4} + \frac{2 \times 5}{2 \times 6}$$

$$= \frac{9}{12} + \frac{10}{12} = \frac{9 + 10}{12} = \frac{19}{12}$$

Otherwise, make a common denominator by multiplying the original denominators together:

$$\frac{2}{17} + \frac{4}{3} = \frac{2 \times 3}{17 \times 3} + \frac{4 \times 17}{3 \times 17}$$

$$= \frac{6}{51} + \frac{68}{51} = \frac{6+68}{51} = \frac{74}{51}$$

Another example:

$$\frac{1}{2} + \frac{1}{3} = \frac{3}{6} + \frac{2}{6} = \frac{5}{6}$$

4 *Solving equations*

It may sound obvious, but the main thing to understand about equations is that the '=' sign means that the two things on either side are *equal* to one another. So whatever you do to one side, you must also do to the other, otherwise they would no longer be equal. (Beware of getting into the bad habit of writing '=' when you really mean 'and so the next step is...'.)

One way to think of an equation is as a 'recipe' for calculating. For example, $F = ma$ tells you how to calculate the net force F if you know the acceleration a that it gives to a mass m. In this example, F is the **subject** of the equation – it is written on its own (usually on the left).

4.1 Rearranging an equation

Quite often, the quantity we want to calculate is wrapped up in the right-hand side of an equation, and we need to make it the subject. When doing this, it helps if you try to understand what you are doing rather than blindly trying to apply a set of rules. It is also wise to write down each step, justifying each one to yourself as you do so. This might sound time-consuming, but it isn't really because it helps you to keep track of what you are doing and, if you do make a slip, it is quite easy to go back and check.

Look at the part of the equation that contains the quantity that you want to know. Think what you need to do to get that quantity on its own, and do the same thing(s) to both sides.

For example, suppose you want to know the acceleration that a force F gives to a mass m:

$$F = ma$$

To get a on its own, you need to divide the right-hand side by m ($ma \div m = a$), so do the same to the left-hand side:

$$\frac{F}{m} = a, \quad \text{or} \quad a = \frac{F}{m}$$

Another example: suppose you want to calculate internal resistance r from

$$V = \mathscr{E} - Ir$$

It is a good idea first to arrange that the thing you are interested in has a positive sign. You can do this by adding Ir to both sides:

$$V + Ir = \mathscr{E}$$

then to get r on its own you subtract V from both sides:

$$Ir = \mathscr{E} - V$$

and then divide by I

$$r = \frac{\mathscr{E} - V}{I} \quad \text{or} \quad r = (\mathscr{E} - V)/I$$

(Notice that you have to divide the *whole* of the right-hand side by I – hence the brackets.)

Maths reference

Brackets and common factors
See Maths note 3.2

4.2 *Simultaneous equations*

Simultaneous equations arise if we have two (or more) different ways of writing a relationship between quantities. If we have two unknown quantities, then they can both be found if we have two simultaneous equations. For three unknown quantities, we'd need three separate equations, and so on.

The trick in solving simultaneous equations is to carry out some algebra and arithmetic to get an expression that involves just *one* of the unknown things, and then use that value to calculate the other one.

For example, the equation $\mathscr{E} = V + Ir$ involves two things that can be measured (V and I). If neither $\mathscr{E}$ nor r is known, then they cannot be found from a single pair of values of V and I. However, if you obtain two *different* pairs of readings (V_1 and I_1, and V_2 and I_2) for the same power supply (using two different external loads), then you can write down two simultaneous equations – two different equations that both describe a relationship between the two unknown things $\mathscr{E}$ and r. These equations let you find both $\mathscr{E}$ and r. So

$$\mathscr{E} = V_1 + I_1 r$$
$$\mathscr{E} = V_2 + I_2 r$$

Since the right-hand side of each equation is equal to $\mathscr{E}$, then they must also be equal to each other:

$$V_1 + I_1 r = V_2 + I_2 r$$

Subtracting V_1 from each side

$$I_1 r = V_2 - V_1 + I_2 r$$

Subtracting $I_2 r$ from both sides (and being careful with signs and with the subscripts 1 and 2)

$$I_1 r - I_2 r = V_2 - V_1$$

Now r is a common factor on the left-hand side, so

$$r(I_1 - I_2) = V_2 - V_1$$

Dividing both sides by $(I_1 - I_2)$ (and using brackets to keep the subtracted things together)

$$r = \frac{(V_2 - V_1)}{(I_1 - I_2)} \qquad \text{or} \qquad r = (V_2 - V_1)/(I_1 - I_2)$$

This value of r can then be used in one of the original equations to find $\mathscr{E}$.

For example: a power supply gives readings of $V_1 = 3\,\text{V}$, $I_1 = 7\,\text{A}$, and $V_2 = 8\,\text{V}$, $I_2 = 2\,\text{A}$. So

$$r = \frac{8\,\text{V} - 3\,\text{V}}{7\,\text{A} - 2\,\text{A}} = \frac{5\,\text{V}}{5\,\text{A}} = 1\,\Omega$$

and

$$\mathscr{E} = V_1 + I_1 r = 3\,\text{V} + 7\,\text{A} \times 1\,\Omega = 3\,\text{V} + 7\,\text{V} = 10\,\text{V}$$

(you would find the same value using V_2 and I_2).

5 *Relationships and graphs*

Graphs are extremely useful in physics for giving us a pictorial representation of how one quantity is related to another. Trends in data are not always clear from a table of results, but become immediately evident when viewing a plot of the two quantities involved.

5.1 *Graphs and proportionality*

Many important relationships in physics involve the idea of direct proportion.

For example, if a conductor obeys Ohm's law, doubling the potential difference produces double the current, tripling the pd triples the current ... and so on. Mathematically, we say that the potential difference is **directly proportional** to the current. In symbols

$$V \propto I \qquad \text{or} \qquad V = kI$$

The symbol $\propto$ means 'is directly proportional to' and k is called a **constant of proportionality** and has a fixed value for a particular set of values of V and I. (The constant k in this example is the same thing as the electrical resistance R.)

If one quantity is directly proportional to another, then a graph of one plotted against the other is a straight line through the origin.

5.2 Linear relationships

The equation $V = \mathscr{E} - Ir$ is an example of a **linear relationship** between two variables, V and I in this case. A graph of V (on the vertical axis, the y-axis) against I (on the horizontal axis, the x-axis) gives a straight line. Linear relationships and graphs are often said to be of the type $y = mx + c$, where y stands for whatever is plotted on the y-axis and x for whatever is plotted on the x-axis, and m and c are constants (they remain fixed when x and y change). This type of graph has two properties that are often useful for doing calculations using experimental results. We can illustrate these with a graph of $y = 2x + 1$, i.e. $m = 2$, $c = 1$ (Figure 2).

On Figure 2, the line cuts the y-axis at $y = 1$ (using the equation, when $x = 0$, $y = c$). The line of such a graph always cuts the y-axis where $y = c$.

If y is directly proportional to x, then the line goes through the origin and $c = 0$.

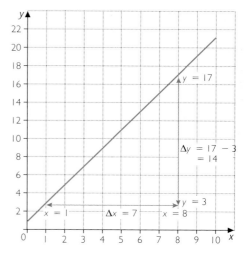

Figure 2 A graph of $y = 2x + 1$

5.3 Gradient of a linear graph

Figure 2 is a graph of the linear relationship $y = 2x + 1$.

The **gradient** (or slope) of the graph is defined as the rise of the graph (the increase in y, Δy) divided by the run (the corresponding increase in x, Δx) found by drawing a right angled triangle as shown in Figure 2. On Figure 2,

$$\Delta y = 14, \qquad \Delta x = 7,$$

$$\text{gradient} = \frac{\Delta y}{\Delta x} = 2.$$

Notice that Δy and Δx are numbers read from the graph scales, and are *not* lengths measured with a ruler, and that any similar triangle drawn on the graph will give the same value of the gradient.

The gradient of a linear graph of y against x is always equal to the value m in the relationship $y = mx + c$.

The graph in Figure 2 has a positive gradient. If m is negative, then the graph slopes down from left to right.

If two variables measured in an experiment are related by a linear equation, then plotting them on a graph enables you to find the values of the constants relating them. It is helpful if you arrange the relationship so that it looks as much like $y = mx + c$ as possible. For example, by subtracting Ir from both sides you can write $\mathscr{E} = V + Ir$ as

$$V = (-r)I + \mathscr{E}$$

which can be compared directly with

$$y = mx + c$$

If you plot measured values of V on the y-axis against corresponding values of I on the x-axis, the graph will be a straight line that cuts the y-axis at $\mathscr{E}$, and with a gradient $m = -r$.

Maths reference

Error bars and error boxes
See Maths note 7.5

5.4 Inverse proportionality

If one quantity is **inversely proportional** to another, then as one increases, the other will decrease. For example, the acceleration produced by a given net force is inversely proportional to the mass on which it acts: doubling the mass halves the acceleration, tripling the mass divides the acceleration by three and so on – and vice versa.

Such a relationship is written using reciprocals and the symbol for direct proportion:

$$a \propto \frac{1}{m} \qquad a = \frac{k}{m}$$

or

$$m \propto \frac{1}{a} \qquad m = \frac{k}{a}$$

(In this case, the constant of proportionality is the same as the net force F.)

If one quantity is inversely proportional to the other (Table 6), the graph of one plotted against the other is curved as in Figure 3.

Maths reference

Reciprocals

See Maths note 3.3

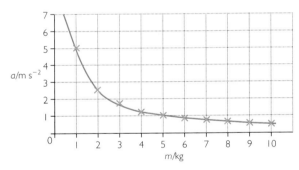

Figure 3 *A graph showing how the acceleration a produced by a constant force F(= 5 N) depends on mass m (data from Table 6)*

m/kg	$(1/m)$/kg^{-1}	a/m s^{-2}
1	1.000	5.00
2	0.500	2.50
3	0.333	1.67
4	0.250	1.25
5	0.200	1.00
6	0.167	0.83
7	0.143	0.71
8	0.125	0.63
9	0.111	0.55
10	0.100	0.50

Table 6 *Data for Figures 3 and 4*

But if one quantity is plotted against the *reciprocal* of the other, then the graph is a straight line through the origin, as shown in Figure 4.

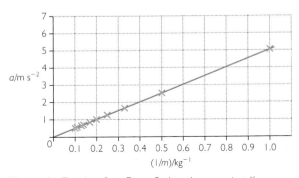

Figure 4 *The data from Figure 3 plotted as a against 1/m*

5.5 Testing mathematical relationships

Sometimes we are interested in finding a mathematical relationship between two measured quantities. This usually involves some educated guesswork, based on ideas about the underlying physics and/or from looking at the numbers. Plotting graphs provides a way of testing the guesses.

Direct proportion

For example, if both quantities increase together, you might guess that one is directly proportional to the other. Plot a graph of one against the other and see whether you can draw a straight line through all the error boxes.

Examples that give straight-line graphs include:

$$s \propto t \text{ for motion at constant speed}$$

$$I \propto V \text{ for an ohmic conductor.}$$

If the plot does not give a straight line, try something else. For example, motion from rest at constant acceleration is described by the equation

$$s = \tfrac{1}{2}at^2$$

$$s \propto t^2$$

A graph of distance s against time t is a curve, but a graph of s against t^2 is a straight line with gradient $a/2$ or $\tfrac{1}{2}a$.

Sometimes you need to use the square root of a quantity to get a straight line. For example, for a simple pendulum a plot of its period T against the square root of its length ℓ gives a straight line:

$$T \propto \sqrt{\ell}$$

Inverse proportion

If one quantity increases as the other decreases, you might guess that you are looking at inverse proportionality, so try plotting a graph using the reciprocal of one quantity.

If this does not give a straight line, try plotting the square, or the square root, of the reciprocal.

For example, suppose you measure the frequency f of the note from a plucked string of mass per unit length μ. Frequency f decreases as you increase μ, but suppose you find that a graph of f against $1/\mu$ is not a straight line.

If a graph of f against $\dfrac{1}{\mu^2}$ is a straight line, then $f \propto \dfrac{1}{\mu^2}$

If you need to plot f against $\dfrac{1}{\sqrt{\mu}}$ to get a straight line, then $f \propto \dfrac{1}{\sqrt{\mu}}$

Maths reference

Experimental uncertainty
See Maths note 7.1

Error bars and error boxes
See Maths note 7.5

Maths reference

Reciprocals
See Maths note 3.3

Inverse proportionality
See Maths note 5.4

6 *Trigonometry and angular measurements*

6.1 *Degrees and radians*

A **radian**, or **rad** for short, is a unit for measuring angles commonly used in physics instead of degrees. Figure 5 shows how the size of an angle, in radians, is defined.

For a full circle, length of arc = length of circumference = $2\pi r$.

Size of angle $= \dfrac{2\pi r}{r} = 2\pi$ radians, i.e. approximately 6.28 rad.

Table 7 lists some useful conversions between radians and degrees.

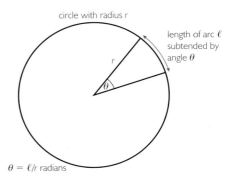

circle with radius r

length of arc ℓ subtended by angle θ

$\theta = \ell/r$ radians

Figure 5   *The size of an angle measured in radians*

Angle	Size in degrees	Size in radians
full circle	360°	2π rad = 6.28 rad
half circle	180°	π rad = 3.14 rad
	114.6°	2.0 rad
quarter circle	90°	$\pi/2$ rad = 1.57 rad
	60°	$\pi/3$ rad = 1.05 rad
	57.3°	1.0 rad
	45°	$\pi/4$ rad = 0.79 rad
	30°	$\pi/6$ rad = 0.52 rad
	28.6°	0.5 rad

Table 7   *Some conversions between radians and degrees*

Note that π is a number (approximately 3.14) that frequently, but not always, appears in angles measured in radians.

6.2 *Sine, cosine and tangent of an angle*

Figure 6 shows a right angled triangle. The sides of the triangle are related by Pythagoras's theorem:

$$c^2 = b^2 + a^2$$
$$c = \sqrt{(a^2 + b^2)}$$

(Care! You can't 'cancel' the squares inside the bracket.)

All similar triangles, i.e. those with the same angle θ, will have sides in the same proportion to one another. The ratios of the sides depend only on the angle θ.

The sine, cosine and tangent of the angle θ are known as **trigonometric ratios**.

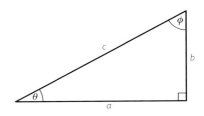

Figure 6   *A right angled triangle*

- Sine of angle θ, $\sin\theta = \dfrac{\text{opposite side}}{\text{hypotenuse}} = \dfrac{b}{c}$

- Cosine of θ, $\cos\theta = \dfrac{\text{adjacent side}}{\text{hypotenuse}} = \dfrac{a}{c}$

- Tangent of θ, $\tan\theta = \dfrac{\text{opposite side}}{\text{adjacent side}} = \dfrac{b}{a}$

We can combine these to give another useful relationship. Since

$$\frac{b}{a} = \frac{b}{c} \div \frac{a}{c} \quad (c \text{ cancels}),$$

we can write

$$\tan\theta = \frac{\sin\theta}{\cos\theta}$$

Also

$$\sin\phi = \frac{a}{c} = \cos\theta \qquad \text{and} \qquad \cos\phi = \frac{b}{c} = \sin\theta$$

i.e. if two angles add up to $90°$, then the cosine of one is equal to the sine of the other.

Using Pythagoras's theorem leads to another useful result. Dividing $c^2 = a^2 + b^2$ by c^2:

$$1 = \frac{a^2}{c^2} + \frac{b^2}{c^2} = \left(\frac{a}{c}\right)^2 + \left(\frac{b}{c}\right)^2$$

$$1 = (\cos\theta)^2 + (\sin\theta)^2,$$

which is true for any angle and is usually written as

$$\cos^2\theta + \sin^2\theta = 1$$

6.3 Graphs of trigonometric functions

For angles greater than $90°$, Figure 7 shows how sin, cos and tan are defined. For some angles, negative numbers are involved. Figure 8 shows how the sin, cos and tan vary with angle θ. Note that we have labelled the axis in degrees and in radians.

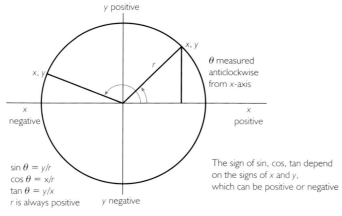

Figure 7   Defining sin, cos and tan for angles greater than $90°$

Maths reference

Degrees and radians
See Maths note 6.1

(a) sin θ

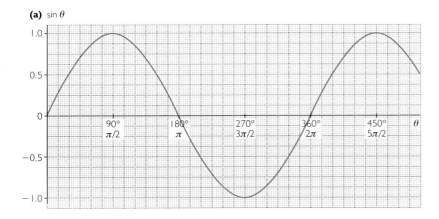

(b) cos θ

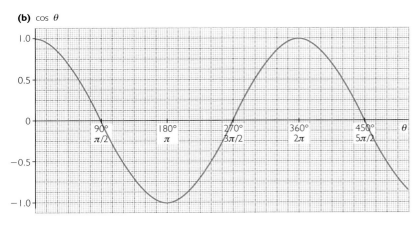

(c) tan θ

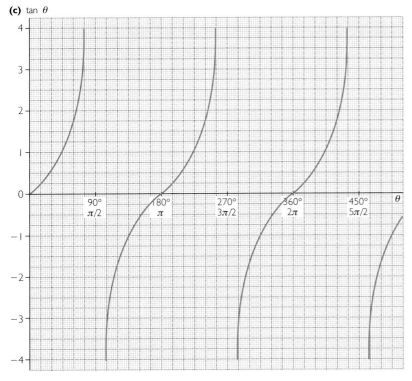

Figure 8 *Graphs of trigonometric functions*

Notice that $\sin\theta$ and $\cos\theta$ are always between $+1$ and -1, but $\tan\theta$ is infinite for some angles (notice the different scale).

Also notice some useful values, e.g. $\sin 30° = \cos 60° = 0.5$. Look at the values of $\sin\theta$ and $\cos\theta$ when θ is a multiple of $90°$.

6.4 Inverse sin, etc.

The angle whose sin is x is written $\sin^{-1} x$ or $\arcsin x$. We can write the relationships from Figure 6 as

$$\theta = \sin^{-1}\frac{b}{c} = \arcsin b/c$$

$$\theta = \cos^{-1}\frac{a}{c} = \arccos a/c$$

$$\theta = \tan^{-1}\frac{b}{a} = \arctan b/a$$

$$\phi = \sin^{-1}\frac{a}{c} = \arcsin a/c$$

Beware! The index -1 here does *not* indicate a reciprocal:

$$\sin^{-1} x \text{ is } not \text{ the same as } \frac{1}{\sin x} = (\sin x)^{-1}$$

6.5 Trigonometry on a calculator

You can find the sine, cosine and tangent of an angle on a calculator. For example, to find $\sin 30°$, type 30 and press sin.

Many scientific calculators can be switched between 'degree' and 'radian' modes. The display will indicate which one you are in.

If you switch your calculator to 'radian' mode, you can find sin, etc., of angles in radians without having to convert to degrees. Check that you know how to do this.

With your calculator in radian mode, type π, $\div$, 2 (you may need to press $=$ as well) and then press sin or cos. You should get $\sin (\pi/2) = 1$, $\cos (\pi/2) = 0$. If you have your calculator in degree mode by mistake, you will find the sin or cos of $1.57°$ ($3.14° \div 2$).

Try finding the sin, cos and tan of some angles in degrees and in radians. Check that you get the same values as shown in Figure 8.

If you know the sin, cos or tan of an angle and wish to determine the size of the angle, use the 'inv' key.

For example, to find the angle whose sin is 0.5, type 0.5, press inv and then press sin. You should get 30 if you have your calculator in degree mode. If you do this with your calculator in radian mode, you will get 0.5236 ($\approx \pi/6$).

6.6 The small angle approximations

There are some useful approximations involving the trigonometric ratios of small angles. These become evident when we express the sine and tangent of an angle θ in terms of the right angled triangles shown in Figure 9.

From the triangle OAC

$$\sin \theta = \frac{AC}{OC} = \frac{AC}{r}$$

and

$$\cos \theta = \frac{OA}{OC} = \frac{OA}{r}$$

From the triangle OBD

$$\tan \theta = \frac{BD}{OB} = \frac{BD}{r}$$

and

$$\cos \theta = \frac{OB}{OD} = \frac{r}{OD}$$

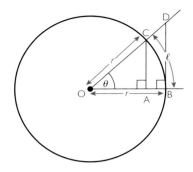

Figure 9   *The sine and tangent of an angle*

Figure 9 shows that $\tan \theta$ is always greater than $\sin \theta$ because BD is greater than AC.

As θ is made smaller, the lines AC and BD become closer together and more equal in length, and the lines OA and OD become closer to r, so *for small angles:*

$$\sin \theta \approx \tan \theta$$

and

$$\cos \theta \approx 1$$

With your calculator in degree mode, try finding the sin, cos and tan of the angles listed in Table 7, and some smaller angles. Notice that the approximations get better as the angles get smaller.

Small angles in radians

Comparison of Figure 9 with Figure 5 shows that the size of θ *measured in radians* (i.e. ℓ/r) lies between $\sin \theta$ and $\tan \theta$ (the arc length ℓ is longer than AC and shorter than OD):

$$\sin \theta < \theta < \tan \theta$$

When θ is small,

$$AC \approx \ell \approx BD$$

and so *for small angles measured in radians* we have some additional approximations:

$$\sin \theta \approx \theta$$

and

$$\tan \theta \approx \theta$$

Switch your calculator into radian mode, and again try finding the sin, cos and tan of various angles. Notice that the approximation gets better at small angles.

6.7 Angular units

Angles can be measured in degrees or radians. Angles smaller than one degree are sometimes expressed in minutes of arc (arcmin) or seconds of arc (arcsec).

Maths reference

Degrees and radians
See Maths note 6.1

$$1° = 60 \text{ arcmin or } 60'$$

$$1' = 60 \text{ arcsec or } 60''$$

$$1 \text{ arcmin} = \frac{1°}{60} = \frac{2\pi}{(60 \times 360)} \text{ rad} = 2.91 \times 10^{-4} \text{ rad}$$

$$1 \text{ arcsec} = \frac{1'}{60} = \frac{1°}{3600°}$$

$$= \frac{\pi}{(3600 \times 180)} \text{ rad} = 4.85 \times 10^{-6} \text{ rad}$$

Table 8 lists some angles expressed in various units.

50°	3000′	180 000″	0.8727 rad
20°	1200′	72 000″	0.3491 rad
10°	600′	36 000″	0.1745 rad
1.0°	60′	3600″	1.745×10^{-2} rad
$1.67° \times 10^{-1}$	10′	600″	2.908×10^{-3} rad
$1.00° \times 10^{-1}$	6.0′	360″	1.745×10^{-3} rad
$1.67° \times 10^{-2}$	1.0′	60″	2.908×10^{-4} rad
$1.00° \times 10^{-2}$	0.6′	36″	1.745×10^{-4} rad
$2.78° \times 10^{-3}$	$1.67' \times 10^{-1}$	10″	4.847×10^{-5} rad
$1.67° \times 10^{-3}$	$1.00' \times 10^{-1}$	6.0″	2.908×10^{-5} rad
$2.78° \times 10^{-4}$	$1.67' \times 10^{-2}$	1.0″	4.848×10^{-6} rad

Table 8 *Angles expressed in various units*

7 Size and precision

7.1 Precision in measurements; experimental uncertainty

In any measurement, there is a limit to the precision of your result. Sometimes this **experimental uncertainty** arises because you get different answers when you repeat the measurement. For example, if you time an athlete running 100 metres, the same athlete will probably record different times on different occasions. The uncertainty in the measurements is indicated by the 'scatter' in the results.

For example, suppose a certain athlete records times of 12.5 s, 12.1 s, 12.6 s, 12.5 s and 12.3 s. The average time is $t = 12.4$ s. The difference between the average and the biggest or smallest value indicates the uncertainty Δt – in this case, $\Delta t \approx 0.3$ s.

Sometimes the uncertainty arises because it is difficult to judge exactly what to measure. For example, if you are measuring the distance from a lens to a clear image it produces on a screen, it might be hard to judge exactly where to put the screen to get the sharpest image. If you measure a distance $v = 24.5$ cm, but are unsure of the sharpest position by 0.5 cm in each direction, then the uncertainty would be $\Delta v \approx 0.5$ cm.

Even if there is no problem deciding exactly what to measure, and you get the same answer each time you repeat the measurement, there is still an uncertainty because the measurement is limited by the instrument you are using. For example, if you use a digital ammeter to measure a current I, and you get 0.357 A each time, you can only be sure that the current is closer to 0.357 A than it is to either 0.356 A or 0.358 A – it could lie anywhere between 0.3565 A and 0.3575 A. So the uncertainty is $\Delta I \approx 0.0005$ A.

Some books refer to **experimental error** rather than uncertainty. Don't be misled into thinking that they mean a mistake. However carefully and correctly you carry out a measurement, there will always be an uncertainty.

Experimental uncertainties apply to *all* measured quantities – including those you look up in a data book, though these values have usually been measured with much greater precision than you can achieve in a school or college laboratory.

7.2 *Calculations with uncertainties; significant figures*

If you carry out a calculation using a measured value, there will always be an uncertainty in your answer. You can use the uncertainties in the measurements to work out the uncertainty in the calculated value.

For example, suppose you measure a current of $I = 0.24$ A $\pm\, 0.01$ A and a corresponding pd of $V = 0.67$ V $\pm\, 0.02$ V.

On a calculator, the resistance found using the 'best' values is

$$R_{\text{best}} = \frac{V}{I} = \frac{0.67\,\text{V}}{0.24\,\text{A}} = 2.791\,6667\,\Omega$$

But, using the largest possible V (0.39 V) and the smallest possible I (0.23 A), the calculated resistance could be as large as

$$R_{\text{max}} = \frac{0.69\,\text{V}}{0.23\,\text{A}} = 3\,\Omega$$

Or, using the smallest V and the largest I, it could be as small as

$$R_{\text{min}} = \frac{0.65\,\text{V}}{0.25\,\text{A}} = 2.6\,\Omega$$

There are several things to notice! First, there are quite large differences between the three values. Second, the first value extends to the full length of the calculator display, whereas the others do not.

The large differences show that you cannot *possibly* say that the resistance is precisely $2.7916667\,\Omega$. This value is close to $2.8\,\Omega$, and the other two differ by $0.2\,\Omega$ in either direction, i.e. the uncertainty in R is $\Delta R \approx 0.2\,\Omega$. The resistance can therefore be written as

$$R = 2.8\,\Omega \pm 0.2\,\Omega.$$

The second figure in this answer (the 8 after the decimal point) is uncertain, and so any further figures are meaningless.

Another way of putting this is to say that the answer has (only) two **significant figures** – the one before the decimal point and the first one after it. The rest of the figures in the original 'best' answer are meaningless. They are *not* significant.

7.3 A useful rule of thumb

In a calculation, the answer cannot be known any more precisely than the values used to calculate it. As a useful rule of thumb, the final answer has no more significant figures than the *least* precise value used in the calculation. (The example in Maths note 7.2 illustrates this.)

Suppose you did a calculation to find the frequency f of light whose wavelength is $468\,\text{nm}$ ($4.68 \times 10^{-7}\,\text{m}$). The speed of light is known very precisely: $2.997925 \times 10^8\,\text{m s}^{-1}$.

Using speed $\div$ wavelength

$$f = \frac{2.997925 \times 10^8\,\text{m s}^{-1}}{4.68 \times 10^{-7}\,\text{m}}$$
$$= 6.4058 \times 10^{14}\,\text{Hz}$$

However, we only knew the wavelength to three significant figures, so we cannot quote the frequency this precisely. We must stick to the three significant figures and write

$$f = 6.41 \times 10^{14}\,\text{Hz}$$

There was in fact no point in using the very precise value for the speed of light. Values listed in data books are often rounded to, say, three significant figures if they are likely to be used only in calculations requiring this precision or less.

7.4 Significant figures and orders of magnitude

The speed of light to seven significant figures is $2.997925 \times 10^8\,\text{m s}^{-1}$; the significant figures are 2997925.

Zeros in front of a number are not significant. The speed of light could be written (rather oddly) as $002.997925 \times 10^8\,\text{m s}^{-1}$ or $0.0002997925 \times 10^{12}\,\text{m s}^{-1}$ without making any difference to its value.

However, zeros at the end of a number are (or at least can be!) significant. If you wrote the speed of light as $299792500\,\text{m s}^{-1}$, that would imply that you knew that the last two figures were definitely zeros and not some other numbers. If they are, in fact, not known, it is better to use standard form so that the meaningless zeros can be dropped.

To five significant figures, the speed of light would be $2.9979 \times 10^8 \, \text{m s}^{-1}$. To three significant figures, it would be $3.00 \times 10^8 \, \text{m s}^{-1}$. Here the zeros *are* significant and should be written down, because 2.997... rounds to 3.00.

To one significant figure the speed of light would be $3 \times 10^8 \, \text{m s}^{-1}$.

If a value is rounded to just the nearest power of 10, then we say we are giving just the **order of magnitude**. Two values are said to have the same order of magnitude if one is between 1 and 10 times the other. For example, the wavelengths of red and blue light (about 400 nm and 700 nm) are within the same order of magnitude. But the wavelengths of infrared radiation range from about 10^{-6} m to about 10^{-3} m, they cover three orders of magnitude.

7.5 Error bars and error boxes

When plotting a graph of experimental data, you should take account of the uncertainties. Rather than representing each measurement by a point, you should draw an **error bar** to represent the range of possible values. Then use the vertical and horizontal error bars to draw an **error box** around each plotted point. Once you have plotted the error boxes, you can then draw a trend line on your graph. It might be possible to draw a straight line passing through all the boxes, even if you could not draw one through all the points.

8 Logarithms

8.1 Logs and powers of 10

If a number can be written as *just* a 'power of 10', then the power is the **logarithm** of that number; strictly speaking, it is the **logarithm to base 10**, or **common logarithm**, of the number, but it is often simply called the **log**.

Table 9 lists some examples using whole-number powers.

Number x	$\log_{10}(x)$
$100\,000 = 10^5$	5
$10\,000 = 10^4$	4
$1000 = 10^3$	3
$100 = 10^2$	2
$10 = 10^1$	1
$1 = 10^0$	0
$0.1 = 10^{-1}$	-1
$0.001 = 10^{-2}$	-2

Table 9 *Some numbers and their common logarithms*

In fact *any positive number* can be expressed as a power of 10, using powers that are not whole numbers. Most whole numbers have logs that are not themselves whole numbers or simple fractions. For example:

$$10^{0.6021} = 4.000$$

so

$$\log_{10} (4.000) = 0.6021$$

All numbers between 1 and 10 have base 10 logs that lie between 0 and 1. For example:

$$10^{0.333} = 2.153$$

so

$$\log_{10} (2.153) = 0.333$$

Similarly, all numbers between 10 and 100 have base 10 logs that lie between 1 and 2; all numbers between 100 and 1000 have base 10 logs between 2 and 3, and so on.

All numbers less than 1 have negative logs. For example:

$$\log_{10} (0.5) = -0.3010$$
$$\log_{10} (0.1) = -1.000$$

Maths reference

Powers that are not whole numbers

See Maths note 1.5

8.2 Logs on a calculator

To find the common log of a number using a calculator, type in the number and then press the key marked log or lg.

This process can be reversed to find the **antilog** of a number. Type in the log whose number you want to find, then press the keys marked INV and log (or lg). By doing this, you can show that 4.000 is the antilog of 0.6021, and 2.153 is the antilog of 0.333.

Notice that using the INV and log keys to find the antilog of a number x gives exactly the same result as using the y^x key to find 10^x.

8.3 Logs; multiplication and division

There is a useful relationship between the logs of x and y and the log of their product xy.

Using the definition of a base 10 log:

$$\text{if } \log_{10} (x) = a, \text{ then } x = 10^a$$
$$\text{and if } \log_{10} (y) = b, \text{ then } y = 10^b$$

So we can write

$$xy = 10^{(a+b)}$$

In other words

$$\log_{10} (xy) = a + b$$

so

$$\log_{10}(xy) = \log_{10}(x) + \log_{10}(y)$$

You can illustrate this relationship using a calculator to look up the logs of various numbers and see how they relate to one another. For example: $\log_{10}(5) = 0.69897$, $\log_{10}(4) = 0.60206$,

$$\log_{10}(5 \times 4) = \log_{10}(20) = 1.30103$$
$$= 0.69897 + 0.60206$$
$$= \log_{10}(5) + \log_{10}(4)$$

There is a similar relationship for division:

$$\frac{x}{y} = 10^{(a-b)}$$

$$\log_{10}\left(\frac{x}{y}\right) = a - b$$

$$\log_{10}\left(\frac{x}{y}\right) = \log_{10}(x) - \log_{10}(y)$$

Maths reference

Combining powers
See Maths note 1.3

Logs and powers of 10
See Maths note 8.1

8.4 Logs and powers

We can extend Maths note 8.3 by considering powers. For example:

$$\log_{10}(x^3) = \log_{10}(x) + \log_{10}(x) + \log_{10}(x) = 3\log_{10}(x)$$

A similar line of reasoning says that for any whole number, n,

$$\log_{10}(x^n) = n\log_{10}(x)$$

This rule also works for powers that are not whole numbers, and for negative powers. For *any* value of y we can write

$$\log_{10}(x^y) = y\log_{10}(x)$$

For example

$$\log_{10}(9^{1/2}) = \log_{10}(\sqrt{9}) = \log_{10}(3)$$

$$\log_{10}(9) = 0.95424$$

$$\log_{10}(3) = 0.47712 = 0.95424 \div 2$$

and

$$\log_{10}(5^{-1}) = \log_{10}\left(\tfrac{1}{5}\right) = \log_{10}(0.2)$$

$$\log_{10}(5) = 0.69897$$

$$\log_{10}(0.2) = -0.69897$$

8.5 Logs to other bases; natural logs

We can define logarithms to base 10 using numbers expressed as power of 10. But there is nothing special about the number 10. We can use any number as the base of logarithms.

Maths reference

Logs and powers of 10
See Maths note 8.1

For example, logarithms to base 2 use the fact that any number can be expressed as a power of 2, as shown in Table 10. Just as with base 10 logs, we are not restricted to whole-number powers.

Number x		$\log_2 (x)$
16	$= 2^4$	4
8	$= 2^3$	3
4	$= 2^2$	2
2	$= 2^1$	1
1	$= 2^0$	0
0.5	$= 2^{-1}$	-1
0.25	$= 2^{-2}$	-2
1.4142	$= 2^{\frac{1}{2}}$	0.5
5	$= 2^{2.32193}$	2.32193
2.567	$= 2^{1.36}$	1.36

Table 10   *Some numbers and their logs to base 2*

By trying some examples using numbers from Table 10, you can demonstrate that the relationships set out in Maths notes 8.3 and 8.4 for base 10 logs also work with logs to base 2. (Notice that in *any* base, the log of 1 is zero.)

We can go further. The number at the base of a system of logs does not itself have to be a whole number. It can be *any* positive number. For *any* system of logs, it is always true that

$$\log (xy) = \log (x) + \log (y)$$

$$\log\left(\frac{x}{y}\right) = \log (x) - \log (y)$$

$$\log (x^y) = y \log (x)$$

Natural logs

Apart from common, base 10, logs, the system of logs most widely used in physics is that of **natural logarithms**. This system uses the number e as its base, where e is the **exponential number** (e $\approx$ 2.718) which arises in the mathematical description of many naturally occurring changes.

The natural logarithm of a number x is written as $\log_e (x)$ or $\ln (x)$. Most calculators have a natural log key, which is usually labelled $\ln x$.

The inverse of a natural log (its antilog) can be found on a calculator using the INV key and the $\ln x$ key. Finding the natural antilog of a number x is the same as finding e^x.

Table 11 lists some examples of natural logs. By picking suitable numbers from Table 11, you can demonstrate that the relationships for multiplication and division and powers also work for natural logs. Notice that $\log_e (e) = 1$, and that $\log_e (1) = 0$.

Maths reference

Exponential changes
See Maths note 9.1

Exponential functions
See Maths note 9.2

Number x	$\log_e(x)$
0.2	−1.69094
0.5	−0.69315
1	0.000000
2	0.69315
2.7183	1.0000
3	1.09861
4	1.38629
5	1.60943
9	2.19722
20	2.99573

Table 11 *Some numbers and their natural logarithms*

8.6 *Using log scales*

When we want to plot a graph of numbers that cover a large range of values, we often use a so-called **logarithmic scale** in order to fit the largest numbers on the graph paper while still being able to distinguish between the smallest numbers. Figure 10 shows such a scale. Notice that the powers of 10 are equally spaced – the scale might be better described as a 'powers scale'. The name 'logarithmic' becomes more obvious when we write the (base 10) logs next to the values of x. The logs of x go up in equal steps just like an ordinary graph scale.

Figure 10 *A logarithmic scale*

When dealing with numbers other than whole-number powers of 10, there are three ways of plotting and reading a log scale – which all amount to the same thing really.

Using logs to plot and read a scale

If you are using ordinary linear graph paper, you need to use logs in order to plot and read a log scale accurately. It can be helpful to write the base 10 logs next to the numbers to be plotted, as was done in Figure 10. Figure 11 shows an expanded view of the part of Figure 10 between $x = 100$ and $x = 1000$, plotted on ordinary graph paper. Table 12 lists some numbers in this range and their base 10 logs.

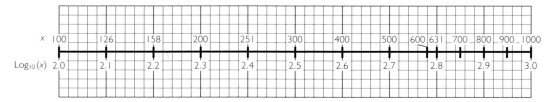

Figure 11   *A log scale covering the range x = 100 to x = 1000*

x	$\log_{10}(x)$
100	2.000
126	2.100
158	2.200
200	2.300
251	2.400
300	2.477
400	2.602
500	2.698
600	2.778
631	2.800
700	2.845
800	2.903
900	2.954
1000	3.000

Table 12   *The numbers plotted on Figure 11 and their logs*

To plot a number x on the scale shown in Figure 11:

use a calculator to find $\log_{10}(x)$

plot $\log_{10}(x)$ on the side of the scale labelled $\log_{10}(x)$.

To read a number from the scale shown in Figure 11:

read $\log_{10}(x)$ from the side of the scale labelled $\log_{10}(x)$

find its antilog using a calculator.

A short cut

If you do not require values to be plotted or read on a log scale very precisely, there is a useful short cut that avoids having to look up logs and antilogs.

From Figure 11, notice that on the side of the scale labelled x:

300 lies roughly half way between 100 and 1000

200 lies roughly one-third of the way along from 100 to 1000

the distance from 100 to 200 is exactly the same as that from 200 to 400 and from 400 to 800

This pattern is repeated between *any* two adjacent whole-number powers (e.g. 30 lies mid-way between 10 and 100 on a log scale, 0.3 lies mid-way between 0.1 and 1.0, etc.).

Bearing these points in mind, it is possible to estimate the value of x just by looking at where it lies on the scale between two whole-number powers.

Log graph paper

Figure 12 shows a piece of logarithmic graph paper. It covers the range of numbers between two adjacent powers of 10. The grid lines are labelled 1, 2, 3 and so on, corresponding to the positions of 100, 200, 300 on the top scale of Figure 11 – or to $1 \times$, $2 \times$, $3 \times \ldots$ any power of 10 that you care to choose.

Plotting and reading values using such a piece of graph paper is just like using ordinary graph paper – the only difference is that the grid spacing varies across the page. There is no need to calculate logs or antilogs, as the paper is already labelled with values of x.

8.7 Using log graphs

There are essentially three reasons for plotting graphs using logarithmic scales:

- to represent a large range of values on a compact scale;
- to see whether data are described by an exponential relationship;
- to see whether data data are described by a power law.

We will deal with each of the last two in turn.

Exponential relationships

An exponential relationship between two variables x and y is one that is described as an equation of the form

$$y = Ae^{kx}$$

where A and k are constants; k is sometimes called the **decay constant** (if negative) or the **growth constant**, but often has a particular name according to the situation being described. For example, the attenuation of a signal in a cable or optical fibre is described by the equation

$$I = I_0\, e^{-\mu x}$$

where I_0 is the initial intensity of the signal, I is its intensity after travelling through a distance x, and μ the attenuation coefficient.

A plot of y against x gives a curve, in which y changes by equal fractions for equal steps in x.

A direct way to determine whether two variables are described by an exponential relationship is to plot a **log–linear graph**. For example, taking logs of the attenuation equation gives

$$\log (I) = \log (I_0) - \mu x \log (e)$$

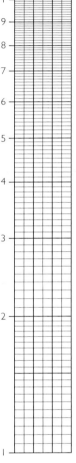

Figure 12 *A piece of logarithmic graph paper*

Maths reference

Exponential changes
See Maths note 9.1

Exponential functions
See Maths note 9.2

This works whichever base of logs we choose. A graph of log (I) on the y-axis against x on the x-axis has the form $y = mx + c$; in other words, it is a straight line.

If we choose to take natural logs, the equation becomes simpler

$$\log_e (I) = \log_e (I_0) - \mu x \log_e(e)$$

i.e.

$$\log (I) = \log (I_0) - \mu x$$

A graph of log (I) against x has a gradient equal to $-\mu$.

This is an example of a general rule: a log-linear graph of an exponential relationship is a straight line whose gradient is equal to the growth or decay constant (see Figure 13).

Maths reference

Gradient of a linear graph
See Maths note 5.3

Logs; multiplication and division
See Maths note 8.3

Logs and powers
See Maths note 8.4

Logs to other bases; natural logs
See Maths note 8.5

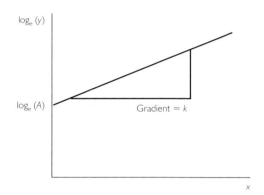

Figure 13 *A log-linear graph of the relationship $y = Ae^{kx}$*

Power-law relationships

Two variables x and y are related by a **power law** if they obey an equation of the form

$$y = Ax^p$$

where A and p and constants; p is called the **exponent** (*not* to be confused with the exponential number e!).

An example of such relationship is Coulomb's law

$$F = \frac{kqQ}{r^2}$$

which describes how the magnitude of the electrostatic force, F, between two charges, q and Q, depends on their separation r.

A graph of x against y gives a curve whose shape depends on the exponent p. A power-law curve can superficially look like an exponential growth or decay curve, but it does *not* follow the 'equal fractions in equal steps' pattern that characterises exponential curves.

One direct way to determine whether variables obey a power law is to plot a **log–log graph.** For example, taking logs (to *any* base) of the Coulomb's law equation gives

$$\log(F) = \log(kqQ) - 2\log(r)$$

A graph of $\log(F)$ against $\log(r)$ has the form $y = mx + c$. It is a straight line with gradient -2.

This is an example of a general rule. A log–log graph of a power-law relationship is a straight line whose gradient is equal to the exponent (see Figure 14).

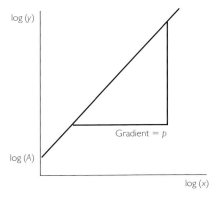

Figure 14   *A log–log plot of the relationship $y = Ax^p$*

Maths reference

Gradient of a linear graph
See Maths note 5.3

Logs; multiplication and division
See Maths note 8.3

Logs and powers
See Maths note 8.4

Logs to other bases; natural logs
See Maths note 8.5

9   *Exponentials*

9.1   *Exponential changes*

Many naturally occurring changes follow a pattern in which the rate of change is proportional to the amount, or number, of something present. Such a change is called an **exponential change**. Such changes are represented by equations of the form

$$\frac{dy}{dt} = kt \qquad \text{or} \qquad \frac{dy}{dx} = kx$$

depending on whether the change takes place over time, t, or over distance, x.

One example of exponential change is radioactive decay, where the number of radioactive disintegrations per second is proportional to the number of unstable nuclei present in a sample. Mathematically, this decay can be represented by an equation

$$\frac{dN}{dt} = -\lambda N$$

where N is the number of unstable nuclei and λ the **decay constant** for the particular isotope involved.

Another example is population growth

$$\frac{dN}{dt} = kN$$

where now N is the number of organisms in a population and k the **growth constant**.

Figure 15 shows graphs of exponential decay and growth. These graphs have certain characteristics that are unique to exponential changes (and which are are related to one another):

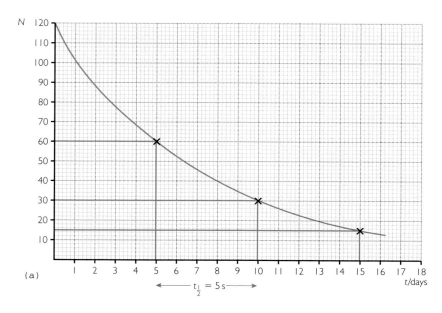

(a)

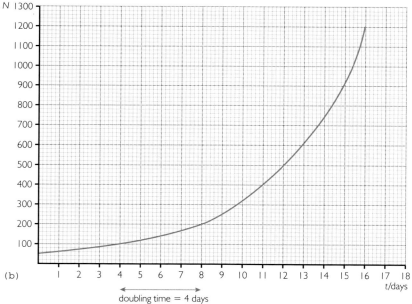

(b)

Figure 15 *Graphs of exponential change: (a) decay, (b) growth*

- the gradient at any point is proportional to the value of y at that point (this is described by the equations stated above)

- equal intervals of time or distance result in equal fractional changes in y

- the time or distance taken for y to halve, or double, is independent of the initial value of y; when dealing with decay over time, this time is called the **half-life** ($t_{1/2}$) of the decay.

9.2 Exponential functions

Exponential changes can always be described by an equation of the form

$$y = y_0 a^{bt} \qquad \text{or} \qquad y = y_0 a^{bx}$$

where a and b are constants and y_0 is the value of y when $x = 0$ or $t = 0$. For growth over time or distance b is positive, for decay b is negative.

For example:

- if $N = 2^t$, then when t increases by 1, N doubles.

- if $y = 3 \times 10^{-x}$, then when x increases by 1, y is divided by 10.

- radioactive decay can be described by the equation

$$N = N_0 \times 2^{-(t/t_{1/2})}$$

where $t_{1/2}$ is the half-life of the decay.

All mathematical functions of the type $y = y_0 a^{bt}$ are called **exponential functions**.

One very commonly used exponential function uses the **exponential number** e (e ≈ 2.718). This number arises from the mathematical description of situations where the constant k in the growth or decay equation is numerically equal to 1.

If

$$\frac{dy}{dx} = y$$

then the change is described by

$$y = y_0 e^x$$

Similarly, if

$$\frac{dy}{dt} = y$$

then

$$y = y_0 e^t$$

The number e can be used to describe *all* exponential changes – and this is the most common way that we write them. If

$$\frac{dy}{dx} = ky$$

then

$$y = y_0 e^{kx}$$

and, similarly, if

$$\frac{dy}{dt} = ky$$

then

$$y = y_0 e^{kt}$$

For example, if a radioactive decay is described by the equation

$$\frac{dN}{dt} = -\lambda N$$

then it is also described by the equation

$$N = N_0 e^{-\lambda t}$$

Some texts write e^x as exp (x), and so on, so our last example would be written

$$N = N_0 \exp(-\lambda t)$$

9.3 *Exponentials and logs*

The exponential number e (e $\approx$ 2.718) is used as the base of so-called natural logarithms. By taking natural logs of exponential growth and decay equations, we arrive at some useful relationships. If

$$y = y_0 e^{kt}$$

then

$$\log_e(y) = \log_e(y_0) + kt$$

This form of the equation is useful as it shows how we can use a log-linear graph to determine whether a change is exponential and, if it is, to determine the value of k.

It also enables us to find the value of k if we know y_0 and y at a given time, t:

$$kt = \log_e(y) - \log_e(y_0) = \log_e\left(\frac{y}{y_0}\right)$$

Similarly, in radioactive decay

$$N = N_0 \exp(-\lambda t)$$

so

$$\log_e(N) = \log_e(N_0) - \lambda t$$

$$\lambda t = \log_e\left(\frac{N_0}{N}\right)$$

This expression leads to a useful relationship between λ and the half-life, $t_{1/2}$, of the decay. If $t = t_{1/2}$, then by definition $N = N_0/2$, so

$$\lambda t_{1/2} = \log_e(2)$$

$$t_{1/2} = \frac{\log_e(2)}{\lambda}$$

Maths reference

Logs to other bases; natural logs

See Maths note 8.5

Maths reference

Using log graphs

See Maths note 8.7

Maths reference

Logs; multiplication and division

See Maths note 8.3

Achievements sections from Salters Horners Advanced Physics AS book

Achievements from Higher, Faster, Stronger (AS book)

After studying this unit you should be able to:

- distinguish between scalar and vector quantities and give examples of each (1.2)*;

- resolve a vector into two components at right angles to each other by drawing and by calculation (2.1, 3.2);

- combine two coplanar vectors at any angle to each other by drawing, and at right angles to each other by calculation (2.1);

- construct displacement–time and velocity–time graphs for uniformly accelerated motion (1.3);

- determine the slope and area of a graph by drawing and (in the case of a straight-line graph) by calculation (1.3, 4.1);

- identify and use the physical quantities derived from the slopes and areas of displacement–time and velocity–time graphs, including cases of non-uniform acceleration (1.3);

- recall and use the expressions $v = \Delta s/\Delta t$ and $a = \Delta v/\Delta t$ (1.2);

- recognise and use the kinematic equations for motion in one dimension with constant velocity or constant acceleration (1.2, 1.3, 5.1, 5.2);

- recognise and make use of the independence of vertical and horizontal motion of a projectile moving freely under gravity (5.1, 5.2);

- recall and use the relationship $F = ma$ in situations where mass is constant (1.4);

- recall and use the independent effect of perpendicular components of a force (2.1, 3.2);

- understand and use the concept of *work* in terms of the product of a force and a displacement in the direction of that force, including situations where the force is *not* along the line of motion (3.1, 3.2);

- calculate power from the rate at which work is done or energy is transferred (3.3);

- recall and use the relationship $E_k = \frac{1}{2}mv^2$ for the kinetic energy of a body (3.1);

- recall and use the fact that the strength of a gravitational field is $g = F/m$ and hence that weight $W = mg$ (1.4, 4.1, 4.2);

- recall and use the relationship $\Delta E_{grav} = mg\Delta h$ for the gravitational potential energy transferred near the Earth's surface (3.1, 4.1, 4.2);

- apply the principle of conservation of energy to examples involving gravitational potential energy and kinetic energy (3.1, 4.1, 4.2).

* Numbers indicate the section(s) that relate to each achievement.

Achievements from Technology in Space (AS book)

After studying this unit you should be able to:

- describe electric current as the rate of flow of charged particles and recall and use the expression $\Delta Q = I\Delta t$ (2.1, 3.2)*;

- recall and use the expression $V = W/Q$ (2.1);

- define and use the concepts of *emf* and *internal resistance* and distinguish between *emf* and *terminal potential difference* (2.1, 2.2, 2.3);

- recall and use the fact that resistance is defined by $R = V/I$ and that Ohm's law is a special case when $I \propto V$ (2.2);

- recognise and use the relationships between current, voltage and resistance, for series and parallel circuits, and appreciate that these relationships are a consequence of the conservation of charge and energy (2.2);

- recall and use the expressions $P = VI$, $W = VIt$ and derive and use related expressions (e.g. $P = I^2R$) (2.3);

- recall and use the fact that the maximum power transfer from a source of emf is achieved when the load resistance is equal to the internal resistance (2.3);

- recognise and use the expression *percentage efficiency* = {[*useful energy* (or power) *output*]/[*total energy* (or power) *input*]} × 100% (2.3, 3.1);

- recall that the resistance of metallic conductors increases with increasing temperature and that the resistance of NTC thermistors decreases with increasing temperature (3.2);

- explain, qualitatively, how changes of resistance with temperature may be modelled in terms of lattice vibrations and number of conduction electrons (3.2);

- recognise and use the expression $\Delta E = mc\Delta\theta$ (3.4)

- explain the principles involved in a continuous flow technique to measure thermal energy transfer (3.4).

* Numbers indicate the section(s) that relate to each achievement.

Achievements from The Sound of Music (AS book)

After studying this unit you should be able to:

- understand and use the terms *amplitude*, *frequency*, *period*, *speed* and *wavelength* (1.2, 2.3)*;

- recall and use the wave equation $v = f\lambda$ (1.3, 2.3);

- recall that a sound wave is a longitudinal wave which can be described in terms of the displacement of molecules or changes in pressure (1.3, 1.5);

- recognise and use the expression $v = \sqrt{(T/\mu)}$ for the speed of a wave on a string or wire (1.5);

- use graphs to represent transverse and longitudinal waves, including standing waves (1.3, 1.4, 1.5);

- explain and use the concepts of *coherence*, *path difference*, *superposition* and *phase* (1.2, 1.4, 1.5, 1.6, 2.2);

- explain what is meant by a *standing wave*, how such a wave is formed, and identify nodes and antinodes (1.4, 1.5);

- identify the physical factors (e.g. length, tension, mass per unit length) which affect the pitch of musical note produced by a string and by a pipe, and hence explain how the pitch may be controlled (1.5);

- distinguish between analogue and digital signals (2.1, 2.2);

- use ray diagrams to trace the path of light through an optical system (2.4, 2.5);

- understand and use the terms *focal length*, *power* (of a lens) and *critical angle* (2.4, 2.5);

- explain how the behaviour of light can be described in terms of waves and photons (2.2, 2.3, 2.6);

- recognise and use the expression $E = hf$ to relate the frequency of radiation to a transition between known energy levels (2.6).

* Numbers indicate the section(s) that relate to each achievement.

Achievements from Digging Up the Past (AS book)

After studying this unit you should be able to:

- recall and use the relationship $R = \rho l/A$, and derive and use related expressions (e.g. $R = l/\sigma A$) (1.2)*;

- express quantities with a very large range, e.g. resistivities of materials, using $\log_{10}$ of those quantities (1.2, 2.1);

- explain how the potential along a uniform current-carrying wire varies with the distance along it and how use can be made of this variation in a potential divider (1.3);

- explain qualitatively how the potential varies with distance in a non-uniform current-carrying wire or other medium (1.3);

- recall that waves can be diffracted and that substantial diffraction occurs when the size of the gap or obstacle is comparable with the wavelength of the radiation (2.3);

- show an awareness of the existence and origin of background radiation, past and present (3.3);

- recognise nuclear radiations (alpha, beta and gamma) from their penetrating power and ionising ability (3.3);

- recall and use the fact that the amount of light emitted in thermoluminescence depends on the number of electrons trapped in 'defect energy levels' and hence on the nuclear radiation to which the material has been exposed (3.2, 3.3);

- recognise and use the expression $E = hf$ to calculate the highest frequency of radiation that could be emitted in a transition across a known energy band gap or between known energy levels (3.2);

- recall that the absorption of a photon can result in the emission of a photoelectron (3.4);

- understand and use the terms *threshold frequency* and *work function* and recognise and use the expression $hf = \phi + \frac{1}{2}mv_{max}^2$ (3.4);

- use the slope and intercept of a graph of a relationship of the form $y = mx + c$ to analyse a physical situation (3.4).

* Numbers indicate the section(s) that relate to each achievement.

Achievements from Good Enough to Eat (AS book)

After studying this unit you should be able to:

- understand and use the terms *density*, *laminar flow*, *streamlined flow*, *terminal velocity*, *turbulent flow*, *upthrust* and *viscous drag* (2.2, 2.3)*;

- recall that the rate of flow of a fluid is related to its viscosity (2.2, 2.3, 2.5);

- recognise and use the expression for Stokes' law, $F = 6\pi r \eta v$ (2.2);

- recall that the viscosities of most fluids change with temperature (2.2);

- distinguish between elastic and plastic deformation of a material (3.3);

- explain what is meant by the terms *brittle*, *ductile*, *hard*, *malleable*, *stiff* and *tough*, use these terms, and give examples of materials exhibiting such behaviour (3.2, 3.3, 5.2);

- explain how to measure the refractive index of a liquid and how this can be used in comparing the concentrations of, for example, sugar solutions (4.1);

- recognise and use the expression for refractive index $\mu = \sin i / \sin r = v_1/v_2$ and predict whether total internal reflection will occur at an interface (4.1);

- explain what is meant by *plane polarised light* (4.2);

- explain how to measure the rotation of the plane of polarisation by a liquid and how this can be used in comparing the concentrations of, for example, sugar solutions (4.2).

* Numbers indicate the section(s) that relate to each achievement.

Achievements from Spare Part Surgery (AS book)

After studying this unit you should be able to:

- explain the meaning of, use and calculate *tensile/compressive stress*, *tensile/compressive strain*, *strength*, *breaking stress*, *stiffness* and *Young modulus* (2.2)*;

- draw force–extension, force–compression, and tensile/compressive stress–strain graphs and identify the *limit of proportionality*, *elastic limit* and *yield point* (2.2);

- calculate the elastic strain energy ΔE_{el} in a deformed material sample, using the expression $\Delta E_{el} = F\Delta x/2$ where applicable, and from the area under its force–extension graph (2.2);

- use electron diffraction images to deduce ordered structure, or lack of it (2.3);

- understand the need for a wave model when explaining electron diffraction (2.3);

- recall that polymers consist of long chain molecules in varying states of order and disorder (2.2, 2.3);

- recognise and use the equation $1/v + 1/u = 1/f$ for a thin lens (with the 'real is positive' sign convention) (3.2);

- recall that, in general, waves are transmitted and reflected at an interface between media (3.3, 4.2);

- explain how different media affect the transmission/reflection of waves travelling from one medium to another (3.3, 4.2);

- explain how a pulse–echo technique can provide details of the position and/or speed of an object (4.2, 4.3);

- explain qualitatively how the movement of a source of sound or light relative to an observer/detector gives rise to a shift in frequency (Doppler effect) (4.3).

* Numbers indicate the section(s) that relate to each achievement.

Index